BAILY'S MAGAZINE
OF
Sports and Pastimes

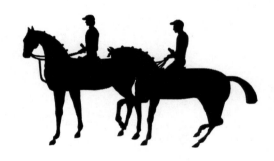

AN INDEX AND
BIBLIOGRAPHY

CHRIS HARTE

**First published in 2017
by Sports History Publishing**

ISBN : 978-1-898010-09-8

Assistant Editor : Susan Lewis

Consultant Editor : Lizzie Mead

Cover : Joseph Brown

Layout : Sarah Evans • sarah@sarahlouisedesigns.co.uk

Contact : chrismedia47@yahoo.co.uk

Printed and bound in Wales

CHAPTERS

	Page
Preface	5
Introduction	9
Some Old Sporting Periodicals	13
Index of Volumes	17
1. Issues 1 - 35	21
2. Issues 36 - 91	30
3. Issues 92 - 140	44
4. Issues 141 - 189	57
5. Issues 190 - 231	70
6. Issues 232 - 266	81
7. Issues 267 - 308	91
8. Issues 309 - 346	102
9. Issues 347 - 370	113
10. Issues 371 - 394	124
11. Issues 395 - 418	135
12. Issues 419 - 442	147
13. Issues 443 - 466	161
14. Issues 467 - 490	175
15. Issues 491 - 514	188
16. Issues 515 - 538	202
17. Issues 539 - 562	217
18. Issues 563 - 586	234
19. Issues 587 - 610	254
20. Issues 611 - 634	274
21. Issues 635 - 658	293
22. Issues 659 - 682	312
23. Issues 683 - 706	325
24. Issues 707 - 730	335
25. Issues 731 - 754	346
26. Issues 755 - 778	357
27. Issues 779 - 796	369
Postscript	379

Recent Books by the Author include

A Season With The Carmarthenshire Hunt (2016)
Old Gold: Carmarthen Town Football Club (2013)
Watching Brief (2010)
Recollections of a Sportswriter (2009)
The History of Australian Cricket (2008)
Rugby Clubs and Grounds (2005)
English Rugby Clubs (2004)
Britain's Rugby Grounds (2003)
Australian Cricket History (2003)
Reminiscences of a Sportswriter (2002)
Menston Actually (2001)
Sports Books in Britain (2000)
Ramblings of a Sportswriter (1999)
A Year in the Sporting Pressbox (1998)
The Twickenham Papers (1997)
A Sportswriter's Year (1997)
Sporting Heritage (1996)
One Day in Leicester (1995)
A History of Australian Cricket (1993)
Cricket Indulgence (1991)
History of South Australian Cricket (1990)
South African International Cricket (1989)
Two Tours and Pollock (1988)
Seven Tests (1987)
Australians in South Africa (1987)
Cricket Safari (1986)
Australian Cricket Journal (1985)
Cricket Rebels (1985)
The History of the Sheffield Shield (1984)
The Fight for the Ashes (1983)
Cathedral End (1979)

In Preparation

A Monograph of the Principal Writers in *Baily's Magazine of Sports and Pastimes, 1860-1926*
(to be published in 2018)

Hunting in Carmarthenshire
(to be published in 2019)

PREFACE

It was during the summer of 1999, when I was working in West Yorkshire, that the idea of compiling a bibliography of *Baily's Magazine of Sports and Pastimes* was first mentioned to me. I had already researched for bibliographies on athletics, cricket, football and rugby union hence the approach.

At the time the publications section of the British Library were very keen to publish as many sporting bibliographies as possible provided they could find a person, or people, willing to undertake such a task.

Cynthia McKinley, based at the Library's Boston Spa complex, was the person who first broached the subject. She, along with her colleague Arthur Cunningham, were the inspirations behind the project. At first I was not too keen to commit myself as, along with two other people, we were soon to launch Britain's first weekly rugby union newspaper.

The point which was made to me was that *Baily's* had been the most prominent sporting magazine of the last half of the Nineteenth Century and the first quarter of the Twentieth Century. As well, I was the only person they knew who had a complete run of all 796 issues.

I gave the matter considerable thought. Fortunately I was then living in a village on the edge of Ilkley Moor so was able to ramble the byways while debating the issue with myself. In the end I decided to accept Cynthia's idea with the proviso that I would do it in between writing books and my various radio commitments.

There really is no excuse for this work to have taken as long as eighteen years to compile. In my defence I have had published thirteen books during this time, with my radio allegiances varying from *BBC Radio Four* to *West Wales Radio*. There have also been magazine and newspaper columns to write as well as to service the new technology which seems to rule the lives of younger generations.

Before I go into too much detail I must explain that once the bibliography had been compiled it has had three very detailed complete checks as more and more information came to hand. Even now I am sure that further detail will be revealed over the passage of time.

Cynthia and Arthur have long since retired from the Library (to go into being involved with an Art Gallery and Antiquarian Bookselling respectively) with the enthusiasm for such bibliographies waning after their departure. Fortunately *Sports History Publishing* has taken over their role.

This work is, therefore, being published in a limited edition of fifty copies most of which I expect will fall into the hands of collectors or University libraries

* * *

There are a number of people to thank for their help, information and assistance in the compilation of this work. I mention them in no particular order. They include Ken Callahan, Diana Chalis, Greg Way, Paul Morgan, Brian Rowlands, Fred Barrett, Andrew King, Walter Gilbey and my wife, Susan, whose ability as a researcher is second to none.

A number of books have been of great help. *Modern English Biography* by Frederic Boase has been essential. Published in six volumes they contain some 30,000 short biographical sketches of persons who died between 1851-1900. Naturally many of those referred to in *Baily's* can be found in these works. Then, of course, came *Who's Who* followed by *Who Was Who*. Although not as detailed as Boase, the information given was useful in gaining a feel for people whose names adorned the 'green covers' of the magazine.

Eileen Loder's enormous research was in continual use. Her book, *Bibliography of the History and Organisation of Horse Racing and Thoroughbred Breeding in Great Britain and Ireland*, is a splendid work. It has as its sub-title: *Books Published in Great Britain and Ireland, 1565-1973*.

Another similar publication came from Anne Grimshaw. *The Horse* had as its sub-title: *A Bibliography of British Books, 1851-1976*, to which she added '*With a Narrative Commentary on the Role of the Horse in British Social History, as Revealed by the Contemporary Literature.*'

Another helpful title was *The Book of the Horse* by Brian Vesey-Fitzgerald which contains a sixty page *Bibliography of Books on Hunting* prepared by Henry Higginson. It is Higginson's work: *British and American Sporting Authors* which initially gave me some of the names of those who had written for *Baily's* under various guises. From this I was put in touch with Ken Callahan in New Hampshire who referred me to his book: *A Dictionary of Sporting Pen Names* which helped me considerably in researching Nineteenth Century *Baily's* contributors.

In 1899, Herbert Slater produced *Illustrated Sporting Books* which was sub-titled: '*A Descriptive Survey of a*

Collection of English Illustrated Works of a Sporting Character.' Slater had previously written a number of similar works but this was the best for checking *Baily's* early contributors.

One book which promised much but gave very little was the *Dictionary of Nineteenth-Century Journalism*, the brainchild of Laurel Brake. The errors in it sent me off on a number of dead ends and I would suggest any researchers give this publication a very wide berth. I met one of the Associate Editors on two occasions in order to point out errors but all I obtained was charm, excuses and two convivial lunches.

The Field 1853-1953 by Robert Rose and *The Story of Your [Sporting] Life 1859-1998* by James Lambie were in continual use as were books written by various *Baily's* contributors. I intend to go into more detail on these in a Monograph to be published shortly.

Obviously various other sporting magazines were consulted. There were quite a few during the life of *Baily's* but most of the relevant detail is noted on the Introduction pages.

*   *   *

It has not been an easy task to research information about Alfred Head Baily; Baily's Magazine; Vinton & Company (the subsequent publishers) or any of the editorial staff.

Alfred served an apprenticeship in the bookselling and publishing house of his maternal grandfather James Richardson which was situated at 23 Cornhill in the City of London. In 1832, Alfred took premises at 83 Cornhill and founded A.H.Baily & Co. He also traded as A.H. & C.E.Baily which later became Baily Brothers who are noted as publishers of the first volumes of *Baily's Magazine*.

With regards to magazines, he published, in 1839, *The Oracle of Rural Life* which, in 1841, became *The Sporting Oracle and Almanack of Rural Life* which, a year later, was retitled *The Sporting Almanack and Oracle of Rural Life*. It ceased in 1844.

The publication on these pages was initially called *Baily's Monthly Magazine of Sports and Pastimes*. However, when Vinton & Co. became the owners they dropped the word 'Monthly' from the title.

None of the 796 issues give any indication as to who edited the magazine, nor the names of any of the staff. Any information has been obtained from, usually, *The Field Magazine, The Illustrated London News* or from books written by contributors.

As far as can be ascertained the editors were Alfred Baily (1860-80); Percy Baily (1880-89); Tresham Gilbey (1889-1915) and George Burrows (1915-26). Assistant editor for a lengthy period was Edward Cuming who, along with James Shepherd, planned and compiled *Baily's Hunting Directory* from its first issue in 1897 until George Burrows took over editing both publications in 1915.

Baily also started *The Live Stock Journal* and *The Bloodstock Review*. The first editor of the Journal was James Sinclair whose subsequent idea of an annual Almanac proved to be highly popular. Alas, it is virtually impossible to obtain copies of the Almanac today. Edward Moorhouse edited the Review and both of them also worked as writers and sub-editors on the Magazine.

In the early days, before photography, the house of Baily employed a number of engravers. George Stodart and Penry Palfrey were the best known and as can be seen within the pages their work was of the highest quality.

The story of Baily's is related on subsequent pages. However, following the takeover by Vinton, A.H.Baily & Co. was sued for bankruptcy on 28 July 1891 and folded shortly afterwards. Vinton & Co. went into liquidation in February 1961.

Baily moved from 83 Cornhill (in November 1843) taking two temporary premises, until in 1846 he took a shop and offices at the other end of the street at 3 Royal Exchange Building. The company stayed here until October 1881 when they moved to 15 Nicholas Lane which then was at the King William Street end of the thoroughfare. Nothing remains today of the Lane's original buildings.

Prior to the sale to Vinton, A H. Baily & Co had a short stay in Suffolk House, Laurence Pountney Hill. From the beginning of January 1889, the Magazine was produced from 9 Bridge Street. In September 1906 new offices were leased at 8 Breams Buildings near to the entrance of Chancery Lane. It was here the Magazine died in 1926.

Vinton & Co continued publishing until 1961, especially the popular Baily's Hunting Directory. They were forced to move in 1942 when a bomb destroyed part of their building. They took up residence at 8 Stratford Place, off Oxford Street, and stayed there until 1955. The final move was to 139 Strand to occupy very cramped third floor offices.

Here a few words of explanation are necessary. All through the text I have used the names by which people were known. Titles came and went, for example there were three Willoughby de Brokes and the same number of Dukes of Beaufort, and in one instance a man had five different titles during his life, stepping up the pecking order each time as those above him "solved the great mystery" (a quote loved by *Baily's* writers). I appreciate that this decision will not please some researchers but I considered it necessary in order to clearly differentiate between generations.

A quirk by the editorial team was their complete dislike of having the name of the same writer attributed more than once in any issue. This led to various pseudonyms or initials being used for one person which caused much angst until it was resolved.

In one instance a military man, John Russell, who was not supposed to write for magazines while a serving officer, used the name 'C.Stein' to cover himself, then different initials to go with his published articles. However, even in modern times, this has led to a number of researchers proudly announcing that they have found the works of 'Stein.'

Some writers who used more than one name are found to have been published many years after their deaths. Henry Pilkington (known as Patrick Perterras, whose pseudonym was 'Homeless') died in 1914 yet his verses were still being used in the final issues of the magazine twelve years later. The same happened with engravings. Penry Palfrey's works were constantly used with some (particularly *The Earth Stopper*) making regular appearances. Other engravers (Frederick Babbage in particular) seemed to make a seamless transition to photography when the need arose.

With engravings I have credited the engraver and not the creator unless, of course, the engraver is not named. With photographs the individual copyright holder is credited but no acknowledgement is given to those supplied by an Agency as the name of the taker is unknown.

The multi-usage, particularly of engravings, emerged following the First World War. *Baily's* lost nearly 90% of its subscribers in the 1914-18 period and the magazine never recovered. The quality of writing went downhill in the 1920s particularly when it came to historical reminiscences. The last few years sometimes saw contributions of only half a page and it is clear that the editorial staff had to fill in the gaps wherever they could.

This is most clearly shown in the 'Our Van' columns. The first three writers Irwin Willes (1860-65), Comyns Cole (1865-90) and Edwin Sachs (1890-1910) provided fifty years worth of detailed news from the worlds of horse-racing and hunting. Charles Richardson did his best until 1920 although his newspaper work about the turf took priority. After that the column became a shadow of its former self and even went through a period where hunting was not mentioned at all.

An eccentricity of the early days when Alfred Baily was in charge was his decision about the make up of volumes. For an unknown reason he adopted the Greek methodology of seven issues per volume. When Vintons took over they moved quickly to the Roman half year system.

Vintons also changed the layout of the text making two columns a page instead of one. Occasionally a purge would take place when old contributors were dropped and new ones came in their place. Sometimes this worked but not always. Working journalists were also tried towards the end of the Magazine's life but they neither had the time nor knowledge to produce essays of substance.

In later years fiction became a page-filler and the thirty plus chapters of stories from the early times just disappeared. The 1920s saw the standard of contributions drop steadily with staff writing being mainly of obituaries or on the promotion of other publications within the publishing house.

Mistakes made in early issues were compounded over the years as writers copied from these secondary sources. The story of *Baily's* is a case in point. It sometimes took me years to find as accurate as possible any detail on the family or firm. It still might not be fully correct so if any further information is found then do, please, contact me.

Finally, with regard to writers using pen-names or initials, the real names were found in the excellent obituaries *Baily's* printed about them. From a personal point of view the revelation that 'Diomed' was Herbert Bromhead (who was also 'Boris' of *The Referee*) meant that I could continue my work on *The Sporting Mirror* which will be my next bibliographical work.

Braemar House
Carmarthen

April 2017

Formerly Richardson's original shop

The Royal Exchange Building at the time of Baily's occupancy

INTRODUCTION

Baily's Magazine of Sports and Pastimes first appeared in March 1860 and was published each month until June 1926. In all, 796 issues appeared in their distinctive 'green covers' over probably the most important period of time for the development of modern sport.

As sports became more codified and disciplined so *Baily's* recorded either the rise in popularity, or the fall from grace, of much of the splendid sporting history which Britain has to offer. The latter part of this was under the editorship of Tresham Gilbey (son of Sir Walter Gilbey, the noted philanthropist) who was in charge from 1889 until 1915, and after him George Burrows until the closure. Prior to that the founder, Alfred Baily (1808-84), had edited the magazine until 1880, after which his son, Percy Baily, took over as editor.

To try to understand the stature in which the magazine was held it is worth going back to the final edition and reading the General Manager's valedictory remarks. He wrote: "It is with unfeigned regret which, it is believed, will be shared by readers at home and abroad, that the proprietors have decided to discontinue the publication of *Baily's Magazine of Sports and Pastimes* as from this issue. This decision has not been made lightly, for the 'green covers' were much more than simply one of the many titles emanating from the publishing house in whose ownership it has been since 1889, and in whose hands the old time traditions of the magazine have been so long maintained."

"The affection in which it has been held by all connected with it, including the many well known contemporary writers on sport whose work is so fully mirrored in its pages, was part of the charm which it held alike for readers and contributors. From a commercial point of view, it was not what our American friends would call 'much of a business proposition' for it was nurtured with a fairly liberal hand and often out of all proportion to the financial return."

"Curiously enough the various attempts made to establish other sporting monthlies never touched *Baily's* which seemed to hold a field peculiarly its own. No doubt the greater and more widespread attention paid to sport in the daily and weekly press, with the rapidity in which results are now available and prominent events described, have militated against the growth of the monthly publications. While as a record of prominent results much of this information now virtually demands a whole volume devoted to the particular sport concerned."

"Then there is another factor which has played an important part in the present decision and that is the great increase in the cost of production as compared with the pre-1914 period. This, combined with the repeated dislocation of business caused by current circumstances [The General Strike] which need not be enumerated here, have all helped to bring about the order to stop publication. The following notes may prove of interest as briefly outlining the history of the magazine."

"From March 1860, *Baily's* has regularly appeared before the public in the shape by which it became so well known and recognised. Its first proprietors were Messrs Baily Brothers of Cornhill who had a small office in that part of the City of London. This was from whence was distributed all that was good in the literature of high class sport and comprising shooting, hunting, racing, cricket, yachting, rowing, fistiana, athletics, walking and professional sculling. Those subjects, let it be explained, were the contents of the first volume of *Baily's* issued in 1860. It began with a March number and ended with the September number of the year. In later times the periods of each volume were changed to the legal half year."

"*Baily's* really took the place of the once famous *Sporting Magazine* which existed from 1792 to 1870. That publication had a curiously chequered career and had become an anachronism long before it expired [as noted elsewhere in this book]. *Baily's Magazine* had cut into it from 1860, the first issue of which carried a number of articles by Henry Rous, Frank Fielding, Francis Francis and others. The first named, of course, was 'The Dictator of the Turf,' Vice Admiral the Hon. Henry John Rous, to give him his correct title. Naturally *Baily's* chose him for its first subject as a sportsman of mark, a feature the magazine sustained to the end of its career."

"The Vice Admiral, in his own contribution, wrote on the subject of 'The English Racehorse.' The author was emphatic that horse racing had been the popular amusement of the people of this country from the time of the Norman Conquest, but he added: 'No mention of horse races are on record before the reign of Henry the Second. This was when the court and nobility attended a tournament at Smithfield, during Lent, where the London citizens disported themselves in martial attire on horseback and races were the order of the day.' In his article for the second issue of *Baily's*, Rous delved deeply into the distinct sources of pure blood of our racehorses. The Duke of Bedford was the subject of the biographical sketch in that edition and in the third number there appeared the life of the Duke of Beaufort of that period."

"Running through the earliest issues of *Baily's* we find such matters as The Battle of Farnborough (the fight between Sayers and Heenan) faithfully recorded. This fist fight was, to the men of the day, an event which ranked high in the British calendar along with the battles of Trafalgar and Waterloo. George Payne, the Earl of Glasgow, the Marquis of Exeter, the Earl of Zetland and George Parr (the Nottinghamshire and All England cricketer) were subjects in the first <u>volume</u> of *Baily's*, and they were followed by the Earls of Derby and Chesterfield, Lord Palmerston, Sir Tatton Sykes, and Messrs James Merry, George Osbaldeston and John Gully."

"Matters such as Tom Cribbs' training; the duties of Masters of the Foxhounds; School life, its sports and pastimes; the treatment of Hunters; Pheasant rearing; and an opening address to Foxhunters were dealt with by scholarly writers. Then there are descriptions of many packs of hounds; including the Oakley, Old Berkshire, South Essex, Middleton, Essex Union and Bramham Moor. And so could one go on recalling the earliest contributions of many excellent writers."

"Head of them all stands the late Major George Whyte-Melville, supported by writers whose pseudonyms were: The Gentleman in Black (Charles Clarke); Amphion (Walter Tyrrell); Argus (Irwin Lewis Willes) and Old Calabar (Count Theobold William de Vismes). No one since has stirred us with such songs as: *The Lord of the Valley; The King of the Kennel* or *The Good Grey Mare*. This, we believe, was the last poem he wrote and there is now added pathos in the concluding lines ... 'I have lived my life, I am nearly done, I have played the game all round.' Lines which today sound strangely prophetic of the empty saddle, which told of the poet's fatal accident in the hunting field. The Cheshire Hunt poet, Rowland Egerton Warburton, contributed most of his earliest verses to *Baily's* and there have been many other writers of great repute attached to the Magazine since."

"The time honoured 'green covers' entered into an altered existence in 1889 when it passed into the hands of Vinton and Co. [Tresham Gilbey was appointed as editor before becoming the General Manager of all Vinton titles]. *Baily's* did not change, however, from the lines laid down by its founder. It continued to hold its high position, opened out to a wider scope and appealed to a larger circle of readers under its new proprietors. It may be recalled that in 1897 the first annual volume of *Baily's Hunting Directory* was published [under Gilbey's direction]. This offshoot has continued to grow and flourish with such remarkable vigour and usefulness that at least it can be claimed that it will worthily continue to carry on the name of the good stock from which it took birth, and maintain its position as the standard annual on hunting. [The Directory continued in book form until 2008, when it then became an electronic publication]."

"The intervening history of *Baily's* is mirrored in the bound volumes of the period, treasured in so many sportsmen's libraries. This is where any volume from a set, picked out at random, will not fail to yield its harvest of joys recalled, and sometimes regrets, of the past. Happy are those fortunate people who possess complete sets of *Baily's* since 1860, for these are a mine of wealth to the sportsman and not likely to decrease in value."

"In less than eight months after *Baily's* celebrated the issue of its one hundredth volume, war descended upon the British Empire and Europe. Regrettably, *Baily's* lost many hundreds of its readers in the first few months of the conflict for hunting men formed a large proportion of the cavalry of that gallant little army which did so much to stem the first onrush of the enemy in Belgium and France. In memory we salute them, those friends and companions of many happy days with horse and hound. We recall the efforts made by those at home to keep the Hunt organisations in being and remember the very thinness of the fields. But what has this to do with the 'green covers?' Memories certainly, but much more, for some part of the old magazine died with them."

"It is with sincere regret that we say farewell to all those who have been brought together within our pages, whether as subjects included in Baily's Portrait Gallery; recalling many of the finest and best of our British sportsmen past and present; or the large band of contributors who gave of their best for the common good of the sports to which they were devoted. Also to business friends, including Messrs Bale who have printed *Baily's* for the past thirty six years (it having previously been William Clowes) and last but not least to readers all over the world to whom, we venture to believe, the `green covers' carried to pioneers at the rim of the Empire."

"It brought them thoughts of good days gone and good days to come amid the green fields and coverts of the homeland; to the veterans, quickened dreams and pleasant memories of bygone days and old time friends; while to all in some measure at least we hope we have helped to nurture and develop that vital healthful spirit and wholesome manhood which is characteristic of all that is best in our British sports and pastimes. And so Baily's has tried to say farewell, and what is not found in the words will be found in the heart, for every good wish to all good sportsmen."

* * *

Prior to Gilbey's valedictory notice and, in fact, even before he took the reins of office, the issue of February 1885 contained notice of the death of the magazine's founder and initial proprietor. What it said showed how unfamiliar the then editorial staff were with events over the first quarter of a century of *Baily's* as they had to guide their way through an obituary. It read in part:

"At a ripe old age, some years beyond the allotted span, Mr Alfred Head Baily passed away at his residence in College Terrace, South Hampstead, on the last day of 1884. He had been in failing health for some time and on the last occasion of our seeing him we were struck with the great change that had taken place in his fine commanding presence and much feared that the end was near."

"The son of a medical man (John Baily); his mother the heiress of Mr James Malcott Richardson the long established bookseller and publisher who had two bookshops in Cornhill, Mr Baily was destined for the publishing business. We believe he served his apprenticeship in that gentleman's establishment."

"It was around 1832 that Mr Baily started in business, initially at 83 Cornhill, London, and soon gathered round him a host of friends. Fond of field sports he kept, as soon as his means would allow, a couple of hunters at Bushey and subsequently had horses at Berkhamsted: his place of business becoming a little rendezvous for sporting men. Charles Apperley, then at the zenith of his fame as a sporting writer; William Maxwell, the author of that charming book *Wild Sports of the West*; Tom Hood, and many others would occasionally drop in at his sanctum for chat and gossip."

"He published for Mr Apperley and Admiral Rous, and brought out Maxwell's *Life of the Duke of Wellington*, which was a great success. He also produced many of Hood's humorous works and his business soon became a flourishing one. And here it may be said that Mr Baily was emphatically a man of business. Though he subsequently saw a good deal of turf life he never allowed his fondness for sport to interfere with the work of his office."

"He began early to take an interest in racing, around the time that *Bloomsbury* beat *Deception* in that memorable snowstorm on Epsom Downs. His was soon a well-known figure. Already intimate with the Admiral, who was then the manager of the Duke of Bedford's stable, they soon became acquainted with Lord George Bentinck, Colonel George Anson, Mr Massey Stanley and most of the leading racing men of that day."

"An intimate friend of John Scott in the palmy days of Whitewall Stables of Malton, he naturally was sure to be on a Whitewall favourite, and in those early days was the means of causing Admiral Rous to win more money (when *The Baron* won the St.Leger) than he had ever won on a race in his life. Later, Mr Baily, from something which came to his knowledge, backed *The Baron* at Goodwood, making the Admiral do likewise. As the price was 40 to 1 they both had a good hedging. Mr Baily was never a commissioner but from his intimacy with the noblemen and gentlemen we have mentioned he and his friends were often asked to put on money by the Admiral, Lord George, Prince Batthyany, Sir Joseph Hawley, Colonel George Anson and others."

"At a later period Mr Baily became connected in business with Baron Rothschild and he also then became in some sense a follower of stocks and shares. It was popularly supposed that he knew when the Baron had 'a good thing' but how true that was we cannot say. However, we know of late years, when he had long since given up active participation in racing, that if Mr Leopold de Rothschild had anything in a big race he fancied then Mr Baily's little stake was generally on."

"In 1860, principally at the suggestions of Henry Rous and Robert Grimston, he commenced the publication of *Baily's Magazine*, which soon took the prominent position it has continued to hold. Mr Baily gathered round him a staff of writers fully qualified to speak with authority on the different branches of sport touched upon in his magazine. He had published a small sporting magazine between 1839-44 (*The Oracle of Rural Life*) but it had not been successful."

"Hunting, racing and breeding were its chief topics but the facile pen and peculiar humour of Irwin Willes (of the *Morning Post*) speedily made the news pages of *Our Van* a leading feature. Frederick Whitehurst, the brilliant Paris correspondent of the *[Daily] Telegraph*, contributed most amusing sketches of life in that gay capital, and Walter Tyrrell discoursed on breeding and wrote some admirable poetic skit on the topics of the town."

"One of the glories of *Baily's* was the fact that most of Major George Whyte-Melville's best hunting songs first saw light in its pages (as did the early works of Adam Lindsay Gordon). How wonderfully stirring they were, while many a good run had its history told in the *Van* by the same hand. Hunting, indeed, in the season was a great feature of the magazine and the Hon. Robert Grimston, a staunch supporter of *Baily's* and a firm friend of its proprietor, once told the present 'Van Driver' that if he had his will the *Van* should be all hunting when it was not cricket: a state of things which, we fear, our readers would have hardly appreciated."

"For the last twenty years or so the racecourse rarely saw Mr Baily. He occasionally went to Newmarket on a Two Thousand Guineas or Cesarewitch day but these visits gradually ceased and in his place of business, in Royal Exchange Buildings, he was content to talk about the sport he had lost the inclination to see."

"Mr Baily was most kind and thoughtful to those engaged in the literary work of the magazine and his death has caused much genuine sorrow amongst all sorts of men associated with him by the ties of friendship and business. He leaves a widow, Louisa Ann Baily and two sons, Alfred Head Baily junior and Percy Head Baily"

*   *   *

There is then a gap prior to the issue of January 1889 when the Baily family sold the magazine to the firm of Vinton & Co., who immediately appointed Tresham Gilbey (1862-1947) as editor. Reading between the lines it would appear that Mrs Louisa Baily had inherited her late husband's company and had continued publication, along with her son Percy, for a further four years. There had been changes of offices and the original printers, William Clowes & Son had, in late 1888, been given notice of a cessation of their arrangements with A.H.Baily & Co.

Gilbey (third son of Sir Walter Gilbey) immediately set out his aims for the magazine in a long-winded editorial which is worth paraphrasing (although slightly repetitive from the valedictory notice). He wrote that there would now be "an altered existence" but "not altered from the lines laid down by its founder that it should be 'a magazine of sports and pastimes, written by gentlemen for gentlemen'." Gilbey stated that *Baily's* "would be taking a higher position and a wider scope, appealing to a larger circle of readers," which he called "that great year by year increasing multitude: the all-round sportsmen." These, he added, were "good over the ridge and furrow, good upon Highland forests and by the banks of Highland rivers," and were "to be found at Lord's, on the Rowley Mile [at Newmarket], at Hurlingham and [along the River Thames] at Ranelagh."

Then Gilbey stated his aspirations, as follows: "Any change of administration is held to involve a necessity of making some statement as to the policy which is to be pursued. The first issue of *Baily's Magazine* after it has passed into the hands of new proprietors [issue 347] seems to require, by way of preface, some declaration of their intentions, aims and hopes."

"They intend to reduce the price of each number to one shilling. They aim at supplying all that has hitherto been provided, and more. They hope that those who have found pleasure in reading the magazine will continue to do so. The wish of the proprietors is to secure the assistance of the very best men upon all the subjects to be dealt with. And they purpose that these subjects shall be, as heretofore, 'British sports and pastimes,' using the phrase in its widest interpretation."

"Whilst neither racing, hunting, shooting, yachting, rowing, cricket, football, golf and athletics will be scanted of the space hitherto devoted to each of them, it will be found that occasional papers can be given upon subjects which do not come under any of these headings, and yet will be found appropriate accompaniments to any on the list."

"At least two pages, of small print, will be allotted each month to correspondence and no criticism by competent folk upon statements made in articles which have appeared in the columns will be excluded. Unless, of course, it be actually ill-natured or dull. Pains will be taken to secure trustworthy replies to any inquiries which may be put and no one will be asked to furnish these answers unless he has given evidence that he has been at least in the position to know."

"Should this old-established magazine deteriorate it shall not be from incapacity or neglect. Whether profit or loss be the result to the proprietors no effort will be spared to sustain, and even to enhance, the established reputation of *Baily's*. The illustrations will be as artistic, the subjects as well chosen, and the treatment of these as complete as the connections and experience of the proprietors will anyhow enable them to provide. This short prologue must be accepted as their assurance to the public. It shall be left to the readers to say whether or not this assurance has been fulfilled."

SOME OLD SPORTING PERIODICALS

(Part of the following appeared in Baily's Magazine in January 1891)

One hundred years ago, bar three, there flourished in Warwick Square by St. Paul's Church Yard, a noted bookseller, John Wheble by name. He had long been associated with Horne Tooke, John Wilkes, and other fiery spirits and politicians of a like kind: in connection with whom he had published several political journals and weekly papers. He also produced *The Middlesex Journal*, the first newspaper which had ever attempted to give in full the Parliamentary debates, which at that time were generally more interesting in the House of Lords than the House of Commons.

As publisher of the *Journal* he soon got into trouble about some satirical sketches of prominent politicians, written by Tooke, and was ordered to appear at the bar of the House of Commons. Wheble refused to obey, and kept in hiding. The House offered a reward for his apprehension, but Wilkes (perhaps the most audacious and irrepressible Member of Parliament that ever faced the Speaker) contrived to get his friend exculpated.

He later hit upon the idea of publishing the *County Chronicle*, which was the first attempt ever made to bring together the town mouse and the country mouse of John Gay's famous fable. Its success led to evolutions little dreamt of at the outset. In 1792 it occurred to Wheble that the rural intelligence supplied to the *Middlesex Journal* was the most interesting and popular feature in that by no means unsuccessful sheet, and that a monthly magazine, devoted to sports, amusements, games, and manly exercises would command extensive support. In this manner *The Sporting Magazine* sprang into existence. The first number appeared on 1 October 1792, with Wheble as editor, and Justins of Brick Lane, Whitechapel, as printers. Its title was *The Sporting Magazine, or Monthly Calendar of the Transactions of the Turf, the Chase, and every other diversion interesting to the Man of Pleasure, Enterprise and Spirit*. The first number also contained the following 'Address to the Public':-

"To relieve the mind from the fatiguing studies of the closet, and preserve the human frame from those afflictions which a sedentary life too frequently occasions, recreation and exercise are found to be essential. This assertion is so self-evident that hardly a single argument can be required in the support of it. What exercise, then, can be equal to that which has athletic rural sports for its object? What recreation can be compared to that in which the mind is pleasingly and anxiously interested concerning the success or failure of an event?"

The address, which deserves passing attention as illustrating the style of writing deemed likely to win favour from our sporting predecessors, winds up with an invocation of *"the disciples of Hoyle, the votaries of Diana, and the frequenters of Newmarket."* It may, perhaps, be unknown to some of our readers that in 1792 *Hoyle's Treatise on Whist* was unrivalled as an authority on that fascinating game.

The Sporting Magazine had not long been in existence before its judicious readers discovered for themselves that its editor, John Wheble, was no sportsman. Nevertheless, for more than twenty-five years he contrived to compile an amusing miscellany, in which spicy and elaborate accounts of prize-fights; of trials for divorce, adultery, seduction and breach of promise; of elopements to Gretna Green and Coldstream; of court-martials, cock-fights, and new dramas constituted the most attractive elements. However, the publication suffered somewhat because of its lateness in detailing its subject matter yet it was extremely valuable as a book of reference and record.

The magazine was supplemented from the first by a really good racing calendar; and, before long, steeplechases over courses (which would have astonished some of our modern Grand National winners) were recorded by what were then regarded as graphic and able pens. Some of the early illustrations may still be observed with interest and instruction. In the first number there is an engraving of George III and his staghounds (after a painting by Thomas Stothard) and also a portrait of Sir Charles Bunbury's horse Diomed, winner of the first Derby. Among the cuts will be found sketches of the Marchioness of Salisbury with a group of young ladies engaged in archery at Hatfield; a couple of famous gamecocks; sketches of the coursing meeting at Swaffham; of Colonel Thomas Thornton hawking for a heron; of the strange death of young Lord Richard Barrymore; of pigeon shooting in Windsor Forest; and of the Welter match at Newmarket imitated in our own times by Sir John Astley and the late Mr. Caledon Alexander, in which the Duke of Bedford on Dragon beat Sir John Lade on Clifden.

In later numbers, George Stubbs, John Francis Sartorious Jr, Samuel Howitt and George Morland contributed specimens of their pictorial talent to the magazine; while excerpts from books, such as Samuel Chifney's *Genius Genuine*, Major Edward Topham's *Life of Elwes the Miser*, and [Peter] *Beckford on Hunting* showed that sporting literature was not neglected by the editor.

In September 1820, Mr Wheble died in his seventy-sixth year at Bromley, in Kent. *The Sporting Magazine* then fell into the hands of his nephew, John Pittman, who continued to publish it at Warwick Square. Among its artists, Ben Marshall, Abraham Cooper and Clifton Tomson began to figure conspicuously in 1821; and in the following year occurred the most notable event in the history of the periodical. Down to that date Mr Charles James Apperley (better known as *Nimrod*) had regarded the magazine with contempt (suggesting it was "a cockney venture") and would have nothing to do with it. In the reign of George the Fourth it was not the fashion for gentlemen to contribute to magazines or newspapers upon sport and country life subjects. *Nimrod* was not only a gentleman by birth but, better still, was a scholar by education. Being, however, in a chronic condition of impecuniosity, *Nimrod* listened to the advice of a friend, who told him that he would make much more money by writing for Pittman than by publishing books of his own.

Accordingly an arrangement was concluded between him and John Pittman at a salary of £1500 a year [£120,000 at today's value] plus all expenses, which proved to be in the highest degree advantageous to the two contracting parties.

At that time, according to one of his intimate friends and associates, Apperley was one of the most fascinating persons ever seen. *"His figure was perfect as regards lightness and activity; his features handsome; his complexion bright and clear; his hair dark and curly; his eyes sparkling with humour and intelligence. He was truly a sunny person – always prompt to oblige, full of harmless fun, and very ready in conversation"*. Apperley was born in 1778 at Plasgronow near Wrexham and educated at Rugby School, of which he always spoke as being in his day a very idle and hard-drinking institution. After marrying Miss Winifred Wynn of Peniarth, Merionethshire, he first settled down at Bilton Hall, near Rugby (formerly the residence of essayist and poet Joseph Addison), and supported himself chiefly by turning raw colts into good hunters, riding them hard across country, and selling them at high prices. He had already sent some good descriptions of runs in Warwickshire, and Sir Watkin Williams-Wynn's hounds in Wales, to local newspapers at a guinea a column, and it was generally known that he wielded an able pen. But the great recommendation which induced Pittman to engage him was that he could ride as well as write. In January 1822 there appeared, therefore, in *The Sporting Magazine* the following *Address to Correspondents*:-

" *Our present number contains the first of a series of interesting letters, descriptive of the most celebrated hunts in the Midland Counties, beginning with the Leicestershire in the time of the late Mr. Meynell and the Earl of Sefton; written by a practical sportsman, and eye-witness of the scenes described. In the succeeding numbers of the Magazine will appear articles, 'On the Choice of Horses Generally', and 'On the Condition of Hunters according to the improved system, by which alone they can keep pace with the present speed of hounds'; also 'Some Remarks on Riding to Hounds'. These will be followed up by 'An Essay on the Art of Driving, and everything belonging to the Road'."*

The following extracts from *Nimrod*'s first letter in a London publication will perhaps be read with interest by some veterans who have accustomed themselves to regard him as the best sporting writer of the present century. In reality he could handle but two subjects effectively – 'The Chase' and 'The Road' and the former very much better than the latter. A more inaccurate and misleading essay, for instance, than that upon the Turf, which appeared from his pen in the July number of *The Quarterly Review* of 1833, was never set up in book print. Upon 'Hunting Horses' he wrote, however, *avec connaissance de cause*, and may be read with profit by hunting men of the present time. He introduces his sketch of 'Fox-hunting in Leicestershire' by a short and modest letter to the editor of *The Sporting Magazine*, which runs as follows:-

"As I know you are always anxious to present your readers with authentic and original information of what is going on in the hunting districts, I have sent you a few remarks founded on my own personal observation, beginning with Leicestershire and, if acceptable, will hereafter furnish you with some particulars relating to other counties. Nimrod"

Therein came a long quotation from *Nimrod* which showed where his strength lay. In style he was inferior to many modern correspondents of *The Field*, especially to 'Brooksby' and 'Arundel.' But he thoroughly understood what he was writing about when the hunting-field was his theme; and his letters (afterwards published in a volume) *On the Condition of Hunters* are as applicable to 1890 as they were to 1825. The result of his connection with *The Sporting Magazine* was an enormous extension of its circulation. The periodical was, in fact, at its apogee from 1822 to 1827 when John Pittman died. Before his death other gentlemen (some of them officers) took to following *Nimrod*'s example, and, like him, found their way as guests to the houses and tables of Masters of Foxhounds because of their writings. The accession of *Nimrod* to the staff of *The Sporting Magazine* marked the opening of a new era in the journalistic history of this country.

Shortly after the death of Pittman a rupture took place between *Nimrod*, editor William Young and widow Mary Ann Pittman. It was caused by the fact that a considerable amount of money had been advanced to Apperley for work not completed and the Pittman estate demanded it be refunded. [All this correspondence is now held in the archives of the University of Virginia].

Robert Smith Surtees, then a London lawyer without practice, saw his opportunity, and resolved to start a *New Sporting Magazine. Nimrod*, being incorrigibly extravagant, had contrived by 1830 to get hopelessly into debt, and was compelled to depart for Calais "for fear of the Jews." Supported by Rudolph Ackermann, the Regent Street printseller, Surtees offered *Nimrod* a very high salary if he would join the *New* (even to the extent of writing under a false name). Terms were made with his creditors, and he returned to England.

For fifteen years from May 1831, when the first number of the new periodical appeared, it was carried on with extraordinary verve and spirit. As 'Sylvanus Swanquill' and 'The Yorkshireman,' Surtees introduced an unexpected vein of humour and drollery into his description of field sports. The first instalment of *Jorrocks* made its appearance in the third number, and simultaneously *Nimrod's Hunting Tours;* his *Life of Jack Mytton* and his letters *On the Condition of Hunters*, kept the ball rolling merrily until 1836, when Surtees retired from the editorship.

Previous to that much-regretted change in the hand which guided its helm, the *New Sporting Magazine* had conferred a lasting boon on sporting connoisseurs for all time by admitting masterful portraits of great race-winners to its pages. They were furnished by Ben Marshall, John Herring, Charles Hancock, and Edwin Cooper – horse painters whose superiors have yet to be discovered, and, in addition, Sir Edwin Landseer and Sir Francis Grant were occasionally represented. They were supplemented by a 'Gallery of Celebrated Sporting Characters,' consisting of pen-and-ink sketches in which Lord Chesterfield; Squire Thornhill; Old General Grosvenor; Jem Bland and Crutch Robinson were portrayed to the life.

Nimrod's connection with the *New* did not long survive the resignation of its editorship by Robert Surtees. In 1839 'Craven,' or Captain John William Carleton of the 2nd Dragoon Guards, undertook to start another new periodical called *The Sporting Review*, with *Nimrod* as the principal contributor. For some years prior to 1839, Carleton had acted as racing editor of the *New*, and was not without such reputation as his hunting and racing books *Records of the Chase* and *Bye-ways and Downs of England*, could confer. On 1 January 1839, the first number of the *Review* was issued, containing a beautiful plate by Herring of Don Juan and the St. Leger field. In May 1843, *Nimrod*, who had become hopelessly careless as to the productions of his pen, and traded solely on his past achievements, died on the day that Cotherstone won the Derby. From that moment all the sporting magazines began to decline, and the last born (*The Sporting Review*) was the first to succumb.

On *Nimrod*'s death it was bought by Messrs. Rogerson & Tuxford, of the Strand; and the following year the *New* also fell into the same hands. Six years later the old *Sporting Magazine*, after more than half a century's residence in Warwick Square, also migrated to the Strand, and all three magazines were owned by the same proprietors and supported by most of the old contributors, to whom were added two new recruits: 'The Druid,' alias 'Gayhurst,' alias 'General Chassé,' alias Henry Hall Dixon (1822-70) and Major George John Whyte-Melville (1821-78). The two new hands were better than any of the old, as may be imagined when it is remembered that Dixon came into the world nearly half a century later than Apperley, and that the author of *Market Harborough* and *The Gladiators* was younger than the creator of *Jorrocks* and *Soapy Sponge* by more than thirty years.

If any writers could have made the three combined magazines (*tria juncta in uno*) a success, Dixon and Whyte-Melville, aided by the best horse-painters in England, and by such contributors as Carleton, Arthur Cecil, Lord William Lennox, 'Actæon,' Surtees, and Robert Vyner (author of *Notitia Venatica*), were the men to do it. But Carleton died in 1856, having signalised himself by writing some clever sketches of sporting celebrities, including Mr. Wyndham Smith, alias 'The Assassin.' It so happened that Captain Carleton owed

'The Assassin' £100 on some bygone race, which provoked the latter to exclaim, "If he would only pay me the £100 that he owes me, I shouldn't care a rush if he painted me black, or green, or white, or yellow, and continued so to paint me until the last hour of his life".

If *Post and Paddock, Silk and Scarlet, Scott and Sebright, and Saddle and Sirloin*, unrivalled classics of the Turf, the Chase, the Leash, the Road, and of country life generally, could not save a magazine, there must have been in it such elements of decay as no ability and no energy could long resist. The fact is that in 1870, which witnessed the death of the last of the sporting magazines associated during any portion of their existence with *Nimrod*, periodicals of that description were already anachronisms.

In 1870 daily sporting newspapers sold for a penny a copy ("the all-conquering penny," as Felix Whitehurst dubbed it) had taken the life out of their slow-going monthly predecessors, which saw their prime when railways were in their infancy and telegraphs unknown. It is almost inconceivable that some who will perchance read these words can remember the day when the issue of The Derby at Epsom was carried all over the island by pigeons, and when a greyhound service was organised – as may be seen from an old number of *The Sporting Magazine* – to convey the result of the St. Leger from Doncaster to Manchester.

When the last of the sporting magazines disappeared from existence after a more or less successful career of seventy-eight years, it had lived its life. Decked in the garb of the penny press, which is the greatest elevator, instructor and enlightener that mankind has yet known, "The Schoolmaster" (to quote Lord Henry Brougham's celebrated phrase) "was universally abroad," illuminating and pouring light into the dark places of earth, and disclosing secrets of which *Nimrod* and his blinded contemporaries passed their lives in abysmal ignorance. To hold its own again against the competition of daily sporting newspapers, it is necessary for a monthly magazine to draw from many sources to which its predecessors had no access. They depended mainly on *Nimrod* as their sheet-anchor, and, in Alexander Pope's words –

"The mouse that only trusts to one poor hole
Can never be a mouse of any soul".

Baily's Magazine, on the contrary, has, during its many years of existence. been so conducted as to command the approval of sportsmen in all countries, as its articles have been contributed by experts in hunting, racing, shooting, fishing, coursing, and every other branch of domestic sports. No less, also, than by others familiar with tiger-shooting in India; with lion-hunting in South Africa; with stalking mountain sheep and elk in the Rockies; with catching devil-fish and tarpon in the Gulf of Mexico, and with pursuing fur, fish, and feather all over the world. In diversity of topics *Baily's* need not fear comparison with any predecessor or contemporary on earth. This magazine, at any rate, will never commit the mistake of riding at single anchor; or, in other words, of depending solely on the supposed attractiveness of one powerful and paramount wielder of the pen.

INDEX

(Vols. 1 - 125, 1860 - 1926, 796 issues)

1	March - September 1860	Issues 1 - 7	(p434)
2	October 1860 - April 1861	Issues 8 - 14	(p420)
3	May - November 1861	Issues 15 - 21	(p376)
4	December 1861 - June 1862	Issues 22 - 28	(p378)
5	July 1862 - January 1863	Issues 29 - 35	(p374)
6	February - August 1863	Issues 36 - 42	(p374)
7	September 1863 - March 1864	Issues 43 - 49	(p374)
8	April - October 1864	Issues 50 - 56	(p376)
9	November 1864 - May 1865	Issues 57 - 63	(p374)
10	June - December 1865	Issues 64 - 70	(p372)
11	January - July 1866	Issues 71 - 77	(p382)
12	August 1866 - February 1867	Issues 78 - 84	(p374)
13	March - September 1867	Issues 85 - 91	(p374)
14	October 1867 - April 1868	Issues 92 - 98	(p366)
15	May - November 1868	Issues 99 - 105	(p378)
16	December 1868 - June 1869	Issues 106 - 112	(p370)
17	July 1869 - January 1870	Issues 113 - 119	(p382)
18	February - August 1870	Issues 120 - 126	(p374)
19	September 1870 - March 1871	Issues 127 - 133	(p406)
20	April - October 1871	Issues 134 – 140	(p430)
21	November 1871 - May 1872	Issues 141 - 147	(p430)
22	June - December 1872	Issues 148 - 154	(p422)
23	January - July 1873	Issues 155 – 161	(p430)
24	August 1873 - February 1874	Issues 162 - 168	(p430)
25	March - September 1874	Issues 169 - 175	(p430)
26	October 1874 - April 1875	Issues 176 - 182	(p430)
27	May - November 1875	Issues 183 - 189	(p430)
28	December 1875 - June 1876	Issues 190 – 196	(p430)
29	July 1876 - January 1877	Issues 197 - 203	(p430)
30	February - August 1877	Issues 204 - 210	(p430)
31	September 1877 - March 1878	Issues 211 - 217	(p430)
32	April - October 1878	Issues 218 - 224	(p430)
33	November 1878 - May 1879	Issues 225 – 231	(p430)
34	June - December 1879	Issues 232 - 238	(p430)
35	January - July 1880	Issues 239 - 245	(p430)
36	August 1880 - February 1881	Issues 246 - 252	(p430)
37	March - September 1881	Issues 253 - 259	(p434)
38	October 1881 - April 1882	Issues 260 - 266	(p430)
39	May - November 1882	Issues 267 - 273	(p430)
40	December 1882 - June 1883	Issues 274 – 280	(p430)
41	July 1883 - January 1884	Issues 281 - 287	(p430)

42	February - August 1884	Issues 288 - 294	(p454)
43	September 1884 - March 1885	Issues 295 – 301	(p446)
44	April - October 1885	Issues 302 - 308	(p510)
45	November 1885 - May 1886	Issues 309 - 315	(p474)
46	June - December 1886	Issues 316 - 322	(p534)
47	January - July 1887	Issues 323 - 329	(p486)
48	August 1887 - February 1888	Issues 330 - 336	(p490)
49	March - September 1888	Issues 337 - 343	(p498)
50	October - December 1888	Issues 344 - 346	(p198)
51	January - June 1889	Issues 347 - 352	(p424)
52	July - December 1889	Issues 353 - 358	(p424)
53	January - June 1890	Issues 359 - 364	(p432)
54	July - December 1890	Issues 365 - 370	(p430)
55	January - June 1891	Issues 371 - 376	(p432)
56	July - December 1891	Issues 377 - 382	(p432)
57	January - June 1892	Issues 383 - 388	(p430)
58	July - December 1892	Issues 389 - 394	(p432)
59	January - June 1893	Issues 395 - 400	(p432)
60	July - December 1893	Issues 401 – 406	(p432)
61	January - June 1894	Issues 407 - 412	(p432)
62	July - December 1894	Issues 413 - 418	(p432)
63	January - June 1895	Issues 419 - 424	(p464)
64	July - December 1895	Issues 425 - 430	(p480)
65	January - June 1896	Issues 431 - 436	(p488)
66	July - December 1896	Issues 437 - 442	(p492)
67	January - June 1897	Issues 443 - 448	(p486)
68	July - December 1897	Issues 449 - 454	(p522)
69	January - June 1898	Issues 455 - 460	(p512)
70	July - December 1898	Issues 461 - 466	(p470)
71	January - June 1899	Issues 467 - 472	(p480)
72	July - December 1899	Issues 473 - 478	(p452)
73	January - June 1900	Issues 479 - 484	(p458)
74	July - December 1900	Issues 485 - 490	(p466)
75	January - June 1901	Issues 491 - 496	(p478)
76	July - December 1901	Issues 497 - 502	(p492)
77	January - June 1902	Issues 503 - 508	(p502)
78	July - December 1902	Issues 509 - 514	(p450)
79	January - June 1903	Issues 515 - 520	(p478)
80	July - December 1903	Issues 521 - 526	(p492)
81	January - June 1904	Issues 527 - 532	(p486)
82	July - December 1904	Issues 533 - 538	(p528)
83	January - June 1905	Issues 539 - 544	(p508)
84	July - December 1905	Issues 545 - 550	(p534)
85	January - June 1906	Issues 551 - 556	(p506)
86	July - December 1906	Issues 557 - 562	(p522)

87	January - June 1907	Issues 563 - 568	(p532)
88	July - December 1907	Issues 569 - 574	(p532)
89	January - June 1908	Issues 575 - 580	(p546)
90	July - December 1908	Issues 581 - 586	(p522)
91	January - June 1909	Issues 587 - 592	(p512)
92	July - December 1909	Issues 593 - 598	(p480)
93	January - June 1910	Issues 599 - 604	(p490)
94	July - December 1910	Issues 605 - 610	(p492)
95	January - June 1911	Issues 611 - 616	(p510)
96	July - December 1911	Issues 617 - 622	(p484)
97	January - June 1912	Issues 623 - 628	(p478)
98	July - December 1912	Issues 629 - 634	(p474)
99	January - June 1913	Issues 635 - 640	(p472)
100	July - December 1913	Issues 641 - 646	(p474)
101	January - June 1914	Issues 647 - 652	(p472)
102	July - December 1914	Issues 653 - 658	(p342)
103	January - June 1915	Issues 659 - 664	(p288)
104	July - December 1915	Issues 665 - 670	(p282)
105	January - June 1916	Issues 671 - 676	(p286)
106	July - December 1916	Issues 677 - 682	(p292)
107	January - June 1917	Issues 683 - 688	(p288)
108	July - December 1917	Issues 689 - 694	(p288)
109	January - June 1918	Issues 695 - 700	(p288)
110	July - December 1918	Issues 701 - 706	(p282)
111	January - June 1919	Issues 707 - 712	(p284)
112	July - December 1919	Issues 713 - 718	(p284)
113	January - June 1920	Issues 719 - 724	(p284)
114	July - December 1920	Issues 725 - 730	(p284)
115	January - June 1921	Issues 731 - 736	(p284)
116	July - December 1921	Issues 737 - 742	(p284)
117	January - June 1922	Issues 743 - 748	(p284)
118	July - December 1922	Issues 749 - 754	(p284)
119	January - June 1923	Issues 755 - 760	(p284)
120	July - December 1923	Issues 761 - 766	(p284)
121	January - June 1924	Issues 767 - 772	(p288)
122	July - December 1924	Issues 773 - 778	(p284)
123	January - June 1925	Issues 779 - 784	(p284)
124	July - December 1925	Issues 785 - 790	(p284)
125	January - June 1926	Issues 791 - 796	(p288)

New Bridge Street in 1891

Volume 1, March - September 1860

Issue 1 : March 1860

Portrait of Alfred Day, jockey	Title page
Portrait and Biography - Henry Rous	(p1-4)
The Experiences of Sydney Godolphin Yahoo esq (parts 1 & 2) by Francis Francis	(p4-14)
The English Race Horse (part 1) by Henry Rous	(p14-20)
Thomas Assheton-Smith by John Eardley-Wilmot	(p21-25)
From Oxford to St.George's (part 1 - College Life) by Edward Bradley	(p25-33)
Cricket in 1860 by Nicholas Wanostrocht	(p33-37)
A Trip to Berkshire by Frank Fielding	(p37-42)
The Leash by John Walsh	(p43-47)
Our Portfolio [inc. *The Sporting Life* Libel Trial; Lord Redesdale's Proposed Bill on Jockey Weights; The Huntsmen's Club]	(p48-51)
The Dramatic and Musical World of London	(p52-55)
Betting on the Derby [and other races]	(p56)

Issue 2 : April 1860

Portrait and Biography - Francis Russell	(p57-59)
The Experiences of Sydney Godolphin Yahoo esq (parts 3 & 4) by Francis Francis	(p60-70)
The English Race Horse (part 2) by Henry Rous	(p70-77)
From Oxford to St.George's (part 2) by Edward Bradley	(p77-92)
Coursing at Waterloo and Ashdown by John Walsh	(p92-98)
A Chapter on Guns by John Walsh	(p98-101)
Our Jockeys (part 1)	(p101-106)
The Bang-Tailed Bay [verses]	(p106-107)
Racing Statistics	(p107-109)
Our Portfolio [inc. Obituary of John Day; Lord Redesdale's Bill; Cricket; Yachting]	(p109-113)
The Dramatic and Musical World of London	(p113-117)
Betting on the Derby [and other races]	(p118)

Issue 3 : May 1860

Portrait and Biography – Henry Somerset	(p119-124)
The Experiences of Sydney Godolphin Yahoo esq (parts 5 & 6) by Francis Francis	(p125-141)
The Battle of Farnborough [Fight: Sayers versus Heenan]	(p141-145)
The Past Fox-Hunting Season (part 1) by George Lane-Fox	(p145-153)
From Oxford to St.George's (part 3) by Edward Bradley	(p153-169)
Oxford and Cambridge University Boat-Race of 1860	(p169-171)
London Rowing Club report	(p171-172)
Our Portfolio [inc. *Bell's Life* Fight Edition; Spring Race Meetings; Surrey County Cricket Club]	(p173-177)
The Dramatic and Musical World of London	(p177-181)
Betting on the Derby [and other races]	(p182)

Issue 4 : June 1860

Portrait and Biography - George Payne	(p183-186)
From Oxford to St.George's (part 4) by Edward Bradley	(p186-200)
Abdel Kader on the Arab by Charles Churchill	(p200-204)
The Experiences of Sydney Godolphin Yahoo esq (part 7) by Francis Francis	(p204-215)
George Parr - A Biography by Nicholas Wanostrocht	(p215-220)
The Past Fox-Hunting Season (part 2) by George Lane-Fox	(p220-228)
[Obituary] Old John Day	(p228-234)

Our Portfolio [inc. The Derby; Yachting; Public Schools Cricket; Royal Thames Yacht Club;
        Review of Lillywhite's Guide for 1860]   (p234-242)
The Dramatic and Musical World of London   (p242-246)

Issue 5 : July 1860

Portrait and Biography - James Carr-Boyle   (p247-250)
From Oxford to St.George's (part 5) by Edward Bradley   (p250-267)
Our Jockeys (part 2)   (p267-272)
The Experiences of Sydney Godolphin Yahoo esq (parts 8 & 9) by Francis Francis   (p273-288)
Henley Royal Regatta   (p288-293)
The Great Match - Horses versus Hounds   (p293-297)
Our Portfolio [inc. Tattersall's Sales; Stockbridge Races; Lord Redesdale's Bill Withdrawn;
        Cricket Reports; Royal Thames Yacht Club]   (p298-308)
The Dramatic and Musical World of London   (p308-310)

Issue 6 : August 1860

Portrait and Biography - Brownlow Cecil   (p311-315)
The English Race Horse (part 3) by Henry Rous   (p315-320)
From Oxford to St.George's (part 6) by Edward Bradley   (p320-334)
My First Insurance Company (part 1)   (p334-338)
The Experiences of Sydney Godolphin Yahoo esq (parts 10 & 11*) by Francis Francis   (p338-354)
The Thames Grand National Regatta   (p355-360)
Kingston-Upon-Thames Regatta   (p360-363)
Cricket [inc. All England Eleven and Marylebone Cricket Club Matches]   (p363-369)
The Dramatic and Musical World of London   (p369-376)

Issue 7 : September 1860

Portrait and Biography - Thomas Dundas   (p377-382)
From Oxford to St.George's (parts 7 & 8) by Edward Bradley   (p383-394)
Cowes Regatta   (p394-398)
The Experiences of Sydney Godolphin Yahoo esq (parts 11* & 12) by Francis Francis   (p398-415)
My First Insurance Company (part 2)   (p415-421)
[Review] *Reminiscences of an Old Sportsman* by John Hamilton   (p421-425)
Cricket [inc. Canterbury Week and Marylebone Cricket Club & Ground Matches]   (p425-430)
Doggett's Coat and Badge [Rowing]   (p430)
The Dramatic and Musical World of London   (p431-434)

Volume 2, October 1860 - April 1861

Issue 8 : October 1860

Portrait of John Wells, jockey   Title page
Portrait and Biography - Edward Stanley   (p1-6)
Sporting and Pheasant Rearing in France [with plans]   (p7-10)
From Oxford to St.George's (part 9) by Edward Bradley   (p10-22)
Angling Haunts (part 1) - Rowsley [Derbyshire] by John Gamgee   (p22-28)
Tom Cribb's Training   (p28-30)
The Experiences of Sydney Godolphin Yahoo esq (part 13) by Francis Francis   (p30-37)
Race for the Championship of the Thames   (p38-39)
Cricket [inc. Gentlemen of Surrey and Surrey County Cricket Club Player Averages]   (p39-47)
Our Van edited by Irwin Willes [inc. Leamington Stakes; Doncaster Races]   (p47-51)
The Dramatic and Musical World of London   (p51-54)

Issue 9 : November 1860

Portrait and Biography - George Stanhope (p55-58)
My First Vacation by Henry Stanley (p59-71)
Her Majesty's Stag Hounds: Season 1860-61 by John Ponsonby (p71)
Lord Lonsdale's Hunt [Tring] by William Lowther (p72)
An Opening Address to all Fox-Hunters by George Lane-Fox (p72-75)
The Experiences of Sydney Godolphin Yahoo esq (part 14) by Francis Francis (p75-84)
Cub Hunting by Knightley Horlock (p85-93)
[Review] *The Tommiebeg Shootings* by Thomas Jeans (p93-97)
Our Van [inc. Jockey Club Meeting; Hunting Reports; Obituary of Charles Gordon-Lennox] (p97-104)
The Dramatic and Musical World of London (p104-106)

Issue 10 : December 1860

Portrait and Biography - John Gully (p107-113)
Fox-Hunting by Knightley Horlock (p114-122)
The Surrey Union Hunt [Leatherhead] by Frederick Hankey (p122)
The Vine Hunt [Overton] by Arthur Whieldon (p123)
The Essex Union Hunt [Ingatestone] by Daniel Scratton (p124)
The Essex Hunt [Harlow] by Joseph Arkwright (p124)
The Essex & Suffolk Hunt [Colchester] by William White (p125)
From Oxford to St.George's (parts 10-11) by Edward Bradley (p125-135)
Bear Shooting in Russia (parts 1 & 2) by Hayward Seton-Karr (p135-145)
Engraving: George Parr, cricketer (facing p139)
The Experiences of Sydney Godolphin Yahoo esq (part 15) by Francis Francis (p145-154)
Our Van [inc. Turkish Baths for Horses; North Devon Hunt;
          Obituary of John Wanless (of *Bell's Life*); Quorn Hunt] (p155-164)
The Dramatic and Musical World of London (p164-168)

Issue 11 : January 1861

Portrait and Biography - Tatton Sykes (p169-174)
Masters of Fox-Hounds by Knightley Horlock (p174-182)
The Oakley Hunt [Bedford] by Robert Arkwright (p183)
The York & Ainsty Hunt by Charles Slingsby (p184)
A Shooting: How to Manage and Mismanage by John Walsh (p184-190)
One More Word on Fox-Hunting by George Lane-Fox (p190-196)
From Oxford to St.George's (part 12) by Edward Bradley (p196-206)
Bear Shooting in Russia (part 3) by Hayward Seton-Karr (p207-213)
Our Van [inc. Hendon National Hunt; Croydon Steeplechases; Gentlemen Jockeys;
          Quorn Hunt; Hursley Hounds] (p213-223)
The Dramatic and Musical World of London (p223-228)

Issue 12 : February 1861

Portrait and Biography - Henry Temple (p229-235)
Independent and Dependent Masters of Fox-Hounds by Knightley Horlock (p235-245)
Wild Sports of the Neilgherry Mountains (part 1) by Henry Leveson (p245-256)
The Horse and his Rider by Charles Clarke (p256-263)
Lord Dacre's Hunt [Welwyn] by Thomas Trevor (p264)
Old Berkshire Hunt [Abingdon] by Charles Duffield (p265)
Mr Hill's Hunt [Pickering] by John Hill (p266)
The Experiences of Sydney Godolphin Yahoo esq (part 16) by Francis Francis (p266-279)
Coursing by Charles Conquest (p279-283)

Our Van [inc. Newmarket Heath Tax; York & Ainsty Hunt;
       Obituaries of Charles White (*Martingale*) and William Justice]   (p283-289)
The Dramatic and Musical World of London   (p289-294)

Issue 13 : March 1861

Portrait and Biography - George Osbaldeston   (p295-306)
A Few Words on the Sagacity of Huntsmen by Thomas Gosden   (p306-311)
The Oakley Hunt 1836 [verses] by Thomas Gosden   (p311-312)
The South Essex Hunt [Romford] by Thomas Lennard   (p312)
Lord Middleton's Fox-Hounds [Malton] by Henry Willoughby   (p313)
The Bramham Moor Hunt [Tadcaster] by George Lane-Fox   (p314)
On the Shape and Make of a Horse [verses]   (p314-315)
The Team and its Drivers by Charles Clarke   (p315-322)
Wild Life (part 1) by Charles Clarke   (p323-329)
Huntsmen, Amateur and Professional by Knightley Horlock   (p329-339)
Cricket: Preview of the Season   (p339-343)
Billiard Entertainments at Brighton by Edward Mardon   (p344-346)
Our Van [inc. Lincoln Meeting; Chester Cup; Hunt Reports;
       Reviews of *The Angler's Register* by Francis Francis, *The Life of a Foxhound*
       by John Mills and *The Stud Book* by James Weatherby]   (p346-353)
The Dramatic and Musical World of London   (p353-356)

Issue 14 : April 1861

Portrait and Biography - James Merry   (p357-363)
On the Roman Bath as Applicable to Training Racehorses by Henry Rous   (p363-369)
School Life: Its Sports and Pastimes by Charles Clarke   (p370-377)
The Treatment of Hunters In and Out of Season by Knightley Horlock   (p377-386)
Wild Life (part 2) by Charles Clarke   (p387-393)
The University Boat Race of 1861   (p393-397)
The Experiences of Sydney Godolphin Yahoo esq (part 17) by Francis Francis   (p398-407)
Coursing by Charles Conquest   (p407-409)
Our Van [inc. Grand National; Ascot Clerk of Course; Reviews of
       The English Sportsman in the Western Prairies by Grantley Berkeley and
       The Imperial Stables in Paris by Hugh Childers; Obituary of John Holmes]   (p410-417)
The Dramatic and Musical World of London   (p417-420)

Volume 3, May - November 1861

Issue 15 : May 1861

Portrait of Sam Rogers, jockey   Title page
Portrait and Biography - Joseph Hawley   (p1-5)
Volunteers and their Views by Charles Clarke   (p5-14)
Summering of Hunters by Knightley Horlock   (p14-21)
Wild Life (part 3) by Charles Clarke   (p22-31)
[Review] *Market Harborough* by George Whyte-Melville   (p31-37)
Our Van [inc. Northampton Races; Jockey Club Meeting; New Forest Hunt; Hunting Dinners]   (p37-46)
The Dramatic and Musical World of London   (p46-50)

Issue 16 : June 1861

Portrait and Biography - John Rous   (p51-53)
The Beauties of Hampton Court Paddocks by Charles Clarke   (p53-63)
Our Fisheries and their Preservation by Francis Francis   (p63-67)

Wild Life (part 4) by Charles Clarke (p67-75)
On Dog Shows (p76-81)
Adventures in Equatorial Africa by Paul du Chaillu (p81-89)
[Review] *Hints on Horsemanship* by George Greenwood (p89-92)
The Late Francis Russell [and the Sale of his Stud] (p92-93)
Our Van [inc. Newmarket Meeting; The Waterwitch Case] (p94-99)
The Dramatic and Musical World of London (p99-104)

Issue 17 : July 1861

Portrait and Biography - Charles Lennox (p105-106)
Rotten Row and its Riders by Charles Clarke (p107-116)
Wild Life (part 5) by Charles Clarke (p117-121)
[Review] *The Autobiography of a Stage-Coachman* by Thomas Cross (p122-127)
Angling Haunts (part 2): Rowsley Revisited by John Gamgee (p127-137)
Cricket [inc. University and Public Schools' Matches] (p137-144)
Our Van [inc. Epsom Derby; Middle Park Sales; Public Schools' Cricket;
            Royal Academy Sporting Pictures; Ascot Stables Company] (p144-155)
The Dramatic and Musical World of London (p156-160)

Issue 18 : August 1861

Portrait and Biography - Charles Towneley (p161-162)
In Season and Out of Season by Charles Clarke (p163-171)
Wild Life (part 6) by Charles Clarke (p172-179)
The Horse Show at Leeds (p180-182)
Our Jockeys (part 3) (p182-188)
[Review] *On House Dogs and Sporting Dogs* by John Meyrick (p188-189)
The Cambridgeshire Gazetteer [verses] (p190)
Wild Sports of the Neilgherry Mountains (part 2) by Henry Leveson (p191-204)
Cricket in June & July by Charlton Lane (p204-210)
Our Van [inc. Stockbridge Cup; Obituaries of Madame La Touche Fay and Edward Irwin] (p210-215)
The Dramatic and Musical World of London (p215-218)

Issue 19 : September 1861

Portrait and Biography - Isaac Wallop (p219-222)
The Agricultural Interest by Charles Clarke (p223-233)
Wild Life (part 7) by Charles Clarke (p233-242)
Arbitration: Francis Rhodes against James Brudenell (p242-245)
Wild Sports of the Neilgherry Mountaind (part 3) by Henry Leveson (p245-256)
Cricket: Close of Marylebone Cricket Club Season; Canterbury Week by Charlton Lane (p256-261)
Our Van [inc. Goodwood Meeting; Brighton Stakes; Yarm Show; Obituaries of
            Justinian Casamajor (aquatic editor *The Field*) and William Oates] (p261-270)
The Dramatic and Musical World of London (p270-272)

Issue 20 : October 1861

Portrait and Biography - Jonathan Peel (p273-278)
Lethifer Auctumnus by Charles Clarke (p278-288)
Fishing and Fishermen by Francis Francis (p288-294)
Hunting in the Himalaya, the Terai and Kashmere (part 1) by Henry Leveson (p294-302)
[Review] *Recollections of a Fox Hunter* by Knightley Horlock (p303-309)
Cricket: Close of the Surrey County Cricket Club Season by Charlton Lane (p309-316)
Our Van [inc. Stockton Meeting; Baden-Baden Races; Great Yorkshire Handicap] (p317-324)
The Dramatic and Musical World of London (p324-326)

Issue 21 : November 1861

Portrait and Biography - George Lane-Fox (p327-329)
Hacks and Hunters by Charles Clarke (p329-339)
Wild Life (part 8) by Charles Clarke (p340-346)
Farming and Fox Hunting by Knightley Horlock (p346-354)
Our Eleven in Winter Quarters [English Cricketers Tour of Australia] by Charlton Lane (p354-357)
Our Jockeys (part 4) (p357-362)
A Few Words With A Legend by Thomas Gosden (p362-363)
A Lay of Glen Lochay [verses] by Thomas Gosden (p363-365)
Our Van [inc. Caesarewich; *Sporting Life* Leader; Quorn Hunt Dispute;
Obituary of Archibald Montgomerie] (p365-372)
The Dramatic and Musical World of London (p372-376)

Volume 4, December 1861 - June 1862

Issue 22 : December 1861

Portrait of Thomas Aldcroft, jockey Title page
Portrait and Biography - Frederic de Lagrange (p1-5)
Woolwich and its Recreations by Charles Clarke (p6-14)
Charlie Thornhill; the Dunce of the Family (parts 1 to 3) by Charles Clarke (p14-31)
Pro Bono Publico by Knightley Horlock (p31-40)
Sporting Notes and Queries (p40-41)
Our Van [inc. Jockeys' Dispute; Worcester Meeting; Vine Hunt; Obituary of George Green;
Continental Races; Painting of the Herefordshire Hunt] (p41-49)
The Dramatic and Musical World of London (p50-54)

Issue 23 : January 1862

Portrait and Biography - William Gratwicke (p55-59)
The Late Prince Consort by Charles Clarke (p59-62)
Charlie Thornhill; the Dunce of the Family (parts 4 to 7) by Charles Clarke (p63-79)
Winter Quarters by Knightley Horlock (p80-87)
Wild Life (part 9) by Charles Clarke (p87-94)
The Biter Bitten (p94-97)
The Pytchley Hunt by John Spencer (p98-99)
Sporting Notes and Queries (p100)
Our Van [inc. Birmingham Cattle Dog Show; *Sporting Life* Inquiry; Quorn Hunt] (p101-107)
The Dramatic and Musical World of London (p107-108)

Issue 24 : February 1862

Portrait and Biography - John Spencer (p109-114)
A Word on Steeplechasing by Charles Clarke (p114-119)
Charlie Thornhill; the Dunce of the Family (parts 8 to 11) by Charles Clarke (p120-136)
Pheasant Shooting by Knightley Horlock (p137-144)
Wild Life (part 10) by Charles Clarke (p144-150)
Fox Hunting Notes of the Past Month by George Lane-Fox (p150-154)
Sporting Notes & Queries (p154)
Our Van [inc. Racing articles in *The Times*; Chantilly Races; Paris Riding School;
Obituaries of Charles Pelham and Thomas Wilkinson] (p155-159)
Art and Dramatic Gossip (p160-162)

Issue 25 : March 1862

Women and their Habits by Charles Clarke (p163-168)
In Season and Out of Season by Knightley Horlock (p168-176)
Charlie Thornhill; the Dunce of the Family (parts 12 to 15) by Charles Clarke (p176-195)
Wild Life (part 11) by Charles Clarke (p195-203)
Fox Hunting Notes of the Past Month by George Lane-Fox (p204-208)
Our Van [inc. Grand Military Steeplechase; Melbourne Races; *Hunting Gazette* reports] (p209-214)
Art and Dramatic Gossip (p215-216)

Issue 26 : April 1862

Portrait and Biography - George Brudenell-Bruce (p217-220)
Alpha and Omega by Charles Clarke (p220-227)
Fox-Hunting Notes of the Past Month by George Lane-Fox (p227-231)
[Review] *Stable Architecture* by Thomas Knightley (p231-232)
Charlie Thornhill; the Dunce of the Family (parts 16 & 17) by Charles Clarke (p232-248)
Portrait and Biography - John Scott (p249-253)
The Turf Market by Irwin Willes (p253-256)
Cricket: Our Eleven in Australia by Charlton Lane (p256-261)
Sporting Notes and Queries (p261-262)
Our Van [inc. Italian Racing; Vatican Foxhunting Banned by Pope Pius IX; Paris Gallops] (p263-268)
Art and Dramatic Gossip (p268-270)

Issue 27 : May 1862

Portrait and Biography - John White (p271-275)
The Pytchley: Hounds, Horses and Men Past and Present (part 1) by Charles Clarke (p275-283)
Ferae Naturae (part 1) [Poachers and Poaching] (p284-290)
Charlie Thornhill; the Dunce of the Family (parts 18 to 20) by Charles Clarke (p290-309)
The University Crews (p309-313)
Sporting Notes and Queries (p313)
A Lay of Modern Rome [verses] (p314)
Our Van [inc. Northampton Meeting; Cheltenham Races; Jockey Club Elections; Craven Hunt; Norfolk Hounds] (p314-322)
Art and Dramatic Gossip (p322-324)

Issue 28 : June 1862

Portrait and Biography - George Grey (p325-333)
The Pytchley: Hounds, Horses and Men Past and Present (part 2) by Charles Clarke (p334-343)
Charlie Thornhill; the Dunce of the Family (parts 21 to 23) by Charles Clarke (p343-362)
Ferae Naturae (part 2) [Poachers and Poaching] (p362-368)
Lament for Old Calabar [verses] by John Davis (p368-369)
The Turf Market by Irwin Willes (p369-372)
Our Van [inc. Newmarket Meeting; Hampton Court Stud; York Races] (p372-378)

Volume 5, July 1862 - January 1863

Issue 29 : July 1862

Portrait of George Thompson, gentleman jockey (Title page)
Portrait and Biography - Richard Bulkeley (p1-4)
John Leech's Gallery of Sketches in Oil by Charles Clarke (p4-12)
Charlie Thornhill; the Dunce of the Family (parts 24 to 26) by Charles Clarke (p12-30)
[Review] *Scott and Sebright* by Henry Hall Dixon (p30-34)

Cricket in June [inc. University Match] by Charlton Lane (p34-39)
Our Van [inc. Epsom Races; Ascot Without The Queen; Tattersall's Sales; Eltham Show; Obituary of Henry Verney] (p39-48)
Art and Dramatic Gossip (p48-50)

Issue 30 : August 1862

Portrait and Biography – Henry Paget (p51-54)
Battersea [International Exhibition] by Charles Clarke (p54-62)
Charlie Thornhill; the Dunce of the Family (parts 27 & 28) by Charles Clarke (p62-77)
Blooming Condition [verses] (p77)
Our Jockeys - John Wells (p77-81)
The Cooperer [verses] by John Davis (p81-82)
The Two Jacobs [verses] by John Davis (p82-83)
Cricket in July [inc. Gentlemen versus Players] by Charlton Lane (p83-91)
The Turf Market by Irwin Willes (p92-94)
Our Van [inc. Stockbridge Races; Great Northern Handicap; Islington Dog Show; Portrait of The Queen and Her Pet Dog Sooty] (p95-102)
Art and Dramatic Gossip (p102-104)

Issue 31 : September 1862

Portrait and Biography – George Byng (p105-108)
Charlie Thornhill; the Dunce of the Family (parts 29 to 31) by Charles Clarke (p108-124)
The Question of the Day [Poaching Prevention Bill] by Charles Clarke (p125-132)
On Otter Hunting (p132-138)
[Review] *Doubtful Crumbs* painted by Edwin Landseer (p138-140)
[Review] *Lillywhite's Cricket Scores and Biographies* by Arthur Haygarth (p140-141)
Cricket in August [inc. Canterbury Cricket Week; John Lillywhite's Law Interpretation] (p141-146)
The Turf Market [inc. Betting in Tottenham Court Road] by Irwin Willes (p147-150)
Our Van [inc. Goodwood Week; Aldershot Military Races; Ebor Meeting; Gainsborough Show] (p150-160)
Art and Dramatic Gossip (p160-162)

Issue 32 : October 1862

Portrait and Biography - Percy Williams (p163-165)
A White Spot in the Black Forest by Charles Clarke (p165-175)
Charlie Thornhill; the Dunce of the Family (parts 32 to 34) by Charles Clarke (p175-193)
Angling Gossip: A Day's Sport in Teviotdale by Francis Francis (p193-199)
Cricket [inc. All England Eleven's Record 503 against Surrey] (p199-203)
Lays of Modern Rome [verses] (p204)
Our Van [inc. Night Poachers' Act; Baden-Baden Steeplechasing; Doncaster Races] (p205-214)
Art and Dramatic Gossip (p214-216)

Issue 33 : November 1862

Portrait and Biography - Henry Villebois (p217-218)
Gentlemen Jockeys by Charles Clarke (p218-227)
Charlie Thornhill; the Dunce of the Family (parts 35 to 37) by Charles Clarke (p227-244)
Shooting in Andalusia by Byng Hall (p244-247)
Cricket: Public School Averages for 1862 (p248-250)
Hunting in the Himalaya, the Terai and Kashmere (part 2) by Henry Leveson (p250-258)
My First Day's Shooting in Brittany by John Kemp (p259-263)
Our Van [inc. Tarragona Affair; Newmarket Meeting; Winchester Grandstand; Obituaries of H.L.Dillon (editor of *Le Sport*), Walter Day and William Chifney] (p263-268)

Art and Dramatic Gossip   (p268-270)

Issue 34 : December 1862

Portrait and Biography - Charles Monck   (p271-274)
Result of the Jockey Club Investigation [Tarragona Affair] by Charles Clarke   (p275-284)
Charlie Thornhill; the Dunce of the Family (parts 38 to 40) by Charles Clarke (p284-300)
The Past, Present and Future of Fox-Hunting (part 1) by George Lane-Fox   (p301-305)
Hunters' Follyes [verses] by Thomas Charretie   (p305-306)
The Tarporley Week by Gage Freeman   (p306-309)
Tarporley Swan-Hopping [verses] by Rowland Egerton-Warburton   (p309-310)
Cricket: Further Public School Averages for 1862   (p311-313)
Our Van [inc. Jockey Club ban on 'Van Driver'; New Masters of Hounds; Hurworth Hunt;
         Winning Stallions Lists; Malton Races Abolished]   (p313-322)
Art and Dramatic Gossip   (p322-324)

Issue 35 : January 1863

Portrait and Biography - Watkin Williams-Wynn   (p325-330)
The Prince of Wales and English Sports and Pastimes by Charles Clarke   (p330-335)
The Tale of the Old Customer   (p336-337)
Charlie Thornhill; the Dunce of the Family (parts 41 & 42) by Charles Clarke   (p338-353)
Gentlemen Riders: George Thompson by Charles Clarke   (p354-356)
A College Fingerpost (part 1)   (p356-364)
Our Van [inc. Croydon Steeplechases; Stud Statistics; Quorn Hunt; West Norfolk
         Hunt Dispute; Obituary of William Gratwicke; Reviews of *Horse Warrantry*
         by William Howlett and *Comic History of England* by Gilbert A'Becket]   (p364-372)
Art and Dramatic Gossip   (p372-374)

George Lane-Fox

Volume 6, February - August 1863

Issue 36 : February 1863

Portrait of Thomas Challoner, jockey   Title page
Portrait and Biography - William Molyneux   (p1-4)
Market Harborough and Steeplechase Reform by Charles Clarke   (p4-14)
Wild Turkey Shooting by Byng Hall   (p14-17)
Charlie Thornhill; the Dunce of the Family (parts 43 & 44) by Charles Clarke   (p18-34)
The Past, Present and Future of Fox-Hunting (part 2) by George Lane-Fox   (p34-42)
Our Van [inc. Quorn Hunt; Suffolk Hounds; Harlestone Stud; Obituaries of James Cresswell
                and Ralph Bullock]   (p43-51)
Art and Dramatic Gossip   (p52-54)

Issue 37 : March 1863

Portrait and Biography - William Selby-Lowndes   (p55-57)
The Master of the Fox Hounds by Charles Clarke   (p57-65)
Charlie Thornhill; the Dunce of the Family (parts 45 to 47) by Charles Clarke   (p65-81)
Thistle Whipping versus Gorse Whipping   (p81-89)
Cricket [inc. Review of *Cricket Scores & Biographies* by Arthur Haygarth]   (p89-91)
Our Van [inc. Carmarthen Steeplechasing; Newmarket Racing; Pytchley Hunt;
                Scarborough Steeplechase; Blackmore Vale Hunt]   (p91-100)
The Turf Market by Irwin Willes   (p100-104)
Art and Dramatic Gossip   (p104-108)

Issue 38 : April 1863

Portrait and Biography - Ernest Duncombe   (p109-110)
The Prince as a Horseman by Charles Clarke   (p111-117)
Snapshots at Snipes   (p117-120)
Charlie Thornhill; the Dunce of the Family (parts 48 & 49) by Charles Clarke   (p120-139)
Ascot by Jeremiah Ives   (p140)
A Night's Fishing on the Toplitz See by William Baillie-Grohman   (p141-148)
Rowing [inc. Chambers versus Everson Championship Race]   (p148-149)
Cricket [inc. Marylebone Cricket Club to Outlaw Throwing] by Charlton Lane   (p150-152)
Our Van [inc. Lincoln Meeting; Isle of Wight Steeplechasing; Crawley & Horsham Hunt;
                Obituaries of John Gully, Tatton Sykes and Henry Fitzroy]   (p152-160)
Art and Dramatic Gossip   (p160-162)

Issue 39 : May 1863

Portrait and Biography - John Brabazon   (p163-164)
A Day with the Quorn by Charles Clarke   (p165-172)
Charlie Thornhill; the Dunce of the Family (parts 50 & 51) by Charles Clarke   (p173-189)
Australian Sketches: Onkaparinga   (p189-195)
The Feathered Game of Texas by Byng Hall   (p195-200)
Rowing [inc. More on Robert Chambers of Newcastle]   (p200-201)
Cricket [inc. Marylebone Cricket Club Debate on Throwing] by Charlton Lane   (p201-206)
Our Van [inc. Punchestown Races; Kildare Hunt; Hambledon Hunt Steeplechases;
                Hampshire Hounds]   (p207-214)
Art and Dramatic Gossip   (p214-216)

Issue 40 : June 1863

Portrait and Biography - Maurice Berkeley   (p217-219)

One More Day with the Quorn by Charles Clarke (p220-233)
Game and Gamekeepers by Hugh Neville (p234-243)
Hampton Court & Middle Park [Sales] by Charles Clarke (p243-253)
Rowing [inc. Henley Regatta Alteration of Dates; Scullers' Races] (p253-254)
Cricket [inc. More on Marylebone Cricket Club Law Changes] by Charlton Lane (p255-258)
Our Van [inc. Chester Cup; Epsom Derby Day; Islington Dog Show;
            Beaufort Hounds in France] (p258-267)
Art and Dramatic Gossip (p267-270)

Issue 41 : July 1863

Portrait and Biography - Charles Manners (p271-273)
On the Breeding of Hunters and Roadsters by Charles Clarke (p273-283)
A College Fingerpost (part 2) (p284-291)
The Dog: English and French by Charles Clarke (p291-299)
Bears: Grizzly and Polar by Grantley Berkeley (p299-307)
The Fur of Texas by Byng Hall (p307-313)
Our Van [inc. Chantilly Races; Wye Meeting; Exeter Agricultural Show;
            Master of Foxhounds Dinner at Boodle's Club] (p313-320)
Art and Dramatic Gossip (p321-324)

Issue 42 : August 1863

Portrait and Biography - Richard Naylor (p325-328)
A Word or Two on The Turf by Charles Clarke (p328-339)
The Four-in-Hand Club by John Timbs (p339-341)
Racing Reforms: Alterations in Rules for Racing (p341-347)
A Week of Forest and Prairie Life (part 1) by Emerson Bennett (p348-353)
Rowing [inc. Thames Races; Chambers versus Green] (p353-357)
[Review] The Angler Naturalist by Henry Cholmondeley-Pennell (p357-359)
Cricket [inc. University and Public Schools Matches] by Charlton Lane (p359-364)
Our Van [inc. The Cremorne Case; Winchester Racing Articles of Agreement; Hamburg
            Agricultural Show; Obituaries of George Manning, Massey Stanley and
            John Daly] (p364-371)
Art and Dramatic Gossip (p372-374)

Volume 7, September 1863 - March 1864

Issue 43 : September 1863

Portrait of George Fordham, jockey Title page
Portrait and Biography - Evelyn Boscawen (p1-3)
Agriculture and Horseflesh in the North of Germany by Charles Clarke (p4-16)
[Review] Fifty Years Biographical Reminiscences by William Lennox (p16-22)
A Week of Forest and Prairie Life (part 2) by Emerson Bennett (p22-29)
Rowing [inc. Tyneside Races; Kew Regatta] (p29-32)
A College Fingerpost (part 3) (p32-35)
Shark Fishing by Grantley Berkeley (p35-43)
Cricket [inc. Canterbury Week; I Zingari/Band of Brothers Match] by Charlton Lane (p44-45)
Our Van [inc. Goodwood Meeting; York Ebor Races; Northern Yearlings Sales] (p45-52)
Art and Dramatic Gossip (p52-54)

Issue 44 : October 1863

Portrait and Biography - William Vane (p55-58)
Autumn Leaves from the Black Forest by Charles Clarke (p58-68)

The Breeding of Hunters and Hacks by Henry Smurthwaite   (p68-73)
The Early Days of a Master of the Fox Hounds (part 1) by George Lane-Fox   (p73-87)
Rowing [inc. Tyne, Kew and Cork Harbour Regattas]   (p88-92)
Cricket [states that '1863 was the Finest ever Season'] by Charlton Lane   (p92-93)
Our Van [inc. Baden-Baden Races; Doncaster Meeting; Cleveland Hound Show; Tatton Sykes'
       Yorkshire Sales; Obituary of James Morrell]   (p94-104)
Art and Dramatic Gossip   (p104-108)

Issue 45 : November 1863

Portrait and Biography - Thomas Egerton   (p109-112)
The Sport of Kings by Charles Clarke   (p113-125)
The Sires of the Day: Newminster by Henry Smurthwaite   (p125-130)
The Early Days of a Master of the Fox Hounds (part 2) by George Lane-Fox   (p130-139)
A College Fingerpost (part 4)   (p139-145)
Rowing [inc. Obituary of Tom Mackinney; London Rowing Club]   (p145-146)
Cricket [inc. Public School Averages; Parr's Team in Australia] by Charlton Lane   (p146-151)
Our Van [inc. Newmarket's Portland Stand; Weighing Room Scandal; Atherstone Hunt]   (p151-159)
Art and Dramatic Gossip   (p159-162)

Issue 46 : December 1863

Portrait and Biography - Carnegie Jervis   (p163-168)
The Recreations of an English Watering Place by Charles Clarke   (p168-177)
The Early Days of a Master of the Fox Hounds (part 3) by George Lane-Fox   (p178-190)
[Review] *Dartmoor Days or Scenes in the Forest* by Edward Davies   (p190-191)
What the Present Generation are Made Of   (p192-195)
Essay on Gambling by Charles Clarke   (p195-199)
The Sires of the Day - Stockwell and Rataplan by Henry Smurthwaite   (p199-205)
Rugby School Cricket Averages   (p205)
Edward Mills Grace   (p206-208)
Cricket Gossip by Charlton Lane   (p208)
Our Van [inc. Shrewsbury Racing; Winning Jockeys' Statistics; Tattersall's New Offices;
       Constantinople Races; Cotswold Hunt]   (p209-216)

Issue 47 : January 1864

Portrait and Biography - Charles Greville   (p217-221)
The Merry Beagles   (p222-224)
The Early Days of a Master of the Fox Hounds (part 4) by George Lane-Fox   (p224-236)
The Late Trespass Case [* Well worth Reading *]   (p236-240)
The Sires of the Day - King Tom, Voltigeur and Blackock by Henry Smurthwaite   (p240-247)
Fox Hunting in South Wales   (p247-255)
Paul Pendril (part 1) by Edward Davies   (p255-262)
Our Van [inc. Newmarket Sales; Cheshire Hunt; German Jockey Club;
       Codification of Football; Obituary of Goodman Levy]   (p262-270)

Issue 48 : February 1864

Portrait and Biography - Charles Slingsby   (p271-272)
The Grand National Hunt Steeplechase by Charles Clarke   (p273-281)
Paul Pendril (part 2) by Edward Davies   (p282-291)
The Early Days of a Master of the Fox Hounds (part 5) by George Lane-Fox   (p291-302)
The Breeding of Hunters by Wellington Cotton   (p302-303)
The Sires of the Day: Sweetmeat, Kingston, Touchstone and Orlando by Henry Smurthwaite   (p304-310)

Our Van [inc. Horse Nomenclature; York & Ainsty Hounds; Berkeley Hunt;
        Trelawney Banquet]   (p310-322)
Art and Dramatic Gossip   (p322-324)

Issue 49 : March 1864

Portrait and Biography - Francis Wemyss   (p325-328)
Mens Sana in Corpore Sano by Charles Clarke   (p328-335)
How the Late Frost was all Owing to Charley Grey   (p335-341)
The Early Days of a Master of the Fox Hounds (part 6) by George Lane-Fox   (p341-355)
The Sires of the Day: Wild Dayrell and Oulston by Henry Smurthwaite   (p355-361)
[Review] *Fish Hatching* by Frank Buckland   (p361-362)
On Steeplechasing and its Bearing on Horse Breeding   (p363-365)
Our Van [inc.National Coursing Club; Lambourn Gallops; Bramham Moor Hunt;
        East Dorset Hounds]   (p365-374)

Volume 8, April - October 1864

Issue 50 : April 1864

Portrait of George Fordham, jockey [error in picture]   Title page
Portrait and Biography - Augustus Bampfylde   (1-6)
University Competition in General and the Boat Race by Charles Clarke   (p6-16)
Paul Pendril (part 3) by Edward Davies   (p17-26)
The Close of the Season [verses]   (p26-27)
The Sires of the Day: Lord of Isles to Flying Dutchman by Henry Smurthwaite   (p27-33)
Woodcock Shooting in Wales   (p33-41)
Cricket, Colonial: The Trip of the Twelve [to Australia] by Charlton Lane   (p42-45)
Our Van [inc. Aintree Meeting; Rugby Steeplechasing; Coursing Season; Isle of Wight Hounds;
        Obituary of James Maxse]   (p45-54)

Issue 51 : May 1864

Portrait and Biography - Richard Ten Broeck   (p55-57)
A Few Words on Sporting Literature and Journalism by Charles Clarke   (p58-68)
The Close of the Hunting Season by Irwin Willes   (p68-71)
The Early Days of a Master of the Fox Hounds (part 7) by George Lane-Fox   (p71-80)
The Sires of the Day [Thoroughbreds] by Henry Smurthwaite   (p80-85)
The Breeding of Hunters by William Cotton   (p85-87)
My Maiden Mount   (p88-90)
Trout Fishing on the Western Waters   (p90-93)
Cricket: Marylebone Cricket Club [Purchase of Lord's Ground] by Charlton Lane   (p94-97)
Our Van [inc. Melton Steeplechase; Northampton Races; Kildare Meeting; Irish Agricultural
        Show; Obituaries of Fitzroy Stanhope and Frederick Magennis]   (p97-108)

Issue 52 : June 1864

Portrait and Biography - Francis Popham   (p109-112)
The National Sport and the National Taste by Charles Clarke   (p112-121)
The Grand Military Steeplechases Near Versailles   (p121-123)
Paul Pendril (part 4) by Edward Davies   (p123-134)
The Early Days of a Master of the Fox Hounds (part 8) by George Lane-Fox   (p134-144)
A Box for the Season by Charles Clarke   (p144-151)
Rowing [inc. Formation of Pride of the Thames Rowing Club]   (p151-153)
The Otter King [mainly verses]   (p153-154)

Our Van [inc. Knavesmire Racing; Epsom Derby; Obituary of Brabason Higgins;
      Reviews of *Hunting Tours* by Cornelius Tongue and *The Fisherman's Magazine*
      edited by Henry Cholmondeley-Pennell] (p155-162)

Issue 53 : July 1864

Portrait and Biography - William Tailby (p163-165)
Admiral Rous and the Irish Turf by Charles Clarke (p165-171)
Provincial Cricket by Charlton Lane (p171-175)
The Early Days of a Master of the Fox Hounds (part 9) by George Lane-Fox (p175-188)
Paul Pendril (part 5) by Edward Davies (p188-195)
The Sires of the Day: Cotherstone and Bay Middleton by Henry Smurthwaite (p195-199)
Rowing [inc. Henley Regatta] (p199-204)
Cricket [inc. More on Purchase of Lord's Cricket Ground] by Charlton Lane (p205-208)
Our Van [inc. Bois de Boulogne Grand Prix; Ascot Meeting; Stockbridge Races;
      Hornsey Wood Pigeon Handicap] (p208-218)

Issue 54 : August 1864

Portrait and Biography - Henry Lowther (p219-221)
Eton and Harrow or Pearls Before Swine by Charles Clarke (p221-228)
Paul Pendril (part 6) by Edward Davies (p228-239)
The Islington Horse Exhibition (p239-245)
On the Plains by Grantley Berkeley (p245-252)
Cricket: The Public Schools Matches of 1864 by Charlton Lane (p252-257)
Rowing [Thames Regattas at Walton, Kingston and Barnes] (p257-261)
Our Van [inc. More on Irwin Willes' Ban; Newcastle Racing; Winchester Meeting;
      Sale of Henry Bentinck's Hunters; Reviews of *Pictures of the Past* by William
      Bradfield, *Sackville Chase* by Charles Collins and *Tales and Traits of Sporting
      Life* by Henry Corbet] (p262-272)
Answers to Correspondents (p272)

Issue 55 : September 1864

Portrait and Biography - Francis Fane (p273-275)
Paul Pendril (part 7) by Edward Davies (p275-282)
The Early Days of a Master of the Fox Hounds (part 10) by George Lane-Fox (p283-296)
Notes on Modern Cricket by James Pycroft (p296-302)
Stag Hunting in Lower Brittany by Frank Featherstone (p302-304)
A College Fingerpost (part 5) (p305-312)
Yachting and Rowing [inc. Cowes Week; Thames Regatta] (p312-316)
Our Van [inc. Wolverhampton Stakes; Darlington Horse Show; Tattersall's Painting by Thomas
      Musgrave Joy; Review of *Game Book for the Season* by William Spiers] (p317-326)

Issue 56 : October 1864

Portrait and Biography - William Craven (p327-329)
Autumnal Leaves by Charles Clarke (p329-340)
Paris Autumn Meeting by Felix Whitehurst (p341-344)
St.Fiacre in the Forest by Frank Featherstone (p344-347)
A Hunting Expedition to the Source of the Ganges (part 1) by Henry Leveson (p348-357)
The Early Days of a Master of the Fox Hounds (part 11) by George Lane-Fox (p357-368)
Our Van [inc. Baden-Baden Races; Doncaster Meeting] (p368-376)

Volume 9, November 1864 - May 1865

Issue 57 : November 1864

Portrait of Jemmy Grimshaw, jockey — Title Page
Portrait and Biography - Henry Paget — (p1-2)
The Death of Pugilism by Charles Clarke — (p3-11)
A Hunting Expedition to the Source of the Ganges (part 2) by Henry Leveson — (p11-20)
A Moot Question - Deterioration in the English Racehorse — (p21-27)
Hare Hunting by Nevill Fitt — (p27-29)
Racing in Paris by Felix Whitehurst — (p30-34)
Shooting at Home and Abroad Contrasted by Byng Hall — (p34-38)
Cricket: Public Schools Averages for 1864 by Charlton Lane — (p38-42)
Our Van [inc. Kelso Races; Fairfield Stud; Coursing; Obituaries of Martin Becher and Samuel Scott; Review of *Sporting Reminiscences of Hampshire* by Nunez Heysham] — (p42-54)

Issue 58 : December 1864

Portrait and Biography - Hugh Lupus — (p55-58)
[Obituary] John Leech by Charles Clarke — (p58-65)
Paul Pendril (part 8) by Edward Davies — (p65-77)
A Few Last Words About Thistle Whipping — (p78-79)
A Hunting Expedition to the Source of the Ganges (part 3) by Henry Leveson — (p79-91)
Cricket: More Public School Averages for 1864 by Charlton Lane — (p92-95)
[Baily's has here devised the now accepted method of calculating batting and bowling statistics, and averages, refining the Eton School attempt of 1852]
Yachting and Rowing [inc. Chambers versus Cooper Match] — (p95-97)
The Davenport Delusions — (p98-100)
The Sporting Gazette [About Plagiarising *Baily's*] — (p100-101)
Our Van [inc. Newspaper Racing Hoax; York & Ainsty Hunt; Obituary of Joseph Maiden; More on Nunez Heysham's book on Hampshire Sport] — (p101-108)

Issue 59 : January 1865

Portrait and Biography - John Trollope — (p109-111)
Over A Country [Market Harborough Steeplechase Rules] by Charles Clarke — (p111-120)
High Steppers and Light Steppers — (p121-128)
On Hounds and Hunting in 1864 by Grantley Berkeley — (p128-136)
Paul Pendril (part 9) by Edward Davies — (p136-145)
[Review] *Which is the Winner* by Charles Clarke — (p145-148)
A Dartmoor Fox [verses] — (p148-149)
Our Van [inc. Owners' Annual Monetary Winnings; Cottesmore Hunt; Winchester Otterhunting] — (p150-159)
Theatrical Gossip — (p159-162)

Issue 60 : February 1865

Portrait and Biography - Edward Hawke — (p163-166)
The Battue by Charles Clarke — (p166-173)
The Championship [Boxing] — (p173-177)
Discursive Notes on Breeding — (p177-185)
The Preservation of Foxes — (p185-191)
Paul Pendril (part 10) by Edward Davies — (p191-200)
The Thames Preservation Society by Francis Francis — (p200-203)
A Law Wanted — (p204-206)
Paris Sport and Paris Life by Felix Whitehurst — (p206-208)

Our Van [inc. Tattersall's Fountain; Puckeridge Hunt; Obituaries of Charles Greville,
      John Crockford (of *The Field*) and John Anderson] (p208-216)

Issue 61 : March 1865

Portrait and Biography - William Poulett (p217-222)
The Manners and Customs of the Public Schools by Charles Clarke (p223-234)
Man, Methodist and Master [Discussion on Foxes] (p234-241)
On the Value of Continued Racing Qualities by Henry Smurthwaite (p241-244)
A Day with Fox Hounds in the Principalities (p245-254)
A Kill on the Garry in February [verses] (p255-256)
Paris Sport and Paris Life by Felix Whitehurst (p256-260)
Our Van [inc. Launch of *The Sporting Times*; Southdown Hounds; South Berks Hunt;
      Monmouthshire Hunt; Boythorpe Stud; Attempted Bribing of Sports Journalists] (p260-270)

Issue 62 : April 1865

Portrait and Biography - Thomas Christie (p271-272)
Servitude and its Fees by Charles Clarke (p272-281)
Our Beckford of the West (p281-291)
The Best Horse That Ever Looked Through a Bridle by Irwin Willes (p291-296)
[Obituary] Charles de Morny (p296-301)
Paul Pendril (part 11) by Edward Davies (p301-307)
Oxford and Cambridge Athletic Games (p307-310)
Paris Sport and Paris Life by Felix Whitehurst (p310-313)
Our Van [inc. *Le Sport* versus *The Sporting Life*; Aintree Races; Pytchley Hunt;
      Bedale Hounds] (p314-324)

Issue 63 : May 1865

Portrait and Biography - Lydston Newman (p325-326)
University Competition by Land and Water by Charles Clarke (p327-333)
The May Fox (p334-342)
The Grand National Hunt Steeplechase (p342-344)
Bow Bells (p344-347)
Punchestown Races by Comyns Cole (p348-353)
The Autumn Meeting at the Valley of Sweet Waters (p353-360)
Yachting and Rowing: The University Boat Race (p360-364)
Paris Sport and Paris Life by Felix Whitehurst (p364-367)
Our Van [inc. Tattersall's Tribute Exhibition; Wetherby Meeting; Northampton Races;
      Dublin Show; Hertfordshire Foxhounds] (p367-374)

Volume 10, June - December 1865

Issue 64 : June 1865

Portrait of Henry Coventry, gentleman jockey Title Page
Portrait and Biography - William Craven (p1-2)
Testimonials in General and One or Two in Particular by Charles Clarke (p3-9)
Osbaldeston and Russell by George Lane-Fox (p10-19)
Paul Pendril (part 12) by Edward Davies (p19-28)
Lord's: Its Past, Present and Future by Charlton Lane (p28-32)
The Royal Albert Veterinary College by John Gamgee (p32-33)
A Word About Grooms (p33-41)
Yachting and Rowing [inc. Royal Western Yacht Club; Sculling Notes] (p41-43)
Paris Sport and Paris Life by Felix Whitehurst (p43-46)

Our Van [inc. Chester Cup; First Yorkshire Grand National; Hampshire Steeplechasing] (p46-53)
Our Derby Prophecy [verses] by Alfred Ainger (p54)

Issue 65 : July 1865

Portrait and Biography - Richard Mitchell (p55-56)
A Few Parting Words on the Late Derby by Irwin Willes (p57-63)
Competition in the Dog Days by Charles Clarke (p63-72)
On Cross Breeding in Horses by Charles Spooner (p72-76)
The Stuff of Which Derby Winners are Made (part 1) by Charles Clarke (p76-80)
Wolf Hunting in the Wilds of Brittany by Frank Featherstone (p80-85)
The Goodwood Cup 1865 [verses] (p86)
The Matches of the Month by James Pycroft (p86-90)
Yachting and Rowing [inc. Harwich Yacht Race; Kings Lynn Rowing; Tyne Cup] (p90-93)
Paris Sport and Paris Life by Felix Whitehurst (p93-96)
Our Van [inc. Epsom Meeting; *The Derby* (verses); Wye Races; Yearling Sales;
          Obituary of Charles Treadwell; Norwegian Fishing] (p97-108)

Issue 66 : August 1865

Portrait and Biography - Henry Moore (p109-110)
The Horse Show of 1865 by Charles Clark (p111-118)
The Old Squire and Grantley Berkeley by George Osbaldeston (p118-124)
The Crustacean by George Lowth (p125-131)
Paul Pendril (part 13) by Edward Davies (p131-138)
Cricket [inc. Gentlemen versus Players; Universities; Public Schools] by Charlton Lane (p139-146)
Yachting and Rowing [inc. Royal Yacht Clubs' Races; Barnes Regatta] (p146-152)
Paris Sport and Paris Life by Felix Whitehurst (p152-154)
Our Van [inc. Stamford Meeting; Obituaries of John Osborne and John Chisholme] (p154-160)

Issue 67 : September 1865

Portrait and Biography - George Coventry (p161-163)
Glacier Promenades (p163-172)
On Beef by Professor John Gamgee (p173-179)
On Art as Connected with Sporting Pictures and Scenes by Henry Smurthwaite (p179-183)
The Mysteries of Otter Hunting by Frank Featherstone (p183-187)
A Long Time Ago by George Lowth (p188-197)
An Afternoon at Aldershot (p197-199)
Yachting and Rowing [inc. Cowes Week; Thames Regatta] (p199-202)
Paris Sport and Paris Life by Felix Whitehurst (p202-205)
Our Van [inc. Goodwood Races; Brighton Meeting; Yorkshire Show; Launch of
          The Sportsman] (p205-214)

Issue 68 : October 1865

Portrait and Biography - Henry Chaplin (p215-217)
After the Season by Charles Clarke (p217-225)
The Stuff of Which Derby Winners are Made (part 2) by Charles Clarke (p226-230)
Paul Pendril (part 14) by Edward Davies (p230-239)
Masters of Hounds: Eton by George Lowth (p240-249)
[Review] *Field and Fern; Scottish Flocks and Herds* by Henry Hall Dixon (p249-250)
Yachting and Rowing [inc. Cornwall Regatta; Obituary of Alfred Julius, sculler;
          Watermen's Races] (p251-254)
Paris Sport and Paris Life by Felix Whitehurst (p255-259)

Our Van [inc. Baden-Baden Races; Doncaster Meeting; Obituaries of Thomas Bowes-Lyon,
        Emmanuel-Jean Gramont-Caderousse and John Herring]   (p259-268)

Issue 69 : November 1865

Portrait and Biography - Henry Willoughby   (p269-271)
Autumnal Leaves by George Lane-Fox   (p271-279)
The Stuff of Which Derby Winners are Made (part 3) by Charles Clarke   (p279-283)
Salmonia by Humphry Davy   (p283-294)
On Clipping and Trimming Horses by John Gamgee   (p294-300)
Thoughts Upon Things [Racing Comment] by Irwin Willes   (p301-304)
[Review] *The Hunting Grounds of the Old World* by Henry Leveson   (p304-307)
[Review] *Blaine's Outlines of the Veterinary Art* by Charles Steel   (p308-309)
Paris Sport and Paris Life by Felix Whitehurst   (p310-314)
Our Van [inc. Cheshire Hunt; The Cesarewitch; Musselburgh Racecourse; Obituary of Henry
        Temple; Review of *The Queen's Messenger* by Byng Hall;
        Jockey Club Handicappers]   (p314-322)

Issue 70 : December 1865

Portrait and Biography - Frederick Johnstone   (p323-324)
A Word on the Past Racing Season by Charles Clarke   (p324-331)
What's What in Paris by Felix Whitehurst   (p331-337)
Reflections of the Racing Season 1865 (part 1) by Irwin Willes   (p337-342)
The Hunter by George Lowth   (p343-351)
[Review] *The Turf and the Racehorse* by Richard Copperthwaite   (p351-354)
Cricket: Public Schools Averages for 1865 by Charlton Lane   (p354-360)
Paris Sport and Paris Life by Felix Whitehurst   (p360-362)
Our Van [inc. Aintree Meeting; Shrewsbury Races; Warwick Steeplechasing; Hambledon Hunt;
        Obituary of Thomas Sayers]   (p362-372)

Volume 11, January - July 1866

Issue 71 : January 1866

Portrait of Henry Custance, jockey   Title page
Portrait and Biography - James Erskine   (p1-2)
Gentlemen Jockeys by Charles Clarke   (p2-11)
What's What in Paris by Felix Whitehurst   (p11-17)
Reflections of the Racing Season 1865 (part 2) by Irwin Willes   (p17-24)
Our Gentlemen Riders: Henry Coventry by George Lane-Fox   (p24-26)
[Review] *Hunting Sketches* by Anthony Trollope   (p26-27)
The Economic Aspects of Horseshoeing by John Gamgee   (p28-29)
Mountain Harriers by George Lowth   (p29-35)
The Death of a Stag   (p36-40)
Paris Sport and Paris Life by Felix Whitehurst   (p40-43)
Our Van [inc. Sayers Auction; Donnington Park Steeplechasing; Frederic de Lagrange's
        English Turf Winnings; Bedale Hunt; Obituaries of Thomas Ball and
        John Malcombe]   (p43-51)
Christmas at the Theatres   (p51-54)

Issue 72 : February 1866

Portrait and Biography - Charles Barnett   (p55-58)
The Stuff of Which Derby Winners are Made (part 4) by Charles Clarke   (p58-70)
Another Day in the Principalities by Teignmouth Melvill   (p71-79)

What's What in Paris by Felix Whitehurst (p79-86)
Blue and Buff by Leonard Taylor (p86-90)
Cricket: Marylebone Cricket Club Season and Statistics by Charlton Lane (p90-100)
Paris Sport and Paris Life by Felix Whitehurst (p101-102)
Our Van [inc. Middle Park Stud; Bicester Hunt; Obituaries of Harry England, Francis Goodricke, Thomas Charretie and Charles Ramsay] (p102-112)

Issue 73 : March 1866

Portrait and Biography - James Farquharson (p113-118)
The New Enemy to Fox Hunting by George Lane-Fox (p118-126)
The Woodcock and the Snipe: The Poacher and Preacher by George Lowth (p126-134)
The Cattle Plague (part 1) by John Gamgee (p134-137)
The Waterloo Run With the Pytchley (plus map) by Anstruther Thomson (p137-140)
What's What in Paris by Felix Whitehurst (p141-149)
A Run for Life (p149-157)
Paris Sport and Paris Life by Felix Whitehurst (p157-159)
Our Van [inc. *Sporting Life* Libel Case; Danebury Stables; South Berkshire Stakes; Retirement of Charles Davis; Obituaries of Joseph Leeson, John White, Henry Peyton, Henry Clifden and Samuel Day] (p159-170)

Issue 74 : April 1866

Portrait and Biography - Anstruther Thomson (p171-174)
The Laws and Practice of Horse Racing by Henry Rous (p174-185)
What's What in Paris by Felix Whitehurst (p185-195)
The Inter-University Sports by John Graham-Chambers (p195-202)
The Oxford and Cambridge Boat Race by Charles Clarke (p202-205)
The Liverpool Steeplechase (p206)
The Cattle Plague (part 2) by John Gamgee (p207-208)
Paris Sport and Paris Life by Felix Whitehurst (p208-211)
Our Van [inc. Grand National Betting; Whitewall Stud; Hambledon Hunt; Obituaries of Caroline Towneley and John Beck] (p211-221)
Death of Captain Parry [verses] by Thomas Charretie (p220)
Theatrical Easter (p222-224)

Issue 75 : May 1866

Portrait and Biography - Richard Sutton (p225-227)
The Mysteries of Otter Hunting by Frank Featherstone (p228-237)
A Day With the Roman Hounds by Byng Hall (p237-243)
Becher and Beechwood: A Run with the Atherstone by Richard Curzon-Howe (p244-248)
Spring Hunting in 1866 (p248-250)
The Last Day with the Prince of Wales' Harriers (p250-252)
How I Won my Wager (p252-256)
What's What in Paris by Felix Whitehurst (p256-263)
Cricket in 1866 [Preview of the Season] by Charlton Lane (p263-266)
Paris Sport and Paris Life by Felix Whitehurst (p266-268)
Our Van [inc. Grand National Hunt Stewards; Punchestown Steeplechasing; Chester Cup; Surrey Staghounds] (p269-278)

Issue 76 : June 1866

Portrait and Biography - Henry Hastings (p279-281)
Ad Montem [Certain Eton Customs] by George Lowth (p281-293)
An Hour at an Ostrich [Ostrich Chasing at Cape Town] by Alfred Wilks-Drayson (p293-299)

Rods and Routes [Fishing in Surrey and Berkshire]   (p299-303)
[Review] *Sporting Sketches Home and Abroad* by Horace Wheelwright   (p303-304)
What's What in Paris by Felix Whitehurst   (p305-313)
Cricket: The May Matches by Charlton Lane   (p314-319)
Paris Sport and Paris Life by Felix Whitehurst   (p319-322)
Our Van [inc. Epsom Races; Islington Horse Show Scandal]   (p322-332)

Issue 77 : July 1866

Portrait and Biography – Ulick de Burgh   (p333-337)
Expenses of Fox Hunting Establishments by George Lane-Fox   (p337-345)
Dartmoor Fishing and an Italian Battue by George Lowth   (p345-354)
The Autobiography of an Old Oak Table (part 1) by Alfred Smith   (p354-363)
[Review] *Researches into the History of the British Dog* by George Jesse   (p363)
Yachting and Rowing [inc. Watermen's Matches; National Thames Regatta]   (p364-368)
Cricket [inc. University Matches; Gentlemen versus Players] by Charlton Lane   (p368-371)
Our Van [inc. Paddock Tax; Middle Park Sales; Admiral Rous Dinner; Obituaries of George
      Stanhope, Bellingham Graham, James Erskine and James Wigram]   (p371-382)

Volume 12, August 1866 - February 1867

Issue 78 : August 1866

Portrait of George Ede, gentleman jockey   Title page
Portrait and Biography - Henry Pelham-Clinton   (p1-3)
Over the Hills   (p3-9)
The Felon Hunt by George Lowth   (p10-22)
Cricket [inc. Gentlemen versus Players; Public Schools' Scorecards] by Charlton Lane   (p22-28)
The Autobiography of an Old Oak Table (part 2) by Alfred Smith   (p28-36)
What's What in Paris by Felix Whitehurst   (p37-43)
Paris Sport and Paris Life by Felix Whitehurst   (p43-46)
Our Van [inc. Northumberland Plate; Palmerston Breeding Association; I Zingari Cricket]   (p46-54)

Issue 79 : September 1866

Portrait and Biography - Thomas Chamberlayne   (p55-59)
Heavy Betting by Charles Clarke   (p59-68)
High Leicestershire [The Quorn, Belvoir & Cottesmore] by George Lowth   (p68-77)
What's What in Paris by Felix Whitehurst   (p77-86)
[Obituary] The Squire: George Osbaldeston   (p86-90)
Yachting and Rowing [inc. Thames Races; Various Regattas]   (p90-96)
Paris Sport and Paris Life by Felix Whitehurst   (p96-98)
Our Van [inc. Goodwood Meeting; Stockton Races; York Foxhound Show]   (p98-108)

Issue 80 : October 1866

Portrait and Biography – George Lambton   (p109-111)
Excited Yorkshire [Doncaster and the St.Leger] by George Wilson   (p111-116)
The Belle of the Hunt [Ellen Lacey]   (p116-121)
Lost and Found: A Bush Adventure [South Africa]   (p121-127)
What's What in Paris by Felix Whitehurst   (p127-138)
A Week at Ballina in July [Angling]   (p138-144)
Up in the Heather   (p144-147)
Yachting and Rowing [inc. Obituary of Gilbert East; Cowes Regatta]   (p147-150)
Paris Sport and Paris Life by Felix Whitehurst   (p150-153)
Our Van [inc. Baden-Baden Meeting; Obituary of Edward Sherman; Hooton Loo Fishing]   (p153-162)

Issue 81 : November 1866

Portrait and Biography - Richard Bourke (p163-164)
Kirby Gate [Quorn Hunt] by George Lowth (p164-169)
The Autobiography of an Old Oak Table (part 3) by Alfred Smith (p169-181)
What's What in Paris by Felix Whitehurst (p181-190)
How the Return Match was Played at Lough Conn [Angling] (p190-194)
The Oaks, AD 802 by George Lowth (p195-203)
[Review] Cricket Quiddities: *Jerks In From Short Leg* by Robert Fitzgerald (p203-205)
Paris Sport and Paris Life by Felix Whitehurst (p205-208)
Our Van [inc. Obituaries of Harry Grimshaw, Charles Martin, Jem Mason and Charles Davis;
      Eastern Counties Handicap; Harrow Cricket Ground; Review of *Life in Tahiti*
      by Dora Hort] (p208-216)

Issue 82 : December 1866

Portrait and Biography - George Howe (p217-218)
What's What in Paris by Felix Whitehurst (p218-229)
[Obituary] James (Jem) Mason (p229-236)
Reflections of the Racing Season, 1866 by Irwin Willes (p236-249)
The Bear Slayer (p249-253)
A Dirge to the Memory of Charles Davis, late Huntsman to Queen Victoria [verses] (p254)
Cricket: Public School Averages for 1866 by Charlton Lane (p255-260)
Paris Sport and Paris Life by Felix Whitehurst (p260-263)
Our Van [inc. Aintree Meeting; Melton Hunt; Carmarthen Steeplechases; Algeria
      Shooting Party] (p263-270)

Issue 83 : January 1867

Portrait and Biography - Harcourt Johnstone (p271-272)
Town and Moor by George Wilson (p272-280)
The Autobiography of an Old Oak Table (part 4) by Alfred Smith (p281-289)
The Thoroughbred Horse (part 1) by Coulson Pitman (p289-293)
The Hunting Doctor (p294-299)
What's What in Paris by Felix Whitehurst (p299-303)
My First Steeplechase by Teignmouth Melvill (p303-308)
Our Van [inc. Croydon Steeplechases; Hertfordshire Foxhounds; Hursley Hunt;
      Belgravia Magazine Trial] (p309-321)
Christmas Amusements (p321-324)

Issue 84 : February 1867

Portrait and Biography - Thomas Parker (p325-326)
[Obituary] Charles Davis by Charles Clarke (p326-336)
Thomas Hughes' Flash in the Pan by George Tyrrell (p336-340)
Thoughts on Stag Hunting by Richard Green-Price (p341-345)
The Thoroughbred Horse (part 2) by Coulson Pitman (p345-351)
Our Gentlemen Riders: George Ede (aka S.M.Edwards) by John Maunsell-Richardson (p351-355)
Wild Shooting Abroad (p355-359)
Paris Sport and Paris Life by Felix Whitehurst (p360-365)
Our Van [inc. RSPCA Croydon Court Case; Vine Hunt; Jockey Club of Vienna; Obituaries of
      Brownlow Cecil and Charles Peek] (p365-374)

Volume 13, March - September 1867

Issue 85 : March 1867

Portrait of William Bevill, gentleman jockey .... Title page
Portrait and Biography - Charles Colville .... (p1-2)
Etiquette in the Hunting Field by George Lane-Fox .... (p3-11)
The Moral Certainty: The Cesarewitch by George Tyrrell .... (p11-18)
En Route to Epsom by Irwin Willes .... (p18-21)
Pencillings in Austria (part 1) by Henry Leveson .... (p21-31)
Gone Away [Foxhunting in Devon] by George Lowth .... (p31-39)
[Review] *The Birds of Middlesex* by James Harting .... (p40-41)
Paris Sport and Paris Life by Felix Whitehurst .... (p41-44)
Our Van [inc. Lincoln Meeting; Quorn Hunt; Isle of Wight Hounds] .... (p45-54)

Issue 86 : April 1867

Portrait and Biography - George Whyte-Melville .... (p55-67)
April Showers [Norseman and The Guineas] by George Wilson .... (p68-77)
A Sporting Trip to Algeria (part 1) by Henry Faulkner .... (p77-89)
Paris Sport and Paris Life by Frederick Whitehurst .... (p90-95)
Our Wagonette [inc. Nottingham Meeting; East Acton Stud; Formation of North
        Cotswold Hunt; Catstock Hounds; Review of *A Fox's Tale* by
        George Rooper] .... (p95-101)
Our Diligence [inc. Roman Hunt; Naples Races; Obituary of John Cust] .... (p101-108)

Issue 87 : May 1867

Portrait and Biography - Francis Conyngham .... (p109-112)
R.M.[Rowley Mile] by George Tyrrell .... (p112-116)
The University Boat Race by Charles Clarke .... (p116-122)
May Flowers [A Visit to Middle Park Stud, Eltham] by George Wilson .... (p122-130)
The Thoroughbred Horse (part 3) by Coulson Pitman .... (p130-135)
Pencillings in Austria (part 2) by Henry Leveson .... (p135-145)
The Chronicles of Heatherthorp (part 1) by Bryon Webber .... (p145-147)
Coursing: The Herefordshire Coursing Club by Victor Gleicken .... (p147-149)
Paris Sport and Paris Life by Felix Whitehurst .... (p149-154)
Our Van [inc. Northamptonshire Stakes; Thirsk Meeting; Raby & Bedale Hounds; Obituaries
        of Billy Bean and William Missing] .... (p154-162)

Issue 88 : June 1867

Portrait and Biography - John Forester .... (p163-165)
A Winter's Tale by George Tyrrell .... (p165-169)
A Lay of Modern Epsom [verses] .... (p169-173)
Hunting on the West Coast of Africa by Henry Leveson .... (p174-184)
A Day With the English Foxhounds at St.Petersburg .... (p184-191)
June Jaunts or Riverside Rambles .... (p192-198)
Yachting and Rowing [inc. New York Yacht Club Races; Newcastle Rowing] .... (p199-202)
Paris Sport and Paris Life by Felix Whitehurst .... (p202-208)
Our Van [inc. Chester Cup; Epsom Meeting; Islington Horse Show] .... (p208-216)

Issue 89 : July 1867

Portrait and Biography - George Wombwell .... (p217-219)
By the Rushes by George Wilson .... (p219-227)

The Broken Blood Vessels by John Gamgee (p227-229)
Leafy June by George Tyrrell (p229-234)
A Sporting Trip to Algeria (part 2) by Henry Faulkner (p234-243)
Cricket in May and June by Charlton Lane (p243-251)
The Duke of Beaufort [*Essential Reading*] (p251-252)
[Review] *The Flying Scud* by Charles Clarke (p252-255)
Yachting and Rowing [inc. Royal London Yacht Club; Thames Rowing] (p255-258)
Paris Sport and Paris Life by Felix Whitehurst (p258-260)
Our Van [inc. Ascot Committee Changes; Shoreham Races; Cambridgeshire Hounds;
          Obituary of Thomas Taylor] (p260-270)

Issue 90 : August 1867

Portrait and Biography - William Douglas-Hamilton (p271-273)
Indian Cavalry Remounts by Charles Clarke (p273-280)
The Rifle Carnival by George Tyrrell (p280-284)
Cricket in July [inc. University match] by Charlton Lane (p284-292)
The Autobiography of an Old Oak Table (part 5) by Alfred Smith (p292-301)
Summer Musings by Charles Batchelder (p301-306)
[Review] *British Rural Sports* by John Walsh (p306-307)
[Review] *The Beauclercs* by Charles Clarke (p307-310)
Yachting and Rowing [inc. Spithead Review; British Regatta in Paris; Wingfield Sculls] (p310-314)
Paris Sport and Paris Life by Felix Whitehurst (p315-318)
Our Van [inc. Hungerford Races; Breeders' Sales; Old Berkeley Hunt;
          Obituary of Charles Monk] (p318-324)

Issue 91 : September 1867

Portrait and Biography - Thomas Smith (p325-330)
Waiting for the Verdict by George Wilson (p330-337)
Goodwood, 1867 by Charles Clarke (p337-343)
The Chronicles of Heatherthorp (part 2) by Bryon Webber (p344-349)
Cricket [inc. Criticism of the Quality of the Sandwiches at Lord's] by Charlton Lane (p349-353)
The September Struggle [Racing Tipsters] (p353-357)
Our Gentlemen Jockeys: William Bevill by John Maunsell-Richardson (p357)
Yachting and Rowing [inc. Cowes Week; Ryde Races; Plymouth Regatta] (p358-361)
Paris Sport and Paris Life by Felix Whitehurst (p361-364)
Our Van [inc. Goodwood Meeting; Ebor Handicap; Yorkshire Agricultural Society; Review of
          Handbook to Scotland by John Murray] (p364-374)

Henry Leveson

Volume 14, October 1867 - April 1868

Issue 92 : October 1867

Portrait of John Daley, jockey	Title page
Portrait and Biography - Henry des Voeux	(p1-2)
By Electric Telegraph [verses] by George Tyrrell	(p2-3)
Japanese Work [Hunting around Yokohama]	(p4-16)
The Autobiography of an Old Oak Table (part 6) by Alfred Smith	(p16-21)
From August to October by George Lane-Fox	(p22-30)
The Chronicles of Heatherthorp (part 3) by Bryon Webber	(p30-35)
Desperate Remedies [Horse Treatment] by John Gamgee	(p35-38)
Yachting and Rowing [inc. Watermen's Races; Barnes Regatta]	(p38-40)
Paris Sport and Paris Life by Felix Whitehurst	(p41-45)
Our Van [inc. Baden-Baden Steeplechases; Doncaster Meeting]	(p46-54)

Issue 93 : November 1867

Portrait and Biography - Orlando Bridgeman	(p55-56)
University Boat Racing by George Tyrrell	(p56-61)
Land and Strand by George Wilson	(p61-72)
An Autumn Walk [Robert Barclay-Allardice]	(p72-76)
The First of November [Hunting and its Culture] by George Lane-Fox	(p76-85)
Desperate Remedies [Horse Blistering and Firing] by John Gamgee	(p85-88)
The Chronicles of Heatherthorp (part 4) by Bryon Webber	(p88-94)
Paris Sport and Paris Life by Felix Whitehurst	(p94-98)
Our Van [inc: Newmarket Meeting; North Warwickshire Hunt; South Essex Hounds; Obituaries of Maurice Berkeley and Frank Dowling (of *Bells Life*)]	(p98-108)

Issue 94 : December 1867

Portrait and Biography - Charles Vivian	(p109-110)
From Dawn to Sunset by George Tyrrell	(p111-117)
On the Sea Coast by Charles Clarke	(p118-123)
The Autobiography of an Old Oak Table (part 7) by Alfred Smith	(p124-131)
Moorwood Hall	(p131-136)
Cricket: The Public Schools Averages for 1867 by Charlton Lane	(p136-142)
Paris Sport and Paris Life by Felix Whitehurst	(p143-150)
Our Van [inc. Shrewsbury Cup; Bramham Moor Huntsman; Hampshire Hunt]	(p151-162)

Issue 95 : January 1868

Portrait and Biography – William Montagu	(p163-164)
An Untrodden Path of Science by Berkeley Porteous	(p165-168)
On the Hearthrug by George Wilson	(p169-178)
Broadbury Moor: The Chase by George Lowth	(p178-187)
The Chronicles of Heatherthorp (part 5) by Bryon Webber	(p187-195)
Athletics and Sport by Charles Clarke	(p195-203)
Paris Sport and Paris Life by Felix Whitehurst	(p204-208)
Our Van [inc. St.Albans Steeplechasing; Obituaries of Edouard Benazet, John Lowther, John Ransom and William Reid; Hursley Hunt]	(p208-216)

Issue 96 : February 1868

Portrait and Biography - Reginald Corbet	(p217-219)
The Lord of the Valley [verses] by George Whyte-Melville	(p220-221)

To 'Dover's' [Berkshire] and Back by George Tyrrell (p221-226)
The Science of Foxhunting by Knightley Horlock (p227-229)
The Autobiography of an Old Oak Table (part 8) by Alfred Smith (p229-238)
When is Foxhunting not Foxhunting by George Lane-Fox (p238-247)
Brighton by Easy Stages (p247-250)
A Chasse in the Mauritius by John Sartorius (p250-254)
The Veteran's Lament [verses] (p254-256)
Paris Sport and Paris Life by Felix Whitehurst (p256-260)
Our Van [inc. Kingsbury Races; York & Ainsty Hounds; Vine Hunt; Obituaries of Alfred Day and Charley Boyce] (p261-270)

Issue 97 : March 1868

Portrait and Biography - Dimitri Soltykoff (p271-272)
The Galloping Squire [verses] by George Whyte-Melville (p272-273)
The North Road by George Wilson (p274-283)
The Dirge of the Defaulter [verses] by George Tyrrell (p283-285)
The Row, the Field and the Circus by Charles Clarke (p285-288)
On Peter Collison's Late Fall [verses] (p289)
When Foxhunting is Foxhunting by George Lane-Fox (p289-296)
A Day on the Downs by Charles Newmarch (p296-302)
The Autobiography of an Old Oak Table (part 9) by Alfred Smith (p302-306)
A Query as to the Science of Foxhunting by Henry Derozio (p306-307)
Paris Sport and Paris Life by Felix Whitehurst (p307-311)
Our Van [inc. Lincoln Meeting; Farmer's Banquet; Rufford Hunt] (p311-324)

Issue 98 : April 1868

Portrait and Biography - John Campbell-Wyndham (p325-327)
The University Boat Race by Charles Clarke (p327-332)
'Baldhead's' reply to 'Juvenis' [Derozio] (p333-334)
The Salmon Fisheries of England by Thomas Ashworth (p334-339)
A Lecture on Foxhunting by Charles Newmarch (p340-344)
A Voice From High Leicestershire [verses] (p345)
Football [Eton version] by George Lowth (p345-356)
Johnny Daley (p356-358)
Paris Sport and Paris Life by Felix Whitehurst (p359-363)
Our Van [inc. Aintree Meeting; Warwick Races; Berkeley Hunt Steeplechases; Obituary of George Swann, James Brudenell and Montgomery Dilly; Sporting Press Changes] (p363-374)

Volume 15, May - November 1868

Issue 99 : May 1868

Portrait of George Knox, gentleman rider Title page
Portrait and Biography - Thomas Drake (p1-2)
The Chronicles of Heatherthorp (part 6) by Bryon Webber (p3-11)
A Glorious Wind-Up by Charles Newmarch (p11-16)
The Autobiography of an Old Oak Table (part 10) by Alfred Smith (p17-24)
Oxford and Cambridge Athletic Sports by Charles Clarke (p24-28)
How I was Cured of Steeplechasing (p28-34)
Cricket: [Preview of the Forthcoming Season] by Thomas Pelham (p34-37)
Paris Sport and Paris Life by Felix Whitehurst (p38-42)
Our Van [inc. Northamptonshire Stakes; Race Fixing Trial; Punchestown Meeting; Quorn Hunt; Obituaries of William Copeland and Fuller Andrews] (p43-54)

Issue 100 : June 1868

Portrait and Biography - [The Late] James Brudenell by George Whyte-Melville (p55-60)
So Early in the Morning [verses] by George Tyrrell (p61-62)
The Two Thousand Day: Extract from Samuel Pepys' Diary (p63-65)
The Abyssinian Expedition by Henry Leveson (p66-71)
The Chronicles of Heatherthorp (part 7) by Bryon Webber (p72-80)
Lustleigh Cleaves [of Dartmoor Forest] by George Lowth (p80-88)
A Day's Pike Fishing in the Light Lands (part 1) (p89-98)
Yachting and Rowing [inc. Royal Thames Yacht Club; University Colleges' Rowing] (p98-100)
Our Van [inc. Chester Meeting; Bogside Races; Obituaries of George Ford, Arthur Edwards and
        John Hobson] (p100-108)

Issue 101 : July 1868

Portrait and Biography - Wellington Stapleton-Cotton (p109-111)
The State of Denmark [Jockey Club Ruling] by George Tyrrell (p111-114)
Rod and Spear by Charles Newmarch (p114-120)
The Derby Day: Extract from Samuel Pepys' Diary (p120-125)
Cricket in June by Thomas Pelham (p125-129)
A Day's Pike Fishing in the Light Lands (part 2) (p130-137)
The Autobiography of an Old Oak Table (part 11) by Alfred Smith (p137-145)
Yachting and Rowing [inc. New Thames Yacht Club; Yachting Congress] (p145-147)
Paris Sport and Paris Life by Felix Whitehurst (p148-153)
Our Van [inc. Admiral Rous/John Day Libel Action; Ascot Meeting; Middle Park Stud] (p153-162)

Issue 102 : August 1868

Portrait and Biography - George Vane (p163-165)
Day versus Rous [Details of the Case] by George Tyrrell (p165-167)
A Summer Evening by George Wilson (p168-175)
Cricket in July by Thomas Pelham (p175-182)
The Chronicles of Heatherthorp (part 8) by Bryon Webber (p182-191)
An Italian Derby: Il Palio di Siena by George Lowth (p191-198)
Yachting and Rowing [inc. Henley Regatta; Sailing Barge Match] (p198-203)
Paris Sport and Paris Life by Felix Whitehurst (p203-207)
Our Van [inc. Alexandra Park Races; Aldershot Camp Meeting; Leicester Agricultural Show;
        Obituary of Artus Talon] (p207-216)

Issue 103 : September 1868

Portrait and Biography - Richard Lumley (p217-218)
The Game of Abyssinia by Henry Leveson (p218-222)
Cruelty in Angling by Henry Cholmondeley-Pennell (p222-228)
The Autobiography of an Old Oak Table (part 12) by Alfred Smith (p229-237)
The Oxford and Cambridge Cricket Match: Samuel Pepys' Diary Extract (p237-239)
Partridge Shooting (p239-246)
Cricket in August [inc. Canterbury Week; Julius Caesar Benefit Match] by Thomas Pelham (p246-254)
Yachting and Rowing [inc. Cowes and Ryde Races; Royal Yacht Squadron,
        Tewkesbury Regatta] (p254-259)
Our Van [inc. Goodwood Cup; Yorkshire Agricultural Show; Obituaries of Robert Munton,
        Arthur Hill, Jacob Omnium, Edward Goulburn and William King] (p259-270)

Issue 104 : October 1868

Portrait and Biography - Alfred de Montgomery (p271-272)

L'Addio [verses] by George Tyrrell   (p273)
The Arabian Horse: The Origin and Antiquity (part 1) by Albert Muntz   (p274-280)
The Autobiography of an Old Oak Table (part 13) by Alfred Smith   (p280-288)
The Chronicles of Heatherthorp (part 9) by Bryon Webber   (p288-297)
Cricket: The Close of the Season by Thomas Pelham   (p297-300)
Red Letter Days   (p300-305)
Head and Hands   (p305-308)
Yachting and Rowing [inc. Thames Rowing]   (p308-309)
Paris Sport and Paris Life by Felix Whitehurst   (p309-314)
Our Van [inc. Prizefighting Ban; Doncaster Meeting; Fairfield Stud; Monmouth Racecourse;
       Obituary of Harry Lamplugh]   (p315-324)

Issue 105 : November 1868

Portrait and Biography - John Douglas   (p325-328)
Newmarket: In Season by George Wilson   (p328-338)
The Arabian Horse: Causes of Decay of Other Breeds (part 2) by Albert Muntz   (p338-345)
The Old Squire [verses]   (p346)
The Autobiography of an Old Oak Table (part 14) by Alfred Smith   (p347-355)
Our Gentlemen Riders: George Knox by John Maunsell-Richardson   (p355-357)
Cricket: The PublicSchool Averages (part 1) by Thomas Pelham   (p357-360)
The Province of Athletics   (p360-365)
[Reviews] *The Boys Own Book* by William Clarke and *A Handbook of Gymnastics & Athletics*
       by Ernst Ravenstein and John Hulley   (p365)
Paris Sport and Paris Life by Felix Whitehurst   (p366-368)
Our Van [inc. Tattersall's Disciplinary Committee; Autumn Handicaps; Hambledon Hunt;
       Epsom Racecourse Land Dispute]   (p368-378)

Volume 16, December 1868 - June 1869

Issue 106 : December 1868

Portrait of Harry Kelley, champion sculler   Title page
Portrait and Biography - Reginald Herbert   (p1-2)
[Obituary] Henry Rawdon-Hastings   (p3)
The Bagman   (p4-11)
Betting and Bettors by George Tyrrell   (p11-15)
The Arabian Horse: On Breeding (part 3) by Albert Muntz   (p15-21)
The Chronicles of Heatherthorp (part 10) by Bryon Webber   (p21-31)
Cricket: The Public School Averages (part 2) [H.M.Grace letter] by Thomas Pelham   (p31-36)
Paris Sport and Paris Life by Felix Whitehurst   (p36-41)
Our Van [inc. Shrewsbury Meeting; Pytchley Hunt; *Bell's Life*; Obituaries of Hugh Somerville,
       James Gilbert and Campbell Wyndham]   (p41-50)

Issue 107 : January 1869

Portrait and Biography - Algernon Peyton   (p51-52)
Newmarket: Out of Season (part 1) by George Wilson   (p53-62)
The Derby Difficulty by George Tyrrell   (p62-65)
1869 [Mainly on Katherine FitzGerald]   (p66-70)
British Sports and Pastimes [Reprints from *St.Pauls Magazine*] by Charles Clarke   (p70-79)
Fox Hunting, Its Future and Prospects by Charles Newmarch   (p80-83)
The Shoeing of Horses by Joseph Shorthouse   (p84-86)
Paris Sport and Paris Life by Felix Whitehurst   (p86-90)

Our Van [inc. Croydon Steeplechases; Epsom Land Problem; York & Ainsty Hunt; Obituary of
      Jack Healy; North Warwickshire Hunt] (p91-104)

Issue 108 : February 1869

Portrait and Biography - John Chaworth-Musters (p105-106)
The Quorn and its New Master by George Lane-Fox (p106-112)
A Rum 'Un to Follow, A Bad 'Un to Beat [verses] by George Whyte-Melville (p112-113)
Stud Prospects by George Tyrrell (p113-120)
Sporting Pictures (p121-122)
The Little Blood Hack [verses] (p122)
Sadler versus Smith [High Court Judgment: Sculling Dispute] (p123-125)
[Review] Observations on Scent: *Memoirs of the Belvoir Hounds* by John Welby (p126-128)
Life Amongst the Bedouins of Tor (part 1) by Henry Leveson (p128-136)
The Autobiography of an Old Oak Table (part 15) by Alfred Smith (p137-144)
Our Van [inc. Turf Reform Bill; Epsom Saga; Grafton Hounds; Obituaries of Edward Hawke,
      Alexander Campbell, John Jackson and John O'Brien; Settlement in Day
      versus Rous] (p145-158)

Issue 109 : March 1869

Portrait and Biography - John Hope (p159-161)
Hunting Song (For the Ladies) by George Whyte-Melville (p161-162)
The University Boat Race by George Tyrrell (p162-167)
A Leap in the Dark [Resolution on Epsom Land Dispute] by Irwin Willes (p167-171)
The Autobiography of an Old Oak Table (part 16) by Alfred Smith (p171-178)
For and Against [verses] (p178-179)
Outdoor Servants: The Gamekeeper by Charles Clarke (p180-184)
The Chronicles of Heatherthorp (part 11) by Bryon Webber (p184-195)
Life Amongst the Bedouins of Tor (part 2) by Henry Leveson (p195-200)
Our Van [inc. Sutton Coldfield Races; Waterloo Cup; York & Ainsty Hunt Tragedy;
      Cheshire Hounds; Obituaries of Charles Slingsby, William Orvice, Edmund
      Robinson, Edward Lloyd, Henry Paget, John Stephenson and William Wardlaw] (p200-212)

Issue 110 : April 1869

Portrait and Biography - Charles Brownlow (p213-216)
Lord James Glasgow [verses] by George Tyrrell (p216-218)
The Trout and Salmon Fisheries of North Wales (p218-227)
The Clipper that Stands in the Stall at the Top [verses] by George Whyte-Melville (p227-228)
Oxford and Cambridge Athletic Sports by Charles Clarke (p228-230)
Coursing by John Walsh (p230-239)
Newby Ferry [verses] by Rowland Egerton-Warburton (p239-241)
Outdoor Servants: The Whippers-In by Charles Clarke (p241-246)
Cricket: Prospects of the Season [inc. Norfolk County Cricket Club and Cambridgeshire
      County Cricket Club both Dissolved] by Thomas Pelham (p246-248)
Harrow School Athletic Sports (p248-251)
Yachting and Rowing [inc. Yacht Congress Regulations; University Boat Race] (p251-255)
Our Van [inc. Grand National; Warwick Races; Essex & Suffolk Hounds; Obituaries of
      Jack Holmes, James Carr-Boyle, William Stebbing, John Johnstone, Arthur
      Heathcote and Jack Robson] (p255-266)

Issue 111 : May 1869

Portrait and Biography - Reginald Graham (p267-268)
Moriturus [verses] by George Tyrrell (p269)

Currant Jelly [On Thistlewhipping]	(p270-273)
The Ward Union Hunt [verses] by George Whyte-Melville	(p273-274)
The Chronicles of Heatherthorp (part 12) by Bryon Webber	(p275-288)
Comparative Merits of Arabian and English Horses by Albert Muntz	(p289-293)
A May Fox or the Forest Vixen by Charles Clarke	(p294-302)
Routed by a Drum [verses]	(p303-304)
[Review] *A System of Figure Skating* by Henry Vandervell	(p305-306)
Yachting and Rowing [inc. Harvard College Rowing Challenge]	(p306)
Paris Sport and Paris Life by Felix Whitehurst	(p307-309)
Our Van [inc. Punchestown Meeting; Newmarket Heath Celebration; Hursley Hunt; Lothian Hounds]	(p310-320)

Issue 112 : June 1869

Portrait and Biography - Alexander Hood	(p321)
Newmarket: Out of Season (part 2) by George Wilson	(p322-328)
On Her Majesty's Service by George Tyrrell	(p329-332)
Cricket [inc. Marylebone Cricket Club Annual General Meeting; Northern Professional Players] by Thomas Pelham	(p332-338)
To Charles Buxton [verses] by Henry Cholmondeley-Pennell	(p338)
Outdoor Servants: The Huntsman by Charles Clarke	(p339-344)
Steeplechasing	(p344-349)
My Cry for Help by George Sims	(p350-356)
Harry Kelley	(p356-358)
Yachting and Rowing [inc. Royal London Yacht Club; London Rowing Club]	(p358-360)
Our Van [inc. Craven Stakes; Epsom Derby; West Fife Hounds; Tattersall's painting by Thomas Musgrave Joy]	(p360-370)

Volume 17, July 1869 - January 1870

Issue 113 : July 1869

Portrait of Harry King, jockey	Title page
Portrait and Biography - Horatio Ross	(p1-4)
Masters' of Fox Hounds Committee Decision on the Grafton and Old Berkeley Hunts	(p4)
How We Spoiled the Egyptians	(p5-10)
Muzzles and Mad Dogs	(p10-14)
Types of Horses: Past and Present by Albert Muntz	(p14-17)
Cricket [inc. University Match; County Reports] by Thomas Pelham	(p18-26)
The Run of the Season [verses]	(p27-28)
Turf Reform [Jockey Club Tribunal] by George Tyrrell	(p28-32)
Outdoor Servants: The Earthstopper by Charles Clarke	(p32-36)
Yachting and Rowing [inc. Royal Thames Schooner Match; Oxford Sculling; Pangbourne Regatta]	(p36-41)
Paris Sport and Paris Life by Felix Whitehurst	(p41-44)
Our Van [inc. Ascot Stakes; Proposed Betting Legislation; New Forest Hounds; Islington Horse Show; Obituary of Robert Clifton]	(p44-54)

Issue 114 : August 1869

Portrait and Biography - Gerard Sturt	(p55-58)
Au Revoir [verses] by George Tyrrell	(p58-59)
The Award: The Sandbeck and Badworth Hunts' Boundary Ruling	(p60-66)
The Chronicles of Heatherthorp (part 13) by Bryon Webber	(p66-76)
Hunting a Bagman by Charles Newmarch	(p77-82)
A Chapter on Speculation	(p83-87)

Cricket [Three Gentlemen versus Players' Matches; Eton versus Harrow] by Thomas Pelham (p87-95)

Who is to Ride Him (part 1) by Theobald de Vismes (p96-102)

Yachting and Rowing [inc. Harwich Regatta; Harvard Rowers] (p102-107)

Our Van [inc. George Knox Case; Tidworth Hounds; Jockey Club Law Courts Decision; Obituaries of George Beers and William Goodwin; Review of *Our Life in Japan* by Richard Jephson] (p107-116)

Issue 115 : September 1869

Portrait and Biography - Charles Yorke ['Champagne Charlie'] (p117)

The Bonnet of Blue [verses] by George Tyrrell (p118-119)

The Stubbles [Partridges and Quail] by Charles Newmarch (p119-125)

Rabies and Hydrophobia by Joseph Shorthouse (p125-131)

A Blank Day (p132-136)

The Pleasures of Cubhunting by Charles Newmarch (p136-142)

Who is to Ride Him (part 2) by Theobald de Vismes (p142-148)

[Reviews] *Veterinary Surgery* by William Dick and *Horses to be Shod* by William Haycock) (p148-149)

Oxford and Harvard [Rowing Challenge] (p150-152)

Yachting and Rowing [inc. Isle of Wight Yachting; Staines Regatta] (p152-156)

Our Van [inc. Sussex Racing; Kilkenny Hunting Dispute; Scottish Grouse Moors; Lincolnshire Agricultural Society; Boulogne Yachting] (p157-170)

Issue 116 : October 1869

Portrait and Biography – James Ker (p171-172)

Leaves From the Journal of our Life at Doncaster by George Tyrrell (p172-179)

Punters-Town Steeplechases (p179-184)

The Galway Salmon Fishery by Theobald de Vismes (p184-188)

The Sires of the Period (part 1) by Charles Race (p188-191)

October Sports (p192-200)

The Leash [Coursing] by Charles Newmarch (p200-204)

A Visit to Elvedon Hall: Seat of Maharajah Duleepsingh (p204-206)

Cricket: The Close of Season by Thomas Pelham (p206-209)

Our Yachts [Cutters and Schooners] (p209-213)

Yachting and Rowing [inc. International Yacht Club; London Rowing Club] (p213-214)

Our Van [inc. Baden-Baden Races; Doncaster Meeting; York & Ainsty Hunt; Obituaries of Charles Taylor and Charles Rushout] (p214-224)

Issue 117 : November 1869

Portrait and Biography - Henry Paget (p225-227)

Lord Derby [verses] by George Tyrrell (p227-229)

[Obituary] Edward Smith-Stanley by Irwin Willes (p229-237)

The Heath: A Sketch (p237-242)

The Sires of the Period (part 2) by Charles Race (p243-246)

Barnet Fair (p246-248)

The Reunion at Melton (part 1) (p248-257)

Outdoor Servants: The Studgroom by Charles Clarke (p257-261)

The Wild West [Staghunting] by Charles Newmarch (p262-266)

Cricket: The Public School Averages (part 1) by Thomas Pelham (p267-269)

Our Van [inc. Autumn Handicaps; Devon & Somerset Staghounds; West Wiltshire Hunt] (p270-278)

Issue 118 : December 1869

Portrait and Biography - Archibald Primrose (p279-280)

At Home [End of the Racing Season] by George Tyrrell] (p280-284)

The Reunion at Melton (part 2)   (p285-294)
The Sires of the Period (part 3) by Charles Race   (p294-299)
The Chronicles of Heatherthorp (part 14) by Bryon Webber   (p299-309)
A Quiet bit of Schooling by Charles Newmarch   (p310-314)
Cricket: The Public School Averages (part 2) by Thomas Pelham   (p314-318)
Rowing [Thames versus Tyne; Rowing and Sculling Matches]   (p318-320)
Our Van [inc. Autumn Meetings; Jockey Club Abolition of Selling Races; Pytchley Hunt;
        Obituaries of Francis Coyle, Richard Grosvenor, Thomas Foley and Charles
        Manners-Sutton]   (p320-332)

Issue 119 : January 1870

Portrait and Biography - Robert d'Orleans   (p333-334)
Suburban Specs [Kingsbury Meetings] by George Tyrrell   (p335-340)
The Coverside Phantom [verses] (part 1) by Rowland Egerton-Warburton   (p340-343)
The Surrey Staghounds by George Lane-Fox   (p343-351)
A Little Horse Talk by George Wilson   (p351-360)
[Review] *Seats and Saddles* by Francis Dwyer reviewed by Charles Clarke   (p360-369)
The Christmas Amusements   (p369-371)
Our Van [inc. Croydon Steeplechasing; North Warwickshire Hunt Testimonial; Bramham Moor
        Hounds; Obituaries of George Foljambe, Thomas Lockyer and Jack Cheswap]   (p372-382)

Volume 18, February - August 1870

Issue 120 : February 1870

Portrait of Thomas French, jockey   Title page
Portrait and Biography - Frederick Delme-Radcliffe   (p1-3)
Foxes or Pheasants: The Cambridgeshire Hunt [verses] by George Tyrrell   (p3-4)
Harry King and the Staghounds by Charles Clarke   (p5-14)
Leighton in 1870 [verses]   (p15)
The Sires of the Period (part 4) by Charles Race   (p16-20)
A Word on the Immorality of Field Sports   (p21-26)
A Wail From Bramham Moor   (p27-32)
The Melbourne Cup: A Lay From the Antipodes [verses] by Adam Lindsay Gordon   (p32-34)
The Dead Heat (part 1) by Theobald de Vismes   (p35-40)
Racing in Upper India by John Spencer   (p41-45)
The Coverside Phantom [verses] (part 2) by Rowland Egerton-Warburton   (p45)
Our Van [inc. Cambridgeshire Hounds; Obituary of Mewyn Marshall; Belvoir Hunt; Letter from
        William Selby-Lowndes regarding Pheasants]   (p46-54)

Issue 121 : March 1870

Portrait and Biography - Henry Deacon   (p55)
Joseph Hawley's Proposals [Turf Reform] by George Tyrrell   (p56-62)
Coursing: The Waterloo Cup by George Wilson   (p62-65)
The Chronicles of Heatherthorp (part 15) by Bryon Webber   (p65-78)
Iris [verses] by Tom Firr, Huntsman, North Warwickshire Hounds   (p79-80)
A Shot at Golden Plover   (p81-87)
On A Tame Fox [verses]   (p88)
The Champion Billiard Match at St.James's Hall   (p89-92)
[Review] *Sea Spray and Smoke Drift* by Adam Lindsay Gordon reviewed by Henry Leveson   (p92-97)
Our Van [inc. Market Harborough Hunt Ball; Atherstone Hunt; Obituary of Nathaniel de
        Rothschild, Thomas Leigh and William Williamson]   (p98-108)

Issue 122 : April 1870

Portrait and Biography - Charles Newton (p109-110)
[Obituary] George Ede [verses] by George Tyrrell (p110-111)
Down Harrow Way (p112-118)
[Obituary] The Druid [Henry Hall Dixon] by Comyns Cole (p119-120)
[Review] *Saddle and Sirloin* by Henry Hall Dixon reviewed by Comyns Cole (p120-122)
The University [Boat] Race by Charles Clarke (p123-126)
The Dead Heat (part 2) by Theobald de Vismes (p126-134)
The Chronicles of Heatherthorp (part 16) by Bryon Webber (p135-144)
A Day in the Meadows by Charles Newmarch (p144-148)
Our Van [inc. Hawley's Turf Reform Bill; Grand National; Rugby Hunt Steeplechase Course;
       Obituaries of Archibald Kennedy, Henry Dixon, George Ede, Samuel Rogers and
       Bingham Jennings] (p149-162)

Issue 123 : May 1870

Portrait and Biography - Frederick Thellusson (p163-164)
Turf Reform [Jockey Club on Hawley's Bill] by George Tyrrell (p165-168)
The Hounds of Augustus Bampfylde (p169-174)
Rogues and Vagabonds (part 1): The Roulette Man by George Sims (p174-179)
A Sporting Story (parts 1 & 2) by Theobald de Vismes (p180-185)
From November to March by Charles Newmarch (p185-190)
Sports Past and to Come [Athletics at Lillie Bridge] by Charles Clarke (p191-197)
The Present Aspect of Athletics (p197-204)
Yachting and Rowing [inc. America's Cup Challengers; University Boat Race] (p204-207)
Our Van [inc. Newmarket Meeting; Northampton Races; South Warwickshire Hunt;
       Dumfriesshire Hounds; Torquay Steeplechase; Reading Racecourse Closure;
       Obituary of George Moore] (p207-216)

Issue 124 : June 1870

Portrait and Biography - Richard Boyle (p217-218)
Flowers in May by George Tyrrell (p218-223)
Cricket in May [inc. Lord's Ground; New Bowling Law] by Thomas Pelham (p224-226)
Some Kentish Beauties [Middle Park Stud] (p226-227)
A Sporting Story (parts 3 & 4) by Theobald de Vismes (p228-234)
The Chronicles of Heatherthorp (part 17) by Bryon Webber (p234-247)
The Cab Horse (part 1) by Charles Newmarch (p247-252)
[Obituary] William Wynne Apperley (p253-255)
Yachting and Rowing [inc. Yankee Clipper Races; Hudson Amateur Rowing Association] (p255-258)
Our Van [inc. Chester Cup; Bath Meeting; Betting Lists Bill Debate; Obituaries of Frederick
       Vyner, Edmund Antrobus, Albert Cox, William Marriott, Stanhope Hawke,
       Richard Tattersall and Robert Johnston] (p259-270)

Issue 125 : July 1870

Portrait and Biography - Albert Craven (p271-272)
Racing Past and Future by Henry Rous (p273-284)
Sir Goathead [verses] by George Tyrrell (p285-286)
The [Rotten] Row in 1870 by Teignmouth Melvill (p287-294)
Cricket [inc. Northern Eleven; Death of George Summers on the Field] by Thomas Pelham (p294-302)
A Sporting Story (parts 5 & 6) by Theobald de Vismes (p302-308)
The Cab Horse (part 2) by Charles Newmarch (p309-314)
Yachting and Rowing [inc. New Thames Yacht Club; Sailing Barge Race] (p314-317)
Our Van [inc. Epsom Meeting; Yearling Sales] (p318-324)

Issue 126 : August 1870

Portrait and Biography - Charles Pelham	(p325)
To Danebury [An Old Hampshire Racecourse] by George Tyrrell	(p326-330)
A Lounge at Lord's	(p330-337)
A Sporting Story (parts 7 & 8) by Theobald de Vismes	(p338-345)
Menus Plaisirs	(p345-352)
[Review] *The Modern Practical Angler* by Henry Cholmondeley-Pennell	(p352-353)
Cricket [inc. University Match; Eton versus Harrow] by Thomas Pelham	(p354-360)
Yachting and Rowing [inc. Royal Cork Yacht Club; Bedford Regatta]	(p360-366)
Our Van [inc. Jockey Club Report; Cumberland Plate; Ham Stakes; Palmerstown Breeding Association; Obituaries of Charles Clarke and James Watt]	(p366-374)

Volume 19, September 1870 - March 1871

Issue 127 : September 1870

Portrait of William Gilbert Grace, cricketer	Title page
Portrait and Biography - Mark Rolle	(p1-4)
The Ocean Race [verses] by George Tyrrell	(p5-6)
Country Quarters: General	(p7-12)
Riding Hobbies (part 1)	(p12-18)
A Sporting Story (parts 9 & 10) by Theobald de Vismes	(p18-26)
Abolition of the Game Laws	(p26-30)
Rogues and Vagabonds (part 2): The Three-Card Man by George Sims	(p30-34)
The Coverts by Nevill Fitt	(p34-37)
National Dog Shows: The Maidstone Show by George Wilson	(p38-40)
Yachting and Rowing [inc. Thames National Regatta; Obituary of Hamilton Verschoyle]	(p41-44)
Our Van [inc. Baden-Baden Racecourse Closure; Goodwood Meeting; Badsworth Hunt Cup; York Races; Obituaries of George Whieldon and William Sadler]	(p44-54)

Issue 128 : October 1870

Portrait and Biography - William Berkeley-Portman	(p55-57)
In Memoriam: Sunlight [verses] by George Tyrrell	(p57)
Country Quarters: Leicestershire	(p58-68)
A Lounge at Tattersall's	(p68-73)
My Match With Quiz by George Sims	(p73-81)
Grouse Driving by Archibald Wortley	(p82-85)
William Gilbert Grace	(p85-87)
A Sporting Story (parts 11 & 12) by Theobald de Vismes	(p88-96)
Thomas French	(p96)
Cricket Retrospect: 1870 Season by Thomas Pelham	(p97-100)
Yachting and Rowing [Anglo-Canadian Rowing Match]	(p101-102)
Our Van [inc. French Racing Prorogued *sine die*; Great Yorkshire Handicap; Obituaries of Thomas Winteringham and Henry Taylor]	(p102-108)

Issue 129 : November 1870

Portrait and Biography - John Russell	(p109-113)
Betting Prosecutions by George Tyrrell	(p113-119)
Country Quarters: Northamptonshire	(p119-132)
Riding Hobbies by George Wilson	(p132-139)
The Royal Deer Drive [at Aultnashellagt, Rossshire]	(p139-140)
Spey Throes by James Bertram	(p140-142)
Hunting Song for November [verses]	(p143)

Our Van [inc. Great Eastern Handicap; Scottish Racing; Hursley Hunt; Brighton Harriers; Obituaries of Joseph Saxon, Arthur Way, George Tuxford (of *The Sporting Magazine*); Picot de Dampierre and Adam Lindsay Gordon] (p144-154)

Hunting: Lists of Hounds, Masters, Huntsmen, Whips, Kennels (p155-170)

Issue 130 : December 1870

Portrait and Biography - George Arundell (p171-172)

Passing Away [verses] by George Tyrrell (p172-173)

Country Quarters: Warwickshire (p174-184)

A Sporting Story (parts 13 & 14) by Theobald de Vismes (p184-194)

Masters of Hounds by George Lane-Fox (p195-198)

Rogues and Vagabonds (part 3): The Welsher by George Sims (p199-203)

Cricket: The Public School Averages for 1870 by Thomas Pelham (p203-213)

Our Van [inc. Worcester Steeplechasing; Hunting Journalism; Blackmore Vale Hunt; Ivybridge Hounds] (p214-224)

Issue 131 : January 1871

Portrait and Biography - Henri d'Orleans (p225-227)

The Place Where the Old Horse Died [verses] by George Whyte-Melville (p227-228)

Deer Stalking (p229-235)

A Tale of the Last Century by Teignmouth Melvill (p235-244)

John Russell [Query on his Biographical Notes] by George Lowth (p245-246)

Country Quarters - Oxfordshire (p247-258)

Breeding and Breeders by George Tyrrell (p259-266)

Rogues and Vagabonds (part 4): The Moneylender by George Sims (p266-271)

Our Van [inc. Birmingham Dog Show; Kingsbury Races; Pytchley Hunt; Review of *Hints to Young Sportsmen* by John Walter] (p272-286)

Issue 132 : February 1871

Portrait and Biography - Jacob Astley (p287-288)

[Obituary] Henry Bentinck: A Memoir (p288-293)

Henry Bentinck on Foxhunting (p293-297)

Under the New Dispensation [Revised Rules of Racing] by George Tyrrell (p298-302)

Country Quarters: Lincolnshire (p303-319)

A Sporting Story (parts 15 & 16) by Theobald de Vismes (p320-330)

Skating in the Fens by Neville Goodman (p331-333)

A Travelling Sketch by Teignmouth Melvill (p334-339)

Our Van [inc. Irish National Hunt; Prosecution of Lord Middleton's Whips; North Warwickshire Hunt; Obituary of Robert Honywood] (p339-348)

Issue 133 : March 1871

Portrait and Biography - William Denison (p349-350)

Over the Hill to Russley by George Tyrrell (p350-357)

Country Quarters: Bedfordshire (p358-367)

To the Distinguished Members of the Oakley Hunt, 1843 [verses] (p367-369)

A Chaunt of Waterloo (p370-371)

Coursing: The Waterloo Cup by George Wilson (p371-377)

A Sporting Story (parts 17 & 18) by Theobald de Vismes (p377-387)

Madras and Calcutta Boat Race by Gordon Loch (p387-393)

Our Van [inc. Tattersall's Sale; Birmingham Steeplechases; Atherstone Hunt; Curraghmore Hounds; Obituaries of George Hodgkinson, Charles Richardson and Thomas Clark] (p394-406)

Volume 20, April - October 1871

Issue 134 : April 1871

Portrait of Richard Daft, cricketer — Title page
Portrait and Biography - William Mortimer — (p1-2)
Country Quarters: Buckinghamshire — (p3-14)
The Greatwood Run with the Beaufort Hounds (with map) by Blair Oliphant — (p14-19)
The Battle of the Blues [verses] by George Tyrrell — (p19-21)
A Race Morning by Comyns Cole — (p21-25)
A Burst with the Baron [verses] — (p26)
A Sporting Story (parts 19 & 20) by Theobald de Vismes — (p27-38)
Wolf Hunting and Wild Sport in Lower Brittany (part 1) by Edward Davies — (p38-45)
Our Van [inc. Lincolnshire Handicap; Obituaries of James Farquharson and William Bishop; Grand Military Hunt Cup; Croydon Races] — (p46-62)

Issue 135 : May 1871

Portrait and Biography - Egon Lamoral — (p63-64)
Harry Hall at Home by George Tyrrell — (p64-69)
A Race Meeting at Malta by Teignmouth Melvill — (p69-72)
Sport and Want of Sport in the Shires (part 1) by Francis Villiers — (p73-83)
Oxford and Cambridge Athletic Meeting by Comyns Cole — (p83-86)
A Sporting Story (parts 21 & 22) by Theobald de Vismes — (p86-99)
Wolf Hunting and Wild Sport in Lower Brittany (part 2) by Edward Davies — (p100-105)
The Fitzwilliam Hunt, 1871 [verses] by William Day — (p106-107)
The Lottery of Breeding by James Cameron — (p108-110)
Yachting and Rowing [inc. Thames Sailing Club; University Boat Race] — (p111-114)
Our Van [inc. Newmarket Handicap; Punchestown Races; North Staffordshire Hunt; Obituary of Thomas Dickens] — (p115-124)

Issue 136 : June 1871

Portrait and Biography - John Goldie — (p125-126)
Turf Vampires and their Victims by George Tyrrell — (p126-132)
The French Contingent by George Lane-Fox — (p133-136)
Sport and Want of Sport in the Shires (part 2) by Francis Villiers — (p136-145)
The Stickleback Papers by George Fleming — (p145-154)
Pussy by George Sims — (p155-163)
A Head Beating (part 1) by Lewis Clements — (p163-167)
Cricket (on James Lillywhite; Heathfield Stephenson and Edgar Willsher) by Thomas Pelham — (p167-172)
Review : *Cricketers in Council* by Herbert Thomas — (p173-174)
A Batch of Yearlings [A Visit to Middle Park, Eltham] by George Wilson — (p174-176)
Our Van [inc. Chester Cup; Newmarket Meeting; Bath Races; Rome Steeplechase; Obituaries of Hugo Meynell-Ingram, Frederick Villiers and George Ongley] — (p176-186)

Issue 137 : July 1871

Portrait and Biography - Alexander Hall — (p187)
A Real Turf Gangrene by George Tyrrell — (p188-194)
Wolf Hunting and Wild Sport in Lower Brittany (part 3) by Edward Davies — (p194-199)
Quiet Ascot by Comyns Cole — (p199-203)
Gone Away over Dartmoor Forest by George Lowth — (p204-206)
Turf Nomenclature (part 1) by John Hotten — (p207-209)
The Crystal Palace Dog Show by George Wilson — (p210-216)
Pigeon Shooting by William Tegetmeier — (p216-219)

Roba di Mare (p219-227)
Cricket [inc. Grace Brothers; Surrey Controversy] by Thomas Pelham (p228-232)
Yachting and Rowing [inc. Royal Harwich Yacht Club; University Oarsmen] (p232-237)
Our Van [inc. Royal Hunt Cup; Stockbridge Races; Prince's Cricket Ground; Obituaries of
    George Stevens and Andrew Arcedeckne; Hunt Servants' Fund] (p238-248)

Issue 138 : August 1871

Portrait and Biography - George Willes (p249)
The Yellow and Black [verses] by George Tyrrell (p250)
The Otter and Otter Hounds (part 1) by Alexander Clark-Kennedy (p251-258)
The Challenge Whip by Teignmouth Melvill (p258-268)
Jack Blake, or Landed at Last (part 1) (p269-275)
Archery - Powderham Castle by George Lowth (p276-283)
Otter Hunting on the Erme, South Devon [verses] (p283-285)
Cricket [inc. University Match; Married versus Singles Fixture] by Thomas Pelham (p285-293)
Yachting and Rowing [inc. Royal Mersey Regatta; Thames Rowing] (p294-299)
Our Van [inc. Public Schools Cricket; Newmarket Week; Coaching Club; Review of
    The Homing or Carrier Pigeon by William Tegetmeier] (p300-310)

* Comyns Cole says Baily's sells 10,000 copies monthly - p301 *

Issue 139 : September 1871

Portrait and Biography - Francis Charteris (p311-312)
The Betting Bill by George Tyrrell (p312-317)
The Otter and Otter Hounds (part 2) by Alexander Clark-Kennedy (p318-324)
The Pool Side (p324-330)
Dozmarye Pool by George Lowth (p330-340)
Sweet Fodder from Mouldy Hay by John Strange (p340)
Jack Blake, or Landed at Last (part 2) (p341-345)
Cricket [inc. Canterbury Week; John Lillywhite Benefit Match] by Thomas Pelham (p345-352)
Yachting and Rowing [inc. Royal Southern Yacht Club; Obituary of James Renforth] (p353-358)
Our Van [inc. Sussex Racing; Birmingham Horse Show; Gravesend Yachting Cup] (p359-372)

Issue 140 : October 1871

Portrait and Biography - Richard Glyn (p373-374)
Wolf Hunting and Wild Sport in Lower Brittany (part 4) by Edward Davies (p374-381)
The Baron Wins [verses] by George Tyrrell (p382)
Jack Blake, or Landed at Last (part 3) (p383-392)
Hunting of the Present Day by George Lane-Fox (p392-394)
This Generation [verses] (p395)
Poaching and its Prevention (p396-398)
A Match at Golf (p398-405)
A Head Beating (part 2) by Lewis Clements (p406-414)
Cricket [inc. Sussex Attendances; Gilbert Grace's Popularity] by Thomas Pelham (p415-420)
Our Van [inc. Depressing Baden-Baden Meeting; Doncaster Races; Cleveland Agricultural
    Show; Obituaries of George Moore, William Blenkiron, Thomas Pedley,
    George Evans, Irwin Willes (of *Baily's*) and Nathaniel Langham] (p420-430)

Volume 21, November 1871 - May 1872

Issue 141 : November 1871

Portrait of Thomas Pickernell, jockey	Title page
Portrait and Biography - Charles Trelawny	(p1-3)
[Obituary] 'Argus` by Alfred Baily	(p3-4)
The Good Grey Mare [verses] by George Whyte-Melville	(p5-6)
Country Quarters - Yorkshire [York & Scarborough]	(p7-20)
Slang Terms and the Gipsy Tongue by John Hotten	(p20-26)
John Scott [verses] by George Tyrrell	(p27-28)
A Cruise to St.Laurence-on-Sea	(p28-32)
Our Van [inc. Newmarket Week; Eggesford Hunt; Tavistock Hounds; Obituaries of William Rigden, Clough Newcome and John Scott]	(p32-44)
Hunting: Lists of Hounds, Masters, Huntsmen, Whips, Kennels	(p45-62)

Issue 142 : December 1871

Portrait and Biography - Jacob Pleydell-Bouverie	(p63-65)
The King of the Kennel [verses] by George Whyte-Melville	(p65-66)
A King in the Vale by George Tyrrell	(p67-75)
The Mare and her Master [verses] by Rowland Egerton-Warburton	(p76-77)
Country Quarters - Yorkshire [Pontefract & Doncaster]	(p77-90)
Wolf Hunting and Wild Sport in Lower Brittany (part 5) by Edward Davies	(p91-99)
Slang Terms and Oriental Roots by John Hotten	(p99-103)
[Review] *Hints On Shore Shooting* by James Harting	(p103)
Cricket: The Public School Averages	(p104-112)
Our Van [inc. Great Shropshire Handicap; Worcester Races; Cheshire Hounds; Durham County Foxhounds; Obituaries of Steere Johnson and Jack Story; Hunting Club Proposal]	(p112-124)

Issue 143 : January 1872

Portrait and Biography - William Oakeley	(p125-126)
A Cheshire Song to an Irish Tune [verses] by Rowland Egerton-Warburton	(p127)
Country Quarters - The Holderness	(p127-141)
A Scenting Day [verses]	(p141-143)
The Days of Old	(p143-149)
Foxes : The Morrices by George Lowth	(p150-156)
November and December in the Shires: Melton by Peter Delme-Radcliffe	(p157-165)
Jack Blake, or Landed at Last (part 4)	(p165-172)
Our Van [inc. Islington Agricultural Show; Kingsbury Races; Obituaries of Wyndham Smith, William Lovell and Hugh Johnstone; Harborough Hunt Dispute]	(p173-186)

Issue 144 : February 1872

Portrait and Biography - William Throckmorton	(p187-188)
Ware Wire [verses] by George Whyte-Melville	(p188-189)
Country Quarters - The North Country Packs	(p189-196)
Master McGrath [verses]	(p196-197)
Slang Terms and their Derivations by John Hotten	(p198-203)
A Decade of Turf Cracks (part 1) by George Tyrrell	(p203-211)
Wolf Hunting and Wild Sport in Lower Brittany (part 6) by Edward Davies	(p212-219)
Jack Blake, or Landed at Last (part 5)	(p219-228)
Deer Stalking in the Highlands by William Wilson	(p228-234)

Our Van [inc. Grand National Hunt Committee; Abergavenny Steeplechasing; Oakley Hunt; Berkeley Hounds; Obituaries of Harry King, George Story and Henry Scott] (p234-248)

Issue 145 : March 1872

Portrait and Biography - John Coupland (p249-250)
Country Quarters - Sinnington, Johnstone's, Cleveland (p250-257)
A Decade of Turf Cracks (part 2) by George Tyrrell (p258-265)
Epigram on a Hard Riding Youth Named Taylor [verses] by Rowland Egerton-Warburton (p265)
Wolf Hunting and Wild Sport in Lower Brittany (part 7) by Edward Davies (p266-271)
Recollections of a Day's Hare Hunting in Surrey by Charles Newmarch (p271-275)
Wild Fowl Shooting in Dutch Waters (part 1) by James Harting (p275-283)
Jack Blake, or Landed at Last (part 6) (p283-290)
My First Lion Hunt by Frederick Bennett (p291-292)
Coursing: The Waterloo Cup by George Wilson (p293-297)
Our Van [inc. South London Harriers; Sutton Coldfield Steeplechase; Cotswold Hounds; Review of *Satanella* by George Whyte-Melville] (p297-310)

Issue 146 : April 1872

Portrait and Biography - John Leigh (p311-312)
Touts by George Tyrrell (p312-318)
Country Quarters - Durham (p318-330)
Turf Nomenclature (part 2) by John Hotten (p330-336)
A Jingle of the Guineas [verses] (p336)
Wolf Hunting and Wild Sport in Lower Brittany (part 8) by Edward Davies (p337-342)
Sailing Away (p343-344)
Paullo Majora Canamus [verses] (p345-348)
Wild Fowl Shooting in Dutch Waters (part 2) by James Harting (p349-355)
Yachting and Rowing [University Boat Race] (p355-359)
Our Van [inc. Windsor Steeplechasing; Croydon Meeting; Tynedale Hunt; Obituaries of Richard Bourke, William Lowther and Frederick des Voeux; Gun Club] (p360-372)

Issue 147 : May 1872

Portrait and Biography - Henry Briscoe (p373-374)
Country Quarters - The Durham Country (p374-394)
Welshers by George Tyrrell (p394-399)
Wolf Hunting and Wild Sport in Lower Brittany (part 9) by Edward Davies (p399-406)
Kangaroo in the Cab Rank [verses] by Comyns Cole (p406)
The Billesdon Coplow by Robert Lowth [A Classic of Sporting Literature] (p407-413)
The Cheshire Hounds [verses] (p414)
Recollections of our Stale Contributor (part 1) by Thomas Groome (p415-417)
Yachting and Rowing [inc. Watermens' Matches; Obituaries of Alfred Shoolbred and Donald Doran] (p417-418)
Our Van [inc. Abergavenny Meeting; Epsom Races; Hambledon Hunt; Obituaries of Algernon Peyton and Thomas Wesley] (p419-430)

Volume 22, June - December 1872

Issue 148 : June 1872

Portrait of Frank Goodall, huntsman Title page
Portrait and Biography - John Astley (p1-3)
The Award [Decision of Masters of Foxhounds Stewards for Whaddon Chase Hunt] (p3)

Our Private View by George Tyrrell (p4-9)

The Song of the Mountain Stream [verses] by John Hotten (p10)

Wolf Hunting and Wild Sport in Lower Brittany (part 10) by Edward Davies (p11-18)

Deer Stalking by William Wilson (p18-24)

How Captain Coverhack took the Wire Fence Foxhounds (p24-35)

Recollections of our Stale Contributor (part 2) by Thomas Groome (p35-39)

The Ostler's Story by Charles Newmarch (p39-43)

Cricket [inc. Reviews of *The Cricketers' Annual* by Charles Alcock and *The Cricket Field* by Frederick Gale] by Thomas Pelham (p43-48)

Yachting and Rowing [inc. Kingston Rowing Club; Professional Rowing Matches] (p48-52)

Our Van [inc. Somerset Stakes; Coaching Club Meeting; Brooksend Harriers; Hunt Servants' Benefit Society; Obituary of Richard Morris] (p53-62)

Issue 149 : July 1872

Portrait and Biography - James Ashbury (p63-65)

The Regeneration of the Thoroughbred by George Tyrrell (p66-71)

Wolf Hunting and Wild Sport in Lower Brittany (part 11) by Edward Davies (p71-79)

Translations From the Greek Anthology [verses] by John Hotten (p79)

The Crystal Palace Dog Show by George Wilson (p80-85)

My Old Horn [verses] by Edward Davies (p86-87)

Shark Fishing at Jamaica by Frederick Bennett (p87-89)

The Brush by George Lowth (p90-94)

Recollections of our Stale Contributor (part 3) by Thomas Groome (p95-97)

Cricket [inc. Leg-Before-Wicket Opinion; University match] by Thomas Pelham (p98-104)

Yachting and Rowing [inc. Royal Thames Yacht Club; Atalanta Boat Club of New York Races] (p104-110)

Our Van [inc. Royal Hunt Cup; Hurlingham Club; Middle Park Closing Sale; Obituaries of William Greenwood, Thomas Scotland, George Delme and John George; Australian Cricket] (p111-124)

Issue 150 : August 1872

Portrait and Biography - George Manners (p125)

The Stud Company [Formed to succeed Middle Park] by George Tyrrell (p126-131)

Wolf Hunting and Wild Sport in Lower Brittany (part 12) by Edward Davies (p131-138)

Scotch Moors and Shooting by Theobald de Vismes (p138-145)

Shakespeare as a Sportsman (part 1) by Thomas Groome (p145-155)

A Night's Shooting in Western Africa by Frederick Bennett (p155-157)

Epitaph to a Huntsman [verses] by Edward Davies (p158-159)

Saddle, Spur and Spear [verses] by Edward Davies (p160-161)

Cock Shooting in Albania by Frederick Bennett (p161-163)

Cricket [inc. Eton versus Harrow; Gilbert Grace's Batting] by Thomas Pelham (p163-168)

The Schools Match [Eton's Coach; Harrow Behaviour] (p169-171)

Yachting and Rowing [inc. Wingfield Sculls; Marlow Regatta] (p171-173)

Our Van [inc. Newmarket Ladies Stand; Alexandra Park Meeting; Melbourne Cricket Club Meeting; Windsor Polo; Nebraska Shooting Party; Obituaries of Ginger Durant and Charles Fitzroy] (p173-186)

Issue 151 : September 1872

Portrait and Biography - George Craven (p187-188)

The Last of Middle Park by George Tyrrell (p188-197)

Shakespeare as a Sportsman (part 2) by Thomas Groome (p197-207)

Wolf Hunting and Wild Sport in Lower Brittany (part 13) by Edward Davies (p207-214)

The Teignbridge Cricket Club by George Lowth (p215-221)

A Reminiscence of Kaffirland (part 1) by Frank Streatfield (p222-227)
Shooting at Sierra Leone by Frederick Bennett (p227-230)
Yachting and Rowing [inc. Isle of Wight Gala; Doggett's Coat & Badge] (p231-237)
Our Van [inc. Goodwood Meeting; Knavesmire Races, Devon Cricket] (p237-248)

Issue 152 : October 1872

Portrait and Biography - Robert Arkwright (p249-250)
Wilton [verses] by George Tyrrell (p250-251)
Wolf Hunting and Wild Sport in Lower Brittany (part 14) by Edward Davies (p251-259)
Recollections of our Stale Contributor (part 4) by Thomas Groome (p259-263)
Snipe Shooting in China by Frederick Bennett (p263-266)
Lays of Many Lands: Ariel's Song by John Hotten (p266-267)
An Adventure with Mexican Hogs by Frederick Bennett (p267-270)
The First of September by George Wilson (p270-274)
After Behemoth by Frederick Bennett (p274-277)
Litho Fracteur Percussion Shells Small Arm Projectile by Henry Leveson (p277-281)
The Brach [refers to Shakespeare as a Sportsman] by George Lowth (p281-282)
Cricket [inc. Surrey Matches; Law Confusion] by Thomas Pelham (p282-286)
Yachting and Rowing [inc. London Rowing Club; Scullers' Races] (p286-288)
Our Van [inc. Baden-Baden Meeting; Devon Cricket; Review of *The Setter* by Edward Laverack; Obituaries of Henley Greaves, Ben Land, Thomas Tryon and Charles Carew] (p288-302)

Issue 153 : November 1872

Portrait and Biography - Francis Scott (p303-305)
Country Quarters - [Wiltshire] Beaufort's Hounds (p305-312)
Wolf Hunting and Wild Sport in Lower Brittany (part 15) by Edward Davies (p313-320)
Letters to Tyro (part 1) by Robert Colton (p320-324)
A Reminiscence of Kaffirland (part 2) by Frank Streatfield (p324-328)
Late Shooting by Charles Newmarch (p328-331)
Our Van [inc. The Cesarewitch; Isle of Thanet Harriers; South Devon Hunt; Jockey Club Scandal] (p331-346)
Hunting: Lists of Hounds, Masters, Huntsmen, Whips, Kennels (p347-364)

Issue 154 : December 1872

Portrait and Biography - Francis Fitzhardinge (p365-366)
To The Editor [verses] by George Tyrrell (p366-368)
Country Quarters - Gloucestershire: Lord Fitzhardinge's Hounds (p368-376)
Farewell to Tarporley [verses] (p376-378)
Letters to Tyro (part 2) by Robert Colton (p378-381)
'Henry Morton Stanley' [real name John Rowlands] and his Book *How I Found Livingstone* (p382-391)
The Vaynol Field Trials by Peter Delme-Radcliffe (p391-397)
Wolf Hunting and Wild Sport in Lower Brittany (part 16) by Edward Davies (p397-404)
Sport at Graytown, Nicaragua by Frederick Bennett (p405-407)
Our Van [inc. Warwick Races; Shrewsbury Meeting; Puckeridge Hunt; East Dorset Hounds; Foxhunting Club Formation] (p407-422)

Volume 23, January - July 1873

Issue 155 : January 1873

Portrait of William Yardley   Title page

Portrait and Biography - Fredrick Brockman (p1-2)
Tally-Ho! [verses] by George Whyte-Melville (p3-4)
Stud Prospects by George Tyrrell (p4-11)
Letters to Tyro (part 3) by Robert Colton (p11-16)
Country Quarters - Cheltenham Staghounds, The Cotswold and the North Cotswold (p16-29)
November and December in the Shires: Rugby by Peter Delme-Radcliffe (p29-39)
Cricket: The Public School Averages by Thomas Pelham (p39-46)
Marylebone Cricket Club North American Tour (p46-48)
Our Van [inc. Bromley Races; Tynedale Hunt; Surrey Union Hounds; Obituaries of William Tollemache, Felix Whitehurst (*Baily's* contributor), John Starkey and Thomas Tedder; New Bristol Racecourse] (p48-62)

Issue 156 : February 1873

Portrait and Biography - Humphrey de Trafford (p63-64)
Letters to Tyro (part 4) by Robert Colton (p64-67)
Country Quarters - The Vale of White Horse (p67-78)
The Pheasant and the Fox [verses] by Rowland Egerton-Warburton (p79)
Wolf Hunting and Wild Sport in Lower Brittany (part 17) by Edward Davies (p80-87)
Lord Kintore on Mr Meynell's System of Hunting (p88-92)
Recollections of our Stale Contributor (part 5) by Thomas Groome (p93-97)
A Dream of the Happy Hunting Grounds by William Cartwright (p97-103)
A Shooting Excursion From Naples by Frederick Bennett (p104-107)
Forest Hunting by Charles Newmarch (p107-110)
Our Van [inc. Cottesmore Hunt; Bicester Hounds; Rothschild's Staghounds; Review of *The Pleasant History of Reynard the Fox* by Henry von Alkmar; Obituaries of James Robinson, Charles Mayo and Charles Bonaparte] (p110-124)

Issue 157 : March 1873

Portrait and Biography - Dudley North (p125)
Wolf Hunting and Wild Sport in Lower Brittany (part 18) by Edward Davies (p126-134)
Recollections of our Stale Contributor (part 6) by Thomas Groome (p134-137)
Coursing: The Waterloo Cup by George Wilson (p138-143)
The Dog Breaker by Charles Newmarch (p144-147)
Country Quarters - [Wiltshire] The Tedworth (p148-161)
[Obituary] Tom Hills, huntsman (p161-164)
A Day's Shooting near Ephesus by Frederick Bennett (p165-167)
A Night's Fishing by the Bay of Biscay by Edward Michell (p168-171)
Our Van [inc. Surrey Union Hunt; South Berkshire Hounds; Bickley Steeplechase] (p172-186)

Issue 158 : April 1873

Portrait and Biography - John Everett (p187)
Country Quarters - The South Wilts (p188-199)
Wolf Hunting and Wild Sport in Lower Brittany (part 19) by Edward Davies (p200-207)
A Man from the Next County (p208-219)
Mr Trelawny's Foxhounds by Peter Delme-Radcliffe (p219-223)
A Day amongst the Ptarmigan (p224-226)
The Fayre One with ye Golden Locks (part 1) by Henry Grattan & Leonard Garston [here as Bryant de Butcherbootes] (p226-232)
The Vixen [verses] (p232)
Our Van [inc. Grand Military Gold Cup; Bristol Racecourse; Tynedale Hunt; Obituaries of Thomas Squires and John Denison; Lillie Bridge Polo Club] (p233-248)

Issue 159 : May 1873

Portrait and Biography - Arthur Annesley	(p249-250)
Country Quarters - Hertfordshire	(p250-269)
Wolf Hunting and Wild Sport in Lower Brittany (part 20) by Edward Davies	(p269-277)
The Shires: Melton by Edward Pennell-Elmhirst	(p277-285)
The Fayre One with ye Golden Locks (part 2) by Bryant de Butcherbootes	(p285-289)
Turtle Turning at Ascension Island by Frederick Bennett	(p289-292)
Our Van [inc. Northamptonshire Stakes; Newmarket Craven Meeting; Conyngham Cup; North Cotswold Hunt; East Sussex Hunt Steeplechase; South of England Coursing Club; Obituaries of John Hope, Henry Coventry and John Welfitt]	(p293-310)

Issue 160 : June 1873

Portrait and Biography - Charles Carington	(p311-312)
Fresh Fields and Pastures New by George Tyrrell	(p312-318)
[Obituary] Lord Zetland [verses] by George Tyrrell	(p318-319)
Wolf Hunting and Wild Sport in Lower Brittany (part 21) by Edward Davies	(p320-327)
Farewell to the Horn [verses]	(p327)
The Fayre One with ye Golden Locks (part 3) by Bryant de Butcherbootes	(p328-337)
The Lovers' Quarrel [verses] by Rowland Egerton-Warburton	(p338-339)
The Road in 1873 (part 1) [History of Modern Coaching] by Charles Newmarch	(p339-343)
Otter Hunting in the West by Alexander Clark-Kennedy	(p343-348)
May Song [verses]	(p349)
A Chapter on Bagmen by Charles Newmarch	(p349-353)
Cricket [inc. County Residential Qualifications; Champions' Cup] by Thomas Pelham	(p353-359)
Yachting and Rowing [inc. Royal London Yacht Club; Tyne Rowing]	(p360-361)
Our Van [inc. Chester Race Meeting; Obituaries of John Smith, Edward Topham and Thomas Dundas; Ivybridge Hunt; Tarporley Hunt Club Poetry]	(p362-372)

Issue 161 : July 1873

Portrait and Biography - Henry Boyle	(p373-374)
Our Contemporary Reviewer by George Tyrrell	(p374-379)
Wolf Hunting and Wild Sport in Lower Brittany (part 22) by Edward Davies	(p379-384)
Vive la Chasse [verses] by Rowland Egerton-Warburton	(p385-386)
The Road in 1873 (part 2) by Charles Newmarch	(p387-395)
Sport in France in 1793 and 1873 by Lewis Clements	(p395-399)
The Old Horse [verses]	(p399)
A Strange Adventure with a Tiger by Frederick Bennett	(p400-403)
Cricket [inc.Yorkshire Matches; University Fixture] by Thomas Pelham	(p403-414)
Yachting and Rowing [inc. Thames Schooner Races; Royal Harwich Yacht Club]	(p414-417)
Our Van [inc. Islington Horse Show; Ascot Races; Hursley Hunt; Cobham Stud; Hunt Servants' Benefit Society]	(p418-430)

Volume 24, August 1873 - February 1874

Issue 162 : August 1873

Portrait of Charles Maidment, jockey	Title page
Portrait and Biography - John Beresford	(p1)
Wolf Hunting and Wild Sport in Lower Brittany (part 23) by Edward Davies	(p2-10)
The Adventures of Octavo Quivery by Ashburnham Bulley	(p10-19)
Country Sketches: My Lord's Herdsman by William Cartwright	(p19-24)
Salmon Farming	(p24-36)
The Legend of Beddgelert by Thomas Groome	(p36-37)

A Night's Shooting at Mahumba Bay, West Africa by Frederick Bennett (p38-40)

Cricket [inc. Canadian Touring Team; Lord's Ground Capacity] by Thomas Pelham (p41-45)

Yachting and Rowing [inc. Royal Cinque Ports Yacht Club; Henley Regatta] (p46-50)

Our Van [inc. Newmarket Week; Worcester Meeting; Lillie Bridge Polo; Review of *Newmarket and Arabia* by Roger Upton; Obituary of Thomas Melrose] (p51-62)

Issue 163 : September 1873

Portrait and Biography - Henry Petre (p63-64)

Queen's Plates [Parliamentary Select Committee Report] by George Tyrrell (p64-68)

The King of the West [verses] by George Whyte-Melville (p69-70)

Wolf Hunting and Wild Sport in Lower Brittany (part 24) by Edward Davies (p70-78)

The Cowes Week by George Hopcroft (p78-84)

The Doncaster Sales by William Tulloch (p84-89)

Lammermuir, 1873 [verses] (p89-90)

The Feast of St.Partridge by George Wilson (p91-95)

Fiesta de Toro [A Bullfight in Madrid] (p95-103)

Cricket [inc. Canterbury week; I Zingari Match] by Thomas Pelham (p104-108)

Yachting and Rowing [inc. Ryde Yachting; Barnes Regatta] (p109-112)

Our Van [inc. Goodwood Cup; Ebor Meeting; Reviews of *Court and Social Life* in France by Felix Whitehurst and *The Book of the Horse* by Samuel Sydney] (p112-124)

Issue 164 : October 1873

Portrait and Biography - Edward Kerrison (p125-126)

Tom French [verses] by George Tyrrell (p126-127)

Wolf Hunting and Wild Sport in Lower Brittany (part 25) by Edward Davies (p127-135)

Brow, Bay and Tray [verses] by George Whyte-Melville (p135-138)

Racket Reminiscences [History of Rackets] by Thomas Groome (p138-144)

The Earl of Portsmouth's Foxhounds by George Lowth (p145-155)

Recollections of an Aristocrat (part 1) by Theobald de Vismes (p156-164)

October Song [verses] (p165)

Partridge Shooting in Sicily by Frederick Bennett (p165-168)

Thoughts on Hunting by George Newmarch (p168-171)

A Lament for John Gallon [verses] by Edward Davies (p172)

Cricket [inc. England Team to Australia; County Reports] by Thomas Pelham (p173-176)

Our Van [inc. Warwick Races; Ayr Meeting; Cottesmore Hunt; Obituary of Tom French] (p176-186)

Issue 165 : November 1873

Portrait and Biography - Richard Lant (p187)

Lord and Laird by George Tyrrell (p188-193)

Wolf Hunting and Wild Sport in Lower Brittany (part 26) by Edward Davies (p194-199)

On the Feeding of Hounds by Wellington Stapleton-Cotton (p200-201)

The Man with One Hunter [verses] by Rowland Egerton-Warburton (p201-202)

Cub Hunting by George Newmarch (p202-205)

Country Quarters - The Old Berkshire (p206-215)

Our Van [inc. Newmarket Meeting; Hunt Changes; South Durham Hunt; New Forest Foxhounds; Thames Sculling] (p216-231)

Hunting: Lists of Hounds, Masters, Huntsmen, Whips, Kennels (p232-248)

Issue 166 : December 1873

Portrait and Biography - Archibald Calvert (p249-250)

A Conservative Reaction by George Tyrrell (p250-256)

Wolf Hunting and Wild Sport in Lower Brittany (part 27) by Edward Davies (p256-265)

Brother Tom [verses] by Rowland Egerton-Warburton (p265-266)
Country Quarters - Berkshire: The Craven (p266-278)
The Country Horse Breaker by George Newmarch (p278-282)
My First Day's Sport in South Africa by Frederick Bennett (p282-284)
Cricket: The Public School Averages by Thomas Pelham (p285-294)
Our Van [inc. Aintree Meeting; Shrewsbury Races; Cotswold Hunt; Yorkshire Hound Show;
    Obituaries of George Laporte (Engraver for *The Sporting Magazine*) and
    Greville Sartoris] (p294-310)

Issue 167 : January 1874

Portrait and Biography - Ralph Nevill (p311-312)
The Prince of the Two Year Course [verses] (p312-314)
Country Quarters - The South Berks and Old Bramshill (p314-327)
On Feeding of Hounds by George Lowth (p327-328)
Recollections of an Aristocrat (part 2) by Theobald de Vismes (p329-338)
Country Sketches: Blyster the Vet by William Cartwright (p338-345)
Won by a Fluke (p345-351)
Duck Decoying in France by Lewis Clements (p351-357)
Sport at Lisbon by Frederick Bennett (p358-361)
Our Van [inc. Smithfield Club Cattle Show; Kingsbury Meeting; National Hunt Committee;
    Obituaries of Chandos Pole and John Haynes; Fife Hounds] (p361-372)

Issue 168 : February 1874

Portrait and Biography - Henry Fitzroy (p373-375)
Cross-Country and Coursing Reform by George Tyrrell (p375-380)
Country Quarters - Hampshire: The Hambledon & Hartley (p380-396)
The Stranger's Story [verses] by Rowland Egerton-Warburton (p397-399)
Frank Raleigh of Watercombe (part 1) by Edward Davies (p399-407)
Trapped [verses] (p407-408)
Ostrich Hunting in South Africa by Frederick Bennett (p409-414)
With Hounds [verses] (p414)
Our Van [inc. Oakley Hunt; Formation of Old Worcestershire Hunt; Life of Tom Olliver;
    Obituary of Richard Bloxsidge; Review of *Pheasants for Coverts and Aviaries*
    by William Tegetmeier] (p415-430)

Volume 25, March - September 1874

Issue 169 : March 1874

Portrait of Henry Constable Title page
Portrait and Biography - Henry Cavendish (p1-2)
Country Quarters - The Hambledon Hunt (p2-15)
[Obituary] A Model Sportsman [Mayer de Rothschild] (p15-21)
Frank Raleigh of Watercombe (part 2) by Edward Davies (p21-30)
Recollections of our Stale Contributor (part 7) by Thomas Groome (p30-36)
A Month in the West [West Country Hunting reports] by Edward Pennell-Elmhirst (p36-40)
Voltigeur [verses] by George Tyrrell (p40-41)
Coursing: The Waterloo Cup by George Wilson (p41-48)
Our Van [inc. Tynedale Hunt; Fife Hounds; Review of *Old Sports and Sportsmen* by John
    Randall; Obituaries of Thomas St.Lawrence, George Hilton and James Randell] (p49-62)

Issue 170 : April 1874

Portrait and Biography - George Fenwick (p63-65)

Mayer de Rothschild [verses]   (p66-67)
Country Quarters - The Vine [Berks, Hants, Oxen]   (p67-85)
Frank Raleigh of Watercombe (part 3) by Edward Davies   (p85-95)
The Bookmaker's Horse [verses] by George Tyrrell   (p95-96)
Recollections of an Aristocrat (part 3) by Theobald de Vismes   (p96-104)
A Leicestershire Burst [verses]   (p105)
Our Van [inc. Aylesbury Steeplechasing; Bristol Meeting; Vale of White Horse Hunt; Forfarshire
           Hounds; Obituaries of George Fitzwilliam and Henry Westenra]   (p106-124)

Issue 171 : May 1874

Portrait and Biography - William Beauclerk   (p125)
Country Quarters - The Hursley [Hampshire]   (p126-139)
Newmarket A.D.1900 [verses]   (p139-142)
Frank Raleigh of Watercombe (part 4) by Edward Davies   (p143-152)
Sensation Sketches by Pen and Pencil by George Tyrrell   (p152-156)
Recollections of an Aristocrat (part 4) by Theobald de Vismes   (p156-165)
Two Day's Shooting in Fatshan Creek, Canton by Frederick Bennett   (p165-170)
Yachting and Rowing [inc. Royal Thames Yacht Club; Thames Rowing]   (p170-172)
Our Van [inc. Punchestown Meeting; Craven Hounds; New Forest Hunt; Obituaries of Ulick
           De-Burgh, William Morritt and Robert Basham]   (p173-186)

Issue 172 : June 1874

Portrait and Biography - Egremont Lascelles   (p187)
Country Quarters - The New Forest and Lord Radnor's   (p188-204)
The Betting Bill by George Tyrrell   (p205-210)
The Fly-Fisher [verses] by Edward Marston   (p210-212)
The First of May in Piccadilly by Charles Newmarch   (p212-215)
The Life and Times of Tommy Coleman by Comyns Cole   (p216-225)
Cricket [inc. England Tour Details; Marylebone Cricket Club Amateur Status] (p225-232)
Our Van [inc. Coaching Reports; Chester Meeting; Carlisle Otterhounds; Westward Ho! Golf;
           Manchester Horse Show; Obituaries of Ouseley Higgins, John Angell and
           Harry Ayris]   (p232-248)

Issue 173 : July 1874

Portrait and Biography - William Morritt [In Memoriam] by George Whyte-Melville (p249-254)
Down and Heath by George Tyrrell   (p254-260)
Frank Raleigh of Watercombe (part 5) by Edward Davies   (p261-269)
A Sporting Cruise to Sardinia (part 1) by Frederick Bennett   (p269-277)
Jinkisson's Duels (part 1) by Thomas Groome   (p277-284)
Cricket [inc. Oxford University Matches; Public Schools' Reports]   (p284-291)
Yachting and Rowing [inc. Royal London Yacht Club; Henley Regatta]   (p291-296)
Our Van [inc. Epsom Meeting; Hurlingham Polo; Totnes Otterhounds; Obituary of Frederick
           Rhodes]   (p296-310)

Issue 174 : August 1874

Portrait and Biography - William Cooper   (p311-313)
Betting in High and Low Places by George Tyrrell   (p313-319)
Frank Raleigh of Watercombe (part 6) by Edward Davies   (p319-330)
Jinkisson's Duels (part 2) by Thomas Groome   (p330-337)
The Old Forester's Story by Charles Newmarch   (p337-341)
Otter Hunting and the Hounds of Geoffrey Hill by George Lowth   (p341-346)
Cricket [inc. Cambridge University Team; Yorkshire Matches]   (p346-353)

Yachting and Rowing [inc. Marlow Regatta; *Sporting Life* Payment; Obituary of John Keen]   (p353-357)
Our Van [inc. Kingsbury Racing Prosecution; Newmarket Land Purchase; Alexandra Park
        Horse Show; Obituary of Jem Hills; Launch of *The World* Magazine]   (p358-372)

Issue 175 : September 1874

Portrait and Biography - Henry Ulick   (p373)
A Pig's Whisper on the St.Leger [verses]   (p374)
Frank Raleigh of Watercombe (part 7) by Edward Davies   (p375-383)
A Day with the Devon & Somerset Staghounds by Comyns Cole   (p384-391)
Recollections of our Stale Contributor (part 8) by Thomas Groome   (p391-397)
A Day's Snipe Shooting Near Palermo by Frederick Bennett   (p397-400)
A Sporting Cruise to Sardinia (part 2) by Frederick Bennett   (p400-411)
Cricket [inc. Nottinghamshire Season; American Baseball Tourists]   (p412-416)
Yachting and Rowing [inc. Victoria Yacht Club; Thames National Regatta]   (p416-418)
Our Van [inc. Brighton Meeting; Obituaries of William Annesley, Sackville Lane-Fox and
        Harry Boulton; Exmouth Cricket; York Races]   (p419-430)

Volume 26, October 1874 - April 1875

Issue 176 : October 1874

Portrait of Henry Jupp   Title page
Portrait and Biography - Granville Leveson-Gower   (p1-3)
A Lame Apology [St.Leger Week] by George Tyrrell   (p3-12)
Frank Raleigh of Watercombe (part 8) by Edward Davies   (p12-19)
A Sporting Cruise to Sardinia (part 3) by Frederick Bennett   (p20-30)
On the Rails [Life in Hyde Park]   (p31-36)
[Review] *Uncle John* by George Whyte-Melville   (p36-38)
Sport in the Far West by Henry Leveson   (p39-45)
Our Van [inc. Warwick Races; Curragh Meeting; Quorn Hunt; Royal Kennels; Obituary of
        Brownlow North; John Corlett of *The Sporting Times*]   (p46-62)

Issue 177 : November 1874

Portrait and Biography - David Roche   (p63)
At the Post by George Tyrrell   (p64-70)
Country Quarters - The Essex   (p70-83)
Frank Raleigh of Watercombe (part 9) by Edward Davies   (p84-93)
Our Van [inc. Newmarket Meeting; West Wilts Hunt; Southwark Court Horse Trial; Obituaries
        of John Weld, John Free, William Blyth and Morgan Williams]   (p93-106)
Hunting: Lists of Hounds, Masters, Huntsmen, Whips, Kennels   (p107-124)

Issue 178 : December 1874

Portrait and Biography - Robert Vyner   (p125)
A Lay of the Ranston Bloodhounds [verses] by George Whyte-Melville   (p126-128)
Country Quarters - The Essex Union   (p128-137)
Carmen Triumphale [verses] by George Tyrrell   (p137-144)
Frank Raleigh of Watercombe (part 10) by Edward Davies   (p144-152)
Cricket: The Public School Averages, 1874   (p152-164)
Behind the Floats by Francis Francis   (p165-170)
Our Van [inc. Worcester Races; Shrewsbury Meeting; Tedworth Hounds; Obituaries of
        John Squires, Cave Humfrey and Thomas Swindell; Opening of *The Road
        Club* Premises]   (p171-186)

Issue 179 : January 1875

Portrait and Biography - Anthony Hamond (p187)
Fashionable Fatlings by George Tyrrell (p188-194)
Frank Raleigh of Watercombe (part 11) by Edward Davies (p195-204)
A Sporting Cruise to Sardinia (part 4) by Frederick Bennett (p205-215)
Recollections of our Stale Contributor (part 9) by Thomas Groome (p215-221)
Stray Recollections of Epping Forest by Edward Buxton (p221-222)
The Game Laws (part 1) by Charles Lefevre (p222-229)
Sport at Jamaica by Frederick Bennett (p230-233)
Our Van [inc. Grove Hunt; South Devon Hounds; Obituaries of John Trollope, Philip
         Honywood, Charles Meek, Harry Feist (of *Sporting Life*), Paddy Green and
         Thomas Marshall] (p233-248)

Issue 180 : February 1875

Portrait and Biography - George Herbert (p249-250)
The Turf in Ireland by George Tyrrell (p250-258)
Country Quarters - The Essex Staghounds (p258-262)
Frank Raleigh of Watercombe (part 12) by Edward Davies (p262-270)
[Review] *The Noble Science* by Peter Delme-Radcliffe (p270-271)
New Year's Day [verses] (p272-273)
The Game Laws (part 2) by Charles Lefevre (p273-281)
Sport in the Italian Alps by Henry Leveson (p282-287)
How We Won the Pony Race by Charles Newmarch (p288-291)
Our Van [inc. Skating in Hyde Park; Pytchley Hunt; Hertfordshire Hunt Club; Review of
         Kennel Stud Book II by Cornelius Tongue; Obituary of Robert Clarke;
         West of England Stud] (p292-310)

Issue 181 : March 1875

Portrait and Biography - Robert Harvey (p311-312)
Racers and Chasers by George Tyrrell (p312-318)
Country Quarters - The East Essex (p318-326)
Frank Raleigh of Watercombe (part 13) by Edward Davies (p326-333)
The Roaring Game [Curling] (p333-342)
Coursing: The Waterloo Cup by George Wilson (p342-356)
Our Van [inc. Sandown Park Racecourse; Market Harborough Hunt Ball; Her Majesty's
         Staghounds; Obituaries of Charles Pelham and Jack Mytton] (p357-372)

Issue 182 : April 1875

Portrait and Biography - Henry Spencer Lucy (p373-375)
Country Quarters - The Essex and Suffolk (p375-383)
'Tis Sixty Years Since [verses] by Rowland Egerton Warburton (p383-385)
Frank Raleigh of Watercombe (part 14) by Edward Davies (p385-394)
Conger-Fishing on the Coast of North Cornwall by George Lowth (p394-402)
Henry Jupp of Dorking by Frederick Gale (p403-405)
Boniface's Benefit [Flintshire Hunters' Cup] (p405-411)
The University Boat Race (p411-413)
Our Van [inc. Holderness Hunt; Hertfordshire Hounds; Croydon Races; Obituaries of Gerard
         Leigh and Sidney Thorp] (p413-430)

Volume 27, May - November 1875

Issue 183 : May 1875

Portrait of John Osborne, jockey	Title page
Portrait and Biography - Charles Stewart	(p1)
Frank Raleigh of Watercombe (part 15) by Edward Davies	(p2-9)
[Obituary] Edward Budd and the Cricket of Earlier Days by James Pycroft	(p9-16)
[Obituary] Joseph Hawley by Comyns Cole	(p17-19)
A Wild Legend of the West by Charles Newmarch	(p19-23)
In Memoriam [verses]: [Great Hopes, Horse]	(p24-25)
Root and Branch (Byerley, Darley, Godolphin) by George Tyrrell	(p26-34)
Kildare Red-Coat Race by Comyns Cole	(p35-39)
A Few Casts with a Fly-Rod by Edward Marston	(p39-43)
Put Away [verses]	(p43)
Yachting and Rowing [inc. New Thames Yacht Club; Tyne Rowing]	(p44-45)
Our Van [inc. Warwick Meeting; Sandown Park Races; Beaufort Hunt; Tedworth Hounds; Lillie Bridge Polo Club; Obituaries of John Salter, Rowland Errington, John Tharp and Hardinge Browne]	(p46-62)

Issue 184 : June 1875

Portrait and Biography - George Glyn	(p63-64)
Gerald Sturt on the Horse Question	(p64-67)
Root and Branch [Byerley Turk & Godolphin Arabian] by George Tyrrell	(p67-75)
How Tom Hall's Fortune was Made by Charles Newmarch	(p75-87)
Frank Raleigh of Watercombe (part 16) by Edward Davies	(p87-94)
Life in the Far West by Henry Leveson	(p94-101)
The Dog-Feeder's Ghost Story by Charles Newmarch	(p101-104)
Cricket [inc. Marylebone Cricket Club Players; Qualification of Colts]	(p105-110)
Yachting and Rowing [inc. Royal London Yacht Club; Oxford University Boat Club]	(p110-111)
Our Van [inc. Chester Cup; Obituary of Peter Withington; Coaching; Cobham Stud]	(p111-124)

Issue 185 : July 1875

Portrait and Biography - Joseph Houldsworth	(p125)
The 'Noble Animal' at the Royal Academy by George Tyrrell	(p125-130)
New Games at Hurlingham [Polo and Lawn Tennis] by Comyns Cole	(p131-140)
Frank Raleigh of Watercombe (part 17) by Edward Davies	(p140-149)
The Road in 1875 (part 1) by Charles Newmarch	(p149-156)
Cricket [inc. Marylebone Cricket Club Fixtures; University Matches]	(p156-166)
Yachting and Rowing [inc. Thames Yacht Races; Henley Regatta]	(p166-171)
Our Van [inc. Islington Horse Show; Ascot Meeting; Hunt Servants' Benefit Society; Hurlingham Polo]	(p171-186)

Issue 186 : August 1875

Portrait and Biography - Henry Tufton	(p187-188)
An Appeal to Stafford Northcote [Horse Breeding]	(p188-191)
Finis Coronat Opus [The Merry Stud] by George Tyrrell	(p192-198)
Frank Raleigh of Watercombe (part 18) by Edward Davies	(p198-208)
The Road in 1875 (part 2) by Charles Newmarch	(p208-215)
Slapton Lea (part 1) [A Devon Lake] by George Lowth	(p216-220)
Cricket [inc. University Match; Representative Teams]	(p220-232)
Yachting and Rowing [inc. Metropolitan Regatta; Wingfield Sculls]	(p233-234)

Our Van [inc. Newmarket Sales; Worcester Racecourse Bookmakers; Alexandra
        Palace Hound Show]   (p235-248)

Issue 187 : September 1875

Portrait and Biography - Gilbert Heathcote   (p249-250)
The Modern 'West' by George Tyrrell   (p250-256)
Provincial Coaching by Charles Newmarch   (p257-262)
Frank Raleigh of Watercombe (part 19) by Edward Davies   (p262-269)
A Pipe in Fuller Pilch's Back Parlour by Frederick Gale   (p270-279)
[Review] Winter in Summer: *A System of Figure Skating* by Henry Vandervell   (p279-283)
Cricket [inc. Marylebone Cricket Club Rules of Cricket; Gloucestershire Matches] (p283-292)
Yachting and Rowing [inc. Southampton Yacht Club; Obituary of James Layton; Ilex
        Swimming Club]   (p293-297)
Our Van [inc. Brighton Races; Carlisle Otterhounds; Yorkshire Horse & Hound Show;
        Devon & Somerset Staghounds; Obituaries of Henry Leigh, Alfred Dyson and
        Edward Baldock]   (p298-310)

Issue 188 : October 1875

Portrait and Biography - Turner Newcomen   (p311-312)
A 'Second October' Acrostic [verses] by Comyns Cole   (p312-313)
Frank Raleigh of Watercombe (part 20) by Edward Davies   (p313-321)
Tom Spring's Back Parlour by Frederick Gale   (p321-336)
Slapton Lea (part 2) by George Lowth   (p336-344)
A Run in the Woldshire Country by George Whyte-Melville   (p344-350)
The Newfoundland Dog and the Bicyclist [verses]   (p350)
A Day in a Punt by Charles Newmarch   (p351-355)
My Last Day's Sport in Africa by Frederick Bennett   (p355-358)
Our Van [inc. Warwick Races; Doncaster Meeting; Obituaries of Richard Bulkeley,
        Henry Leveson (*Baily's* contributor) and John Markwell]   (p359-372)

Issue 189 : November 1875

Biography - Harcourt Capper   (p373)
Friends in Council [Revised Laws of Racing] by George Tyrrell   (p374-380)
From Knavesmire to Penhill by George Wilson   (p380-392)
The Sporting Gent by Frederick Gale   (p392-399)
Our Van [inc. Newmarket Races; Cambridgeshire Hounds; Hertfordshire Hunt; Obituary of
        Walter Lyndon; Sandown Park Polo]   (p399-412)
Hunting: List of Hounds, Masters, Huntsmen, Whips, Kennels   (p413-430)

River Tyne Rowing

Volume 28, December 1875 - June 1876

Issue 190 : December 1875

Portrait of John Francis Clark, racing judge	Title page
Portrait and Biography - Spencer Compton	(p1-2)
Assumed Names [Racing] by George Tyrrell	(p3-7)
[Obituary] Frederick Miller [Cricketer] by Frederick Gale	(p7-10)
Frank Raleigh of Watercombe (part 21) by Edward Davies	(p10-18)
Stag Hunting by Charles Newmarch	(p19-25)
A New Era for Man and Beast [Electro-Magnetism] by Joseph Shorthouse	(p25-27)
Reclaimed by Charles Newmarch	(p27-35)
Cricket: The Public School Averages	(p36-48)
Our Van [inc. Worcester Races; Liverpool Cup; Salopian Hurdle; Quorn Hunt; Obituary of Henry Dence]	(p48-62)

Issue 191 : January 1876

Portrait and Biography - George Chetwynd	(p63-64)
For the Season 1876 by George Tyrrell	(p64-71)
Frank Raleigh of Watercombe (part 22) by Edward Davies	(p72-81)
Carpe Diem [verses]	(p81)
Experiences of Thomas Coleman (part 1) by Comyns Cole	(p82-92)
The 'Sell' Last Shooting Season	(p92-98)
On Cloutsham Ball by Charles Newmarch	(p98-106)
How to Restore County Elevens by Frederick Gale	(p106-112)
Our Van [inc. London Cattle Show; Royal Huntsman; Hampshire Hunt; Obituaries of George Greenwood and Peter Delme-Radcliffe; Worcestershire Agricultural Society]	(p112-124)

Issue 192 : February 1876

Portrait and Biography - Josslyn Pennington	(p125-126)
A Character [William Graham] by George Tyrrell	(p126-130)
Frank Raleigh of Watercombe (part 23) by Edward Davies	(p131-140)
Country Quarters - Cambridgeshire	(p140-149)
Hunting and Shooting [verses]	(p149)
Experiences of Thomas Coleman (part 2) by Comyns Cole	(p150-158)
Storms in Butter-Boats (part 1) by Robert Grimston	(p158-167)
About Several Men who went a-Angling by Frederick Gale	(p167-171)
Our Van [inc. Her Majesty's Buckhounds; Madras Hounds; Obituaries of Anthony Rothschild, Tommy Ward; Theobald de Vismes (*Baily's* contributor) and William Graham; Review of *Sister Louise* by George Whyte-Melville]	(p171-186)

Issue 193 : March 1876

Portrait and Biography - George Spencer-Churchill	(p187)
The First Grey Hair [verses] by George Whyte-Melville	(p188-189)
The Ring and the Book by George Tyrrell	(p189-194)
Frank Raleigh of Watercombe (part 24) by Edward Davies	(p194-202)
Country Quarters - The Old Surrey (part 1)	(p202-209)
How to do it [verses]	(p209)
Coursing: The Waterloo Cup by George Wilson	(p210-220)
A Reminiscence of the Brighton Downs by Charles Newmarch	(p220-226)
Thomas Coleman on Breeding and Training (part 3) by Comyns Cole	(p226-234)
The Macadamizer [verses] by Thomas Vigors	(p235)

Our Van [inc. Birmingham Steeplechases; Hambledon Hunt; Rufford Hounds; Obituaries of
        George Curzon, George Arundel, Edward Pellew, Daniel Berkshire, George
        Darby and Frederick Brockman]   (p236-248)

Issue 194 : April 1876

Portrait and Biography - Samuel Reynell   (p249-250)
Sire and Son by George Tyrrell   (p250-256)
The Close of the Season [verses] by Rowland Egerton-Warburton   (p256-257)
Fox Hunting Reminiscences of Hertfordshire (part 1)   (p258-262)
In the Forest by Comyns Cole   (p263-265)
Frank Raleigh of Watercombe (part 25) by Edward Davies   (p265-273)
Unpretending and Pretending Sports by Frederick Gale   (p274-281)
Country Quarters - The Old Surrey (part 2)   (p281-289)
With the Old Southern Hounds by Charles Newmarch   (p289-294)
Our Van [inc. Sandown Park Meeting; Bristol Races; Vale of White Horse Hunt; Ascot
        Racecourse Buildings; Review of *The Octopus* by Henry Lees; Obituary of
        John Barton]   (p295-310)

Issue 195 : May 1876

Portrait and Biography - Arthur Sumner   (p311-312)
Holiday Soldiers by William Alden   (p312-317)
William Augustus, Soldier and Sportsman   (p317-321)
Oxford and Cambridge Boat Race, 1876 [verses] by Frederick Gale   (p321)
Fox Hunting Reminiscences of Hertfordshire (part 2)   (p322-330)
Frank Raleigh of Watercombe (part 26) by Edward Davies   (p330-339)
Number One on his Trial by Frederick Gale   (p339-341)
On the Grass round Rugby by Charles Newmarch   (p342-350)
Recollections of Thomas Coleman (part 4) by Comyns Cole   (p350-361)
Our Van [inc. Bogside Races; Beaufort Hunt Steeplechases; New Newmarket Stand; Hursley
        Hunt; Petre Staghounds]   (p361-372)

Issue 196 : June 1876

Portrait and Biography - Henry Armitage   (p373-375)
Between the Showers by George Tyrrell   (p375-378)
Reminiscences of a Fox Hunter in Essex   (p379-384)
John Francis Clark [Racing Judge] by Joseph Shorthouse   (p385-388)
Storms in Butter-Boats (part 2) by Robert Grimston   (p388-392)
Half-Hours at Hatchett's by Thomas Taunton   (p392-400)
The Common Sense of Touting by William Alden   (p400-404)
Sport under Difficulties by Frederick Gale   (p404-410)
Cricket [Marylebone Cricket Club Annual Report; University Matches]   (p410-417)
Our Van [inc. Newmarket Spring Meeting; Obituaries of James Montgomery, William Hay,
        John Gore and Henry Poole; Manchester Horse Show; Mentmore Staghounds] (p418-430)

Volume 29, July 1876 - January 1877

Issue 197 : July 1876

Portrait of Robert Peck, horse trainer   Title page
Portrait and Biography - Alexander Baltazzi   (p1-2)
In the Park [Hyde Park]   (p2-8)
Round Whittlebury Forest by Charles Newmarch   (p8-14)

North versus South at Lord's by Frederick Gale (p14-20)
The Distemper of Dogs by William Hunting (p20-24)
Quail Shooting Near the Pyramids (p24-34)
Cricket [inc. Obituary of Charles Wynch; Oxford University Matches] (p35-47)
Our Van [inc. Introduction of Lacrosse; Hunt Servants' Benefit Society; Ascot Meeting; Review of *Sport in Abyssinia* by Dermot Bourke; Obituary of Charles Barnett] (p48-62)

Issue 198 : August 1876

Portrait and Biography - Cristobel de Murrieta (p63-64)
A Brown Study in the Midlands by George Tyrrell (p64-69)
Frank Raleigh of Watercombe (part 27) by Edward Davies (p69-79)
Shows Considered in their Relation to Sport by Thomas Taunton (p79-83)
How Tom Stretcher lost the Big Pike by Charles Newmarch (p83-89)
Cricket [inc. Marylebone Cricket Club Members; Career of Tom Box] (p89-104)
Yachting and Rowing [inc. Channel Yacht Race; Royal Cinque Ports Regatta] (p104-111)
Our Van [inc. Exeter Stakes; Obituaries of Francis Conyngham, Harry Goater and Thomas Box; Wimbledon Prize Shooting; The Badminton Club] (p112-124)

Issue 199 : September 1876

Portrait and Biography - Mark Wood (p125-126)
Sheffield Lane by George Tyrrell (p126-131)
Frank Raleigh of Watercombe (part 28) by Edward Davies (p131-141)
Recollections of Thomas Coleman (part 5) by Comyns Cole (p141-150)
Reminiscences of Mr Honywood's Beagles (p150-155)
Cricket [inc. North versus South Matches; Canterbury Week] (p156-167)
Yachting and Rowing [Thames Regatta; London Rowing Club] (p167-172)
Our Van [inc. Brighton Meeting; Knavesmire Racing; Horncastle Fair; Obituaries of Henry Lowther and Michael Dunne; Newcastle Rowing] (p173-186)

Issue 200 : October 1876

Portrait and Biography - Samuel Nicoll (p187)
Lines [verses] by Vernon Delves-Broughton (p188)
[Obituary] Nicholas 'Felix' Wanostrocht by Frederick Gale (p188-191)
An Early Ashdown Meeting by Charles Newmarch (p191-197)
Frank Raleigh of Watercombe (part 29) by Edward Davies (p197-205)
The Old Fashioned First of September by Frederick Gale (p206-213)
American Trotters by John Fullerton (p213-222)
[Obituary] Percy Williams (p223-226)
The Run Nobody Ever Saw by John Fullerton (p226-230)
Yachting and Rowing [Philadelphia Regatta; Oarsmen of America] (p230-233)
Our Van [inc. Doncaster Meeting; Radnor's Hounds; Dublin Horse Show; Obituary of Arthur Ridding] (p233-248)

Issue 201 : November 1876

Portrait and Biography - James Dear (p249-250)
On Winchester Racecourse by Comyns Cole (p250-254)
The Top of the Town by George Tyrrell (p254-259)
Lines [verses] by Vernon Delves-Broughton (p259)
Frank Raleigh of Watercombe (part 30) by Edward Davies (p259-268)
Country Quarters - The Surrey Union (p269-277)
Our Van [inc. Newmarket Races; Masters of Foxhounds Changes; North Shropshire Hunt; Hamburg Rowing; Obituary of George Lawrence] (p277-292)

Hunting: List of Hounds, Masters, Huntsmen, Whips, Kennels (p293-310)

Issue 202 : December 1876

Portrait and Biography - Lawrence Dundas (p311-312)
The Dream of an Old Meltonian [verses] by William Bromley-Davenport (p312-315)
Recollections of Thomas Coleman (part 6) by Comyns Cole (p315-323)
The Straight Tip by Thomas Vigors (p323-332)
With the Brookside Harriers by Charles Newmarch (p332-338)
Cricket: The Public School Averages (p338-356)
Our Van [inc. Worcester Races; Aintree Meeting; North Warwickshire Hounds; Her Majesty's
    Staghounds] (p356-372)

Issue 203 : January 1877

Portrait and Biography - Dudley Carleton (p373-374)
The Decline of the English Horse by Robert Grimston (p374-377)
Stud Gossip by George Tyrrell (p377-387)
A Fogey's Kaleidoscope by Frederick Gale (p387-399)
Robert Peck by Comyns Cole (p399-403)
Amateur or Gentlemen Huntsmen by John Maunsell-Richardson (p403-410)
A September Holiday by Comyns Cole (p410-415)
Our Van [inc. Islington Cattle Show; Kingsbury Racing; Quorn Hunt; Obituaries of John Rolt
    and Edward Godsell; Review of *Irish Hunting History* by O'Connor Morris
    (of *The Field*); Grand Military Meeting] (p415-430)

Volume 30, February - August 1877

Issue 204 : February 1877

Portrait of Thomas Cannon, jockey Title page
Portrait and Biography - William Pleydell-Bouverie (p1-2)
The New Laws of Racing by George Tyrrell (p2-7)
How the Fenians Stopped the Battue by Frederick Gale (p8-13)
By the Sad Sea Waves by Charles Newmarch (p13-20)
Frank Raleigh of Watercombe (part 31) by Edward Davies (p20-29)
Hunters' Certificates by Edward Pennell-Elmhirst (p29-34)
Glimmers From Limmer's by Charles Batchelder (p34-40)
Review: *Sport in Many Lands* by Henry Leveson (p40-42)
Our Van [inc. Quorn Hunt; Fife Hounds; Review of *The Great Run* by George Winter; Obituaries
    of Samuel Reynell and Robert Wormald; Road Club Dinner] (p43-62)

Issue 205 : March 1877

Portrait and Biography - John Marjoribanks (p63)
A Chapter of Trainers by George Tyrrell (p63-69)
A Word with Pedagogues by Frederick Gale (p69-77)
The Recollections of Thomas Coleman (part 7) by Comyns Cole (p78-88)
Frank Raleigh of Watercombe (part 32) by Edward Davies (p88-98)
Coursing: The Waterloo Cup by George Wilson (p98-107)
Our Van [inc. Birmingham Races; Tedworth Hounds; Tynedale Hunt; Obituaries of James
    Merry, John Verrall, Frederick Byng, Joseph Little, Henry Willis, John Eden and
    William Coulthurst; Review of *Bound to Win* by Hawley Smart] (p108-124)

Issue 206 : April 1877

Portrait and Biography - Henry Verney (p125-126)
Turf Reciprocity by George Tyrrell (p126-132)
William Gladstone on the Boat Race [verses] (p132)
Real Gentlemen Players by Frederick Gale (p133-134)
Samuel Pepys on Cricket by Frederick Gale (p134-138)
A Letter to George Anderson (p139)
Our Mares by Albert Muntz (p140-143)
Frank Raleigh of Watercombe (part 33) by Edward Davies (p143-151)
The Biography of a Huntsman (part 1) by John Squires (p151-161)
Athletics and Aquatics [inc. Inter-University Sports; Boat Race Dead-Heat] (p161-164)
Our Van [inc. Croydon Races; Badminton Hounds; Cottenham National Hunt; Ivybridge
        Meet; Obituaries of James Rait and Jerry Goodlake; Forfarshire Hounds;
        Ranelagh House Polo] (p164-186)

Issue 207 : May 1877

Portrait and Biography - Sewallis Shirley (p187)
Man or Monkey [verses] by George Tyrrell (p188-189)
The Great Walking Match by Charles Batchelder (p189-191)
Abuse of Public Sports (p191-194)
From Belvoir to Brixworth by Edward Pennell-Elmhirst (p194-207)
The Biography of a Huntsman (part 2) by John Squires (p207-215)
Fish Murder (part 1) by Frederick Gale (p215-220)
The Recollections of Thomas Coleman (part 8) by Comyns Cole (p220-226)
Another Cricket Season [New Marylebone Cricket Club Secretary; Public Schools' Captains] (p226-232)
Our Van [inc. Northampton Races; Bristol Meeting; Bedale Hounds; Beaufort Hunt
        Steeplechases] (p233-248)

Issue 208 : June 1877

Portrait and Biography - William Gerard (p249)
Scarlet versus Yellow [verses] by Rowland Egerton Warburton (p250)
A Blank Day with the Belle Vue by Frederick Gale (p250-262)
The Biography of a Huntsman (part 3) by John Squires (p262-270)
Some Phases and Peculiarities of Irish Hunting by Comyns Cole (p270-276)
A Good Run and its Consequences (part 1) by Charles Newmarch (p277-285)
Strange Incidents in the History of a Hunter by Charles Newmarch (p286-288)
Cricket [inc. Marylebone Cricket Club Annual Meeting; Oxford University Record Low Score] (p288-295)
Yachting and Rowing [inc. Thames Valley Sailing Club; Walton Regatta] (p295-297)
Our Van [inc. Chester Cup; Manchester Horse Show; Coaching Club; Tattersall's Sales;
        Review of *Juliet* by Lovett Cameron; Obituary of Morgan Vane] (p297-310)

Issue 209 : July 1877

Portrait and Biography - John Mitford (p311-313)
Admiral Rous [verses] by George Tyrrell (p313-314)
Memoir of Reverend John Russell (part 1) by Edward Davies (p314-323)
The Pride of our Village by Frederick Gale (p323-331)
A Good Run and its Consequences (part 2) by Charles Newmarch (p331-339)
On the Breeding and Feeding of Horses and Cattle by William Macdonald (p339-342)
The Recollections of Thomas Coleman (part 9) by Comyns Cole (p342-348)
Cricket [inc. Cambridge University Matches] (p349-353)
Rowing [inc. Henley Regatta; Thames Rowing] (p353-358)

Our Van [inc. Islington Horse Show; Ascot Meeting; Review of *The English Game of Cricket* by Charles Box; Obituaries of William Clayton, Alfred Hedges and Henry Rous] (p358-372)

Issue 210 : August 1877

Portrait and Biography - Leonard Morrogh (p373-374)
Black Sheep in the Fold by George Tyrrell (p374-378)
Memoir of Reverend John Russell (part 2) by Edward Davies (p378-387)
Fish Murder (part 2) by Frederick Gale (p388-393)
The Horse that Jones Rejected by Edward Pennell-Elmhirst (p393-398)
Thomas Cannon by Comyns Cole (p398-399)
Getting out of a Screw (p399-404)
Cricket [inc. Cricketer's Fund; Harrow School Fixture Change] (p405-414)
Aquatics [inc. Maidenhead Regatta; Henley Diamond Sculls] (p415-417)
Our Van [inc. Newmarket Week; Cahirmee Green Fair; Doncaster Agricultural Show; Obituaries of James Hall, William Gaskell and Thomas Crommelin] (p417-430)

Volume 31, September 1877 - March 1878

Issue 211 : September 1877

Portrait of Fred Archer, jockey Title page
Portrait and Biography - Georg Munster (p1)
A Word With Our Contemporary Reviewer by George Tyrrell (p2-8)
Memoir of Reverend John Russell (part 3) by Edward Davies (p8-18)
Neology in the Veterinary Art by Joseph Shorthouse (p18-23)
Scraps From the Supper Table [Cricket Dinners] by Frederick Gale (p24-31)
Cricket [inc. Gilbert Grace's Record Score; Canterbury Week] (p32-40)
Yachting and Rowing [inc. Royal Yacht Squadron; Kingston Rowing Club] (p40-47)
Our Van [inc. Brighton Race Club; Stockton Races; Ebor Meeting; Review of *Hunting Songs* by Rowland Egerton-Warburton ; Obituaries of Edward Studd; Charles Henderson and Williamson Booth] (p47-62)

Issue 212 : October 1877

Portrait and Biography - Francis Hastings (p63-64)
A Turf Acrostic [verses] by George Tyrrell (p64-66)
Memoir of Reverend John Russell (part 4) by Edward Davies (p66-78)
Social Life in the Last Century by Frederick Gale (p78-89)
Ad Montem: A Reminiscence by Nevill Fitt (p89-96)
Ireland's Hunting Resources and Capabilities by Comyns Cole (p96-104)
Tom Stretcher Amongst the Trout by Charles Newmarch (p104-110)
Our Van [inc. Doncaster Meeting; Gloucestershire Cricket; Holderness Hounds; Obituary of John Tyssen; Decline of Horse Fairs] (p110-124)

Issue 213 : November 1877

Portrait and Biography - John Hargreaves (p125-126)
The Fight for the Championship [verses] by George Tyrrell (p127-130)
Solution of George Tyrrell's Double Acrostic (p130)
One Day in Ireland by Comyns Cole (p130-140)
Memoir of Reverend John Russell (part 5) by Edward Davies (p141-149)
Yachting and Rowing [inc. Tyne Rowing; London Rowing Club Regatta] (p149-151)

Our Van [inc. Orleans Club; Curragh Meeting; Reviews of *The Art of Horse Breaking* by
      Robert Moreton and Records of *The Chase* by Cornelius Tongue; *The Tin
      Trumpet* Sporting Newspaper; Review of the Play *The Lady Gay Spanker*]   (p151-168)
Hunting: List of Hounds; Masters, Huntsmen, Whips, Kennels   (p169-186)

Issue 214 : December 1877

Portrait and Biography - George Arundell   (p187-188)
A Turf *Annus Mirabilis* by George Tyrrell   (p188-193)
Farming and Fox-Hunting [verses] by Rowland Egerton-Warburton   (p194-195)
Memoir of Reverend John Russell (part 6) by Edward Davies   (p195-208)
Newmarket by Frederick Gale   (p208-214)
[Obituary] Thomas Coleman by Comyns Cole   (p214-217)
Down the Great South Road by Comyns Cole   (p217-224)
From Hand to Mouth   (p224-228)
Our Van [inc. Worcester Races; Sefton Steeplechase Congress; Pytchley Hunt;
      Thanet Harriers; Obituaries of William Leamon and Morton Stubbs;
      Essex Union Hounds; Reviews of *Horses and Riding* by George Neville and
      Shooting, Yachting & Sea-Fishing Trips by Lewis Clements]   (p229-248)

Issue 215 : January 1878

Portrait and Biography - George Hamilton   (p249-250)
Trying Back by George Tyrrell   (p250-256)
Memoir of Reverend John Russell (part 7) by Edward Davies   (p256-268)
Men of Metal [Cricket in Sheffield] by Frederick Gale   (p268-273)
Meadow and Pasture Lands: Their Renovation and Repair (part 1) by Joseph Shorthouse   (p273-281)
A Cockney Holiday by Comyns Cole   (p281-285)
Cricket: The Public School Averages   (p285-295)
Our Van [inc. International Polo Club Ball; Vine Hunt; Whaddon Chase Hounds;
      Obituaries of Henry Willoughby, Henry Fitzroy and Robert Campbell]   (p295-310)

Issue 216 : February 1878

Portrait and Biography - Edward Chaplin   (p311-312)
Departed Worth [Review of Thirteenth Stud Book] by George Tyrrell   (p312-317)
Perfection [verses] by George Whyte-Melville   (p318)
Idlers in Autumn   (p319-325)
Memoir of Reverend John Russell (part 8) by Edward Davies   (p325-337)
Meadow and Pasture Lands: Their Renovation and Repair (part 2) by Joseph Shorthouse   (p338-343)
Tempora Mutantur [verses]   (p343)
Clubs [Gentlemen's Clubs] by Frederick Gale   (p344-348)
The Last Leap by Edward Pennell-Elmhirst   (p348-354)
All About the Crack of a Whip by Frederick Gale   (p355-358)
Our Van [inc. Quorn Hunt; Obituaries of Oliver Jones, George Brudenell-Bruce, William
      Summers and Thomas Day; Marden Deer Park Stud]   (p359-372)

Issue 217 : March 1878

Portrait and Biography - Albert Brassey   (p373)
The Right Man in the Right Place [verses]   (p374-375)
Memoir of Reverend John Russell (part 9) by Edward Davies   (p375-386)
Justice to Ireland by Frederick Gale   (p386-393)
Tiger Shooting in the Deccan by George Collins   (p393-405)
Coaching for the Million by Comyns Cole   (p405-411)
Country Umpires by Frederick Gale   (p412-415)

Our Van [inc. Pytchley Hunt; Craven Hounds; Surrey Staghounds; Obituary of Henry
        Bowyer; Kingsbury Race Fixing]   (p416-430)

Volume 32, April - October 1878

Issue 218 : April 1878

Portrait of Thomas Firr, huntsman	Title page
Portrait and Biography - James Lowther	(p1-3)
In Nuptias [verses] by William Alden	(p3-4)
A Dream of the Past by James Roche	(p4-5)
A Peck of March Dust by George Tyrrell	(p6-11)
Memoir of Reverend John Russell (part 10) by Edward Davies	(p11-22)
Epidemic, Endemic, Infectious and Contagious Diseases by Joseph Shorthouse	(p22-28)
Eurydice [verses] by Frederick Gale	(p28-29)
Old England and Young England by Frederick Gale	(p29-34)
Gossip From Grass Lands (part 1) by Edward Pennell-Elmhirst	(p34-42)
Coursing: The Waterloo Cup by George Wilson	(p42-47)
Our Van [inc. Grand Military Gold Cup; Kingsbury Racing; Billesdon Hunt; Rothschild's Staghounds; Aylesbury Hunt Steeplechases; Obituaries of William Cooper and Reginald Greville-Nugent; Edmund Tattersall's Speech]	(p47-62)

Issue 219 : May 1878

Portrait and Biography - Mosse Robinson	(p63-65)
The Passing of Beauclerc [verses] by Digby Willoughby	(p65-66)
[Review] *Riding Recollections* by George Whyte-Melville	(p66-68)
The Quorn [verses]	(p68-70)
Memoir of Reverend John Russell (part 11) by Edward Davies	(p70-81)
A Substitute for the Tobacco Tax [verses]	(p82)
Let Her Paint An Inch Thick [verses]	(p82)
[Obituary] Fothergill Rowlands by Joseph Shorthouse	(p83)
The Town and Country Mouse by Frederick Gale	(p84-88)
Gossip From Grass Lands (part 2) by Edward Pennell-Elmhirst	(p89-100)
The Cricket Season [Australian Tour; Prince's Ground]	(p100-108)
Athletics and Aquatics [Nore Yacht Club; Amateur Athletic Club]	(p108-113)
Our Van [inc. Hereford Steeplechases; Beaufort's Hounds; Brocklesby Hunt; British Empire Horse Supply Association]	(p113-124)

Issue 220 : June 1878

Portrait and Biography - William Beach	(p125-126)
Marden Deer Park by George Tyrrell	(p126-130)
Memoir of Reverend John Russell (part 12) by Edward Davies	(p130-142)
Gossip From Grass Lands (part 3) by Edward Pennell-Elmhirst	(p143-151)
The Expenses of Coaching by Charles Newmarch	(p152-160)
Cricket [inc. Marylebone Cricket Club Rule Change; Australians on Tour]	(p160-166)
Yachting and Rowing [inc. Lloyd's Yacht Register; Definition of Amateur Rowers]	(p166-169)
Our Van [inc. Sandown Park Lawn; Launceston Hounds; Colindale Hunt; Calcutta Cricket Club; Manchester Horse Show; Obituary of (the other) Thomas Smith; Review of *The Moor and The Loch* by John Colquhoun]	(p169-186)

Issue 221 : July 1878

Portrait and Biography - Laurence Palk	(p187)
Memoir of Reverend John Russell (part 13) by Edward Davies	(p188-198)

Polo in India (p198-199)
The Female Slave by Frederick Gale (p199-205)
The Treatment of Sprains, Break-Down and Other Injuries [Horses] by Joseph Shorthouse (p206-207)
[Review] *Thirteen Years Among the Wild Beasts of India* by George Sanderson (p207-211)
Falconry: The Prospects of its Revival by James Harting (p211-218)
The Bachelor Master of Foxhounds by Charles Newmarch (p218-221)
Cricket [inc. Australian Tour Matches; Cambridge University Eleven] (p222-228)
Yachting and Rowing [inc. Thames Cutter Matches; Obituary of Frederick Arthur;
     Ilex Swimming Club] (p229-235)
Our Van [inc. Epsom Week; Hunt Servants' Benefit Society Annual General Meeting;
     Cobham Stud Sale; Ranelagh Pony Steeplechases] (p235-248)

Issue 222 : August 1878

Portrait and Biography - Charles Russell (p249-253)
Our Goodwood Saturday by George Tyrrell (p254-257)
Memoir of Reverend John Russell (part 14) by Edward Davies (p257-270)
Bought and Sold [verses] by Rowland Egerton-Warburton (p271-273)
The Economy of a Grouse Moor by Archibald Wortley (p273-279)
The Cradle of Cricket by Frederick Gale (p279-285)
A Model Puppy Show by Nevill Fitt (p286-292)
An Old Stager on the Australian Cricketers (p292-293)
Yachting and Rowing [inc. Henley Regatta; Wingfield Sculls] (p294-298)
Our Van [inc. Stockbridge Cup; Peterborough Hound Show; Review of *Tally Ho!* by
     Frederick Whitehurst; Devon & Somerset Staghounds] (p298-310)

Issue 223 : September 1878

Portrait and Biography - Douglas Whitmore (p311-312)
Round-Arm Recollections by Charles Russell (p312-314)
Hunting Red Deer on Exmoor by Nevill Fitt (p314-319)
Peas in One's Shoes by Frederick Gale (p320-327)
The Sportsman's Commissariat (p328-339)
A Strange Wolf Hunt by Charles Newmarch (p339-344)
Cricket [inc. University Match; Middlesex Championship] (p344-353)
Yachting and Rowing [inc. Weymouth Regatta; Royal Albert Yacht Club] (p353-359)
Our Van [inc. Brighton Races; Stockton Meeting; Halifax Racecourse; Obituary of
     Tommy Nevill] (p359-372)

Issue 224 : October 1878

Portrait and Biography - Gerald Goodlake (p373-374)
George Payne by George Tyrrell (p374-378)
[Review] *Hunting Songs* by Rowland Egerton-Warburton (p379-386)
Private Billiards (part 1) by Joseph Bennett (p387-391)
Tom Firr by Comyns Cole (p391-393)
My Dentist [verses] (p393)
The Sound of an Old Bell by Frederick Gale (p394-400)
Major Battle's Opinion on Play (p401-406)
Cricket [inc. Australian Matches; Prince's Ground] (p406-416)
Yachting and Rowing [inc. *The Sportsman* Challenge Cup; *Newcastle Chronicle* Cup] (p416-418)
Our Van [inc. Doncaster Racing; Obituary of George Payne] (p418-430)

Volume 33, November 1878 - May 1879

Issue 225 : November 1878

Portrait of William Puttock, deer-cartman	Title page
Portrait and Biography - Barnard Hankey	(p1)
The 'Little Pedlingtons' of the Turf by George Tyrrell	(p2-7)
Lines Suggested by the Will of the Late George Payne [verses] by Rowland Egerton-Warburton	(p7)
Private Billiards (part 2) by Joseph Bennett	(p7-9)
The Blue Coat and Brass Buttons Era by Frederick Gale	(p10-15)
Concerning the Capercailzie by Archibald Wortley	(p16-21)
Tom Stretcher Looks over a Manor by Charles Newmarch	(p21-28)
Our Van [inc. Kempton Park; Newmarket Oaks; Quorn Hunt Boundary; West Street Harriers; Review of *The Battle of the Roosters* by Wallis Mackay]	(p28-44)
Hunting: Lists of Hounds, Masters, Huntsmen, Whips, Kennels	(p45-62)

Issue 226 : December 1878

Portrait and Biography - Francis Foljambe	(p63-64)
The Cock of the Woods [verses] by George Tyrrell	(p64-65)
Corkey and Blower Brown on the Brain by Frederick Gale	(p65-72)
Vale of White Horse [verses] by George Tyrrell	(p73)
A Riverside Sketch by Charles Newmarch	(p74-80)
The Grouse Harvest by Archibald Wortley	(p80-88)
About Some Future Wellingtons [Rugby Football]	(p89-90)
Rook Hawking by Charles Newmarch	(p90-95)
Cricket: The Public School Averages	(p95-107)
Our Van [inc. Worcester Meeting; Shrewsbury Racing Incidents; New Jockey Club Rules; Billesdon Hunt; Radnor's Hounds]	(p107-124)

Issue 227 : January 1879

Portrait and Biography - Bache Cunard	(p125)
G.J.Whyte-Melville [verses] by George Tyrrell	(p126-127)
Down or Woodland by Edward Pennell-Elmhirst	(p128-133)
On the Death of Major Whyte-Melville [verses] by Rowland Egerton-Warburton	(p133-134)
[Review] *Hunting Songs and Verses* by George Whyte-Melville, by Edward Davies	(p134-143)
When We Middle-Aged Fogeys Were Boys by Frederick Gale	(p143-153)
Scotland's Most Famous Fish by James Bertram	(p153-159)
Deal and Back for Two Hundred Pounds by Frederick Gale	(p159-163)
Deer and Deer Parks by Joseph Shorthouse	(p164-169)
Our Van [inc. Sandown Park Stewards; Funeral of George Whyte-Melville; Tedworth Hounds; *The World* Hunting Story; *Vanity Fair* Article]	(p170-186)

Issue 228 : February 1879

Portrait and Biography - Frank Chaplin	(p187)
The Future of Epping Forest by Edward Buxton	(p188-192)
The Manager's Ball [verses]	(p192-193)
Stud Farms: Their Aspects and Prospects by Joseph Shorthouse	(p194-201)
[Review] *Sketches of the Wild Sports and Natural History of the Highlands* by Charles St.John	(p201-213)
Gleanings From the Grass (part 1) by Edward Pennell-Elmhirst	(p214-221)
Pike Fishing in Winter by John Keene	(p221-225)
Improving the Occasion by Frederick Gale	(p226-231)
Song [verses]	(p232)

Our Van [inc. North Warwickshire Hunt; Southdown Hounds; Review of *Covert Side Sketches* by Nevill Fitt; Norfolk Staghounds; Obituaries of William Treen and Charles Brindley]   (p233-248)

Issue 229 : March 1879

Portrait and Biography - Stirling Crawfurd   (p249-250)
General Jonathan Peel [verses]   (p251)
Studies From the Stud Book (part 1): The Newminster Family by George Tyrrell   (p251-259)
About a Thoroughbred by Frederick Gale   (p259-264)
Tom Stretcher Amongst the Dog Dealers by Charles Newmarch   (p264-272)
[Review] *Wild Life in a Southern County* by Richard Jefferies   (p272-273)
The Staghounds of Thomas Lyon Thurlow by Edward Pennell-Elmhirst   (p273-278)
A Night on the South Platte   (p279-283)
Coursing: The Waterloo Cup by George Wilson   (p283-291)
Our Van [inc. South Berkshire Hunt; South Devon Hounds; Fife Foxhounds; Reviews of *The Hunting Counties of England* by Edward Pennell-Elmhirst and Pigskin and Willow by Byron Webber; Obituaries of Jonathan Peel and Henry Pelham-Clinton]   (p291-310)

Issue 230 : April 1879

Portrait and Biography - Richard Streatfield   (p311)
Early Entries and Lapsed Liabilities by George Tyrrell   (p312-315)
The Salmon as an Object of Sport and Natural History by James Bertram   (p316-326)
A Sermon From the Stage by Frederick Gale   (p326-332)
The Thames Trout and its Capture by John Keene   (p332-339)
The Empress in Ireland by Comyns Cole   (p339-348)
Sport for Bad Seasons by Charles Newmarch   (p348-353)
Yachting and Rowing [inc. Professional Rowing; University Boat Race Preview]   (p354-356)
Our Van [inc. Derby Steeplechases; Billesdon Hunt; Dartmoor Hounds; Boxing; Review of *Columbarium* by John Moore]   (p356-372)

Issue 231 : May 1879

Portrait and Biography - Henry Vigne   (p373-374)
Members of the Committee of Tattersall's   (p374-375)
Baily's Advice to the Bookmakers [verses]   (p375-377)
Gleanings From the Grass (part 2) by Edward Pennell-Elmhurst   (p377-385)
The Abbotsford Hunt: Scottish Border Sports by James Bertram   (p385-395)
William Puttock: A Biographical Sketch by Joseph Shorthouse   (p396-400)
The University Boat Race   (p400-402)
Bankruptcy in Arcadia by Frederick Gale   (p402-409)
Championship and University Athletics   (p410-412)
Our Van [inc. Obituary of John Frail; Northampton Meeting; Punchestown Races; Essex Union Hunt; New Forest Hounds; Jersey Steeplechases; Marden Deer Park Stud]   (p413-430)

Florence Baillie-Grohman

Volume 34, June - December 1879

Issue 232 : June 1879

Portrait of John Fricker, huntsman	Title page
Portrait and Biography - Hayes St.Leger	(p1-2)
Russley Revisited by George Tyrrell	(p2-9)
The Great Lake Trout Interviewed by James Bertram	(p9-18)
Gleanings From the Grass (part 3) by Edward Pennell-Elmhirst	(p18-27)
The Revival of the Box Hill Coach by Septimus Berdmore	(p27-34)
Racing in Red Coats by Comyns Cole	(p34-38)
The Cobham Menu by Comyns Cole	(p38-40)
Cricket [inc. Colts Matches; Cambridge University Players]	(p40-48)
Yachting and Rowing [inc. Royal London Cutter Match; Tyne Rowing]	(p48-50)
Our Van [inc. Chester Meeting; Manchester Horse Show; Dartmoor Foxhounds; Colindale Hounds; Obituary of Teignmouth Melvill (*Baily's* contributor); Metropolitan Racecourse Bill]	(p50-62)

Issue 233 : July 1879

Portrait and Biography - Robert Erskine	(p63-64)
[Obituary] Owen Swift by George Tyrrell	(p64-69)
Summer Scarlet [Peterborough Hound Show]	(p69-75)
Some Notes on Coarse Fish Angling by John Keene	(p76-81)
Gossip About Poachers and Poaching by Richard Jefferies	(p81-90)
The Driving Clubs by Septimus Berdmore	(p90-98)
Cricket [inc. Cricketers' Fund Benefit Match; County Reports]	(p99-107)
Yachting and Rowing [inc. New Thames Yawl Match; Henley Regatta]	(p107-111)
Our Van [inc. Ascot Races; Alexandra Park Horse Show; Whyte-Melville Memorials; Review of *Sussex Cricket Past and Present* by Charles Trower]	(p111-124)

Issue 234 : August 1879

Portrait and Biography - Henry Eaton	(p125)
Rara Avis [verses] by George Tyrrell	(p126-128)
The Evening Standard on Owen Swift	(p128-130)
Fishing Stations on the Thames by John Keene	(p130-140)
How the Grouse have Wintered by James Bertram	(p140-146)
[Obituary] Lionel de Rothschild	(p146-150)
Gilbert Grace Testimonial by Charles Russell	(p150-151)
A Day with the Pytchley in 1900 by Edward Pennell-Elmhirst	(p151-155)
Pons Asinorum by Frederick Gale	(p155-158)
Cricket [inc. Cambridge University Team; Marylebone Cricket Club Playing Rules]	(p158-168)
Yachting and Rowing [inc. Le Havre Regatta; Wyfold Cup]	(p168-174)
Our Van [inc. Newmarket Meeting; Kilburn Horse Show; Cobham Stud Company; Cricket in Paris]	(p174-186)

Issue 235 : September 1879

Portrait and Biography - Richard Oswald	(p187-188)
Changing Pastures by George Tyrrell	(p188-196)
Our Sport Upon the Sea by John Keene	(p196-203)
Sport at Rugby School	(p204-208)
Four Years of Road Work by Septimus Berdmore	(p208-217)
The Irish Wolfhound by James Harting	(p218-223)
Cricket [inc. Canterbury Week; Cheltenham Festival]	(p223-232)

Yachting and Rowing [inc. Royal Southampton Yacht Club; Barnes & Mortlake Regatta]   (p232-237)
Our Van [inc. Brighton Meeting; Redcar Racing; The Coaching Season; Review of
         Hark Away by Frederick Whitehurst]   (p237-248)

Issue 236 : October 1879

Portrait and Biography - Francis Egerton   (p249-250)
The Jests of John Warde by Edward Pennell-Elmhirst   (p250-252)
The Past Salmon Season: The Disease by James Bertram   (p252-258)
Cub Hunting in Meath by Comyns Cole   (p258-263)
De Senectute by Frederick Gale   (p263-270)
A Dead Sell by George Tyrrell   (p271-278)
Jamaica Jottings (part 1) by Frank Streatfield   (p278-284)
The Old Dover Road by Frederick Gale   (p284-292)
Tom Stretcher Buys More Dogs by Charles Newmarch   (p292-297)
Yachting and Rowing [inc. Dartmouth Regatta; Yacht Racing Association; Neuilly Rowing] (p297-298)
Our Van [inc. Great Yorkshire Handicap; Devon & Somerset Staghounds; Tattersall's Auction;
         Cobham Stud Sale; Obituary of Henry Padwick]   (p298-310)

Issue 237 : November 1879

Portrait and Biography - William Fitzroy   (p311-312)
A Plague Spot in our Racing System by George Tyrrell   (p312-318)
A Gossip about the Grouse Family by James Bertram   (p318-325)
Nullum Tetigit Quod Non Ornavit by Frederick Gale   (p325-334)
Jamaica Jottings (part 2) by Frank Streatfield   (p334-338)
[Review] *Kaffir Land* by Frank Streatfield   (p338-340)
Our Van [inc. Newmarket Autumn Meeting; Old Berkeley Hunt; Isle of Wight Hounds;
         Hunt Subscriptions; Jockey Club Betting Rule; Reviews of *Book of Sketches*
         by Finch Mason and *The Amateur Poacher* by Richard Jefferies   (p340-354)
Hunting: List of Hounds; Masters, Huntsmen, Whips, Kennels   (p355-372)

Issue 238 : December 1879

Portrait and Biography - Arthur Longman   (p373-374)
Every Inch a King [verses] by George Tyrrell   (p374-376)
The Scottish Deer Forests by James Bertram   (p377-384)
A Battered Portmanteau (part 1) by George Wilson   (p384-391)
Deer Coursing in Parks by Comyns Cole   (p391-399)
Arscott of Tetcote [Hunting Song] *trad.*   (p399-401)
John Fricker Huntsman to the Tedworth by Comyns Cole   (p401-402)
Cricket: The Public School Averages   (p402-413)
Our Van [inc. Shrewsbury Races; Kempton Park Handicap; Bicester Hounds; Burton Hunt;
         Review of *Sketches at Home and Abroad* by Horace Wheelwright; Grand
         National Hunt Committee]   (p413-430)

Volume 35, January - June 1880

Issue 239 : January 1880

Portrait of Frederick Cox, huntsman   Title page
Portrait and Biography - George Luttrell   (p1-2)
Tom Jennings's Jubilee [verses] by George Tyrrell   (p2-7)
Woodman, Spare that Tree [Epping Forest] by Edward Buxton   (p7-9)
Rummager : The Autobiography of a Hound by Finch Mason   (p9-13)
The Perplexities of Salmon Growth by James Bertram   (p13-26)

An Indian Scare (p26-29)
Thermometer Below Zero [verses] by Frederick Gale (p29-30)
Old Hampshire Hunt Songs (p30-38)
[Review] *History of the British Turf* by James Rice (p38-46)
[Review] *The Gamekeeper at Home* by Richard Jefferies (p46-47)
Our Van [inc. Islington Cattle Show; Grand National Hunt Committee Ruling; Essex &
      Suffolk Hunt; Surrey Staghounds; Jockey Club Declaration; Jersey Draghounds] (p47-62)

Issue 240 : February 1880

Portrait and Biography - Talbot Clifford-Constable (p63-64)
Turf Undertakers by George Tyrrell (p64-67)
A Battered Portmanteau (part 2) by George Wilson (p68-75)
Beasts and Birds of Sport (part 1): Hares and Rabbits by James Bertram (p75-84)
Sport in Zululand by Frank Streatfield (p84-89)
The Law of Leg-Before-Wicket by Frederick Gale (p90-95)
A Day at the Cross Roads by Finch Mason (p95-104)
Our Van [inc. Quorn Hunt; North Warwickshire Hounds; Berkhamsted Buckhounds;
      Obituary of Thomas Parr; Launch of *Life* Magazine; Whyte-Melville Memorials] (p104-124)

Issue 241 : March 1880

Portrait and Biography - Edward Stracey-Clitherow (p125-126)
One of the Old School by George Tyrrell (p126-130)
Beasts and Birds of Sport (part 2): Fox and Badger by James Bertram (p130-138)
Richardson's Show by Frederick Gale (p139-142)
The Law of Leg-Before-Wicket Further Considered by William Ford (p142-144)
Hunting in Waltham Forest by Edward Buxton (p144-148)
Jamaica Jottings (part 3) by Frank Streatfield (p148-152)
A Strange Dog Story by Charles Newmarch (p152-159)
Some Notes on Trout and Fly-Fishing by John Keene (p159-167)
Coursing: The Waterloo Cup by George Wilson (p167-172)
Rowing [inc. Obituary of Alfred Trower; University Boat Race Preparations] (p172-173)
Our Van [inc. Rufford Hunt; Fife Hounds; Obituary of John Walker; Gentlemen Riders;
      Review of *Green Ferne Farm* by Richard Jefferies] (p173-186)

Issue 242 : April 1880

Portrait and Biography - Charles Beresford (p187-188)
[Review] *The Racehorse in Training* by William Day (p189-195)
Beasts and Birds of Sport (part 3): Pheasants and Partridges by James Bertram (p195-204)
The Empress of Austria in Meath by Comyns Cole (p204-213)
Incidents in Fox Life by Charles Newmarch (p213-221)
The Law of Leg-Before-Wicket Further Considered by Frederick Gale (p221)
Hunting Hospitality by Charles Newmarch (p222-226)
The University Boat Race (p227-231)
Aquatic Notes [inc. Nice Riviera Regatta; Twickenham Rowing Club] (p232)
Our Van [inc. Household Brigade Steeplechase; Lincolnshire Handicap; Aintree Grand
      National; Lamerton Hounds; Obituary of Ben Morgan] (p233-248)

Issue 243 : May 1880

Portrait and Biography - William Cavendish (p249-250)
In a Country Village by Frederick Gale (p250-258)
Beasts and Birds of Sport (part 4): Peewits and Plovers by James Bertram (p258-266)
Fragmenta Pugnatoria (part 1) by Thomas Groome (p266-274)

Hunting in Ireland (part 1) by Comyns Cole (p274-280)
African Pig-Sticking (p280-287)
Cricket in 1880 [Canadian Tourists; Scarborough Festival] (p287-294)
Yachting and Rowing [inc. Nice/Ajaccio Yacht Race; Obituary of Allan Morrison] (p294-295)
Our Van [inc. Epsom Meeting; Hertfordshire Hunt; Tedworth Hounds; Reverend John Russell Testimonial; Obituary of William Milner] (p295-310)

Issue 244 : June 1880

Portrait and Biography - George Harris (p312)
Beasts and Birds of Sport (part 5): Rooks and Ravens by James Bertram (p313-321)
Roaring [*Critique of The Racehorse in Training* by William Day] (p321-323)
Fragmenta Pugnatoria (part 2) by Thomas Groome (p323-331)
Some Fishing Reminiscences by John Keene (p332-340)
Pre-Railway Life in London by Frederick Gale (p340-347)
Cricket [inc. Cambridge University Matches; Australian Tour Schedule] (p347-355)
Yachting and Rowing [inc. New Thames Cutters; Obituary of Robert Jewitt] (p355-357)
Our Van [inc. Chester Meeting; Manchester Racecourse Company; New Forest Hunt; Manchester Horse Show] (p357-372)

Issue 245 : July 1880

Portrait and Biography - Henry Meysey-Thompson (p373-374)
A Timely Concession by George Tyrrell (p374-379)
Beasts and Birds of Sport (part 6): Otters and Salmon by James Bertram (p379-388)
Frederick Cox by Comyns Cole (p388-389)
Beer and Some of its Counterfeits by Joseph Shorthouse (p389-398)
A Chapter on Falls by Charles Newmarch (p398-403)
Cricket [inc. Australian Fixtures; County Match Curtailed] (p403-413)
Yachting and Rowing [inc. Harwich Regatta; Amateur Rowing Championships] (p413-417)
Our Van [inc. Ascot Stakes; Peterborough Hound Show; Huntsmen/ Jockey's Cricket Match] (p417-430)

Volume 36, August 1880 - February 1881

Issue 246 : August 1880

Portrait of Joseph Cannon, jockey Title page
Portrait and Biography - Henry Stapylton (p1-2)
Omne Exit in Fumo [Jockey Club inquiry *in camera*] by George Tyrrell (p2-6)
Beasts and Birds of Sport (part 7): Grouse by James Bertram (p6-14)
Masters of Hounds by Charles Newmarch (p14-20)
[Review] *The Moor and the Loch* by John Colquhoun (p21-22)
Reason or Instinct by Frederick Gale (p22-29)
A Lost Link [Obituary of John Barr, falconer] by Nevill Fitt (p30-34)
Copt Hall [Life of Henry Conyers] by Edward Buxton (p34-39)
Cricket [inc. University Match; Nottinghamshire Players] (p39-47)
Yachting and Rowing [inc. Cinque Ports Club Regatta; Royal Clyde Yacht Club] (p47-51)
Our Van [inc. Ranelagh Floodlit Polo; Tedworth Hound Show; Obituaries of George Bryan and Joseph Dawson; Goodwood Meeting] (p51-62)

Issue 247 : September 1880

Portrait and Biography - Douglas Graham (p63-64)
Northern Lights and Shadows by George Tyrrell (p64-70)
'Christopher North' [John Wilson] in his Sporting Jacket by James Bertram (p70-78)
Carp and Carp-Fishing by John Keene (p78-85)

About Breeches and Boots by Frederick Gale (p85-93)

Tom Stretcher Shows his Dogs by Charles Newmarch (p93-98)

[Review] *English Trees and Tree-Planting* by William Ablett (p99-101)

Yachting and Rowing [inc. Royal Southampton Yacht Club; Barnes Regatta] (p101-106)

Our Van [inc. Brighton Stakes; Lewes Meeting; York & Ainsty Hunt; John Russell Presentation] (p107-124)

Issue 248 : October 1880

Portrait and Biography - Algernon Rushout (p125)

Beasts and Birds of Sport (part 8): Deer by James Bertram (p126-134)

The New Route to Box Hill by Charles Newmarch (p135-140)

Haunts of the Wild Red Deer (p140-145)

The Dublin Horse Show by Comyns Cole (p145-150)

The Foraging Fox; or Reynard in Pursuit (p151-155)

Chained in the Yard [verses] (p155-157)

Literature : *Treatyse of Fysshynge with an Angle* [1496] by Juliana Berners; *Englishe Dogges* [1576] by John Caius; *Notes on Game and Game Shooting* by John Manley (p157-159)

Cricket [inc. Australian Tour Matches; Obituary of Frederick Grace] (p159-168)

Yachting and Rowing [inc. Torbay Regatta; Milford Haven Yachting; Obituary of Henry Weston] (p169-172)

Our Van [inc. Sandown Park Rustics; Doncaster St.Leger; Belvoir Hunt; Review of *Cricket Scores and Biographies 1874-76* by Frederick Lillywhite] (p172-186)

Issue 249 : November 1880

Portrait and Biography - George Astley (p187)

The Devil, His Due [verses] by George Tyrrell (p188-189)

The Scottish Angling Season by James Bertram (p189-198)

Hunting Song (p198-201)

Hunting in Ireland (part 2) by Comyns Cole (p201-206)

Gipsy Kettle by Frederick Gale (p206-214)

Rowing: Thames Challenge Matches (p214-215)

Our Van [inc. Newmarket Meeting; East Essex Hunt; Whyte-Melville Fountain at St.Andrews; Australian Cricketers' Banquet; Tring Harriers; Review of *My Day with the Hounds* by Finch Mason] (p215-230)

Hunting: List of Hounds; Masters, Huntsmen, Whips, Kennels (p231-248)

Issue 250 : December 1880

Portrait and Biography - Frederick Villiers (p249-250)

The Sinews of Racing Warfare by George Tyrrell (p250-255)

Beasts and Birds of Sport (part 9): Wild Fowl by James Bertram (p256-265)

Fragmenta Pugnatoria (part 3) by Thomas Groome (p265-276)

The Irish Hunting Season by Comyns Cole (p276-281)

Forewarned, Forearmed by Frederick Gale (p281-285)

Cricket: The Public School Averages (p286-290)

Rowing: Thames Sculling Regatta (p291-292)

Our Van [inc. Brighton Races; Sefton Steeplechase; Queen's Staghounds; Rugby Hunt; Penllergare Foxhounds; Obituary of George Rice] (p292-310)

Issue 251 : January 1881

Portrait and Biography - Derrick Westenra (p311-312)

Sporting Parody [verses] by Rowland Egerton-Warburton (p312-313)

A Missing Chapter of Boxiana by Henry Miles (p313-316)

The National Game Harvest by James Bertram (p316-325)
Hunting Quarters in Ireland by Comyns Cole (p325-330)
First and Second Class by Frederick Gale (p330-336)
An Adventure on a Footpath by Elim d'Avigdor (p337-342)
Stage Pictures by Old Painters: Sir George Etherege by Thomas Groome (p343-349)
With the Great Rough Hounds by Charles Newmarch (p349-355)
Wolf Hunting in a Waggon by Frederick Gale (p355-356)
Our Van [inc. Sandown Park Meeting; South Cheshire Hunt; Eridge Castle Hounds; Brighton Harriers; Review of *The Silver Greyhound* by Edward Haworth; Obituaries of James Southerton, George Grace and Mark Cattley] (p356-372)

Issue 252 : February 1881

Portrait and Biography - Charles Pelham (p373)
William I'Anson by George Tyrrell (p374-379)
Medical Science versus Veterinary Medicine by Joseph Shorthouse (p379-386)
Beasts and Birds of Sport (part 10): Wild Ducks by James Bertram (p386-395)
Exeter by George Rooper (p395-400)
[Obituary] Frank Buckland by Comyns Cole (p400-402)
Striking Ile: Denver, Colorado (p402-407)
The Three F's [verses] (p408)
Retrospection by Charles Newmarch (p408-413)
Rowing [inc. Thames Rowing; Review of *The Rowing Almanack* by Edwin Brickwood] (p413-414)
Our Van [inc. Quorn Hunt Ball; Pytchley Woodland Hunt; Berkhamsted Buckhounds; Tom Spring's Grave Restoration; Obituary of Edward Sothern; Epping Forest Lament] (p414-430)

Volume 37, March - September 1881

Issue 253 : March 1881

Portrait of Charles Ward, huntsman Title page
Portrait and Biography - Michael Shaw-Stewart (p1)
Studies From the Stud Book (part 2) by George Tyrrell (p2-9)
Drawing or Designing [verses] (p9)
Scotch Angling Quarters by James Bertram (p10-18)
Sport in the North Pacific Ocean (p18-23)
Notes From the Stag Hunting Country (part 1) by Charles Newmarch (p24-30)
Hounds near Cambridge by Edward Pennell-Elmhirst (p31-34)
Cross Country Riding in Ireland (part 1) by Comyns Cole (p34-40)
Joseph Cannon by Comyns Cole (p40-42)
Coursing: The Waterloo Cup by George Wilson (p42-46)
Yachting and Rowing: Rowing Challenge Matches (p46-48)
Our Van [inc. Obituaries of Henry Hill, Harry Constable and Grantley Berkeley; South Berkshire Hunt; South Durham Hounds; Old Berkeley Hunt] (p48-62)

Issue 254 : April 1881

Portrait and Biography - Walter Long (p63-64)
Studies From the Stud Book (part 3) by George Tyrrell (p64-71)
[Obituary] Grantley Berkeley by Comyns Cole (p71-73)
Beasts and Birds of Sport (part 11): Miscellaneous Birds by James Bertram (p74-81)
The Fox Hunt on Ben Lomond (part 1): The Meet by John Verrall (p81-88)
Sport in the Marshes by George Wilson (p88-94)
Cross Country Riding in Ireland (part 2) by Comyns Cole (p94-98)

Notes From the Stag Hunting Country (part 2) by Charles Newmarch (p98-106)
Yachting and Rowing [inc. Yacht Building; Grove Park Rowing Club] (p107-110)
Our Van [inc. Grand Military & Household Brigade Steeplechase; Lincoln Cup; East Essex Hunt; North Warwickshire Huntsman; Review of *The Sportsman's Year Book for 1881*] (p111-124)

Issue 255 : May 1881

Portrait and Biography - Anthony Maynard (p125)
[Review] *The Horse Breeders' Handbook* by Joseph Osborne (p126-131)
Habited Habituees of Irish Happy Hunting Grounds by Comyns Cole (p131-136)
The Fox Hunt on Ben Lomond (part 2): The Hunt by John Verrall (p137-144)
Horses of Arabia by Ritter von Vincenti (p144-149)
Notes From the Stag Hunting Country (part 3) by Charles Newmarch (p150-158)
The Oxford and Cambridge Boat Race (p158-162)
Cricket [inc. Purchase of Trent Bridge; Surrey Coaching Staff] (p162-169)
Yachting and Rowing [inc. Professional Rowers; American Sculling Design] (p169-170)
Our Van [inc. Lillie Bridge University Sport; Northampton Races; Quorn Hunt; New Forest Hounds; Dumfriesshire Hunt Dinner] (p170-186)

Issue 256 : June 1881

Portrait and Biography - William Eden (p187)
Waste of Nature by Frederick Gale (p188-195)
The Birthplace of Kisber by James Bertram (p196-200)
Devonshire [On Fishing] by George Rooper (p200-207)
Punchestown Past Present and Prospective by Comyns Cole (p207-214)
The Three H's [verses] (p215)
Spring Hunting in the New Forest by Edward Pennell-Elmhirst (p216-221)
Cricket [inc. New Parks Ground in Oxford; Marylebone Cricket Club Matches] (p221-228)
Yachting and Rowing [inc. Royal Thames Yacht Club; Thames Rowing Club] (p228-231)
Our Van [inc. Chester Meeting; Manchester Horse Show; Reviews of *Riding on the Flat and Across Country* by Horace Hayes and *In Luck's Way* by Byron Webber] (p231-248)

Issue 257 : July 1881

Portrait and Biography - Edward Frewen (p249-250)
Trout Breeding in Scotland by James Bertram (p250-257)
A Word in Season by Frederick Gale (p257-260)
Summer Meets by William Day (p261-266)
Hunting in America by Nevill Fitt (p266-268)
Master of the Horse in a Circus (p269-277)
[Reviews] *Blair Athol* by William Allison; *Fancy Pigeons* by James Lyell; *The Practical Fisherman* by John Keene; *The Gun and its Development* by William Greener; *Encounters with Wild Beasts* by Parker Gillmore; *Horses and Stables* by Sir Frederick Fitzwygram; *A Treatise on Diseases of the Ox* by John Steele (p277-281)
Cricket [inc. Oxford University Pitches; Nottinghamshire Professional Players] (p281-289)
Yachting and Rowing [inc. Obituary of William Rudge; Cornell University Rowing Team] (p289-292)
Our Van [inc. Epsom Meeting; Ascot Races; Islington Horse Show; Obituary of Nat Cook; Hunt Servants Benefit Society New Offices; Reviews of *Book of the Horse* by Samuel Sydney and *Country Sketches* by Finch Mason; James Southerton Memorial] (p292-310)

Issue 258 : August 1881

Portrait and Biography - Adrian Hope (p311-312)
Game Bird Gossip and Fish Tattle by James Bertram (p312-319)
Cahirmee Great Horse Fair by Comyns Cole (p319-325)
Striking a Balance by Frederick Gale (p325-333)
The Future of Sport in Disturbed Ireland by Comyns Cole (p334-340)
The Ground Game Act and Fox Hunting by Charles Newmarch (p341-344)
Cricket [inc. Representative Matches; Schools' Reports] (p344-353)
Yachting and Rowing [inc. Royal Cornwall Yacht Club; Ottawa Regatta] (p353-358)
Our Van [inc. Jockey Club Regulations; Goodwood Cup; Obituary of Jonathan Carter; Cheltenham Horse Show] (p358-372)

Issue 259 : September 1881

Portrait and Biography - George Cadogan (p373-374)
[Review] *Lays of the Deer Forest* by John Stuart, reviewed by James Bertram (p374-382)
The Pleasures of Shooting with a Cockney by Charles Newmarch (p382-387)
The Hunt Club Meeting (part 1) by Edward Pennell-Elmhirst (p388-395)
Kangaroo Hunt at Gournama [Northern New South Wales] (p395-401)
Cricket [inc. Canterbury Week; James Lillywhite's Benefit Match] (p401-409)
Yachting and Rowing [inc. Yacht Racing Association; Cowes Week; *The Sportsman* Challenge Cup Rowing] (p409-414)
Our Van [inc. Brighton Meeting; Lewes Racing; Stockton Races; Ebor Meeting] (p414-434)

* This month Baily's moved their offices a few hundred yards from 3 Royal Exchange Buildings, Cornhill to 15 Nicholas Lane, off King William Street.

Volume 38, October 1881 - April 1882

Issue 260 : October 1881

Portrait of George Champion, huntsman Title page
Portrait and Biography - Walter Long (p1)
The Dublin Horse Show by Comyns Cole (p2-7)
[Review] *Pugilistica* by Henry Miles (p7-10)
A Chat about Pike and Pike-Fishing by John Keene (p10-16)
The Hunt Club Meeting (parts 2 & 3) by Edward Pennell-Elmhirst (p16-25)
[Reviews] *The Book of the Rabbit* by Leonard Gill and *The ABC Poultry Book* by Mary Wilson (p25-28)
Visions of the Past by Charles Newmarch (p28-33)
About Two Cricket Grounds by Frederick Gale (p33-42)
Yachting and Rowing [inc. Royal Dorset Regatta; French Rowing Championships] (p42-45)
Our Van [inc. Doncaster Racing; New Forest Hunt; Hertfordshire Kennels; Obituaries of Henry Savile and Joseph Radcliff; Frederick Gale's lecture on *Modern Sports; Their Use and Their Abuse*] (p45-62)

Issue 261 : November 1881

Portrait and Biography - Harvey Bayly (p63-65)
Scattered Abroad by George Tyrrell (p65-69)
The Hunt Club Meeting (parts 4 to 7) by Edward Pennell-Elmhirst (p69-78)
[Reviews] A Gossip About Game and its Cookery: *Modern Domestic Cookery* by Jenny Wren; *The Cook and Housewife's Manual* by Meg Dods; *Cookery* by Margaret Sims reviewed by James Bertram (p78-87)

The Guards A Cheval by Comyns Cole (p88-91)
Yachting and Rowing: French Rowing Championships (p91-92)
Our Van [inc. Stud Farm at Woodburn, Kentucky; Middle Park Plate; Quorn Hounds;
        Burton Hunt; Ballynahinch Staghounds; Obituary of Henry Briscoe] (p92-106)
Hunting: List of Hounds; Masters, Huntsmen, Whips, Kennels (p107-124)

Issue 262 : December 1881

Portrait and Biography - Marcus Beresford (p125-126)
Jumping Jottings From Paddyland by Comyns Cole (p127-134)
[Obituary] Two Blanks in the Marylebone Cricket Club: Frederick Bathurst by Frederick Gale (p135-139)
[Obituary] Robert Fitzgerald by Chandos Leigh (p139-140)
Woodcock-Snipe-Ptarmigan by James Bertram (p140-146)
Charles 'Bob' Ward, Huntsman by Comyns Cole (p146-147)
Sport of the Past and Present with the Greenland Whale by George Greville (p148-155)
Cricket: The Public School Averages (p155-164)
Rowing [inc. The Stewards' Cup; Bewdley Regatta Court Case] (p165-166)
Our Van [inc. Worcester Races; Aintree Meeting; Obituary of William Macdonald; Newmarket
        Drag Hounds; Southwold Hunt; The Badminton Club] (p167-186)

Issue 263 : January 1882

Portrait and Biography - Robert Price (p187)
The Balance of Nature in Relation to Sport by James Bertram (p188-197)
The Thoroughbred in America by Comyns Cole (p197-201)
I Preach to the Parson by Frederick Gale (p201-208)
Scotch Grouse and Other Game in '81 by James Bertram (p208-214)
Breeding Hunters by Richard Green-Price (p214-216)
Warned Off by John Verrall (p217-223)
Hibernia Anti-Venatica [Fox Hunting in Ireland] by Comyns Cole (p223-229)
The Storm Drum by Frederick Gale (p229-234)
Our Van [inc. Racing Statistics; Belvoir Hunt; Radnor's Hounds; Hunting in Kildare; Review
        of Road Scrapings by Martin Haworth] (p235-248)

Issue 264 : February 1882

Portrait and Biography - David Carrick-Buchanan (p249)
To the Fund [Jockey Club Levy] by George Tyrrell (p250-254)
John Warde by Edward Pennell-Elmhirst (p254-257)
Concerning Monaco by Edouard Beaumont (p258-265)
Winter Coaching by Septimus Berdmore (p266-270)
The Fate of Fox Hunting in Ireland by Comyns Cole (p270-274)
On the Welsh Border (part 1) by Richard Green-Price (p274-278)
The Teign by Thomas Boosey (p279-285)
Animal Life in the Forests of Venezuela by Georg Gothe (p285-288)
Under the Greenwood Tree by Henry Herbert(p288-293)
Our Van [inc. Rising Popularity of Foxhunting; Review of Concrete Buildings for Landed
        Estates by John Birch; Old Berkshire Hunt; Ward Union Staghounds; Obituaries
        Bob Rear, Pack Beresford, James Macdonald, Robert Goff and Charles
        Brownlow] (p294-310)

Issue 265 : March 1882

Portrait and Biography - Edward Hartopp (p311-312)
More Frightened than Hurt by George Tyrrell (p312-318)
Tweed Celebrities of the Rod by James Bertram (p318-326)

A Chat with Peter Beckford by Charles Newmarch (p326-331)
Notes on Wild Fowl in Two Hemispheres by Elim d'Avigdor (p331-337)
Groomiana by Comyns Cole (p338-342)
An Unequal Match [Cricket] by Frederick Gale (p342-346)
Coursing: The Waterloo Cup by George Wilson (p346-353)
On the Welsh Border (part 2) by Richard Green-Price (p353-356)
Rowing: Professional Matches (p357-358)
Our Van [inc. Sportsman's Exhibition; Frederick Gale Lecture; Holderness Hounds; Bedale Hunt; Essex Union Hunt Ball; Limerick Staghounds; Obituary of St.George Lowther] (p358-372)

Issue 266 : April 1882

Portrait and Biography - William Rigden (p373-374)
The Earl of Wilton by George Tyrrell (p374-378)
The Otter (part 1) by George Lowth (p378-386)
The Bearing-Rein Question [verses] (p386)
Spring Sport in Ireland by Comyns Cole (p387-392)
Leaves From a Rugby Scorebook [Cricket] by William Seton (p392-396)
Qualified Hunters: How to Deal with Them by Edward Pennell-Elmhirst (p397-401)
George Champion by Comyns Cole (p401-403)
The Finish of the Season by Nevill Fitt (p403-408)
Yachting and Rowing [inc. Yacht Racing Association; Boat Race Preview] (p408-409)
On the Winner of the Liverpool Steeplechase [verses] (p410)
Our Van [inc. Cart Horse Show; Grand Military Steeplechase; Pytchley Hunt Point-to-Point; Whaddon Chase Hounds; Reviews of *Worth Winning* by Caroline Lovett and *Rebecca* by Richard Green-Price] (p410-430)

The Grave of George Whyte-Melville in Tetbury

Whyte-Melville Plinth at St. Andrews

Volume 39, May - November 1882

Issue 267 : May 1882

Portrait of George Carter, huntsman	Title page
Portrait and Biography - George Pritchard-Rayner	(p1-3)
A Dip into The Derby [verses] by George Tyrrell	(p3-6)
The Otter (part 2) by George Lowth	(p6-14)
Melton in 1830: [verses] by Bernal Osborne with comments by Comyns Cole	(p14-20)
The Sport of Kings: A Retrospect of the 1881-82 Season by Edward Pennell-Elmhirst	(p20-25)
The Stud Groom's Story by Charles Newmarch	(p25-31)
Nerve by Frederick Gale	(p31-35)
Second Horsemen: Their Use and Abuse by Charles Newmarch	(p36-40)
The Cricket Season of 1882: Preview of the Australian Tour	(p40-47)
Yachting and Rowing [inc. Royal Yacht Squadron Commodore; Tyne Rowing]	(p48-49)
Our Van [inc. Vale of White Horse Point-to-Point; Newmarket Turf Club; Launch of *The Winning Post* Newspaper; Worcestershire Hounds Sale; Obituary of Henry Hall]	(p48-62)

Issue 268 : June 1882

Portrait and Biography - Thomas [Leslie-] Slingsby	(p63-64)
The Otter and the Hound (part 3) by George Lowth	(p64-73)
The Salmon Disease, and the Salmon Supply by James Bertram	(p73-82)
A May Fox [Fox Hunting in Glamorganshire] by Edward Pennell-Elmhirst	(p83-86)
The Ward Union Hunt by Comyns Cole	(p87-95)
Manners Makyth Man [Sporting Etiquette] by Frederick Gale	(p95-100)
Cricket [inc. Australian Tour Matches; Betting Scandal]	(p100-106)
Yachting and Rowing [inc. Royal London Yacht Club Clubhouse at Cowes; Chinnery Competitions]	(p106-107)
Our Van [inc. Chester Cup; Obituaries of William Fitzroy, William Roden and Joseph Radcliff; Hunt Servants' Benefit Society Annual General Meeting; Review of *Country Sketches* by Finch Mason]	(p107-124)

Issue 269 : July 1882

Portrait and Biography - Henry Selwin-Ibbetson	(p125-126)
The Gold of Arabia by George Tyrrell	(p126-131)
Between Two Flags by Comyns Cole	(p131-138)
Anglers' Exhibits at the Edinburgh Fishery Exhibition by James Bertram	(p138-146)
Summer Meets by William Day	(p146-152)
A Day on the Monnow with Geoffrey Hill by Richard Green-Price	(p152-155)
Bricket Wood [Hertfordshire] by William Day	(p156-158)
A Mission From the Red Indians by Frederick Gale	(p159-161)
Cricket [inc. More on Australian Matches; County Reports]	(p162-169)
Yachting and Rowing [inc. Harwich Race; New Thames Schooner Match]	(p170-172)
Our Van [inc. Ascot Meeting; Stockbridge Racing; Cambridge University Polo Club; National Hunt Steeplechase Committee Report; Obituary of John Shafto]	(p172-186)

Issue 270 : August 1882

Portrait and Biography - John Cookson	(p187-188)
The Coming Grouse Drives and Pheasant Battues by Guy Mannering	(p188-196)
The Otter and the Hound (part 4) by George Lowth	(p196-205)
A Summer's Ramble, Rod in Hand by Joseph Wheeldon	(p205-211)
Polo in Ireland by Comyns Cole	(p212-216)
Borneo and its Wild Sport	(p216-222)

Cricket [inc. Continuing Australian Tour Matches; University Reports]   (p222-231)
Yachting and Rowing [inc. Royal Mersey Yacht Club; Amateur Rowing Association]   (p231-236)
Our Van [inc. Newmarket Meeting; Obituary of Thomas Harrison; Coaching Season]   (p236-248)

Issue 271 : September 1882

Portrait and Biography - William Forbes   (p249-250)
The New Dispensation [Grand National Hunt Committee] by George Tyrrell   (p250-254)
A Battered Portmanteau (part 3) by George Wilson   (p255-262)
A Gossip about the Grouse of the Period by Guy Mannering   (p262-266)
A Midshipman's Life (part 1) by Cecil Sloane-Stanley   (p266-271)
Half Hours with Dan Seffert by Charles Newmarch   (p271-277)
Cricket [inc. Australians at Canterbury; Throwing Controversy]   (p278-287)
Yachting and Rowing [inc. Isle of Wight Yachting; Wingfield Sculls]   (p287-292)
Our Van [inc. Brighton Races; Yorkshire Oaks; New Forest Hounds]   (p292-310)

Issue 272 : October 1882

Portrait and Biography - Richard Howell   (p311)
Seal Slaying as a Means of Sport by James Bertram   (p312-319)
A Midshipman's Life (part 2) by Cecil Sloane-Stanley   (p319-327)
Carp Fishing on the Priory Water by Joseph Wheeldon   (p327-335)
Veterinary Surgeons by Charles Newmarch   (p335-343)
A Lion Story   (p344-350)
An Irish Horse Deal by Charles Newmarch   (p350-354)
Cricket [inc. Oval Test Match; Gloucestershire Season]   (p354-360)
Yachting and Rowing [inc. Michigan Rowing Team; Obituary of Thomas Bone]   (p360-362)
Our Van [inc. St.Leger Meeting; Obituaries of Peter Rolt and Thomas Hartopp; The New Turf
        Club at Newmarket; Review of *On The Grampian Hills* by Frederick Whitehurst   (p362-372)

Issue 273 : November 1882

Portrait and Biography - William Onslow   (p373-374)
The Loch Leven Fishing Controversy by James Bertram   (p374-382)
A Midshipman's Life (part 3) by Cecil Sloane-Stanley   (p382-387)
George Carter by John Gale   (p387-389)
About an Old Cricket Ball by Frederick Gale   (p389-394)
Our Van [inc. Press Facilities at Newmarket; Warnham Hounds; Bedale Hunt Servants; East
        Devon Hunt; Reviews of *Records of the Fife Foxhounds* by John Babbington
        and *Harriers* by Septimus Berdmore; West Kensington Agricultural Hall]   (p394-412)
Hunting: List of Hounds; Masters, Huntsmen, Whips, Kennels   (p413-430)

Volume 40, December 1882 - June 1883

Issue 274 : December 1882

Portrait of Arthur Coventry, gentleman rider   Title page
Portrait and Biography - James Sawrey-Cookson   (p1-2)
Pastures New by George Tyrrell   (p3-9)
Sketches in the Soudan (part 1): On the March by Willoughby Verner   (p9-17)
A Midshipman's Life (part 4) by Cecil Sloane-Stanley   (p17-23)
A Lay of the Blackmore Vale [verses] by Alexander Clark-Kennedy   (p23-24)
Half-Hours with Dan Seffert by Charles Newmarch   (p25-30)
Prospects and Retrospects of the Chase in Ireland by Comyns Cole   (p31-36)
Mine Ease at Mine Inn by Frederick Gale   (p36-41)
Cricket: The Public School Averages 1882   (p41-46)

Our Van [inc. Aintree Meeting; Derby Steeplechasing; Quorn Hunt; Obituaries of
      Frank Turton, Charles Marlow, Clare Vyner and Frederick Gretton]   (p47-62)

Issue 275 : January 1883

Portrait and Biography - Geoffrey Hill   (p63-64)
Reminiscences of John Day by Ralph Payne-Gallwey   (p64-72)
By Sedge and Stream in Winter Time by Joseph Wheeldon   (p72-81)
Some Memories of Midlothian Meets by James Bertram   (p81-89)
Out in the Snow by John Verrall   (p89-92)
The Modern Master of the Foxhounds by George Lowth   (p92-100)
On the Fords by Richard Green-Price   (p100-105)
The Best Music [verses] by Alexander Clark-Kennedy   (p105-106)
Rowing: Professional Rowing   (p107)
Our Van [inc. Bedford Lodge Stable Scandal; Jockey Club Reforms; London Agricultural Fair;
      Pytchley Hunt; Grafton Hounds; Obituaries of John Day and Anthony Trollope;
      Review of *Old Coaching Days* by Stanley Harris]   (p107-124)

Issue 276 : February 1883

Portrait and Biography - Francis Ford   (p125-126)
Fences and No Fences: An Irish Controversy by Comyns Cole   (p126-131)
The Spoiling of Sport by the Pollution of Streams by William Young   (p131-138)
A Day's Pleasure by George Wilson   (p138-146)
Sketches in the Soudan (part 2): A Day in the Jungle by Willoughby Verner   (p146-156)
A Cricket Chat with William Murdoch by Frederick Gale   (p156-164)
A Lay of the Dorsetshire Hills [verses] by Charles D'Oyly   (p164-166)
Our Van [inc. Obituaries of Ralph Etwall, Dudley Milner, Case Walker, George Grey,
      Samuel Martin, William Prime, George Fenwick and John Tautz; Atherstone Hunt;
      Stratton Hounds; Reviews of *Carriages, Roads and Coaches* by Septimus
      Berdmore and *The Fowler in Ireland* by Ralph Payne-Gallwey]   (p166-186)

Issue 277 : March 1883

Portrait and Biography - Henry Leach   (p187-188)
Tottering Thrones by George Tyrrell   (p188-194)
A Day with the Foot Hounds by John Verrall   (p194-199)
Gleanings From the Notebook of a Gambler by Edouard Beaumont   (p200-208)
Old Landmarks of Sport by Richard Green-Price   (p208-214)
Our Canadian Cousins by Frederick Gale   (p214-218)
Sketches in the Soudan (part 3/1): The Arab Village by Willoughby Verner   (p218-222)
The Sport of Old England [verses] by Alexander Clark-Kennedy   (p223-224)
Coursing: The Waterloo Cup by George Wilson   (p224-232)
Our Van [inc. The Sportsman's Exhibition; Review of *Harness* by John Philipson; York &
      Ainsty Hunt; Steeplechase Horses; Obituary of Stirling Crawfurd]   (p232-248)

Issue 278 : April 1883

Portrait and Biography - Charles Gordon-Lennox   (p249-251)
Beenham House [Stud] by George Tyrrell   (p251-256)
The Debate Upon George Anderson's Bill [Pigeon Shooting]   (p256-259)
About Driving Four Horses   (p259-270)
Pigeon Pastimes by James Bertram   (p270-278)
Sketches in the Soudan (part 3/2): The Arab Village by Willoughby Verner   (p278-282)
Macheath's Complaint by Richard Green-Price   (p283-286)
Pigbury's Pond by Joseph Wheeldon   (p286-295)

Our Van [inc. Cart Horse Show; Edmund Tattersall on Void Nominations; Cambridge
    University Steeplechases; Morpeth Hounds; Obituary of Mark Wood; Review
    of *The Record of The Boat Race* by George Treherne]   (p295-310)

Issue 279 : May 1883

Portrait and Biography - John Froude-Bellew   (p311-312)
The Great Fisheries Exhibition by James Bertram   (p312-320)
Echoes of the Past Season by Richard Green-Price   (p320-326)
Sketches in the Soudan (part 4): Days at Keren by Willoughby Verner   (p326-334)
Reminiscences of Bygone Days by Joseph Wheeldon   (p334-342)
Turf Recollections (part 1) by William Day   (p342-347)
This Year's Cricket [Marylebone Cricket Club President Robert Grimston; Yorkshire Matches]   (p348-353)
Yachting and Rowing [inc. Nice Yacht Club; Nore Club Match]   (p354-356)
Our Van [inc. Punchestown Meeting; Rugby Hunt Point-to-Point; Obituary of Gustavus
    Batthyany; South Staffordshire Hunt]   (p357-372)

Issue 280 : June 1883

Portrait and Biography - Albert Saxe-Coburg   (p373-377)
Summer Saturdays by George Tyrrell   (p378-385)
Reverend John Russell (part 1): In Memoriam by Mohun Harris   (p385-390)
Prospects of Sport in Scotland by James Bertram   (p390-395)
Spring Hunting in the New Forest by William Day   (p396-401)
Rook Shooting by John Verrall   (p401-407)
May Cricket [Cambridge University Matches; Marylebone Cricket Club on Throwing]   (p407-413)
Yachting and Rowing [inc. Yacht Racing Association Guidelines; Obituary of James Moxton   (p413-415)
Our Van [inc. Roodee Racecourse; Coaching Club Meet; Reviews of *Foils and Counterfoils*
    by Richard Green-Price and *Indian Racing Reminiscences* by Horace Hayes]   (p416-430)

Volume 41, July 1883 - January 1884

Issue 281 : July 1883

Portrait of Charles Wood, jockey   Title page
Portrait and Biography - Park Yates   (p1-2)
A Fish Dinner at the Fishery Exhibition by James Bertram   (p2-9)
A Battered Portmanteau (part 4) by George Wilson   (p10-18)
An Idyll of the Thames by Joseph Wheeldon   (p18-23)
Hunters and Hounds at Peterborough by William Day   (p24-28)
Reverend John Russell (part 2): In Memoriam by Mohun Harris   (p29-33)
Sketches in the Soudan (part 5/1): A Trip into Terra Incognita by Willoughby Verner   (p33-38)
Cricket [inc. Orleans Club Match; Oxford University Players]   (p38-45)
Yachting and Rowing [inc. Yachting Reports; Obituary of George Kent]   (p45-49)
Our Van [inc. Ascot Meeting; Stockbridge Races; Reviews of *Foxhunting* by William
    Bromley-Davenport and *Kelvington* by Alfred White; Obituary of Joseph
    Shorthouse]   (p49-62)

Issue 282 : August 1883

Portrait and Biography - Walter Powell   (p63-64)
The Story of the Eglinton Tournament Re-told by James Bertram   (p64-72)
Oliver Lumby: The Cool Hand (part 1)   (p72-84)
The Song of the Grouse [verses] by Alexander Clark-Kennedy   (p84-85)
Sketches in the Soudan (part 5/2): A Trip into Terra Incognita by Willoughby Verner   (p85-91)
Turf Recollections (part 2) by William Day   (p91-96)

Cricket: Public School Matches (p96-105)

Yachting and Rowing [inc. Obituary of Matthew Webb; Geneva International Regatta] (p105-110)

Our Van [inc. The Newmarket Club; Kempton Park Races; Review of *The Cream of Leicestershire* by Edward Pennell-Elmhirst; Ward Union Hunt; Obituary of Thomas Howe] (p110-124)

Issue 283 : September 1883

Portrait and Biography - Thomas Peyton (p125-127)

This Year's Sport on the Heather by James Bertram (p127-135)

Oliver Lumby: The Cool Hand (part 2) (p135-148)

Turf Recollections (part 3) by William Day (p148-157)

Cricket [inc. Canterbury Week; County Reports] (p157-166)

Yachting and Rowing [inc. Cowes Week; Provincial Regattas] (p166-172)

Our Van [inc. Lewes Races; Redcar Meeting; Ebor Handicap; Obituary of Charles Trelawney] (p172-186)

Issue 284 : October 1883

Portrait and Biography - Lowry Cole (p187-188)

Reminiscences of Bygone Days: Padgington Wood by Joseph Wheeldon (p188-197)

Oliver Lumby: The Cool Hand (part 3) (p197-209)

Falling Leaves by Charles Newmarch (p209-214)

Amongst the Tigers (p214-221)

The River Monarch [verses] by Alexander Clark-Kennedy (p221-223)

Cricket: The Past Season (p223-229)

Yachting and Rowing [inc. Solent Regatta; Thames-side Rowing Clubhouses] (p229-233)

Our Van [inc. Doncaster Meeting; Ayr Racecourse; New Forest Foxhounds; Hertfordshire Hunt] (p233-248)

Issue 285 : November 1883

Portrait and Biography - Rowland Hill (p249-250)

Cheerless, Chill November by Joseph Wheeldon (p250-261)

Oliver Lumby: The Cool Hand (part 4) (p261-270)

Obstacles by Richard Green-Price (p270-276)

Our Van [inc. The Cesarewitch; Jockey Club Cup; Obituary of William Brice; Devon & Somerset Staghounds; Review of *Records of the Fife Foxhounds* by Stephen Babington (p276-292)

Hunting: List of Hounds; Masters, Huntsmen, Whips, Kennels (p293-310)

Issue 286 : December 1883

Portrait and Biography - Charles Wicksted (p311-312)

Hunting Reflections by Edward Pennell-Elmhirst (p312-319)

[Review] *An Autobiography* by Anthony Trollope (p319-322)

Uncle John by Joseph Wheeldon (p322-331)

At the Fall of the Year [verses] by Alexander Clark-Kennedy (p331-334)

Oliver Lumby: The Cool Hand (part 5) (p334-342)

An Unpreserved Manor by John Verrall (p342-346)

The Importation of Foreign Cattle by William Hunting (p346-350)

Our Van [inc. Brighton Meeting; Derby Racing; Hertfordshire Harriers; Rothschild's Staghounds; Reviews of *The Right Sort* by Mary Kennard and *Hunting Songs and Poems* by John Musters; Obituaries of John Laurenson, Alan Gardner, Frederic de Grange and Robert Hanbury] (p351-372)

Issue 287 : January 1884

Portrait and Biography - Herbert Langham	(p373-374)
The Irish Hunting Horizon by Comyns Cole	(p374-383)
Greybeard at Home	(p383-390)
The Gamest Fox in the Vale [verses] by Alexander Clark-Kennedy	(p390-392)
An Old Fashioned Christmastide by Joseph Wheeldon	(p392-401)
English and Australian Cricket [Tour Preview]	(p401-406)
In Mid-Season [Hunting Round-Up] by Edward Pennell-Elmhirst	(p406-414)
Our Van [inc. Islington Agricultural Show; Obituaries of Thomas Leedham, Alfred Smith, George Craven and William Hurman; Testimonial Dinner to Joseph Wheeldon; Review of *The Architecture of The Stable* by John Birch; Dissolution of Grand National Hunt Committee]	(p415-430)

Volume 42, February - August 1884

Issue 288 : February 1884

Portrait of William Murdoch, cricketer	Title page
Portrait and Biography - Thomas Nickalls	(p1-2)
Wild Sport in the Orkney Isles (part 1): Amongst the Seals by Alexander Clark-Kennedy	(p3-12)
Hunting From London by Edward Pennell-Elmhirst	(p13-19)
Life in the Deer Forests by James Bertram	(p19-26)
Roach Fishing in Western Waters by Joseph Wheeldon	(p26-35)
The West Midland Shires by Richard Green-Price	(p35-43)
An Evening in the Woods by John Verrall	(p43-46)
Our Van [inc. North Warwickshire Hunt; Garth's Hounds; Obituaries of John Russell, Charles Trelawny, Reginald Trelawny, George Brendon, Richard Grosvenor and Henry Buck (*Hotspur* of the *Daily Telegraph*); Jockey Club Licences]	(p47-62)

Issue 289 : March 1884

Portrait and Biography – Hugh Lowther	(p63-64)
Wild Sport in the Orkney Isles (part 2): Amongst the Wildfowl by Alexander Clark-Kennedy	(p64-72)
A Chat about English Trotters and their Use by Charles Newmarch	(p72-79)
The Last Day in the Woods by Joseph Wheeldon	(p79-91)
For'ard [Hunt Reports; Obituary of Ferdinand Fairfax] by Richard Green-Price	(p91-98)
The Ground Game Act by James Bertram	(p98-102)
The Foxhunter's Widow [verses] by Sybil Maxwell	(p102-103)
The Fishery Exhibition's Legacy of Literature [inc. reviews of *The Sea Fisheries and Fishing Population* by Alfred Saxe-Coburg; *Life of the Fisher Folk* by Leoni Levi; *Harvest of the Sea* by James Bertram; *British Marine and Freshwater Fishes* by Saville Kent; *The Preservation of Fish Life in Rivers* by Massey Mainwaring; *The Salmon Fisheries* by Charles Fryer; *Coarse Fish Culture* by Robert Marston; *On the Culture of Salmonidae* by James Maitland; *Angling Societies* by Joseph Wheeldon; *Fish Culture* by Francis Day] by Comyns Cole	(p103-110)
Coursing: The Waterloo Cup by George Wilson	(p111-121)
Yachting and Rowing [inc. Double Sculling; London Rowing Club]	(p121-124)
Our Van [inc. Meynell Hunt; Brighton Harriers; Berkhamsted Buckhounds; South Devon Hunt; Obituary of Alister James; Grand Military Steeplechase]	(p124-140)
The Days When I Rode With the Quorn [verses] by Charles Barstow	(p140)

* The first time in an issue that a female contributor has been named. However, it is highly likely that unnamed female writers have previously been published anonymously *

Issue 290 : April 1884

Portrait and Biography - William Cuffe (p141-142)
Three Days on Loch Tay by Three of Us by James Bertram (p142-151)
Hunters by Richard Green-Price (p151-158)
Wild Sport in the Orkney Isles (part 3): Wildfowl, Snipe, Plover, Hawks by Alexander
        Clark-Kennedy (158-168)
On Training Animals by Gage Freeman (p169-172)
Past and Present by Joseph Wheeldon (p172-182)
Yachting and Rowing [inc. Nice Yacht Club; Irish Rowing] (p182-186)
Our Van [inc. Reconstitution of Grand National Hunt Committee; The Sportsman's
        Exhibition; Pytchley Hunt Point-to-Point; Cambridge University Steeplechase] (p186-202)

Issue 291 : May 1884

Portrait and Biography - Henry Dent (p203-204)
Facile Princeps [Hunt Reports] by Richard Green-Price (p204-213)
Dreams and Omens of the Derby by Edouard Beaumont (p213-223)
Wild Sport in the Orkney Isles (part 4): A Whale Hunt (i) by Alexander Clark-Kennedy (p223-229)
The Last of the Prize-Fighters by Frederick Gale (p230-237)
Oxford and Cambridge Athletics by Comyns Cole (p237-240)
This Year's Cricket: Preview (p240-246)
Yachting and Rowing [inc. Cercle Nautique Regatta; Henley Course] (p247-248)
Our Van [inc. New Leicester Racecourse; Epsom Meeting; Obituaries of Robert Grimston,
        Hamilton Williamson, Francis Scott, John Wisden and Edwin Scobell] (p248-264)

Issue 292 : June 1884

Portrait and Biography - Owen Williams (p265-266)
Are the Deer Forests in Danger by James Bertram (p266-273)
Wild Sport in the Orkney Isles (part 5): A Whale Hunt (ii) by Alexander Clark-Kennedy (p273-280)
Coaching by Septimus Berdmore (p280-290)
Daniel Darnall's Difficulties by Joseph Wheeldon (p290-300)
L'Envoi [Hunt Reports; Obituary of Walter Montagu] by Richard Green-Price (p300-304)
May Cricket: Start of Australian Tour (p304-311)
Yachting and Rowing [New Thames Yacht Club; Thames Rowing Club] (p311)
Our Van [inc. New Forest Hunt; Ludlow Hunt Club; Manchester Horse Show] (p311-326)

Issue 293 : July 1884

Portrait and Biography - Percy Wyndham (p327-328)
Rusticus Expectat [Racing Calendar Changes] by Richard Green-Price (p328-333)
Thames Trouting on the Derby Day by Joseph Wheeldon (p334-343)
On Horse Shows by Comyns Cole (p343-349)
Wild Sport in the Orkney Isles (part 6): Among the Sea Fowl by Alexander Clark-Kennedy (p350-357)
The Old Road: An Angler's Lay [verses] by Alexander Clark-Kennedy (p357-359)
Hunters and Hounds at Peterborough by William Day (p359-364)
The Dream of an Old Meltonian by William Bromley-Davenport (p364-367)
Cricket [inc. Australian Tour Matches; Cambridge University Players] (p367-373)
Yachting and Rowing [inc. Royal Northern Yacht Club; New Thames Rowing Club] (p373-375)
Our Van [inc. Islington Horse Show; Ascot week; Obituaries of William Bromley-Davenport,
        Henry Thompson, Thomas Carlyon and Tass Parker] (p375-388)

Issue 294 : August 1884

Portrait and Biography - Ivo Bligh (p389-390)

On Highland Heather by James Bertram   (p390-398)

Arab Horses by Comyns Cole   (p399-406)

Wild Sport in the Orkney Isles (part 7): More Sea Fowl by Alexander Clark-Kennedy   (p406-414)

About Racing Touts and Tipsters by Edouard Beaumont   (p414-423)

Notes on Riding Tours (part 1) by William Day   (p424-428)

July Cricket [inc. Old Trafford Test; Philadelphians' Tour]   (p428-437)

Yachting and Rowing [inc. Mudhook Yacht Club; Ostend Regatta]   (p437-441)

Our Van [inc. Danebury Meeting; Tattersall's Newmarket Sales; Shrewsbury Agricultural Show; South Durham Horse Show; Review of [Sporting] *Holiday Haunts* by Bernard Becker; Obituaries of Fenwick Bisset and Caledon Alexander]   (p441-454)

Volume 43, September 1884 - March 1885

Issue 295 : September 1884

Portrait of Matthew Dawson, trainer   Title page

Portrait and Bibliography - Henry Howard   (p1-3)

Wild Sport in the Orkney Isles (part 8): De Omnibus Rebus by Alexander Clark-Kennedy   (p3-11)

Lions and Lion Tamers by Edouard Beaumont   (p11-20)

Notes on Riding Tours (part 2) by William Day   (p21-25)

The Scottish Angler's Round 1884 by James Bertram   (p25-32)

Alumnus [Sport at Eton] by Richard Green-Price   (p32-35)

The First of September [verses] by Alexander Clark-Kennedy   (p36-38)

August Cricket [inc. Canterbury Week; Australian Tour]   (p38-45)

Yachting and Rowing [inc. Plymouth Corinthian Yacht Club; Oxford Regatta]   (p46-48)

Our Van [inc. Redcar Meeting; Stockton Handicap; Devon & Somerset Staghounds]   (p49-62)

Issue 296 : October 1884

Portrait and Bibliography - Algernon Greville   (p63-64)

The Philosophy of Big Bags [Grouse Shooting] by James Bertram   (p64-69)

The Dublin Horse Show 1884 by Comyns Cole   (p69-75)

The Progress of Sport by Frederick Gale   (p75-84)

Do Fish Feel Pain by John Keene   (p84-88)

Giant Strides by Richard Green-Price   (p88-94)

Shall I [Hunting Fiction] by William Day   (p94-101)

Close of the Cricket Season: Conclusion of Australian Tour   (p101-105)

Yachting and Rowing [inc. Royal Dorset Regatta; Obituaries of Robert Risley and George Purdue]   (p106-108)

Our Van [inc. Huntingdon Racing; Bath Horse Show; Obituary of William Oldaker]   (p108-124)

Issue 297 : November 1884

Portrait and Biography - Dudley Stanhope   (p125)

Invalided Sportsmen by George Lowth   (p126-132)

The Opening Hunting Season by Richard Green-Price   (p132-140)

The Bird of the Battues by James Bertram   (p140-149)

Notitia Venatica by William Blew   (p150-158)

Now and Then: Irish Sport in the Past and Present by Comyns Cole   (p158-167)

Guilty or Not Guilty by Joseph Wheeldon   (p167-178)

Yachting and Rowing [inc. Yacht Racing Association; Australian Rowing]   (p178-180)

Our Van [inc. Kempton Park Meeting; Dewhurst Plate; West Kent Hunt; Kildare Hounds; Obituary of Arthur Ward]   (p180-194)

Issue 298 : December 1884

Portrait and Biography - William Rayer	(p195-196)
Horse and Hound by Edward Pennell-Elmhirst	(p196-204)
Jumping Powder by Richard Green-Price	(p204-211)
How Hunters Can Be Bred to Pay by Charles Newmarch	(p211-219)
Defective Wind in Horses by William Hunting	(p219-223)
About Tips to Gamekeepers and Others	(p223-230)
Sporting Recollections by Finch Mason	(p230-235)
The Growth of Sport in Scotland by James Bertram	(p235-239)
Our Van [inc. Aintree Meeting; Manchester Racing; Cunard's Hounds; North Cheshire Hunt; Tredegar Hunters' Show]	(p240-256)

Issue 299 : January 1885

Portrait and Biography - Thomas Byrne	(p257-258)
Sporting Statesmen and Senators À Cheval	(p258-264)
"Hounds, Please, Gentlemen!" by Richard Green-Price	(p264-270)
About Wagering and Gambling by Edouard Beaumont	(p270-278)
The Reciprocities of Fox Hunting by Edward Pennell-Elmhirst	(p279-287)
A New Training Experience by Frederick Gale	(p287-292)
Gentlemen Huntsmen and Hunt Servants by Charles Newmarch	(p292-300)
A Tale About a Dog by Lewis Clement	(p300-302)
Do Not Ride Over Them Now [verses] by Alexander Clark-Kennedy	(p303-304)
Our Van [inc. Smithfield Club; Reviews of *The Russell Album* by Thomas Marshall, *Robert the Bruce* by Alexander Clark-Kennedy and *From Post to Finish* by Hawley Smart; Limerick Hunt; York Gimcrack Club; Obituaries of William Hugh and Richard Lumley]	(p305-318)

Issue 300 : February 1885

Portrait and Biography - Andrew Knowles	(p319-320)
Fox Hunting Fallacies by Edward Pennell-Elmhirst	(p320-327)
Lord [George] Cadogan's State of the Turf by Frederick Gale	(p327-332)
Bent Forelegs by William Hunting	(p333-337)
At Home by Richard Green-Price	(p337-344)
The Four Stages of Salmon Life by Charles Fryer	(p345-355)
Bits, Bridles and Hands by Charles Newmarch	(p355-363)
About Circuses	(p363-372)
Our Van [inc. Berkhamsted Buckhounds; Hertfordshire Hunt; Old Berkeley Hunt; Obituaries of Arthur Egerton, Heneage Finch and Alfred Head Baily]	(p373-388)

* Report on the death of Alfred Baily on 31 December 1884 at his home in South Hampstead *

Issue 301 : March 1885

Portrait and Biography - Hugh Fortescue	(p389-390)
Ladies in the Hunting Field by Frederick Gale	(p390-398)
The Game Laws and the Poachers by Richard Jefferies	(p398-405)
Gone to Ground by Richard Green-Price	(p405-412)
Coursing: The Waterloo Cup by George Wilson	(p412-418)
Gags and Martingales by Charles Newmarch	(p419-425)
A Plea for the Deer-Cart by Charles Newmarch	(p425-431)
Our Van [inc. Kempton Park Steeplechasing; Belvoir Hunt; Whaddon Chase Hounds; Bicester Hunt Ball; Obituary of Thomas McGeorge; Review of *The Life of Robert Grimston* by Frederick Gale]	(p431-446)

Volume 44, April - October 1885

Issue 302 : April 1885

Portrait of Edward Hanlan, rower ... Title page
Portrait and Biography - George Parker ... (p1-2)
What Should Sportsmen Eat and Drink by James Bertram ... (p2-10)
Over [Farmers using Barbed Wire] by Richard Green-Price ... (p10-15)
Irish Hunters Past and Present (part 1) by Comyns Cole ... (p15-21)
Horse Breeding by Gerard Wallop ... (p21-27)
Saddles by Charles Newmarch ... (p27-33)
Unnerving Hunters by William Hunting ... (p33-36)
Hunting Correspondence by Comyns Cole ... (p36-44)
Yachting and Rowing [inc. Obituaries of Charles Thellusson and Curtis Lampson; Henley Towpath] ... (p44-46)
Our Van [inc. Shire Horse Society Show; Aylesbury Steeplechases; Bramham Moor Hunt; Whaddon Chase Hunt; Dear's Harriers; Ranelagh Club at Barn Elms] ... (p46-62)

Issue 303 : May 1885

Portrait and Biography - Edward Clayton ... (p63-65)
Jockeys (part 1) by Charles Newmarch ... (p65-71)
Turf Nomenclature by William Tulloch ... (p71-80)
The Sporting Resources of Dublin by Comyns Cole ... (p80-87)
Financial Aspects of the Derby by Edouard Beaumont ... (p87-96)
Rook Hawking by James Harting ... (p96-104)
The Derby: A Picture Founded on Facts by Frederick Gale ... (p104-110)
Irish Hunters Past and Present (part 2) by Comyns Cole ... (p110-114)
The Cricket Season of 1885: County Previews ... (p115-121)
Yachting and Rowing [inc. Teddington Sailing Club; University Boat Race] ... (p121-123)
Our Van [inc. The Badminton Club; Northampton Meeting; Punchestown Races; Oakley Hunt; South Staffordshire Hounds] ... (p123-140)

Issue 304 : June 1885

Portrait and Biography - Richard Curzon-Howe ... (p141)
The Dukes and Lords of the Derby by Frederick Gale ... (p142-153)
Jockeys (part 2) by Charles Newmarch ... (p154-160)
A Saunter Through Shropshire Haras by Richard Green-Price ... (p160-165)
Racing by Henry Valoynes ... (p165-175)
Horsemanship [Riding Schools] by Gerard Wallop ... (p175-183)
Bumping Races: A Reminiscence of Oxford Days ... (p184-190)
Spring Hunting in the New Forest by William Day ... (p190-195)
The Past Hunting Season by Richard Green-Price ... (p195-204)
Yachting and Rowing [inc. Yacht Racing Association; Amateur Swimming Union; Obituary of Thomas Talfourd] ... (p204-208)
Our Van [inc. Chester Cup; Old Berkeley Hunt; Reviews of *Harrow School* by Percy Thornton, *The History of Newmarket* Volume I by John Hore and *Hound and Horn: The Life of George Carter* by John Gale; Obituary of Frederick Swindell ... (p209-226)

Issue 305 : July 1885

Portrait and Biography - Allan Steel ... (p227-228)
Jockeys (part 3) by Charles Newmarch ... (p229-236)
[Reviews] Scrope Redivivus : Reprints of *Days of Deer Stalking* and *Days and Nights of Salmon Fishing* both by William Scrope ... (p236-244)

How They Roar by Richard Green-Price   (p244-248)

Amateur Training by Frederick Gale   (p249-258)

A Turf Notability: Frederick Swindell by Ralph Payne-Gallwey   (p258-266)

On Spavin by William Hunting   (p266-271)

A Tall Angling Yarn by Alexander Clark-Kennedy   (p271-275)

Cricket in 1885 [inc. Nottinghamshire Matches; Obituary of John Juniper]   (p275-281)

Our Van [inc. Epsom Meeting; Ascot Races; Obituaries of Philip Bishop, George Edwards, William Hawtin, William Pender, George Ferrot, George Barrow, James Wilson, Francis Hastings and Burton Persse; Badminton Club Dinner]   (p281-296)

Issue 306 : August 1885

Portrait and Biography - Guy Paget   (p297-298)

O'er the Muir, Amang the Heather by James Bertram   (p298-305)

Pleasant Pastures: A Peep at the Eaton Stud by Richard Green-Price   (p305-311)

The Annals of Lawn Tennis by Henry Jones   (p312-317)

The Defence of Field Sports   (p317-327)

The Descent of the Foxhound by Charles Newmarch   (p327-336)

On Taking a Holiday   (p336-343)

Summer Meets by William Day   (p343-351)

Modern Phaetons (part 1) by Frederick Gale   (p351-354)

Yachting and Rowing [inc. Royal Thames Yacht Club's Channel Match; Le Havre Regatta; Obituary of William Jessop]   (p354-359)

Our Van [inc. Newmarket Summer Meeting; Leicester Races; Oakley Hunt; Reviews of *Hunting Songs and Sport* by Lina Chaworth-Musters and *Modern English Sports* by Frederick Gale]   (p359-374)

Issue 307 : September 1885

Portrait and Biography - Patrick Carnegy   (p375-376)

Notes of the Earlier St.Legers by William Day   (p376-385)

Glanders in Horses by William Hunting   (p385-390)

The Breeder's Companion by Richard Green-Price   (p390-397)

A Peasant Proprietary and Game Preservation by Charles Newmarch   (p397-405)

Australian Horses by William Lamonby   (p405-409)

Modern Phaetons (part 2) by Frederick Gale   (p409-412)

Fencing Masters by Henry Dunn   (p413-418)

Cricket in 1885 [inc. Obituary of William Blackman; County Reports]   (p418-423)

Yachting and Rowing [inc. Cowes Week; Barnes Regatta]   (p424-427)

Our Van [inc. Jockey Club Fixtures List; Brighton Races; Redcar Meeting; Scarborough Tennis; Hertfordshire Hunt Boundaries; Buxton Horse Show; Obituary of John Walker]   (p427-444)

Issue 308 : October 1885

Portrait and Biography - Thomas Boughey   (p445-446)

Doncaster and the St.Leger by William Day   (p446-456)

The Old Southern Hound by Charles Newmarch   (p456-465)

Running Men and Pedestrians by Charles Butcher   (p465-472)

The Season's Yachting by Dixon Kemp   (p473-481)

The Horse Fair by Richard Green-Price   (p481-487)

Foot Lameness in Horses by William Hunting   (p488-491)

Edward Hanlan by Comyns Cole   (p492-494)

Yachting and Rowing [inc. America's Cup Races; River Tyne Rowing]   (p494-496)

Our Van [inc. Derby Meeting; Great Yorkshire Handicap; Barnet Fair; Enfield Staghounds; Hursley Hunt]   (p496-510)

Volume 45, November 1885 - May 1886

Issue 309 : November 1885

Portrait of John Roberts, billiards — Title page
Portrait and Biography - George Middleton — (p1-2)
The Staghound by Charles Newmarch — (p2-13)
A Memorable Salmon Year by James Bertram — (p14-21)
Property in Game by John Verrall — (p22-29)
Steeplechasing by Comyns Cole — (p29-38)
Cubs and Cub-Hunting by Richard Green-Price — (p38-46)
Our Van [inc. Leicester Races; Middle Park Stakes; Hertfordshire Hunt; Marylebone Cricket Club in America; Obituaries of Richard Webster, John Tregonwell and John Bowes] (p46-62)

Issue 310 : December 1885

Portrait and Biography - Douglas Baird — (p63)
Sporting Lessees by Edward Michell — (p64-72)
The Bloodhound (part 1) by Charles Newmarch — (p72-79)
Burning the Waters by James Bertram — (p79-84)
[Review] *Hunting* by Mowbray Morris reviewed by Richard Green Price — (p84-89)
[Review] *Field Sports in the North of Europe* by Llewellyn Lloyd — (p89-94)
The Alleged Increase of Racing by John Verrall — (p94-96)
Hunting Notes by Edward Pennell-Elmhirst — (p97-104)
Shoe-Lameness in Horses by William Hunting — (p105-108)
Shots: Bad and Good by John Tennant — (p109-113)
Our Van [inc. Brighton Races; Aintree Meeting; Atherstone Hunt; Whaddon Chase Hounds; North Warwickshire Hunt; Review of *Tales for Sportsmen* by Simpkin Marshall] (p114-132)

Issue 311 : January 1886

Portrait and Biography - Charles Tyrwhitt — (p133-134)
Men May Come and Men May Go by Richard Green-Price — (p134-140)
Banished and Vanished Sports by John Verrall — (p140-147)
The Winning Sires by Ralph Payne-Gallwey — (p147-155)
Wanted: A Horse Institute by William Hunting — (p156-159)
The Bloodhound (part 2) by Charles Newmarch — (p160-165)
The Old Squire by Joseph Wheeldon — (p165-174)
Modern Chess by William Steintz — (p174-180)
Our Van [inc. Islington Horse Show; Leicester Cross-Country Meeting; Oakley Hunt; Chorleywood Hounds; Obituaries of Dudley North and Charles Brewer; Reviews of *The Pytchley Book of Refined Cookery* by Herbert Langham and [William] *Ruff's Guide to the Turf*] — (p181-202)

Issue 312 : February 1886

Portrait and Biography - Henry Wombwell — (p203-205)
What Parliament Can Do for Sport by Richard Green-Price — (p205-211)
The Beagle by Charles Newmarch — (p211-220)
Musings in the Frost by Edward Pennell-Elmhirst — (p220-227)
A Fox Chase [verses] — (p227-228)
Eels: How to Breed, Feed, Catch and Cook Them by James Bertram — (p228-237)
English Skating by Henry Vandervell — (p237-241)
Fen Shooting at Huggins Carr Farm by Joseph Wheeldon — (p241-253)
On Feeding Horses by William Hunting — (p253-257)

Our Van [inc. Quorn Hunt; Berkhamsted Buckhounds; Limerick Hounds; Meynell Hunt;
        Obituary of William Mortimer]   (p257-272)

Issue 313 : March 1886

Portrait and Biography - Ferdinand de Rothschild   (p273)
The Royal Company of Archers by James Paul   (p274-282)
Rough Hounds: The Welsh Harrier and Otter Hound (part 1) by Charles Newmarch   (p283-290)
A Bounty to Horse Breeding and Turf Reform by Richard Green-Price   (p291-296)
Coursing: The Waterloo Cup by George Wilson   (p296-306)
A Bush Race Meeting in Australia by George Darley   (p306-309)
Whiting and Whiting Fishing by Edward Stone   (p310-313)
Our Van [inc. Prize Fighting; Rothschild's Staghounds; Hertfordshire Hunt; Hursley Hounds;
        Review of *Masters of Foxhounds 1885* by William Tuck]   (p313-334)

Issue 314 : April 1886

Portrait and Biography - John Browne   (p335-336)
The New Rules of Betting by Richard Green-Price   (p336-341)
The Salmon in Parliament by James Bertram   (p341-349)
Rough Hounds: The Welsh Harrier and Otter Hound (part 2) by Charles Newmarch   (p349-359)
Modern Billiards by Benjamin Garno   (p359-365)
Forage: Its Varieties and Values by William Hunting   (p365-371)
A Brief Glance at the Counties by Frederick Gale   (p371-377)
Yachting and Rowing [inc. University Boat Race Preview; Henley Regatta Changes]   (p377-379)
Our Van [inc. Croydon Steeplechasing; Reviews of *Reminiscences of the Turf* by William Day
        and *The History of Newmarket* Volumes II & III by John Hore; Whaddon Chase
        Hounds; Grafton Hunt; Obituaries of Charles Colville, George Dupplin, Charles
        Tyrwhitt, Harry Villebois and Frederick Barne; Hackney Stud Book Society]   (p379-400)

Issue 315 : May 1886

Portrait and Biography - John Trotter   (p401-402)
The Meath Hunt by Comyns Cole   (p402-411)
[Review] *Reminiscences of the Turf* by William Day reviewed by John Kent   (p411-425)
A Turf Partnership by Ralph Payne-Gallwey   (p425-434)
King Nip by Richard Green-Price   (p434-441)
Punchestown: Past, Present and Prospective by Comyns Cole   (p441-448)
Yachting and Rowing [inc. America's Cup Preparations; Thames Conservancy Charges]   (p449-452)
Our Van [inc. Ranelagh Club; Epsom Meeting; Enfield Staghounds; South Staffordshire Hunt;
        Reviews of *Racing* by William Craven and *Steeplechasing* by Arthur Coventry;
        Obituary of Samuel Pitman]   (p452-474)

Volume 46, June - December 1886

Issue 316 : June 1886

Portrait of Thomas Jennings, trainer   Title page
Portrait and Biography - Cromartie Leveson-Gower   (p1-2)
Sporting Literature [Analysis of Books from 1486]   (p2-9)
Rejoinder to John Kent's Reply by William Day   (p9-22)
The Eccentricities of Sport by Richard Green-Price   (p22-28)
Carp Culture at Home and Abroad by Edward Marston   (p28-36)
Prince's Club by Frederick Gale   (p36-43)
The Ordinary Harrier by Charles Newmarch   (p43-53)
Turf Tyranny or British Boycotting by Comyns Cole   (p53-57)

Yachting and Rowing [inc. New Thames Yacht Club; Obituaries of Charles Plunkett,
        William Paton, Charles Bush and William Leverell of *Bell's Life*]   (p57-61)
Our Van [inc. Chester Cup; Ward Union Staghounds; Meath Hunt; Duhallow Hounds;
        Obituaries of Edward St.John, George Brooks, James McBride and John
        Mitford; Review of *Hunting Notes in the West Midlands* by Richard Green-Price]   (p62-78)

** This volume starts with a larger type; is better laid out and uses a number of different fonts.
The articles are longer and some give the impression of being written in-house instead of using those
from contributors. The Annual Hunting Lists have been transferred to other Baily's titles **

Issue 317 : July 1886

Portrait and Biography - John Carter-Wood   (p79-80)
The Paddock by Richard Green-Price   (p80-87)
The Modern Foxhound (part 1) by Charles Newmarch   (p87-94)
The Royal Buckhounds and their Masters (part 1) by John Hore   (p94-103)
Game Farming and Fowl Breeding by Herbert Atkinson   (p103-112)
The Apotheosis of Tom and Jerry [Closure of *Bell's Life in London*, 1822-86] by Frederick Gale   (p113-121)
Our Horse Supply by William Craven   (p121-130)
A Summer Meet by William Day   (p130-136)
The Australian Team of 1886 by Frederick Gale   (p136-140)
Yachting and Rowing [inc. Clyde Yachtsmen; Putney Tidal Rowing]   (p140-144)
Our Van [inc. Islington Horse Show; Ascot Meeting; Rothschild's Cricket Ground]   (p144-156)

Issue 318 : August 1886

Portrait and Biography - Shipley Stuart   (p157-158)
The Grouse, Deer and Salmon of the Period by James Bertram   (p158-166)
The Modern Foxhound (part 2) by Charles Newmarch   (p166-173)
The Tout by Richard Green-Price   (p173-179)
The Coaches of 1886 by Nevill Fitt   (p179-185)
Horse Taming and Breaking by William Craven   (p186-192)
The Royal Buckhounds and their Masters (part 2) by John Hore   (p192-201)
Horseshoe Pads by William Hunting   (p202-205)
Yachting and Rowing [inc. Royal Mersey Yacht Club; Royal Ulster Regatta; Obituary of
        Hugh Cowie]   (p205-211)
Our Van [inc. Newmarket Meeting; Liverpool Racing; Obituaries of William Selby-Lowndes
        and John Booth; South Staffordshire Hunt]   (p212-226)

Issue 319 : September 1886

Portrait and Biography - George Nevill   (p227-228)
The Royal Game of Golf by Robert Clark   (p228-237)
The Eclipse by Richard Green-Price   (p237-244)
Man and Horse by William Craven   (p244-253)
Midsummer Angling by Frederic Halford   (p253-259)
The Royal Buckhounds and their Masters (part 3) by John Hore   (p259-267)
Bookmakers and Betting by Ralph Payne-Gallwey   (p267-277)
Cricket in 1886 [Review of the Season] by Frederick Gale   (p277-282)
Yachting and Rowing [inc. Royal Cornwall Regatta; Thames Rowing Club]   (p282-288)
Our Van [inc. Goodwood Racing; Lewes Blackballing; Stockton Handicap; Obituary of
        Rudston Read; Reviews of *Shooting: Field & Covert* and *Shooting: Moor &
        Marsh* both by Ralph Payne-Gallwey]   (p288-304)

Issue 320 : October 1886

Portrait and Biography - Robins Bolitho (p305-306)
The Future of The Derby by Edouard Beaumont (p306-313)
The Survival of the Fittest by Richard Green-Price (p313-319)
Tandem-Driving as a Pastime by Charles Newmarch (p319-326)
Sporting in Hampshire by Nunez Heysham (p326-335)
Celebrities at Home: The Arab Steed in the Desert of Sahara by William Craven (p336-342)
The Feast of St.Partridge by George Wilson (p342-347)
The Dublin Horse Show of 1886 by Comyns Cole (p347-354)
The Royal Buckhounds and their Masters (part 4) by John Hore (p354-360)
Yachting and Rowing [inc. Royal Highland Yacht Club; Twickenham Rowing Club Regatta] (p360-366)
Our Van [inc. Huntingdonshire Stakes; Doncaster Meeting; Oakley Hunt; Obituaries of Welsh
        Thornton, Henry Dixon, George Goddard and William Coleman; Opening of
        the Constitutional Club] (p366-382)

Issue 321 : November 1886

Portrait and Biography - George Cholmondeley (p383-384)
We'll all go A-Hunting Today by Richard Green-Price (p384-391)
The Roaring Game and its Surroundings [Curling and its Literature] by James Bertram (p392-399)
Terriers and their Uses (part 1) by Charles Newmarch (p400-406)
Hunting in Hibernia [verses] by Rowland Egerton-Warburton (p407)
Touts and Tipsters by Ralph Payne-Gallwey (p407-414)
Chantilly by Coulson Pitman (p414-423)
[Review] *Sport in Eastern Bengal* by Frank Simson (p423-429)
The Royal Buckhounds and their Masters (part 5) by John Hore (p429-436)
Our Van [inc. Epsom Meeting; Newmarket Racing; Grafton Hunt; Whaddon Chase Hounds] (p436-452)

Issue 322 : December 1886

Portrait and Biography - Watkin Williams Wynn (p453-454)
Acclimatisation and Crossing by James Bertram (p455-463)
My Brilliant and I [Ladies Hunting] by Richard Green-Price (p463-469)
Fish Fighting in Siam by Edward Marston (p469-476)
[Obituary] Frederick Archer by Comyns Cole (p477-482)
Terriers and their Uses (part 2) by Charles Newmarch (p483-491)
Mange in Foxes by Harding Cox (p491-494)
Riders in Red [verses] (p494)
Recollections and Incidents of a Highland Holiday by Joseph Wheeldon (p495-504)
The Royal Buckhounds and their Masters (part 6) by John Hore (p505-513)
Yachting and Rowing [inc.Yacht Racing Association; Oxford University Fours] (p514)
Our Van [inc. Brighton Meeting; Memories of Fred Archer; Obituaries of John Bastard and
        Martin Haworth-Leslie; Cottesmore Hounds; South Berkshire Hunt] (p515-534)

Volume 47, January - July 1887

Issue 323 : January 1887

Portrait of George Barrett, jockey Title page
Portrait and Biography - Frederick Ames (p1)
The Jockey Club: Its History and Work by John Hore (p2-9)
Fox Hunting in the Last Century by Edward Pennell-Elmhirst (p9-19)
[Obituary] Horatio Ross (1801-86) by Comyns Cole (p19-24)
Weights by Richard Green-Price (p24-30)
Unfair Riding in the Hunting-Field by Charles Newmarch (p31-38)

First and Second Turn Out by Frederick Gale (p39-46)
The Royal Buckhounds and their Masters (part 7) by John Hore (p46-56)
Rough Terriers by Charles Newmarch (p56-57)
Our Van [inc. Smithfield Club Show; York Gimcrack Club; Westover Harriers; Obituaries of Henry Cartwright, Barton Powlett, Henry Paulet and Horatio Ross; Building of Olympia] (p57-78)

Issue 324 : February 1887

Portrait and Biography - William Warner (p79)
Proposed Close Time for Hares by James Bertram (p80-87)
The Sires of the Season by Richard Green-Price (p87-96)
The Cleveland Bays by Charles Newmarch (p96-106)
An Economical Hunt by Edward Pennell-Elmhirst (p107-113)
The Royal Buckhounds and their Masters (part 8) by John Hore (p114-122)
Our Van [inc. Obituaries of George Broke-Middleton, Erle Drax and Edward Burbage; Vale of Aylesbury Hunt; Quorn Huntsman; The Pink 'Un [John Corlett] Libel Trial; Fred Archer's Will] (p122-140)

Issue 325 : March 1887

Portrait and Biography - Charles Esdaile (p141-142)
Do Deer Eat their Horns? (p142-150)
Woodcraft by Charles Newmarch (p150-159)
Harry Highclere by Richard Green-Price (p159-165)
National Athletics by Frederick Gale (p165-171)
Reply to the Author of 'Riders in Red' [verses] (p172)
Coursing: The Waterloo Cup by George Wilson (p172-184)
The Royal Buckhounds and their Masters (part 9) by John Hore (p184-193)
Our Van [inc. Kempton Park Races; Bedale Hunt; Oakley Hounds; South Devon Hunt] (p193-210)

Issue 326 : April 1887

Portrait and Biography - Henry Daly (p211-212)
The Jubilee of King George III: Sport Then and Now by William Beloe (p212-223)
What Hunting Does for the Country by Richard Green-Price (p223-230)
Black and White [Sporting Parsons] by Frederick Gale (p230-236)
Sport in the South of France by Coulson Pitman (p236-247)
Some Masters of Hounds by Edward Pennell-Elmhirst (p247-253)
Francis Doyle's St.Leger of 1886 Contrasted with his St.Leger of 1827 [verses] (p254-259)
The University Boat Race (p259-262)
The Royal Buckhounds and their Masters (part 10) by John Hore (p263-270)
Our Van [inc. Hunters Improvement Society; Derby Meeting; Aylesbury Hunt Steeplechases; Old Surrey Hunt Dinner; Obituary of Robert Bateson-Harvey] (p271-288)

Issue 327 : May 1887

Portrait and Biography - Henry Hungerford (p289-290)
The Saddling Bell by Richard Green-Price (p290-297)
The Effect of Shows and Field Trials on Pointers and Setters by Charles Newmarch (p297-304)
Owners, Name Your Foals by William Craven (p304-311)
A Nimrod of the Streams by Edward Marston (p312-320)
Shooting in Burmah by Vesey Stockley (p321-324)
Cricket in 1887 [County and Canadian Tour Preview] by Frederick Gale (p324-332)
Yachting and Rowing [Cape May Challenge Cup; Metropolitan Regatta] (p332)

Our Van [inc. Northampton Racing; Epsom Meeting; Sportsman's Exhibition; Fitzwilliam
          Hounds; Obituaries of Charles Newdigate, John Halliday and George Tyrrell
          (*Baily's* Contributor 'Amphion')]   (p332-354)

Issue 328 : June 1887

Portrait and Biography - Harding Cox   (p355-357)
Betting Systems Dissected by Edouard Beaumont   (p357-367)
Fish Culture by Richard Green-Price   (p367-372)
Spring Poachers by Charles Newmarch   (p373-380)
Racing and its Surroundings by Ralph Payne-Gallwey   (p380-388)
New Forest Spring Hunting by William Day   (p388-394)
The Royal Buckhounds and their Masters (part 11) by John Hore   (p395-400)
Yachting and Rowing [inc. Royal Thames Yacht Club; Obituary of William Mackie]   (p400-403)
Our Van [inc. Kempton Park Jubilee Meeting; Olympia Horse Show]   (p403-416)

Issue 329 : July 1887

Portrait and Biography - William Legh   (p417-418)
The Ascot Jubilee by Richard Green-Price   (p418-426)
Among the Scottish Grouse by James Bertram   (p426-434)
Conjuring   (p434-443)
Under the Willows by Charles Newmarch   (p443-450)
The Military Tournament by Comyns Cole   (p451-455)
Hunters and Hounds at Peterborough by William Day   (p455-461)
Pastime for Princes [verses] by Rowland Egerton-Warburton   (p461-462)
Yachting and Rowing [inc. Royal Harwich Regatta; Royal Thames Channel Match;
          Cambridge University Rowing; Ilex Swimming Club]   (p462-468)
Our Van [inc. Manchester Racing; Ascot Meeting; Royal Counties Agricultural Show;
          Obituary of George Finch-Hatton; Review of *The Game of Cricket* by
          Frederick Gale]   (p469-486)

Volume 48, August 1887 - February 1888

Issue 330 : August 1887

Portrait of John Porter, huntsman   Title page
Portrait and Biography - Charles Talbot   (p1-2)
Turf Laws: Written and Unwritten by Ralph Payne-Gallwey   (p2-10)
A Pillar of Salt by Richard Green-Price   (p10-17)
Aquatics Old and New by Wilfred Pocklington   (p17-25)
Wild Sport on Exmoor by Charles Newmarch   (p25-34)
Cricket in 1887 by Frederick Gale   (p34-41)
Yachting and Rowing [inc. Royal Clyde Yacht Club Regatta; Obituary of Robert Boyd;
          Henley Regatta]   (p41-47)
Our Van [inc. Tattersall's Sales; Liverpool Cup; Leicester Races; Obituary of Henry Hargreaves;
          Newcastle Agricultural Show]   (p48-62)

Issue 331 : September 1887

Portrait and Biography - Allen Bathurst   (p63-64)
On Ponies by Richard Green-Price   (p64-72)
Up-Stream with the Salmon; Down-Stream with the Smolts by Edward Marston   (p72-80)
Otter-Hunting by Charles Newmarch   (p80-89)
The Dublin Horse Show of 1887 by Comyns Cole   (p89-95)
Cricket: The End of the Season by Frederick Gale   (p96-103)

Yachting and Rowing [inc. Royal Western Yacht Club; Amateur Punting Club; Taff Rowing
        Club]   (p103-109)
Our Van [inc. Southdown Racing Club Blackballing; Redcar Races; Ebor Meeting; Yorkshire
        Society Show; Bramham Moor Hunt Luncheon; Obituary of Richard
        Green-Price senior]   (p109-128)

Issue 332 : October 1887

Portrait and Biography - Arthur Wilson   (p129-130)
Doncaster by Richard Green-Price   (p130-137)
Country Craft by Margaret Oliphant   (p137-147)
The Hunting Outlook by Edward Pennell-Elmhirst   (p147-155)
The Partridge by Charles Newmarch   (p155-165)
Trotters   (p165-174)
The Black Fox by Harding Cox   (p175-189)
Yachting and Rowing [inc. Torbay Yachting; London Rowing Club]   (p190-191)
Our Van [inc. Derby Meeting; Devon & Somerset Staghounds; New Forest Hunt; Obituaries of
        James Martin and Hayes St.Leger]   (p191-210)

*This issue marked the retirement of the magazine's sole engraver, Joseph Brown, who had
contributed some 665 portraits to the magazine since the first number. He had also provided
numerous engravings to other Baily's publications*

Issue 333 : November 1887

Portrait and Biography - Henry Boden   (p211-212)
Newmarket by Richard Green-Price   (p212-218)
About the Unprofitable Prophets by Edouard Beaumont   (p219-227)
Turf Reforms and Legislation (part 1) by Ralph Payne-Gallwey   (p227-234)
Poultry Breeding for Pastime and Profit by Margaret Oliphant   (p235-243)
The Haute-Ecole or Manege: Is it Useful? by Charles Newmarch   (p243-253)
Hunting Annotations by Edward Pennell-Elmhirst   (p253-261)
Our Van [inc. Jockey Club Hearing; Newmarket Meeting; Hursley Hounds; Obituaries of
        Walter Gilmour and George Fordham; Winter Coaching]   (p261-280)

* In this issue Baily's announced the successor to engraver Joseph Brown. It was George Stodart
who had his first contribution published on the page following the Contents*

Issue 334 : December 1887

Portrait and Biography - Richard Moore   (p281-282)
The Realities of Hunting by Richard Green-Price   (p283-289)
Financial Aspects of Sport by Frederick Aflalo   (p289-299)
Between the Flags by Albert Muntz   (p299-307)
Turf Reforms and Legislation (part 2) by Ralph Payne-Gallwey   (p307-314)
Tank Shooting in Ceylon by Harry Storey   (p314-317)
North Country Sport by John Radcliffe   (p317-326)
Our Van [inc. Brighton Racing; Grand Sefton Steeplechase; Hampshire Hunt; Obituary of
        Mohun Harris]   (p326-346)

Issue 335 : January 1888

Portrait and Biography - Edmund Tattersall   (p347-350)
A Good Hunter by Richard Green-Price   (p350-356)
Racing Finance by Frederick Aflalo   (p357-364)
Hound Breeding by Charles Newmarch   (p364-375)

Jumping Blood by Albert Muntz (p376-383)
Cricketers in Council (part 1) by Frederick Gale (p383-391)
Sport in Bengal by Charles Buckland (p391-398)
The Dethronement of the Foxhound by Edward Pennell-Elmhirst (p398-405)
Our Van [inc. Middlesex Steeplechase; Gimcrack Club Speech; South Berkshire Hunt;
    Bicester Hounds; Obituaries of Charles Ward and Newcombe Mason;
    Conviction of Two Ascot Welshers] (p406-424)

Issue 336 : February 1888

Portrait and Biography - Hedworth Barclay (p425-427)
Sunshine Ahead by Richard Green-Price (p427-433)
Salmon Life and Growth by Edward Marston (p434-441)
English Saddles and English Seats by Charles Newchurch (p441-450)
Kingsclere by Comyns Cole (p450-452)
Dairying as Work for Country Gentlemen by Margaret Oliphant (p452-460)
The Horse Supply of England by Albert Muntz (p461-468)
Hackles Up (part 1): Men Who Hunt to Ride by Harding Cox (p468-473)
Elephant Shooting in Ceylon by Harry Storey (p473-478)
Our Van [inc. Jockey Club on Gimcrack Speech; Grafton Hunt; Obituary of John Holman;
    Review of *Wisden's Cricket Almanac*] (p479-490)

Volume 49, March - September 1888

Issue 337 : March 1888

Portrait of Jack Watts, jockey Title page
Portrait and Biography - Harry Fetherstonhaugh (p1-2)
The Queens Premiums by Richard Green-Price (p2-7)
About Heather-Burning by John Radcliffe (p7-15)
The Grand National by Albert Muntz (p15-22)
Ensilage for Brood Mares by Charles Newmarch (p22-29)
Hackles Up (part 2): Covert Owners and Gamekeepers by Harding Cox (p29-33)
Turf Reforms and Legislation (part 3) by Ralph Payne-Gallwey (p33-38)
Shooting by Moonlight in Ceylon by Harry Storey (p38-44)
Cricketers in Council (part 2) by Frederick Gale (p45-50)
Yachting and Rowing [inc. London Model Yacht Club; Obituaries of John Walsh and Hector
    McLean] (p51-54)
Our Van [inc. Jockey Club Stewards' Meeting; Staines Hurdle Plate; Badminton Hounds;
    Quorn Hunt; Obituaries of William Miles and Charles Symonds] (p54-70)

Issue 338 : April 1888

Portrait and Biography - John Watson (p71-72)
Landed Interests by Richard Green-Price (p72-78)
Charles Kingsley as an Angler by Richard Glover (p79-84)
Luke the Labourer by Luke Williams (p85-93)
Our Harness Horses by Albert Muntz (p94-101)
Snipe Shooting in Ceylon by Harry Storey (p101-105)
Hunting in Snow by Charles Newmarch (p106-113)
Coursing: The Waterloo Cup by George Wilson (p114-122)
The University Boat Race by Wilfred Pocklington (p122-124)
Yachting and Rowing [inc. America's Cup Challenge; Henley Regatta Programme] (p124)
Our Van [inc. Kempton Park Stewards' Steeplechase; Derby Meeting; Obituaries of William
    Standish and John Darby; Atherstone Huntsman] (p124-140)

Issue 339 : May 1888

Portrait and Biography - Chandos Leigh (p141-143)
Poaching and Game-Law Cases by Harrington Keene (p143-150)
Turf Gossip by Richard Green-Price (p151-155)
The Wood Pigeon by Charles Newmarch (p156-163)
A Morning on the Mere [Suffolk] by Tom Markland (p164-167)
A Retrospect of the Hunting Season by Edward Pennell-Elmhirst (p167-174)
Turf Reforms and Legislation (part 4) by Ralph Payne-Gallwey (p174-178)
The Cricket Season of 1888 [inc. Australian Tourists; Death of Frederick Lucas] by Frederick Gale (p178-185)
Yachting and Rowing [inc. Madeira Race; London Rowing Club] (p185-187)
Our Van [inc. Northampton Racing; Esher Stakes; Obituaries of Edward Tredcroft and Joseph Anderson; Belvoir Hunt] (p187-202)

Issue 340 : June 1888

Portrait and Biography - George Rodney (p203-204)
Market Gardening for Country Gentlemen by Margaret Oliphant (p204-214)
The Taxation of Horses and Vehicles by Frederick Aflalo (p214-221)
Vermin and How to Trap Them (part 1) by Charles Newmarch (p221-229)
Angling for Tigers (p230-234)
The Carp and his Cousins by Edward Marston (p234-242)
The Origin of Racing Colours by Edward Bunbury (p243-246)
The Cricket Season of 1888 [inc. Marylebone Cricket Club Laws; University Matches] by Frederick Gale (p246-253)
Yachting and Rowing [inc. Holyhead Regatta; Obituary of Thomas Ewing; French Rowing Championship] (p254-256)
Our Van [inc. Newmarket Meeting; Chester Cup; New Forest Hunt; Obituaries of Allen McDonough and Frederick Field Whitehurst (*Baily's* Contributor)] (p256-272)

* In June 1888, Baily's moved their offices from 15 Nicholas Lane, King William Street, where they had been for the previous seven years, to new premises a few hundred yards away.
They took two offices in Suffolk House, Laurence Pountney Hill, which is situated off Cannon Street.
This move turned out to be for just four months *

Issue 341 : July 1888

Portrait and Biography - Henry Fitzwilliam (p273-275)
Ascot by Richard Green-Price (p275-282)
Modern Angling by James Bertram (p282-291)
Vermin and How to Trap Them (part 2) by Charles Newmarch (p291-299)
Coaching by Comyns Cole (p299-306)
Polo in Paddy Land: Its Past and Its Prospects by Comyns Cole (p307-313)
Field Trials Come of Age (part 1) by Richard Lloyd-Price (p314-321)
Hunters and Hounds at Peterborough by William Day (p321-326)
The Cricket Season of 1888 [inc. Parsees' Tour; Australian Matches; County Comments] by Frederick Gale (p326-332)
Yachting and Rowing [inc. Thames Cutter Matches; Cambridge University Rowing] (p333-336)
Our Van [inc. Ascot Meeting; Obituary of Francis Doyle; Olympia Cattle Show] (p337-350)

Issue 342 : August 1888

Portrait and Biography - John Lambton (p351-352)
How the Birds and Beasts of Sport have Wintered by James Bertram (p353-361)
The Brighton Road in 1888 by Charles Newmarch (p361-371)

Portraits of Celebrated Racehorses by Richard Green-Price (p371-377)
Field Trials Come of Age (part 2) by Richard Lloyd-Price (p377-385)
Tobacco Farming as Work for Country Gentlemen by Margaret Oliphant (p386-394)
Breeding Classes at Horse Shows by Albert Muntz (p394-399)
The Cricket Season of 1888 [inc. Representative and Public Schools Matches] by
       Frederick Gale (p400-408)
Yachting and Rowing [inc. Amsterdam International Regatta; Upper Thames Sailing] (p408-414)
Our Van [inc. Tattersall's Sales; Liverpool Cup; Sandown Park Meeting; South Berkshire Hunt;
       Obituary of Thomas Drake] (p415-428)

Issue 343 : September 1888

Portrait and Biography - Henry Hawkins (p429-431)
Over the Hills and Far Away by Richard Green-Price (p431-439)
Shorthorn Breeding by James Bertram (p439-446)
The Resuscitation of Nearly Obsolete Sports by Charles Newmarch (p447-454)
Midsummer Meanderings in Meath by Comyns Cole (p454-458)
Some Racing Topics by Ralph Payne-Gallwey (p458-465)
Sport in the Dacca Country by Charles Buckland (p465-471)
The Cricket Season of 1888 [inc. High Scoring; Large Attendances; Poor Pitches] by
       Frederick Gale (p472-479)
Yachting and Rowing [inc. Cowes Week; Thames' Regattas] (p479-481)
Our Van [inc. Goodwood Meeting; Lewes Handicap; Stockton Races; New Forest Hounds] (p482-498)

* In September 1888, Baily's Magazine, and other Baily's titles, were sold to Vinton & Co., Limited. The office moved once again, this time to Vinton's at 9 New Bridge Street, a distance eastwards of half a mile. The owner of Vinton's, Walter Gilbey, who had been mentioned frequently in the magazine, was a wine merchant who gave his name to Gilbeys Gin *

Volume 50, October - December 1888

Issue 344 - October 1888

Portrait of George Dawson, huntsman Title page
Portrait and Biography - Arthur Plunkett (p1-3)
Seabreeze by Richard Green-Price (p3-9)
The Gamekeeper of the Period: His Duties and Responsibilities by James Bertram (p10-18)
The Shire Horse by Charles Newmarch (p18-27)
Huntsmen Past and Present by Edward Pennell-Elmhirst (p27-36)
The Dublin Horse Show Week 1888 by Comyns Cole (p36-41)
The Cricket Season of 1888 [inc. Parsees' Tour; Surrey County Champions] by Frederick Gale (p42-50)
Yachting and Rowing [inc. Obituaries of Alfred Paget and John Wylie; Royal Dorset Yacht Club
       Regatta; Formation of Thames Boating Union] (p50-52)
Our Van [inc. Doncaster Races; Manchester Racecourse Company; Devon & Somerset
       Staghounds; Reviews of *En Deplacement Chasse a Courre en France et en
       Angleterre* and *Les Grandes Guides* both by Donatien Levesque, and *Brakes* by
       William Philipson] (p53-66)

Issue 345 : November 1888

Portrait and Biography - Frederick Bradburne (p67-68)
Pink Again by Richard Green-Price (p68-74)
The Fish Egg Harvest by James Bertram (p74-80)
The Bloodhound: Is he any use as a Detective by Charles Newmarch (p81-89)
In the Days of Crockford and the Bonds by Henry Mannering (p89-97)

Chat About Chasers by Albert Muntz (p97-103)

Football by Frederick Gale (p103-110)

Yachting and Rowing [inc. Amateur Rowing Association; Obituary of Tom King] (p111-112)

Our Van [inc. Newmarket Meeting; Hertfordshire Hounds; Whaddon Chase Hunt; Jockey Club Fixtures' List] (p112-128)

Issue 346 : December 1888

Portrait and Biography - George Douglas-Pennant (p129-131)

Fortune's Frolics on the Turf by Edouard Beaumont (p131-140)

Our Poor Chalk Hill Lands by Frederick Aflalo (p140-149)

The Fall of the Curtain by Richard Green-Price (p150-156)

The Progress of Sport in Scotland by James Bertram (p157-164)

The Sheep Culture of the Century by Charles Newmarch (p165-174)

Harness and Saddlery by James Cameron (p175-181)

Our Van [inc. Aintree Meeting; South Nottinghamshire Hunt; Warwickshire Hounds; Atherstone Huntsman Presentation; Review of *The Horse: How to Breed and Rear Him* by William Day] (p182-198)

* This shortened Volume had the intention of bringing the magazine into line with the accepted legal half-year. Originally the former owners had gone for the Greek seven-monthly volume; now, under the new proprietors, this changed to the Roman six-monthly version *

Walter Gilbey

Volume 51, January - June 1889

Issue 347 : January 1889

Portrait [sculp. Stodart] of William Robinson, jockey — Title page
The History of Baily's Magazine by Comyns Cole — (p1-3)
Portrait [sculp. Stodart] and Biography - Charles Cavendish — (p4-5)
The Racing Season of 1888 by Edwin Sachs — (p5-16)
Some Phases of the Economy of Sport by Frederick Aflalo — (p16-22)
A Hunt Question [Injunction by Puckeridge Farmers] — (p22)
Catching Tigers Alive by Charles Buckland — (p23-27)
The Cricket Season of 1889 [inc. Initial Cricket Council Meeting] by Frederick Gale — (p27-31)
Engraving [sculp. Stodart]: *Dick Simpson* — (facing p31)
Dick Simpson, huntsman — (p31-33)
The Oakley Hounds and Country by Charles Newmarch — (p33-40)
Newmarket in the Reign of Queen Anne (part 1) by John Hore — (p40-46)
Our Van [inc. Kempton Park Meeting; Old Berkeley Hunt; Obituaries of John Arkwright, Richard King-Wyndham, John Trotter and James Selby; Review of *Ruff's Guide*; Tattersall's Winter Sales] — (p47-66)
Summary of Results for December 1888 — (p67-68)

** There are a number of changes from this issue onwards. The layout has received attention and the font increased in size; further **Illustrations** are provided; the **Contents Page** is broken down by additional subject headings with **Correspondence** and **Summary of Results** making their debut **

Issue 348 : February 1889

Portrait [sculp. Stodart] and Biography - Richard Burke — (p69-71)
Coursing by George Wilson — (p71-74)
The Rowing Season of 1888 by Claude Holland — (p74-79)
Enquiry into the Migration of Woodcock by William Tegetmeier — (p79-85)
The Grafton Hounds and Country by Charles Newmarch — (p85-93)
Opening of the Hunting Season in Ireland by Comyns Cole — (p93-98)
Harness Horses by James Cameron — (p99-100)
Engraving [sculp. Pratt]: *The Return* — (facing p101)
Review of *The Return* by Henry Alken — (p101-102)
A Merry Christmas with the Pike by Henry Cholmondeley-Pennell — (p102-107)
Newmarket in the Reign of Queen Anne (part 2) by John Hore — (p107-113)
Viva! la Chasse: A Hunting Toast [verses] by Alexander Clark-Kennedy — (p114-115)
The Royal Agricultural Society [Fiftieth Anniversary] — (p115)
A Plan to Popularise Hunting by Robert Lockwood — (p116)
Our Van [inc. Bathurst's Hounds; Puckeridge Farmers at Court of Appeal; Shropshire Hounds; Obituaries of Cornelia Prittie and Leonard Morrogh; Review of *Wisden's Cricketers' Almanack*] — (p117-134)
Correspondence [Lord Charles Russell on the Oakley Hounds] — (p134-138)
Book Reviews: *Hunting in Hard Times* by Georgina Bowers and *Powder, Spur and Spear* by James Moray-Brown — (p138)
Summary of Results for January 1889 — (p139-140)

George Stodart engraved all illustrations for the past sixteen issues. From now on all engravings will be individually credited, if the name of the creator is known

Issue 349 : March 1889

Portrait [sculp. Stodart] and Biography - James Machell (p141-143)
Football and its Critics by Charles Alcock (p143-147)
Lord Rothschild's Staghounds by Charles Newmarch (p148-156)
Sale of Pedigree Farm Stock [Shorthorns] (p156)
The Visitors' Day [verses] by Philip Blair-Oliphant (p157-159)
Newmarket in the Reign of Queen Anne (part 3) by John Hore (p159-164)
Hunting Countries Physically Considered by William Blew (p164-173)
Engraving [sculp. Pratt]: *Hark Forrard* (facing p173)
Review of *Hark Forrard* by Henry Alken (p173)
Coursing: The Waterloo Cup by George Wilson (p174-180)
Pheasant Rearing by William Tegetmeier (p180-185)
The Three-Year-Olds of 1889 (part 1) by Henry Valoynes (p185-190)
The University Boat Race by Claude Holland (p190-192)
Our Van [inc. Kempton Park Meeting; Shire Horse Society; Grafton Hunt; Obituaries of Harvey Bayly, James Snowden and Richard Oliver; Badminton Club Dinner; Quorn Hounds] (p192-209)
Correspondence [Woodcocks and Suffolk Mares] (p210)
Summary of Results for February 1889 (p211-212)

Issue 350 : April 1889

Portrait [sculp. Stodart] and Biography - John Harvey, huntsman (p213-215)
A Plea for Falconry by Thomas Mann (p215-220)
Bicycling and Tricycling by Hewitt Griffin (p220-226)
Caveat Emptor [verses] (p227-229)
The Three-Year-Olds of 1889 (part 2) by Henry Valoynes (p229-236)
Cricket Reminiscences (p237-239)
American Baseball [A.G.Spalding's Tour] by Frederick Gale (p240-243)
Yachting and Rowing [Monaco Regatta; London Rowing Club] by Brooke Heckstall-Smith (p243-244)
Engraving [sculp. Pratt]: *Blue Grass* (facing p244)
Hunter Sires by William Trench (p244-250)
Salmon Fishery Legislation by James Bertram (p251-255)
Newmarket in the Reign of Queen Anne (part 4) by John Hore (p256-258)
A Mountain Fox Hunt by Alexander Clark-Kennedy (p259-264)
Our Van [inc. Croydon Steeplechases; Hursley Hounds; Meynell Hunt; Royal Agricultural Society State Banquet] (p265-277)
Racing Prophecies (p278-279)
Correspondence [Woodcocks and Welsh Hunting] (p280-282)
Book Review: *Driving* by Mowbray Morris (p282)
Summary of Results for March 1889 (p283-284)

Issue 351 : May 1889

Portrait [sculp. Stodart] and Biography - Robert Townley-Parker (p285-287)
Summering Hunters by William Trench (p287-289)
Blair Athol by Ralph Payne-Gallwey (p290-298)
Harrow School by Manley Kemp (p298-302)
Won by a Head [verses] (p303-304)
A Doubtful Case of Roaring (p304-306)
The Bicester and Pytchley New Rules by Edward Pennell-Elmhirst (p307-309)
Lawn Tennis by Nicholas Jackson (p310-313)
My Dog Snooks by Hugh deBurgh Daly (p314-316)
English Horse Show Society (p316)

Engraving [sculp. Pratt]: *Hunter Stallions*   (facing p317)
Hunter Stallions at Grass   (p317-318)
The Boat Race 1889 by Claude Holland   (p319-321)
The Coaching Season by Comyns Cole   (p322-326)
Thames Trouting by Henry Cholmondeley-Pennell   (p327-330)
Newmarket in the Reign of Queen Anne (part 5) by John Hore   (p330-332)
The Cricket Season of 1889 [England in South Africa; Obituary of Harry Jupp] by
      Frederick Gale   (p333-335)
Our Van [inc. Northampton Meeting; Vale of Aylesbury Steeplechasing; Review of *Some
      Incidents in the Life of a Foxhound* by Myra Swan; The Royal Buckhounds]   (p336-351)
The End of the Season [verses] by Guy Selby   (p351)
Racing Prophecies   (p352-353)
Reply to Cricket Reminiscences by Frederick Gale   (p354)
Summary of Results for April 1889   (p355-356)

Issue 352 : June 1889

Portrait [sculp. Stodart] and Biography - Charles Green   (p357-359)
Reminiscences of Albert Gate [Tattersall's]   (p359-363)
Sporting Quarters in Scotland by James Bertram   (p364-367)
Fox Hunting in the United States   (p368-369)
Book Review: *Ten Years Wild Sports* by Heywood Seton-Karr   (p369)
A Horse-dealing Vet's Dodges [verses]   (p370-371)
The Cricket Season of 1889 [Perambulators versus Etcaeteras Match; Spofforth Qualification]
      by Frederick Gale   (p371-377)
The Duke of Beaufort's Hounds   (p377)
Public School Sports: Eton by Albert Brassey   (p378-387)
Some Notes on Welbeck and its Stud by John Kent   (p387-395)
Engraving [sculp. Pratt]: *St.Simon*   (facing p388)
Newmarket in the Reign of Queen Anne (part 6) by John Hore   (p396-400)
Spring Hunting in the New Forest by Abel Chapman   (p401-404)
Yachting and Rowing [inc. The Island Sailing Club, London Model Yacht Club] by Brooke
      Heckstall-Smith   (p405-407)
Our Van [inc. Kempton Park Meeting; Newmarket Stakes; English Horse Show Society;
      Review of *Three Great Runs* by John Anstruther-Thomson]   (p407-419)
Racing Prophecies   (p420-421)
Correspondence [Falconry, Horse Shoes and Blair Athol]   (p422)
Summary of Results for May 1889   (p423-424)

** Three further engravers are now being used for internal issue use.
They are Edward Hacker, Joseph Bishop Pratt and William Roffe. Also, **Our Van** temporarily ceased
noting general Obituaries as from the March 1889 issue. It also lost a lot of its 'gossipy oomph.'**

Volume 52, July - December 1889

Issue 353 : July 1889

Portrait [sculp. Stodart] of Frederick Barrett, jockey   Title page
Portrait [sculp. Roffe] and Biography - John Straker   (p1-2)
A Swan-Song   (p2-8)
An Old Racing Club by William Scarth-Dixon   (p8-13)
Foemen Worthy of Our Steel by Walter Gallichan   (p13-21)
The Summer Meet at Peterborough by William Day   (p21-26)
Field Sports Protection Society: Annual General Meeting Report   (p26)

The New Rules of Racing by Ralph Payne-Gallwey (p27-32)
Engraving [sculp. Hacker]: *Blue Gown* (facing p33)
The Derby of 1868: A Reminiscence by Thomas Pinch (p33-38)
The Cricket Season of 1889 by Frederick Gale (p38-44)
Yachting and Rowing [inc. New York Yacht Club; Royal Cork Club] by Brooke Heckstall-Smith (p45-48)
North versus South [verses] (p49)
Our Van [inc. Epsom Meeting; Islington Horse Show; Ascot Racing] (p50-67)
Racing Prophecies (p68-69)
Correspondence [Falconry and Blair Athol] (p70)
Summary of Results for June 1889 (p71-72)

Issue 354 : August 1889

Portrait [sculp. Stodart] and Biography - John North (p73-75)
Death of Sire 'Camballo' (p75)
Judging at Horse Shows by Wellington Combermere (p76-79)
The Grouse Shooter's Song by Alexander Clark-Kennedy (p80-81)
The Chetwynd versus Durham Case by Comyns Cole (p81-88)
Book Review: *Angling Songs* by Thomas Stoddart (p88)
A Ride in the Lebanon [Illustrated] (p89-104)
After the Battle [Horse Deaths] (p104)
Engraving [sculp. Pratt]: *Fond of Timber* (facing p104)
The Cricket Season of 1889 by Frederick Gale (p105-113)
Newmarket in the Reign of Queen Anne (part 7) by John Hore (p114-117)
Henley Regatta 1889 by Claude Holland (p117-123)
Yachting [inc. Royal Ulster Yacht Club; Cinque Ports Yacht Club Regatta] by Brooke
    Heckstall-Smith (p123-124)
Our Van [inc. Windsor Park Show; Tattersall's Newmarket Sales; Portland Stakes; Kendal
    Otterhounds; Review of *In the North Countree* by William Scarth-Dixon] (p124-139)
Racing Prophecies (p140-141)
Summary of Results for July 1889 (p142-144)

This issue has, for the first time, illustrated sketches throughout an article

Issue 355 : September 1889

Portrait [sculp. Roffe] and Biography - Thomas Tyrwhitt-Drake (p145-146)
A Glimpse at Sport in Norway (part 1) by Fraser Sandeman (p146-152)
What's in a Name by Ralph Payne-Gallwey (p153-157)
Adam Lindsay Gordon (p158-163)
Red-Legged Partridges and Quail by Frank Bonnett (p164-168)
Some Notes on Sporting Dogs by Frederick Gresham (p168-173)
Cricket: Hitting - A Lost Art (p173-177)
Engraving [sculp. Pratt]: *Good on the Road* (facing p177)
[Review] *Good on the Road* by Henry Alkin (p177-178)
Highland Shepherds and their Dogs by Alexander Stewart (p178-183)
The Sweet of the Year [verses] (p183)
Yachting and Rowing [inc. Royal London Yacht Club; Maidenhead Rowing Club] by
    Brooke Heckstall-Smith (p184-187)
The National Pony and Galloway Racing Club by William Blew (p187-192)
Riding a Runaway by George Underhill (p192-196)
The Lay of the Gunner [verses] (p197)
Our Van [inc. Goodwood Meeting; Redcar Racing; Stockton Races; North Staffordshire Hunt;
    Yorkshire Grouse Moors] (p197-209)
Racing Prophecies (p210-211)

Late Parcels [Devonshire Stag Hunting] by Comyns Cole (p212)
Summary of Results for August 1889 (p213-216)

Issue 356 : October 1889

Portrait [sculp. Roffe] and Biography - Alan Cathcart (p217-219)
The Last of the Fools [James Hirst] (p219-225)
A Glimpse at Sport in Norway (part 2) by Fraser Sandeman (p225-232)
Notes on *The History and Antiquities of Hawsted* by John Cullum (p232)
After the Cricket Season [verses] (p233-234)
The Early Days of Goodwood Races by John Kent (p234-238)
[Henry] Searle versus [William] O'Connor: The Championship [Rowing] by John Jacobs (p238-242)
Norfolk Fishing by Henry Dunster (p242-247)
Champion Counties [Cricket] by Frederick Gale (p247-249)
Engraving [sculp. Pratt]: *A Norfolk Hunter and Trotter in the Olden Time* (facing p249)
A Norfolk Trotter by Edward Cooper (p249-250)
The Revived Interest in Half-Bred Horse-Breeding by Alan Cathcart (p250-259)
Wasting [Jockeys] by Horace Hutchinson (p260-263)
[Review] *Cricketing Saws and Stories* by Horace Hutchinson (p263)
My First Salmon [verses] (p264-265)
The Sewage Problem (p265)
Our Van [inc. Portsmouth Park Racecourse; Dublin Horse Show; Horse Show Judging;
    Review of *My Friend the Bloodhound* by Percy Lindley] (p266-281)
Correspondence [Adam Lindsay Gordon and Stable Management] (p282-283)
Racing Prophecies (p284-285)
Summary of Results for September 1889 (p286-288)

Issue 357 : November 1889

Portrait [sculp. Roffe] and Biography - John Maunsell Richardson (p289-292)
Records of a Summer Excursion (p292-299)
Wanted: An Instructor by Hugh deBurgh Daly (p299-303)
Coach-Horses [Notes of Walter Calverley] (p303)
The Sweetest of Sounds [verses] (p304)
A Decidedly Fishy Story by William Senior (p305-309)
On the Downs and in the Woodlands by Frederick Gale (p309-313)
Stud Lore by Richard Green Price (p313-320)
Lightening the Draught of Four-Wheel Carriages by Thomas Brigg (p320)
Engraving [sculp. Pratt]: *Away! Away!* (facing p321)
Away! Away! (p321)
Sport and Sporting Writers 150 Years Ago by John Kent (p321-324)
The First in the Van [verses] (p325-326)
Hunting: The Dispute in the Puckeridge Country by Edward Pennell-Elmhirst (p326-330)
Our Van [inc. Cesarewitch Meeting; Croydon Racecourse Licence; South Berkshire Hunt;
    Essex Hounds] (p330-345)
Correspondence [County Cricket Championship] (p346-348)
[Review] *Travels in France* by Arthur Young (p348-349)
Racing Prophecies (p350-351)
Summary of Results for October 1889 (p352)

Issue 358 : December 1889

Portrait [sculp. Roffe] and Biography - Edward Walker (p353-354)
A Brush or a Wife by George Underhill (p354-361)
Anecdotes and Shooting Adventures of the Tsar Alexander II (p362-377)

Jessie [verses]   (p378)
Winning Sires by Richard Green-Price   (p378-384)
Engraving [sculp. Pratt]: *Coursing Scene*   (facing p385)
Coursing by George Wilson   (p385-388)
Another Australian Invasion by Frederick Gale   (p388-390)
Miss Martha   (p391-401)
'Ware Wire' by Edward Pennell-Elmhirst   (p401-404)
The Thoroughbred Pet [verses]   (p405)
Our Van [inc. Obituary of Evelyn Boscawen; Croxteth Cup; Cotswold Hounds; Whaddon
          Chase Hunt]   (p405-419)
Correspondence [Frederick Gale on County Cricket]   (p420-421)
Racing Prophecies   (p422-423)
Summary of Results for November 1889   (p424)

Volume 53, January - June 1890

Issue 359 : January 1890

Portrait [sculp. Stodart] of Thomas Loates, jockey   Title page
Portrait [sculp. Roffe] and Biography - Blundell Maple   (p1-4)
A Visit to Whitewall by Coulson Pitman   (p4-9)
Seaside Shooting in the Tropics   (p9-14)
Riding Accidents by Horace Hutchinson   (p14-19)
Karine   (p19-29)
A Lowland Grilse Water   (p29-31)
Diana [verses]   (p32)
Engraving [sculp. Pratt]: *That Will Shut Out Many and Make the Thing Select*   (facing p33)
That Will Shut Out Many and Make the Thing Select by Richard Green-Price   (p33)
Cricketers in Council [Report on Meeting] by Frederick Gale   (p34-35)
A Night with the Eels   (p35-36)
A Fox by Richard Green-Price   (p37-43)
Our Discussion Forum (part 1) [On Cattle Shows]   (p44-49)
Our Van [inc. Gimcrack Club Speech; Elsenham Paddocks; Gosling's Hounds; Warwickshire
          Hunt; Calpe Hunt]   (p49-69)
[Valedictory] Comyns Cole's Twenty-Five Years as 'Van Driver'   (p69)
Review of Books: *Sporting Anecdotes* by James Bertram; *A Nasty Cropper* by George Underhill;
          East Africa and its Big Game by John Willoughby; *The Habits of the Salmon* by
          John Traherne, and *Hindu-Koh* by Donald MacIntyre   (p70-71)
Summary of Results for December 1889   (p72)

** The owner of Vinton & Co. Ltd., the publishers, Mr (later Sir) Walter Gilbey is starting to get his
Elsenham Stud and horses mentioned regularly in the magazine **

Issue 360 : February 1890

Portrait [sculp. Roffe] and Biography - Graham Foster-Pigott   (p73-75)
Handicapping by Richard Green-Price   (p75-80)
Current Football by Charles Alcock   (p80-83)
Saddles and Sore Backs   (p83-85)
Stable Secrets [verses]   (p85-87)
Days to Memory Dear (part 1): With the Pike by Thomas Mann   (p87-90)
The American Buffalo by Robert Auld   (p90-97)
Our Old Quartermaster   (p98-100)
Art and Sport at the Grosvenor (part 1) by Comyns Cole   (p100-104)

Our Discussion Forum (part 2) [Hunting]   (p104-111)
The Arabian Horse by William Kerr   (p111-122)
Engraving [sculp. Palfrey]: *Khaled*   (facing p113)
Engraving [sculp. Palfrey]: *Speed of Thought*   (facing p117)
In the Provinces: A Hunting Story by George Underhill   (p122-126)
The Puckeridge Country by Edward Pennell-Elmhirst   (p127-128)
Our Van [inc. Belgian Prize-Fight; Cottesmore Hunt; Essex Hounds; Worsley Shire Horses;
        Obituary of Joseph Sadler; Review of *Wisden's Cricketer's Almanack*]   (p129-141)
Correspondence [Irish Land Question and the Tinamou]   (p142-143)
Review of Books: *A Thousand Miles on an Elephant* by Holt Hallett; *Hunting in Craven* by
        William Gomersall, and *Old Country Life* by Sabine Baring-Gould   (p144)

** With this issue starts a comprehensive Contents Page at the beginning of each magazine.
Advertising pages are increased while the sections **Sporting Diary for the Month** and **Summary of Results**
[the latter temporarily] are removed from the main text and inserted on, and by, the internal covers **

Issue 361 : March 1890

Portrait [sculp. Mote] and Biography - William Wharton   (p145-147)
A Visit to a West Country Stud by Coulson Pitman   (p147-152)
My First and Last [Rugby] Football Match   (p152-156)
The Horse of the Steel-Clad Warrior   (p156-157)
Engraving [sculp. Palfrey]: *Horse of the Steel-Clad Warrior*   (facing p156)
Art and Sport at the Grosvenor (part 2) by Comyns Cole   (p158-162)
My Favourite Salmon Rod [verses] by Alexander Clark-Kennedy   (p162-163)
The Breeder's Outlook by Richard Green-Price   (p164-168)
Damage Funds by William Fawcett   (p169-172)
The Coming Boat Race by Claude Holland   (p172-174)
Tandem Driving   (p175-179)
Engraving [sculp. Pratt]: *Tandem Team – Princess and Brunette*   (facing p177)
Bicycling and Tricycling by Hewitt Griffin   (p179-181)
The Shires by Edward Pennell-Elmhirst   (p182-186)
The National Regatta by Dixon Kemp   (p187)
Our Discussion Forum (part 3) [Country Shows]   (p188-194)
Days to Memory Dear (part 2): Dry Fly Fishing by Thomas Mann   (p194-199)
The Waterloo Cup by George Wilson   (p199-200)
Our Van [inc. Lincolnshire Handicap; Cheshire Hunt; Portal's Harriers; Deerstalking in the
        Highlands; River Test Fishing; Obituary of Mackworth Praed]   (p201-214)
Roundabout County Papers [inc. London County Council Sporting Licences and County
        Hunt Balls]   (p215-216)

* Two other engravers being used are Henry William Mote and Penry Palfrey *

Issue 362 : April 1890

Portrait [sculp. Roffe] and Biography - Roderic Owen   (p217-219)
Indian Birds   (p219-225)
Our Lost Aquatic Supremacy by Brooke Heckstall-Smith   (p226-231)
That Fox Again by Richard Green-Price   (p231-237)
A Day in the Great Blast by Thomas Markland   (p237-241)
Old Lady Bunting (part 1)   (p242-247)
Engraving [sculp. Palfrey] *Suleiman*   (facing p248)
Falls and Fair Fences by Edward Pennell-Elmhirst   (p248-251)
Days to Memory Dear (part 3): Tweed Salmon Fishing by Thomas Mann   (p251-256)
Over-Riding Hounds by William Fawcett   (p257-260)

A New Pursuit by Hugh deBurgh Daly (p260-264)
Our Van [inc. Opening of Hurst Park Racecourse; Hertfordshire Hunt; East Sussex Foxhounds;
          Obituary of Arthur Brook; Review of *Flowers of the Hunt* by Finch Mason;
          University Boat Race] (p264-281)
Roundabout County Papers [inc. Forests; County Histories, Wheat; Angus Cattle; Sussex
          Butter] (p282-284)
Correspondence [Hunting Horses] (p285-286)
The Beacon Course [verses] (p286)
Odds and Ends [Selected Paragraphs From Old Publications] (p287-288)

Issue 363 : May 1890

Portrait [sculp. Roffe] and Biography - Charles Russell (p289-292)
The Little Grey Mare by Richard Green-Price (p293-298)
Training for Boat Races by Claude Holland (p298-302)
Mistakes in Breeding Racehorses by William Day (p302-308)
Golf and its Attractions by Gordon McPherson (p309-313)
Old Lady Bunting (part 2) (p313-318)
Trainers: New and Old by Francis Lawley (p319-330)
Engraving [sculp. Stodart]: *John Dawson* (facing p321)
The Cricket Season of 1890 by Frederick Gale (p330-333)
Fast Hounds and Faulty Hounds by Edward Pennell-Elmhirst (p333-336)
The Coaching Season by Coulson Pitman (p337-338)
Our Discussion Forum (part 4) [Women's Cricket] (p339-343)
Our Van [inc. House of Commons Point-to-Point; Savernake Staghounds; Biggleswade
          Harriers; Obituaries of Gerald Goodlake and Joseph Tollit] (p343-354)
Roundabout County Papers [inc. Victoria Park Cricket Association] (p354-355)
Correspondence [Hunt Steeplechase Meetings] (p356-357)
Lowlander and Galopin [Verses] (p357)
Odds and Ends [inc. Cricket in 1789; Devizes Beagles] (p358)
Summary of Results for April 1890 (p359-360)

Issue 364 : June 1890

Portrait [sculp. Roffe] and Biography - Albert Hornby (p361-363)
Sport and Pastime at the Universities by Charles Oakley (p364-370)
Aquatics at Eton by Claude Holland (p371-376)
Engravings: *Stanley Muttlebury* and *Claude Holland* (on p374)
The Late Earl of Derby by Francis Lawley (p376-386)
Tangier, and Pig-Sticking in Morocco (p386-392)
Sir Bevys by Richard Green-Price (p392-393)
Engraving [sculp. Palfrey]: *Sir Bevys* (facing p392)
Red Deer and the Chester Cup by John Kent (p393-398)
Stud Farms, Public and Private by Richard Green-Price (p398-404)
The Cricket Season of 1890 by Frederick Gale (p405-409)
In Memoriam: Gerald Goodlake [verses] by Alexander Clark-Kennedy (p410-412)
On the Origin and Early History of Polo Among the English by James Moray-Brown (p412-417)
Our Van [inc. Chester Races; Newmarket Meeting; Obituary of Tom Wallace] (p417-428)
Roundabout County Papers [inc. Golf in Sussex; Cock Fighting] (p428-429)
Odds and Ends [inc. Cricket in Paris 1785] (p430-431)
Summary of Results for May 1890 (p432)

** The magazine's editor, Tresham Gilbey, is starting to get his personal interests, such as Polo and
the Essex Foxhounds, mentioned regularly as well as his father's horses. **

Volume 54, July - December 1890

Issue 365 : July 1890

Portrait [sculp. Stodart] of James Bailey, huntsman   Title page
Portrait [sculp. Roffe] and Biography - William Henry Grenfell   (p1-3)
The Past and Present of Lawn Tennis by Nicholas Jackson   (p3-7)
Accidental Discovery of a Racehorse's Merits by John Kent   (p7-9)
An Amateur's Idea of Fishing by John Bullock   (p9-14)
The *Live Stock Journal* Summer Number   (p14)
Alfred Shaw by Frederick Gale   (p15-18)
Engraving [sculp. Pratt]: *Alfred Shaw*   (on p15)
The View that Beats them All [verses] by George Williams   (p19-20)
Sport in the Southern States by Francis Lawley   (p20-30)
The Broadside Measurements of Ormonde by Penry Palfrey   (p31-34)
Outline Diagram of *Ormonde* [sculp. Palfrey]   (on p32)
Engraving [sculp. Palfrey]: *Ormonde*   (facing p33)
The Royal Commission on Horse Breeding by Richard Green-Price   (p34-39)
Yachting by Brooke Heckstall-Smith   (p39-42)
The Road [Stage Coaching] by William Blew   (p43-48)
The Cricket Season of 1890 by Frederick Gale   (p48-51)
Our Van [inc. Carthorse Parade; Epsom Meeting; Hunt Cup; Hunt Servants Benefit Society; Gilbey Testimonial Committee]   (p52-63)
Roundabout County Papers [inc. Horse Shows; Coaching Clubs]   (p64-65)
Odds and Ends [inc. Northampton races 1778; Duke of Grafton's Hounds 1745]   (p65-67)
Correspondence [Adam Lindsay Gordon from Edwin Blackmore; The New Rules of Racing from Richard Green-Price]   (p68-70)
Summary of Results for June 1890   (p71-72)

The Live Stock Journal and Almanac now start to get reviewed as Vinton's, through Walter Gilbey, had purchased both titles. They joined the growing number of various sporting books and magazines now emanating from this publishing house

Issue 366 : August 1890

Portrait [sculp. Roffe] and Biography - Charles Legard   (p73-75)
The Roedeer   (p75-79)
Lion Hunting at the Cape Sixty Years Ago (part 1) by Henry Eyre   (p79-83)
Jonathan Peel by Francis Lawley   (p83-94)
In the Gulf of Arta   (p94-105)
Engraving [sculp. Palfrey]: *Miss Elis*   (facing p105)
Further Reminiscences of Goodwood Races by John Kent   (p105-111)
Turf Jottings by Richard Green-Price   (p112-116)
Peterborough Hound Show by William Day   (p116-119)
Henley Regatta 1890 by Claude Holland   (p120-124)
The Cricket Season of 1890 by Frederick Gale   (p124-127)
Amongst the Grouse by Alexander Clark-Kennedy   (p127-129)
Our Van [inc. Leicester Meeting; South Berkshire Hunt; South Oxfordshire Cricket; Obituaries of John Joyce and Robert Morley]   (p129-140)
Roundabout County Papers [inc. Old Rugbeians Society (Beginning of Webb-Ellis Myth); Richard Jefferies Memorial]   (p141)
Odds and Ends [inc. Kendal Races 1822]   (p142)
Summary of Results for July 1890   (p143-144)

Issue 367 : September 1890

Portrait [sculp. Roffe] and Biography - William Kemmis (p145-146)
September on Mountain and Stubble by Alexander Clark-Kennedy (p147-151)
Lion Hunting at the Cape Sixty Years Ago (part 2) by Henry Eyre (p151-155)
Slows! And How to Play Them by Frederick Gale (p155-160)
Out and About [Bank Holiday Hunting] by Richard Green-Price (p160-164)
[Obituary] John Fremont (p164-174)
Our Grand Old Game [verses] (p175-176)
Carlo and Carlist [Pointers] (p176-177)
Engraving [sculp. Lucas]: *Carlo and Carlist* (facing p177)
The Turf in Scotland (part 1) by Coulson Pitman (p177-182)
A Day's Sport in Jamaica (p183-190)
The Cricket Season of 1890 by Frederick Gale (p190-193)
Our Van [inc. Lewes Meeting; Redcar Races; Devon & Somerset Staghounds; Canterbury Cricket Week; Thames National Regatta] (p194-208)
Roundabout County Papers [inc. Royal Hunt Club; Cricket Council County Status] (p209-211)
Review of Books: *The Art of Riding* by Herbert English; *Golf* by Horace Hutchinson; *Tennis* by John Heathcote; *Handbook of Athletic Sports* by Ernest Bell; *The Scientific Education of Dogs for the Gun* by Nevill Fitt; *Sketches of British Sporting Fishes* by John Watson (p212-213)
Odds and Ends [inc. Gambling at Cricket 1792] (p214)
Summary of Results for August 1890 (p215-216)

Issue 368 : October 1890

Portrait [sculp. Roffe] and Biography - Philip Muntz (p217-219)
What we Saw at Kisber by Henry Freeman (p219-229)
Lion Hunting at the Cape Sixty Years Ago (part 3) by Henry Eyre (p230-235)
The Turf in Scotland (part 2) by Coulson Pitman (p235-240)
October With the Gun by Alexander Clark-Kennedy (p240-245)
Engraving [sculp. Pratt]: *Duck Decoy* (facing p245)
Duck Decoying in Norfolk by Henry Dunster (p245-249)
Fortuitus Cespes by Francis Lawley (p249-256)
What's the Price [Horses] by Richard Green-Price (p257-263)
The Cricket Season of 1890 by Frederick Gale (p263-266)
Bicycling and Tricycling by Hewitt Griffin (p266-269)
Our Van [inc. Doncaster Racing; Newmarket Meeting; Dublin Horse Show; Obituary of Wyndham Portman (editor *Horse & Hound*)] (p269-283)
Roundabout County Papers [inc. West Kent Hounds; Royal Southampton Yacht Club] (p283-285)
Odds and Ends [inc. Prize Fight, Ben versus Johnson 1791] (p286)
Summary of Results for September 1890 (p287-288)

Issue 369 : November 1890

Portrait [sculp. Roffe] and Biography - Randolph Churchill (p289-293)
Winter Sports in the Engadine [illustrated] (part 1) by Sarah Prideaux (p293-298)
November Shooting by Alexander Clark-Kennedy (p298-303)
A Peep at French Sport by Richard Green-Price (p303-309)
Sylvanus Damson's Great Adventure (part 1) (p309-318)
Fox Hunting by Edward Pennell-Elmhirst (p318-321)
Engraving [sculp. Palfrey]: *A Good Hunter* (facing p319)
The Thoroughbred in Argentina (p321-324)
Lion Hunting at the Cape Sixty Years Ago (part 4) by Henry Eyre (p324-327)
Touts and Tipsters by Francis Lawley (p327-335)

David Edward Jones (p336-337)
Hunts and their Masters by William Blew (p338-342)
Our Van [inc. Twickenham Plate; Cesarewitch Week; Bicester Hunt; Oakley Hounds] (p343-354)
Roundabout County Papers [inc. Suffolk Sheep; Swimming Horses] (p354-355)
Odds and Ends [inc. Knutsford Races 1790] (p356)
Summary of Results for October 1890 (p357-358)

Issue 370 : December 1890

Portrait [sculp. Roffe] and Biography - Arthur Heywood-Lonsdale (p359-362)
Coursing: The Opening of the Season by George Wilson (p362-363)
River Yacht Racing by Brooke Heckstall-Smith (p364-367)
Winter Sports in the Engadine [illustrated] (part 2) by Sarah Prideaux (p367-373)
The Endurance of Racehorses by John Kent (p373-380)
Sylvanus Damson's Great Adventure (part 2) (p380-390)
Danebury and The Cannons by Comyns Cole (p390-393)
Engraving [sculp. Stodart]: *Tom Cannon jr, Tom Cannon sr, Mornington Cannon, Joe Cannon* (facing p390)
Stalking Duck (p393-395)
Blood versus Bone by Horace Hutchinson (p395-400)
A Blank Day on the Tweed by Victor Gleichen (p401-406)
Yearling Sales 1890 (p407-412)
Our Van [inc. Lincoln Meeting; Lingfield Racing; Manchester Races; South Molton Harriers; Cheshire Hunt] (p413-426)
Roundabout County Papers [inc. Game returns in Badenoch] (p427)
Odds and Ends [inc. Betting on Single Horse races] (p428)
Summary of Results for November 1890 . (p429-430)

Comyns Cole

Volume 55, January - June 1891

Issue 371 : January 1891

Portrait [sculp. Stodart] of Frederick Allsopp, jockey	Title page
Portrait [sculp. Roffe] and Biography - Frederick Marshall	(p1-3)
Tally Ho Back! by Richard Green-Price	(p4-9)
The Angler in January by William Senior	(p9-11)
Some Old Sporting Periodicals by Francis Lawley	(p11-17)
Football Accidents by John Bullock	(p17-19)
Cricket Council, Deceased by Ogle Moore	(p20-22)
The Flea-Bitten Grey [verses] by William Phillpotts-Williams	(p23-25)
The Rough and the Smooth of Hunting by Edward Pennell-Elmhirst	(p25-28)
Review: *The Livestock Journal Almanac 1891*	(p28)
What Have the Societies done for Horse-Breeding by William Blew	(p29-32)
Duck and Mallard by John Hill	(p32-35)
Engraving [sculp. Pratt]: *A Startled Mallard*	(facing p32)
Amongst the Lapps by Abel Chapman	(p36-43)
A Cinche: A Tale of the American Turf	(p43-51)
A Winter Day with Wild Swans by Alexander Clark-Kennedy	(p51-54)
Our Van [inc. Carmarthenshire Steeplechasing; Manchester Meeting; Gimcrack Club Speech; South Berkshire Hunt; Obituaries of James Dear and John Phelps; County Cricket Council]	(p54-68)
Roundabout County Papers [inc. Obituary of John Tollemache; Horse Climates]	(p69-70)
Odds and Ends [inc. Ennis Racing; York Tipsters 1790]	(p71)
Summary of Results for December 1890	(p72)

* From this issue the magazine is presented with two editorial columns per page and printed in a smaller type *

Issue 372 : February 1891

Portrait [sculp. Roffe] and Biography - Auguste Lupin	(p73-76)
Some Problems of the Chase	(p76-80)
The Turf: Its Position and Prospects by John Corlett	(p80-86)
Spurs: Their Use and Abuse by Richard Green-Price	(p86-90)
Uncle Sam's First Salmon	(p91-95)
Lord Lamington on Crockford's Club by Francis Lawley	(p96-104)
Engraving [sculp. Parr]: *The Squire*	(facing p105)
The Squire by Charles Batchelder	(p105-106)
The Old Fisherman [verses] by Frederick Doveton	(p106-107)
Steeplechase Reform by William Howth	(p108-115)
Capercailzie Stalking in Snow by Alexander Clark-Kennedy	(p115-119)
Engraving [sculp. Stodart]: *The Beech Marten*	(facing p120)
Capture of a Beech Martin by William Tegetmeier	(p120-121)
Foxes and Hounds by Edward Pennell-Elmhirst	(p121-124)
A Bear Hunt in Nova Scotia by Parker Gillmore	(p124-125)
Our Van [inc. Albrighton Hounds; Lanarkshire & Renfrewshire Hunt; Grafton Hounds; Obituary of Edward Courtenay; Reviews of *Wisden's Cricketers' Almanack 1891* edited by Sydney Pardon; *Letters to Young Shooters* by Ralph Payne-Gallwey; *Handbooks of Athletic Sports: Boxing, Wrestling, Fencing, Broadsword & Single-Stick* by Ernest Bell; *Annals of a Fishing Village* by Denham Jordan; *Sport and Adventures Among the North American Indians* by Charles Messiter; and *Autobiography of a Gipsy* by Arthur Way]	(p126-140)

Correspondence [Breeding of Horses]   (p140)
Roundabout County Papers [inc. Fen Skating; Devon & Somerset Staghounds]   (p141-142)
Odds and Ends [inc. Longhorn Prices 1792; Curragh Ride 1791]   (p143)
Summary of Results for January 1891   (p144)

Issue 373 : March 1891

Portrait [sculp. Roffe] and Biography - Charles Fernie   (p145-146)
The Midlands by Edward Pennell-Elmhirst   (p146-148)
The Angler in March by William Senior   (p148-151)
A Bagman by Richard Green-Price   (p152-157)
Irish Football Association by John Bullock   (p157-161)
A Fighting Tiger by John Fife-Cookson   (p161-168)
My Old Horse and I [verses]   (p169-170)
Bicycling and Tricycling by Hewitt Griffin   (p170-172)
Jumping Sires by Charles Newmarch   (p172-176)
A Rest by the Way by Comyns Cole   (p176-179)
Engraving [sculp. Beckwith]: *A Rest by the Way*   (facing p176)
Survivors (part 1) by Abel Chapman   (p179-181)
Grigg's Mare by Armiger Barczinsky   (p182-191)
The Horse Shows by Comyns Cole   (p191)
Henry Bethune by Comyns Cole   (p192-193)
Engraving [sculp. Stodart]: *Henry Bethune*   (facing p192)
The Waterloo Cup by George Wilson   (p193-195)
The Ethics of Field Sports by John Caton   (p195-198)
Fashionable Sporting Literature by Herbert Slater   (p198-200)
Our Van [inc. Sefton Steeplechase; Reviews of *Racing Reminiscences* by George Chetwynd
         and *First Flight* by Myra Swan; Lingfield Racecourse; Obituary of Mackenzie
         Grieves]   (p201-209)
Roundabout County Papers [inc. Middlesex Woodcocks; Obituary of Walter Arbuthnott]   (p209-212)
Correspondence [inc. Beech Martens; Use of Spurs]   (p212-213)
Odds and Ends [inc. Oxford to London Rowing 1822]   (p214-215)
Summary of Results for February 1891   (p216)

Issue 374 : April 1891

Portrait [sculp. Roffe] and Biography - Nigel Kingscote   (p217-219)
Hawking in Algeria by James Harting   (p219-224)
Hounds by Richard Green-Price   (p224-228)
Gossamer by Edward Pennell-Elmhirst   (p228-230)
Engraving [sculp. Babbage]: *Gossamer*   (on p229)
An Omitted Napoleonic Chapter by Francis Lawley   (p230-238)
Engraving [sculp. Babbage]: *Marengo - Napoleon's Charger*   (facing p230)
Steeplechase Reform by Harry Sargent   (p238-240)
The Allingley Whips (part 1)   (p240-246)
The Squire [verses] by William Phillpotts-Williams   (p247-248)
The Angler in April by William Senior   (p248-251)
Engraving [sculp. Adel]: *Common and Brandling Trout*   (facing p248)
On Middleham Moor by Coulson Pitman   (p251-256)
The Horse's Hoof [Illustrated] by George Fleming   (p256-261)
Racing in the West of England by William Allison   (p262-263)
Between the Seasons by Knight Horsfield   (p263-265)
Horse Breeding: Systematic and Continuous by Reginald Mainwaring   (p265-267)
Elephant and Buffalo Shooting in Ceylon by William Jesse   (p267-270)

Our Van [inc. Shire Horse Show; Lincolnshire Handicap; University Boat Race; Review of *Turf Celebrities* by William Day and *The General Stud Book* by John Butler] (p270-281)

Roundabout County Papers [inc. Lord Harris on Cricket; Fen Horses] (p281-283)

Correspondence [inc. Jumping Sires; Martens] (p283-286)

Odds and Ends [inc. York and Brighton Races 1790] (p286-287)

Summary of Results for March 1891 (p288)

Issue 375 : May 1891

Portrait [sculp. Roffe] and Biography - William Burdett-Coutts (p289-291)

After the Season by Edward Pennell-Elmhirst (p292-294)

The Angler in May by William Senior (p295-297)

The Cricket Season of 1891 by Frederick Gale (p297-299)

Survivors (part 2) by Abel Chapman (p299-301)

A Happy Thought by Comyns Cole (p301-304)

On the Mole and Arun by Sylvanus Urban (p305-307)

The Allingley Whips (part 2) (p307-314)

The Top of the Tree by Charles Batchelder (p314-320)

Francis Doyle by Francis Lawley (p320-329)

Engraving [sculp. Stodart]: *Francis Doyle* (facing p320)

[Review] *Cricket* by Gilbert Grace (p329-330)

My First Leopard by William Jesse (p331-334)

The Road Coaches by Coulson Pitman (p334-336)

Aquatics in 1891by Claude Holland (p336-338)

Thoroughbred Horses as Hacks and Hunters by Horace Hutchinson (p338-342)

Scent in Dogs by Gordon McPherson (p342-345)

Engraving [sculp. Babbage]: *King Herod & Flying Childers* (facing p342)

Our Van [inc. Leicester Meeting; Epsom Races; Craven Week; Frederick Gale to Canada; Hertfordshire Point-to-Point; Essex Hunt Steeplechase; Reviews of *Country House Sketches* by Charles Rhys and *Golf and Golfers* by Gordon McPherson] (p345-356)

Correspondence [Use of Spurs; Middleham Moor] (p356-357)

Odds and Ends [inc. Weight of Sheep Breeds 1791] (p357-359)

Summary of Results for April 1891 (p359-360)

Issue 376 : June 1891

Portrait [sculp. Roffe] and Biography - Henry James (p361-362)

The Cricket Season of 1891 by Frederick Gale (p363-365)

The Angler in June by William Senior (p365-368)

The Turf in France by Coulson Pitman (p368-371)

The Championship Golf Tournament by Gordon McPherson (p371-373)

From Oxford to Ascot, and Back by Charles Kent (p373-381)

[Review] *Riding* by Alfred Watson, reviewed by Richard Green-Price (p381-385)

The Keeper's Kennels (p385-386)

Engraving [sculp. Holm]: *Ali, Napoleon's Battle Charger* (facing p387)

Napoleon's Chargers by Francis Lawley (p387-396)

The Islington Horse Show by Comyns Cole (p396-398)

A Few Notes on Victorian Racing by Henry Beddington (p398-403)

Old Days in the Mediterranean (part 1) (p403-411)

[Obituaries] Capel Hanbury-Williams and Geoffrey Hill by Richard Green-Price (p411-412)

May on the Moor [verses] by Frederick Doveton (p413)

Our Van [inc. Chester Cup; Gatwick Racecourse; Review of *Hints to Huntsmen* by Anstruther Thomson; Buckinghamshire & Bedfordshire Otterhounds; Surrey Farmers' Staghounds] (p414-427)

Roundabout County Papers [inc. Yachting Fixtures; Dumfriesshire Otterhounds] (p428-429)

126

Correspondence [inc. Point-to-Point Committee; Use of Spurs]   (p429)
Odds and Ends [inc. Walking distances 1791]   (p430-431)
Summary of Results for May 1891   (p431-432)

On 29 June 1891, A.H.Baily & Co., and Alfred Head Baily junior, were both issued with an order for bankruptcy. It was stated that Baily junior "had continued to trade after knowing himself to be insolvent and, on a previous occasion, been adjudged bankrupt."

Volume 56, July - December 1891

Issue 377 : July 1891

Portrait [sculp. Stodart] of Charles Leedham, huntsman   Title page
Portrait [sculp. Roffe] and Biography - Thomas Mann   (p1-3)
Our New Llyn by Richard Green-Price   (p3-8)
Long Distance Shooting by Thomas Fremantle   (p8-12)
The Cricket Matches of Fiction by Edmund Christian   (p12-17)
The Angler in July by William Senior   (p17-20)
Engraving [pinx. Chalon]: *Flora*   (facing p21)
Some Raby Records by William Scarth-Dixon   (p21-27)
A Real Good Horse [verses] by John Trew-Hay   (p28)
The Road in 1891 by William Blew   (p29-32)
The Two Racing Dukes of Grafton by Ralph Payne-Gallwey   (p32-41)
The Cricket Season of 1891 by Frederick Gale   (p41-43)
Old Days in the Mediterranean (part 2)   (p43-46)
The [Peterborough] Hound Show of 1891 by William Day   (p46-48)
The Big Stag of Ben Vhui by James Bertram   (p49-55)
The Keeper's Story of the Poachers' Capture   (p55-57)
Our Van [inc. Coaching Meets; Ascot Meeting; Hurlingham Shots; St.Andrews Golf] (p57-66)
Roundabout County Papers [inc. Doncaster Agricultural Meeting; July Regattas]   (p67-68)
Correspondence [Future of Ascot Racecourse]   (p68)
Odds and Ends [inc. Marylebone Cricket Club match 1790; Bath & West Agricultural Society
        1768]   (p69-70)
Summary of Results for June 1891   (p70-72)

Issue 378 : August 1891

Portrait [sculp. Roffe] and Biography - Thomas Parrington   (p73-78)
After Ibex in Afghanistan by Charles Yate   (p78-82)
Grouse Shooting by James Bertram   (p82-89)
Bream and Tench Fishing in Surrey by Elim d'Avigdor   (p89-93)
A Morning in Kingston Harbour   (p94-98)
The Thames National Regatta by John Jeffery   (p99-102)
Sailor [Verses]   (p102-103)
James Jewitt by Comyns Cole   (p104-105)
Engraving [sculp. Roffe]: *James Jewitt*   (facing p104)
The Cricket Season of 1891 by Frederick Gale   (p105-106)
In Mid-Season by Richard Green-Price   (p107-111)
Olden Cricketts by Charles Alcock   (p111-113)
Engraving [pinx. Hayman]: *Cricket in 1740*   (on p112)
Lighthouses by Francis Lawley   (p113-122)
Henley Regatta 1891 by Claude Holland   (p123-125)
Where the Congers do 'Conger-egate' by Goulter Wood   (p126-128)
Up the Cam in a Canadian Canoe   (p128-131)

Our Van [inc. Leicester Racing; Obituary of Charles Blake (of *Sporting Life*); Review of
     Baseball by Newton Crane] (p132-140)
Odds and Ends [inc. A Staffordshire Ox 1776] (p141-142)
Summary of Results for July 1891 (p142-144)

Issue 379 : September 1891

Portrait [sculp. Roffe] and Biography - Thomas de Grey (p145-146)
From Daybreak to Sundown by Richard Green-Price (p147-151)
A Brief Reminiscence of a Partridge Shoot by George Grey (p151-153)
The Jubilee of Canterbury Cricket Week by Ogle Moore (p153-156)
Engraving [sculp. Babbage]: *Carbine* (facing p157)
Carbine [Melbourne Cup Winner 1890] by Nat Gould (p157-163)
The Duel by William Fox-Russell (p163-168)
The Angler in September by William Senior (p168-172)
Wild Turkey Shooting: *Ornithological Biography* by John Audubon (p172-181)
[Review] *Through the Stable and Saddleroom* by Arthur Fisher (p182-184)
The Cricket Season of 1891 by Sydney Pardon (p184-185)
Sport in Scandinavia by Fraser Sandeman (p186-193)
Military Riding by William Fife (p193-199)
Our Van [inc. Brighton Racing; Lewes Meeting; Thursby's Foxhounds; Obituary of Francis
     Fane; Thames National Regatta; Reviews of *Riding for Ladies* by William Kerr
     and *The Double Event* by Nat Gould] (p200-213)
Odds and Ends [inc. *Le Figaro* publishing Lawley's articles on Napoleon] (p213-214)
Summary of Results for August 1891 (p214-216)

Issue 380 : October 1891

Portrait [sculp. Roffe] and Biography - Charles Basset (p217-218)
Hunters and their Values by Charles Tindall (p219-223)
The Past Rowing Season by Claude Holland (p223-227)
Letters to my Friends: A Week at Newmarket by Alfred Watson (p228-230)
The Quorn Hunt Song by John Brodie (p230-232)
Engraving [sculp. Babbage]: *George Byng* (facing p233)
[George Byng] Earl of Strafford by Francis Lawley (p233-242)
The Angler in October by William Senior (p243-245)
Glimpses at Coon Hunting by George Grey (p245-246)
A Keeper's Confession by Ogle Moore (p246-248)
Engraving [sculp. Babbage]: *Common* (facing p249)
Doncaster: Common's Year by Richard Green-Price (p249-254)
In a Quandary (p255-262)
The Wild Duck by Bosworth Smith (p262-271)
Our Van [inc. Doncaster Meeting; Ayrshire Handicap; Atherstone Hounds; Canadian Rugby
     Tourists; Reviews of *Practical Horsemanship* by William Kerr; *The Horse: Its
     Keep and Management* by William Cook; *Driving as I Found It* by Frank Swales;
     Riding on the Flat and Across Country and *Veterinary Notes for Horse Owners*
     both by Horace Hayes; Royal Western Yacht Club Regatta] (p271-283)
Odds and Ends [inc. Yorkshire Shorthorns 1736; Birmingham Prize-Fight 1791] (p284-286)
Summary of Results for September 1891 (p286-288)

Issue 381 : November 1891

Portrait [sculp. Roffe] and Biography - Henry Brougham (p289-291)
The Foibles of Hunting by Richard Green-Price (p291-295)
Dreams over an Old Diary (p295-300)

A Shooting Cruise on the Albanian Coast (p300-306)
Richard Watt [Illustrated] by Francis Lawley (p307-319)
The Hunting Season by Edward Pennell-Elmhirst (p320-325)
The Angler in November by William Senior (p325-329)
A Pearl of Great Price [verses] by John Trew-Hay (p329-330)
Lynn Stream! A Tragedy (p330-332)
Coursing: The Opening Season by George Wilson (p332-333)
About a Mule (p334-337)
The Feeding of Horses by George Fleming (p337-342)
Our Van [inc. Gatwick Racecourse; Newmarket Meeting; Cottesmore Hunt; Woodnorton
          Harriers; Obituaries of Omer Talon, Archer Houblon and Isaac Wallop;
          English Cricketers in Philadelphia] (p342-357)
Odds and Ends [inc. Carlisle Races 1761] (p358)
Summary of Results for October 1891 (p359-360)

Issue 382 : December 1891

Portrait [sculp. Roffe] and Biography - John Talbot-Crosbie (p361-364)
The Code of Honour by Francis Lawley (p364-372)
A Tardy Confession by Henry Cholmondeley-Pennell (p373-377)
The Trophies of Hunting by Richard Green-Price (p377-382)
Rowing by Claude Holland (p383-384)
Partridge Driving [verses] by Frederick Duprey (p384)
The Angler in December by William Senior (p385-388)
The Steeplechase Match [verses] by Alan Duncan (p389-390)
[Review] Twelve Packs of Hounds by John Charlton, reviewed by Comyns Cole (p391-392)
My Shoot by Thomas Fremantle (p392-396)
A Scotch View of Scotch Fish and Fishermen by Abel Chapman (p396-398)
Bicycling and Tricycling by Hewitt Griffin (p399-402)
The Prospects of Steeplechasing by Herbert Bromhead (p402-407)
The Hackney Horse by Anthony Hamond (p407-410)
Engraving [sculp. Palfrey]: Hackney Mares (facing p408)
A Badger Hunt (p411-412)
Our Van [inc. Trotting Stud Book; Aintree Meeting; Cambridgeshire Hunt; Reviews of A
          Century of Foxhunting with the Warwickshire Hounds by Theophilus Puleston,
          On Surrey Hills by Jordan Denham, Saddles and Saddlery by Frederick Smith
          and Hindu-Koh by Donald MacIntyre; Obituaries of Robert Lawley, John Gosden
          and John Nightingall; Military Riding; English Cricket Team to South Africa] (p413-429)
Odds and Ends [inc. Connaught Trout; Betting at York Races] (p429-430)
Summary of Results for November 1891 (p430-432)

Volume 57, January - June 1892

Issue 383 : January 1892

Portrait [sculp. Stodart] of George Lohmann, cricketer Title page
Portrait [sculp. Roffe] and Biography - Philip Barthropp (p1-3)
The Prairie Bred Hunter by Frederick Lambart (p4-5)
The Exploits of Hunting by Richard Green-Price (p6-9)
In the Far West by Frederick Gale (p10-15)
A Battue (p15-18)
Engraving [sculp. Beckwith]: The Battue (facing p16)
Hunting Reminiscences by William Blew (p18-24)
[Obituary] Rowland Egerton-Warburton by Francis Lawley (p25-35)

Some Waterside Acquaintances by William Senior (p36-39)
Cricket [Marylebone Cricket Club matters] by Sydney Pardon (p40-42)
Rowing [Tyne Races; University Trials] by Claude Holland (p42-43)
[Review] *Foxhound, Forest and Prairie* by Edward Pennell-Elmhirst (p44-45)
Roaring in Horses by George Fleming (p45-50)
Leaves From an Indian Shikar Diary (part 1) by James Moray-Brown (p51-52)
Our Van [inc. Newmarket Sales; Reviews of *Notitia Venatica* (revised edition) by William Blew, *The White Hat* by Finch Mason, *Livestock Journal Almanac 1892*, and *That Piebald Pony* by James Bailey; Obituaries of Wellington Stapleton-Cotton, Arthur Mesham, Victor Brooke and William Cavendish; Blankney Hunt; Southwold Hounds] (p53-69)
Summary of Results for December 1891 (p70-72)

On 28 January 1892, the High Court in Bankruptcy suspended Baily junior's discharge from bankruptcy for two years and three months "until 28 April 1894."

Issue 384 : February 1892

Portrait [sculp. Roffe] and Biography - James Weatherby (p73-76)
Accidents and Emergencies in the Hunting Field [Illustrated] by Thomas Bond (p76-84)
Among the Wildfowl on the Coast of Jutland by Fraser Sandeman (p85-90)
Golf by Gordon McPherson (p90-92)
The Difficulties of Hunting by Richard Green-Price (p92-97)
Connemara and White Trout by Richard Lloyd-Price (p97-101)
Breeding Hunters by Charles Tindall (p101-104)
Engraving [sculp. Babbage]: *A Hunter Sire* (facing p104)
The Horse and the Hound [verses] by Scudamore Argove (p105)
[Review] *Life of Pitt* by Archibald Primrose, reviewed by Francis Lawley (p106-114)
Rowing by Claude Holland (p114-116)
The Horse's Hock by George Fleming (p116-119)
[Obituary] Thomas Statter by Comyns Cole (p120-123)
The Dog: A Tale of the American Turf (p123-129)
Our Van [inc. Reviews of *The Jockey Club* by Robert Black and *In the Days When We Went Hog Hunting* by James Moray-Brown; Obituary of Victor Gleichen (*Baily's* contributor); Ledbury Hunt; Kildare Hounds; Meath Hunt; Eastbourne Hounds; East Kent Huntsman; Fen Skating] (p130-142)
Summary of Results for January 1892 (p142-144)

Issue 385 : March 1892

Portrait [sculp. Roffe] and Biography - John Leigh (p145-147)
The Turf Outlook for 1892 by Richard Green-Price (p147-153)
The Inland Fisheries of Norway by Fraser Sandeman (p153-158)
'Ware Wheat' by Victor Gleichen (p158-161)
Sale of Partridges' Eggs by William Tegetmeier (p161-164)
Horses with Shoes and Horses Without Them [Illustrated] by George Fleming (p165-170)
Scent: What is it? [Illustrated] by Frederick Gresham (p170-174)
Hunting Song [from *Hunting Songs and Poems*] by John Campbell (p175)
Polo Ponies by James Moray-Brown (p176-180)
Engraving [sculp. Bradley]: *Well Played – A Goal* (facing p176)
The Admiral's Punt by William Senior (p180-183)
The Stud of Thoroughbreds at Sledmere by John Radcliffe (p183-187)
The Royal Artillery Draghounds by William Fox-Russell (p187-190)
Coursing: The Waterloo Cup by George Wilson (p191-193)
Country Football by Thomas Pellat (p194-200)
Rowing by Claude Holland (p200-202)

Our Van [inc. Kempton Park Meeting; Brocklesby Hounds; Obituary of Henry Armstrong;
        English Cricketers in Australia]   (p202-213)
Summary of Results for February 1892   (p214-216)

* Pagination error *

Issue 386 : April 1892

Portrait [sculp. Roffe] and Biography - Gerald Ricardo   (p215-216)
Notes on Breeding by William Day   (p216-220)
The Capercailzie and its Ways by Frederick Whishaw   (p220-224)
Crib-Biting by George Fleming   (p224-229)
Steeplechasing by Alfred Watson   (p230-235)
Engraving [sculp. Babbage]: *Roman Oak*   (facing p230)
[Obituary] Georgina de Ros by Francis Lawley   (p235-244)
A Profitable Entertainment by William Fox-Russell   (p244-249)
[Reviews] Some Books on Horses: *The Horse* by William Flower; *Saddles and Sore Backs* by
        Frederick Smith; *The Art of Riding* by Herbert English and *Practical Horsemanship*
        by William Kerr reviewed by Comyns Cole   (p249-254)
The Nestors of Hunting by Richard Green-Price   (p254-259)
The Popularity of Polo by James Moray-Brown   (p260-264)
The Hackney Horse Society and the Inspection Question by Comyns Cole   (p265-269)
Rowing by Claude Holland   (p269-271)
Our Van [inc. Hurst Park Steeplechasing; Fitzwilliam Hunt; Ludlow Hounds; Obituaries of
        William Gregory and John Cookson]   (p272-284)
Summary of Results for March 1892   (p284-286)

Issue 387 : May 1892

Portrait [sculp. Roffe] and Biography - Noel Fenwick   (p287-289)
The Summering of Hunters (part 1) by Charles Tindall   (p289-293)
My Old Creel by William Senior   (p294-298)
To, and In, Mashonaland (part 1) by Frederick Selous   (p299-304)
Rowing by Claude Holland   (p304-307)
Engraving [sculp. Clydon]: *Rowing*   (on p307)
Cycling Under Three Heads (part 1) by Hewitt Griffin   (p307-310)
Normandy Field Trials by Frederick Gresham   (p310-313)
The Sporting Parson [verses] by William Phillpotts-Williams   (p313-314)
Engraving [sculp. Clydon]: *Polo*   (on p315)
Strategy, Tactics and Danger in Polo by James Moray-Brown   (p315-321)
Coaching Days on the Great North Road by Francis Lawley   (p321-331)
Engraving [sculp. Babbage]: *Coaching in the Olden Days*   (facing p327)
Steeplechasing Before 1820 by Herbert Bromhead   (p331-335)
Cricket in 1892 by Sydney Pardon   (p336-338)
A Private Training Ground by Richard Green-Price   (p338-342)
The Protection of the Horse's Hoof (part 1) by George Fleming   (p342-344)
Our Van [inc. Steeplechasing; Obituaries of George Middleton, Nicholas Cornish and James
        Goater; West Norfolk Hunt; Eggesford Hounds; Inter-Varsity Sports]   (p345-356)
Summary of Results for April 1892   (p357-358)

Issue 388 : June 1892

Portrait [sculp. Roffe] and Biography - Arthur Tempest   (p359-361)
Cricket: In Rain or Sunshine by Richard Green-Price   (p361-366)
Thames Trout Fishing by Herbert Bromhead   (p367-371)

The Summering of Hunters (part 2) by Charles Tindall (p371-373)
To, and In, Mashonaland (part 2) by Frederick Selous (p373-379)
The Protection of the Horse's Hoof (part 2) by George Fleming (p379-381)
George Lohmann by Comyns Cole (p381-382)
A Polo Song by George Rimington (p383-384)
The Month's Cricket by Sydney Pardon (p384-386)
The Sportsman's Library: Reviews of *The Life of a Foxhound* by John Mills; *Examples of Stables, Hunting Boxes and Racing Establishments* by John Birch, and *Autobiography of an English Gamekeeper* by John Wilkins (p386-389)
Rowing by Claude Holland (p389-391)
Cycling Under Three Heads (part 2) by Hewitt Griffin (p392-397)
On Nobbling Horses by Francis Lawley (p398-407)
Polo in May by James Moray-Brown (p408-414)
Our Van [inc. Kempton Jubilee Handicap; Chiddingfold Hunt; Stevenstone Hunt; Southampton Yacht Club; Obituaries of Thomas Pearson, William Beasley and James Scarlett] (p415-429)
Summary of Results for May 1892 (p429-430)

Volume 58, July - December 1892

Issue 389 : July 1892

Portrait [sculp. Collaph] of Frank Gillard, huntsman — Title page
Portrait [sculp. Roffe] and Biography - John Drake-Smith (p1-4)
Salmon and Grayling Fishing on the Russo-Norwegian Frontier by Fraser Sandeman (p5-11)
Hambledon and its Cricketers of Long Ago by Burnett Fallow (p12-18)
Engraving [sculp. Clydon]: *Hambledon Cricket* (on p18)
Hereditary Unsoundness by Charles Tindall (p18-22)
To, and in, Mashonaland (part 3) by Frederick Selous (p22-29)
Engraving [sculp Bradley]: *Loose Boxes* (facing p29)
Summering Hunters: How Shall We House Them by John Birch (p29-34)
The Blue Doctor by Stephen Leydhen (p34-39)
Troubles of a Shore Shooter by Gregory Benoni (p39-45)
The Sportsman's Library: Reviews of *The Angler's Companion* by Thomas Stoddart (new ed); *Wild Sports of the West of Ireland* by William Maxwell (new ed); *Schools and Masters of Fence* by Egerton Castle (new ed); *Sporting Sketches in South America* by William Kennedy; *Camping Out* by Arthur Macdonell; *The Handbook of Poker* by William Florence; *The Racehorse* by Robert Warburton and *Hints on Colt-Breaking* by William Hutchison (p45-50)
After Bears in Kullu by Richard Tyacke (p50-54)
Rowing by Claude Holland (p54-57)
The Month's Cricket by Sydney Pardon (p57-60)
Our Van [inc. Carthorse Parade; Manchester Cup; Ascot Hunt Cup; Polo Champion Cup] (p60-70)
Summary of Results for June 1892 (p70-72)

Issue 390 : August 1892

Portrait [sculp. Roffe] and Biography - Thomas Fremantle (p73-74)
A Reverie on Cricket by Herbert Hewett (p75-78)
Sport in the Lews by Thomas Fremantle (p79-87)
Trainers of the Day by Comyns Cole (p87-90)
Engraving [sculp. Babbage]: *James Ryan* (facing p89)
Modern Improvements in Guns and Rifles by Thomas Fremantle (p90-92)
The Peterborough Show by William Day (p92-98)
The Ascot Cup by Francis Lawley (p98-109)

Two Polo Tournaments by James Moray-Brown (p109-115)
Are Horse Breeders Encouraged by Richard Green-Price (p115-119)
The Month's Cricket by Sydney Pardon (p120-123)
Rowing by Claude Holland (p123-126)
Grouse Shooting by William Tegetmeier (p127-131)
Leaves From an Indian Shikar Diary (part 2) by James Moray-Brown (p131-132)
Our Van [inc. Bibury Stakes; Obituaries of Henry Moore, Nicholas Charlton and Robert Coney; Review of *Hints on Racing* by William Day; Four-in-Hand Club; Norfolk Hackneys] (p132-142)
Summary of Results for July 1892 (p142-144)

Issue 391 : September 1892

Portrait [sculp. Roffe] and Biography - Alexander Webbe (p145-147)
September Leaves by Richard Green-Price (p147-152)
Two Days' Woodcock Shooting in the West of Ireland by Josslyn Gore-Booth (p153-158)
The Detection of Lameness in Horses by George Fleming (p158-162)
Bicycling by Hewitt Griffin (p162-164)
Thoroughbred Horses in War by Francis Lawley (p164-175)
A Plea for the Polecat by James Harting (p175-177)
Rowing by Claude Holland (p178-179)
The Month's Cricket by Sydney Pardon (p180-182)
Yachting by Brooke Heckstall-Smith (p182-186)
The Silent Depths by Stephen Leydhen (p186-192)
Game Law Vagaries and Game Law Reform by Leonard West (p192-195)
The Big Stag of Cairn Leadh by Coulson Pitman (p195-198)
A Lion Adventure in Somaliland by Blair Lodgian (p198-202)
Our Van [inc. Redcar Meeting; Stockton Racecourse; Devon & Somerset Staghounds; East Suffolk Foxhounds; Goodwood Hounds; East Sussex Agricultural Society] (p202-213)
Summary of Results for August 1892 (p214-216)

Issue 392 : October 1892

Portrait [sculp. Roffe] and Biography - John Lawrence (p217-219)
Autumnal Tints by Richard Green-Price (p219-224)
The Faults of Foxhunters by Guy Gravenhill (p224-227)
Among the Reindeer on the High Fjelds by Abel Chapman (p227-231)
The Detection of Lameness in Horses by George Fleming (p231-235)
[Memoir] Joseph Hawley by Francis Lawley (p235-246)
[Review] *Angler's Literature* by Fraser Sandeman (p246-247)
Plaisanterie by Penry Palfrey (p248)
Engraving [sculp. Babbage]: *Plaisanterie* (facing p248)
The All-Ireland Polo Club Cup by James Moray-Brown (p249-251)
The Close of the Cricket Season by Sydney Pardon (p251-254)
Captain Jack (p255-260)
Engraving [sculp. Palfrey]: *John Skipworth* (on p255)
Rowing by Claude Holland (p261-263)
A Day with the Dromores by Stephen Leydhen (p263-269)
After Big Game in Albania (p269-274)
Our Van [inc. Doncaster Meeting; Ayrshire Handicap; Cricket in Canada; Compton Stud Show; Brighton Comet Coach] (p275-286)
Summary of Results for September 1892 (p287-288)

Issue 393 : November 1892

Portrait [sculp. Roffe] and Biography - Richard Green-Price   (p289-291)
Literature and the Turf by John Doyle   (p291-296)
A Canadian Winter by Frederick Gale   (p296-299)
As You Were by Richard Green-Price   (p299-307)
Commencement of the Coursing Season by George Wilson   (p307-309)
The Dolliad [Satire 1814, with verses] by Francis Lawley   (p309-311)
The Anglo-French Boat Race by Claude Holland   (p311-313)
Pike Fishers and Pike Fishing by Herbert Bromhead   (p313-319)
A Reminiscence by Frederick Whitehurst   (p319-321)
Glanders by George Fleming   (p321-326)
Johnny Rond (part 1) by Stephen Leydhen   (p326-334)
A Chat About Steeplechasing by William Fox-Russell   (p334-337)
List of Hounds 1892-93 [Large folded page]   (facing p336)
The Merlin and Other Hawks by James Harting   (p337-342)
Leaves From an Indian Shikar Diary (part 3) by James Moray-Brown   (p343-344)
The Hunting Season [With Mastership Changes] by Edward Pennell-Elmhirst   (p344-348)
Our Van [inc. Review of *The Racing Life of Lord George Bentinck* by John Kent; Middle Park Plate; Gatwick Meeting; Stanmore Chase]   (p349-357)
Summary of Results for October 1892   (p358-360)

Issue 394 : December 1892

Portrait [sculp. Roffe] and Biography - Charles Wright   (p361-362)
[Review] *The History of White's* by Algernon Bourke reviewed by Francis Lawley   (p363-373)
The Brocklesby Rallywood and Will Goodall by Richard Green-Price   (p373-380)
A Word on Cricket: Second Class Counties by Herbert Hewett   (p380-384)
The Art of Salmon Poaching by Alfred Burden   (p384-387)
The Cavalry Horses of France, Germany and England by William Fife   (p387-395)
Black Collars: The Epwell Hunt [verses from 1807]   (p395-399)
Squire Osbaldeston by William Blew   (p400-404)
Navicular Disease [Illustrated] by George Fleming   (p405-410)
Frank Gillard by Comyns Cole   (p410-411)
Johnny Rond (part 2) by Stephen Leydhen   (p411-418)
Our Van [inc. Portsmouth Park Meeting; Paris Horse Sales; Cambridgeshire Hunt; Puckeridge Hounds; Wimbledon Chase; National Skating Association; Essex County Cricket Club Finances]   (p418-430)
Summary of Results for November 1892   (p430-432)

Amy Menzies

Volume 59, January - June 1893

Issue 395 : January 1893

Portrait [sculp. Palfrey] of Edwin Fownes, coachman	Title page
Portrait [sculp. Roffe] and Biography - Cecil Legard	(p1-3)
A Terrible Christmas by Francis Lawley	(p4-14)
Farmers and Foxes [Illustrated] by Henry Davenport	(p14-15)
Ladies' Riding by Alice Hayes	(p16-19)
Some Recollections of Shooting by John Cordeaux	(p20-25)
A Hunting Christmas Log by Richard Green-Price	(p25-30)
Two Old Hands by Arthur Grey	(p30-32)
La Fleche by Penry Palfrey	(p32-33)
Engraving [sculp. Babbage]: *La Fleche*	(facing p32)
The Pleasures of Fishing by Herbert Bromhead	(p33-36)
Navicular Disease [Illustrated] by George Fleming	(p36-40)
Johnny Rond (part 3) by Stephen Leydhen	(p41-51)
Lines to My Rod [verses] by John Halifax	(p51)
The Sportsman's Library: Reviews of *Horn Measurements* by Rowland Ward, *Sporting Sketches in South America* by William Kennedy, *The Horsewoman* by Alice Hayes, *Coursing* by Harding Cox, *Falconry* by Gerald Lascelles and *Five Years' Hunting in South Africa* by Ronaleyn Cumming	(p52-56)
Our Van [inc. Bicester Hunt; Birmingham Cattle Show; Tredegar Horse Show; National Skating Association; Obituary of Samuel Darbishire and Review of *The Live Stock Journal Almanac for 1893*]	(p56-70)
Correspondence [Best Colt]	(p70-71)
Summary of Results for December 1892	(p71-72)

Issue 396 : February 1893

Portrait [sculp. Roffe] and Biography - Algernon Freeman-Mitford	(p73-75)
An Old Sporting Worthy by Richard Green-Price	(p76-81)
The Balance of Nature by Frederick Gale	(p82-87)
Steeplechase Riders, Past and Present by Herbert Bromhead	(p88-92)
Rugby versus Association Football by Michael Flynn	(p93-96)
The Circus by Thomas Frost	(p96-100)
The Treatment of Navicular Disease [Illustrated] by George Fleming	(p100-104)
Some Huntsmen of Today: Thomas Whitemore (Oakley); Benjamin Capell (Blankney); Richard Stovin (Heythrop); Charles Fox (Blackmoor Vale); Thomas Perry (Craven); Frank Bartlett (Fitzwilliam); Charles Travess (Cotswold); Thomas Smith (Bramham Moor); Edward Woodcock (Surrey); George Gillson (Cottesmore) and Charles Littleworth (Eggesford)	(p105-114)
Photograph [Swain]: *Thomas Whitemore*	(on p105)
Photograph [Swain]: *Benjamin Capell*	(on p106)
Photograph [Swain]: *Richard Stovin*	(on p107)
Photograph [Swain]: *Charles Fox*	(on p108)
Photograph [Syse]: *Thomas Perry*	(on p109)
Photograph [Syse]: *Frank Bartlett*	(on p110)
Photograph [Syse]: *Charles Travess*	(on p111)
Photograph [Syse]: *Thomas Smith*	(on p112)
Photograph [Swain]: *Edward Woodcock*	(on p113)
Photograph [Swain]: *George Gillson*	(on p114)
Photograph [Swain]: *Charles Littleworth*	(on p114)
The Peregrine Falcon [Illustrated] by Henry Evans	(p115-119)
A Reminiscence [verses]	(p119-120)

Stuck Up By Tommy Clarke the Bushranger by Guy Eden (p121-126)

Winter Sport in Norway by Fraser Sandeman (p126-131)

Our Van [inc. Rothschild's Hounds; Quorn Hunt; Obituaries of William Grayson, Frederick Watson, Lydston Newman, Hawley Smart, Alexander Barclay and Charlton Lane (*Baily's* contributor); Unregistered Bookmakers; Cockfighting Judgment; New York Yacht Club] (p131-143)

Summary of Results for January 1893 (p144)

Issue 397 : March 1893

Portrait [sculp. Roffe] and Biography - Rowland Hunt (p145-146)

English Deer Parks by Francis Lawley (p147-155)

Letters to Young Polo Players (part 1) by James Moray-Brown (p156-160)

A Coursing Chat by Herbert Bromhead (p160-167)

An England Eleven and the Australians by Herbert Hewett (p167-171)

An East Riding Foxhunter [some verses] by William Kidson (p172-173)

The Ethics of Football by Gordon McPherson (p174-176)

Engraving [sculp. Palfrey]: *Nicholas Charlton* (facing p177)

[Obituary] Nicholas Charlton by Lionel Musters (p177-178)

A Highland Fete (p178-181)

Shuckburgh Hill [verses] by Reginald Wyverne (p181-186)

A Hunting Country by Richard Green-Price (p187-191)

[Review] *A Famous Foxhunter* (5th edition) by John Eardley-Wilmot (p192-196)

Rowing by Claude Holland (p197-199)

Some Diseases of the Horse's Feet (part 1) by George Fleming (p200-203)

Our Van [inc. Old Steeplechase Courses; South & West Wiltshire Point-to-Point; Pembrokeshire Hunt; Obituaries of John Watson, Henry Stansfeld and Philip Carter] (p204-215)

Summary of Results for February 1893 (p215-216)

Issue 398 : April 1893

Portrait [sculp. Roffe] and Biography - Comyns Cole (p217-219)

Hunting Songs by William Blew (p219-226)

Riding at Fences by Robert Weir (p226-230)

Letters to Young Polo Players (part 2) by James Moray-Brown (p230-235)

The Ides of March by Charles Batchelder (p235-240)

Coursing: The Waterloo Cup by George Wilson (p241-245)

The Sportsman's Library: Reviews of *L'Elevage du Pur Sang en France* by Georges des Farges; *A History and Description of the Modern Dog* by Rawdon Lee; *The Young Squire* by Richard Green-Price; *Oriental Field Sports* (new ed.) by Thomas Williamson; *Turf, Tent and Tomb* by Bernard Tauchnitz and *The Gun and its Development* by William Greener (p245-248)

Some Trainers of Today: Matthew Dawson; John Porter; Robert Sherwood; James Jewitt; James Ryan; Percy Peck; Thomas Leader and Richard Marsh (p249-260)

Photograph [Syse]: *Matthew Dawson* (on p249)

Photograph [Syse]: *John Porter* (on p251)

Photograph [Swain]: *Robert Sherwood* (on p253)

Photograph [Syse]: *James Jewitt* (on p254)

Photograph [Syse]: *James Ryan* (on p255)

Photograph [Syse]: *Percy Peck* (on p256)

Photograph [Syse]: *Thomas Leader* (on p258)

Photograph [Syse]: *Richard Marsh* (on p259)

Engraving [sculp. Palfrey]: *Training* (on p260)

Hunting From Oxford by John Green (p261-265)

Over Warwickshire Grass [verses] (p266)

Some Diseases of the Horse's Feet (part 2) by George Fleming (p267-270)

Rowing by Claude Holland (p270-273)

Engraving [Palfrey]: *Frank Clark* (on p271)

Our Van [inc. Gatwick Races; Grand Military Meeting; Lingfield Steeplechasing; Review of *Trotting Stud Book* by Frederick Cathcart; Obituaries of John Craven and Abington Baird; University Boat Race] (p273-285)

Correspondence [Marylebone Cricket Club by Frederick Gale] (p285-286)

Summary of Results for March 1893 (p287-288)

Issue 399 : May 1893

Portrait [sculp. Roffe], Biography and Illustration - Herbert Hewett (p289-291)

Yachting Prospects by Brooke Heckstall-Smith (p292-294)

Letters to Young Polo Players (part 3) by James Moray-Brown (p294-300)

Cricket Reporting: New Style by Edmund Christian (p301-304)

Scraps From Alken's Notebook by Penry Palfrey (p304-305)

Engraving [sculp. Colls]: *Scraps From Alken's Notebook* (facing p304)

Bicycling by Hewitt Griffin (p305-308)

Some Modern Stage Coachmen: Charles Webling (Excelsior); Edwin Fownes (Rocket); Arthur Fownes (Vivid and Venture); Walter Samson (New Times) and Henry King (Magnet) (p308-312)

Engraving [sculp. Palfrey]: *Charles Webling* (on p309)

Engraving [sculp. Palfrey]: *Edwin Fownes* (on p309)

Engraving [sculp. Palfrey]: *Arthur Fownes* (on p310)

Engraving [sculp. Palfrey]: *Walter Samson* (on p311)

Engraving [sculp. Palfrey]: *Henry King* (on p311)

The Sports of Yesterday by Stephen Leydhen (p312-318)

Rowing by Claude Holland (p319-321)

Sport in Kullu by Richard Tyacke (p321-328)

A Rough Day in the Hebrides (p329-335)

Ballade of the Turnpike [verses] by Alfred Cochrane (p335)

Golf [Illustrated] by Gordon McPherson (p336-338)

[Review] *Handbook on Dogs and Hunting* (1544 ed.) by Michael Biondo (p339-344)

Our Van [inc. Epsom Meeting; Essex Hunt Steeplechases; Badminton Hunt Point-to-Point; Obituary of James Philcox; Polo in India; Amateur Racquet Championship] (p344-357)

Correspondence (Spur Straps] (p358)

Summary of Results for April 1893 (p358-360)

Issue 400 : June 1893

Portrait [sculp. Roffe] and Biography - Francis Grenfell (p361-363)

Three Famous Horse Matches by Francis Lawley (p363-372)

Summer Sports in Canada by Frederick Gale (p372-377)

University Cricket by Charles Smith (p378-380)

The Trial: A Sketch (part 1) by Richard Green-Price (p380-384)

Rowing by Claude Holland (p384-386)

Epsom and its Derby by Herbert Bromhead (p387-392)

Some Polo Players of Today: Charles Stanhope; Francis Herbert; William Jenner; Francis Mildmay; Arthur Peat; James Peat; Toby Rawlinson and John Watson (p393-403)

Engraving [sculp. Palfrey]: *Charles Stanhope* (on p393)

Engraving [sculp. Palfrey]: *Francis Herbert* (on p395)

Engraving [sculp. Palfrey]: *William Jenner* (on p396)

Engraving [sculp. Palfrey]: *Francis Mildmay* (on p397)

Engraving [sculp. Palfrey]: *Arthur Peat* (on p399)

Engraving [sculp. Palfrey]: *James Peat* (on p400)

Engraving [sculp. Palfrey]: *Toby Rawlinson* (on p401)

Engraving [sculp. Palfrey]: *John Watson* (on p402)
A Day on a Sea Loch by John Russell (p404-411)
Engraving [sculp. Adel]: *Salmon and Trout* (on p411)
Edwin Fownes by Comyns Cole (p412)
The Sportsman's Library: Reviews of *Ecuyers et Ecuyeres* by Baron de Vaux; *Canoeing with Sail and Paddle* by John Hayward; *Recreation* by William Odell and *Short Stalks* by Edward Buxton (p413-415)
Our Van [inc. Chester Race Company; Newmarket Stakes; Australian Cricket Tour; Amateur Golf Championship; Obituary of William Burton] (p416-431)
Summary of Results for May 1893 (p431-432)

Volume 60, July - December 1893

Issue 401 : July 1893

Portrait [sculp. Palfrey] of Arthur Nightingall, jockey (Title page)
Portrait [sculp. Roffe] and Biography - Reginald Mainwaring (p1-2)
Chargers by John Russell (p3-9)
A Chapter on Cricket in Australia by Charles Fernival (p9-13)
A Forgotten Field Sport by Henry Doughty (p13-15)
Real Yorkshire by Richard Green-Price (p16-19)
Engraving [sculp. Romney]: *Real Yorkshire* (facing p16)
Pigeon Shooting by John Williams (p20-23)
The Decline of Irish Humour by Francis Lawley (p24-32)
The Coaches in the Park by Comyns Cole (p33-36)
Racing in 1848 and 1893 by Frederick Wingfield (p36-40)
The Oldest Cricket Guide by Michael Flynn (p41-43)
The Sportsman's Library: Reviews of *Horses, Sound and Unsound* by James Lupton; *The Farrier* by Arthur Fisher; *Practical Flyfishing* (new ed.) by John Beever and *Kennel Nomenclature* by Morgan Lloyd-Price (p44-46)
Rowing by Claude Holland (p47-50)
Engraving [sculp. Palfrey]: *Charles Kent* (on p47)
Cricket Notes by Sydney Pardon (p50-52)
A Tale of the Tournament [verses] by Harry Cumberland-Bentley (p53)
Pig-Sticking by Edward Lloyd (p54-58)
Our Van [inc. Richmond Horse Show; Ascot Meeting; Sandwich Golf; Royal Thames Yacht Club; West Kent Hunt] (p59-70)
Summary of Results for June 1893 (p70-72)

Issue 402 : August 1893

Portrait [sculp. Roffe] and Biography - Windham Wyndham-Quin (p73-75)
Bookmaking in the United States by William Gilpin (p75-78)
Forage by George Fleming (p78-83)
The Favourite: A Sketch (part 2) by Richard Green-Price (p84-89)
Engraving [sculp. Greig]: *Otter Hunting* (facing p89)
Otter Hunting by Alexander Clark-Kennedy (p89-91)
Thomas Thornton by Francis Lawley (p91-99)
Colours, Yellow, Black Cap by John Brown (p100-105)
Sporting Associations of Rutlandshire by Herbert Bromhead (p105-114)
The Sportsman's Library: Reviews of *The Young Cricketer's Tutor* (new ed.) by John Nyren; *Cricket* by William Murdoch; *On English Lagoons* by Peter Emmerson; *Whips and Whip-Making* by William Ashford and *Songs & Verses* by Harry Cumberland-Bentley (p114-118)

Rowing by Claude Holland (p119-121)
Polo: The Soldiers' Tournament by James Moray-Brown (p121-126)
Horses and Hounds at Peterborough by Comyns Cole (p126-130)
Cricket in July by Sydney Pardon (p130-132)
Our Van [inc. Stockbridge Meeting; County Cup Polo Tournament; Obituaries of Fownes
        Luttrell, Frederick Gough-Calthorpe and Thomas Holmes] (p133-141)
Summary of Results for July 1893 (p142-144)

Issue 403 : September 1893

Portrait [sculp. Roffe] and Biography - Andrew Stoddart (p145-147)
Voltigeur's First Race by John Smith (p147-151)
Thames Gudgeon Fishing by Herbert Bromhead (p152-156)
Two Days' Sport at Chicago by Frederick Gale (p156-160)
Engraving [sculp. Engleheart]: *The Spicy Screw* (facing p161)
The Spicy Screw by Richard Green-Price (p161-165)
Indian Dacoity and Thuggee by Francis Lawley (p166-175)
England Past and Present [verses] by Alfred Cochrane (p175)
The Cricket Match that was not Played (p176-177)
The Doctor's Horse and Stable (part 1) by Robert Collyns (p178-182)
Indian Ponies for English Polo Players by Thomas Dale (p183-186)
The Sportsman's Library: Reviews of *The Jamaica Stud Book with Historical Sketch of the Turf*
        by Thomson Palache; *Back to the Land* by Harold Moore; *The Autobiography of
        an Old Passport* by Alfred Smith; *The Dog in British Poetry* by Maynard Leonard;
        The Atlantic Ferry by Arthur Maginnis and *The Art and Pastime of Cycling* (3rd ed.)
        by Richard Mecredy (p186-191)
Cricket in August by Charles Smith (p191-194)
Rowing by Claude Holland (p194-197)
Our Van [inc. Redcar Meeting; Colwick Park; Obituaries of George Pritchard-Rayner and
        George Hills; Devon & Somerset Staghounds; Furzedown Golf Course] (p197-212)
Correspondence [Breeding Polo Ponies] (p212-214)
Summary of Results for August 1893 (p214-216)

Issue 404 : October 1893

Portrait [sculp. Roffe] and Biography -Thomas Lister (p217-219)
The Chincoteague Ponies by Francis Lawley (p220-226)
The Sportsman's Cabinet by John Slater (p226-229)
The Doctor's Horse and Stable (part 2) by Robert Collyns (p229-232)
Engraving [sculp. Engleheart]: *A Distressed Mother* (facing p233)
A Distressed Mother by Richard Green-Price (p233-236)
Quiet Angling by Robert Marston (p236-241)
Some British Game Birds by Fraser Sandeman (p241-246)
A Hunting Problem by Henry Davenport (p246-249)
[Review] *The Stud Book* [Volume 17] by Richard Green-Price (p250-251)
Two Dogs of Mine by Frederick Gresham (p252-254)
The End of the Cricket Season by Sydney Pardon (p254-256)
The Sportsman's Library: Reviews of *Long Casts and Sure Rises* by Edgar Shrubsole; *Notes of
        Sport in the Levant* by Dayrell Davies; *Harry Dale's Jockey* by Nat Gould; *Hints
        to Horsewomen* by Harriet Allbutt and *Stray Sport* by James Moray-Brown (p257-260)
After Markor Amongst the Kagnag Mountains, Kashmir by William Alexander (p260-265)
The Earliest Traces of Cricket by Michael Flynn (p265-268)
[Obituary] William Llewelyn of Penllergaer (p269-270)
Our Van [inc. Doncaster Races; New Birmingham Racecourse; Prestwick Golf Championship;
        Cardiff Horse Show; Brenton Reef Yachting Challenge Cup] (p270-284)

Correspondence [Cricket and Breeding Polo Ponies]   (p284-286)
Summary of Results for September 1893   (p287-288)

Issue 405 : November 1893

Portrait [sculp. Roffe] and Biography - William Inge   (p289-292)
Prescott Hewett by Francis Lawley   (p292-299)
The Early Days of Stage Coaches (part 1) by William Blew   (p299-303)
A Hunting Problem by John Brock   (p304)
Some Gentlemen Huntsmen of Today: Henry Somerset; Reginald Corbet; George Monckton-
        Arundell; Henry Verney; Reginald Chandos-Pole, Preston Rawnsley and Edward
        Lycett-Green by Richard Green-Price   (p305-312)
Engraving [sculp. Palfrey]: *Henry Somerset*   (on p305)
Engraving [sculp. Palfrey]: *Reginald Corbet*   (on p307)
Engraving [sculp. Palfrey]: *George Monckton-Arundell*   (on p308)
Engraving [sculp. Palfrey]: *Henry Verney*   (on p309)
Engraving [sculp. Palfrey]: *Reginald Chandos-Pole*   (on p309)
Engraving [sculp. Palfrey]: *Preston Rawnsley*   (on p310)
Engraving [sculp. Palfrey]: *Edward Lycett-Green*   (on p311)
Anglers' Sociability by Alfred Burden   (p312-316)
Letters on Whist (part 1) by William Deane   (p316-318)
Rugby Football Union by Charles Smith   (p318-319)
Cricket: A Suggestion for the Counties by Ivo Bligh   (p320-323)
Keillor [verses]   (p323-324)
The Sportsman's Library: Review of *Travel and Adventure in South East Africa* by
        Frederick Selous   (p325-328)
Jack Mytton by Ernest Rhys   (p328-335)
Miss Marchmont's Mare by Finch Mason   (p336-339)
The Hunting Season by Edward Pennell-Elmhirst   (p340-343)
Our Van [inc. Nottingham Racecourse; Lowther Stakes; America's Cup Yachting; St.Andrews
        Golf; Cricket in Vienna]   (p344-357)
Summary of Results for October 1893   (p357-360)

Issue 406 : December 1893

Portrait [sculp. Roffe] and Biography - Walter Selby   (p361-363)
[Review] *A History of Foxhunting in the Wynnstay Country* by Gresley Puleston reviewed by
        Francis Lawley   (p364-372)
A French Breeding Stud by Coulson Pitman   (p373-378)
Letters on Whist (part 2) by William Deane   (p378-380)
Cricket by Frederick Gale   (p381-384)
County Cricket by Edward Grace   (p384)
American Racing in 1893   (p385-391)
Orme by Penry Palfrey   (p392-393)
Engraving [sculp. Babbage]: *Orme*   (facing p392)
Round the Decoy by Harry Cumberland-Bentley   (p393-395)
Football at the Universities by Charles Smith   (p396-397)
The Sportsman's Library: Review of *American Big-Game Hunting* by Theodore Roosevelt (p398-400)
Shall We Save The 'Follow-on' by Herbert Hewett   (p400-404)
Steeplechasers and the Law of Objections by Richard Green-Price   (p404-408)
The Early Days of Stage Coaches (part 2) by William Blew   (p409-413)
Arthur Nightingall by Comyns Cole   (p413-414)
Our Van [inc. Aintree Meeting; The French Turf (article by Georges des Farges in *La Vie
        Contemporaine*); Hertfordshire Hunt; University Sport; Durham County Cricket
        Club]   (p415-429)

Summary of Results for November 1893 (p430-432)

Volume 61, January - June 1894

Issue 407 : January 1894

Portrait [sculp. Stodart] of Arthur Shrewsbury — Title page
Portrait [sculp. Roffe] and Biography - Clayton Swan (p1-3)
Newmarket in Olden Times (part 1) by John Kent (p4-8)
On Berkshire Downs by Herbert Bromhead (p9-14)
Letters on Whist (part 3) by William Deane (p15-16)
Snipe Shooting by James Harting (p16-19)
Engraving [sculp. Scott]: *Snipe Shooting in January* (facing p16)
A Word for Pugilism by Francis Lawley (p19-28)
Our Nimrods by Richard Green-Price (p28-32)
How They Took Their Winnings by Frederick Aflalo (p33-35)
Cornish Cockshooting at Christmastide by Alfred Burden (p35-38)
Cricket: That Hated World Championship by Charles Calverley (p39-42)
My First Run with the Royal Artillery Drag by William Fox-Russell (p42-45)
A Day at Niagara by William Senior (p45-49)
The Sportsman's Library: Reviews of *Hunting Maps* by Arthur Swiss; *The Book of the Horse* (new ed.) by Samuel Sidney; *Forays Among Salmon and Deer* by James Conway and *The Horse World of London* by William Gordon (p49-51)
Our Van [inc. Steeplechase Meetings; South Dorset Hounds; North Herefordshire Hunt; University Sport; Golf Review; Obituary of Thomas Edwards-Moss; Review of *The Live Stock Journal Almanac 1894*] (p52-70)
Correspondence [Stage Coaches] (p70)
Summary of Results for December 1893 (p71-72)

Issue 408 : February 1894

Portrait [sculp. Josey] and Biography - Humphrey de Trafford (p73-75)
Encouragement of Horse Breeding by Richard Green-Price (p75-80)
Newmarket in Olden Times (part 2) by John Kent (p81-86)
Letters on Whist (part 4) by William Deane (p86-88)
Engraving [sculp. Beckwith]: *Pike* (facing p89)
Pike and Pike Fishing by Herbert Bromhead (p89-94)
Punting by Henry Herbert (p94-96)
[Review] *The Pamirs* by Charles Murray reviewed by Francis Lawley (p96-104)
Engraving [sculp. Palfrey]: *Frederick Gale* (facing p105)
Frederick Gale by Comyns Cole (p105-106)
Hunting Reflections by William Blew (p107-113)
The Sportsman's Library: Reviews of *Wisden's Cricketer's Almanack 1894* by Sydney Pardon; *With Horse and Hound in Worcestershire* by Alexander McNeill and *Riding Recollections* by Henry Custance (p113-117)
A Plea for English Golfers by Charles Smith (p117-118)
The Ethics of Coursing by Gordon MacPherson (p118-121)
On Hunting Foxes in France by Coulson Pitman (p122-124)
The Future of Hunting by Mavis Enderby (p125-128)
Our Van [inc. General Stud Book Supplement; Sinnington Hounds; Obituaries of Charles Payne, Scott Browne and William Sherley; University Sport; Royal Norwich Golf Club] (p129-142)
Correspondence [Stage Coaches] (p142)
Summary of Prominent Results for January 1894 (p142-144)

Issue 409 : March 1894

Portrait [sculp. Roffe] and Biography - Herbert Williams-Wynn (p145-147)
Inns and Inn Signs by William Blew (p148-152)
Letters on Whist (part 5) by William Deane (p153-155)
Sportsmen and Tobacco (p156-159)
His Favourites by Richard Green-Price (p159-164)
Engraving [sculp. Engleheart]: *East Essex Fox Hounds* (facing p161)
Barbs as Polo Ponies for English Players (p164-167)
Skaters, Skating and Skates by Edwin Sachs (p167-170)
From a Queensland Station: Horse Breaking (p170-172)
Shooting on Norwegian 'Ski' by Edward Kennedy (p173-177)
Xenophon on Horsemanship by Francis Lawley (p177-185)
Was Walter Scott an Angler by William Senior (p185-192)
Hunting in the Tropics by John Green (p192-196)
Our Van [inc. Lancashire Steeplechase; Sandown Park Meeting; North Cheshire Hounds;
          Mid-Kent Staghounds; Obituaries of George Whitemore and Thomas Adams;
          University Sport; Ladies Golf Union; Gamekeepers' Benefit Society; National
          Whippet Racing Club] (p197-214)
Summary of Results for February 1894 (p215-216)

Issue 410 : April 1894

Portrait [sculp. Alais] and Biography - Walter Gilbey (p217-221)
The Hunting Season by Richard Green-Price (p221-225)
Trout Culture (part 1) by Thomas Andrews (p225-229)
The Football Season of 1893-94 by Charles Smith (p229-230)
Science and the Turf (part 1) by Henry Herbert (p231-233)
Gentlemen Riders : Frank Atkinson, Percival Bewicke, Charles Thompson, William Moore
          and Gerald Milne by Herbert Bromhead (p233-241)
Engraving [sculp. Palfrey]: *Frank Atkinson* (on p234)
Engraving [sculp. Palfrey]: *Percival Bewicke* (on p235)
Engraving [sculp. Palfrey]: *Charles Thompson* (on p237)
Engraving [sculp. Palfrey]: *William Moore* (on p239)
Engraving [sculp. Palfrey]: *Gerald Milne* (on p240)
Letters on Whist (part 6) by William Deane (p242-249)
The Story of Appomattox by Francis Lawley (p250-257)
Some Oxford Recollections [Steeplechasing] (p257-260)
The Army and Quorn versus Pytchley Point-to-Point Races (p260-264)
Two Sporting Kings of France by Coulson Pitman (p264-267)
Our Van [inc. Gatwick Meeting; Grand Military Steeplechase; Rothschild's Staghounds;
          Waterloo Cup; University Boat Race; Obituaries of George Knox plus Herbert
          Bromhead and Edward Davies (both *Baily's* contributors)] (p267-286)
Summary of Results for March 1894 (p286-288)

Issue 411 : May 1894

Portrait [sculp. Roffe] and Biography - John Thursby (p289-291)
The Philosophy of Driving by Septimus Berdmore (p291-295)
Greensward Sermons (part 1): The Amateur Cricketer by Frederick Gale (p295-300)
On a Norwegian Lake by Henry Bryden (p301-304)
Engraving [sculp. Engleheart]: *Touchstone* (facing p305)
Touchstone by Richard Green-Price (p305-311)
Are Trout Educated by Frederic Halford (p311-316)

Broncho Days [verses] by Bertram Tennyson (p316-317)

A Narrow Squeak by Thomas Whimbrel (p318-320)

Sportsman's Library: Reviews of *L'Elevage du Pur Sang en France* by Georges Des Farges; *The Education of the Horse* by Esli Crocker; *Modern Dogs* by Rawdon Lee; *Cricket* (5th ed.) by Allan Steel (p321-325)

Bicycling Politics by Hewitt Griffin (p325-327)

Unlucky Racehorses by William Pooley (p328-330)

Trout Culture (part 2) [Illustrated] by Thomas Andrews (p331-335)

Billiards: Past, Present and Future by Sydenham Dixon (p336-341)

Our Van [inc. Northampton Races; Aylesbury Steeplechases; The Nimrod Club; Puckeridge Hunt Settlement; Obituaries of Andrew Miles, George Baird and George Brudenell-Bruce; University Sport; County Golf] (p342-358)

Summary of Results for April 1894 (p358-360)

Issue 412 : June 1894

Portrait [sculp. Allingham] and Biography - Sammy Woods (p361-363)

Our June Racing by Richard Green-Price (p364-368)

About Some Polo Clubs (part 1) by James Moray-Brown (p368-375)

Fox and Cox [verses] (p375-376)

Engraving [sculp. Parr]: *Bond's Norfolk Phenomenon* (facing p377)

The Norfolk Hackney by Romer Williams (p377-380)

Accidents and Wounds by Francis Lawley (p380-387)

Some Old-Time Athletes (part 1) by Sydenham Dixon (p387-391)

Before the Curtain (p391-395)

Opening of the Cricket Season by Sydney Pardon (p395-399)

London Coaches and Their Routes (part 1) by William Blew (p399-404)

Rowing by Claude Holland (p405-407)

The Sportsman's Library: Reviews of *Modern Dogs: Terriers* by Rawdon Lee; *The Arabian Horse* by William Tweedie and *Fifty Years of My Life* by John Astley (p407-413)

Arthur Shrewsbury by Comyns Cole (p413-414)

Our Van [inc. Chester Meeting; Lingfield Racecourse; Manchester Cup; Cart Horse Society; Royal Liverpool Golf Club; Suffolk Hunt] (p414-430)

Summary of Results for May 1894 (p431-432)

Volume 62, July - December 1894

Issue 413 : July 1894

Portrait [sculp. Stodart] of Edmund Bentley, huntsman Title page

Portrait [sculp. Roffe] and Biography - Maurice de Hirsch (p1-3)

Horse Breeding in Two Hemispheres by George Lynes (p3-7)

The Lounger by Richard Green-Price (p7-12)

A Dialogue on Driving by Thomas Dale (p12-15)

The King of Games [verses] (p15)

Dogs and Their Training by Rawdon Lee (p16-20)

Engraving [sculp. Engleheart]: *Dog Breaking* (facing p16)

Greensward Sermons (part 2): The Cricket Club by Frederick Gale (p21-26)

About Some Polo Clubs (part 2) by James Moray-Brown (p26-33)

Cricket by Sydney Pardon (p34-38)

London Coaches and Their Routes (part 2) by William Blew (p38-43)

Rowing by Claude Holland (p44-47)

Some Old-Time Athletes (part 2) by Sydenham Dixon (p47-51)

The Sportsman's Library: Reviews of *Sport in Somaliland* by Frederic Glyn; *The Manual of Drill and Physical Education* by Thomas Chesterton; *The Lower and Mid-Thames* by Frederick Amphlett; *Thames and Tweed* by George Rooper, and *Thrown Away* by Nat Gould (p51-54)

Our Van [inc. Epsom Meeting; Richmond Horse Show; Review of *Shallows* by Myra Swan; University Sport; Sandwich Golf; Launch of *Polo Magazine*] (p55-70)

Summary of Results for June 1894 (p70-72)

Issue 414 : August 1894

Portrait [sculp. Allingham] and Biography - Martin Hawke (p73-75)
Fish and Fishing at the English Lakes by Rawdon Lee (p75-81)
A Famous Yacht by Brooke Heckstall-Smith (p82-83)
The Rules of Polo by Thomas Dale (p83-85)
The Early Days of English Sculling by John Jeffery (p85-88)
Engraving [sculp. Topham]: *Starting for the Cup* (facing p89)
Starting for the Cup by Penry Palfrey (p89-90)
London Coaches and Their Routes (part 3) by William Blew (p90-97)
Cricket by Sydney Pardon (p98-102)
Trout Culture (part 3) by Thomas Andrews (p102-108)
Are Racehorses Overtrained by Francis Lawley (p109-116)
Rowing by Claude Holland (p116-119)
The Peterborough Hound Show by Comyns Cole (p120-125)
Some Old Time Athletes (part 3) by Sydenham Dixon (p126-130)
Our Van [inc. Newmarket Racing; Hurst Park Meeting; University Sport; Hampton Court Stud; Tooting Bec Golf Club] (p130-142)
Summary of Results for July 1894 (p142-144)

Issue 415 : September 1894

Portrait [sculp. Roffe] and Biography - William Patterson (p145-147)
How Long Will Foxhunting Live by Francis Lawley (p148-153)
Red and Black Grouse by Frank Bonnett (p154-157)
An Indian Sky Meeting by Francis Harvey (p157-161)
Engraving [sculp. Woodman]: *Partridge Shooting* (facing p161)
Partridge Shooting by Penry Palfrey (p161-162)
Cricket by Sydney Pardon (p163-171)
Bradley's Little Game (p172-176)
Sport on Exmoor by Maud Wynter (p176-181)
Photograph: *Arthur Heal – Huntsman Devon & Somerset Staghounds* (facing p176)
Greensward Sermons (part 3): Forming an Eleven by Frederick Gale (p181-186)
The Sportsman's Library: Reviews of *At the Sign of the Wicket* by Edmund Christian; *Among Men and Horses* by Horace Hayes; *Hints on Driving* by Morley Wright; *The Grouse* by Hugh Macpherson; *Shooting* by Archibald Stuart-Wortley; *History of the English Landed Interest* by Russell Garnier; *The Tidal Streams of the West Coast of Scotland* by Howard Collins; *North Again Golfing This Time* by William Raston; *Humerous Golf Sketches* by Charles Edmondson; *The Norfolk Cricket Annual 1894* by Robin Legge (p187-196)
Engraving [pinx. Thorburn]: *Old Grouse on the Tops* (facing p192)
The Public School Cricket Season 1894 by Charles Smith (p197-198)
The Totalisator in New Zealand by Cunningham MacGregor (p199-202)
Our Van [inc. Stockton Cricket Club; Bramham Moor Hunt; Haydon Hounds; Woodnorton Harriers; Belfast Regatta; Norfolk County Golf; Cheltenham Archery] (p202-213)
Correspondence [Soil in Horse Breeding] (p213-214)

Summary of Results for August 1894   (p214-216)

Issue 416 : October 1894

Portrait [sculp. Allingham] and Biography - Algernon Borthwick   (p217-218)
Is Racehorse Breeding a Lottery by John Doyle   (p218-223)
Through the Bracken by Richard Green-Price   (p224-228)
September Cricket by Sydney Pardon   (p229-232)
Engraving [sculp. Beckwith]: *A Precipitate Leap*   (facing p233)
A Precipitate Leap by Penry Palfrey   (p233-234)
An Old-Fashioned Trainer by Francis Lawley   (p234-241)
Bicyclists and the Roads by Hewitt Griffin   (p242-244)
The Norwegian Salmon Fishery Report by Fraser Sandeman   (p245-248)
Farm Buildings [Illustrated] by Charles Curtis   (p249-255)
Engraving [sculp. Spring]: *Amongst the Firs and Larches*   (facing p257)
The Sportsman's Library: Reviews of *Game Birds and Shooting Sketches* by John Millais;
        Collecting and Preserving Trophies by Rowland Ward; *Poems in Pink* by
        William Philpotts-Williams; *The Match of the Season* by John Trew-Hay and
        Cruising in the Netherlands by Christopher Davies   (p257-262)
Engraving [sculp. Sleigh]: *Varieties of Greyhen*   (on p258)
At the Shearers' Shed by Guy Eden   (p263-270)
Tiger Incidents in Assam by John Fife-Cookson   (p271-272)
Our Van [inc. Doncaster Meeting; Derby Horse Show; East Sussex Hounds; Mid-Devon Hunt;
        Royal Dublin Golf Club; Obituary of Frank Beers]   (p272-286)
Correspondence [Horse Breeding in Virginia]   (p286)
Summary of Results for September 1894   (p287-288)

Issue 417 : November 1894

Portrait [sculp. Roffe] and Biography - Frederick Lort-Phillips   (p289-290)
Old Coaching Days by Francis Lawley   (p291-298)
Our New Pink by Richard Green-Price   (p298-302)
The Chiddingfold Hunt by Frederick Gale   (p302-305)
Engraving [sculp. Alais]: *Graham Cooper and the Chiddingfold Hounds*   (facing p304)
Our Subsidiary Winter Games: Hockey and Lacrosse by Edwin Sachs   (p305-310)
A Kennel Dialogue by Rawdon Lee   (p311-315)
Some Big Jumps by Edward Spencer   (p315-321)
The Fleece of Victory [verses] by Norman Gale   (p321)
Some New Masters of Foxhounds: Penn Sherbrooke (Sinnington); George Bowen (Newmarket
        & Thurlow); Seymour Dubourg (South Berks); Lancelot Bathurst (Puckeridge)
        and Henry Lambe (Eggesford)   (p322-325)
Photograph [Hadley]: *Penn Sherbrooke*   (facing p322)
Photograph [Downey]: *Lancelot Bathurst*   (facing p324)
Photograph [Yeo]: *Henry Lambe*   (facing p326)
Photograph [Elliott]: *Seymour Dubourg*   (facing p328)
Photograph [Edwards]: *George Bowen*   (facing p330)
Opening of the Hunting Season by Edward Cuming   (p326-330)
The Three Jonahs in British Columbia by Charles Wolley   (p330-338)
The County Cricket Championship by Sydney Pardon   (p339-341)
Mahaseer Fishing in the Kurram River by William Davis   (p342-343)
Our Van [inc. Kempton Park Meeting; Gatwick Races; Obituaries of John Astley, Robert
        Sherwood, Frederick Fane, Thomas Corrigan and Francis Dougles; Association
        Football; Bournemouth Golf Club; Carbery Hunt Club; Blankney Hounds]   (p343-357)
Correspondence [Fox Hunting]   (p358)
Summary of Results for October 1894   (p358-360)

Issue 418 : December 1894

Portrait [sculp. Roffe] and Biography - Henry Nevill (p361-363)
Racehorses and Their Friends by John Kent (p364-368)
Some Past Masters of Foxhounds (part 1): William Vane by William Blew (p368-373)
Sport in Kumaon and Ghurwal, Himalayas by Richard Tyacke (p374-377)
Engraving [sculp. Kernot]: *The Tout* (facing p376)
About Touts by Edward Spencer (p377-382)
The Sportsman's Library: Reviews of *Les Courses en France et a l'Etranger* by Georges des Farges; *Heavy Horses* by Herman Biddell and *Sporting Days in Southern India* by Arthur Pollock (p383-390)
Engraving [sculp. Virol]: *French Racecourses I* (facing p385)
Engraving [sculp. Virol]: *French Racecourses II* (facing p387)
A Veteran Sportsman: Robert Watson by Daly Devereux (p391-393)
Engraving [sculp. Palfrey]: *Robert Watson* (on p391)
William Gregory's Autobiography by Francis Lawley (p393-400)
Our Hunting Coffers by Richard Green-Price (p401-405)
Land at Last by Frederick Gale (p405-409)
Golf in 1894 by Charles Smith (p409-412)
Edmund Bentley by Comyns Cole (p412-413)
Our Van [inc. Aintree Meeting; Obituaries of Caroline Graham and Dudley Persse; Whaddon Chase Hunt; Cambridgeshire Hounds; Enfield Chace Staghounds; Rugby Union and Professionalism] (p413-428)
Correspondence [Steeplechase Jumps] (p429-430)
Summary of Results for November 1894 (p430-432)

Fraser Sandeman

Volume 63, January - June 1895

Issue 419 : January 1895

Portrait [sculp. Palfrey] of Johnny Briggs, cricketer	Title page
Portrait [sculp. Alais] and Biography - George Saxe-Coburg	(p1-4)
Phasianus Colchicus by Francis Lawley	(p4-11)
Modern Hound Breeding by Gerald Ricardo	(p12-15)
Woodcocks by James Harting	(p15-18)
Engraving [sculp. Beckwith]: *A Pied Woodcock*	(facing p17)
Sport: Its Assailants and Defenders by John Doyle	(p18-25)
Schooling by Edward Spencer	(p25-31)
Science and the Turf (part 2) by Henry Herbert	(p31-33)
Seasonable Advice by Horace Hayes	(p33-36)
Shoulder to Shoulder by Richard Green-Price	(p36-41)
Some Past Masters of Foxhounds (part 2): Ralph Lambton by William Blew	(p41-47)
Cricket Arrangements by Sydney Pardon	(p47-49)
Polo Ponies by Edward Miller	(p49-55)
Engraving [sculp. Palfrey]: *Arab Stallion Sir Robert*	(on p50)
Engraving [sculp. Palfrey]: *Thoroughbred Stallion Rosewater*	(on p51)
Engraving [sculp. Stodart]: *Barb Stallion Awfully Jolly*	(on p53)
The Sportsman's Library: Reviews of *African Hunting and Adventure* by William Baldwin; *Cheshire Hunt* by John Cornish; *Sir Victor Brooke: Sportsman and Naturalist* by Leslie Stephen; *The Life of Admiral Lord Collingwood* by Clark Russell and *Live Stock Journal Almanac 1895*	(p56-61)
Our Van [inc. Newmarket Steeplechasing; Obituaries of James Weatherby, James Moray-Brown (*Baily's* contributor), William Sensier, Charles Meyer, John Hart, Charles Sarderson and John Lomax; Association Football; Mid-Kent Staghounds; England Cricketers in Australia]	(p62-78)
Summary of Results for December 1894	(p79-80)

Issue 420 : February 1895

Portrait [sculp. Alais] and Biography - Merthyr Guest	(p81-84)
The Gentleman Troller by William Senior	(p85-90)
Some Past Masters of Foxhounds (part 3): John Farquharson by William Blew	(p90-96)
Engraving [sculp. Wells]: *Thomas Kennedy*	(facing p97)
One in Ten Thousand by Charles Stanhope	(p97-98)
Hunting Reminiscences by Charles Gordon-Lennox	(p98-101)
Cross Country Cracks by Edward Spencer	(p102-108)
Good Runs and Great Hunts [Illustrated] by Harry Sargent	(p108-116)
Looking Ahead by Frederick Gale	(p116-120)
To a Favourite Hunter [verses] by Hanbury Williams	(p120-121)
English Thoroughbreds in the United States by William Gilpin	(p122-125)
The Poet Sportsman of the Eighteenth Century	(p125-128)
The Sportsman's Library: Reviews of *Wisden's Cricketers' Almanack 1895* by Sydney Pardon and *Thoughts Upon Sport* by Harry Sargent	(p129-132)
Sporting Parsons by John Kent	(p132-133)
Our Van [inc. The Sporting League; Obituaries of Thomas Andrews, Alexander Clark-Kennedy (*Baily's* contributor), Frederick Barrett, Joseph Watson and William Tailby; Bicester Hunt; Teme Valley Hounds; Australian Cricket]	(p133-149)
Correspondence [A Tiger Story]	(p149-151)
Summary of Results	(p151-152)

Issue 421 : March 1895

Portrait [sculp. Allingham] and Biography - Hugh Dawnay	(p153-154)
Old Days at Baden Baden (part 1) by Comyns Cole	(p155-156)
Fox Hunting in Bechuanaland by Henry Bryden	(p157-163)
Veterinary Surgeons and Horse Owners by Horace Hayes	(p163-166)
The Pruning of Forest Trees	(p166-169)
Engraving [sculp. Bright]: *Thoroughbred Stallion Wisdom*	(facing p169)
Wisdom by Richard Green-Price	(p169-173)
Two Great Players of Ball-Games by William Clews	(p174-183)
Told in 1894 [verses] by Harry Cumberland-Bentley	(p183-184)
The Red Light	(p184-186)
Rabies and Hydrophobia by Gregory Benoni	(p186-188)
A Famous Run [part verses] by Richard Green-Price	(p189-190)
Looking Back by Frederick Gale	(p191-194)
The Rubber Game [Melbourne Test Match] by Sydney Pardon	(p195-196)
The Sportsman's Library: Review of *An Angler's Paradise* by Joseph Armistead	(p196-198)
Some Past Masters of Foxhounds (part 4): Sir Tatton Sykes by William Blew	(p199-204)
Steeplechase Courses of the Past: Bromley, Croydon and Eltham by William Fox-Russell	(p204-207)
The Huntsman's Dodge by Finch Mason	(p207-210)
Our Van [inc. Ice Skating; Llangibby Hunt; Obituary of Elim D'Avigdor; West Norfolk Hounds; Holderness Hunt; Isle of Wight Agricultural Society]	(p211-223)
Summary of Results for February 1895	(p223-224)

Issue 422 : April 1895

Portrait [sculp. Roffe] and Biography - Charles Hylton	(p225-227)
[Obituaries] Two Blanks in the Cricket World: Frederick Ponsonby and James Pycroft by Frederick Gale	(p227-232)
Old Days at Baden Baden (part 2) by Comyns Cole	(p232-235)
Veterinary Progress (part 1) by Horace Hayes	(p235-237)
Retrospect of Sport in Cachar	(p238-240)
At Beche Wood [verses] by Bruce Lowsley	(p240)
Engraving [pinx. Mathews]: *Cloister*	(facing p241)
Some Owners and Riders: Charles Duff, Walter Beevor, Albert Ripley, Herbert Ripley, Cecil Grenfell, Cuthbert Slade and Henry Powell by John Maunsell-Richardson	(p241-253)
Engraving [sculp. Palfrey]: *Charles Duff*	(on p241)
Engraving [sculp. Palfrey]: *Walter Beevor*	(on p243)
Engraving [sculp. Palfery]: *Albert Ripley*	(on p245)
Engraving [sculp. Palfrey]: *Herbert Ripley*	(on p247)
Engraving [pinx. Haigh]: *Father O'Flynn*	(facing p249)
Engraving [sculp. Palfrey]: *Cecil Grenfell*	(on p249)
Engraving [sculp. Palfrey]: *Cuthbert Slade*	(on p250)
Photograph [Hailey]: *The Midshipmite*	(facing p251)
Engraving [sculp. Palfrey]: *Henry Powell*	(on p251)
Engraving [pinx. Jones]: *Van der Berg*	(facing p252)
The Charlton Hunt and the Goodwood Hounds by William Blew	(p253-259)
An Unbearable Recollection	(p260-266)
The Sportsman's Library: Reviews of *Hints on Billiards* by John Buchanan; *Sketches in the Hunting Field* by Alfred Watson; *The Tetcott Hunt Week* by John Wollocombe, and *A History of the Fox-Terrier* by Rawdon Lee	(p267-269)
The Shooting Season of 1894 in Norway by Fraser Sandeman	(p269-273)
In Dotterel Land by John Cordeaux	(p274-278)

Our Van [inc. Gatwick Meeting; Waterloo Cup; Newmarket & Thurlow Hunt; Welsh Hounds;
          South Berkshire Harriers; Obituary of Jack Treadwell; Hampshire & Isle of Wight
          Golf Association; Rugby Union County Championship]   (p278-294)
Correspondence [Wisdom ownership]   (p295)
Summary of Results for March 1895   (p295-296)

Issue 423 : May 1895

Portrait [sculp. Roffe] and Biography - Harry McCalmont   (p297-299)
The Cream of the Racing Season by Richard Green-Price   (p300-304)
Hitting Below the Belt by Frederick Gale   (p305-308)
Wild-Fowling on the Shannon by Charles Hickie   (p308-312)
Engraving [sculp. Yates]: *The Fox's Head*   (facing p313)
Kennels (part 1) [Illustrated] by Harry Sargent   (p313-319)
The Coming Polo Season by Thomas Dale   (p319-325)
Engraving [sculp. Palfrey]: *Snorter*   (facing p321)
Engraving [sculp. Bradley]: *A Backhander*   (facing p323)
The Sportsman's Library: Reviews of *Life and Times of The Druid* by Francis Lawley; *Birds,
          Beasts and Fishes of the Norfolk Broadland* by Peter Emerson; *Through a Field
          Glass* by George Underhill; *Polo* by James Moray-Brown, and *Thirty Years of
          Shikar* by Edward Braddon   (p325-333)
Engraving [sculp. Babbage]: *From the Orkneys to Kensington*   (on p326)
Point-to-Point Steeplechases by Edward Spencer   (p333-338)
On the Art of Driving a Team by Henry Hothfield   (p339-341)
Veterinary Progress (part 2) by Horace Hayes   (p341-344)
Alton Strip [verses] by Norman Innes   (p344-345)
Soldiers in the Saddle 1895 by Frederick Gresham   (p346-348)
Polo in India by Charles Newmarch   (p348-349)
A Cambridge Town and Gown by Cuthbert Bradley   (p350-355)
An Anecdote of John Press by Henry Festing   (p355-356)
With the Devon Minnow by Alfred Burden   (p356-359)
Our Van [inc. The Druid Library; Newmarket Meeting; Obituaries of Thomas Towneley and
          John Cowan; Cheshire Farmers; Puckeridge Hunt; Eggesford Hounds; University
          Boat Race; Yorkshire Union Golf]   (p359-373)
Correspondence [Ladies on Horseback]   (p373-374)
Summary of Results for April 1895   (p375-376)

Issue 424 : June 1895

Portrait [sculp. Roffe] and Biography - Stanley Jackson   (p377-380)
Eccentricities of Horse-Breeding by Francis Lawley   (p380-386)
Notes on the Rifle (part 1) by Thomas Fremantle   (p387-390)
The Long Dogs [verses] by Bertram Tennyson   (p391)
The Tennis Championship by Charles Heathcote   (p391-393)
Engraving: *John Herring*   (facing p393)
Animal Painters: John Frederick Herring senior by Walter Gilbey   (p393-395)
Engraving [sculp. Scott]: *Elis*   (facing p395)
Hound Music, Hound Language by Edward Pennell-Elmhirst   (p396-398)
Drawing [pinx. Birch]: *Stallion Stables*   (facing p399)
Boxes for Stallions [Illustrated] by John Birch   (p399-405)
Engraving [sculp. Palfrey]: *Hunter Brood Mares Scarlet and Dorothy*   (facing p405)
Hunter Prizes at Horse Shows by William Blew   (p405-411)
Engraving [sculp. Babbage]: *Swallow*   (facing p409)
A Famous Gentleman Rider: Thomas Townley by Finch Mason   (p411-415)

Engraving [sculp. Palfrey]: *Thomas Townley*	(on p413)
Mules and Mule Breeding by William Tegetmeier	(p416-422)
Engraving [sculp. Werrotrawl]: *Poitou Mule Brunette*	(facing p419)
Engraving [sculp. Werrotrawl]: *English Mule*	(facing p421)
Cricket by Sydney Pardon	(p423-427)
Sporting Pictures at the Royal Academy by Comyns Cole	(p428-430)
That Mayfly Day by William Senior	(p430-434)
Kennels (part 2) by Harry Sargent	(p435-440)
W.G. [verses]	(p440)
Johnny Briggs by Comyns Cole	(p441-442)
Our Van [inc. Obituaries of William Douglas-Hamilton and Robert Peel; Old Berkshire Hunt West; Hurlingham Polo; Amateur Golf Championship; Continental Rowing; University Sport]	(p443-462)
Summary of Results for May 1895	(p462-464)

Volume 64, July - December 1895

Issue 425 : July 1895

Portrait [sculp. Palfrey] of Richard Yeo, huntsman	Title page
Portrait [sculp. Alais] and Biography - John Corlett	(p1-3)
Ocean Lanes by Francis Lawley	(p4-11)
Notes on the Rifle (part 2) by Thomas Fremantle	(p11-15)
Neque .. Post Equitem Sedet Atra Cura [verses] by Roland Rivington	(p15-16)
Hound Breeding by Richard Green-Price	(p16-20)
Photograph [pinx. Natsteaval]: *The Craven Vagabond*	(facing p16)
Engraving: *Abraham Cooper*	(facing p21)
Animal Painters: Abraham Cooper by Walter Gilbey	(p21-23)
Engraving [pinx. Cooper]: *Thomas Waring*	(facing p22)
The Best of the Best by Frederick Gale	(p23-26)
The Bicycle for Ladies by Hewitt Griffin	(p26-29)
Veterinary Progress (part 3) by Horace Hayes	(p29-32)
Engraving [pinx. Gilbert]: *Priam Winning The Gold Cup*	(facing p33)
A Great Racehorse: Priam by John Kent	(p33-38)
A Mail Coach by William Blew	(p38-41)
Engraving [sculp. Swain]: *A Glimpse of the Past*	(facing p38)
Cricket by Ogle Moore	(p42-46)
Grandfather Pike by Harry Cumberland-Bentley	(p47-49)
Racing in the Antipodes by Henry Verney	(p49-52)
The Sportsman's Library: *Reviews of A Mixed Bag* by William Senior; *The Horse Breeder's Handbook* by Joseph Osborne and *La Race Pure en France* by Georges des Farges	[p53-56)
Days in Norway by William Senior	(p57-61)
Racing Subalterns by Peter Prince	(p61-64)
Our Van [inc. Cart-Horse Parade; Manchester Cup; Richmond Horse Show; Ranelagh Polo Pony Show; University Sport; East Midlands Golf Union]	(p64-77)
Correspondence [Horse Breeding]	(p77)
Summary of Results for June 1895	(p78-80)

* A statement from the publishers reads: "Baily's Magazine is the only periodical of its class that every month presents to its readers a steel engraved plate. In future this feature will be continued while the other illustrations will be increased and the size of the Magazine enlarged."*

Issue 426 : August 1895

Portrait [sculp Allingham] and Biography - Philip Le Gallais (p81-83)
Mr Gladstone's Coaching Days by Francis Lawley (p84-91)
An Otter Hunt by Arthur Hussey (p91-95)
Buying and Hiring Hunters for Leicestershire by Horace Hayes (p95-96)
Engraving [sculp. Fry]: *Benjamin Marshall* (facing p97)
Animal Painters: Benjamin Marshall by Walter Gilbey (p97-99)
Notes on the Rifle (part 3) by Thomas Fremantle (p99-106)
Engraving [pinx. Baker]: *Rifleman Presenting - Prone Position* (facing p101)
Engraving [pinx. Baker]: *Rifleman Presenting - Back Position* (facing p103)
The Close of the Polo Season by Thomas Dale (p106-108)
Amateur Cricket at the Universities by Frederick Gale (p109-112)
An Autocrat of the River (p112-114)
Engraving [sculp. Beckwith]: *Salmon* (facing p113)
Pigeon Shooting by Harry Cumberland-Bentley (p114-120)
Perrott: The Dartmoor Guide by Frederick Doveton (p120-125)
Photograph [Swain]: *James Perrott* (facing p120)
A Cotswold Trout Stream by Joseph Gibbs (p125-130)
Cricket by Ogle Moore (p130-135)
There is Only One Cure for all Malady Sure [verses] (p136)
Engraving [sculp. Babbage]: *The Oakley Dandy* (facing p137)
Peterborough Hound Shows by Gerald Ricardo (p137-143)
The Sportsman's Library: Reviews of *Rifle and Spear with the Rajpoots* by Nora Gardner and
    The Polo Pony Stud Book by William Baxter (143-145)
Our Van [inc. Stockbridge Meeting; Henley Regatta; University Sports; St.Andrews Golf;
    Bisley Shots] (p146-157)
Correspondence [Hound Breeding] (p157)
Summary of Results for July 1895 (p158-160)

Issue 427 : September 1895

Portrait [sculp. Roffe] and Biography - Francis Alexander (p161-163)
A Day's Sea-Fishing by John Russell (p163-166)
Partridge-Shooting Gossip by George Teasdale-Buckell (p166-170)
Notes on the Rifle (part 4): by Thomas Fremantle (p170-174)
Photograph: *Rifle Bullets Showing Rifling Marks* (facing p173)
Public School Cricket in 1895 by Charles Smith (p174-176)
Animal Painters: Charles Henderson by Walter Gilbey (p176-178)
Photograph: Charles Cooper Henderson (facing p176)
Engraving [sculp. Babbage]: *Going to the Fight* [Correct title is *Returning from the Fight*] (facing p178)
St.Leger Favourites (p178-182)
Engraving: *Launcelot and Maroon* (facing p180)
Where is the Old Mill Wheel by Frederick Gale (p182-186)
Our New Legislators by Richard Green-Price (p186-190)
Engraving [sculp. Birch]: *Stud Farm* (facing p191)
The Stud Farm by John Birch (p191-195)
Engraving [sculp. Birch]: *Plan of Stud Farm* (facing p192)
Hack Hunters (p196-199)
Engraving [sculp. Babbage]: *The Hack Hunter* (facing p196)
Falling In by George Sams (p199-203)
Frank Beers: In Memoriam [verses] (on p202)
Autumn Polo by Thomas Dale (p204-207)
Cricket by Ogle Moor (p207-216)

Some Yachting Notes by Brooke Heckstall-Smith (p216-222)

[Obituary] John Jones: Cheshire Huntsman by Richard Green-Price (p223)

Our Van [inc. Goodwood Meeting; Birmingham Racecourse; Nimrod Club; Exmoor Hunting; Obituaries of Henry Daly and William Goodall; Hound Culture in Ireland; Wingfield Sculls; Dublin Horse Show] (p224-238)

Summary of Results for August 1895 (p238-240)

Issue 428 : October 1895

Portrait [sculp. Alais] and Biography - Charles Bulkeley (p241-244)

The Imprisoned Cub by Richard Green-Price (p244-250)

October Sport by George Teasdale-Buckell (p250-253)

The Drop Scene on a Great Success by Frederick Gale (p253-257)

Engraving [sculp. Engleheart]: *The Chase and the Road* (facing p257)

Animal Painters: Samuel Alken, Henry Alken and Henry Gordon Alken by Walter Gilbey (p257-261)

Engraving: *Red Deer* [Horse] (facing p261)

The Chester Cup of 1844 by John Kent (p261-264)

The America's Cup by Brooke Heckstall-Smith (p265-267)

Lepping Lucubrations by Claremont Clare (p267-271)

Stock-Riding in Australia as it Was (p271-272)

Engraving [sculp. Hacker]: *Running a Muck* (facing p273)

Running Amuck by Septimus Berdmore (p273-275)

The Last Race [verses] by Diane Chasseresse (p275-276)

Notes on the Rifle (part 5) by Thomas Fremantle (p276-281)

An Outsider Wins (p281-287)

Mimi by Penry Palfrey (p288-289)

Engraving [sculp. Babbage]: *Mimi* (facing p288)

Humber Shore-Shooting by Leonard West (p289-290)

The Sportsman's Library: Reviews of *Sport on the Pamirs and Turkistan Steppes* by Charles Cumberland; *History of a Hundred Centuries* by Gilbert Grace; *Angling Travels in Norway* by Fraser Sandeman, and *Rugby Cricket Club 1844-94* by David Buchanan (p290-294)

Some Curious Habits of Wildfowl (p295-299)

Single to Oblige by Stephen Gayler (p299-304)

The Hare in Norway by Fraser Sandeman (p305-307)

Our Van [inc. Derby Racing; Doncaster Meeting; Obituaries of James Ashbury, Robert Gosling and Peter McEwan; Midland Horse Show; New York Athletic Club; Cheshire Hunt; Irish Golf Championship] (p308-317)

Correspondence [Rugby Union versus Rugby League] (p317-318)

Summary of Results for September 1895 (p319-320)

Issue 429 : November 1895

Portrait [sculp. Roffe] and Biography - Edward Pennell-Elmhirst (p321-323)

Two London Bankers by Francis Lawley (p323-331)

An Apotheosis of Hunting by Hugh Henry (p331-335)

Animal Painters: John Wootton by Walter Gilbey (p336-339)

Engraving [sculp. Babbage]: *Waiting for the Master* (facing p337)

Engraving [pinx. Wootton]: *The Chase is Over* (facing p338)

Drawn Matches by Frederick Gale (p339-342)

Notes on the Rifle (part 6) by Thomas Fremantle (p343-347)

On the Wrong Side by Edward Spencer (p348-353)

Photograph [Reid]: *Lily Agnes* (facing p353)

Some Noted Stallions and Mares (p353-357)

Photograph [Reid]: *Shotover* (facing p354)

Photograph [Reid]: *Donovan* (facing p356)
Jumping at Horse Shows by Horace Hayes (p357-360)
Photograph [Reid]: *Orme* (facing p358)
Yachting Notes by Brooke Heckstall-Smith (p360-361)
Photograph [Reid]: *Bend Or* (facing p360)
The Willows that Fringe the Brook [verses] by Geoffrey de Holden-Stone (p362-363)
Baseball [with Sketch] (p364-367)
Moonlighting of Cattle in Australia (p367-369)
Up a Tree by Albany de Fonblanque (p369-374)
November for Grayling by William Senior (p374-377)
International Athletics by Archibald Sinclair (p378-380)
The Hunting Season 1895-96 by William Blew (p380-385)
The Sportsman's Library: Reviews of *A Dream's Fulfilment* by Harry Cumberland-Bentley,
    and *The Art of Horse Shoeing* by William Hunting (p385-388)
Our Van [inc. Middle Park Stakes; Ridgway Coursing Club; Corinthians Football Club;
    Midland Counties Golf] (p389-398)
Summary of Results for October 1895 (p398-400)

Issue 430 : December 1895

Portrait [sculp. Alais] and Biography - Evelyn Wood (p401-405)
Some of the Troubles of the Master of Foxhounds by Charles McNeill (p405-407)
A Great Cavalry Soldier [Banastre Tarleton] by Francis Lawley (p408-415)
A Wild Fox by Richard Green-Price (p416-421)
Animal Painters: Samuel Howitt by Walter Gilbey (p421-424)
Engraving [sculp. Howitt]: *Taking Wild Horses on the Plains of Moldavia* (facing p423)
Engraving [sculp. Howitt]: *The Chase* (facing p424)
Can't You Leave it Alone by Frederick Gale (p425-427)
Who-Whoop [verses] by Horace Field (p427)
Sport and Sportsmen in the United States by Albany de Fonblanque (p428-432)
Engraving [sculp. Palfrey]: *Richard Lawley* (facing p433)
Hunting in the Neilgherries (p433-437)
Notes on the Rifle (part 7) [with Sketch] by Thomas Fremantle (p437-441)
A Muddling Run [verses] (p442)
How Do Our Sires Work Out by Richard Green-Price (p443-448)
Billiards by William Broadfoot (p448-451)
The Sportsman's Library: *Reminiscences of a Redcoat* by William Heron-Maxwell (p451-452)
Two Bad Shots by John Halifax (p453-458)
The Cod Fisheries of Lofoden by Fraser Sandeman (p458-461)
Richard Yeo by Comyns Cole (p461)
Our Van [inc. Obituaries of Edwin Weever, James Ryan and George Elliot; Aintree Meeting;
    Bicester Hunt; Eastbourne Harriers; East Kent Foxhounds and London Football
    Association] (p462-478)
Summary of Results for November 1895 (p478-480)

Volume 65, January - June 1896

Issue 431 : January 1896

Portrait [sculp. Palfrey] of Mornington Cannon, jockey Title page
Portrait [sculp. Allingham] and Biography - Vincent Calmady (p1-4)
A Lost Sport by Francis Lawley (p5-13)
A Sportsman Malgre Lui (p13-20)
Animal Painters: James Seymour by Walter Gilbey (p20-22)

Engraving [sculp. Babbage]: *Brushing into Cover* (facing p20)
Notes on the Rifle (part 8) [with Diagrams] by Thomas Fremantle (p23-30)
Yachting by Brooke Heckstall-Smith (p30-31)
Thirteen-Two [verses] by Geoffrey de Holden-Stone (p31-32)
Photograph: *Grace Lowther* (facing p33)
Fair Huntresses (part 1) by William Blew (p33-39)
Photograph [Swain]: *Elizabeth Egerton* (facing p34)
Photograph: *Helen Gerard* (facing p36)
Photograph: *Eleanor Hornsby* (facing p38)
Photograph: *Violet Harter* (facing p39)
[Review] *Breeding Racehorses by the Figure System* by Bruce Lowe reviewed by John Doyle (p40-49)
A Chapter in the History of the Quorn Hounds by William Blew (p49-55)
Fox-Hunting by Edward Pennell-Elmhirst (p55-58)
Tit for Tat (p58-60)
The Sportsman's Library: *Famous Horses* by Theodore Taunton; *Hockey* by Henry Battersby, and *An Idol's Passion* by Irene Osgood (p61-63)
Our Van [inc. Royal Rock Beagle Hunt; The Military Tournament; Croome Hunt; New Forest Deerhounds; Blackheath Rugby; Golf Historians; University Sport] (p63-78)
Summary of Results for December 1895 (p79-80)

Issue 432 : February 1896

Portrait [sculp. Roffe] and Biography - Hugh Browning (p81-82)
Doctors and Sport by Francis Lawley (p83-90)
Animal Painters: Sawrey Gilpin by Walter Gilbey (p90-94)
Painting: *Sawrey Gilpin* (facing p90)
Engraving [sculp. Babbage]: *John Parkhurst* (facing p93)
Fair Huntresses (part 2) by William Blew (p94-100)
Photograph: *Frances Bingham* (facing p95)
Photograph: *Edith Kenyon-Slaney* (facing p96)
Photograph: *Robina Falkiner* (facing p97)
Photograph: *Matilda Joyce* (facing p98)
Notes on the Rifle (part 9) [with Diagram] by Thomas Fremantle (p100-107)
Both Sides of the Shield by Frederick Gale (p107-111)
The Reverie by Harry Cumberland-Bentley (p112-113)
Engraving [sculp. Goodman]: *The Reverie* (facing p112)
Gentleman Charles by George White (p113-119)
Horse, Hound and Horn [verses] (p119-120)
In the Old Coaching Days by William Blew (p121-128)
Early Salmon Fisheries of Scotland by William Murdoch (p128-133)
The Sportsman's Library: Reviews of *In Haunts of Wild Game* by Frederick Kirby; *Wisden's Cricketers' Almanack 1896* by Sydney Pardon; *Practical Wildfowling* by Henry Sharp; *A Cheval* by Baron Charles de Vaux; *Les Grands Veneurs de France* by Baron Charles de Vaux; *The Food of Crops* by Charles Aikman, and *Practical Veterinary Advice for Stockowners* by Alfred Archer (p133-141)
The Spaniel by Frederick Gresham (p141-145)
Our Van [inc. Long Distance Racing; John Thursby's Testimonial; Obituary of James Dougall; Barnton Golf; London Football Association Charity Cup] (p146-159)
Summary of Results for January 1896 (p159-160)

Issue 433 : March 1896

Portrait [Roffe] and Biography - Henry Seymour (p161-163)
The Fashions of Hunting by Richard Green-Price (p163-167)
Engraving [sculp. Scott]: *Breaking Cover* (facing p167)

Animal Painters: Philip Reinagle by Walter Gilbey (p167-171)
Engraving [sculp. Mackenzie]: *Thomas Thornton* (facing p169)
Early Trout Fishing by Michael Watkins (p171-175)
Dimple [Verses] by Harry Cumberland-Bentley (p175-176)
Notes on the Rifle (part 10) [with Diagrams] by Thomas Fremantle (p177-185)
Cross-Country Running by Archibald Sinclair (p185-190)
A Spring Fishing Adventure by William Senior (p190-195)
The Sportsman's Library: Review of *Illustrated Horse Breaking* by Horace Hayes (p196-197)
Photograph: *Margaret de Freville* (facing p197)
Fair Huntresses by William Blew (p197-202)
Photograph: *Kathleen Gott* (facing p198)
Photograph: *Marie Hargreaves* (facing p199)
Photograph: *Lilian Browning* (facing p200)
Photograph: *Marion Green* (facing p201)
Photograph: *Foster Townsend* (facing p202)
Lanercost by Ernest Smith (p202-206)
Photographs: *Elspeth & Cannie Lad* (facing p207)
About Dandies by Edward Spencer (p207-212)
Hunting Incidents by William Blew (p212-217)
Fishing in the Ardennes and Black Forest by Abel Chapman (p217-219)
Where the Ash-Plants Grow [verses] by Geoffrey de Holden-Stone (p219-220)
Hunting in India by Charles Newmarch (p220-223)
Our Van [inc. Gatwick Steeplechasing; Castle Bromwich Meeting; Pytchley Hunt; Cairo Horse
            Show; West Somerset Hounds; University Sport; Waterloo Cup] (p223-238)
Summary of Results for February 1896 (p239-240)

Issue 434 : April 1896

Portrait [sculp. Allingham] and Biography - Charles Cunningham (p241-243)
Engraving [sculp. Babbage]: *Why Not* (facing p242)
St.James's Square by Francis Lawley (p243-252)
Animal Painters: Stephen Elmer by Walter Gilbey (p252-254)
Engraving [sculp. Alais]: *Woodcock* (facing p252)
Trojan by Stephen Elmer (p254-255)
Engraving [sculp. Smith]: *Trojan* (facing p254)
The Season in the Shires by Thomas Dale (p255-258)
Photograph [Robinson]: *The Ireland Ladies Hockey Team* (facing p259)
Ladies Hockey by Edwin Smith (p259-261)
Photograph [Robinson]: *The England Ladies Hockey Team* (facing p260)
Folklore of Indian Animals by John Russell (p261-270)
The Keeper's Zong [verses] by Bernard Lowsley (p270-271)
Engraving [sculp. Bradley]: *The Belvoir Hunt – John Manners and Frank Gillard* (facing p273)
The Belvoir Hunt Changes by Cuthbert Bradley (p273-275)
Bicycling by Hewitt Griffin (p275-278)
A Dream in India [verses] by John White (p279)
A Popular Tobogganer by Arthur Perry (p280-281)
Photograph: *A Famous Tobogganer* (facing p280)
Celebrated Equine Duels by Richard Green-Price (p281-286)
Vincent Calmady [verses] by William Collins (p286)
The Sportsman's Library: Reviews of *The Essex Foxhounds* by Richard Ball; *Modern Polo* by
            Edward Miller; *The Courser's Guide* by Thomas Jones (p287-294)
An Express Journey Fifty Years Ago by Frederick Gale (p294-300)

Our Van [inc. Surrey Steeplechase; Review of *The Memoirs of Claude Champion de Crespigny*;
      Cairo Sports; Obituaries of Vincent Calmady, Edmund Park-Yates, John Jones,
      George Bragg, Charles Peachey and Edwin Neave; Hunters' Improvement Society;
      Essex Hunt Point-to-Point; Pau Golf]   (p300-319)
Photograph [Maull]: Edmund Park-Yates   (facing p306)
Summary of Results for March 1896   (p319-320)

Issue 435 : May 1896

Portrait [sculp. Alais] and Biography - George Leatham   (p321-323)
[Review] Bartholomew Sulivan by Henry Sulivan reviewed by Francis Lawley   (p323-332)
The Row by Richard Green-Price   (p332-336)
Engraving [sculp. Babbage]: *Badger and Dogs*   (facing p337)
Animal Painters: Luke Clennell by Walter Gilbey   (p337-339)
Engraving [sculp. Babbage]: *Riding in a Storm*   (facing p339)
Two-Year-Old Racing by John Kent   (p340-342)
Rooks and Rook Shooting by Thomas Fremantle   (p343-348)
Polo Players: John Watson by Cuthbert Bradley   (p348-350)
Lithograph [sculp. Bradley]: *John Watson on Fritz*   (facing p348)
The Royal Military Tournament by John Russell   (p351-358)
An Old Sportsman to His Old Gun [verses] by Robert Gibbs   (p359)
Creslow: A Famous Fixture of Foxhounds by John Kersley-Fowler   (p360-363)
Photograph [Payne]: *Creslow House*   (facing p360)
The Australians 1896 by Herbert Hewett   (p363-367)
A Modern Roundabout Paper by Frederick Gale   (p368-372)
Whitetail Deer in Rocky Mountains, Alberta [verses] by Michael Holland   (p372-373)
The Sportsman's Library: Reviews of *Hunting in the Golden Days* by Hubert Garle and *Snakes*
      by Herbert Tichborne   (p373-374)
Engraving [sculp. Babbage]: *Changing Horses*   (facing p375)
Posting in all its Branches by John Bluett   (p375-378)
Ponies and Galloways by George Harper   (p378-382)
Our Van [inc. Aintree Pressbox; Althorp Stakes; Obituaries of Henry Stapylton and Gerard
      Hoare; Brocklesby Hunt Week; Belvoir Hounds; North Cotswold Hunt; Olympic
      Games in Athens]   (p382-398)
Summary of Results for April 1896   (p399-400)

Issue 436 : June 1896

Portrait [sculp. Allingham] and Biography - John Hill   (p401-403)
The Hundred Best Patterns of Floating Flies (part 1) by Frederic Halford   (p403-408)
Engraving [sculp. Babbage]: *The Ninth Duke of Hamilton on a Cover Hack*   (facing p409)
Animal Painters: George Garrard by Walter Gilbey   (p409-412)
Engraving [sculp. Palfrey]: *Walter Smythe*   (facing p413)
Hurlingham and Ranelagh by Thomas Dale   (p413-416)
Engraving [sculp. Palfrey]: *Edward Miller*   (facing p415)
The Old Coaching Days by William Blew   (p416-423)
Engraving [sculp. Babbage]: *After a Heavy Stage*   (facing p416)
Racing near the Equator   (p423-427)
Some Curious Horses by Bird Thompson   (p427-435)
Polo Players: William Walker by Cuthbert Bradley   (p436-438)
Lithograph [sculp. Bradley]: *William Walker on Bedouin*   (facing p436)
Photograph: *Magic, A High-Caste Nejd Arab*   (facing p438)
The Olympic Games by Frederick Webster   (p439-441)

Ponies by William Blew (p442-445)
Engraving [sculp. Babbage]: *The First Leap* (facing p442)
Engraving [sculp. Babbage]: *Pony Stallion* Berkeley Model (facing p444)
Cricket by Sydney Pardon (p446-450)
Salmon Records by Augustus Grimble (p450-455)
Fin, Fur and Feather in Ireland by Thomas Poole (p455-458)
Golf on the Sea Links of Scotland by Gordon McPherson (p458-461)
Coaching in Ceylon by Robert Dunkin (p462-467)
Mornington Cannon by Comyns Cole (p467-468)
Our Van [inc. Chester Races; Newmarket Meeting; Hoylake Ladies Golf; Hurlingham Polo; Richmond Horse Show] (p468-486)
Summary of Results for May 1896 (p487-488)

Volume 66, July - December 1896

Issue 437 : July 1896

Portrait [sculp. Palfrey] of Harry Bonner, huntsman Title page
Portrait [sculp. Roffe] and Biography - Rudolph Lehmann (p1-3)
[Review] *A Manual of Forestry* by William Schlich reviewed by Francis Lawley (p3-14)
Royalty and Sport by Richard Green-Price (p14-18)
Animal Painters: Dean Wolstenholme snr by Walter Gilbey (p18-22)
Engraving [sculp. Babbage]: *Gray Pilot* and *Sally* (facing p18)
Engraving [sculp. Babbage]: *Dean Wolstenholme snr* (facing p22)
The Hundred Best Patterns of Floating Flies (part 2) by Frederic Halford (p23-30)
The Irish Eclipse by Edward Spencer (p30-35)
Engraving [sculp. Engleheart]: *Harkaway* (facing p30)
Gibraltar Revisited by Arthur Griffiths (p36-43)
Rowing in 1896 by Reginald Rowe (p44-51)
Photograph*: Douglas McLean* (on p45)
Photograph: *Stanley Muttlebury* (on p46)
Photograph: *Harcourt Gold* (on p47)
Photograph: *William Fernie* (on p49)
Memories of an Old Soldier (part 1): Oakapple by Arthur Griffiths (p52-60)
Polo Players: Alfred 'Toby' Rawlinson by Cuthbert Bradley (p60-63)
Lithograph [sculp. Bradley): *Toby Rawlinson 'Riding Off'* (facing p60)
Our Van [inc. Epsom Meeting; Obituary of Nevill Fitt (*Baily's* contributor); Test Match at Lord's; Ladies' Kennel Association; Sandwich Golf; Dublin Lawn Tennis; Hurlingham Polo Pony Show] (p63-82)
Summary of Results for June 1896 (p82-84)

* From this issue the quality of the magazine's paper improves: it being coated and thicker. There is also a point size increase, a new font and a different printing technique *

Issue 438 : August 1896

Portrait [sculp. Allingham] and Biography - Timothy O'Brien (p85-88)
The Appreciation of Thoroughbred Stock by Francis Lawley (p89-97)
Animal Painters: Dean Wolstenholme jnr by Walter Gilbey (p97-104)
Lithograph: *Dean Wolstenholme jnr* (facing p98)
Engraving [sculp. Babbage]: *The Burial of Tom Moody* (behind p101)
The Death of Tom Moody [Music & Verses] (behind p104)
Memories of an Old Soldier (part 2): Commandant Stirling by Arthur Griffiths (p105-116)
Warlike Archery in England by Walter Sparrow (p116-123)

Sketch: *Early English Archery* (facing p116)
Sketch: *Norman and Early English Archers* (facing p118)
Sketch: *English Archery* (facing p120)
Engraving [sculp. Engleheart]: *Royal Toxopholite Ground, 1836* (facing p122)
The Hundred Best Patterns of Floating Flies (part 3) by Frederic Halford (p123-128)
A Song of the Rod [verses] by Robert Gibbs (p128-129)
The Affair at Abu-Simbel by Arthur Griffiths (p130-135)
Polo Players: Gerald Hardy by Cuthbert Bradley (p136-139)
Lithograph [sculp. Bradley]: *Gerald Hardy on Sailor* (facing p136)
The Lesson of the Varsity Cricket Match by Sydney Pardon (p139-144)
The Sportsman's Library: *Kingsclere* by John Porter (p144-149)
Our Van [inc. Stockbridge Meeting; Lingfield Races; Obituary of Roderic Owen; Peterborough Hound Show; Henley Regatta; Inter-Regimental Polo Cup] (p149-169)
Lithograph: *Tancred*, Champion at Peterborough (facing p157)
Summary of Results for July 1896 (p170-172)

Issue 439 : September 1896

Portrait [sculp. Roffe] and Biography - James Platt (p173-175)
The Noble Art of Self-Defence by Francis Lawley (p175-182)
Trainers and Training by Richard Green-Price (p182-186)
Old-Time Partridge Shooting (p186-189)
Engraving [sculp. Engleheart]: *Old Time Partridge Shooting* (facing p186)
Engraving [sculp. Babbage]: *Pointers and Gamekeeper* (facing p191)
Animal Painters: Henry Chalon by Walter Gilbey (p191-195)
Memories of an Old Soldier (part 3): Bill Thorburn's Last Chance by Arthur Griffiths (p195-201)
The Lament of an Old Cab Horse [verses] by John Wilson (p201-202)
Polo Players: Charles Stanhope by Cuthbert Bradley (p202-205)
Lithograph [sculp. Bradley]: *Charles Stanhope on Ali Baba* (facing p202)
Public School Cricket 1896 by Charles Smith (p205-207)
Some Turf Casualties (part 1) by Edward Spencer (p207-211)
Breeding and Rearing Pheasants as a Profitable Industry (p212-216)
Professional Cricketers of the Past and Present by Frederick Gale (p217-221)
The Sportsman's Library: Reviews of *The Horse-Breeder's Handbook* by Joseph Osborne; *Notes on the Rifle* by Thomas Fremantle; *Dolomite Strongholds* by Sanger Davies; *Modern Dogs: The Terriers* by Rawdon Lee; *Cricket Scores & Biographies* by Arthur Haygarth and *With Boat and Gun in the Yangtze Valley* by Henling Wade (p221-226)
The Strange History of a Doncaster Cup (p227-230)
Our Van [inc. Goodwood Meeting; Redcar Races; Warwickshire Polo; Devon & Somerset Staghounds; Oval Test Match; Walton Regatta; North Berwick Golf Club; Obituaries of Moritz von Zedtwitz and John Millais; Yorkshire Hackneys] (p231-249)
Summary of Results for August 1896 (p250-252)

Issue 440 : October 1896

Portrait [sculp. Roffe] and Biography - Allan Maclean (p253-255)
Australian Bushrangers by Francis Lawley (p255-262)
Engraving [pinx. Barenger]: *Doll* (facing p263)
Animal Painters: James Barenger by Walter Gilbey (p263-265)
Coaching in Ireland at the Time of the Rebellion by William Blew (p265-272)
Some Turf Casualties (part 2) by Edward Spencer (p272-279)
The Cachar Races 1882 (p279-280)
The Family Fox Covert by Cuthbert Bradley (p280-287)
Lithograph [sculp. Bradley]: *The Promising Litter at Home* (facing p280)

Women and Sport (part 1) by Florence Baillie-Grohman (p287-292)
My Charger [verses] by John Wilson (p293)
Memories of an Old Soldier (part 4): The Luck of Sergeant Davis by Arthur Griffiths (p293-304)
The Sportsman's Library: Reviews of *Sport in the Alps* by William Baillie-Grohman;
    Handbook for Lady Cyclists by Lillias Campbell-Davidson, and *Tales of South
    Africa* by Henry Bryden (p304-306)
The Last of the Mohocks by Arthur Griffiths (p306-312)
In the Bayons of the Mexican Gulf by Albany de Fonblanque (p313-315)
Our Van [inc. Doncaster Meeting; Westmeath Polo; Dublin Horse Show; Obituary of John
    Scott; Johannesburg Hunt Club; Windsor & Eton Regatta; Welsh Golf Union;
    Puckeridge Hunt] (p316-330)
Photograph: *Royal Meath* (facing p321)
Summary of Results for September 1896 (p331-332)

Issue 441 : November 1896

Portrait [sculp. Allingham] and Biography - Robert Crewe-Milnes (p333-335)
Two Famous War Chargers by Francis Lawley (p335-345)
Engraving [sculp. Babbage]: *Copenhagen* (facing p337)
Engraving [sculp. Babbage: *Copenhagen* [head] (facing p339)
Engraving: General Lee on *Traveller* (facing p343)
A Hunting Lecture by Richard Green-Price (p346-350)
New Newmarket by Edward Spencer (p350-352)
Engraving [sculp. Hollay]: *Turkeys* (facing p353)
Animal Painters: Francis Barlow by Walter Gilbey (p353-355)
Engraving [sculp. Babbage]: *A View Over the Long Course at Newmarket* (facing p355)
Animal Painters: Peter Tilleman by Walter Gilbey (p355-356)
The Berkeley Hunt by William Blew (p356-360)
Women and Sport (part 2) by Florence Baillie-Grohman (p360-366)
November [verses] by William Phillpotts-Williams (p366-367)
Memories of an Old Soldier (part 5): The Crosses of Fortune by Arthur Griffiths (p367-376)
Will Goodall [verses] by Frederick Kingston (p376-377)
Engraving [sculp. Babbage]: *Jack Stevens* (facing p379)
Huntsmen Past and Present (part 1) by Thomas Dale (p379-382)
Improvements in Bicycles by Edward Trendall (p383-386)
Foot Beagles by Walter Crofton (p386-390)
Photograph: *Prima Donna and Opera* [Beagles] (on p388)
A Day's Wolf-Hunting by Bertram Tennyson (p390-393)
The Hunting Season 1896-97 [with Masters of Foxhounds changes] by Edward Cuming (p394-398)
Our Van [inc. Testimonial for Joseph Osborne (*Baily's* contributor); Kempton Park Meeting;
    Badminton Hunt; Devon & Somerset Staghounds; Corinthian Football Club;
    Irish Golf Championship] (p399-409)
Correspondence [Old Berkeley West Hunt; Amateur Rugby Union] (p409-410)
Summary of Results for October 1896 (p411-412)

Issue 442 : December 1896

Portrait [sculp. Allingham] and Biography - Arthur Balfour (p413-416)
Apology to Deputy-Inspector Joseph Jee (p416)
Influence of Weather Upon Sport by Francis Lawley (p417-423)
Huntsmen and Whippers-In (part 2) by Thomas Dale (p423-428)
The Music of the Pack [verses] (p428)
Engraving: *James Ward* (facing p429)
Animal Painters: James Ward by Walter Gilbey (p429-434)
Engraving: *Monitor* (facing p433)

The Huntsman in Green [verses] by William Phillpotts-Williams (p435)
[Obituary] George Lane-Fox by Comyns Cole (p436-439)
Photograph [Maffett]: *George Lane-Fox* (facing p436)
A Sequence of Elizabethan Sonnets: George Lane-Fox by Eliza Middleton (p440)
Memories of an Old Soldier (part 6): A Loss to the Service by Arthur Griffiths (p441-448)
A Suggestion to Cricketers: The Follow-On by Herbert Hewett (p448-453)
Some Garrison Theatricals by Arthur Griffiths (p454-458)
Learning to Hit a Polo Ball by George Fothergill (p459-461)
Photograph: *Female Pike* (facing p463)
The Lady of the Lake by Michael Goulter-Wood (p463)
When They Wore Tall Hats by Frederick Gale (p464-469)
The Sportsman's Library: *The Life of a Fox* and *Extracts From the Diary of a Huntsman* both by Thomas Smith (p470-472)
Harry Bonner by William Blew (p473-474)
Our Van [inc. George Lane-Fox as a *Baily's* contributor; Aintree Meeting; Quorn Hunt; Border Hounds; Salt Water Angling; University Sport; Romford Golf] (p474-489)
Summary of Results for November 1896 (p489-492)

Abel Chapman

Volume 67, January - June 1897

Issue 443 : January 1897

Portrait [sculp. Palfrey] of Nat Robinson	Title page
Portrait [sculp. Allingham] and Biography - Thomas Bunbury	(p1-5)
Frank Buckland by Francis Lawley	(p5-14)
Engraving: *Frank Buckland*	(facing p11)
Engraving [sculp.Engleheart]: *Loyal Foxhunters*	(facing p15)
Loyal Foxhunters by Richard Green-Price	(p15-19)
The Irish Horsedealer [verses] by William Phillpotts-Williams	(p19)
Engraving [sculp. Babbage]: *Looby at Full Stretch*	(facing p21)
Animal Painters: John Sartorius by Walter Gilbey	(p21-23)
Engraving [pinx. F.Sartorius]: *Mr Bishop's Celebrated Trotting Mare*	(facing p23)
Animal Painters: Francis Sartorius by Walter Gilbey	(p23-24)
Memories of an Old Soldier (part 7): The Wantiga of Madipur by Arthur Griffiths	(p24-33)
Playing Trout in Weedy Rivers by Frederic Halford	(p33-38)
An Appeal [verses] by Harry Cumberland-Bentley	(p38-39)
[Review] *Annals of the Warwickshire Hunt, 1795-1895* by Charles Mordaunt	(p39-46)
Horse-Taming Extraordinary by Edward Spencer	(p46-50)
Heathfowl Shooting on Dartmoor by Edward Caswall	(p50-53)
Huntsmen Past and Present (part 3) by Thomas Dale	(p53-57)
Engraving [pinx. Turner]: *Major-General Wyndham's Foxhounds Breaking Cover*	(facing p55)
The Sportsman's Library: *Records and Reminiscences of Goodwood* by John Kent; *Mr Spinks and His Hounds* by Frederick Lutyens; *The Poetry of Sport* by Hedley Peek; *Plain Poems* by William Phillpotts-Williams; *The Live Stock Journal Almanac 1897* by James Sinclair	(p57-63)
Our Van [inc. Obituary of John Baldwin; Newmarket Steeplechasing; Jockey Club Handicapping; Warwick Racing Club; Snainton Hounds; Rugby Union County Championship]	(p64-78)
Summary of Results for December 1896	(p79-80)

Issue 444 : February 1897

Portrait [sculp. Roffe] and Biography - Charles Lewis	(p81-83)
Scent by Richard Green-Price	(p83-87)
Engraving [sculp. Babbage]: *Coursing - Epsom Downs*	(facing p89)
Animal Painters: John Nott Sartorius by Walter Gilbey	(p89-92)
Animal Painters: John Francis Sartorius by Walter Gilbey	(p92-96)
Engraving [sculp. Babbage]: *Coursing at Hatfield Park*	(facing p95)
Hackney Mare 'Phenomena' by Walter Gilbey	(p97)
Photograph [Gerrard]: *John Bligh*	(facing p99)
The Earl of Darnley by Francis Lawley	(p99-105)
Memories of an Old Soldier (part 8): Private Stubbs of C Troop by Arthur Griffiths	(p106-113)
Two Old London Coaching Inns by William Blew	(p114-116)
October Flighting by Harry Cumberland-Bentley	(p117-119)
Huntsmen Past and Present (part 4) by Thomas Dale	(p119-125)
Engraving [pinx. Prior]: Meet *of Her Majesty's Staghounds*	(facing p121)
We are an Athletic People by Charles Smith	(p125-127)
Gentleman Jack [verses] by Peter Ditchfield	(p127-128)

The Sportsman's Library: Reviews of *Rugby Football* by Fletcher Robinson; *Records of Big Game* by Rowland Ward; *Wisden's Cricketers' Almanack 1897* by Sydney Pardon; *The Chant of a Lonely Soul* by Irene Osgood; *Tales of South Africa* by Henry Bryden; *The Game Laws of England* by George Warry; *A Sporting Tour* by Thomas Thornton; *Points of the Horse* by Horace Hayes]   (p128-138)
The Valley of Orotava and Adjacent Lands by Eric Knight   (p138-141)
Our Van [inc. Lincolnshire Handicap; Windsor Steeplechasing; Fernie Hounds; York & Ainsty Hunt; The Literature of Sea Angling]   (p141-159)
Summary of Results for January 1897   (p159-160)

Issue 445 : March 1897

Portrait [sculp. Allingham] and Biography - William Hine-Haycock   (p161-163)
Some Goodwood Recollections by John Kent   (p163-165)
Salmon Migrations and Angling in Scotland by William Murdoch   (p165-172)
The True Story of 'D'ye Ken John Peel' by Hardwicke Rawnsley   (p173-191)
Lithograph: *John Peel*   (facing p175)
Lithograph: *Old John Peel and his Hounds*   (facing p177)
Photograph [Wilkinson]: *Young John Peel*   (facing p179)
Photograph [Wilkinson]: *John Woodcock Graves*   (facing p181)
Photograph [Wilkinson]: *Ruthwaite*   (facing p183)
Photograph [Wilkinson]: *Kennel of the Famous Pack*   (facing p183)
Photograph [Wilkinson]: *John Peel's Tombstone*   (facing p185)
Photograph [Wilkinson]: *John Peel's Hunting Tackle*   (facing p187)
Engraving [sculp. Lydon]: *John Warde*   (facing p193)
Animal Painters: William Barraud by Walter Gilbey   (p193-196)
Photograph [Barrauds]: *Henry Barraud*   (facing p195)
Animal Painters: Henry Barraud by Walter Gilbey   (p196-198)
Told in the Train by Harry Cumberland-Bentley   (p198-201)
Huntsmen and Whippers-in (part 5) by Thomas Dale   (p201-207)
Memories of an Old Soldier (part 9): The King of Chipanga by Arthur Griffiths   (p207-216)
On Buying Polo Ponies by John Radcliffe   (p216-220)
The Death of the Red Stag [verses] by Robert Gibbs   (p221-222)
Our Van [inc. Sandown Racing; Quorn Hunt Capping; Puckeridge Hounds; Waterloo Cup; Gulf of Genoa Yachting; University Golf; Piscatorial Society Annual Dinner; Obituary of William Duncum]   (p222-238)
Summary of Results for February 1897   (p238-240)

Issue 446 : April 1897

Portrait [sculp. Roffe] and Biography - Henry Tomkinson   (p241-243)
Will 'Capping' Answer by Richard Green-Price   (p243-247)
The Evolution of the Modern Carriage by William Blew   (p247-253)
Away to the River [verses] by Frederick Doveton   (p254)
Engraving [sculp. Babbage]: *British Birds*   (facing p255)
Animal Painters: Luke Cradock by Walter Gilbey   (p255-256)
Animal Painters: William Shepard by Walter Gilbey   (p256)
Animal Painters: Charles Collins by Walter Gilbey   (p256)
Animal Painters: Peter Casteels by Walter Gilbey   (p256-257)
Animal Painters: Thomas Spencer by Walter Gilbey   (p257-258)
Animal Painters: Anthony Walker by Walter Gilbey   (p258)
Whyte-Melville [verses] by William Phillpotts-Williams   (p259)
Engraving [sculp. Babbage]: *The Death of the Fox*   (facing p261)
The Death of the Fox by Walter Gilbey   (p261)
The Chase [verses] by William Somervile   (p261-263)

A Voice from the Bush by Frederick Gale (p263-266)
Old Mess Days and Ways by Arthur Griffiths (p267-271)
In Praise of Number One: Polo by Thomas Dale (p272-275)
Frank Forester by Arthur Bradley (p275-282)
Engraving: *Henry Herbert* (facing p277)
A Racing Retrospect [verses] by Geoffrey de Holden Stone (p283-284)
Memories of an Old Soldier (part 10): Troublous Times by Arthur Griffiths (p285-294)
The Last Run [verses] by Peter Ditchfield (p294)
The London Horse Shows by Comyns Cole (p295-300)
Engraving [sculp. Babbage]: [Hackney Mare] *Orange Blossom* (facing p297)
Photograph [Gibbs]: [Hunter Gelding] *Gendarme* (facing p299)
Our Van [inc. Grand Military Meeting; Hurst Park Court Appeal; Obituary of Henry Linde; Old Berkeley West Hunt; Essex Point-to-Point Races; Tooting Bec Golf Club] (p300-318)
Sporting Intelligence [inc. Obituaries of Arthur Heywood-Lonsdale, John Codling, George Hayhurst-France, James Younge, Harry Linde and Vincent McSwiney; Cannes Yachting; *The Sportsman* Twenty-First Anniversary; Llangibby Foxhounds; Cheshire Hunt] (p318-320)
Summary of Results for March 1897 (p320-322)

* Sporting Intelligence is now incorporating Summary of Results *

Issue 447 : May 1897

Portrait [sculp. Roffe] and Biography - Frederick Stanley (p323-324)
The Angler at Sea by Frederick Aflalo (p325-329)
Some Punchestown Pictures by William Forbes (p329-333)
Lithograph [pinx. Hayes]: *Corinthian Cup, Punchestown 1854* [with Key Plate] (facing p330)
Animal Painters: Richard Barrett Davis by Walter Gilbey (p334-338)
Engraving [sculp. Babbage]: *Luxury* (facing p334)
Engraving [sculp. Babbage]: *Tom Grant* (facing p339)
Huntsmen of Byegone Days: Tom Grant, Goodwood Hunt by George Garrow-Green (p339-341)
Cricket by Sydney Pardon (p341-344)
The Mystery of the Eel by John Bickerdyke (p344-347)
Boxing and Fencing at Cambridge University by Sidney Gillum (p347-349)
You Bet by Richard Green-Price (p349-353)
The Polo Season by Thomas Dale (p353-355)
Orme and Other Savage Thoroughbreds by Francis Lawley (p355-361)
Memories of an Old Soldier (part 11): The Black Mamba by Arthur Griffiths (p361-369)
The Sportsman's Library: *Golf in Theory and Practice* by Harry Everard; *Pheasants* by William Tegetmeier; *A Year in the Fields* by John Burroughs; *Hints for the Hunting Field* by William Wharton; *Hints on Stable Management* by Michael Rimington; *Ferrets* by Nicholas Everitt; *Wild Sports in Ireland* by John Bickerdyke, and *The Tame Fox* by Finch Mason (p370-377)
A Cricket Song [verses] by Peter Ditchfield (p377)
Our Van [inc. Lincoln Handicap; Northampton Meeting; Doveridge Handicap; Bevendean Plate; Whitton Park Cycling Club; Callaly Hounds; Crystal Palace Horse Show; Thames Punting Club; Obituary of Hugh Kirkcaldy] (p378-399)
Sporting Intelligence [inc. Obituaries of Samuel Blake, Hugh Dalziel, John Hodson and William Newcome; Tattersall's Ring Court Ruling; Wore Hunt Steeplechases; Hertfordshire Hounds; Baumber Chases; Liverpool Football] (p399-404)

Issue 448 : June 1897

Portrait [sculp. Roffe] and Biography - Reynold Clement (p405-407)
[Review] *The Stud Book* by Richard Green-Price (p407-412)

Three Days by Arthur Griffiths (p412-417)
Animal Painters: James Pollard by Walter Gilbey (p418-420)
Engraving [sculp. Babbage]: *Fly Fishing* (facing p418)
Engraving [pinx. Green]: *John Warde* (facing p421)
Hunt Masters of Byegone Days: John Warde by Charles Harper (p421-423)
[Obituary] Henry Forester by Francis Lawley (p424-432)
Lithograph [sculp. Bradley]: *Foiled - Number One Caught the Back* (facing p433)
The Opening of the Polo Season by Thomas Dale (p433-436)
Memories of an Old Soldier (part 12): A Bad Lot by Arthur Griffiths (p436-444)
[Obituary] John de Heley Chadwick by Finch Mason (p444-447)
Cricket by Sydney Pardon (p447-450)
The Sportsman's Library: Reviews of *Wild Norway* by Abel Chapman; *The Sportsman in
          Ireland* by Herbert Maxwell (p450-451)
A Day on the Gloucestershire Coln by Stanley Dennis (p451-455)
Bowling by Antony Guest (p455-457)
The Black Panther of Ootcha-Mulla by Edward Almack (p458-463)
Nat Robinson by Comyns Cole (p463-464)
Our Van [inc. Roodee Racing; Obituary of Charles Yorke; Southampton Yacht Club; Muirfield
          Golf; Corinthians Football Club Tour of South Africa; Queens Club Tennis;
          Ladies Hockey in British Columbia] (p465-482)
Sporting Intelligence [inc. Cattistock Hunt; Obituaries of Nicolas Esterhazy, Abraham Bartlett,
          Thomas Gratrex and Henry Brudenell; Review of *Australian Racing Chronicle*] (p482-486)

Volume 68, July - December 1897

Issue 449 : July 1897

Portrait [sculp. Palfrey] of Evan Williams, huntsman Title page
Portrait [sculp. Allingham] and Biography - Debonnaire Monson (p1-3)
Napoleon and Wellington as Sportsmen by John Russell (p3-11)
Animal Painters: David Dalby by Walter Gilbey (p12-14)
Lithograph [pinx. Dalby]: *Lord Harewood's Hunt* (facing p12)
Huntsmen of Byegone Days: John Hoitt by George Garrow-Green (p14-18)
Sketch: *Manor House, Edstone, Warwickshire* (facing p17)
Reminiscences of the Staff College by Arthur Griffiths (p19-26)
Amongst the Downs by Richard Green-Price (p26-30)
Croquet Redivivus by Gerald Hayward (p30-35)
Photograph [Singer]: *Thomas Gratrex* (facing p35)
Thomas Gratrex by Francis Lawley (p35-41)
The Open Champion Cup [Polo] by Thomas Dale (p42-45)
Lithograph [sculp. Bradley]: *Fight for the Open Champion Polo Cup* (facing p42)
Cricket by Sydney Pardon (p45-48)
The Angler's Flies by William Senior (p49-56)
The Sportsman's Library: Reviews of *The Complete Cyclist* by Arthur Pemberton;
          The Migration of Birds by Charles Dixon; *The Encyclopaedia of Sport* by
          Hedley Peek; *In the Land of the Bora* by Robert Dunkin; *Cakes and Ale* by
          Edward Spencer (p57-61)
The Gallery Ride [verses] by Thomas Dale (p61)
Our Van [inc. Epsom Meeting; Ascot Races; Yacht Racing Association; Football Association
          Annual General Meeting; Hoylake Golf; Irish Tennis Championship] (p62-81)
Sporting Intelligence [inc. Obituaries of Frank Silcock and Frank Ward; Kempton Park Betting
          Case; Eskdaile Hunt] (p81-88)

Issue 450 : August 1897

Portrait [sculp. Alais] and Biography - Denis Daly (p89-91)
How to Make a Racehorse by Richard Green-Price (p92-96)
My Grandfather's Journals (part 1): How I won my Commission by Arthur Griffiths (p96-104)
The Deer Paddock by William Jenkins (p104-105)
Engraving [sculp. Engleheart]: *The Deer Paddock* (facing p104)
In an Eastern County by John Russell (p105-114)
The Coming Grouse Season by George Wilson (p115-117)
The Soldiers' Tournaments [Polo] by Thomas Dale (p118-122)
Engraving [sculp. Fry]: *John Scott* (facing p123)
Animal Painters: John Scott by Walter Gilbey (p123-129)
Engraving [pinx. Scott]: *Death of the Dove* (facing p126)
Peterborough Horse and Hound Show by Gerald Ricardo (p129-136)
Cricket by Sydney Pardon (p136-140)
The Old Hostelries by Frederick Gale (p140-144)
The Sportsman's Library: Reviews of *The Game of Polo* by Thomas Dale; *The Trout and Fly-Fishing* by Albert Petit and various reprints (p144-147)
Engraving: *Polo in India* (facing p144)
Sea Fly-Fishing in Scotland by John Milne (p147-150)
Our Van [inc. Stockbridge Races; Hawkstone Otterhounds; Henley Regatta; Inter-University Swimming; Dieppe Golf] (p151-164)
Sporting Intelligence [inc. Obituaries of William Molyneux, William Bell-Irving, Samuel Allsopp, Henry Croker and Francis Stonor; Newmarket Starting Gates; West Cumberland Otterhounds] (p165-172)

Issue 451 : September 1897

Portrait [sculp. Allingham] and Biography - Charles Wright (p173-175)
Some Famous War-Horses by Francis Lawley (p175-184)
In Sutherland by John Bickerdyke (p184-187)
Animal Painters: John E Ferneley by Walter Gilbey (p188-192)
Engraving [sculp. Babbage]: *Captain Ross on Clinker* (facing p188)
Animal Painters: John Ferneley by Walter Gilbey (p192-193)
My Grandfather's Journals (part 2): A First Night at Mess by Arthur Griffiths (p193-200)
Engraving [sculp. Babbage]: *Napoleon Le Grand* (facing p201)
Some Holderness-Bred Horses by John Radcliffe (p201-205)
The Close of the Polo Season by Thomas Dale (p206-210)
Public School Cricket 1897 by Charles Smith (p210-213)
Entrance to the Army by John Russell (p213-220)
Aquatics Past and Present by William Blew (p221-226)
Cricket by Sydney Pardon (p226-229)
To a Foxhound Puppy [verses] by Peter Ditchfield (p229-230)
A Day with the Indian Grouse (p230-232)
The Sportsman's Library: Reviews of *The Book of the Dry Fly* by George Dewar; *The Jubilee Book of Cricket* by Kumar Ranjitsinhji; *The Paper Boat* by John Inglis (p233-235)
Our Van [inc. Redcar Races; Devon & Somerset Staghounds; Shooting at Bisley; Sherborne & Compton Stud Show; Metropolitan Regatta; Obituary of Charles Finlay; East Lothian Golf] (p236-250)
Sporting Intelligence [inc. Obituaries of William Spillane, Thomas Glover and James O'Donoghue; Goodwood Cup] (p250-258)

Issue 452 : October 1897

Portrait [sculp. Roffe] and Biography - Austin Mackenzie (p259-261)

The Derbyshire Wye by Frederic Halford (p262-267)

Doncaster Reflections by Richard Green-Price (p267-272)

[Obituary] Francis Roche by Eric Parker (p272-273)

Animal Painters: Francis Turner by Walter Gilbey (p274-278)

Engraving [pinx. F.Turner]: *The Find 'Hark to Rallywood'* (facing p274)

Animal Painters: George Turner by Walter Gilbey (p278-279)

My Grandfather's Journals (part 3): India by Arthur Griffiths (p279-286)

Polo and Ponies at Dublin by Thomas Dale (p286-289)

Ernest Balfour by Claude Holland (p290-291)

Photograph [Luny]: *Ernest Balfour* (facing p290)

War Correspondents by John Russell (p291-299)

The Conventional Bore by Frederick Gale (p299-300)

Training in Theory and Practice by William Blew (p300-305)

Deer Stalking by James Harting (p306-309)

Cricket by Sydney Pardon (p309-312)

A Yachting Colonial Governor by Francis Lawley (p312-321)

Material versus Pasture (p321-323)

Our Van [inc. Berks & Bucks Farmers' Harriers; West Somerset Hounds; Dublin Horse Show;
King of Siam's Yacht; Welsh Rugby Union; Penarth Golf] (p324-337)

Sporting Intelligence [inc. Obituaries of Lionel Rickards, George Scott, Thomas Hale,
Ian Keith-Falconer, Thomas Rook and Henry Smith; World Pacing Record;
Hartington Handicap; West Carbery Hunt Club] (p338-346)

* Retirement by Comyns Cole from his position as the second 'Van Driver' *

Issue 453 : November 1897

Portrait [sculp. Allingham] and Biography - Gilbert Greenall (p347-350)

Belvoir Reminiscences by William Blew (p350-356)

How to Show Foxes by Stanley Dennis (p356-363)

Engraving [sculp. Babbage]: *From Scent to View* (facing p363)

An Old Hunting Diary by Delme Radcliffe (p363-366)

Engraving [sculp. Babbage]: *The End* (facing p364)

Sketch [sculp. Radcliffe]: *Full Cry* (on p365)

The Rod and Gun in Norway by Abel Chapman (p367-369)

Animal Painters: John Boultbee by Walter Gilbey (p370-371)

Lithograph [pinx. Boultbee]: *The Death* (facing p370)

Animal Painters: John Best by Walter Gilbey (p371-373)

Engraving [sculp. Cook]: *Ginger Red* (facing p372)

Engraving [sculp. Cook]: *Birchin Yellow* (facing p372)

Animal Painters: Thomas Gooch by Walter Gilbey (p373-374)

Engraving [sculp. Babbage]: *Goldfinder* (facing p374)

My Grandfather's Journals (part 4): Egypt and High Wycombe by Arthur Griffiths (p375-381)

A Small English Shooting by John Russell (p381-389)

Mange in Foxes by Richard Green-Price (p390-394)

With the Stag on Exmoor by George Garrow-Green (p395-399)

Coursing by George Wilson (p399-401)

Old Memories [verses] by Peter Ditchfield (p402)

Telegony by Richard Hollett (p403-405)

The Sportsman's Library: *Scores and Annals of the West Kent Cricket Club* by Philip Norman (p405-408)

The Hunting Season by William Blew (p409-412)

Our Van [inc. Birmingham Races; Manchester Meeting; Launch of *Baily's Hunting Directory*
by Edward Cuming; Craven Hunt; Bexhill Harriers; North Surrey Golf Club] (p412-427)

Sporting Intelligence [inc. Obituaries of William Noble, William Yates, William Martingell
       and Thomas Fielden; Enfield Chace Stag Hunt; Old Berkshire Hounds]   (p427-434)

Issue 454 : December 1897

Portrait [sculp. Roffe] and Biography - Edward Wynyard   (p435-437)
The Army Medical Service by John Russell   (p437-447)
Autumn Quail in Egypt by Hugh Martin   (p447-451)
The Earth-Stopper by Penry Palfrey   (p452)
Engraving [sculp. Babbage]: *The Earth Stopper*   (facing p452)
My Grandfather's Journals (part 5): The Story of Hatim Tai by Arthur Griffiths   (p453-460)
Engraving [sculp. Babbage]: *The Shoeing Forge*   (facing p461)
Animal Painters: Edmund Bristowe by Walter Gilbey   (p461-463)
Engraving [pinx. Blake]: *Dead Game*   (facing p463)
Animal Painters: Benjamin Blake by Walter Gilbey   (p463-464)
Old Memories by Frederick Gale   (p465-469)
Fox-Hunting in the Olden Time by Edward Cuming   (p470-473)
The Old Mare's Story [verses] by William Phillpotts-Williams   (p474-475)
Cricket by Sydney Pardon   (p475-478)
Sporting Bores by Charles Smith   (p478-481)
The Motor Car of the Past by Edwin Campbell   (p481-485)
The Sportsman's Library: Reviews of *The Queen's Hounds and Stag Hunting Recollections*
       by Thomas Ribblesdale; *Reminiscences of a Huntsman* by Grantley Berkeley;
       Guide to Fish Culture by James Armistead; *Over the Open* by William
       Phillpotts-Williams   (p485-490)
Evan Williams by Comyns Cole   (p491)
Our Van [inc. Gatwick Handicap; Curragh Meeting; Grand Sefton Steeplechase; Quorn Hunt;
       Reviews of *Baily's Hunting Directory* and *History of Blackheath Golf Club* by
       William Hughes; Eastbourne Hounds; Obituary of Ellis Gosling; Anglesey Hunt
       Steeplechase; Wimbledon Golf Club]   (p492-514)
Sporting Intelligence [inc. Obituaries of Hercules Robinson, Panton Priestley, George
       Masterman, John Fleming, Joseph Morgan and John Middleton; Eskdaile Hunt
       Club; Hurlingham Polo Manager]   (p514-522)

Volume 69, January - June 1898

Issue 455 : January 1898

Portrait [sculp. Palfrey] of John Hearne, cricketer   Title page
Portrait [sculp. Roffe] and Biography - Garnet Wolseley   (p1-5)
The College Grinds by Thomas Dale   (p5-11)
The Conyers Testimonial by Robert Ball   (p11-12)
Photograph: *Henry Conyers Testimonial Silver*   (facing p11)
A Chat with a Whipper-In by Robert Collins   (p12-14)
Engraving [sculp. Meyer]: *Thomas Stothard*   (facing p15)
Animal Painters: Thomas Stothard by Walter Gilbey   (p15-18)
The Song of the Shires [verses]   (p19)
Our Army's Future Leaders by John Russell   (p20-29)
Photograph [Bennett]: *Dorothy Coventry on Sixpenny*   (facing p29)
Dianas of Today: With Hounds in Worcestershire by Frances Slaughter   (p29-38)
Photograph: *Lily Wrangham*   (facing p33)
Photograph: *Monica Peel on Black Jack*   (facing p37)
Photograph: *Helen Martin*   (facing p38)
My Grandfather's Journals (part 6): A Prisoner of War by Arthur Griffiths   (p41-48)

The Sportsman's Library: Reviews of *Sporting & Athletic Records* by Hubert Morgan-Browne; *The Haughtyshire Hunt* by William Fox-Russell; *Hunting* by George Underhill; *Sea Fish* by Frederick Aflalo, and *Racing & Chasing* by Alfred Watson (p48-52)

The Two-Year-Olds of 1897 by Richard Green-Price (p52-55)

Glove Fighting by Frederick Gale (p55-57)

Jorrocks Statuette by Comyns Cole (p57-58)

Photograph [Lutyens]: *Jorrocks on Arterxerxes* (on p57)

Our Van [inc. Warwick Racing; Manchester Meeting; Llangibby Hounds; Kilkenny Hunt; East Sussex Hunt; Review of *Livestock Journal Almanac 1898* by James Sinclair; Sydney Test Match; Obituaries of Walter Crofton, Stanley Williams, Frederick Middleton and William Pownall] (p58-83)

Sporting Intelligence [inc. Obituaries of Thomas Skipworth, James Hastie, Walter Powell, Mark Howcutt, Harold Freeman, Dudley Carleton and Vaughan Jenkins; Colneis Harriers; Essex Staghounds] (p84-88)

Issue 456 : February 1898

Portrait [sculp. Allingham] and Biography - Owen Williams (p89-90)

Sketch [pinx. Hunter]: Chester Races, May 1791 (facing p91)

Racing a Century Ago by Richard Green-Price (p91-95)

Dianas of Today: With Hounds From Badminton and Berkeley by Frances Slaughter (p95-104)

Photograph: *Louise Worcester* (facing p96)

Photograph [Bullingham]: *Gertrude Hoare* (facing p96)

Photograph [Lambert]: *Adelaide Holmes-a-Court* (facing p100)

Photograph [Lamb]: *Constance Rolt* (facing p100)

Photograph: *Mary Matthews* (facing p100)

Engraving [sculp. Babbage): *Deer Stalking* (facing p105)

Animal Painters: Charles Hancock by Walter Gilbey (p105-109)

Some Old Irish Hunting Notes by William Blew (p109-116)

Hunting Sonnets (p117-118)

Gebhard Blucher von Wahlstatt (p118-122)

Engraving [sculp. Palfrey]: *Prince Blucher* (facing p118)

The Emperor of Elba by John Russell (p122-129)

Empty Thrones by Frederick Gale (p130-135)

My Grandfather's Journals (part 7): Still A Prisoner of War by Arthur Griffiths (p135-143)

Keepers and Fox Preserving by George Upton (p143-147)

The Sportsman's Library: Reviews of *Wisden's Cricketers' Almanack* by Sydney Pardon; *The Badminton Diary* by Fitzalan Manners; *The Angler's Library* by Herbert Maxwell (p148-150)

Our Van [inc. Obituaries of Seymour Egerton and Rice Meredith; Devon & Somerset Staghounds; Belvoir Hunt; Fife Hounds; Meath Hunt; Tipperary Hounds; Melbourne Test Match; Northern Rugby Union] (p150-168)

Correspondence: The Army Medical Staff (p169-172)

Sporting Intelligence [inc. Obituaries of Herbert Arkwright, Robert Chambers, Charles Lea, Marcus Lewis and William Farnell-Watson; West Kent Hunt; South Cheshire Hounds; County Down Staghounds; Brighton Harriers] (p173-176)

Issue 457 : March 1898

Portrait [sculp. Allingham] and Biography - Edward Barclay (p177-180)

The Racehorse: How to Rear Him by Walter Gilbey (p181-185)

A Heather Fox by Frederick Lutyens (p185-188)

Lithograph [pinx. Lutyens]: *A Heather Fox* (facing p187)

Monte Carlo by Richard Green-Price (p188-192)

Engraving [sculp. Babbage]: *Jesse Curling* (facing p188)

Dianas of Today: With Hounds in the Old Dorset Country by Frances Slaughter (p192-203)

Photograph [Clarke]: *Dorothy Parke* (facing p192)

Photograph [Day]: *Elizabeth Guest* (facing p192)

Photograph [Copeman]: *Alys Serrell on Colleen* (facing p196)

Lithograph: *Theodora Guest on Pembroke* (facing p200)

The Army Medical Service by John Russell (p204-209)

Both Sides of the Shield by Thomas Dale (p210-214)

Cricket in Australia by Ivo Bligh (p214-218)

John Hargreaves [verses] by William Phillpotts-Williams (p219)

My Grandfather's Journals (part 8): More A Prisoner of War by Arthur Griffiths (p220-228)

Sport in Angoni Land (p228-235)

Quickstep [verses] (p235)

The Sportsman's Library: *The Art of Deer-Stalking* by William Scrope (p236-237)

Our Van [inc. Gatwick Steeplechasing; Birmingham Racecourse; Brooklyn Jockey Club; Obituaries of Erasmus Barrowes, Hodgson Wright and John Ewen; Waterloo Cup; Southdown Hunt; Galway Blazers; Brighton Beagles; Felixstowe Golf Course] (p238-257)

Correspondence: Arab Horses from Emile Dillon (p258-259)

Sporting Intelligence [inc. Obituaries of William Winn; Charles Winn, Windham Carmichael-Anstruther, Abel Smith, John Atkinson and John Selwyn; Thames Angling Preservation Society; Belvoir Foxhounds; South Cheshire Hunt] (p259-264)

Issue 458 : April 1898

Portrait [sculp. Allingham] and Biography - Thomas Miller (p265-267)

Is Not Steeplechasing Deteriorating by Richard Green-Price (p268-271)

The Coming Polo Season by Thomas Dale (p272-274)

Lithograph [pinx. Agasse]: *Mail Coach* (facing p275)

Animal Painters: Jacques Agasse by Walter Gilbey (p275-278)

Rosemary [verses] by William Phillpotts-Williams (p279)

The Early Trout by Paul Taylor (p280-282)

Hounds on the Show Bench by Walter Crofton (p282-288)

Desire [verses] by Harry Cumberland-Bentley (p288-289)

Staghounds at Bath and Cheltenham by William Blew (p289-295)

Photograph [Fall]: *Edmund Tattersall* (facing p295)

[Obituary] Edmund Tattersall by Francis Lawley (p295-298)

The Tattersall Family by Francis Lawley (p298-306)

Lithograph: *Old Tatt* (facing p298)

Lithograph: *Richard Tattersall* (facing p300)

The Early Days of the Highland Regiments (part 1) by John Russell (p306-314)

Mostly About Snakes by Harry Cumberland-Bentley (p315-317)

The Thruster's Song [verses] by Stanley Dennis (p318-319)

A Word on Behalf of Umpires by Otho Paget (p320-322)

The Sportsman's Library: Reviews of *Cycling* by Frederick Graves; *A Bibliography of Skating* by Frederick Foster; *A Sketch of the Natural History Vertebrates* by Frederick Aflalo; *Pike and Perch* by Alfred Jardine; *The Secret of a Hollow Tree* by Naunton Covertside (p322-323)

Tom Whitemore in Retirement by Edward Cuming (p324-325)

Photograph [Reid]: *Thomas Whitemore* (on p324)

Our Van [inc. Grand Military Meeting; Obituaries of George Barrett and Orlando Bridgeman; Essex Staghounds; North Middlesex Polo Club; University Sport; Cottesmore Hunt; Lytham St.Anne's Golf Club] (p325-345)

Correspondence: Arab Horses from Charles Oakeley (p345)

Sporting Intelligence: [inc. Obituaries of John Trotter, George Barrett, Travers Allan, George Robson, Isaac Mitchell, Carleton Cowper and John Tremlett; Gogerddau Hunt; Harrington's Foxhounds]   (p346-352)

Issue 459 : May 1898

Portrait [sculp. Allingham] and Biography - Daniel Cooper   (p353-355)
A Sketch of Aylesbury Steeplechases by William Blew   (p355-360)
Engraving [sculp. Lewis]: *John Chapman*   (facing p361)
Animal Painters: Francis Grant by Walter Gilbey   (p361-363)
Is Polo Expensive by Thomas Dale   (p364-366)
On the Ladies Links by May Hezlet   (p366-370)
Trout Fishing by Alexander Mackie   (p370-375)
Turf Nomenclature by Edward Spencer   (p375-381)
My Grandfather's Journals (part 9): Ciudad Rodrigo by Arthur Griffiths   (p381-390)
An Interesting Old Cricket Match by William Seton   (p390-391)
Woodstock's Race [verses] by Geoffrey de Holden-Stone   (p392-393)
The Early Days of the Highland Regiments (part 2) by John Russell   (p394-402)
Photograph: *Eyre Powell*   (facing p403)
Eyre Powell by Edward Cuming   (p403-404)
Our Van [inc. Newmarket Steeplechasing; Folkestone Racecourse Company; Essex Hunt Club Steeplechasing; Burstow Hunt; Hawkestone Otterhounds; Obituaries of Henry Howard, Hamar Bass, Goodrich Allfrey and Richard Council; Polo in India, Oxford Draghounds]   (p404-425)
Sporting Intelligence [inc. Wheatland Hounds; Obituaries of John Campbell, John Calder, Richard Johnson, Thomas Browne, William Monson, Reuben Hunt and George Ure; North Cornwall Hunt; Melbourne Club Cricket; Cattistock Hounds]   (p426-432)

Issue 460 : June 1898

Portrait [sculp. Allingham] and Biography - William Fife   (p433-436)
Condition by Richard Green-Price   (p436-440)
Engraving [sculp. Babbage]: *Fox-Hounds in Full Cry*   (facing p441)
Animal Painters: George Laporte by Walter Gilbey   (p441-442)
Remarkable Match Against Time by William Lamonby   (p443-444)
The World it goes Round Upon Wheels by Frederick Gale   (p444-456)
Engraving [sculp. Lewis]: *The Night Mails Leaving The General Post Office 1836*   (facing p444)
Engraving: *Steam Motor Carriage 1823*   (on p445)
Engraving: *Old Cabriolet [Front] 1823*   (on p446)
Engraving: *Old Cabriolet [Rear] 1823*   (on p446)
Engraving: *Sign of Old White Horse Cellar*   (on p447)
Engraving: *Card of the Old Canterbury Tally Ho! 1828*   (on p448)
Engraving: *Card of the Eagle Dover Coach 1828*   (on p449)
Piscator-Viator by James Mullen   (p456-461)
Midget by John Radcliffe   (p461-466)
Country Life at Burlington House by Penry Palfrey   (p466-471)
The County Cup and the Hurlingham Polo Committee by Thomas Dale   (p471-474)
Cricket by Sydney Pardon   (p474-476)
My Grandfather's Journals (part 10): Badajoz & Salamanca by Arthur Griffiths   (p477-483)
The Sportsman's Library: *With Bat and Ball* by George Giffen   (p483-485)
John Hearne by Edward Cuming   (p485-486)
Our Van [inc. Epsom Meeting; Gatwick Racing; Ranelagh Polo; Eden Park Polo Club; Tetcott Hunt; Eastbourne Hounds; London Playing Fields Committee]   (p486-507)

Sporting Intelligence [inc. Obituaries of Alexander Williamson, Francis Tuke, John Robinson, Frederick Milbank, Edward Bleackley (of *Sporting Chronicle*), William Beauclerk, John Barry and James Scott; Surrey County Cricket; Old Hawking Club; Surrey Union Foxhounds]   (p507-512)

Volume 70, July - December 1898

Issue 461 : July 1898

Portrait [sculp. Palfrey] of Jim Cockayne, huntsman   Title page
Portrait [sculp. Allingham] and Biography - Alfred Lyttelton   (p1-3)
Jockeyship by Richard Green-Price   (p4-9)
Photograph [Kilkenny]: *Beatrice and Constance Butler*   (facing p9)
The Gentle Craft by Frances Slaughter   (p9-12)
Rising to Order by Frederick Gale   (p12-14)
The County Polo Club Association by Thomas Dale   (p14-17)
Our Gypsy Visitors by John Russell   (p17-23)
By Order of the Czar by John Doyle   (p24-27)
Photograph [Hailey]: *Galtee More*   (facing p24)
Salmon Studies by William Murdoch   (p27-33)
Superstitions of the Turf by Ernest Smith   (p33-36)
Bounties on Vermin in America   (p36-39)
A Last Century Episode by Arthur Stuart   (p39-43)
County Councils and Wild Birds by Watkin Watkins   (p44-48)
Cricket by Sydney Pardon   (p49-51)
Animal Painters: List of Artists' Dates of Birth by Walter Gilbey   (p52)
Our Van [inc. Knavesmire Meeting; Epsom Races; Obituaries of Comyns Cole (of *Baily's*) and George Ulyett; Polo Hunt Cup; Paris Polo Club; Roscommon Staghounds; Stevenstone Hounds; Mid-Devon Hunt; Yarmouth Golf]   (p52-81)
Sporting Intelligence [inc. Obituaries of Pybus Sellon, Harry Herbert, Walter Maule, Leeds Paine, Thomas Acland and Richard Donaldson; Belvoir Hunt; Brighton Races; Quorn Hunt; Tynedale Foxhounds]   (p81-88)

Issue 462 : August 1898

Portrait [sculp Allingham] and Biography - John Rolls   (p89-92)
Salmo Fontinalis by John Russell   (p92-99)
Shall We Have Shorter Periods at Polo by Thomas Dale   (p99-101)
The Dead Men's Steeplechase [verses] by Geoffrey de Holden-Stone   (p101-103)
Hunter Sires by Walter Gilbey   (p104-110)
Engraving [pinx. Ferneley]: *Hunter Sire Cognac*   (facing p104)
Photograph: *Ellesmere by New Oswestry*   (facing p108)
My Grandfather's Journals (part 11): A Second Visit to Madrid by Arthur Griffiths (p110-116)
Horses and Hounds at Peterborough by Gerald Ricardo   (p116-122)
Cricket by Sydney Pardon   (p123-125)
Spoiling the Egyptians by George White   (p126-131)
The Sportsman's Library: Reviews of *The Breeders' Handbook* by Joseph Osborne; *New and Old Chips* by Robert Mansfield; *A Pink 'Un and a Pelican* by Arthur Binstead & Ernest Wells; *From Tonquin to India* by Henri D'Orleans; *Trouting in Norway* by Edmund Burton; *The Salmon* by Alfred Gathorne-Hardy; *Polo* by Thomas Drybrough   (p131-136)
Experiences in Falls from Horseback by Frederick Wedge   (p137-141)
A Day in the Highlands by James Mullen   (p141-145)

Our Van [inc. Hurst Park Foal Plate; Final Stockbridge Meeting; Old Berkshire Hounds;
     Carmarthenshire Hunt; Masters of Harriers & Beagles Association; Polo
     County Cup; Shanghai Polo; Obituaries of Edwin Fownes and Isaac Walker;
     Henley Regatta] (p146-164)
Sporting Intelligence: [inc. University Athletics; Suffolk Hounds; Amateur Athletic
     Championships; Obituaries of Michael Ellison, Edwin Parr and Joseph Oates] (p164-170)

Issue 463 : September 1898

Portrait [sculp. Allingham] and Biography - Herbert Maxwell (p171-173)
In Cotton's Country by John Bickerdyke (p173-176)
The First of September by Harry Stannard (p177-179)
Lithograph [sculp. Stannard]: *A Winged Bird for a Sovereign* (facing p178)
Turf Topics by Richard Green-Price (p179-182)
Chargers by John Russell (p182-190)
Photograph [Chancellor]: *Lord Roberts on his Arab Charger* (facing p182)
Photograph [Gibbs]: *Captain Peel's Charger Sultan* (facing p188)
The Revised Laws of Billiards by John Buchanan (p190-193)
My Grandfather's Journals (part 12): Cecile by Arthur Griffiths (p193-200)
Cricket Centuries by Edward Bligh (p200-204)
The Polo Season 1898 by Thomas Dale (p204-207)
The Sportsman's Library: Reviews of *The Golfing Pilgrim* by Horace Hutchinson and *Wisden's*
     Public School Matches by Sydney Pardon (p208-211)
Public School Cricket in 1898 by Sydney Pardon (p211-214)
Our Van [inc. Goodwood Plate; Brighton Races; Obituaries of Samuel Hyde and Matthew
     Dawson; East Kent Hunt; Wirral Polo; Musselburgh Golf] (p214-238)
Sporting Intelligence [inc. Obituaries of Edgar Pardon, Frank Rutledge, John Bibby, Robert
     Exshaw and Herbert Gillman; Tattersall's Sales; Doggett's Coat and Badge;
     Hawkstone Otterhounds; Muskerry Foxhounds (p238-244)

Issue 464 : October 1898

Portrait [sculp. Allingham] and Biography - Leonard Brassey (p245-247)
On the Moors in Autumn by Thomas Cuthell (p247-249)
Notes on the Rough Welsh Hound by Cambridge Phillips (p249-251)
The Black Sheep of Sport by Richard Green-Price (p251-255)
Polo in Ireland 1898 by Thomas Dale (p255-257)
Tom Moody, The Willey Squire and Bachelor's Hall by Henry Archer (p258-264)
Photograph [Bartlett]: *The Needle's Eye on the Wrekin* (facing p258)
Photograph [Bartlett]: *The Acton Arms, Morville* (facing p261)
Photograph of Engraving [Bartlett]: *The Death of Tom Moody* (facing p263)
Photograph of Engraving [Bartlett]: *The Jolly Old Squire* (facing p264)
My Grandfather's Journals (part 13): Waterloo by Arthur Griffiths (p265-272)
The Mausoleum at Tedworth [verses] by William Phillpotts-Williams (p273)
Conditions in Hunters: Human & Equine by Hugh Henry (p274-276)
Trout Fishing in the Taunus by Henry Cholmondeley-Pennell (p277-282)
The Chaunt of Achilles [with verses by Patroclus] (p283-289)
The Sportsman's Library: Reviews of *Northward over the Great Ice* by Robert Peary; *Rowing*
     and Punting by Douglas McLean & William Grenfell, and *Old Flies in New*
     Dresses by Charles Walker (p290-293)
Notes on Croquet by Walter Peel (p293-295)
Our Van [inc. Great Ebor Handicap; Review of *The Turf* by Alfred Watson; Obituary of George
     Egerton; Grafton Hunt; Eastbourne Rowing Club; Bangalore Polo; Cardiff Horse
     Show] (p296-313)

Sporting Intelligence [inc. East Kent Hounds; County Cricket; Obituaries of Paul Esterhazy, Colin Byrne, Hugh Baillie and Hubert Howard; Ashdown Forest Golf; Cheriton Otterhounds] (p314-320)

Issue 465 : November 1898

Portrait [sculp. Mote] and Biography - Kenelm Pepys (p321-322)
Jumping by Richard Green-Price (p323-327)
Foraging on the Kapochi by Thomas Nicholson (p327-331)
Engraving [pinx. Smith]: *Hugo Meynell, 1794* (facing p331)
Sporting Celebrities: Hugo Meynell by George Underhill (p331-335)
Warwickshire First [verses] by William Phillpotts-Williams (p336)
Spots on the Cricket Sun by Frederick Gale (p337-339)
Dianas of Today: Our Lady Masters by Frances Slaughter (p340-343)
Saddles [with Sketches and Photographs] by Thomas Dale (p343-348)
A Reminiscence [verses] by William Clements (p349-350)
The Boone and Crockett Club by John Russell (p351-357)
A Lament [verses] (p358-359)
Judging at Horse Shows by Gerald Ricardo (p359-361)
The Hunting Season by William Blew (p361-365)
The Sportsman's Library: *The Sportswoman's Library* by Frances Slaughter; *Cambridge and its Colleges* by Hamilton Thompson; *Owd Bob* by Alfred Ollivant; *Records of Hunting in Westmeath* by Gerald Dease, and *A Near Thing* by Harry Cumberland-Bentley (p365-367)
In a Hampshire Wood by George Dewar (p367-370)
Our Van [inc. Manchester Meeting; Obituaries of John Clark, John Browne and Henry Paget; Cheshire Hounds; Dumfriesshire Hunt; Review of *Baily's Hunting Directory* by Edward Cuming; Poona Polo Tournament; County Down Golf Club] (p370-389)
Sporting Intelligence [inc. Obituaries of Charles Tebbutt and John Cottle; Llangibby Foxhounds; Newmarket Sales; Shooting Parties] (p390-394)

Issue 466 : December 1898

Portrait [sculp. Mote] and Biography - William Dunn (p395-396)
The Etiquette of Hunting by Richard Green-Price (p397-399)
The Captain's Story: An Episode of the China Seas (p399-404)
A Day with The Bedfordshire by Frederick Lutyens (p404-407)
Lithograph [pinx. Lutyens]: *Yoicks Wind Him* (facing p404)
Our Racehorses by Edward Clayton (p407-408)
Lifting the Curtain of the Past by Frederick Gale (p408-412)
An Interview with an Old Huntsman by William Phillpotts-Williams [verses] (p412)
Engraving [pinx. Cooper]: *Thomas Assheton Smith* (facing p413)
Sporting Celebrities: Thomas Assheton Smith by George Underhill (p413-418)
The Tennis Championship by Wallis Myers (p418-419)
Docking Horses by Wortley Axe (p420-422)
The Phantom Ride [verses] (p423)
The Irish Bone-Setter by Henry Devereux (p424-430)
The Sportsman's Library: Reviews of *The Egyptian Soudan* by Henry Alford; *The Life of George Stubbs* by Walter Gilbey, and *The Romance of a Grouse Moor* by Mary Stevenson (p430-433)
Valour in the Hunting Field by Hugh Henry (p434-437)
Jim Cockayne by Edward Cuming (p437-438)
Our Van [inc. Newmarket Houghton Meeting; South Notts Hunt; Rufford Hounds; North Cotswold Hunt; Hurworth Hounds; Seavington Harriers; University Sport] (p439-462)

Sporting Intelligence [inc. Atherstone Hounds; Obituaries of John Beasley, Christopher Topham and William Smith; Holderness Hunt; Southdown Foxhounds; Great Yarmouth Harriers; River Tay Salmon Fishing]   (p462-470)

Rowland Egerton-Warburton

Volume 71, January - June 1899

Issue 467 : January 1899

Portrait [sculp. Palfrey] of Robert Abel, cricketer	Title page
Portrait [sculp. Alais] and Biography - John Fock	(p1-4)
Hunt Servants - Their Benefits by Richard Green-Price	(p5-8)
Don't - To Ingenuous Polo Players by Thomas Dale	(p8-11)
The Farmer [verses] by William Phillpotts-Williams	(p11)
Hunting in Devonshire by Edward Cuming	(p12-17)
Badger Digging	(p18-19)
The Hunt Ball by Henry Archer	(p19-21)
Northamptonshire in 1827 [verses] by Matthew Fortescue	(p21-23)
A Mixed Bag on the East Coast by Henry Stannard	(p24-25)
Lithograph [pinx. Stannard]: *Crumpled in the Air*	(facing p24)
Bits and Bitting [with Photographs]	(p26-32)
Sam's Message by Frederick Lutyens	(p32-34)
The Blackcock and Capercailzie in Scotland by John Mullen	(p34-38)
The Sportsman's Library: Reviews of *A Summer on the Rockies* by Rose Price; *The Campaign in Tirah* by Horace Hutchinson; *Fishing and Fishers* by Paul Taylor; *The Reminiscences of Frank Gillard* by Cuthbert Bradley; *From Morn till Eve* by John Wollocombe	(p39-42)
Our Van [inc. Derby Racing; Manchester Meeting; Woodland Pytchley Hounds; North Staffordshire Hunt; Obituaries of William Gregory, William Hurrell and Bernard Heygate; Tynedale Hounds; West Kent Hunt; Mid-Kent Staghounds; East Galway Hunt; Ullswater Hounds; Polo in India; Worsley Golf Club]	(p43-71)
Sporting Intelligence [inc. Obituaries of Burton Bingham, Robert Spurway and Christopher Sykes; Limerick Foxhounds; United Cork Hunt]	(p71-76)

Issue 468 : February 1899

Portrait [sculp. Alais] and Biography - Frederick Glyn	(p77-79)
Nerve in Man by Richard Green-Price	(p79-83)
Oxford Revisited by John Russell	(p84-93)
Terriers for the Hunting Field by George Lowe	(p93-94)
Gaudeamus Igitur [verses] by Geoffrey de Holden-Stone	(p94-95)
The White Horse, Fetter Lane by William Fradgley-Moore	(p96-97)
Engraving [pinx. Pollard]: *The Cambridge Telegraph*	(facing p96)
Hares by Theodore Cook	(p97-99)
Englishwomen and their Sports and Games (part 1) by Walter Sparrow	(p99-104)
The Grey Fox of Rubers Law [verses]	(p104-105)
Breaking Dogs for the Gun by Frederick Gresham	(p106-109)
Photograph [Reid]: *English Setters*	(facing p106)
Photograph [Reid]: *Pointer*	(facing p108)
Photograph [Reid]: *Curly Coated Retriever*	(facing p108)
Character and Characters in the Hunting Field by Hugh Henry	(p109-114)
The Knockout Blow at Schools by Frederick Gale	(p114-116)
County Cricket: Qualification of Players by Ivo Bligh	(p116-118)
Northamptonshire in 1828 [verses] by Matthew Fortescue	(p119-120)
The Sportsman's Library: Reviews of *The Quorn Hunt* by William Blew; *Estate Fences* by Arthur Verson	(p120-127)
Our Van [inc. Worcestershire Hounds; Carlow Hunt; Grafton Hounds; Salkeld Hounds; Sporting Spaniel Club; Leasowe Golf Club]	(p128-152)

Sporting Intelligence [inc. South Devon Hunt; Obituaries of James Collings, Robin Lubbock, Algernon Percy, Edward Kitchener and Samuel Clowes; Essex Union Hounds; East Kent Hunt; West Surrey Staghounds]   (p152-156)

Issue 469 : March 1899

Portrait [sculp. Alais] and Biography - Robert Watson   (p157-160)
Perquisites and Tips   (p160-168)
Coming Events by Richard Green-Price   (p168-172)
March Trout by Henry Cholmondeley-Pennell   (p173-175)
Antony and Cleopatra by Frederick Lutyens   (p176-181)
Lithograph [pinx. Lutyens]: *Slowly but Surely*   (facing p176)
The Colour of Horses by John Radcliffe   (p182-184)
A Word in Season [verses] by John Williams   (p184)
Saddle Bars and Stirrups [with Sketches and Photographs] by John Russell   (p185-191)
Inter-County Cricket and The County Championship by Ivo Bligh   (p192-195)
Attractions and Advantages of Sport by Jonathan Pim   (p196-201)
Gone Away [verses] by Robert Cochrane   (p201)
Polo Pony Shows by Thomas Dale   (p202-203)
The Sportsman's Library: Reviews of *Kings of the Turf* by William Willmott-Dixon; *The House on Sport* by William Morgan; *A Cotswold Village* by Arthur Gibbs; *Ten Days at Monte Carlo* by Victor Bethell   (p203-205)
Luxuries and Necessaries in Hunting Establishments by William Blew   (p206-210)
Sensational Ballooning by William Lamonby   (p210-212)
Our Van [inc. National Hunt Committee; North Cotswold Hounds; Kildare Hunt; Templemore Staghounds; Retirement of Tom Firr; Obituaries of Charles Shrubb and George Davidson; Wimbledon Polo Club; University Sport]   (p213-232)
Sporting Intelligence [inc. Shropshire Hounds; Obituaries of Thomas Lyon, William Poulett, Edwin Mills, Henri Say, Thomas Walker, William Forbes, Henry Jones, Joseph Chitty, Lon Myers, Thomas Longmire, Charles Trail and William Holloway; Tipperary Foxhounds]   (p232-236)

Issue 470 : April 1899

Portrait [sculp. Mote] and Biography - Frank Bibby   (p237-238)
The Hunting Season by Richard Green-Price   (p239-242)
The Flying Childe by Henry Archer   (p242-249)
Engraving [sculp. Babbage]: *William Childe*   (facing p242)
Photograph: *Kinlet House and Park*   (on p244)
Photograph: *Bewdley Bridge*   (facing p246)
After Twenty-Three Years [verses] by Henry Lucy   (p249-250)
The Death of Marshal Ney by John Russell   (p251-257)
At the Wall [verses] by Geoffrey de Holden-Stone   (p257-258)
Englishwomen and their Sports and Games (part 2) by Walter Sparrow   (p259-265)
Woodcut: *Treatise on Fishing with an Angle*   (on p261)
The Preservation of African Game by Frederick Selous   (p265-268)
Some Breeding-Stud Reminiscences by William Blew   (p269-275)
The Coming Polo Season by Thomas Dale   (p276-279)
Northamptonshire in 1829 [verses] by Matthew Fortescue   (p280-281)
Why Not Try It? [Cricket] by Frederick Gale   (p282-284)
The Sportsman's Library: Reviews of *Stonehenge on the Horse* by Harold Leeney; *The Great Horse* by Walter Gilbey; *The Flowing Bowl* by Spencer Mott; *On Plain and Peak* by Randolph Hodgson   (p285-287)
Our Van [inc. French Pari-Mutuel; Brocklesby Hunt; Eglinton's Hounds; County Down Staghounds; Four Burrow Foxhounds; Indian Polo Championship; Waterloo Cup] (p287-313)

Sporting Intelligence [inc. Obituaries of Robert Kearney, Crowther Harrison, David Moore,
   Henry Persse and Vivian Champion de Crespigny; Army Racquet Championship;
   Percy Hounds; Westmeath Harriers; West Surrey Staghounds]   (p313-318)

Issue 471 : May 1899

Portrait [sculp. Mote] and Biography - George Herbert   (p319-321)
Two and a Half Centuries of Betting Legislation by Laurence Duckworth   (p321-327)
Spring Salmon Angling by Alexander Mackie   (p328-330)
Fred Cox by John Reid   (p330-331)
Photograph [Reid]: *Frederick Cox*   (facing p330)
Sprudelheim by John Russell   (p331-340)
A Plea for Half-Bred Sires by Richard Green-Price   (p340-343)
My Hobby [verses] by William Alderton   (p344-345)
Game Preservation in the Middle Ages by John Russell   (p345-351)
The Chances of the Game: De Soto's System by Arthur Griffiths   (p352-357)
Faute de Mieux [verses] by Charles Beaumont   (p358)
Engraving [sculp. Fogg]: *Robert Forfeit*   (facing p359)
Bob Forfeit by Penry Palfrey   (p359)
Bicester and Warden Hill Hunt by Henry Tubb   (p359)
Anecdotal Sport by William Willmott-Dixon   (p360-365)
The Sportsman's Library: *Dry Fly Fishing* by Frederick Halford   (p366)
Engraving: *Landing a Trout*   (facing p366)
The Turf and its Tipsters by William Blew   (p367-370)
Our Van [inc. Lincoln Meeting; Lancashire Steeplechase; Eastbourne Hounds; Hambledon
   Hunt; Wimbledon Park Polo Club; Irish Partridge Shooting; Obituaries of
   Frederick Hobson and Francis Wilson; Piscatorial Society Dinner]   (p371-394)
Sporting Intelligence [inc. Obituaries of John Wilkinson, Leonard Shiel, William Barnes,
   Richard Carruthers, Frederick Wilson, LeGendre Starkie and Monier
   Monier-Williams; Meynell Hunt Finances; Croome Hunt Point-to-Point; East
   Essex Hunt Steeplechases; Eamont Harriers]   (p394-400)

Issue 472 : June 1899

Portrait [scalp Alais] and Biography – Evelyn Boscawen   (p401-404)
Scotland and Wild Birds by Watkin Watkins   (p404-409)
The Only Appeal Left by Frederick Gale   (p409-410)
The Hard Case of Number Two [Polo] by Thomas Dale   (p411-412)
The Man-Hunting Bloodhound by John Russell   (p413-417)
The Chances of the Game: The Play at Halesworth House by Arthur Griffiths   (p418-423)
On Hunt Races by Richard Green-Price   (p423-426)
Anecdotal Sport by William Willmott-Dixon   (p426-430)
Sport at the Royal Academy by Edward Cuming   (p431-432)
Photograph [Dickinson]: *The Eighth Duke of Beaufort* (Henry Somerset)   (facing p433)
The Duke of Beaufort by Francis Lawley   (p433-429)
Cricket Song [verses] by William Blew   (p439-440)
Herling Fishing in South Scotland by Paul Taylor   (p440-442)
The Sportsman's Library: Reviews of *The Law Affecting The Turf* by Laurence Duckworth;
   Riding and Polo by Thomas Dale, and *Records of Big Game* by Rowland Ward   (p443)
A Coaching Chapter by William Blew   (p444-451)
Robert Abel by Edwin Smith   (p451-452)
Our Van [inc. Epsom Meeting; Chester Races; Calcutta Polo; Culmstock Otterhounds; Enfield
   Chase Staghounds; Scottish Trout Anglers' Association]   (p452-474)

Sporting Intelligence [inc. Dumfriesshire Hunt; Rugby Polo Club; Obituaries of Robert
          Stevens, Michael Widger, Tom Nickalls and Henry Raphael; South London
          Harriers; East Galway Hounds]   (p474-480)

Volume 72, July - December 1899

Issue 473 : July 1899

Portrait [sculp. Palfrey] of Will Dale, huntsman   Title page
Portrait [sculp. Alais] and Biography - Gregor MacGregor   (p1-4)
Photograph [Hawkins]: *MacGregor and Stoddart*   (on p3)
Memories of my Horses by John Russell   (p4-12)
All Nature looks Smiling and Gay by Richard Green-Price   (p12-15)
Working Spaniels by Frederick Gresham   (p16-19)
Photograph [Reid]: *Working Spaniels*   (facing p16)
The Studs in France by Laurent DuReste   (p19-21)
Anecdotal Sport by William Willmott-Dixon   (p22-28)
Dard Fishing in Normandy by Abel Chapman   (p29-34)
Photograph: *Where the Dard Lie*   (facing p30)
Photograph: *Spoilsports in the Shallows*   (on p33)
The Chances of the Game: Ivo Treherne by Arthur Griffiths   (p35-39)
After the Inter-Regimental [Polo] by Thomas Dale   (p40-41)
The Arab Horse as a Racer by Charles Oakeley   (p41-43)
Trout Fishing in Norway by Harry Lupton   (p43-45)
The Fowler [verses] by Robert Gibbs   (p46-47)
The Sportsman's Diary: Reviews of *Our Lady of the Green* by Louie Mackern; *The Book of
          Cricket* by Charles Fry; *Giants of the Game* by Robert Lyttelton; *An Exiled Scot* by
          Henry Bryden; *Sport in East Central Africa* by Vaughan Kirby   (p47-48)
Our Van [inc. Ascot Meeting; London Polo Club; Hunt Servants Benefit Society; Boulogne
          Horse Show; Lord's Test Match; Henley Regatta; Sandwich Golf]   (p49-71)
Sporting Intelligence [inc. Obituaries of William Watts, William Brett, Rosa Bonheur, Arthur
          Hardinge and Isaac Stordy; Thurstonfield Hounds; Queen's Cup Yachting]   (p71-80)

Issue 474 : August 1899

Portrait [sculp. Alais] and Biography - Cuthbert Quilter   (p81-83)
The Bibury Club by Edward Cuming   (p83-88)
Anecdotes of an Old Turfite by John Kent   (p88-89)
The Teal and Green: A Dee Problem   (p90-93)
The Measurement of Ponies by John Hill   (p94-96)
White Heather by Cuthbert Bradley   (p96-101)
Lithograph [sculp. Bradley]: *The Fiery Ordeal*   (facing p96)
A Race Meeting in China by Randolph Chester   (p102-103)
The Chances of the Game: Hammer Hume by Arthur Griffiths   (p103-107)
A Twelfth of August in the Irish Midlands by Mackay Wilson   (p107-110)
A Century's Coach-Building by John Bluett   (p111-114)
Peterborough Horse & Hound Show by Edward Cuming   (p114-118)
Photograph: *Champion Foxhounds at Peterborough*   (facing p114)
The Poisoning of Vermin and its Results   (p118-120)
Shades of Henley by Walter Woodgate   (p121-122)
My Mayfly Diary by John Bickerdyke   (p123-128)
Anecdotal Sport by William Willmott-Dixon   (p128-133)
Our Van [inc. Newmarket Meeting; Bibury Club Racing; Ranelagh Polo Cup; Simla Polo;
          University Sport; Chicago Golf]   (p133-151)

Sporting Intelligence [inc. Obituaries of William I'Anson, Edward Hanraham and Lee
       Steere; Heligoland Yacht Race; Thames Swimming Championships; Warnham
       Staghounds] (p151-156)

Issue 475 : September 1899

Portrait [sculp. Roffe] and Biography - Robert Sanders (p157-159)
African Horse-Sickness by John Russell (p159-166)
Racing: Sport of the Autumn by Richard Green-Price (p167-170)
The Past Polo Season by Thomas Dale (p170-174)
The Chances of the Game: Father and Son by Arthur Griffiths (p174-178)
Public School Cricket by Charles Smith (p179-181)
Game Legislation in Norway by Harry Lupton (p181-183)
Photograph [Short]: *New Forest Ponies- Mares* (facing p185)
Photograph [Short]: *Forest Ponies* (facing p185)
Photograph [Short]: *New Forest Ponies* (facing p187)
Photograph [Short]: *New Forest Ponies and Foal* (facing p187)
Horses of the Wildwood by George Dewar (p185-187)
The Salmon in the Statute Book by Abel Chapman (p187-192)
Vain Glory and Egotism by Frederick Gale (p193-195)
Anecdotal Sport by William Willmott-Dixon (p195-200)
Gendarme and Goldflake (p200-201)
Photograph [Reid]: *Gendarme* (facing p200)
Photograph [Reid]: *Goldflake* (facing p200)
The Black Wood of Rannoch by Michael Watkins (p201-205)
Recollections of Racing in India by Charles Oliver (p205-209)
Our Van [inc. Goodwood Meeting; Lewes Handicap; Obituary of Jack Drybrough;
       Johannesburg Polo Club; Neuadd Fawr Hounds; Public Schools Cricket;
       London Rowing Club] (p209-225)
Sporting Intelligence [inc. North Staffordshire Hunt; Wingfield Sculls; Obituaries of John
       Drake-Smith, Albert Menier, Thomas Ramshay, Percy Hope-Johnstone and
       Robert Peck; Brampton Harriers; Avon Vale Hunt; Doggett's Coat & Badge] (p225-230)

Issue 476 : October 1899

Portrait [sculp. Allingham] and Biography - Robert Poore (p231-233)
In East Anglia by Richard Green-Price (p233-237)
The Pointer by Walter Gilbey (p238-239)
Engraving [sculp. Babbage]: *The Spanish Pointer* (facing p238)
Racehorses from Australia by John Doyle (p239-247)
Engraving: *Meets of the Belvoir Hounds* (facing p247)
[Review] *History of the Belvoir Hunt* by Thomas Dale (p247-250)
Photograph [pinx. Nightingale]: *Gambler* (on p249)
Lithograph: *John Houson, Rector of Brant Broughton* (facing p250)
Deadly Snakes of India by John Russell (p251-258)
Curiosities of Shooting by Thomas Fremantle (p258-261)
Head-Stalls and Halters [with Photographs] by Horace Hayes (p262-264)
Percy Brown [verses] by William Phillpotts-Williams (p265)
A Day with the Otter Hounds (p266-267)
Bowls by James Pretsell (p267-268)
The Chance of the Game: Faro's Daughter by Arthur Griffiths (p269-273)
Music and Morals in the Kennel by Thomas Dale (p273-275)

The Sportsman's Library: Reviews of *After Big Game in Central Africa* by Edouard Foa; *Old Raby Hunt Club Album* by George Fothergill; *Bearers of the Burden* by William Drury; *Retrievers and How to Break Them* by Henry Smith; *Flat Racing Explained* by Francis Higgins; *Kennel Nomenclature* by Michael Lloyd-Price; *The Golfers' Guide* by James Fairbairn, and *Hedges & Hedge-Making* by William Malden (p275-278)

Life's Run [verses] by Harry Lupton (p278)

Anecdotal Sport by William Willmott-Dixon (p279-283)

The Veterinary Profession by Charles Batchelder (p284-288)

Our Van [inc. Stockton Meeting; Leopardstown Races; Oakley Hunt; Bath & County Harriers; Obituaries of Charles Leedham and William Bartlett; Wells Hounds; Dublin Inter-Regimental Polo; Irish Golf Championship] (p288-300)

Sporting Intelligence [inc. Obituaries of Arthur Budd and Ernest Renshaw; Blackpool Athletics; Albrighton Hounds; Kildare Hunt] (p300-304)

Issue 477 : November 1899

Portrait [sculp. Mote] and Biography - Nathaniel Cockburn (p305-307)

What Shall I Subscribe by William Blew (p307-312)

Some Spanish Mules by Arthur Griffiths (p312-317)

Photograph: *Charles Leacroft* (facing p317)

The Bishop of Brackenfield (p317-320)

Hands [verses] by William Phillpotts-Williams (p320)

What is a Sportsman by Richard Green-Price (p321-325)

Engraving [sculp.Babbage]: *The Shoeing Forge* (facing p325)

The Village Forge (p325-326)

Snipe by John Russell (p326-334)

Land on the Starboard Bow by Frederick Gale (p334-338)

Hind Shooting (p338-341)

Spaniel and Pheasant by Frederick Gresham (p342-344)

Lithograph [pinx. Cooper]: *Spaniel and Pheasant* (facing p342)

Anecdotal Sport by William Willmott-Dixon (p344-349)

The Hunting Season by William Blew (p349-353)

Review: *Baily's Hunting Directory* by Edward Cuming (p353)

Our Van [inc. Manchester Meeting; Amory's Staghounds; Ledbury Hunt; Castlecomer Hounds; Limerick Hunt; American Polo; Scottish National CoursingClub] (p354-374)

Sporting Intelligence [inc. Shropshire Hounds; Obituaries of Frederick Charsley, John Gretton and Thomas Anson; Blencathra Hunt; Cheshire County Cricket Club; Tedworth Hunt; Ormond Hounds] (p375-378)

Issue 478 : December 1899

Portrait [sculp. Allingham] and Biography - George Osborne (p379-381)

Twenty-One Years of a Chalk-Stream Diary by Frederic Halford (p381-386)

Lithograph [pinx. Ross]: *Robert Luther of Acton Salop* (facing p387)

Amateur Huntsmen by Richard Green-Price (p387-391)

Sportsmen to the Front by Thomas Dale (p392-395)

Hunting in France by John Russell (p395-400)

More about Mules by Arthur Griffiths (p401-405)

What Next by Ivo Bligh (p405-409)

Review Essay: *Side-Saddle Riding* [with Photographs] by Eva Christy (p411-413)

The Foxhunter's Widow [verses] by William Phillpotts-Williams (p413)

Modern Marksmanship [with Photograph] by Thomas Fremantle (p414-419)

Hunting: Ancient and Modern by William Blew (p420-425)

Engraving [sculp. Scott]: *Hunter - Duncombe* (facing p420)

Anecdotal Sport by William Willmott-Dixon (p425-427)

The Sportsman's Library: Reviews of *Lays of the Chase* by Harry Lupton; *The Trout-Fly Dressers Cabinet of Devices* by Harry McClelland (p427)

Will Dale by Edwin Smith (p428-429)

Our Van [inc. Aintree Meeting; Obituary of James Jewitt; Cottesmore Hunt; Rufford Hounds; Galway Blazers; Kildare Hunt; University Sport; Brancaster Golf] (p429-448)

Sporting Intelligence [inc. Yorkshire County Cricket Club; Heythrop Hunt; Obituaries of Arthur Puttick, George Rumbold, William Tharp, Stanley Dendy and Charles Dalley; Cheshire Beagles; South Union (Cork) Hunt; Clare Harriers] (p448-452)

Volume 73, January - June 1900

Issue 479 : January 1900

Portrait [sculp. Palfrey] of Otto Madden, jockey — Title page

Portrait [sculp. Alais] and Biography - William Beresford (p1-5)

Woodcock by John Russell (p5-13)

Verses by George Whyte-Melville: To an Old Schoolfriend (p13-14)

Millais the Sportsman by John Bickerdyke (p14-18)

Hunting Dress, Ancient and Modern by William Blew (p19-23)

Cavalry Horsemanship by Francis Dashwood (p24-25)

Rattler [verses] by William Phillpotts-Williams (p25)

[Review] *Manual on Coaching* [with Musical Score] by Fairman Rogers (p26-30)

Shooting in Egypt by George Heathcote (p30-34)

Fair Play [with Diagram] by Edward Bligh (p35-37)

Photograph [Newman]: *Walter Rothschild's Team of Zebras* (facing p39)

The Zebra in Harness by Abel Chapman (p39-40)

Anecdotal Sport by William Willmott-Dixon (p40-43)

The Sportsman's Library: Reviews of *The History of the York & Ainsty Hunt* by William Scarth-Dixon; *Colonel Botcherby MSH* by William Fox-Russell; *Lady Barbarity* by John Snaith; *Thomas's Hunting Diary* by James Clair-Erskine; *Holloas from the Hills* by Scott Anderson (p44-48)

Cross-Country Meetings by Richard Green-Price (p49-51)

Our Van [inc. Lancashire Handicap; Obituaries of Richard Naylor, Anchitel Ashburnham and William Gregory; South Dorset Hunt; South Quorn Hunt; Meath Hounds; Cambridge University Boat Club] (p51-76)

Sporting Intelligence [inc. Llangibby Hounds; Obituaries of Thomas Stevens, Charles Ward, Philip Williams and Arthur Fortescue; South Cheshire Hunt; West Surrey Staghounds] (p77-80)

Issue 480 : February 1900

Portrait [sculp. Allingham] and Biography - William Ward (p81-85)

Sport and the War (part 1) by Richard Green-Price (p85-89)

Natural Fly Preservation by Wilson Pope (p90-94)

The Duke of Westminster by Edward Cuming (p94-96)

Engraving [sculp. Palfrey]: *Hugh Grosvenor* (facing p94)

An Old Wykehamist [Cricket] by Alfred Lowth (p97-100)

Missing [verses] by Harry Lupton (p100)

Transport and Supply in South Africa by John Russell (p101-107)

Cross-Country Meetings by Tresham Gilbey (p107)

Photograph: *Civilisation's Progress* (facing p109)

[Review] On the Pacific Slope: *Fifteen Years' Sport and Life in the Hunting Grounds of Western America and British Columbia* by William Baillie-Grohman (p109-111)

Photograph: *The Largest Moose Antlers on Record* (facing p111)

The Winter Exhibition at The Royal Academy by Edward Cuming (p111-112)
Charles Ward by William Blew (p113-119)
The Sportsman in the Transvaal [verses] by William Phillpotts-Williams (p120)
Spurs, Ancient and Modern [with Photographs] by George Burrows (p121-127)
National Hunt Rules by Henry Powell (p127-128)
Anecdotal Sport by William Willmott-Dixon (p129-132)
The Sportsman's Library: Reviews of *Riding, Driving and Kindred Sports* by Thomas Dale; *Wisden's Cricketers' Almanack 1900* by Sydney Pardon; *Amongst the Jockeys 1899* by Edmund Searle (p132-134)
Our Van [inc. Vine Hounds; Isle of Wight Hunt; Obituaries of Archibald Blackwood and William Bates; North Cheshire Hounds; South Coast Staghounds; Carlow Hounds; Lucknow Polo] (p135-153)
Sporting Intelligence [inc. Shropshire Hounds; Obituaries of David Turner, George Watson, Elliott Hodgkin, William Brancker, Arthur Mansfield, Henry Meux, Margrave Pallavicini, Pryse Pryse, John Levett and John Thewlis; Gogerddan Hounds; Kent County Cricket Club Presentations; Essex Hunt] (p153-156)

Issue 481 : March 1900

Portrait and Biography - John Bulteel (p157-160)
Lithograph [pinx. Babbage]: *Manifesto* (facing p158)
Game Preservers and Peregrines by Edmund Mitchell (p160-166)
Lithograph [pinx. Babbage]: *Drogheda* (facing p160)
Sport and the War (part 2) [with verses] by Richard Green-Price (p166-170)
Verses by George Whyte-Melville [second set] (p170-171)
The Position of Provincial Countries by William Phillpotts-Williams (p171-172)
Modern Steeplechasing by William Scarth-Dixon (p173-176)
Lithograph [pinx. Palfrey]: *Royal Horse Artillery Team Horse* (facing p177)
The Transport of Army Horses to South Africa by Henry Powell (p177-179)
Stet Fortuna Domus by Frederick Gale (p180-182)
The Yeoman and the Hunting Man as Soldiers by Hugh Henry (p183-185)
Fractures in Horses Limbs [with Sketches] by George Fleming (p186-192)
Fashions in Card Games by Henry Allen (p192-200)
Hunting Recollections by Daly Devereux (p200-204)
A Shoot on Dartmoor by Edward Caswall (p204-207)
The Sportsman's Library: Reviews of *Among Horses in Russia* by Horace Hayes; *Football, Hockey & Lacrosse* by John Fegan and *The Foxhunter's Vade Mecum* by Richard Ord (p208-209)
Our Van [inc. Gatwick Meeting; Obituary of Harry Bull; Dartmoor Hounds; Silverton Harriers; Tipperary Hunt; Punjab Polo Tournament; North Wiltshire Polo Club] (p209-227)
Sporting Intelligence [inc. Tiverton Hunt; Obituaries of William Brougham, Samuel Marsland, Losey Wilkinson, Thomas Phillips and Richard Bevan; Braes of Derwent Foxhounds; Tenby Hunt Steeplechases; Pontefract Farmers' Club; Glamorganshire Hounds] (p227-230)

Issue 482 : April 1900

Portrait [sculp. Mote] and Biography - Edward Portman (p231-232)
An Imperial Corps of Guides by Henry Allen (p233-238)
Veteran Masters of Harriers by John Russell (p239-247)
Photograph [Elliott]: *John Vaughan-Price* (on p239)
Photograph [Chaffin]: *William Chorley* (on p241)
Photograph [Tuck]: *George Race* (on p243)
The Coming Polo Season by Thomas Dale (p247-249)
Lithograph [pinx. Palfrey]: *Flying Fox* (facing p249)

The Kingsclere Sale by Richard Green-Price (p249-254)
The Hireling [verses] (p255-256)
Racket: A Belvoir Beauty by Cuthbert Bradley (p256-259)
Lithograph [pinx. Bradley]: *Racket* (facing p256)
Neotinea Intacta by Matthew Joyce (p260)
Some Curious Veterinary Receipts by Clayton Morrell (p261-262)
A Foot-Follower's Song [verses] by John Russell (p263)
Ten Days' Shooting Leave in India by Herbert Fanshawe (p264-268)
Women in the Hunting Field by Clifford Cordley (p269-273)
Hunting on the Modder (p274)
Anecdotal Sport by William Willmott-Dixon (p275-278)
Amputation of Limbs in Animals by Joshua Nunn (p279-280)
The Position of Provincial Countries (p280-281)
Our Van [inc. Sandown Park United Services Meeting; Taunton Vale Hunt; Royal Buckhounds; Ludlow Hounds; Kilkenny Hunt; The Etiquette of Huntsmen; Waterloo Cup; Obituaries of Edward Peate and James Maclaren] (p282-302)
Sporting Intelligence [inc. Shropshire Hounds; Obituaries of John Channons and George Cole; South Cheshire Hunt; Warnham Staghounds; Ullswater Foxhounds] (p302-306)

Issue 483 : May 1900

Portrait and Biography - Cyril Stacey (p307-309)
The Liabilities of Stakeholders by Harry Sargent (p310-312)
Lithograph [pinx. Palfrey]: *Fifteen-Hand Hunter* (facing p313)
The Horse for Mounted Infantry by William Fife (p313)
Hands and Seat by Hugh Henry (p314-317)
Is Pigeon Shooting on the Decline by Thomas Fremantle (p317-320)
Remounts for the English Army at Home by John Russell (p320-328)
Told by a Polo Stick [verses] by Harry Cumberland-Bentley (p329-331)
Old-Time Tandem-Matches by George Hardwick (p331-333)
Lithograph [pinx. Lucas]: *Puff and Piff* (facing p333)
White Dachshunds by Frederick Gresham (p333-334)
The Lady Cricketers [Illustrated] by Herbert Hewett (p334-340)
Revised Laws of Whist by William Whitfield (p340-342)
Bowls by James Pretsell (p343-344)
The Sportsman's Library [Illustrated]: Reviews of *Pink and Scarlet* by Edwin Alderson; *Among Horses in South Africa* by Horace Hayes; *The Game Birds* by Charles Dixon; *The Stallion Register* by William Walker (p344-347)
The Cricket Season by Sydney Pardon (p348-351)
Anecdotal Sport by William Willmott-Dixon (p352-355)
Our Van [inc. Lincolnshire Handicap; Alexandra Park Meeting; Blackmore Vale Hunt; Meath Hounds; Warwickshire Polo Club; Singapore Polo; Sandwich Golf] (p355-376)
Sporting Intelligence [inc. Blankney Foxhounds; Newry Harriers; Obituaries of Thomas Hornby, Frederick Milligan, William Denison and Robert Coombe; Suffolk Hunt Point-to-Point; Burstow Hounds] (p376-382)

Issue 484 : June 1900

Portrait [sculp. Allingham] and Biography - Edward Lycett-Green (p383-385)
The Meridian of Racing by Richard Green-Price (p385-388)
Photograph: *The Nimrod* [Coach] (facing p389)
Keep in the Middle of the Road by William Blew (p389-394)
Lithograph [pinx. Palfrey]: *Royal Mail Coach* (facing p392)
Horses and the War by John Russell (p394-397)
A Marylebone Muddle by Sydney Pardon (p397-399)

The Scotch Fishery Board's Marine Hatchery (p399-403)
Sporting Pictures at the Royal Academy by Edward Cuming (p403-405)
Ireland and Wild Birds by Watkin Watkins (p405-409)
[Review] *Boxers and their Battles* by William Willmott-Dixon (p409-413)
Lithograph: *Tom Sayers* (facing p411)
Lithograph: *Tom Spring* (facing p413)
Polo and the Measurement Question by Thomas Dale (p413-414)
Great Transformation Scene by Frederick Gale (p415-417)
    (* First Time in Baily's that it is stated "the Editor may not accept the writer's views" *)
Photograph: *Trained Goshawk 'Gaiety Gal'* (facing p419)
The Sportsman's Library: Reviews of *The Art and Practice of Hawking* [with Sketches] by
    Edward Michell; *Experts on Guns and Shooting* by George Teasdale-Buckell;
    Cricket in Many Climes by Pelham Warner; *Side Saddle Riding* by Eva Christy (p419-423)
Anecdotal Sport by William Willmott-Dixon (p423-426)
Herbert Otto Madden by Edwin Smith (p426-427)
Our Van [inc. Newmarket Craven Meeting; South & West Wiltshire Hunt; Obituaries of
    Gordon Mackenzie, Charles Rose and William Wright; Rugby Hounds; Plymouth
    Polo Club; Pembrokeshire Hounds] (p427-454)
Sporting Intelligence [inc. Sport at Kafir River Bridge; Obituary of Edmund Peel; Quorn Hunt;
    Holderness Hounds; Beaufort Hunt] (p454-458)

Volume 74, July - December 1900

Issue 485 : July 1900

Portrait [sculp. Palfrey] of Ben Capell, huntsman Title page
Portrait [sculp. Allingham] and Biography - James Russel (p1-3)
Reminiscences of Coaching Seventy Years Ago by Frederick Toms (p3-7)
[Review] *Small Horses in Warfare* by Walter Gilbey (p7-10)
Lithograph [pinx. Taylor]: *On the Alert* (facing p9)
The Height of Polo Ponies by Richard Green-Price (p10-11)
The Law of Averages & Chance by Henry Allen (p11-18)
Photograph [Haidinger]: *Avoiding the Grip* (facing p19)
Wrestling in the Salzburg Mountains by Lukas Eisenmann (p19-23)
Photograph [Haidinger]: *A Leg Grip* (facing p21)
Photograph [Haidinger]: *A Decisive Moment* (facing p22)
A Gap in the Pavilion at Lord's by Frederick Gale (p24-25)
The Johnsonian Angler by John Mullen (p25-29)
Frederick Marshall by Frederick Gale (p29-31)
Cricket by Sydney Pardon (p31-36)
Engraving: *The Royal Stand [Ascot] in 1842* (facing p37)
[Review] *Royal Ascot* by George Cawthorne (p37-40)
Engraving: *The Royal Stand [Ascot] in 1822* (facing p39)
Some Bets and their Subjects by William Blew (p40-44)
The Sportsman's Library: Reviews of *Poems* by Harry Cumberland-Bentley and *Songs of the
    Edinburgh Angling Club* by David Douglas (p45-46)
Imperial Yeomanry Hospital Fund by Andrew Fielding (p46-47)
Our Van [inc. Ascot Meeting; Ranelagh Polo Hunt Cup; Wirral Polo Club; Obituaries of Henry
    L'Estrange, David Ogilvy, Charles Lowman, Henry Dalbiac and William
    Pleydell-Bouverie; Cork Park Racing; Richmond Horse Show; Waterford
    Foxhounds] (p47-72)
Sporting Intelligence [inc. Sligo Polo Club; Obituaries of James Orr-Ewing, William Wilson,
    William Stout, David Buchanan, Cecil Boyle and Marshal Porter; Mid-Kent
    Staghounds; Rufford Foxhounds] (p73-78)

Issue 486 : August 1900

Portrait [sculp. Allingham] and Biography - Walter Buckmaster	(p79-82)
The Salmon Question by Frederic Halford	(p82-86)
Sledmere by Richard Green-Price	(p86-90)
Foxhounds, Ancient and Modern by William Blew	(p90-94)
Lithograph [pinx. Barraud]: *Betsy*	(facing p90)
Engraving [sculp. Babbage]: *Trojan*	(facing p92)
Lithograph [pinx. Bradley]: *Pytchley Potentate*	(facing p94)
A Queen's Cup Yacht Race by Brooke Heckstall-Smith	(p95-100)
On a Welsh Bog by Eric Parker	(p100-102)
The Ethics of the Prize Ring by George Murdoch	(p102-106)
Relieved [verses] by Harry Lupton	(p106-107)
Young Hawks by Edwin Moore	(p108-113)
Cricket by Sydney Pardon	(p114-118)
Otter Hunting by Lionel Jervis	(p119-121)
Anecdotal Sport by William Willmott-Dixon	(p122-126)
Another German Trout River by John Wheeldon	(p126-129)
The Sportsman's Library [A Diary and a Novel]	(p130)
Our Van [inc. Colombo Polo Club; Obituaries of Debonnaire Monson, William Edwardes, Thomas Conolly and Richard Daft; Stevenstone Hounds; Curragh Meeting; Henley Regatta]	(p131-147)
Sporting Intelligence [inc. Pretoria Steeplechase; Obituaries of John Shaw and John Wynn-Griffith; Stamford Bridge Athletics; Cheriton's Otterhounds]	(p147-152)

Issue 487 : September 1900

Portrait [sculp. Mote] and Biography - Archibald MacLaren	(p153-155)
General Seydlitz by John Russell	(p156-163)
A Gunroom Causerie (part 1) by Thomas Fremantle	(p164-165)
Prominent Members of Our Jockey Club by Cyril Luckman	(p166-169)
How Are We to Breed Cavalry Horses by Richard Green-Price	(p170-173)
David Buchanan by Frederick Gale	(p174-176)
Photograph [Speight]: *David Buchanan*	(facing p174)
The Thill-Dog in Belgium and France by Abel Chapman	(p177-180)
Photograph: *Vegetable Woman, Dinant*	(facing p179)
Photograph: *Baker's Cart at Dinant*	(facing p179)
How it all Came About [Canterbury Cricket Week] by Frederick Gale	(p180-183)
Billiards by John Buchanan	(p183-186)
Cricket by Sydney Pardon	(p186-189)
The Sportsman's Library: Reviews of *Stable Management* [with Photographs] by Horace Hayes; *Notes on Reconnoitring in South Africa* by Richard M.; *Annals of Sandhurst* by Mockler Ferryman; *All About Dogs* by Charles Lane; *Sporting Sketches* by Nat Gould; *The Young Sportsman* by Alfred Watson	(p189-196)
A Battle Royal by William Murdoch	(p197-200)
Public Schools Cricket in 1900 by Charles Smith	(p200-202)
Some of my Father's Stories by Frederick Toms	(p203-206)
Athletic Training in America by Charles Batchelder	(p206-208)
Our Van [inc. Goodwood Meeting; Warwickshire Polo; Obituaries of Horace Twiss, Charles Lowman, Frederick Church and David Mahony; Hawkstone Otterhounds; Drogheda Memorial Plate; Duhallow Hounds; Molesey Regatta]	(p209-222)
Sporting Intelligence [inc. North Cheshire Hunt; Obituaries of John Burnup, Henry Simpson, Alfred Ollivant and Thomas Ashton; Cowes Yachting; Punting Championships; Rugby Cricket Club]	(p222-228)

Issue 488 : October 1900

Portrait [sculp. Mote] and Biography - Henry Manners	(p229-231)
Hunting Sounds by Richard Green-Price	(p231-234)
Soldiering and Sport by John Russell	(p235-240)
Engraving [sculp. Babbage]: *The Leicestershire Steeplechase*	(facing p241)
[Review] *Animal Painters of England* by Walter Gilbey	(p241-243)
Engraving [sculp. Babbage]: *Wild Horses of Moldavia*	(facing p242)
A Gunroom Causerie (part 2) by Thomas Fremantle	(p243-245)
Reminiscences of Oxford Life and Sport (part 1) by John Hill	(p245-252)
Photograph: *John Hill*	(facing p247)
Photograph: *Henry Neville*	(facing p249)
Unsatisfied Umpires by Otho Paget	(p252-255)
Croquet Notes by Walter Peel	(p255-257)
Spurs at Polo by Thomas Dale	(p257-259)
The Game of Bridge by Ernest Bergholt	(p259-265)
Baily's Hunting Directory by Edward Cuming	(p266)
Irish Notes by Thomas Vigors	(p266-269)
Photograph [Lafayette]: *Hunter Gelding - Canon Arthur*	(facing p269)
[Review] *The Walkers of Southgate* by William Bettesworth	(p270-272)
The Farmer's Shooting Party by Edward Miller	(p273-277)
Staghunting History by William Blew	(p277-286)
Our Van [inc. York Ebor Meeting; Review of *Indian Polo Calendar*; Bedford Polo; Montreal Hunt Club; Dart Vale Harriers; East Cornwall Hunt; Swaffam Coursing]	(p286-301)
Sporting Intelligence [inc. Grouse Shooting; Obituaries of George Dawson-Damer, Richard Flower, Alfred Knowles and Edward Woodcock; Dublin Polo]	(p301-308)

Issue 489 : November 1900

Portrait [sculp. Allingham] and Biography - Digby Willoughby	(p309-312)
Shore Shooting in November by Edward Almack	(p312-315)
Whips [with Photographs] by George Burrows	(p315-324)
A Gunroom Causerie (part 3) by Thomas Fremantle	(p324-326)
Experiences of Horses in the War by Lester Arnold	(p326-330)
Reminiscences of Oxford Life and Sport (part 2) by John Hill	(p331-338)
Photograph: *William Jenkins*	(on p331)
Photograph: *John Hampton-Jones and Dairymaid*	(on p333)
Hunting Song [verses] by George Whyte-Meville	(p338)
Notes of a Yachting Cruise (part 1) by Thomas Plowman	(p339-346)
Photograph: *George Hart on The Knight*	(facing p347)
[Review] *Leaves from a Hunting Diary in Essex* by Beauchamp Yerburgh	(p347-349)
Lithograph [pinx. Abole]: *Willingate Spain and Willingate Doe*	(facing p349)
A Dream of the Happy Hunting Fields	(p350-354)
The Sportsman's Library: Reviews of *Hunting* by Otho Paget, and *Wild Sports of Burma and Assam* by Fitzwilliam Pollok and William Thom	(p354-356)
Welsh Blood [inc. verses]	(p357-358)
The Hunting Season's Arrangements by William Blew	(p358-365)
Our Van [inc. Old Manchester Racecourse; Obituary of William Chorley; Quarme Harriers; East Devon Hounds; Pembrokeshire Hunt; Manchester Polo Club; New Ross Hounds]	(p365-380)
Sporting Intelligence [inc. Obituaries of Henry Stanley, Edward Stracey-Clitheroe, Thomas Bennett, Richard Curzon-Howe, Reginald Partridge, James Porter, George Lister and Frederick Tait; Dumfriesshire Otterhounds; Deer-Stalking at Lillechonate; Great Yarmouth Swimming; Culmstock Otterhounds]	(p381-386)

Issue 490 : December 1900

Portrait [sculp. Mote], Biography and Obituary - Joseph Hanwell (p387-389)
The Reserve Squadrons by John Russell (p390-397)
The Successful Sires of the Racing Season by William Tegetmeier (p397-400)
Retriever Trials on Game by George Teasdale-Buckell (p401-404)
Reminiscences of Oxford Life and Sport (part 3) by John Hill (p405-411)
Photograph: *Henry Brassey* (facing p407)
Photograph: *Edward Hanmer* (facing p407)
Photograph: *Hicks Beach* (facing p407)
Photograph: *Charles Ashton* (facing p407)
Two Remedies [verses] by Robert Gibbs (p411-412)
Notes of a Yachting Cruise (part 2) by Thomas Plowman (p412-420)
About the Turf in 1900 by Richard Green-Price (p420-425)
Photograph [Edwards]: *Philip Le Gallais* (facing p425)
Philip Le Gallais by Edward Cuming (p425)
Sport and Feasting by William Blew (p426-430)
[Reviews] *Horses Past and Present* & *Ponies Past and Present* both by Walter Gilbey (p430-433)
Photograph: *Arab Horse Mesaoud* (facing p430)
A Favourite [verses] by Richard Clapham (p433-434)
A Gunroom Causerie (part 4) by Thomas Fremantle (p434-436)
The Cream of the Itchen by James Englefield (p436-439)
Ben Capell by Edwin Smith (p440-441)
Our Van [inc. Liverpool Autumn Cup; South Berkshire Hunt; Percy Hounds; Cleveland Hunt; Hunt Servants' Benefit Society; Sportsmen in the House of Commons; Galway Blazers; Obituary of William Yardley] (p441-460)
Sporting Intelligence [inc. Cotswold Foxhounds; Obituaries of Gordon Wood, Charles Paget, Rajinder Singh, Charles Hamblin, Arthur Swanston and Nicholas Calvert; North Buckinghamshire Harriers] (p461-466)

Frederick Gale

Volume 75, January - June 1901

Issue 491 : January 1901

Portrait [sculp. Palfrey] of Thomas Hayward, cricketer	Title page
Portrait [sculp. Allingham] and Biography - John Crozier	(p1-3)
With the Blencathra Foxhounds by Madeleine Campbell	(p3-5)
The Fox and his Enemies by Richard Green-Price	(p6-10)
Thoroughbreds and their Grassland by Adrian Peacock	(p10-15)
The Starting Gate in England by Roope Reeve	(p16-18)
The Make of Polo Sticks by Thomas Dale	(p18-21)
Lithograph: *Robert Nesfield*	(facing p21)
The Old Master of the High Peak Harriers	(p21-26)
Old Haunts Revisited	(p26-31)
An Usk Trout by Eric Parker	(p32-33)
The Workman's Motto [verses] by William Alderton	(p33-34)
Pheasant and Partridge Shooting by Thomas Fremantle	(p34-36)
The Sportsman's Library: Reviews of *The Livestock Journal Almanac* by James Sinclair; *A History of Steeplechasing* by William Blew; *Publicans and Sinners* by George Bosville	(p36-38)
Engraving: *Trotting Mare Phenomena*	(facing p36)
Cricket Topics by Sydney Pardon	(p39-40)
Some Steeplechase Comparisons by Arthur Meyrick	(p40-46)
A Gunroom Causerie (part 5) by Thomas Fremantle	(p46-48)
Practical Earth-Stopping	(p48-51)
Our Van [inc. Manchester Meeting; Jockey Club Inquiry; Obituaries of Thomas Jennings, Robert Hanbury, Jack Ferris and William Campbell; Essex Foxhounds; Quorn Hunt Finances; Cleveland Hunt; Jerez Polo]	(p51-75)
Sporting Intelligence [inc. Westmeath Foxhounds; Oxenholme Staghounds; Obituaries of Neil MacVicar, Emily Vicars and Charles Barrett; Hambledon Hunt]	(p75-78)

Issue 492 : February 1901

Portrait [sculp. Allingham] and Biography - Richard Lane-Fox	(p79-80)
Small Notes from a Small Shooting by Eric Parker	(p81-86)
Our Boys by Richard Green-Price	(p87-90)
Lithograph [pinx. Ferguson]: *Edgar Reynolds*	(facing p91)
Edgar Reynolds, Master of the Coniston Hounds by Edward Cuming	(p91-92)
The Coniston Hounds by Edward Cuming	(p92-97)
Sketch [pinx. Ferguson]: *Henry Lancaster, huntsman, Coniston Foxhounds*	(facing p95)
Lithograph [pinx. Ferguson]: *Henry Lancaster's Tackle*	(on p96)
From the Front: In the Orange River Colony	(p97-98)
Loch Leven with Rod and Skates by John Mullen	(p99-103)
Cricket Topics by Sydney Pardon	(p103-105)
Some Sportive Notes (part 1) by Thomas Plowman	(p105-111)
Winter Exhibition at The Royal Academy by Edward Cuming	(p112-113)
The Sportsman's Library: *Notes From The Diary* by George Fothergill; *Tales of Pink and Silk* by George Collins; *Wisden's Cricketers' Almanack 1901* by Sydney Pardon; *The Golden Circle* by William Philpotts-Williams, and *A Century of Foxhunting* by George Underhill	(p113-116)
Sketch [pinx. Alland] : *"Why I've Got a Croon on Muster Foswith you Feul"*	(facing p115)
Cricketomachia by Frederick Gale	(p117-123)
A Gunroom Causerie (part 6) by Thomas Fremantle	(p124-125)
Hunting a Century Ago by William Blew	(p126-130)

Cavalry Horses for India by William Fife (p130-134)

Our Van [inc. Obituary of William Beresford; National Hunt Rules; Warwickshire Hunt;
Worcestershire Foxhounds; Welsh Hounds for India; Badsworth Hunt;
Waterford Hounds; Lucknow Polo] (p134-152)

Queen Victoria [with Photograph] (p153)

Sporting Intelligence [inc. North Cheshire Hunt; Obituaries of Ernest Walford, Henry
Wyndham, James Rose, John Jones, Thomas Redford and Courtenay Clack;
Glamorganshire Hounds; Weston-super-Mare Harriers] (p154-156)

Issue 493 : March 1901

Portrait [sculp. Alais] and Biography - John Gilmour (p157-159)
The Future of the Yeomanry by John Russell (p160-167)
Salmonology by William Murdoch (p167-170)
Photograph [Johnstone]: *George Watson* (facing p171)
George Watson, Master of Foxhounds, Melbourne Hunt (p171-172)
After Woodcock in the Mediterranean (p172-175)
Some Sportive Notes (part 2) by Thomas Plowman (p175-178)
Our Girls by Richard Green-Price (p178-182)
A Panacea [verses] by Frederick Lutyens (p182-185)
Lithograph [pinx. Lucas]: *Roughside* (facing p185)
Some Curious Backs by Coulson Pitman (p185-188)
Lithograph [pinx. Babbage]: *Gradient* (facing p187)
Retrievers by Leonard Willoughby (p188-192)
Flyfisher's Fever by Paul Taylor (p192-193)
Royalty and Sport by William Blew (p193-201)
A Dream [verses] by Harry Cumberland-Bentley (p201-202)
The Sportsman's Library: *Riding and Hunting* by Horace Hayes (p202-204)
The Reintroduction of the Great Bustard by George Teasdale-Buckell (p205-206)
Anecdotal Sport by William Willmott-Dixon (p206-208)
Our Van [inc. Sandown Park Steeplechasing; National Hunt Rules; Obituaries of John
Hamilton, Henry Burrowes, Frederick Greenfield, William Reddie-Waddell and
Douglas Maclean; Croome Hounds; Lanarkshire & Renfrewshire Hunt;
Cambridgeshire Hounds; Meath Hunt; University Boat Race; International Rugby;
Skiff Racing Association] (p209-233)
Sporting Intelligence [inc. Abe Bailey Stud Sale; Obituaries of William Pochin, John Traherne,
George Bourne, Richard Harmer, John Nickolls, Vernon Drew, Alan Stewart and
John Banks; Middleton Park Harriers; Holderness Hunt] (p234-236)

Issue 494 : April 1901

Portrait [sculp. Allingham] and Biography - Richard Waldie-Griffith (p237-239)
Some Stray Notes: Foxhunting by Scott Plummer (p240-245)
Cavalry in War Time by John Russell (p245-252)
Engraving [pinx. Marshall]: *Heads Up and Tongues Going* (facing p253)
A Puppy Hunting by Ernest Middleton (p253-257)
Photograph [Thompson]: *Cecil Boyle* (facing p257)
[Obituary] Cecil Boyle by William Verney (p257-261)
Ars Scribendi by Richard Green-Price (p262-265)
Lithograph [pinx. Pridniss]: *The Moment to Pull* (facing p267)
The Sportsman's Library: Reviews of *The Wildfowler in Scotland* by John Millais; *The Laws
and Principles of Vint* by Frank Haddan (p267-269)
Lithograph: *Mallard Feeding* (on p267)
A Requiem [verses] by Harry Parker (p269)
Polo Prospects in 1901 by Thomas Dale (p270-273)

Names for Hounds by Alexander Wilson (p273-279)
Sport with the Army in South Africa by Charles Harper (p279-282)
The Autobiography of a Polo Pony by Frederick Rouse (p282-284)
Our Van [inc. Hurst Park Meeting; Obituaries of John Thursby and Richard Rawle; Royal
        Buckhounds; Barnstaple Staghounds; Dartmoor Hunt; Catterick Bridge Polo
        Club; Carlow Hunt; Scottish Grouse Shooting; Waterloo Cup; Oxford University
        Point-to-Point Races; England Rugby at Blackheath] (p285-313)
Sporting Intelligence [inc. Wheatland Hounds; Ullswater Foxhounds; Obituaries of Michael
        Church, Francis Phillips, Robert Boulton, Gerald Fitzgerald, Charles Ashworth,
        John Marriott and Joseph Lowe; Willenhall Harriers; Puckeridge Hounds;
        Thanet Harriers; Pendle Forest Harriers] (p313-316)

*The article <u>Ars Scribendi</u> contains the only known description of the magazine's founder
and first editor Alfred Head Baily *

Issue 495 : May 1901

Portrait [sculp. Allingham] and Biography - Lionel Palairet (p317-319)
Thoroughbreds and their Grassland by Adrian Peacock (p319-323)
Monmouthshire by Richard Green-Price (p324-327)
Two Old Family Packs of Harriers by John Russell (p327-332)
Photograph [Waldron]: *Thomas Eames* (on p328)
Photograph [Higgins]: *Edward Eames* (on p329)
Photograph [Elliott]: *William Bragg* (on p330)
Photograph: *Two Couple and a Half of the Furlong Harriers* (on p331)
The Leg-Before-Wicket Question by Courtenay Boyle (p332-336)
The Leading Cross-Country Stallions by Abel Chapman (p336-340)
Old Time Coach Driving by William Blew (p340-346)
The Lament of an Old Hound [verses] (p347)
Cricket Bar One by Frederick Gale (p348-350)
Comte Leon-Louis Tresvaux de Berteux by Charles Squire (p350-353)
Engraving: *Leon-Louis de Berteux* (facing p350)
Country Parsons by John Russell (p353-359)
The Sportsman's Library: Reviews of *The English Turf* by Charles Richardson; *John Wisden's
        Cricketers' Notebook* by Frederick Ashley-Cooper (p359-361)
Our Prospective Racing Yacht by Thomas Dale (p361-365)
The Royal Buckhounds by Edward Cuming (p365-366)
The Gauntlet by George Maunsell (p367-369)
Our Van [inc. Melton Mowbray Meeting; Lincoln Racing; Obituaries of Edward Thornewill,
        Douglas Lane and Edward Bastard; Ledbury Hunt; Belvoir Hounds; California
        Polo; Baldoyle Racing; Carlow & Island Hounds] (p369-392)
Sporting Intelligence [inc. Glamorgan Hunt; Isle of Man Harriers; Obituaries of John Hamer
        and Henry Wilmot; North Hereford Hounds; Huntingdon Steeplechase; Louth
        Hounds] (p392-396)

Issue 496 : June 1901

Portrait [sculp. Allingham] and Biography - James Larnach (p397-400)
Cavalry Charges in South Africa by John Russell (p400-406)
A Working Leg-Before-Wicket Majority by Edward Bligh (p407-413)
On Field Trials by George Teasdale-Buckell (p414-417)
Inclination to Try by William Phillpotts-Williams (p417-419)
To An Old Trout [verses] by Stephen Hiney (p419)
Photograph: *Old Joe by Decider* (facing p421)
Curious Backs by William Fawcett (p421)

The Pari Mutuel and its Rivals by Charles Squire (p422-426)

Cricket Reform by Otho Paget (p427-428)

The Champion Athlete of India by Charles Batchelder (p429-430)

Photograph [Mowll]: *Norman Pritchard* (on p429)

Sporting Pictures at The Royal Academy by Edward Cuming (p430-432)

Experiences among the Norwegian Trout by Abel Chapman (p432-438)

The Hunt Button in France [from *Annuaire de la Venerie Francaise*] (p439)

The Sportsman's Library: Reviews of *The Eighth Duke of Beaufort and the Badminton Hunt* by Thomas Dale; *Shots From a Lawyer's Gun* by Nicholas Everett, and *Cricket and Golf* by Robert Lyttelton (p440-443)

Lithograph [pinx. Grant]: *Eighth Duke and Duchess of Beaufort* (facing p440)

Automatons by William Blew (p443-446)

The Sportsman-Soldier's Lament [verses] by Reginald Wyverne (p447-448)

A Night in a Somali Karia by Henry Pilkington (p448-449)

Thomas Hayward by Edwin Smith (p450)

Our Van [inc. Epsom Meeting; Liverpool Polo Club; Hawkstone Otterhounds; Enfield Chace Hunt; Punchestown Racing; Berkeley Stud; Obituaries of Douglas Forbes and Daniel Legge; Deal Golf] (p451-472)

Sporting Intelligence [inc. Cottesmore Hunt; Obituaries of Andrew Johnstone and William Dore; Association of Masters of Harriers & Beagles; Penton Harriers; Lancashire County Cricket Club; Crawley & Horsham Point-to-Point Races] (p472-478)

Volume 76, July - December 1901

Issue 497 : July 1901

Portrait [sculp. Palfrey] of John Isaac, huntsman — Title page

Portrait [sculp. Allingham] and Biography - Oswald Mosley (p1-3)

Shropshire: Old Landmarks of Sport by Richard Green-Price (p3-7)

The Varsity and Afterwards (part 1) by Thomas Wells (p8-13)

Cricket Topics by Sydney Pardon (p13-15)

On Don-side by John Russell (p16-21)

A Plea for the Postboy by John Bluett (p21-26)

On a Welsh Stream by Abel Chapman (p26-29)

Judging at Shows by Gerald Ricardo (p29-31)

Photograph: *Tuner and Tippler – Rough Welsh Hounds* (facing p33)

Two Rough Welsh Hounds by Cambridge Phillips (p33)

Sport in Monmouth: Lord Tredegar's Hounds (p34-35)

From a Shooting Hut on the Norwegian Fjelds by Abel Chapman (p35-38)

On the Instinct of Animals by Gage Freeman (p38-41)

The Sportsman's Library: Reviews of *Sixty Years of the Turf* by George Hodgman; *How to Box to Win* by Terry McGovern; *Dogs Tales Wagged* by Richard Lloyd-Price; *The Lighter Side of Cricket* by Philip Trevor; *Tales of the Stumps* by Horace Bleackley (p41-45)

Old Sporting Magazines by George Hardwick (p46-49)

The Origin of Cricket by Charles Woodruff (p50-54)

Photograph [Rouch]: *Volodyovski* (facing p55)

Our Van [inc. Epsom Meeting; Masters of Foxhounds Association; Hunt Servants Benefit Society; Essex Staghounds; Eggesford Hounds; Oxford University Polo Club; Cork Park Racing; Dundalk Hurdles; Obituaries of Joseph Osborne and O'Connor Morris (*Triviator* of *The Field*); Muirfield Golf] (p55-76)

Sporting Intelligence [inc. Obituaries of Thomas Robinson, Courtenay Boyle, William Scott-Elliot and John Tait; Queen's Club Tennis; Irish Athletics; Dartmoor Foxhounds, Chiddingfold Hunt] (p76-82)

Issue 498 : August 1901

Portrait [sculp. Allingham] and Biography - Edgar Vincent (p83-84)
Photograph: *Perdita II* (facing p85)
The Royal Stud by Richard Green-Price (p85-89)
West Argyllshire Sport by Mackay Wilson (p90-93)
From Fort Jameson to Fort Rosebery by Hubert Harrington (p94-102)
The Varsity and Afterwards (part 2) by Thomas Wells (p102-105)
Troubadour [verses] by Reginald Wyverne (p105-106)
Maimed Warriors by John Russell (p107-111)
The Decline of Wrestling by Percy Longhurst (p111-114)
Horses and Hounds at Peterborough by Cuthbert Bradley (p114-121)
Lithograph [pinx. Bradley]: *Warwickshire Pedlar* (facing p114)
Salmon Culture in Norway by Abel Chapman (p121-123)
Feathered Friends and Foes by Watkin Watkins (p124-128)
The Evolution of the Phantom Minnow by George Maunsell (p128-131)
The Sportsman's Library: *Bird Watching* by Edmund Selous (p131-132)
Small Men as Soldiers by Robert Light (p132-134)
Our Van [inc. Auteuil Steeplechases; Ascot Meeting; Gosforth Park Racing; Obituaries of Pierre Lorillard and Matthew Maher; Public Schools Polo; Curragh Meeting; Henley Regatta] (p135-156)
Sporting Intelligence [inc. Cottesmore Hounds; Swimming Championships; University Tennis; Obituaries of Robert Carpenter and Stephen Phillpott; Blackmore Vale Hunt] (p156-162)

Issue 499 : September 1901

Portrait [sculp. Allingham] and Biography - Charles Newton (p163-166)
Scottish Fishing Inns by John Russell (p166-172)
Engraving [pinx. Topham]: *The Fly-Fisher* (facing p166)
The New Volume of The Stud Book by Richard Green-Price (p172-176)
My Small Moor by Eric Parker (p176-179)
The Past Season at Polo by Thomas Dale (p179-183)
Highland Holiday Angling by William Murdoch (p184-186)
Public Schools Cricket in 1901 by William Ford (p187-190)
Doggett's Coat and Badge by William Blew (p190-196)
Seventy-One Years in the Cricket Field by Frederick Gale (p196-200)
The Sportsman's Library: *The British Thoroughbred Horse* by William Allison reviewed by John Doyle (p200-206)
The First Shot of the Season by Thomas Fremantle (p206-208)
A Norman Horse Fair by John Russell (p209-214)
Photographs: *Types of Horses at a Norman Fair* (facing p211)
Cricket by Sydney Pardon (p214-216)
The Australian Horse and Rider by Hugh Henry (p216-220)
Our Van [inc. Goodwood Meeting; Devon & Somerset Staghounds; North Cotswold Hunt; Essex Otterhounds; Obituary of William Hicks-Beach; Burghley Park Polo Club; Galway Steeplechasing; Kingston Rowing Club] (p220-238)
Sporting Intelligence [inc. Bisley Rifle Competition; Wingfield Sculls; Punting Championships; Obituaries of Thomas Lane, George Lepper, Buchanan Baird, James Howard and Jack Boden] (p239-244)

Issue 500 : October 1901

Portrait [sculp. Allingham] and Biography - Ernest Cassel (p245-246)
Recruiting for Light Cavalry by John Russell (p247-252)
Ptarmigan Shooting by George Herbert (p253-254)

Retrievers: Some Difficult Problems by George Teasdale-Buckell (p254-259)
Photograph [Reid]: *Flat-Coated Retriever* (facing p254)
Photograph [Reid]: *Curly-Coated Retriever* (facing p254)
Map: Part of North-Eastern Rhodesia (facing p261)
Sport and Work on an African Station by Hubert Harrington (p261-263)
Mark Over by Richard Green-Price (p263-267)
County Cricket in 1901 by Sydney Pardon (p267-274)
A Criticism on Condition of Army Horses by John Hill (p274-276)
A Horse's Experience (part 1) by John Hill (p276-282)
The Sportsman's Library: Reviews of *Athletics of Today* by Harold Graham; *The State Breeding Studs of Austria and Hungary* by Georges Des Farges, and *Billiards for Everybody* by Charles Roberts (p282-283)
Hunting Counties by William Blew (p284-288)
The Selection of a Shot by Leonard Willoughby (p289-296)
Our Van [inc. Redcar Meeting; Clare Harriers; Norwich Staghounds; York & Ainsty Hunt; Indian Cavalry Polo; Obituary of Francis Lawley; New Dublin Racecourse; Royal Dublin Golf Club] (p297-320)
Sporting Intelligence [inc. Eggesford Hunt; Essex Union Foxhounds; Obituaries of Alexander Forbes and Arthur Dale; Grouse Shooting] (p321-326)

Issue 501 : November 1901

Portrait [sculp. Allingham] and Biography - Charles Pierrepont (p327-328)
Gone Away by Richard Green-Price (p329-332)
Kennels for Foxhounds [with Diagram] by Thomas Young (p332-339)
A Morning's Cubbing [verses] (p339-340)
Reminiscences of a Voyage by John Russell (p340-345)
Lithograph [pinx. Fothergill]: *Ruler* (facing p345)
Trail Hounds by George Fothergill (p345-348)
Reflections on Cricket by Otho Paget (p348-352)
A Trip to Lake Bangweulu by Hubert Harrington (p352-356)
Map: Another Part of North-Eastern Rhodesia (facing p352)
St.Hubert's Mass by Charles Squire (p356-357)
Photograph [Delton]: *Blessing the Hounds* (facing p356)
Salmonology by William Murdoch (p357-360)
A Horse's Experience (part 2) by John Hill (p361-367)
The Yachting Season of 1901 by Geoffrey de Holden-Stone (p367-370)
A Cure for the Bluedevils by Frederick Gale (p370-374)
The Sportsman's Library: Reviews of *Horse Breeding in England and India* by Walter Gilbey; *Mad Lorrimer* by Finch Mason, and *East of Suez* by Alice Perrin (p375-376)
The New Masters of Hounds by Edward Cuming (p377-381)
Our Van [inc. Newmarket Meeting; East Kent Hunt; Limerick Racing; Tipperary Hunt; Ormonde Hounds; Crystal Palace Polo Club; Royal & Ancient Golf Club (p381-401)
Sporting Intelligence [inc. Cranleigh Cricket Dinner; Woodland Pytchley Huntsman; West Surrey Staghounds; Eridge Foxhounds; Tullamore Harriers; Jedforest Hunt; Cheshire Dairy Show; Obituaries of Andrew Murray and Edward De Freville; Medway Rowing] (p401-406)

Issue 502 : December 1901

Portrait [sculp. Allingham] and Biography - William Wroughton (p407-408)
Our Riding Horses by Richard Green-Price (p409-412)
Sketchy Thoughts on Hunting (part 1) by William Blew (p413-416)
Exmoor at Night [verses] by William Phillpotts-Williams (p416-418)
Honorary Secretaries of Fox Hunts (part 1) by William Blew (p418-419)

Photograph [Salmon]: *John King*	(facing p418)
Photograph [Hughes]: *Henry Allfrey*	(facing p418)
The Sport of a Dry-Fly Purist by James Englefield	(p420-423)
The Leg-Before-Wicket Question [with Sketch] by Henry Palairet	(p423-430)
Long Reigning Masters of Hounds by William Blew	(p430-437)
The Progress of Grouse Preservation by George Teasdale-Buckell	(p437-442)
Evenings Sport along the Luapula River (part 1) by Hubert Harrington	(p442-444)
Kitchen Hippics [verses] by Henry Hall Dixon	(p444-445)
The Position of Foxhunting in Game Preserving Counties by Frank Bonnett	(p445-448)
The Sportsman's Library: Reviews of *Light Freights* by William Jacobs; *Reminiscences of a Gentleman Horse Dealer* by Harold Treherne	(p448-450)
A Disciple of Diana [verses] by Reginald Span	(p450-451)
Fox and Hare Hunting in the Middle Ages by John Russell	(p451-457)
John Isaac by Edwin Smith	(p457-458)
Our Van [inc. Newmarket Meeting; *The Racing Calendar*; Market Harborough Residents; Staintondale Hounds; Croome Hunt; Barnstaple Staghounds; Ranelagh Polo Club; Waterford Hounds; Obituary of John Jackson]	(p458-485)
Sporting Intelligence [inc. Obituaries of Archibald Smith, Alfred Tysoe, Wilford Brett, Lionel Barlow, John Lawrence, Culme Seymour and John Quickfall; Meynell Hounds; North Cotswold Hunt]	(p485-492)

Volume 77, January - June 1902

Issue 503 : January 1902

Portrait [sculp. Palfrey] of Kempton Cannon, jockey	Title page
Portrait [sculp. Allingham] and Biography - George Lehndorff	(p1-5)
The Oldest Hunt in England by Jack Fairfax-Blakeborough*	(p5-8)
Moving Spirit of Foxhunting by Lionel Lambart	(p8-10)
Our Riding Ponies by Richard Green-Price	(p10-14)
Honorary Secretaries of Foxhounds (part 2) by William Blew	(p14-16)
Photograph: *David Lascelles*	(facing p14)
Photograph [Watson]: *George Whitcombe*	(facing p14)
The Sportsman's Wardrobe by William Blew	(p16-21)
South African Horses by Horace Hayes	(p22-28)
Photograph [Hayes]: *Thick-Set Transvaal Gelding*	(facing p25)
Photograph [Hayes]: *Cape Pony - Arab Blood*	(facing p25)
Photograph [Hayes]: *Cape Pony - Well-Bred*	(facing p27)
Photograph [Hayes]: *Basuto Pony - Ordinary*	(facing p27)
Photograph [Hayes]: *Basuto Pony - Well-Bred*	(on p27)
No Critics but the Dogs by George Teasdale-Buckell	(p28-31)
Bloodstock Sales and the Breeding Question by Arthur Coaten	(p32-35)
Grass Countries [verses] by William Alderton	(p35)
Old Coaching Tokens by Septimus Berdmore	(p35-37)
Photographs: *Coaching Tokens*	(on p36)
The Sportsman's Library: Reviews of *Staghunting on Exmoor* by Philip Evered; *Hunting Journal of the Blackmore Vale Hounds* by Theodora Guest; *Livestock Journal Almanac* by James Sinclair; *Notes for Hunting Men* by Gordon Mackenzie; *Ice Sports* by Fletcher Robinson; *Monte Carlo Anecdotes* by Victor Bethell	(p37-42)
Photograph: *Culbone Stables*	(facing p39)
Amongst Indian Jheels by Henry Pilkington	(p42-44)
Operation for Broken Knees in Horses by Joshua Nunn	(p45-48)
The Red Horse Vale by Henry Allen	(p49-52)
Photograph: *Middleton Memorial Stone*	(on p51)

Ferreting by Eric Parker (p52-54)
William on Hunting [verses] by Stanley Hiney (p54)
Shooters and Shots by Leonard Willoughby (p55-58)
Our Van [inc. Steeplechasing; Shropshire Hunt; Ashburton Harriers; Obituaries of Charles Legard, Thomas Bligh, John Power and George Lohmann; Ledbury Hunt; Market Harborough Polo Club; Meath Hounds; Roscommon Staghounds; Sydney Test Match] (p58-83)
Sporting Intelligence [inc. Yorkshire Cricket; Essex Foxhounds; Obituaries of William Hanbury, Charles Molyneux, Percy Ormrod, James Napier and William Osborne; Henley Regatta Accounts; Minor Counties Cricket; South Oxfordshire Hunt] (p84-88)

* This is the earliest known freelance essay from the pen of Jack Fairfax-Blakeborough who, at the time, was an eighteen-year-old racing and hunting reporter for The North Eastern Daily Gazette in Middlesbrough *

Issue 504 : February 1902

Portrait [sculp. Allingham] and Biography - Peter Ormrod (p89-90)
Shooting Babblement by Thomas Fremantle (p91-95)
How American Polo Ponies are Trained by Thomas Dale (p96-98)
Fencing in England and France by Theodore Cook (p99-101)
Sport on the Luapula River (part 2) by Hubert Harrington (p101-106)
Map: *Lower Luapula District of Rhodesia* (facing p103)
Belvoir Past and Present by Cuthbert Bradley (p106-108)
Lithograph [pinx. Bradley]: *Belvoir* (facing p106)
A New Polo Ground for London by Thomas Dale (p109-113)
Drawing: *Plan of Roehampton Club Grounds* (facing p111)
The Crabber [verses] by William Phillpotts-Williams (p113-115)
Sketchy Thoughts on Hunting (part 2) by William Blew (p115-118)
Photograph [Byrne]: Francis Lawley (facing p119)
[Obituary] Francis Lawley by Edward Cuming (p119-122)
The Sportsman's Library: Review of *Deer Stalking and the Deer Forests of Scotland* by Augustus Grimble; *Wisden's Cricketers' Almanack* by Sydney Pardon; *Tales of Pink and Silk* by George Collins (p122-124)
Photograph: Henry Selwin (facing p125)
[Obituary] Lord Rookwood by Edward Cuming (p125-126)
Tandem Driving by William Blew (p126-132)
[Obituary] Another Landmark Removed [William Burrup] by Frederick Gale (p133-135)
Reminiscences of Thames Perch-Fishing by James Englefield (p135-142)
The Vulpicide's Dream (p142-150)
His Last Run [verses] (p150-151)
Our Van [inc. The Reformation of Racing; American Racing Scams; Quorn Hunt Huntsman; Portman's Hounds; South Coast Harriers; Baldoyle Meeting; Obituaries of Sackville Phelps, Louisa Devereux, Edward Bligh, Georgina Langford, James Harriss, Daniel Fraser and John Briggs; Carlow & Island Hunt] (p151-173)
Sporting Intelligence [inc. *The Racing Calendar*; Obituaries of William Liddell, Frank Smith and Leonard Netherton; Glamorgan Hounds; Tedworth Hunt] (p173-176)

Issue 505 : March 1902

Portrait [sculp. Alais] and Biography - Arthur Cecil (p177-179)
Fences by John Russell (p180-186)
Sketchy Thoughts on Hunting (part 3) by William Blew (p186-191)
A Journey of Exploration to the Liposhosi and Bangweulu by Hubert Harrington (p191-195)
Map: *Luapula District of Rhodesia* (facing p193)
Photograph [Yates]: *George Wilson* (facing p195)

Photograph [Lamb]: *Francis Henry*   (facing p195)
Honorary Secretaries of Foxhounds (part 3) by William Blew   (p195-197)
Salmon Angling by William Murdoch   (p197-201)
Light-Horse Breeding by Richard Green-Price   (p201-205)
Reynard's Reverie [verses]   (p205-206)
Risks in the Hunting Field by Hugh Henry   (p206-209)
Progress with the Partridge by George Teasdale-Buckell   (p209-212)
The Sportsman's Library: Reviews of *A History of the Meynell Hounds* by James Randall; *Horses on Board Ship* by Horace Hayes; *Transport of Horses by Sea* by Edward Martin; *Athletics* by William Beach-Thomas; *Athletic Sports* by William Burke; *A North Country Album* by George Fothergill; *The Fish River Bush, South Africa* by William Black; *Ping Pong* by Arnold Parker   (p212-216)
Sport with Horse and Hound on the South African Veldt by Burton Durham   (p216-220)
A Sportsman of Long Ago [Thomas Parkyns]   (p220-223)
The Haunt of the Huchen by Edwin Sachs   (p223-227)
The Oldest Hunt in the World by John Dransfield   (p227-228)
Shooters and Shots [Breach of Copyright]   (p228)
Our Van [inc. Kempton Park Steeplechasing; Melton Hunt Ball; Beaufort's Hunt; Tremlett Hounds; Cleveland Hunt; Worcester Park Polo Club; Obituaries of Derrick Power and William Fitzwilliam; Reviews of *The Fox-Hunter's Vade-Mecum* by Richard Ord; *Saddles and Harness* by John Nunn]   (p229-253)
Sporting Intelligence [inc. Obituaries of Ellis Ashmead-Bartlett and John Harbottle; Minehead Harriers; National Skating Association; Farndale Hunt Ball; Burma Pony Races]   (p253-256)

Issue 506 : April 1902

Portrait [sculp. Allingham] and Biography - Horace Brand   (p257-258)
How to Bet by Richard Green-Price   (p258-261)
The Town Plate by John Hill   (p262-265)
Honorary Secretaries of Foxhounds (part 4) by William Blew   (p266-267)
Photograph [Lafayette]: *Steuart Duckett*   (facing p266)
Photograph [Brown]: *George Wade*   (facing p266)
The Coming Polo Season by Thomas Dale   (p267-272)
[Obituary] William Fitzwilliam by Edward Cuming   (p272-273)
After Moorland Trout by Paul Taylor   (p274-276)
North-Eastern Rhodesia by Hubert Harrington   (p276-278)
The Remount Question by Frederick Dashwood   (p278-284)
Some Varied Shooting Scenes by Leonard West   (p284-286)
Riding Schools and Bits by Frederick Dashwood   (p287-288)
Coursing - The Waterloo Cup by George Wilson   (p289-291)
Photograph: *Tennis Ball* [Horse]   (facing p291)
The London Horse Shows by Gerald Ricardo   (p291-298)
Photograph: *Mademoiselle* [Horse]   (facing p297)
What is Cruelty in Sport by Abel Chapman   (p299-301)
Shooting Notes by George Teasdale-Buckell   (p301-303)
The Sportsman's Library: Reviews of *Shooting, Salmon Fishing and Highland Sport* by Augustus Grimble; *New Ideas on Bridge* by Archibald Dunn; *Shooting* by Alexander Shand   (p303-305)
Our Van [inc. Kempton Park Steeplechasing; South Staffordshire Hunt; North Warwickshire Hounds; Nantwich Farmers' Club; Obituaries of Arthur Dunn and Henry Haywood; Oxford University Point-to-Point Races]   (p305-332)
Sporting Intelligence [inc. Obituaries of William Drage, Frank Behrens and Thomas Bradburn; Radnorshire & West Herefordshire Hunt; Wells Harriers; Albrighton Hounds]   (p332-336)

Issue 507 : May 1902

Portrait [sculp. Allingham] and Biography - Powlett Milbank (p337-338)
Society and Sport in Tangier by Arthur Griffiths (p338-343)
Spring Thoughts by Richard Green-Price (p343-346)
The Australian Cricketers by Sydney Pardon (p346-349)
The Licensing of Firearms by Max Baker (p349-351)
Hunting Accidents of the Season by William Blew (p351-356)
How I Shot My Christmas Dinner by Hubert Harrington (p356-357)
Successful Sires of the Steeplechase Season by Arthur Coaten (p358-361)
To Generals MWW & JFW [verses] (p362-363)
The Grind - An Oxford Institution (p364-367)
Engraving [pinx. Marshall]: *Roan Billy* (facing p367)
[Review] *The History and Delineation of the Horse* by John Lawrence (p367-369)
Rook Shooting New and Old (p369-372)
A Retrospection [verses] (p373-374)
The Sportsman's Library: Reviews of *The Fox Terrier* by Rawdon Lee; *Breaking and Riding*
       by James Fillis (p374-375)
The Sports of Our Ancestors by Abel Chapman (p375-380)
Old Coaching Days by William Blew (p380-386)
Eheu Fugaces [verses] by Robert Gibbs (p386-387)
Coiling and Casting from the Reel by Alfred Burden (p388-389)
Our Van [inc. Lincoln Meeting; New Manchester Racecourse; Northampton Races; Essex
       Staghounds; Southwold Hounds; Percy Hunt; Hailsham Harriers; Obituary of
       Power O'Shea; Brookside Harriers] (p390-412)
Sporting Intelligence [inc. Meynell Hunt Point-to-Point; Henham Harriers; Obituaries of
       William Langley*, Ernest Brown and Richard Fry; Cheshire Beagles; High
       Peak Harriers; Cattistock Hounds] (p412-418)

** Bill Langley, who died in Florence aged 79, had been a sporting writer for over half a century.
For many years he was the editor of Bell's Life and in 1862 took up the editor's chair of The Sporting
Gazette. Under the pseudonym of 'Pavo' he wrote articles on The Turf for The Morning Post **

Issue 508 : June 1902

Portrait [sculp. Allingham] and Biography - Charles Fry (p419-421)
The Horse: Its Senses and Disposition by Richard Green-Price (p422-426)
Some Lessons in Polo from America by Thomas Dale (p426-429)
Photograph [Webster]: *Reginald Corbet* (facing p429)
[Obituary] Henry Reginald Corbet by Edward Cuming (p429-432)
To A Leicestershire Fox [verses] by Stephen Hiney (p432)
Sport at the Royal Academy by Edward Cuming (p432-436)
New Guns and Old Theories on Gunnery by George Teasdale-Buckell (p436-439)
The Rubaiyat of the Turf [verses] (p440-441)
A Retrospect of Thames Trout-Fishing by James Englefield (p441-447)
Impressions of the International Golf Match by Gordon McPherson (p447-449)
A Hundred Years Ago: From *The Sporting Magazine* (p449-450)
The Sportsman's Library: Reviews of *Sporting Pictures* by Fletcher Robinson; *International*
       Polo Club Guide by Josiah Newman (p450-453)
Engraving [sculp. Engleheart]: *The Steward's Stand after the Derby* (facing p453)
An Old Derby Picture by Edward Cuming (p453-454)
School Riding in the Hunting Field by William Blew (p454-459)
The Battered Brigade [verses] by William Oliver (p459-460)
Light-Horse Breeding by Lionel Foster (p460-463)
Somervile's Land (part 1) by Frederick Bramston (p463-466)

Kempton Cannon by Edwin Smith   (p467-468)

Photograph [Dickinson]: *James Machell*   (facing p468)

Our Van [inc. Newmarket Meeting; American Polo Tour; York Polo Club; Obituaries of
   James Machell and Evan Williams; Punchestown Meeting; Cork Park Racing;
   Irish Ladies Golf]   (p468-495)

Sporting Intelligence [inc. Blackmore Vale Hunt; Obituaries of Bertram Drage, James
   Hopwood and Thomas Dunn; Manchester Tennis Club; Hursley Foxhounds] (p495-502)

Volume 78, July - December 1902

Issue 509 : July 1902

Portrait [sculp. Alais] of Thomas Bishopp, huntsman   Title page

Portrait [sculp. Colls] and Biography - Foxhall Keene   (p1-3)

What Have We Learned From The War by John Russell   (p3-8)

Some Reminiscences of the Road by William Blew   (p8-15)

Photograph [Rouch]: *Hurlingham Cup Polo Team*   (facing p15)

Our Polo Players of Today by Thomas Dale   (p15-19)

Photograph: *Frederick Freake*   (facing p16)

Photograph: *Walter Buckmaster*   (facing p16)

Photograph: *Patrick Nickalls*   (facing p16)

Photograph: *Cecil Nickalls*   (facing p16)

Photograph [Rouch]: *The Inniskilling Team*   (between p16-17)

Photograph: *Francis Egerton-Green*   (between p16-17)

Photograph: *Edward Miller*   (between p16-17)

Photograph: *John Hargreaves*   (between p16-17)

Photograph: *Gerald Fitzgerald*   (between p16-17)

Photograph: *Charles Stanhope*   (between p16-17)

Photograph: *John Watson*   (between p16-17)

Photograph: *Alfred Rawlinson*   (between p16-17)

Photograph: *John Phipps-Hornby*   (between p16-17)

Photograph: *Henry Fitzroy*   (between p16-17)

Photograph: *Humphrey de Trafford*   (between p16-17)

Photograph: *Edward Sheppard*   (between p16-17)

Photograph: *Jack Tyrwhitt-Drake*   (between p16-17)

Photograph: *Godfrey Heseltine*   (facing p17)

Photograph: *Robert Hudson*   (facing p17)

Photograph: *Jean de Madre*   (facing p17)

Photograph: *Frank Mackay*   (facing p17)

Some Gossip on Irish Horsebreeding by Claremont Clare   (p20-24)

[Review] A Solution of the Remounts Question: *Horses for the Army* by Walter Gilbey (p24-26)

Sea Trout: Fishing and Fisheries (part 1) by William Murdoch   (p27-31)

The New Proposals for Field Trials by George Teasdale-Buckell   (p31-35)

A Hundred Years Ago: Cricket from *The Sporting Magazine*   (p35-36)

Lithograph [pinx. Bradley]: *England versus America*   (facing p36)

International Polo by Thomas Dale   (p36-38)

The Sportsman's Library: *Surrey Cricket: Its History and Associations* by Richard Webster (p39-41)

Cricket - Futile Test Matches by Otho Paget   (p41-45)

School Riding in the Hunting Field: A Reply   (p45-46)

Our Van [inc. Castle Irwell Racecourse; Doncaster Spring Handicap; International Polo Matches;
   Obituaries of Thomas Whitemore, Robert Dawson and Henry Latham; Richmond
   Horse Show; Hoylake Golf]   (p47-65)

Sporting Intelligence [inc. Carmarthenshire Hunt; Obituaries of George Gregson, Charles
Earle-Marsh, Geoffrey Austin and Harry Goodbun; Cambridgeshire Hunt; Melbrake
Hounds; Longford Harriers]   (p65-72)

*From this issue there is a new style to Our Van. There are now lengthy comments on various
sporting issues. However, records do not indicate that there is a new 'Van Driver'*

Issue 510 : August 1902

Portrait [sculp. Allingham] and Biography - James Butler   (p73-74)
The Decay of Riding by Hugh Henry   (p75-77)
Eclipse by Walter Gilbey   (p78-82)
Lithograph [pinx. Stubbs]: *Eclipse*   (facing p78)
The Report of the Betting Committee by William Blew   (p82-84)
A Mixed Bag at Fort Rosebery by Hubert Harrington   (p85-86)
Lithograph [pinx. Marshall]: *Tom Oldaker*   (facing p87)
The Old Berkeley Country by Otho Paget   (p87-91)
Cricket by Sydney Pardon   (p92-98)
The Golf Championships by Gordon McPherson   (p98-100)
A Hundred Years Ago: Shooting from *The Sporting Magazine*   (p101-102)
[Review] The Sportsman's Library: *Modern Polo* by Edward Miller   (p102-107)
Horse and Hound at Peterborough by Cuthbert Bradley   (p108-113)
Lithograph [pinx. Bradley]: *The Champion Dog Hound*   (facing p108)
On the Choice Among Many Powders by George Teasdale-Buckell   (p114-117)
Puppy Judging by George Collins   (p117-119)
In the Gloaming by Eric Parker   (p119-121)
Our Van [inc. Ascot Racecourse; Ranelagh Polo Cup; Carlisle Light Horse Show; York Polo
Club; University Sport; Henley Regatta]   (p121-140)
Sporting Intelligence [inc. Beenham House Stud; Heythrop Hunt; Fitzwilliam Hounds;
Obituary of John Dennis; Southwold Hunt]   (p140-148)

Issue 511 : September 1902

Portrait [sculp. Allingham] and Biography - Aldred Lumley   (p149-152)
Some St.Leger Annals by Richard Green-Price   (p152-156)
Scentless Birds and their Enemies by George Teasdale-Buckell   (p157-159)
The Past Polo Season by Thomas Dale   (p160-163)
Photograph: *Eleanor 1801*   (facing p163)
Photograph: *Blink Bonny 1857*   (facing p163)
Eleanor and Blink Bonny at Epsom by Arthur Meyrick   (p163-168)
Reminiscences of Thames Fishing by James Englefield   (p168-172)
Public School Cricket in 1902 by William Ford   (p173-176)
Autumn Trouting in the Luxemburg Ardennes by Edwin Sachs   (p176-183)
Photograph [Hawkins]: *Gilbert Jessop*   (facing p183)
Cricket: The Match of the Season by Otho Paget   (p183-186)
A Hundred Years Ago: Dogget's Annual Coat & Badge from *The Sporting Magazine* (p187-188)
The Sportsman's Library: Reviews of *More Tales of the Stumps* by Horace Bleackley;
Sporting Scotland by Thomas Dykes   (p188-189)
Annals of the Road by William Blew   (p189-196)
Our Van [inc. Lingfield Park Plate; Goodwood Meeting; Obituary of Anthony Maynard;
York & Ainsty Hunt; Hurlingham Polo; Warwickshire Polo Club; London
Rowing Club; Cork Regatta; Newquay Golf]   (p196-215)
Sporting Intelligence [inc. Cobham Stud; Obituaries of John Watts, William Gerard, Frederick
Bartlett and George Vernon; Crystal Palace Athletics; Wingfield Sculls;
Wynnstay Hunt]   (p215-222)

Issue 512 : October 1902

Portrait [sculp. Colls] and Biography - John Lumley-Savile (p223-226)
Salmon Lore by William Murdoch (p226-230)
Photograph [Ernst]: *Penry Palfrey* [*Baily's* Engraver] (facing p231)
[Obituary] Penry Powell Palfrey by Edward Cuming (p231-233)
Lithograph [pinx. Palfrey]: *Pulling up to Unskid* (facing p232)
Engraving [sculp. Palfrey]: *Horse and Foal* (on p233)
A Very Rough Day by Eric Parker (p234-235)
The Classics of Old Venery (part 1) by William Baillie-Grohman (p236-241)
The Future of Grouse Shooting by George Teasdale-Buckell (p242-245)
The Horse: Its Action and Deportment by Richard Green-Price (p246-250)
Blue and White Hoops [verses] by William Ogilvie (p250)
Some United States Partridges by Robert Shufeldt (p251-255)
Lithograph [Shufeldt]: *Texan Bob-White Partridge* (on p251)
Lithograph [Shufeldt]: *Mountain Partridge* (on p252)
Lithograph [Shufeldt]: *Chestnut-Bellied Scaled Partridge* (facing p252)
Lithograph [Shufeldt]: *Gambel's Partridge* (facing p252)
Engraving [pinx. Shufeldt]: *Massena Partridge* (on p254)
A Chant from North Cheshire [verses] by John Brown (p255-256)
[Obituary] A Famous Huntsman: John Dale by Edward Cuming (p257-260)
Photograph [Hills]: *John Dale* (on p257)
A Hundred Year Ago: Shooting in Scotland from *The Sporting Magazine* (p261)
The Cricket Season of 1902 by Otho Paget (p262-266)
Sport Obtainable near Aden by Henry Pilkington (p266-269)
The Sportsman's Library: Review of *Scottish Hunts* by Harry Judd (p270-271)
Our Van [inc. Pontefract Racecourse; Knavesmire Rent; Quorn Hunt; Melton Horse Show; London Polo Club; Coursing; Obituaries of George Vernon and Jack Russell; Portrush Golf] (p271-289)
Sporting Intelligence [inc. Hampshire Cricket; Doncaster Sales; Pytchley Hounds; Upham Draghounds; Obituary of James Lyall; Pretoria Polo] (p289-296)

Issue 513 : November 1902

Portrait [sculp. Allingham] and Biography - Luke White (p297-298)
Hunt Wants by Richard Green-Price (p298-301)
Dry-Fly Prospects by Frederic Halford (p301-305)
The Rules of Polo by Edward Miller (p305-308)
Lithograph [pinx. Lewinn]: *Thomas Rounding* (facing p309)
Some Old-Fashioned Sportsmen (part 1): Thomas and Richard Rounding by Walter Gilbey (p309-310)
Hacking to Covert by Austin Mackenzie (p310-312)
Heavyweight Hunters by Albert Muntz (p312-313)
What a Good Huntsman Ought to Possess by William Sumners (p314-315)
Photograph [Piggott]: *Galeazzo* (facing p315)
Photograph [Piggott]: *St.Frusquin* (facing p315)
A Model Stud Farm by Abel Chapman (p315-320)
An Interrupted Query [verses] by John Brown (p320-321)
The Playgoer's Autumn (p321-326)
Jack and Joe of the Imperial Yeomanry [verses] by Walter Yeldham (p327)
A Hundred Years Ago: The Prince's Harriers from *The Sporting Magazine* (p328)
The Sportsman's Library: Reviews of *A History of the Cambridge University Cricket Club* by William Ford, and *Dry-Fly Fishing* by Frederic Halford (p329-332)
The Classics of Old Venery (part 2) by William Baillie-Grohman (p333-337)
A Review of the River Season by Reginald Rowe (p337-340)
The Yachting Season of 1902 by Geoffrey de Holden-Stone (p340-343)

The Betting Question [Debate from Carlisle Conference] by Edward Cuming   (p344-345)
The Hunting Season by William Blew   (p345-350)
Polo and the Price of Ponies by Edward Sawrey-Cookson   (p351)
Our Van [inc. Newmarket Racecourse Development; Cottesmore Hunt; Melton Chummery;
    Furlong Harriers; *Baily's Hunting Directory 1902-03*; Market Harborough Polo;
    Pytchley Hunt Horse Show; Obituaries of Edward Hardcastle and George
    Davenport; Highgate Swimming Gala]   (p352-367)
Sporting Intelligence [inc. Quantock Staghounds; Obituaries of James Gribble, Thomas Hughes,
    Daniel Neilson, Henry Poe, Richard Moir, Robert Gurdon, Thomas Erskine and
    Hubert Vernon; Neuaddfawr Foxhounds; Eridge Hounds; Barnstaple Staghounds;
    Cambo Harriers]   (p367-372)

Issue 514 : December 1902

Portrait [sculp. Allingham] and Biography - William Curtis   (p373-375)
A Few Suggestions as to Wire and Poultry Funds by Edward Cuming   (p375-379)
Umpiring at Polo by Denis Daly   (p380-381)
Among the Grayling by Paul Taylor   (p381-382)
How to Make a Partridge-Shoot by Arthur Blyth   (p383-386)
Photograph: *Difficult Shots - Low Behind*   (on p384)
Photograph: *Difficult Shots - High Behind*   (on p385)
Polo: America versus England 1902 by Edward Miller   (p386-389)
Photograph: *Edward Bowlby*   (facing p389)
[Obituary] Edward Salvin Bowlby   (p389-390)
The Bloodhound by Cyril Stacey   (p391-398)
Photograph: *The Homeleigh Bloodhounds*   (facing p393)
Photograph: *Brindisi, Regent and Black Marcus*   (on p395)
Polo Topics by William Ball   (p399-400)
[Obituary] Henry Chandos-Pole by Edward Cuming   (p400-401)
The Memories of Sport by Knight Horsfield   (p401-404)
Sold [verses] by William Ogilvie   (p404)
A Hundred Years Ago: Foxhounds from *The Sporting Magazine*   (p405)
The Rules of Polo by Thomas Dale   (p406-408)
The Difficulties of a Master of Hounds   (p409-411)
The Sportsman's Library: Reviews of *Crag and Hound in Lakeland* by Claude Benson; *The
    Spell of the Jungle* by Alice Perrin; *The Credit of the County* by William Norris
    and *The Heart of the Ancient [Canadian] Wood* by Charles Roberts   (p411-413)
Riding to Hunt and Hunting to Ride by Hugh Henry   (p413-417)
Thomas Bishopp by Edwin Smith   (p417)
Our Van [inc. Middle Park Plate; Jockey Club Cup; Obituaries of Lewis Flower, Frederick
    Dugdale and Arthur Appleby; North Cotswold Hunt; Bath Harriers; Cumberland
    Hounds; England Polo Team to India; Sunningdale Golf; Oxford University
    Authentics Cricketers in India]   (p418-444)
Sporting Intelligence [inc. Dart Vale Harriers; Obituaries of Henry Deacon, William Pinder,
    Esme Harrison, Robert Luxton and John King; Newmarket Sales; North
    Cheshire Foxhounds; Brocklesby Hunt]   (p444-450)

Volume 79, January - June 1903

Issue 515 : January 1903

Portrait [sculp. Alais] of Danny Maher, jockey	Title page
Portrait [sculp. Colls] and Biography - Hugh Grosvenor	(p1-2)
Hunting Pages by Richard Green-Price	(p2-6)
Foxhunting Damages by Edward Cuming	(p6-8)
Qualifications in County Cup Polo by Edward Miller	(p8-9)
[Review] Memoirs of a Famous Schoolmaster: *Edward Bowen* by William Bowen	(p9-15)
Heads of the Belvoir Kennel 1902-03 by Cuthbert Bradley	(p16-19)
Drawings [pinx. Bradley]: *Heads of the Belvoir Kennel*	(facing p16)
The Ballade of Blankley Rough [verses] by Stephen Hiney	(p19)
The Advances of Medicine by Hammond Smith	(p20-25)
The Stag [verses]	(p25)
Concluding Reminiscences of Thames Fishing by James Englefield	(p26-30)
Tips and Tipping	(p30-31)
Cricket Problems by Otho Paget	(p32-34)
A Hundred Years Ago: Hounds from *The Sporting Magazine*	(p35)
Principal Polo Tournaments 1902 [Results Spreadsheet]	(p36-37)
Spaniels by George Teasdale-Buckell	(p38-40)
Engraving [sculp. Scott]: *Spaniel and Pheasant*	(facing p38)
Sketchy Thoughts on Hunting (part 4) by William Blew	(p40-44)
The Sportsman's Library: Reviews of *Racquets, Tennis and Squash* by Eustace Miles; *Livestock Journal Almanac* by James Sinclair; *Across Country with Horse and Hound* by Frank Peer; *The Englishwoman's Yearbook* by Francis Slaughter	(p44-48)
The Woodcock [verses] by Evelyn Lewes	(p49)
[Obituary] Tom Firr by Edward Cuming	(p50-51)
Our Van [inc. Obituary of Harry McCalmont; Quorn Hunt; Atherstone Hounds; Meerut Polo; Calcutta Polo Club; Newport Horse Show]	(p52-72)
Sporting Intelligence [inc. Warwickshire Hounds; Obituaries of George Anderson, Robert Jefferson, William Abdale and William Fane; Newmarket Sales; Garth Hunt; Belvoir Hunt Secretary]	(p72-76)

Issue 516 : February 1903

Portrait [sculp. Colls] and Biography - George Thursby	(p77-80)
Mementoes of Sport by Lester Arnold	(p80-87)
No Scent by Richard Green-Price	(p87-90)
Racing in South Africa by Leroy Scott	(p90-96)
Some Old-Fashioned Sportsmen (part 2): Francis Astley by Walter Gilbey	(p96-97)
Engraving [sculp. Woodman]: *Francis Astley and his Harriers*	(facing p96)
Quiet to Ride and Drive by William Blew	(p97-104)
Ireland [verses] by Reginald Wyverne	(p104-105)
Players That I Have Seen Play by John Bluett	(p105-109)
The Position of the Medical Profession by Hammond Smith	(p109-114)
Bend Or by Abel Chapman	(p114-116)
Foxhunting in Ireland Before the New Year by Edward Cuming	(p116-122)
The Sportsman's Library: Reviews of *History of the Brocklesby Hounds* by George Collins; *A History of The North Staffordshire Hounds* by Charles Blagg	(p122-124)
Proposed Alterations in Polo Rules by Edward Miller	(p125-127)
A Hundred Years Ago: Wildfowl from *The Sporting Magazine*	(p127-128)
Photograph [Dickinson]: *Henry Verney*	(facing p129)
[Obituary] Lord Willoughby de Broke of Compton Verney (part 1) by William Verney	(p129-133)

The Whip [verses] by Richard Clapham (p133)
Our Van [inc. Obituaries of Richard Fry, Edward Weatherby and George Champion; National Hunt Committee; Cottesmore Hunt; Morpeth Hounds; University Sport; Henley Regatta Rules] (p134-150)
Sporting Intelligence [inc. Obituaries of Lucius Gwynn, Harry Sidney, Charles Mason, Louis Bryne, Harriett Turnbull (daughter of C.J.Apperley), John Sparrow, George Pinder, William Hine-Haycock, Ashley Crompton and Edmond de la Haye-Jousselin; Exeter Harriers; Oxford Authentics in Delhi; Carmarthenshire Hunt Incident; Meath Hunt; Australian Cricket Finances; Teme Valley Foxhounds] (p151-154)

Issue 517 : March 1903

Portrait [sculp. Allingham] and Biography - Washington Singer (p155-157)
The Show Season by Richard Green-Price (p157-160)
Polo Ponies by Edward Miller (p160-164)
The Present Law on Gambling by William Blew (p165-167)
The Cap by John Douglas (p168-169)
Notes and Sport of a Dry-Fly Purist by James Englefield (p170-176)
Some Old-Fashioned Sportsmen (part 3): Philip Payne by Walter Gilbey (p176-177)
Lithograph: *Philip Payne* (facing p176)
Mainly About the National Hunt and its Members by Arthur Meyrick (p177-185)
Horses on Board Ship by Horace Hayes (p185-190)
Photograph: *End View of the Portable Horsebox* (on p186)
Photograph: *Stalls With Single Breastboards* (on p187)
Photograph: *Disembarking Sling* (on p188)
Photograph: *Disembarking Horses* (on p189)
A West Country Hunt by William Blew (p191-193)
The Trout Season by Paul Taylor (p193-195)
Cricket Reform by Edward Bligh (p195-197)
[Obituary] Lord Willoughby de Broke of Compton Verney (part 2) by William Verney (p197-203)
The Sportsman's Library: Reviews of *Veterinary Notes for Horse Owners* by Horace Hayes; *Hunting in Couples* by Godfrey Bosvile; *Hints on Billiards* by John Buchanan (p203-205)
Some Rare British Birds by Watkin Watkins (p205-210)
Our Van [inc. Kempton Park Meeting; Fernie Hunt; Atherstone Hounds Purchase; South Oxfordshire Hunt; Essex Staghounds; East Sussex Otterhounds; Obituary of Daniel French; Polo Ponies Register] (p210-231)
Sporting Intelligence [inc. Obituaries of John Fletcher, Oswald Park and William Bishop; Haydon Hunt; Eskdaill Foxhounds; Southern Counties Cross-Country Championships; Muskerry Hunt; East Kent Foxhounds] (p232-236)

Issue 518 : April 1903

Portrait [sculp. Colls] and Biography - Arthur Coventry (p237-239)
Who Wrote England's Oldest Hunting Book by William Baillie-Grohman (p240-246)
With Polo Players at Burlingame, California by Thomas Drybrough (p247-252)
Photograph [Drybrough]: *Ponies and Pavilion at Burlingame* (on p249)
Rebecca by Richard Green-Price (p252-255)
Hambledon - The Cradle of Cricket by Walter Bettesworth (p255-258)
Engraving [sculp. Rhodes]: *William Somervile* (facing p259)
Somervile's Land (part 2) by Frederick Bramston (p259-262)
Photograph: *Somervile Church Tablet* (facing p261)
Hansom Cabs by William Hill-James (p262-266)
Hunting on Wheels by Robert Cochrane (p266-268)
The Hare [verses] by Alan Haig-Brown (p268)

Polo: The Coming Season by Edward Miller (p269-275)
Photograph [Babbage]: *Polo Pony Larky* (facing p275)
The Spring Horse Shows by Gerald Ricardo (p275-279)
Gloaming Salmon Angling by William Murdoch (p280-284)
A Hundred Years Ago: Easter Sports from *The Sporting Magazine* (p284-285)
The Breeding of Hunters by Herbert Rowland (p285-288)
With the Border Mew by William Ogilvie (p288-291)
Robin Hill by Edward Cuming (p291-292)
Photograph [Grabham]: *Robin Hill* (on p291)
Our Van [inc. Manchester Racecourse Company; Cottesmore Hunt; Obituaries of Edward
        Manners and Harry Pocklington; Tredegar's Hounds; Bramham Moor Hunt;
        Waterloo Cup; Inter-Varsity Point-to-Point Steeplechase; North Berwick Golf] (p292-311)
Sporting Intelligence [inc. Grafton Hunt; Obituaries of Thomas Lindsay, John Crozier,
        Charles Landon; Hely Hutchinson-Almond, Robert Brereton, Isabella Hudson
        (John Peel's daughter), William Vincent and Edward Gabbetis; Muskerry Hounds;
        Grand Military Racquets; Kildare Harriers; River Tay Angling] (p312-316)

Issue 519 : May 1903

Portrait [sculp. Allingham] and Biography - George Montgomerie (p317-319)
Some Animal Life in the West Indies by John Russell (p319-325)
Polo Hopes and Fears by Thomas Dale (p326-329)
The Wider Wicket by Otho Paget (p329-331)
Cottenham Memories 1883-1903 by Cuthbert Bradley (p332-334)
Lithograph [pinx. Bradley]: *Cottenham Cambridge University Meeting* (facing p332)
Averages in Horse Racing (p334-337)
Otter Hunting by Maud Wynter (p337-339)
Polo in India by Lester Arnold (p339-340)
Successful Steeplechase Sires by Abel Chapman (p341-344)
Ichthyonomologia by John Glenhest (p344-347)
A Hundred Years Ago: Rotten Row from *The Sporting Magazine* (p348)
Engraving [pinx. Sartorius]: *Rotten Row* [in 1803] (facing p348)
About the Drag by William Blew (p349-354)
Cricket in 1903 by Otho Paget (p355-357)
The Sportsman's Library: Reviews of *Exmoor Streams* by Claude Wade; *The Horsewoman*
        by Alice Hayes (p358-361)
A Race meeting near Lucknow in Indian Mutiny Days by Lester Arnold (p361-364)
The Great Quorn Run from Barkby Holt [with Map] by Edward Cuming (p364-366)
Alone on the Prairies by Frederick Gale (p367-372)
Our Van [inc. Lincolnshire Handicap; Northampton Meeting; Hunt Capping; Obituary of
        Eliot Zborowski; Essex Otterhounds; Portmarnock Golf] (p373-391)
Sporting Intelligence [inc. Obituaries of Charles Shepherd, Richard Garth, Charles Nepean,
        William Alderson and Frederick Higgins; North Staffordshire Hunt;
        Warwickshire Hounds; Wilton Foxhounds] (p392-398)

Issue 520 : June 1903

Portrait [sculp. Colls] and Biography - William Walker (p399-401)
Duelling by John Russell (p402-408)
Horses versus Motors by Richard Green-Price (p408-411)
Sea Trout - Fishing and Fisheries (part 2) by William Murdoch (p412-416)
Kershaw's Hitchin Coach by Stephen Kinglake (p416-417)
Lithograph: *Kershaw's Hitchin Coach* (facing p416)
Polo: The New Hurlingham Committee by Thomas Dale (p417-418)
Sport and Animal Life at The Royal Academy by Edward Cuming (p419-423)

Our Twelve Best of Today by Edward Cuming   (p423)
Things I Have Seen and Heard (part 1) by Robert Lowth   (p424-429)
Cricket Reforms by Sydney Pardon   (p429-431)
A Hundred Years Ago: Ranelagh from *The Sporting Magazine*   (p432-433)
The Sportsman's Library: Reviews of *Daily Training* by Edward Benson; *A Stretch off the
        Land* by Stewart Bowles   (p433-435)
An Invitation [verses]   (p435)
The Polo Season by Edward Miller   (p436-438)
Long Distance Walking by William Chinnery   (p438-442)
Otter Hunting in Wales by John Ditchfield   (p443-444)
The Status of Racing in the State of New York by Belmont Purdy   (p444-446)
Oorial Shooting: The Muckle Ram by Lester Arnold   (p447-450)
Danny Maher by Edwin Smith   (p450-451)
Our Van [inc. Hooton Park Club Steeplechasing; Great Metropolitan Handicap; Cumberland
        Hunt; Reviews of *Hunter Sires* and *Early Carriages and Roads*, both by Walter
        Gilbey; Cardiff Polo Club; Obituaries of Samuel Butler, Robert Menzies and
        Robert Hanbury; University Golf]   (p451-471)
Sporting Intelligence [inc. Essex County Cricket Club; Foxbush Harriers; Norwich
        Staghounds; Obituaries of Cecil Howard, Arthur Haygarth and Thomas Lawley;
        Tattersall Foxhounds Sale]   (p472-478)

Volume 80, July - December 1903

Issue 521 : July 1903

Portrait [sculp. Alais] of James Beavan   Title page
Portrait [sculp. Coles] and Biography - Cuthbert Burnup   (p1-3)
All Among the Loughs by Richard Green-Price   (p4-8)
Racehorses or Race Horses by Alan Haig-Brown   (p8-10)
Our Twelve Best of Today: Polo Players by Walter Buckmaster   (p10-15)
The Progress of Swordsmanship in England by Theodore Cook   (p16-22)
Cricket by Sydney Pardon   (p23-27)
Lithograph [pinx. Henderson]: *Travelling Post*   (facing p27)
Early Carriages by William Blew   (p27-28)
The Golf Amateur Championship by Gordon McPherson   (p29-33)
A Hundred Years Ago: Foot Racing from *The Sporting Magazine*   (p33-34)
The Sportsman's Library: Reviews of *Thoroughbred and Other Ponies* by Walter Gilbey;
        Riding, Driving and Kindred Sports by Thomas Dale; *How to Buy a Gun* by
        Henry Bryden; *Lawn Tennis at Home and Abroad* by Wallis Myers; *The Law of
        Pleasure Yachts* by Charles Jemmett; *A Girl's Life in a Hunting Country* by
        Emily Buchanan   (p34-37)
To A Great Cricketer by Stephen Hiney   (p37)
The Polo Season by Edward Miller   (p38-42)
Notes and Sport of a Dry-Fly Purist by James Englefield   (p42-47)
Things I Have Seen and Heard (part 2) by Robert Lowth   (p48-52)
Fire Risks at Schools [Eton College Fire]   (p53-55)
Our Van [inc. Gatwick Meeting; Salisbury Racing; County Polo; Hurlingham Gun Club;
        Obituaries of Arthur Shrewsbury and Robert Thoms; Muirfield Golf]   (p55-74)
Sporting Intelligence [inc. Obituaries of William Williams, Henry Etheridge, Francis Soames,
        John Everett and Thomas Kingsbury; North Warwickshire Hunt; Northern
        Otterhounds; Herne Hill Harriers]   (p75-80)

Issue 522 : August 1903

Portrait [sculp. Allingham] and Biography - Henry Stonor (p81-83)
Tweeny Days [Salmon Fishing] by Elisha Walton (p83-90)
Stray Notes on Breeding (part 1) by Philip Muntz (p90-93)
Physical Training: Its Application to Sport by Charles Batchelder (p93-96)
Polo Ponies and their Value by Edward Miller (p96-98)
Our Twelve Best of Today: Amateur Cricketers by Herbert Hewett (p98-102)
Things I Have Seen and Heard (part 3) by Robert Lowth (p102-107)
Champions of English Billiards by John Buchanan (p108-111)
Cricket by Sydney Pardon (p111-115)
A Hundred Years Ago: A Turf Affair from *The Sporting Magazine* (p116)
The Polo Season by Edward Miller (p117-124)
The Sportsman's Library: *Cricket Across the Seas* by Pelham Warner (p124-127)
Lithograph [pinx. Bradley]: *Earl Bathurst's Stentor* (facing p127)
Horses and Hounds at Peterborough by George Lowe (p127-133)
The Vaccination of Dogs Against Distemper by Henry Gray (p134-135)
Our Van [inc. Ascot Meeting; Newcastle Races; Blackmore Vale Polo; Obituary of John Tonge; Henley Regatta; Wimbledon Lawn Tennis; Tooting Bec Golf Club] (p136-156)
Sporting Intelligence [inc. Obituaries of George Gillson, Charles Colville and John Hetherington; Jockey Club Election; Huntsman Jack Carr; Cricketers' Fund Meeting] (p156-164)

With this issue opening Portraits are being printed in Sepia

Issue 523 : September 1903

Portrait [sculp. Colls] and Biography - Edward Guinness (p165-167)
Duelling in France by John Russell (p167-174)
The Marylebone Cricket Club Team for Australia by Otho Paget (p174-178)
The Offside Rule at Polo (p178-180)
Some Recent Impressions of Spain by Charles Squire (p180-184)
Notes Upon Horses' Heads [with Sketches] by George Fothergill (p184-192)
Lithograph [pinx. Fothergill]: *Head of a White Hunter* (facing p184)
Public Schools Cricket in 1903 by William Ford (p192-195)
The Motor Cars Bill (p195-197)
Our Twelve Best of Today: Game Shots by Eric Parker (p198-208)
Photograph: *Charles Greenwood* (Hotspur of *The Daily Telegraph*) (facing p209)
[Obituary] Charles Greenwood by Edward Cuming (p209-210)
Cricket by Sydney Pardon (p210-212)
A Hundred Years Ago: Partridge Shooting from *The Sporting Magazine* (p212-213)
Polo by Edward Miller (p213-218)
The Sportsman's Library: Reviews of *A Book of Golf* by James Braid; *The Cricket of Abel, Hirst and Shrewsbury* by Eustace Miles (p218-220)
Things I Have Seen and Heard (part 4) by Robert Lowth (p221-224)
Our Van [inc. Goodwood Meeting; Devon & Somerset Staghounds; Sinnington Hounds; London Rowing Club; Cork Regatta; Davis Cup Tennis] (p224-241)
Sporting Intelligence [inc. Newmarket Sales; Atherstone Foxhounds; Obituaries of Arthur Smeaton and Jack Todd; Doggett's Coat & Badge; Vale of White Horse Hunt; Cottesmore Hounds; Seine Swimming] (p241-246)

Issue 524 : October 1903

Portrait [sculp. Colls] and Biography - John Brocklehurst (p247-248)
The Amateur (p249-252)

Photograph [pinx. Babbage]: *Old Dutch Gig* (facing p253)
Photograph [pinx. Babbage]: *Gipsy Living Van* (facing p253)
Curious Carriages by Abel Chapman (p253-257)
Photograph [pinx. Babbage]: *French Station Brougham* (facing p256)
Photograph [pinx. Babbage]: *Boat Carriage* (facing p256)
Discrimination Between Different Scents by George Teasdale-Buckell (p258-261)
The Yeoman and the Empire (p261-263)
Woodpigeon Shooting by Eric Parker (p264-266)
The Early Life of the Foxhound by Frederick Gresham (p267-269)
Polo in India - The Station Game by Lester Arnold (p269-271)
Things I Have Seen and Heard (part 5) by Robert Lowth (p271-275)
Our Twelve Best of Today: Fly Fishermen by George Dewar (p276-280)
Cricket by Sydney Pardon (p280-283)
A Hundred Years Ago: A Racing Book from *The Sporting Magazine* (p284-285)
The Sportsman's Library: *Cricket* by Horace Hutchinson (p285-287)
Impression of Wild Stag Hunting by William Bruette (p287-292)
Rainbows or Grayling by Paul Taylor (p292-293)
Polo by Edward Miller (p294-301)
Our Van [inc. Redcar Racing; Stockton Meeting; Great Ebor Handicap; Belvoir Hunt;
            Philadelphia Cricketers; Irish Open Golf Championship] (p302-322)
Sporting Intelligence [inc. Obituaries of William Holmes-A'Court, Thomas Elwon, William
            Orr-Ewing, Charles Nugent, Thomas Slingsby and William Claxon; Jedforest
            Hunt; Buckinghamshire Otterhounds; Doncaster Sales; Vine Hunt] (p322-328)

Issue 525 : November 1903

Portrait [sculp. Colls] and Biography - Charles Brand (p329-331)
Exercise [Polo Ponies] by Edward Miller (p331-334)
The Hunter Shows of 1903 by Gerald Ricardo (p334-338)
Photograph [pinx. Babbage]: *Hunter Gelding Red Cloud* (facing p334)
Our Twelve Best of Today: Amateur Huntsmen by Edward Cuming (p338-341)
Australian Cricket Tours by Otho Paget (p341-343)
Roads Improvement (p344-348)
Lithograph [pinx. Ellis]: *Old Berkeley West Country* (facing p349)
In the Old Berkeley West Country [Wynn Ellis] by Edward Cuming (p349)
Flapper Shooting by Edwin Arnold (p350-353)
A Lady's Hunter by William Scarth-Dixon (p353-355)
A Dry-Fly Fisherman in South Wales by James Englefield (p355-358)
The Sportsman's Library: Reviews of *The Best of the Fun* by Edward Pennell-Elmhirst;
            Foxhunting in the Shires by Thomas Dale; *Hunting, Racing and Polo Things*
            by Harold Dale; *Shooting* by Horace Hutchinson, and *Birkenhead and its*
            Surroundings by Henry Aspinall (p358-362)
A Hundred Years Ago: Foxhounds from *The Sporting Magazine* (p363)
Tally Ho! [verses] by Frank Hallsworth (p364-365)
Things I Have Seen and Heard (part 6) by Robert Lowth (p365-370)
On the Road in Norway by Abel Chapman (p371-375)
American Polo by Belmont Purdy (p376-377)
The Hunting Season by William Blew (p378-384)
Our Van [inc. Newmarket Meeting; Quantock Staghounds; Quorn Hunt Committee;
            Furlong Harriers; Meath Hunt; Review of *Baily's Hunting Directory*;
            Obituary of John Crossland] (p384-403)
Sporting Intelligence [inc. South London Harriers; Obituaries of Oscar Heriot, Llewellyn
            Turner, Alexander Buller and Walter Kynaston; Radnorshire & West Hereford
            Hounds; Medway Rowing; Scottish Water Polo] (p403-410)

Issue 526 : December 1903

Portrait [sculp. Colls] and Biography - John Munro	(p411-413)
Collars and Saddles by Wortley Axe	(p413-417)
Engraving [pinx. Laporte]: *Hold Hard*	(facing p417)
Riding to Hounds by William Blew	(p417-423)
Successful Stallions in 1903 by Abel Chapman	(p423-426)
Our Twelve Best of Today: Amateur Golf Players by Gordon McPherson	(p427-431)
Australian Cricket Legislature by Otho Paget	(p431-433)
Partridge Shooting at a Country House in the Fifties by Frederick Corrance	(p433-435)
The Foxhound [verses] by Alan Haig-Brown	(p435)
Drawing [pinx. Fothergill]: *George Robinson*	(facing p437)
George Robinson: A North Country Character by John Radcliffe	(p437-438)
Notes and Sport of a Dry-Fly Purist: Trout Season by James Englefield	(p438-445)
Friends in the Hunting Field by Hugh Henry	(p445-447)
Things I Have Seen and Heard (part 7) by Robert Lowth	(p448-454)
A Hundred Years Ago: Cavalry from *The Sporting Magazine*	(p455)
The Sportsman's Library: Reviews of *Points of a Racehorse* by John Hills; *Hare Hunting and Harriers* by Henry Bryden; *Sporting Sonnets* by Alan Brown; *Snipe and Woodcock* by Leonard de Visme Shaw; *Horses, Guns and Dogs* by Otho Paget; *Sketch Book* by George Fothergill; *Slipper's Foxhunting* by Enone Somerville	(456-461)
Round the Theatres	(p461-464)
Sport at the Universities by Pack Ford	(p464-467)
James Beavan by Edwin Smith	(p467-468)
Our Van [inc. Sandown Park Meeting; Northampton Racecourse; Aintree Racing; Melton Hunting; York & Ainsty Hunt; Dunhallow Hounds; Association of Hunt Secretaries; Essex Cricket; Obituaries of Charlotte Spencer and George Nash]	(p468-485)
Sporting Intelligence [inc. Cinque Ports Golf Club; Obituaries of John Cust and John Vaughan-Pryse; Ystrad & Pentyrch Hunt; Yorkshire Cricket; Zetland Hunt; Muirfield Golf]	(p486-492)

Volume 81, January - June 1904

Issue 527 : January 1904

Portrait [sculp. Alais] of Leonard Braund, cricketer	Title page
Portrait [sculp. Colls] and Biography - Francis Baring	(p1-2)
Hunting by Scent by Christian Cecil	(p3-7)
Covert Shooting by Hugh MacPherson	(p7-10)
Some Steeplechasing Odds and Ends by William Blew	(p11-16)
The Fascination of Fishing by Clifford Cordley	(p17-21)
Hunters at Coedkernew by Edward Cuming	(p21-23)
Pig-Sticking by George Miller	(p23-25)
The Capercailzie by Abel Chapman	(p26-27)
Engraving [pinx. Turner]: *The Capercailzie*	(facing p26)
The Passing of the Starting Gate in American Racing by Belmont Purdy	(p27-29)
A Hundred Years Ago: Curious Horse Race from *The Sporting Magazine*	(p30)
Polo Tournaments in 1903 by Edward Miller	(p31-33)
The Proposed County Cricket Tournament by Otho Paget	(p34-36)
Our Twelve Best of Today: Gentlemen Riders by John Richardson	(p37-43)
The Christmas [Stock] Shows by Gerald Ricardo	(p43-46)

The Sportsman's Library: Reviews of *An Angler's Autobiography* by Frederic Halford; *Livestock Journal Almanac* by James Sinclair; *The Racing Year* by Edward Moorhouse; *The Arcadian Calendar* by Edward Cuming; *The Racecourse Atlas of Great Britain* by Frederick Bayliss; *Nyasaland Under the Foreign Office* by Hector Duff; *Feathered Game* by Dwight Huntington; *The Master of Hounds* by George Underhill; *Horse Breeding and Management* by Frederick Adye   (p46-53)

Things I Have Seen and Heard (part 8) by Robert Lowth   (p54-59)

The Romance of a Migrant by George Teasdale-Buckell   (p59-62)

In the City [verses] by William Ogilvie   (p62-63)

Sketchy Thoughts on Hunting (part 5) by William Blew   (p63-67)

Our Van [inc. Derby Gold Cup; Obituaries of Dimitri Soltykoff and Blundell Maple; Bramham Moor Hunt; Carlow & Island Hounds; Westmeath Hunt; New Ross Hounds]   (p68-80)

Sporting Intelligence [inc. Obituaries of John Kershaw, Thomas Kemble, Thomas Tyrwhitt-Drake and John Penn; Taunton Vale Harriers; Holm Hill Hunt; Romney Marsh Harriers; Four Burrow Hunt; St.Andrews Golf Links]   (p80-84)

Issue 528 : February 1904

Portrait [sculp. Colls] and Biography - Frederic Halford   (p85-87)

The Temperament of Hounds by Richard Green-Price   (p88-91)

Aids in Horsemanship by Edward Miller   (p91-93)

The Stable - The Bush - The Hunting Field   (p93-98)

Foxhunting in the Lake District by Leonard West   (p98-100)

Photograph [West]: *Watching Hounds*   (facing p98)

Photograph [West]: *On the Lake's Fells*   (facing p98)

Photograph [Daniels]: *Itchen above Twyford*   (facing p101)

[Review] *An Angler's Autobiography* by Frederic Halford   (p101-102)

Photograph [Daniels]: *On Candover Brook*   (facing p102)

Horse Dealing for Amateurs by Maud Wynter   (p103-105)

The Test Matches in Australia by Sydney Pardon   (p106-107)

Sport at the Universities: Retrospective and Prospective by Pack Ford   (p107-110)

Our Twelve Best of Today: Gentlemen Riders to Hounds by Edward Clayton   (p110-119)

The Poetry of the Chase by Hugh Henry   (p119-126)

The Abuse of Angling Privileges by Carter Platts   (p126-128)

The Sportsman's Library: Reviews of *Angling Anecdotes* by Robert Stanley and *Names for Hounds* by Alexander Wilson   (p128-129)

A Hundred Years Ago: Pedestrianism from *The Sporting Magazine*   (p129-130)

Revised Polo Rules by Edward Miller   (p131-134)

Hints about Hunters by George Harper   (p134-139)

Walnuts and Wine [verses] by William Ogilvie   (p139-140)

Stray Notes on Breeding (part 2) by Philip Muntz   (p140-145)

Our Van [inc. Woodland Pytchley Hunt; Quorn Hunt Kennels; West Somerset Hounds; West Norfolk Hunt; Gentlemen Riders]   (p146-163)

Sporting Intelligence [inc. Holderness Hounds; Obituaries of Gage Freeman (*Baily's* contributor), Edward Haworth, Thomas Petch, Humphrey Rocklington-Senhouse, James Welland, Henry Keppel and Michel Conturie; Monmouthshire Hunt; Southdown Hunt; Blencathra Foxhounds]   (p164-168)

Issue 529 : March 1904

Portrait [sculp. Collis] and Biography - John Hargreaves   (p169-171)

Ancient Hunting Horns and Hunting Music (part 1) by Florence Baillie-Grohman   (p171-174)

The Wettest Season on Record by Richard Green-Price   (p175-178)

The Trout in Spring by Paul Taylor   (p178-180)

Pig-Sticking: The Old Grey Boar by George Miller   (p180-182)

Two Old Sporting Books [*Oracle of Rural Life and Sportsman's Almanac for 1840* published
   by Alfred Baily and [Donald] *Walker's Manly Exercises* by John Carleton]   (p182-187)
Engraving [pinx. Barraud]: *Rabbit Shooting*   (facing p185)
Cricket at Some Schools by Otho Paget   (p187-188)
Notes and Sport of a Dry-Fly Purist by James Englefield   (p189-195)
Our Twelve Best of Today: Professional Huntsmen by Edward Cuming   (p196-200)
About Foxes by Edward Cuming   (p200-208)
Horsemanship by Edward Miller   (p209-210)
A Hundred Years Ago: Bear-Hunting from *The Sporting Magazine*   (p211)
The Snipe [verses] by Stephen Hiney   (p212)
The Sportsman's Library: Reviews of *Billiards Expounded* by John Mannock; *Points of the
   Horse* by Horace Hayes; *The Keepers' Book* by Stodart Walker; *Sound and
   Unsound Horses* by Frank Barton   (p213-216)
Photograph [Elliott]: *Henry Sturt*   (facing p217)
[Obituary] Lord Alington by Edward Cuming   (p217)
Golf at Continental Health Resorts by Horace Wyndham   (p218-220)
Some Ancient Racing Epitaphs by Arthur Meyrick   (p220-224)
After Wildfowl on the Alde by Henry Pilkington   (p224-226)
Sport in Wales Thirty Years Ago by Newton Apperley   (p226-231)
Our Van [inc. Hurst Park Races; Lamerton Hounds; Quorn Hunt; Obituary of William Hearn;
   Bedale Hunt; Sinnington Hounds]   (p232-243)
Sporting Intelligence [inc. Cambridgeshire Foxhounds; Anglesey Harriers; Obituaries of
   Robert Baker, Albert Ripley, William Sales, David Carrick-Buchanan and
   Samuel Skinner; Bentley & Willenhall Harriers; West Surrey Staghounds;
   Sandwich Golf Championships; Coniston Hounds]   (p244-248)

Issue 530 : April 1904

Portrait [sculp. Colls] and Biography - William Selby-Lowndes   (p249-251)
Old Sporting Tools   (p251-258)
[Review] *Eighty Years Reminiscences* by John Anstruther-Thomson   (p258-263)
Lithograph: *John Anstruther-Thomson on Iris 1870*   (facing p258)
Ancient Hunting Horns and Hunting Music (part 2) [with Sketches] by Florence
   Baillie-Grohman   (p263-267)
Crooked Powder by Eric Parker   (p267-269)
Timber Measurement and Sale by Claremont Clare   (p270-273)
Come Along Coronet [verses] by William Ogilvie   (p273-274)
Some Features of Recent Test Matches by Otho Paget   (p274-277)
A Hundred Years Ago: Epping Hunt from *The Sporting Magazine*   (p277-278)
Our Twelve Best of Today: All-Round Sportsmen   (p278-282)
The Sportsman's Library: Reviews of *Trout Fishing* by Earl Hodgson; *Game of British
   Columbia* by John Babcock; *The Birds of Tennyson* by Watkin Watkins   (p283-285)
The Horse Shows by Gerald Ricardo   (p285-290)
Photograph [Babbage]: *Hunter Gelding, Red Ruby*   (facing p290)
An Impossible Wicket by Edward Bligh   (p291-293)
To A Fox [verses] by Robert Churchill   (p293-294)
Low-Lying Roads by Athol Maudslay   (p295-296)
The Board of Green Cloth by Sydenham Dixon   (p296-298)
Hands by Maud Wynter   (p298-301)
With a Nine-Foot Rod in Wales by Arthur Johnson   (p301-305)
Spring Products at the Theatres   (p305-308)
[Obituary] Duke of Cambridge   (p309)

Our Van [inc. Grand Military Meeting; Cheltenham Races; North Warwickshire Hunt; Kildare Hounds; Wexford Hunt; Association of Hunt Secretaries; Obituary of Reginald Ward; Waterloo Cup; Davis Cup Tennis; Nuneaton Point-to-Point] (p309-323)
Sporting Intelligence [inc. North Cornwall Hounds; Cambridge University Athletics; Obituaries of Edward Moon, William Mills, John O'Neill and Alexander Shand; Monmouthshire Hunt; Barnstaple Staghounds; Golf in Biarritz] (p324-328)

Issue 531 : May 1904

Portrait [sculp. Colls] and Biography - Charles Rose (p329-331)
Foxhounds: The Best of All by George Lowe (p331-336)
Prospects of Polo by Edward Miller (p336-338)
The Hunter: The Right and Wrong Sort by Hugh Henry (p338-340)
Winning Steeplechase Stallions by Abel Chapman (p341-345)
Cricket Prospects [South African Tourists] by Sydney Pardon (p345-348)
Lithograph [pinx. Woodward]: *The Worcestershire Foxhounds* (facing p349)
Old Worcestershire by Richard Green-Price (p349-351)
The End of the Hunting Season by William Blew (p352-358)
Lion Hunting in East Africa (p358-360)
A Four-Footed Friend by John Maxtee (p360-362)
Drawing: *One of the Real Old Sort* (facing p361)
A Hundred Years Ago: *Berlin Gazette* story from *The Sporting Magazine* (p363)
The Development of the Motor Car by Edwin Campbell (p364-367)
The Sportsman's Library: Reviews of *Poultry Keeping on Farms* by Walter Gilbey; *The Collie* by Hugh Dalziel (p367-369)
Two Tiger Stories and an Ibex by Edward Almack (p369-372)
Wild Turkeys by Frank Bonnett (p372-375)
Saithe Fishing in a Norwegian Fjord by Abel Chapman (p375-379)
Sport at the Universities by Pack Ford (p379-382)
The Australian as a Horseman by William Ogilvie (p382-386)
Our Van [inc. Lincolnshire Handicap; Blankney Hounds; Cheriton Otterhounds; Tetcott Hunt; Obituary of William Ford (*Baily's* contributor); Wharfedale Otterhounds; Cross-Country Running] (p386-401)
Sporting Intelligence [inc. Meynell Hunt Point-to-Point; Obituaries of Preston White and William Wright; Taunton Foxhounds; County Polo Association; Formby Golf Club] (p402-408)

Issue 532 : June 1904

Portrait [scalp. Colls] and Biography - Pelham Warner (p409-411)
The Horse and his Rider by John Russell (p411-417)
Sport with Beagles by Walter Crofton (p417-421)
The Gamekeeper - Old Style by Carter Platts (p421-425)
Cricket Reform by Sydney Pardon (p425-426)
Lithograph [pinx. Herring]: *Walton* (facing p427)
The Tap-Root of Polo-Pony Breeding by Richard Green-Price (p427-430)
A Dry-Fly Purist's Advice by James Englefield (p431-435)
[Obituary] Frederick Gale by Edward Cuming (p436-437)
[Frederick Gale] A Tribute by Arthur Mursell (p437-439)
A Hundred Years Ago: Cricket from *The Sporting Magazine* (p439-440)
Polo by Edward Miller (p440-442)
Photograph [Graham]: *Henry Torre* (facing p443)
[Obituary] Henry John Torre by Walter Venn (p443-449)
Sport and Animal Life at The Royal Academy by Edward Cuming (p449-452)
Kennel Huntsmen by George Lowe (p453-457)

The Sportsman's Library: Reviews of *First Favourites* by Nathaniel Gubbins [Edward
      Spencer Mott]; *A Fairy in the Pig Skin* by George Harper; *The Unlucky Golfer*
      by Maurice Hime   (p457-459)

The Derby [verses] by Alan Haig-Brown   (p459-460)

Muchee Bawan: The Home of Fish by Peter Bairnsfather   (p460-464)

Leonard Braund [Cricketer] by Edwin Smith   (p464-465)

Our Van [inc. Epsom Meeting; Chester Races; Essex Union Hunt; Obituary of Wilfred
      Marshall; Salmon & Trout Association; Covered Tennis Courts; Harrogate
      Cycling]   (p466-478)

Sporting Intelligence [inc. Hussars Polo Club; Lanarkshire & Renfrewshire Hunt; Obituaries
      of Thomas Horsfall and Henry Stanley; Rugby Tour of New South Wales; Fife
      Hounds; Royal Liverpool Golf Club; West Kent Foxhounds; Bedale Hunt]   (p478-486)

Volume 82, July - December 1904

Issue 533 : July 1904

Portrait [sculp Alais] of Bridger Champion, huntsman   Title page

Portrait [Lafayette] and Biography - Michael Rimington   (p1-3)

Engraving [sculp. Turner]: *William Adams, Master of the Ludlow Hounds*   (facing p5)

Old Shropshire by Richard Green-Price   (p5-7)

Golf [Championship Reports] by Gordon McPherson   (p7-9)

Angling in the West of Ireland by Edgar Shrubsole   (p9-12)

Photograph: *Palmerstown River, Below Bridge*   (on p10)

Photograph: *A Stream in the Finny River*   (on p11)

Otter Hunting by Payne Collier   (p13-18)

Photograph [Gay]: *Pack of Otter Hounds*   (facing p15)

Photograph: *Devon Otterhounds*   (on p18)

[Review] Healthy Stables: *Horse Breeding in England and India* by Walter Gilbey
      [with Sketches]   (p19-29)

Current Cricket by Sydney Pardon   (p29-33)

Foxhounds: Making a Pack by Gordon Lowe   (p34-38)

Sport at the Universities by Pack Ford   (p38-40)

A Master of Fence [verses] by William Ogilvie   (p41)

Lithograph [pinx. Palfrey]: *The Old Bell, Stansted*   (facing p43)

[Review] A Road in the Eastern Counties: *The Newmarket, Bury, Thetford and Cromer Road*
      by Charles Harper   (p43-47)

Lithograph [pinx. Palfrey]: *The White Bear, Stansted*   (facing p45)

Lithograph [pinx. Cordery]: *The Expedition Newmarket & Norwich Coach*   (facing p47)

Association of Hunt Secretaries (with list of members)   (p48-50)

Polo in London by Edward Miller   (p51-54)

Photograph: *The Old Cantabs' Polo Team*   (facing p53)

A Hundred Years Ago: Carriages from *The Sporting Magazine*   (p55)

Aquatics [Regatta reports] by Claude Holland   (p56-58)

The Sportsman's Library: Reviews of *How We Recovered The Ashes* by Pelham Warner;
      Sport and Adventure in the Indian Jungle by Mervyn Smith   (p58-61)

The Finest Game Bird in the World by George Teasdale-Buckell   (p62-65)

Lithograph: [American] *Sizes of Quail*   (on p63)

The Champion Polo Cup of 1904 by Edward Miller   (p66-70)

Our Van [inc. Salisbury Cup; Epsom Meeting; Carlow Hunt Club; County Down Staghounds;
      Obituary of Alexander Hood; Richmond Horse Show; Surrey County Tennis;
      I Zingari Presentation Dinner]   (p70-84)

Photograph [Rouch]: *St.Amant*   (facing p73)

Photograph [Rouch]: *Pretty Polly*   (facing p75)

Sporting Intelligence [inc. Rochdale Harriers; Reigate Horse & Hound Show; Obituaries of
        Walter Carpenter, Charles Dillon, Edward Pilkington and James Youl; Surrey
        Union Hounds]   (p84-90)

From this Issue Portraits are no longer Engraved

Issue 534 : August 1904

Portrait [Elliott] and Biography - Reginald Rimington-Wilson   (p91-94)
Grouse Driving by Harold Macfarlane   (p94-98)
Summer Trouting on the North Country Rivers by Carter Platts   (p98-105)
Photograph [Inman]: *Come to my Corner*   (facing p101)
Photograph [Inman]: *Unhook the Fish*   (facing p101)
Photograph [Inman]: *Hang of the Stream*   (facing p103)
Photograph [Inman]: *Kneeling in the Water*   (facing p103)
The Progress of Swordsmanship by Theodore Cook   (p105-116)
Photograph [Russell]: *Close Play for the Wrist*   (facing p107)
The Amateur Golf Championships for 1904 by Gordon McPherson   (p117-121)
Mr Romer Williams' 'Happy Man' by George Fothergill   (p121-124)
Lithograph [Fothergill]: *Happy Man*   (facing p123)
A Morning in the Park by John Russell   (p124-131)
A Hundred Years Ago: Betting from *The Sporting Magazine*   (p131-132)
[Obituary] Edward Tyrwhitt-Drake   (p132-134)
Aquatics: Henley Regatta by Claude Holland   (p134-138)
Photograph [Rouch]: *Racing Past Phyllis Court*   (facing p137)
Horses and Hounds at Peterborough by George Lowe   (p138-145)
Lithograph [pinx. Bradley]: *Warwickshire Traveller*   (facing p143)
Lithograph [pinx. Bradley]: *Rufford Furrier*   (facing p145)
Polo-Bred Stallions by Stanley Burke   (p146-148)
Gentlemen versus Players by Otho Paget   (p148-152)
The Sportsman's Library: Reviews of *The Twentieth Century Dog* by Herbert Compton;
        The Brocklesby Hounds Lists by George Collins   (p152-153)
Sport at the Universities by Pack Ford   (p154-156)
Polo by Edward Miller   (p156-159)
Our Van [inc. Ascot Meeting; Gosforth Park Races; Obituaries of Reginald Mainwaring,
        Richard Boyle, William Blew (*Baily's* contributor) and Thomas Emmett;
        Wimbledon Tennis; West Hertfordshire Golf Club]   (p160-174)
Sporting Intelligence [inc. Obituaries of George Garth, William Redfern and Richard Sale;
        Worcester Races; Cricketers' Fund Friendly Society; Bombay Hunt Dinner;
        Transvaal Game Protection Association]   (p174-184)

Issue 535 : September 1904

Portrait [Lafayette] and Biography - Arthur James   (p185-186)
The Migrations of the Salmon by William Calderwood   (p187-193)
Some Great Sportsmen of Past Times   (p193-197)
Engraving [pinx. Mayall]: *Horatio Ross*   (facing p194)
Engraving [sculp. Brown]: *George Osbaldeston*   (facing p195)
The First by Eric Parker   (p197-200)
Lithograph [pinx. Loduc]: *Partridges*   (facing p199)
The Turf of Today by Richard Green-Price   (p201-204)
Public School Cricket in 1904 by William Seton   (p205-207)
Moorland Trout by Clifford Cordley   (p207-210)
Doncaster and the St.Leger by Charles Richardson   (p210-216)
Engraving [pinx. Turner]: *Blue Bonnet*   (facing p213)

Photograph [Rouch]: *St.Leger Horses*   (facing p215)
Polo by Edward Miller   (p216-220)
Mat Dawson and Master Kildare by George Lowe   (p221-224)
Cricket in August by Otho Paget   (p225-228)
A Hundred Years Ago: Racing Accidents from *The Sporting Magazine*   (p228-229)
Pointers & Setters and Field Trials by George Teasdale-Buckell   (p229-234)
Photograph: *Bragg of Keir Pointing*   (on p231)
To Barmaid [verses] by Robert Churchill   (p234-235)
Lithograph [pinx. Fothergill]: *A Bit of Old Yorkshire*   (facing p237)
John Carr of Ruswarp by George Fothergill   (p237)
The Sportsman's Library: Reviews of *Africa from South to North through Marotseland* by
        Alfred Gibbons; *Rowing & Sculling* by Guy Rixon   (p238-239)
The Horse of Northern China by Joshua Nunn   (p240-241)
Hunting Sires of the Past by William Trench   (p241-246)
Lithograph [pinx. Thomson]: *Orville*   (facing p245)
Bonnie Ireland [verses] by William Ogilvie   (p247)
Our Van [inc. Goodwood Grandstand; Brighton Races; Obituaries of Reginald Mainwaring,
        John Kent (*Baily's* contributor) and Herbert Jenner-Fust; Devon & Somerset
        Staghounds; Grouse Shooting; Salmon & Trout Association; Thames Punting
        Club Regatta; International Athletics]   (p247-262)
Sporting Intelligence [inc. Newmarket Sales; Wingfield Sculls; Obituaries of John Evans,
        Anthony Stokes and John Thorogood; County Down Staghounds; West
        Cumberland Otterhounds; Holmleigh Bloodhounds; Grafton Hunt]   (p263-270)

Issue 536 : October 1904

Portrait [Howard] and Biography - John French   (p271-274)
The Salmon & Sea-Trout Rivers by Augustus Grimble   (p274-278)
The Agnes Family of Racehorses by Charles Prior   (p278-290)
Lithograph [pinx. Herring]: *Priam*   (facing p281)
Engraving [sculp. Turner]: *Sam Chiffney*   (facing p283)
Lithograph: *Emilius*   (facing p285)
Once Again by Eric Parker   (p290-292)
Trout Fishing in Norway by Abel Chapman   (p292-300)
Photograph: *Vinje Lake, Telemark*   (facing p295)
Photograph: *Vaagsli Lake, Old Telemark House*   (facing p295)
Photograph: *Red and the Bredheim Lake*   (facing p297)
Photograph: *The Kjosnaes Fjord on the Jolster Lake*   (facing p297)
Photograph: *Stolkjaerre*   (facing p299)
Photograph: *Cariole*   (facing p299)
On the Right Way to Beat a Grouse Moor by George Teasdale-Buckell   (p301-304)
A Hundred Years Ago: Harriers from *The Sporting Magazine*   (p305)
Lithograph: *Tregonwell Frampton as a Young Man*   (facing p307)
[Review] The History of English Racing: *A History of the English Turf* by Theodore Cook   (p307-313)
Lithograph: *The Welter Stakes at Bibury 1821*   (facing p309)
Lithograph: *Tommy and Toddy*   (facing p311)
Engraving: *West Australian*   (facing p313)
Irish Polo by Edward Miller   (p313-316)
The Sportsman's Library: Reviews of *The Sportsman's Book for India* by Frederick Aflalo;
        Cricket by Frederick Holland; *Wrestling* by Walter Armstrong; *Notes of an
        East Coast Naturalist* by Arthur Patterson   (p316-318)
Cricket Notes by Sydney Pardon   (p319-320)
The Planting of Trees and Shrubs for Ornament [with Photographs]   (p321-326)
The Migration of British Game Birds by Watkin Watkins   (p326-331)

Our Van [inc. Great Ebor Meeting; Staghunting on Exmoor; Old Berks Hunt; Obituaries of
     James Lowther; John Moore, John Fock; Horace Hayes (*Baily's* contributor),
     George Darby and William Renshaw; Dublin Horse Show; Irish Golf
     Championship]   (p331-349)
Sporting Intelligence [inc. Obituaries of Hilda McNeill, Anthony Huxtable, Josiah Cartledge,
     George Parker, William Bulmer and Michael Hartigan; Teviotdale Angling
     Association; Blankney Hunt; Doncaster Sales; Transvaal Trout Society]   (p349-358)

Issue 537 : November 1904

Portrait [Hall] and Biography - William Fitzwilliam   (p359-361)
Scriptural Hunting, Fowling and Fishing by John Russell   (p361-368)
The Thames Salmon Experiments by William Boulton   (p368-377)
Photograph: *Catching up Smolt*   (facing p371)
Photograph: *Crosbie Gilbey*   (facing p372)
Photograph: *William Grenfell*   (facing p374)
The Colour of Horses by Richard Green-Price   (p377-381)
The Sportsman's Library: *With Hound and Terrier in the Field* by Alys Serrell   (p381-386)
Lithograph: *Harvey Yeatman*   (facing p383)
Photograph: *James Farquharson*   (facing p385)
[Review] *Baily's Hunting Directory 1904-05* by Edward Cuming   (p386)
A Hundred Years Ago: Racing from *The Sporting Magazine*   (p387)
Tom Parr and his Times by George Lowe   (p388-392)
[Obituary] George Darby by George Fothergill   (p392-395)
Photograph [Darby]: *George Darby*   (facing p395)
Polo 1904 by Edward Miller   (p396-399)
Photograph [Gay]: *John Anstruther-Thomson*   (facing p401)
[Obituary] Colonel John Anstruther-Thomson   (p401-403)
Engraving [pinx. Turner]: *Cheering in Covert*   (facing p405)
The Sport of Kings [verses] by William Ogilvie   (p405)
The Sportsman in the Hunting Field by Hugh Henry   (p406-409)
Hunt Changes by Edward Cumings   (p410-415)
Our Van [inc. Ayr Meeting; Jockey Club Stewards; Obituaries of George Astley and Owen
     Williams; Cottesmore Hunt; Middleton's Hounds; University Sport; Mid-Surrey
     Golf Club]   (p416-435)
Sporting Intelligence [inc. Obituaries of John LaTouche, Alex Goodman, Charles Harvey,
     John Parnell, William Rigden, William Cartmell, Benjamin Cleave, James Bibby
     and Arthur Anstruther-Thomson; Yorkshire County Cricket Club; Tickham Hounds;
     Glamorganshire Golf Club; Australian Turf Winnings; Amory's Staghounds]   (p436-444)

Issue 538 : December 1904

Portrait [Elliott] and Biography - Edwyn Francis   (p445-447)
A Good Hunter by Richard Green-Price   (p448-451)
Lanercost and Beeswing by George Lowe   (p451-456)
Foxhunting on the Fells by Charles Benson   (p456-462)
Photograph [Abraham]: *Sharp Edge, Saddleback*   (on p457)
Photograph [Abraham]: *Head of Newlands*   (facing p459)
Photograph [Abraham]: *Thirlmere, Looking North*   (facing p461)
The Oldest English Hunting Book: *The Master of Game* translated by William
     Baillie-Grohman   (p463-465)
The Breeding Honours of the Year by Abel Chapman   (p466-471)
Photograph [Rouch]: *Gallinule*   (facing p469)
Photograph [Haley]: *Cyllene*   (facing p471)
A Worthy Veteran by William Fawcett   (p471-477)

Photograph: *Johnny Ryan* (facing p472)

Winter Fishing by Ernest Phillips (p477-483)

A Hundred Years Ago: Foxhounds from *The Sporting Magazine* (p483-485)

Lithograph [sculp. Dunkerton]: John Monk (facing p485)

An Old Hertfordshire Huntsman by William Fawcett (p485)

Lithograph: *Gone Away* (facing p487)

The Sportsman's Library: Reviews of *The Sedgefield Country* by Jack Bevans; *Nature and Sport in Britain* by Henry Bryden; *Fifty Leaders of British Sport* by Ernest Elliott (p487-490)

Winter Shooting in Scotland by Hector Macpherson (p490-493)

The Bitting of Polo Ponies and Hunters by Edward Miller (p494-497)

The Foxhounds of the Old Slave States by George Teasdale-Buckell (p497-501)

Bridger Champion by Edwin Smith (p501)

Hacking Home [verses] by William Ogilvie (p502)

Our Van [inc. Gatwick Races; Grand Sefton Steeplechase; Bramham Moor Hunt; Master of Foxhounds Association; Obituaries of Thomas Merthyr-Guest, George Watson and Jack Brown; Wembley Park Polo Club] (p503-522)

Sporting Intelligence [inc. West Kent Foxhounds; Barnstaple Staghounds; Tynedale Foxhounds; Obituaries of Astley Paston-Cooper, Christopher Fawcett, John Holroyd-Smith and Stanley Richardson-Cox; Lamerton Foxhounds; Bedale Hunt] (p522-528)

Walter Buckmaster

Volume 83, January - June 1905

Issue 539: January 1905

Portrait [sculp. Sherborn] of William Lane, jockey	Title page
Portrait [Bassano] and Biography - Arnold Keppel	(p1-5)
Old Soldier Servants and Old Regimental Ways (part 1) by John Russell	(p5-11)
Harriers in Kennel by Henry Bryden	(p11-14)
Photograph [Coater]: *Southern Hound Blood*	(on p12)
Photograph [Coater]: *Blue Mottled Puppies*	(on p13)
The Hunting Farmer by Richard Green-Price	(p15-18)
Bait Fishing for Grayling by Carter Platts	(p18-24)
Photograph [Inman]: *The Deeper Gentle Stream*	(facing p21)
Photograph [Inman]: *Water Pours Over the Sharp Ledge*	(facing p23)
Women and Sport by Alan Haig-Brown	(p25-27)
The Chakore of the Himalayas by Lester Arnold	(p27-31)
Photograph: *Chakore*	(facing p29)
Engraving [pinx. Cooper]: *William Worley of The Royal Paddocks*	(facing p31)
Portrait of an Old Retainer by Edward Cuming	(p31)
A Hundred Years Ago: Harriers from *The Sporting Magazine*	(p32-33)
Wildfowling in North-West Donegal by Edgar Shrubsole	(p33-36)
Photograph [Shrubsole]: *Lough Fern, Donegal*	(on p34)
Photograph [Shrubsole]: *Mulroy Bay, Donegal*	(on p35)
Bush Memories [verses] by Guy Eden	(p36-37)
The Discard at Bridge by Ernest Bergholt	(p38-40)
A Dry-Fly Purist's Advice to a Beginner (part 2) by James Englefield	(p41-45)
From Orville to Carbine by George Lowe	(p46-49)
Cricket Notes by Otho Paget	(p49-53)
Photograph: *War Ambulance Dogs*	(facing p53)
Major Richardson's War Dogs by Nicol Simpson	(p53-54)
The Sportsman's Library: Reviews of *Big Game* by Dwight Huntington; *Livestock Journal Almanac* by James Sinclair; *A Book of the Snipe* by Robert Gibbs; *Guide to Horsemanship and Horse Training* by Coombe Williams	(p54-60)
Lithograph [pinx. Shayer]: *Going to the Fair*	(facing p57)
Our Van [inc. Belper Selling Handicap; Gimcrack Dinner; Blackmore Vale Hunt; Louth Hounds; Dart Vale Harriers; Birmingham Cattle Show; Obituary of James Cranston; University Sport]	(p61-80)
Sporting Intelligence [inc. Obituaries of William Riall, Duff Assheton-Smith, Daniel Lascelles, Albert Yorke, Walter Shoolbred and Frederick Fitzwygram; Tipperary Foxhounds; Bentley Harriers; Essex Staghounds; Surrey Union Hunt]	(p80-84)

Issue 540 : February 1905

Portrait [Weston] and Biography - Evan Hanbury	(p85-87)
Old Soldier Servants and Old Regimental Ways (part 2) by John Russell	(p87-93)
Woodcock and Snipe by Edward Caswall	(p93-99)
Photograph: *Some of the Ground*	(facing p95)
Engraving [sculp. Turner]: *Woodcock Shooting in the Olden Time*	(facing p97)
The Llama and its Relations	(p99-106)
Photograph: *Llamas at Huanuni*	(facing p101)
Photograph: *Huanuni Village, Bolivia*	(facing p101)
Photograph: *Llama Laden*	(facing p103)
Photograph: *Llamas Feeding*	(facing p103)
Etiquette in the Hunting Field by Hugh Henry	(p106-110)

Lithograph [pinx. Wolstenholme]: *Crossing Country* (facing p109)

Rough Shooting in Connemara by Henry Wade (p110-112)

Polo Prospects for 1905 by Edward Miller (p113-114)

The Watts Exhibition at Burlington House by Edward Cuming (p114-115)

Nerve (p116-118)

A Hundred Years Ago: Illegal Hunting in Guildford from *The Sporting Magazine* (p118-119)

The Two Greatest Golfers (part 1): Allan Robertson by Gordon McPherson (p119-122)

Photograph [Downie]: *Allan Robertson* (on p120)

The Sportsman's Library: *The Roedeer* by Charles Payne; *Wisden's Cricketers' Almanack* by Sydney Pardon; *Angling Observations of a Coarse Fisherman* by Charles Marson (p122-126)

The Marar Prairie, Somaliland by Henry Pilkington (p126-129)

Photograph [Dunning]: *Irish Wolfhound* (facing p129)

The Irish Wolfhound by Cyril Stacey (p129-131)

Small Horses by George Lowe (p131-135)

The Shooting Club System of America by George Teasdale-Bucknell (p135-138)

After Oorial by Roger Kennion (p138-143)

Diana's Vengeance by Francis King (p144-148)

Hints About Hacks by Charles Harper (p148-153)

Our Van [inc. National Hunt Committee; Quorn Hunt; Ledbury Hounds; Obituaries of Henry Sebright, Cecil Foljambe and John Easterby; Army Golf Cup] (p153-163)

Sporting Intelligence [inc. Obituaries of Stephen Dobson, George Lambert, John Paterson, Young Graham, Robert Biscoe, Harold Brunwin and William Tombs-Dewe; North Warwickshire Hounds; South Devon Hunt] (p164-168)

Issue 541 : March 1905

Portrait [Lafayette] and Biography - Frank Shuttleworth (p169-171)

Fashion in Breeding by George Lowe (p171-175)

The Frozen-Out Foxhunter by Richard Green-Price (p176-179)

Early Trouting by Clifford Cordley (p179-182)

Grey Thoroughbred Horses by Charles Pitman (p183-193)

Photograph [Legoupy]: *Le Sancy* (facing p185)

Photograph: *Grey Leg* (facing p187)

Photograph [Cartwright]: *Darkie* (facing p189)

Kilworth Sticks [verses] by Harry Cumberland-Bentley (p194-195)

Engraving: *Quorndon Hall* (facing p197)

A Hundred Years Ago: Quorndon Hall from *The Sporting Magazine* (p197)

Decadence of Sport (p198-202)

The Two Greatest Golfers (part 2): Tommy Morris by Gordon McPherson (p202-205)

Photograph [Hardie]: *Tommy Morris* (on p203)

Polo by Edward Miller (p205-208)

How to Win at Cricket by Otho Paget (p208-209)

The Bob-Tailed Fox [verses] by Robert Churchill (p210)

Notes and Sport of a Dry-Fly Purist by James Englefield (p211-214)

The Sportsman's Library: Reviews of *The Gun-Room* by Alexander Innes-Shand; *A Modern Campaign* by David Fraser (p214-217)

Horse Bandages [with Diagrams] by Joshua Nunn (p217-219)

Regulations for International Cricket by Sydney Pardon (p220-221)

Sport at the Universities by Pack Ford (p221-223)

Race Lotteries in India by David Fraser (p223-228)

Old Hunting Songs by William Parlour (p229-233)

Lithograph [pinx. Laporte]: *Made A Cast* (facing p231)

The Rural Economy of Game by George Teasdale-Bucknell (p233-236)

Our Van [inc. Quorn Hunt Master; West Somerset Hounds; Quantock Staghounds; York & Ainsty Hunt; Argentine Polo; Obituary of James Phillips; North Berwick Golf]   (p236-247)

Sporting Intelligence [inc. Obituaries of Joseph Bennett, Henry Vane-Tempest, John Cooper, Charrington Nicholl and Frederick Gosden; Lanarkshire & Renfrewshire Hounds; East Kent Hounds]   (p247-250)

Issue 542 : April 1905

Portrait [Maull] and Biography - James Cross   (p251-252)
An Old Squire's Diary by William Wilmott-Dixon   (p253-256)
Brothers Banded as Sportsmen by Ralph Nevill   (p257-261)
The Rabbits of the Rocks by Carter Platts   (p262-266)
Photograph: *The Edge of the Scars*   (facing p265)
Photograph: *On the Scree*   (facing p265)
Farewell to Manifesto [verses]   (p267)
How to Become a Bowler by Otho Paget   (p268-270)
On the Opening of the Trout Season 1905 by James Englefield   (p270-272)
On Hirelings by Maud Wynter   (p272-275)
The London Horse Show by George Lowe   (p275-283)
Photograph [Babbage]: *Mark For'ard*   (facing p279)
Photograph [Babbage]: *Battlement*   (facing p281)
The Sportsman's Library: Reviews of *A History of the Old Berks Hunt* by Frederick Loder-Symonds; *A Driving Tour in the Isle of Wight* by Hubert Garle; *The Harness Horse* by Walter Gilbey   (p283-289)
Photograph: *Old Berkshire Hounds*   (facing p285)
Engraving: *Rycott House*   (facing p287)
Photograph: *Grey Mare Motor*   (facing p289)
The Coming-On Trout by Paul Taylor   (p290-291)
A Hundred Years Ago: Pugilism from *The Sporting Magazine*   (p292-293)
The Polo Ponies at the Polo Pony Show by Edward Miller   (p293-298)
Photograph [Babbage]: *Gownboy*   (facing p295)
Photograph [Babbage]: *Early Dawn*   (facing p297)
The First Trout [verses] by Christopher Cassels   (p298-299)
What is the Most Difficult Shooting by George Teasdale-Bucknell   (p299-302)
The American Jockey's Seat by Belmont Purdy   (p303-306)
The Bengali Baboo on Horsemanship and Sport   (p306-310)
More Sporting Ancient Epitaphs by Arthur Meyrick   (p310-314)
Our Van [inc. Sandown Park Meetings; Cottesmore Hunt; Bramham Moor Hounds; University Sport; Obituary of William Grace; Cross-Country Running]   (p315-329)
Sporting Intelligence [inc. Obituaries of Archibald Livingstone, Robert Jardine, William Gething, George Hustler, William Furnival, Robert Robertson, Alexander Findlay and William Pugh; Radnorshire & West Herefordshire Hounds; Surrey Staghounds; Burstow Hounds]   (p329-334)

Issue 543: May 1905

Portrait [Elliott] and Biography - John Wallington   (p335-336)
Have Our Racehorses Deteriorated by John Doyle   (p337-344)
A Reminiscence of Yester by William Fox- Russell   (p345-351)
Photograph [Gordon]: *Yester House*   (facing p347)
Photograph [Gordon]: *The Old Castle of Yester*   (facing p349)
Photograph [Brown]: *Dumfriesshire Otterhounds*   (facing p351)
Tips by Frederick Aflalo   (p352-356)
The Management of Trout Waters by Rowden Bridge   (p357)
The Hunting Parson by Richard Green-Price   (p358-362)

Engraving [sculp. Browne]: *Reverend John Russell* (facing p361)
The Art of Gentle Batting by Otho Paget (p362-366)
Successful Sires of the Steeplechase Season by Arthur Coaten (p366-372)
Photograph [Rouch]: *Hackler* (facing p369)
Polo by Edward Miller (p372-376)
A Hundred Years Ago: Epping Hunt from *The Sporting Magazine* (p376-377)
Sport at the Universities by Pack Ford (p377-380)
A Plea for Better Fielding by Herbert Jenner-Fust (p380-384)
The Lions of the Gir by Lester Arnold (p384-387)
Photograph [Tadman]: *The Water Jump at Sandown* (facing p389)
Elliman Taking the Water at Sandown Park (p389)
The Sportsman's Library: Review of *Miss Lavinia Badsworth MFH* by Eyre Hussey (p389-390)
Etiquette of the Shooting Field by George Teasdale-Buckell (p390-394)
Our Van [inc. Lincoln Meeting; Nettlecombe Harriers; Middleton's Hounds; Salisbury
          Plain Bloodhounds; Edward Lyttelton at Eton; County Cricket Preview;
          Edinburgh Golfers] (p395-414)
Photograph [Rouch]: *Kirkland* (facing p399)
Sporting Intelligence [inc. Obituaries of Edward Sworder, Fletcher Menzies, Thomas Plumb,
          William Chinnery, Beatty Ball, John Massey and James Muscroft;
          Puckeridge Hunt; Cranbrook Game Farm; North Warwickshire Hunt;
          Surrey Union Foxhounds] (p414-420)

Issue 544 : June 1905

Portrait [Edwards] and Biography - Gerald Lascelles (p421-423)
The Blackmail System (part 1) by Frederick Aflalo (p424-427)
Remarkable Racing Dreams by William Wilmott-Dixon (p427-434)
Ne Quid Nimis by Richard Green-Price (p434-437)
A Stock Farm in Lincolnshire by George Lowe (p438-444)
Photograph [Dickinson]: *Taylor Sharpe* (facing p441)
The Mightiest Lion Hunter by Christopher Cassels (p444-451)
Photograph: *Roualeyn Gordon-Cumming* [Portrait] (facing p447)
Lithograph: *Roualeyn Gordon-Cumming* [Action] (facing p449)
Weed Cutting in Trout Streams by Rowden Bridge (p451-452)
How to Encourage Wild Pheasants by Frederick Millard (p452-456)
The Vale of White Horse's Worcester by George Lowe (p456-459)
Photograph: *Worcester* (facing p459)
In Defence of Coarse Fishing by Ernest Phillips (p460-467)
Engraving [sculp. Beckwith]: *Pike* (facing p463)
Engraving [sculp. Beckwith]: *Perch* (facing p463)
Ladies' Races by Charles Greswell (p467-470)
Photograph [Arcade]: *Sylvia Day* (facing p469)
Sport and Animal Life at The Royal Academy by Edward Cuming (p471-474)
A Hundred Years Ago: Otter Hounds from *The Sporting Magazine* (p474-475)
Walking a Puppy [verses] by William Ogilvie (p475)
Polo by Edward Miller (p476)
Two Fine Polo Matches by Cecil Nickalls (p477-478)
Polo Ponies in Ireland by George Miller (p478-480)
The Grosvenors on the Turf by Ralph Nevill (p480-484)
The Sportsman's Library: Reviews of *Rifle and Romance in the Indian Jungle* by Alexander
          Glasfurd; *An Angler's Hours* by Hugh Sheringham (p484-488)
Lithograph: *At Home* (facing p487)
William Lane by Edwin Smith (p488)

Our Van [inc. Epsom Meeting; Chester Cup; Obituaries of George Mulcaster and Richard Mitchell; Craven Hounds; Amateur Rowing Association; Australian Cricket Tour; Donegal Golf]   (p489-501)
Sporting Intelligence [inc. Obituaries of James Boote, John Elloitt, Thomas Weldon, John Welby and Frank Lord; Worcestershire Hounds; Richmond Horse Show; Wells Harriers; North Warwickshire Hunt]   (p501-508)

Volume 84, July - December 1905

Issue 545 : July 1905

Portrait of John Boore, huntsman   Title page
Portrait [Lafayette] and Biography - Edward Baird   (p1-4)
Then and Now by John Russell   (p4-11)
The Moorland Beck by Carter Platts   (p11-15)
Photograph: *The Rugged Slopes of the Heath Clad Ravines*   (facing p13)
Photograph: *The Roystering Burn Through the Hamlet*   (facing p13)
An Old Coaching Road by Newton Apperley   (p16-24)
Photograph [Pearce]: *Llyfnant Valley*   (facing p19)
Photograph [Pearce]: *Royal House, Machynlleth*   (facing p19)
Photograph [Frith]: *Shrewsbury Welsh Bridge*   (facing p21)
Photograph [Pearce]: *Wynnstay Arms*   (facing p21)
The Decline of the Wager (part 1) by Frederick Aflalo   (p24-29)
The Byeways of Sport by Richard Green-Price   (p29-32)
The Golf Amateur Championship by Gordon McPherson   (p33-35)
The Sportsman's Library: Reviews of *Polo Past and Present* by Thomas Dale; *Modern Carriages* by Walter Gilbey; *The Complete Golfer* by Harry Vardon   (p35-41)
Photograph: *Pace* [Polo]   (facing p37)
Photograph: *Stopping a Run* [Polo]   (facing p39)
Engraving [sculp. Dickinson]: *Princess Victoria's Pony Carriage*   (facing p41)
[Obituary] John Earle Welby (*Baily's* contributor)   (p42-43)
A Hundred Years Ago: Racing from *The Sporting Magazine*   (p44-45)
Samuel Chifney by Edward Spencer   (p45-50)
Photograph [Devereux]: *Samuel Chifney's Tombstone at Hove*   (facing p47)
Engraving [sculp. Woodman]: *Samuel Chifney*   (facing p49)
A Dry-Fly Purist's Advice to a Beginner (part 3) by James Englefield   (p50-54)
Epsom Paddock on Derby Day by George Lowe   (p55-59)
Polo in London by Edward Miller   (p59-61)
The May-Fly Season by George Dewar   (p62-64)
Wild Pigeons by George Teasdale-Buckell   (p64-67)
Our Van [inc. Newmarket Stakes; Epsom Meeting; Australian Test Matches; Dumfriesshire Foxhounds; Scottish Golf]   (p68-81)
Photograph [Rouch]: *Cicero*   (facing p71)
Sporting Intelligence [inc. Hunting Court Case (*important*); Tattersall's Sales; Obituaries of John Arkwright, Henry Bull, William Cant, Charles Garnett, William Ashby, Charles Samways, Gipsy Cooper and George Woodley; Austrian Jockey Club; Croome Hunt]   (p81-88)

Issue 546 : August 1905

Portrait [Lafayette] and Biography - John Cotterell   (p89-90)
Are We A Horsey Nation by Richard Green-Price   (p91-94)
The Blackmail System (part 2) by Frederick Aflalo   (p95-99)
Salmon-Fishing in North-West Donegal by Edgar Shrubsloe   (p99-104)

Photograph [Shrubsole]: *On the Stranacorkagh River* (facing p101)
Photograph [Shrubsole]: *An Upper Reach of the Clady River* (facing p103)
The Great Northern Diver in Canada by Bonny Dale (p105-109)
Photograph [Dale]: *The Loon* (on p105)
Photograph [Dale] *Loon's Nest and Egg* (on p107)
After Cornish Conger by Edwin Arnold (p110-112)
The Decline of the Wager (part 2) by Frederick Aflalo (p113-117)
Open Golf Championship by Gordon McPherson (p117-119)
Large Flies and Small by Rowden Bridge (p119-121)
The Sportsman's Library: Reviews of *Oxford and Cambridge Cricket Scores* by John Betham;
          Going to West Africa by Alan Field (p121-122)
A Hundred Years Ago: Cricket from *The Sporting Magazine* (p122)
The Peterborough Shows by George Lowe (p123-131)
Lithograph [sculp. Bradley]: *Harper* (facing p127)
Polo [Cup Competitions] by Edward Miller (p131-135)
Photograph [Rouch]: *Inniskilling Dragoons Polo Team* (facing p133)
Can We Breed to Type: A Polo Pony Sale by John Hill (p135-138)
Photograph: Saddle Pony *Greek Boy* (facing p137)
Photograph: Saddle Pony *Paul Pry* (facing p137)
An Ancient Race Meeting by William Scarth-Dixon (p139-141)
The Opening Day [verses] by Carter Platts (p141-145)
Photograph: *The Shot* (facing p143)
Photograph: *The Drivers* (facing p143)
A Sensational Varsity [Cricket] Match (p145-147)
Henley Royal Regatta by Pack Ford (p147-149)
The Twelfth [verses] by Christopher Cassels (p150)
The Experienced Fowler by Abel Chapman (p151-155)
Our Van [inc. Manchester Meeting; Ascot Races; Eton versus Harrow Cricket; University
          Sport; Obituary of Harold Mahony; Wimbledon Tennis; Stock Exchange Golf] (p155-167)
Sporting Intelligence [inc. Obituaries of Benjamin Chaston and William Higgins; North
          Bucks Harriers; North Cheshire Kennels; Old Berkshire Hunt] (p167-176)

Issue 547 : September 1905

Portrait [Dickinson] and Biography - Richard Webster (p177-178)
Foxhounds: How to Draft Them by George Lowe (p179-183)
Engraving [sculp. Beckwith]: *West Australian Turf Club's Tote* (facing p185)
The Totalisator by Richard Green-Price (p185-188)
The Gentle Art of Missing by George Teasdale-Buckell (p188-196)
Angling in Badenoch by Hector Macpherson (p196-203)
Photograph [Valentine]: *Adverikie Lodge from Loch Laggan* (facing p199)
Photograph [Wilson]: *The Osprey's Nest Loch-An-Eilein* (facing p201)
Sculling in 1905 by Guy Nickalls (p204-205)
Engraving [pinx. Lyon]: *Newcomb's Bay Arabian* (facing p207)
Newcomb's Bay Arabian by James Cameron (p207-208)
Public Schools Cricket in 1905 by William Seton (p208-210)
French Horses in the St.Leger by Charles Richardson (p210-214)
Polo Tournaments by Edward Miller (p214-218)
A Dry-Fly Purist's Advice to a Beginner (part 4) by James Englefield (p218-221)
Photograph [Rouch]: *Thomas Beasley* (facing p223)
[Obituary] Tommie Beasley by Edward Cuming (p223-225)
Croquet Without Curates by Charles Locock (p225-230)
Photograph [Maull]: *Walter Peel* (facing p226)
Photograph [Jaques]: *Henry Needham* (facing p227)

Photograph [Maull]: *Jarvis Kenrick* (facing p229)
A Hundred Years Ago: York Racecourse Dispute from *The Sporting Magazine* (p231)
Fishing in the Lake District by Ernest Phillips (p232-237)
Riding by the Sea by Hugh Henry (p238-240)
Our Van [inc. Lingfield Park Plate; Goodwood Meeting; Brighton Races; Lewes Stakes; Great Yorkshire Show; Exmoor Staghunting; Obituary of Elliot Hutchins; Fifth Cricket Test Match; Calcutta Cup Golf] (p240-259)
Photograph [Rouch]: *Val D'Or* (facing p243)
Sporting Intelligence [inc. Bisley Rifle Shoot; Real Tennis; Wingfield Sculls; Obituaries of Richard Dunn and Edgar Varney; North Wales Otterhounds] (p259-266)

Issue 548 : October 1905

Portrait [Maull] and Biography - Alexander Henderson (p267-269)
Pines and Bracken by John Russell (p269-276)
Foxhounds by George Lowe (p276-281)
Two Norwegian Trout Streams by Abel Chapman (p281-288)
Photograph: *A Cast in the Evening* (facing p283)
Photograph: *Landing a Trout* (facing p283)
Photograph: *The Foss Pool* (facing p285)
Photograph: *Best Bit of the Rauma* (facing p285)
Photograph: *Lake Molmen* [n.b. name may not be correct] (facing p287)
Photograph: *Below the Mouths of the Gron* [n.b. name may not be correct] (facing p287)
A Fencing Tournament at Etretat by Theodore Cook (p289-293)
Some Firsts of October by Charles Batchelder (p293-297)
Engraving [pinx. Turner]: *Pheasant Shooting in the Olden Time* (facing p295)
The Burn [verses] by Christopher Cassels (p297-298)
Photograph: *A Scottish Burn* (on p298)
The County Championship by Sydney Pardon (p299-302)
Half a Century's Hunting Recollections (part 1) by Francis King (p302-307)
Mares and the St.Leger by William Scarth-Dixon (p307-311)
Engraving [sculp. Meisenbach]: *Caller Ou* (facing p309)
The Sportsman's Library: Reviews of *The Practical Angler* by William Stewart; *Cricket on the Brain* by Harry Furniss; *The Winning Rules Roulette* by Angelo Contarini; *Golf Faults Illustrated* by George Beldham; *The Newfoundland Guide Book* by Daniel Rowse; *Diversions Day by Day* by Edward Benson (p312-314)
A Hundred Years Ago: Pontefract Races from *The Sporting Magazine* (p314-315)
Polo in Ireland by Edward Miller (p315-319)
Sport in the City by George Fleming (p319-322)
Growth and Homing of the Salmon by Henry Cholmondeley-Pennell (p322-324)
A Tramp through Limerick Bogs by Henry Pilkington (p324-326)
With the Otterhounds by Gilbert Mott (p327-330)
Welsh Sewin Fishing by Walter Gallichan (p330-333)
Our Van [inc. Gimcrack Stakes; Doncaster Racing; Staghunting on Exmoor; Grouse Driving; Banquet to Lord Hawke; Harry Vardon Golf] (p334-349)
Sporting Intelligence [inc. Vale of White Horse Huntsman; Bexhill Harriers; Warwickshire Hunt; Obituaries of Robert Nesfield, Charles Perkins, Nicholas Spink, Charles Saunders, Philip Dunne and Robert Martin (Ballyhooley of *The Sporting Times*); Carlisle Otterhounds] (p350-358)

Issue 549 : November 1905

Portrait [Bassano] and Biography - Fiennes Cornwallis (p359-360)
Ars Venatica by Richard Green-Price (p361-364)
Foxhounds - Entering Puppies by George Lowe (p365-370)

Lithograph [pinx. Alken]: *Gone Away Forward* (facing p367)
The Minnow and the Fly-Rod by Carter Platts (p370-375)
Photograph: *The Treacherous Edge* (facing p373)
Photograph: *The Old Grey Bridge* (facing p373)
Short Shoots in November by Charles Batchelder (p376-379)
Photograph: *Young Prejvalsky Horses and their Mongolian Foster-Mothers* (facing p381)
[Reviews] *Origin and Influence of the Thoroughbred Horse* by William Ridgeway; *The Arab the Horse of the Future* by James Boucaut (p381-385)
Lithograph [pinx. Herring]: *Queen Victoria's Favourite Arab and Dogs* (facing p385)
Half a Century's Hunting Recollections (part 2) by Francis King (p385-388)
Rowing in 1905 by Pack Ford (p388-390)
The Sportsman's Library: Reviews of *Big Game Shooting* by Horace Hutchinson; *Wildfowl* by De Visme Shaw; *Retrievers and Retrieving* by William Eley; *The Little Farm* by Walter Copeland (p390-394)
Photograph: *Captain Radclyffe's Record Bear* (facing p393)
Notes and Sport of a Dry-Fly Fisherman by James Englefield (p395-398)
Horses [verses] by William Scarth-Dixon (p398-399)
Polo 1905 by Edward Miller (p399-402)
Claims Upon Hunt Poultry Funds by Frederick Millard (p402-405)
In Memory of His Heaviness [verses] by Christopher Cassels (p405-407)
Photograph: *We Confirmed Him Thirty-Pounder* (facing p407)
Sport in the City by George Fleming (p408-411)
Distemper in 1905 by Edward Cuming (p412-414)
Is Hunting a Rich Man's Luxury by Charles Richardson (p414-418)
Hunt Changes by Edward Cuming (p419-423)
[Review] *Baily's Hunting Directory 1905-06* by Edward Cuming (p424)
Our Van [inc. Newbury Racecourse; Jockey Club Stakes; Obituaries of Hugh Fortescue, Edward Rawnsley and William Oscroft; Fitzwilliam Hunt; Cheriton Otterhounds; University Sport; Marylebone Cricket Club Tour to South Africa; St.Andrews Golf] (p424-441)
Sporting Intelligence [inc. Obituaries of Reynold Clement, Archibald Stuart-Wortley and Edmond Mildmay; Eastbourne Foxhounds; Craven Harriers; Llangibby Foxhounds; West Surrey Hunt; Wormit Bowling Club; Hurworth Foxhounds; Isle of Man Harriers] (p441-448)

Issue 550 : December 1905

Portrait [Coe] and Biography - Robert Fellowes (p449-451)
Foxhounds - The Type to Follow by George Lowe (p452-456)
Lithograph [pinx. Nightingale]: *Gambler* (facing p455)
Engraving: *Fox's Head* (on p456)
The Influence of Sport Upon Character by Hugh Henry (p457-461)
Hunt Runners (part 1) by Edward Cuming (p462-468)
Photograph [Starling]: *Jack Grimsdell* (facing p465)
Lithograph [pinx. Ellis]: *Coe Piggott* (facing p467)
The Stud Book by Richard Green-Price (p468-471)
Successful Sires of the Racing Season by Arthur Coaten (p471-477)
Photograph [Hailey]: *Isinglass* (facing p473)
Photograph [Rouch]: *Count Schomberg* (facing p475)
[Review] *An Australian Cricketer on Tour* by Frank Laver (p478-481)
Sport in the City by George Fleming (p481-486)
Foxhunting by John Cooper (p487-489)
Some Further Experiences with Grayling by Paul Taylor (p489-490)
A Hundred Years Ago: Edinburgh Racecourse from *The Sporting Magazine* (p490-491)

Half a Century's Hunting Recollections (part 3) by Francis King (p491-496)

The Sportsman's Library: Reviews of *Outdoor Pastimes of an American Hunter* by Theodore Roosevelt; *The Horse* by Wortley Axe; *Half a Century of Sport in Hampshire* by Frederick Aflalo; *Nature in Eastern Norfolk* by Arthur Patterson; *Garden City and Agriculture* by Thomas Adams; *The Golliwogg's Fox Hunt* by Florence Upton (p496-503)

Photograph: *The Pack Baying the Bear* (on p497)

Photograph: *Upright Pasterns* (facing p499)

Photograph: *Good Quarters and Gaskins* (facing p501)

Some Autumn Productions at the Theatres by Otho Paget (p503-506)

The Gimcrack Stakes by William Scarth-Dixon (p507-511)

John Boore by Edward Cuming (p511-512)

Our Van [inc. Newmarket Meeting; Gatwick Stakes; Grand Sefton Steeplechase; French Bookmakers; Quorn Hunt; Obituary of Florence Dixie; West Somerset Hounds; Tiverton Hunt; New Zealand Rugby Tour; Bournemouth Golf Club] (p512-527)

Sporting Intelligence [inc. Obituaries of Henry East, Henry Mildmay, Richard Gillow, Thomas Webber and Peter Ronalds; East Kent Hounds; Tanatside Harriers; Blackmore Vale Hunt] (p527-534)

Volume 85, January - June 1906

Issue 551 : January 1906

Portrait [Hawkins] of George Hirst, cricketer — Title page

Portrait [Lafayette] and Biography - Warner Hastings (p1-3)

A Christmas Dream on Sport by Richard Green-Price (p3-7)

Foxhounds: Their Ancestry by George Lowe (p7-13)

Lithograph [pinx. Reinaele]: *Foxhounds* (facing p9)

The Development of the Modern Motor by Edwin Campbell (p13-15)

Becking by Charles Batchelder (p15-18)

Hunt Runners (part 2) by Edward Cuming (p19-26)

Photograph [Morel]: *David Swinton* (facing p21)

Lithograph [pinx. Thompson]: *Dick Baker* (facing p25)

Sport in the City by George Fleming (p26-31)

Half a Century's Hunting Recollections (part 4) by Francis King (p31-35)

A Hundred Years Ago: Partridge shooting from *The Sporting Magazine* (p36-37)

Cricket Topics by Sydney Pardon (p37-40)

Is Foxhunting Doomed by John Jacobs (p40-45)

Lithograph [Shayer]: *Returning From Market, 1838* (facing p45)

The Sportsman's Library: *Live Stock Journal Almanac* by James Sinclair; [Hunting] *Sketch Book* by George Fothergill; *Hunting Diary* by William May; *Badminton Diary* by Alfred Watson (p45-47)

In Pursuit of the Pike by Ernest Phillips (p47-55)

A Gossip on Hunting Men by William Wilmott-Dixon (p56-65)

Photograph: *Monaul Pheasants* (facing p65)

Photograph: *Koklass Pheasants* (facing p65)

Pheasant Shooting in the Himalayas by Allan Davis (p65-67)

Our Van [inc. Derby Races; Manchester Meeting; Devon & Somerset Staghounds; North Cotswold Bitches; Sinnington Hunt; University Sport; Sandwich Golf; London Playing Fields Society] (p67-84)

Sporting Intelligence [inc. Obituaries of Harvey Combe, Ralph Brassey, Edward Meyricke, Worsley Worswick, Charles Seymour, Alfred Stokes, Albert Clear and Edwin Brickwood (rowing editor of *The Field*); Ystrad & Pentyrch Hounds; Bexhill Harriers; West Norfolk Hunt; Southdown Hounds] (p85-90)

Issue 552 : February 1906

Portrait [Howard] and Biography - William Cardwell (p91-92)
Collection of Indian Weapons (part 1) by Lester Arnold (p92-99)
What Next by Richard Green-Price (p100-103)
Foxhounds: The Sires of the Day by George Lowe (p103-109)
Photograph [Paith]: *Colonist & Cardinal* (facing p105)
Hunt Runners (part 3) by Edward Cuming (p109-113)
Lithographs [Bradley]: *Leicestershire Runners - Quorn and Cottesmore* (facing p111)
Oxford and Cheltenham Coach by Stanley Kingslake (p113-115)
Lithograph: *Oxford and Cheltenham Coach* (facing p115)
The Broads as a Sporting Centre (p115-120)
Photograph [Clarke]: *Casting a Net for Small Line Bait* (facing p117)
Photograph [Clarke]: *A Broadland Sportsman With His Punt* (facing p119)
Notes and Sport of a Dry-Fly Purist by James Englefield (p120-126)
A Hundred Years Ago: Foxhounds from *The Sporting Magazine* (p127)
A Farewell to a Hunter [verses] by Charles Batchelder (p128)
The New Year at the Theatres by Otho Paget (p129-132)
Racing at Gibraltar in 1905 (p133-137)
Half a Century's Hunting Recollections (part 5) by Francis King (p138-143)
Rugby Football by Charles Harris (p143-147)
The Thoroughbred by William Scarth-Dixon (p147-151)
[Obituary] Vyell Edward Walker by Sydney Pardon (p151-154)
Our Van [inc. Racehorse Owners Association; Obituary of William Craven; Albrighton Hunt; Fitzhardinge Hounds; Bedale Hunt; Army Polo Committee; Marylebone Cricket Club in South Africa; Hoylake Golf Course] (p155-171)
Sporting Intelligence [inc. Sinnington Hounds; Obituaries of Courtenay Knollys, Hugh Browning, William Hanway, Clervaux Saunders, Richard Fitzherbert, Robert Hutton-Squire, Nunez Heysham (*Baily's* contributor) and Henry Schreiber; Eglinton Hounds; Bovicott Otterhounds] (p171-174)

Issue 553 : March 1906

Portrait [Spalding] and Biography - Edward Mashiter (p175-176)
Distemper in Hounds by Edward Cuming (p176-183)
Recollections of Seventy-Five Years' Sport (part 1) by Robert Fellowes (p183-187)
The Education of the Puppy by William Fawcett (p187-192)
Lithograph [Bradley]: *The Mother* (facing p189)
Lithograph [Bradley]: *Sent to Walks* (facing p191)
A Few Cocks and Some Rabbits by Arthur Blyth (p192-195)
Breeds of British Salmon by William Murdoch (p195-197)
Lithograph: *Vanguard Running a Fox to Ground* (facing p199)
[Review] *The Foxhounds of Great Britain* by Humphrey de Trafford, by Richard Green-Price (p199-203)
Lithograph: *Viscount Galway with Hounds* (facing p201)
Hind-Hunting by Charles Hely-Hutchinson (p204-209)
Photographs: Famous Liverpool Riders - *Alec Goodman, Thomas Olliver, Thomas Pickernell, John Page, George Stevens, Maunsell Richardson, Edward Wilson, Arthur Nightingall, Thomas Beasley* (facing p211)
Famous Grand National Riders by Arthur Meyrick (p211-216)
A Hundred Years Ago: Deer Stealing from *The Sporting Magazine* (p217)
The Sportsman's Library: Reviews of *Wisden's Cricketers' Almanack* by Sydney Pardon; *The Horse: Its Treatment* by Wortley Axe (p218-223)
Two Noted Hunting Sires by Edward Cuming (p223-227)
The University Boat Race by Pack Ford (p228-230)
Goose Shooting in Manitoba by Robert Green-Price (p230-234)

Hunting Ladies by Maud Wynter (p234-237)

Some Theories on Acquiring a Seat by Harold Leeney (p237-241)

Our Van [inc. Tantivy Steeplechase; Middlesex Hurdle Race; Cottesmore Hunt; East Cornwall Hounds; Hurworth Hunt; Obituaries of Charles Littleworth, Isabella Howe and Evan Nepean; Walton Heath Golf Club] (p241-253)

Sporting Intelligence [inc. West Norfolk Foxhounds; Obituaries of John Thornton, John Blanshard, Thomas Hughes, James Miller, George Shiffner, Alfred Landon, Charles Cornish (Field Sports Editor of *The Spectator*), William Hozier, John Hill, John Bell-Irving, Charles Littleworth, Thomas Preston, John Arkwright and Philip Blake; Croome Hounds] (p254-258)

Issue 554 : April 1906

Portrait [Elliott] and Biography - Henry Hawkins (p259-260)

Recollections of Seventy-Five Years' Sport (part 2) by Robert Fellowes (p260-265)

[Obituary] Richard Lane-Fox by Richard Green-Price (p265-266)

Spring Trout and Spring Weather by Paul Taylor (p266-268)

The Towered Bird by George Teasdale-Buckell (p268-271)

Hunt Runners (part 4) by Edward Cuming (p272-276)

Lithograph [pinx. Bradley]: *With the North Cotswold* (facing p275)

The Old Horse by Hugh Henry (p276-278)

Some Novelties in the Laws of Croquet [with Diagrams] by Otho Paget (p279-283)

True Fishing Stories by Hugh Sheringham (p283-286)

A Hundred Years Ago: Pugilism from *The Sporting Magazine* (p287-288)

Photograph [Dexter]: *Borzoi Sandringham Moscow* (facing p289)

The Borzoi by Frederick Gresham (p289-292)

Photograph [Bowden]: *Borzoi Puilai* (facing p291)

Some Sport in the Transvaal in 1878 by Alsager Pollock (p292-299)

A Song of Homage [verses] by Cyril Stacey (p299)

Herod Blood by Stanley Burke (p300-303)

The Last of the Bitterns by Allan Johnson (p303-305)

Spring Horse Shows by George Lowe (p305-317)

Photograph [Babbage]: *King II* [Champion Stallion] (facing p307)

Photograph [Babbage]: *Diplomatist* [Hackney] (facing p309)

Photograph [Babbage]: *Menella* [Harness Champion] (facing p311)

Photograph [Babbage]: *Pinderfields Horace* [Pony Champion] (facing p313)

Photograph [Babbage]: *Wales* [Premium Champion] (facing p315)

Photograph [Babbage]: *King Edward* [Hunter's Improvement Society Champion] (facing p317)

The Sportsman's Library: *Modern Dogs* by Rawdon Lee; *The Country Cottage* by George Morris; *Through Race Glasses* by Francis Vincent (p317-320)

Lithograph: *Kerry Beagles* (facing p319)

Our Van [inc. Grand Military Gold Cup; Warwick Races; Holderness Hunt; Old Berkeley West Hounds; Bramham Moor Hunt; American Polo; Marylebone Cricket Club in South Africa; Obituaries of Richard Humphrey, Edward Buckland and Evan Nepean; University Boat Race; Cross Country Running] (p320-339)

Sporting Intelligence [inc. Kennel Club Secretary; South Berks Hunt; Obituaries of Arthur Jeffreys, Hutchinson Hunt and Frank Goodall; Garth Hounds; Football Association Presentation; South Cheshire Foxhounds; East Essex Hunt] (p339-342)

Issue 555 : May 1906

Portrait [Elliott] and Biography - Assheton Biddulph (p343-346)

Englishmen's Sport in Future Years by Alfred Watson (p346-350)

A Plea for the Hare by Alan Haig-Brown (p350-353)

Pelota by Edwin Sachs (p353-357)

Lithograph [pinx. Lucas]: *Jack Shepherd on Whitethorn* (facing p357)

Jack Shepherd: An Old Hunt Servant by Edward Cuming (p357-358)

The Preparatory School by William Seton (p358-362)

[Obituary] John Gubbins by John Smith (p362-366)

Photograph [Walery]: *John Gubbins* (facing p365)

Dressing Flies by Henry Cholmondeley-Pennell (p367-368)

Navicular Disease [with Sketches] by Wortley Axe (p369-375)

Photograph: *The Beech* (facing p375)

The Beech as a Commercial Tree by Charles Curtis (p375-376)

The Hermit Family by George Lowe (p377-381)

Sport at the Universities by Pack Ford (p381-385)

Photograph [Subercaze]: *Henry Ridgway* (facing p385)

Foxhunting in France by Charles Squire (p385-387)

South African Tour: Marylebone Cricket Club Comment by Sydney Pardon (p387-391)

Some Fables on Horses by Richard Green-Price (p391-395)

Photograph [Noble]: *Hot on the Trail* (facing p397)

Photograph [Noble]: *The Worry* (facing p397)

The Advent of the Otter-Hunting Season by Theodore Cook (p397)

A Hundred Years Ago: Cockings from *The Sporting Magazine* (p398)

The Sportsman's Library: Review of *The Fox* by Thomas Dale (p399-402)

Lithograph [Thorburn]: *When All is Quiet* (facing p401)

Polo in 1906 by Edward Miller (p402-404)

Our Van [inc. Lincolnshire Handicap; Newbury Meeting; Grand Prix de Nice; Quorn Hunt Kennels; Exmoor Staghunting; Obituary of Edward Bovill; Mid-Surrey Golf Club] (p405-420)

Photograph [Rouch]: *Ascetic's Silver* (facing p407)

Sporting Intelligence [inc. Obituaries of Stanley Arnold, Hopton Williams, Richard Woodland and James Darrell; Newmarket & Thurlow Foxhounds; Taunton Vale Hunt; Colne Valley Harriers] (p420-426)

Issue 556 : June 1906

Portrait [Bassano] and Biography - Charles Duncombe (p427-429)

Sport at Westminster by Richard Green-Price (p429-432)

Education at the Public Schools by William Seton (p433-437)

Successful Steeplechase Sires by Arthur Coaten (p437-442)

Photograph [Rouch]: *Red Prince II* (facing p439)

The Billiard Cue by John Buchanan (p442-443)

A Country Fair by Albert Muntz (p443-446)

Lithograph [pinx. Agasse]: *A Country Fair in 1819* (facing p445)

The Judging of Polo Ponies by Walter Buckmaster (p447-449)

Sport and Animal Life at the Royal Academy by Edward Cuming (p449-452)

Notes and Sport of a Dry-Fly Purist by James Englefield (p452-456)

Hound Sales Past and Present by George Lowe (p456-462)

The Olympic Games by Theodore Cook (p462-463)

Lithograph [pinx. Sharpin]: *Punt Gunning* (facing p465)

A Clever Shot by Herbert Sharp (p465-467)

Cricket Notions by Otho Paget (p467-469)

The Salmon's Visual Apparatus by Allan Stewart and Marcus Gunn (p469-477)

A Hundred Years Ago: A Foot Race from *The Sporting Magazine* (p477-478)

The Sportsman's Library: Reviews of *Horses for the Army* by Walter Gilbey; *Practical Hints for Hunting Novices* by Charles Richardson; *The Sporting Spaniel* [with Photograph] by Chester Phillips; *Game and Foxes* by Frederick Millard; *Seventy Years Fishing* by Charles Barrington; *Rambles with a Fishing Rod* by Edward Roscoe (p478-485)
Engraving [sculp. Scott]: *Cocker Spaniels* (facing p481)
Photograph: *Clumber Spaniel* (on p481)
George Hirst by Otho Paget (p485-486)
Our Van [inc. Newmarket Matters; Chester Meeting; Stoke D'Abernon Polo Club; St.Andrews Golf; Hunt Secretaries' Association; Shropshire Field Trials] (p487-499)
Photograph [Rouch]: *Gorgos* (facing p489)
Photograph [Rouch]: *Flair* (facing p491)
Sporting Intelligence [inc. Queen's Club Tennis; Obituaries of George Jones and William Murray; Hunt Servants' Benefit Society; Tattersall's Sales; Hursley Hunt] (p500-506)

Volume 86, July - December 1906

Issue 557 : July 1906

Portrait [Elliott] of George Shepherd, huntsman Title page
Portrait [Lafayette] and Biography - Eustace Loder (p1-5)
Discipline at the Public Schools by William Seton (p5-9)
Polo by Thomas Dale (p9-12)
The Other Mayfly by Carter Platts (p13-18)
Photograph: *On His Way to the Landing Net* (facing p15)
Photograph: *Youngsters Have Gathered the Fly* (facing p15)
Photograph: *Creeper Fishing* (facing p17)
Photograph: *Female Shore Fly; Two Hook Tackle; Creeper Baited* (facing p17)
First Steps in Cricket Reform by Edward Bligh (p18-22)
Hunt Servants' Horses by Edward Cuming (p22-25)
The Lesson of the Olympic Games by Theodore Cook (p25-36)
An Appeal for Light [Marylebone Cricket Club Ruling] (p36-39)
Photograph: *The Oak* (facing p39)
The Oak as a Commercial Tree by Charles Curtis (p39-41)
London Polo by Edward Miller (p41-48)
Photograph [Rouch]: *Worcester* (facing p43)
Photograph [Rouch]: *Miss Haig* (facing p45)
Photograph [Rouch]: *New Boy* (facing p47)
The Derby and its National Use by George Lowe (p48-53)
Current Cricket by Sydney Pardon (p53-56)
A Hundred Years Ago: Cricket from *The Sporting Magazine* (p57)
The Amateur Golf Championship by Gordon McPherson (p58-60)
The Sportsman's Library: Reviews of *Recollections of a Bison & Tiger Hunter* by Felix Seebee; *The Art of Shooting* by Charles Lancaster; *The Cricketers' Autograph* by Broadbent Trowsdale; *A Collection of Hunting Songs* by John Reeve (p60-61)
Angling as a Sport for Ladies by Ernest Phillips (p62-66)
Our Van [inc. Newmarket Stakes; Epsom Meeting; Racehorse Owners Association; Reigate Hound Show; Berks & Bucks Farmers Staghounds; The Angling Association; Milford, Godalming & District Harriers; Obituaries of Thomas Brocklebank and George Brendon; Ladies Golf Union; Calcutta Racecourse] (p66-82)
Sporting Results (p83-86)

Issue 558 : August 1906

Portrait [Bassano] and Biography - Charles Rolls (p87-90)
On Midland Streams by John Bickerdyke (p90-94)
Staghunting on Exmoor (p94-97)
Sports and Pastimes at the Public Schools by William Seton (p97-102)
Rosapenna by Richard Green-Price (p102-109)
Photograph [Welch]: *Rosapenna Hotel and Golf Links* (facing p105)
Photograph [Welch]: *Glen Lough, Donegal* (facing p107)
The Open Golf Championship by Gordon McPherson (p109-112)
Lawn Tennis Progress by Edward Michell (p112-116)
The Ash as a Commercial Tree by Charles Curtis (p117-119)
Photograph: *The Ash* (facing p119)
Grouse Prospects by George Teasdale-Buckell (p120-121)
A Hundred Years Ago: Pigeon Shooting from *The Sporting Magazine* (p122)
Cricket: Two Fine Games at Lord's by Otho Paget (p123-129)
Henley Royal Regatta by Pack Ford (p129-132)
The Horse and Hound Shows at Peterborough by George Lowe (p132-143)
Photograph [Babbage]: *Nugget* (facing p135)
Lithograph [pinx. Bradley]: *Warwickshire Wizard* (facing p139)
Photograph [Rouch]: *The English Polo Team* (facing p143)
A Notable Polo Month by Archibald Charlton (p143-149)
Photograph [Rouch]: *Twentieth Hussars Polo Team* (facing p145)
Photograph [Rouch]: *Little Playmate* (facing p147)
The Sportsman's Library: Review of *The Science of Dry Fishing* by Frederick Shaw; *Polo* by Thomas Drybrough (p149-151)
Our Van [inc. Ascot Meeting; Lingfield Park Plate; Carlisle Otterhunting Club; North Durham Hunt; Hunt Secretaries Association; Llangibby Hounds; Cruden Bay Golf Club; Mysore Polo; Ootacamund Hounds; Melbourne Hunt] (p151-167)
Sporting Results (p167-174)

* In late August 1906, Baily's Magazine and their publishers Vinton & Co. moved to new premises at 8 Breams Buildings, Chancery Lane, City of London. In 2014 the offices were converted into six luxury flats, each selling at in excess of £2,150,000. *

Issue 559 : September 1906

Portrait [Lafayette] and Biography - Osbert Molyneux (p175-176)
A Collection of Indian Arms (part 2) by Lester Arnold (p177-184)
The Horse for Exmoor by Thomas Dale (p184-187)
Photograph [Lafayette]: *Benjamin Gosling* (facing p189)
[Obituary] Captain G.B.Gosling by Edward Cuming (p189)
The Future of Horsebreeding by George Lowe (p190-194)
The Spread of the Dry-Fly Cult by Carter Platts (p194-199)
Photograph: *In a Devotional Attitude* (facing p197)
Photograph: *A Dry Fly Pool in a Wet Fly River* (facing p197)
Photograph: *The Long Deeps* (facing p199)
Photograph: *Through Level Pastures* (facing p199)
An Old Sportsman by Richard Green-Price (p200-203)
Cricket by Sydney Pardon (p204-209)
Photograph [Collis]: *Kent Cricket Team* (facing p207)
Polo in July and August by Edward Miller (p210-214)
Photograph: *Typical Polo Ponies* (facing p213)
English Yacht Clubs by Horace Wyndham (p214-218)
Photograph [Rouch]: *Schooners Racing for the Emperor's Cup* (facing p217)

Public School Cricket in 1906 by William Seton (p219-222)
A Hundred Years Ago: Single Sticks from *The Sporting Magazine* (p223)
Partridge Rearing by George Teasdale-Buckell (p224-229)
Engraving [pinx. Turner]: *First Day of the Season* (facing p227)
Sport at the Universities by Pack Ford (p229-231)
The Longbow by Henry Walrond (p231-234)
The Sportsman's Library: Reviews of *Bombay Ducks* by Douglas Dewar; *Mr Baxter, Sportsman* by Charles Marsh (p234-235)
Our Van [inc. Newmarket Meetings; Goodwood Races; French Racing; Quantock Staghounds; Obituaries of John Manners, John Bramston, Lucy Standish, Bertram Edwards and Archibald Palmer; Craigmillar Park Golf Club; Hamilton Otterhounds; Ormond Hunt; Bangalore Polo; Simla Tennis] (p236-254)
Sporting Results (p255-260)

Issue 560 : October 1906

Portrait [Illingworth] and Biography - Romer Williams (p261-263)
Riding to Staghounds over Exmoor by Cyril Stacey (p264-270)
The Gentleman Farmer by Richard Green-Price (p270-273)
How to Become a Good Game Shot by Thomas Fremantle (p273-276)
The Form of the Foxhound by George Lowe (p276-281)
Photograph: *Elm Tree* (facing p283)
The Elm as a Commercial Tree by Charles Curtis (p282-284)
Lancashire and Some of its Rivers by Ernest Phillips (p285-292)
Photographs: *Views on the Lune* (facing p287)
Photographs: *Views on the Wyre* (facing p289)
The Cambridge and Harvard Boat Race by Pack Ford (p292-294)
The Grouse Season of 1906 by George Teasdale-Buckell (p295-297)
Photograph [Lafayette]: *Greater Britain* (facing p299)
Hunters at the Dublin Show by George Lowe (p299-301)
Photograph [Lafayette]: *Redshank* (facing p301)
Worm Fishing in Brooks by George Garrow-Green (p301-303)
A Hundred Years Ago: Bull-Baiting from *The Sporting Magazine* (p304)
To a Gentleman in Search of a Horse [verses] by David Montefiore (p305-306)
Cricket by Sydney Pardon (p306-311)
Some Critics on Horse Breeding by William Scarth-Dixon (p311-314)
Plover by Eric Parker (p314-317)
The Sportsman's Library: Reviews of *The Forests and Deer Parks of Somerset* by William Greswell; *A Girl of Resource* by Eyre Hussey; *Tally Ho!* by Helen Mathers; *Wild Life in East Anglia* by William Dutt; *Salmon Fishing* by Earl Hodgson; *How to Punch the Bag* by Young Corbett (p317-320)
A Famous Old Sporting Work by John Buchanan (p320-325)
Photograph [Rouch]: *Slieve Gallion* (facing p327)
Our Van [inc. Great Ebor Handicap; Doncaster Racing; Dieppe Races; Baden-Baden Meeting; Bloodhound Hunt Club; Culmstock Otterhounds; Obituaries of Thomas Boughey, Charles Lewis and George Watson; Sparkford Vale Harriers; Queensland Turf Club] (p327-342)
Photograph [Rouch]: *Troutbeck* (facing p329)
Sporting Results (p343-348)

Issue 561 : November 1906

Portrait [Fry] and Biography - Robert McKergow (p349-350)
The Outlook of Hunting 1906-07 by Richard Green-Price (p351-355)
Engraving [pinx. Barraud]: *Who-Whoop* (facing p353)

Tracking Game by Richard Cobbold (p355-358)
Photograph [Dyal]: *Beasts Killed in Central India* (facing p357)
The Foxhound Entries for the Season (part 1) by George Lowe (p359-365)
[Review] *The Old Surrey Foxhounds* by Humphrey Taylor (p365-369)
Engraving [pinx. Wolstenholme]: *Run to Earth* [at Walton Heath] (facing p367)
Photograph: *Edmund Byron* (facing p369)
Notes and Sport of a Dry-Fly Purist by James Englefield (p370-372)
Pearl Diver by George Lowe (p373-374)
Captain Barclay of Ury (p375-378)
Lithograph: *Robert Barclay of Ury* (facing p377)
Autumn Evenings in London by Otho Paget (p378-383)
Lithograph [pinx. Cutler]: *Equality with Henry Boden up* (facing p385)
Henry Boden and his Hunter by Edward Cuming (p385)
A Hundred Years Ago: The Berkeley Hounds from *The Sporting Magazine* (p386)
The Scotch Pine as a Commercial Tree by Charles Curtis (p387-389)
Photograph: *Wind-Blown Scotch Pines in the New Forest* (on p387)
Caravans for Sportsmen by Ludovick Cameron (p389-393)
Photograph: *Caravan Adapted for Sporting Purposes* with Interior Floor-Plan (facing p391)
The Sportsman's Library: Reviews of *The Complete Rugby Footballer* by David Gallaher;
         The Autobiography of Robert Standish-Sievier (p393-395)
[Review] *Baily's Hunting Directory 1906-07* by Edward Cuming (p395)
Cricket Reform: A Suggestion by John Buchanan (p396-398)
A Day on the North Tyne by Charles Benson (p398-403)
Photographs: *Fishing on the North Tyne* (facing p401)
The Evolution of the Outrigger by John Jeffrey (p403-407)
Hunt Changes by Edward Cuming (p407-413)
Our Van [inc. Manchester Meeting; Newmarket Charges; Longchamps Racing; Cattistock
         Hunt; East of Scotland Otterhounds; Obituaries of George Brendon, Addams
         Williams, Charles Wicksted, Francis King (*Baily's* contributor) and St.John
         Spackman; Professional Golfers Association; Calcutta Turf Club; Burma Polo;
         Australasian Turf Register] (p413-431)
Sporting Results (p432-436)

Issue 562 : December 1906

Portrait [Elliott] and Biography - William Bass (p437-438)
On Some Abuses in Foxhunting by Thomas Dale (p439-444)
The Racing Season of 1906 by Richard Green-Price (p444-448)
The Overestimation of Athletics by Eustace Miles (p449-450)
Rock-Fishing on the Yorkshire Coast by Carter Platts (p451-457)
Photograph: *Filey Brig - The Sea Anglers Incomparable Platform* (facing p453)
Photograph: *Broken Lines of White Horses* (facing p455)
Photograph: *A Nice Codling* (facing p455)
The Black Cock [verses] by Alan Haig-Brown (p457)
Photograph [Bourne]: *The Poonah Hounds* (facing p459)
The Sportsman's Paradise by George Cecil (p459-463)
Photograph [Bourne]: *Tent Pegging at Poonah* (facing p461)
Photograph: *The Hyderabad Racecourse* (facing p463)
The Retriever and His Trials by George Teasdale-Buckell (p464-467)
Successful Stallions of the Year by Arthur Coaten (p468-474)
Photograph [Parsons]: *Persimmon* (facing p471)
Photograph [Parsons]: *Carbine* (facing p471)
Winter Evenings in London by Otho Paget (p475-477)
The Foxhound Entries for the Season (part 2) by George Lowe (p477-485)

A Hundred Years Ago: A Fighting Dog from *The Sporting Magazine* (p485-486)

The Sportsman's Library: Reviews of *Campfires in the Canadian Rockies* by William Hornaday; *Practical Rowing* by Arthur Stevens; *Golf Greens and Green-Keeping* by Horace Hutchinson; *The Pointer and His Predecessors* by William Arkwright (p486-494)

Photograph: *Mr Hornaday's First Mountain Goat* (on p487)

Lithograph [pinx. Earl]: *Aldin Fluke and Bride II* (facing p491)

Snipe Shooting by George Garrow-Green (p495-497)

Cairo and its Surroundings (p497-499)

Lithograph: *An Eastern Charger* (facing p499)

George Shepherd by Edward Cuming (p500)

Our Van [inc. Gatwick Meeting; Newbury Races; French Racing Tax; Kildare Hunt; Horsham Golf Club; University Rugby; Obituaries of George Hunt, Arthur Brown, Charles Cunningham and John Worthington; Indian Racing Scandals; Indian Cricket; Queensland Turf Club] (p501-518)

Sporting Results (p518-522)

Richard Green-Price

Theodore Cook

Volume 87, January - June 1907

Issue 563 : January 1907

Portrait [Foster] of Albert Trott, cricketer	Title page
Portrait [Elliott] and Biography - Charles Godman	(p1-2)
Driving the Moss by Arthur Browne	(p3-5)
The Rules of Racing by Charles Richardson	(p5-9)
Lithograph [pinx. Shayer]: *Brighton Day Mails Passing on Hookwood Common*	(facing p11)
The Old Coaching Days by Lilian Bland	(p10-18)
Lithograph [pinx. Henderson]: *Road Scrapings*	(facing p13)
Lithograph [pinx. Henderson]: *A Night Team*	(facing p15)
Lithograph [pinx. Pollard]: *The White Horse, Fetter Lane*	(on p15)
Hunters Past and Present by Thomas Dale	(p18-23)
Photograph [Van der Weybe]: *George Hunt*	(facing p23)
[Obituary] Captain George Warwick Hunt	(p23-26)
Pursuits of a Gentleman of the Fourteenth Century	(p26-28)
The Last Fence [verses] by William Ogilvie	(p29)
A Word About Card Games by Matthew Moser	(p30-34)
Photograph: *Historical Pack - Rump Parliament Suite 1657*	(facing p30)
Photograph: *French Pack - Seventeenth Century*	(facing p30)
Photograph: *Spanish Pack 1735*	(facing p30)
Photograph: *Indian Pack*	(on p32)
Photograph: *Italian Pack - Jester or Joker*	(on p33)
Photograph: *Old German Pack - King of Acorns*	(on p33)
The Experienced Angler by Abel Chapman	(p35-38)
December in London by Otho Paget	(p39-41)
Photograph: *A Larch Plantation in the New Forest*	(facing p43)
The Larch as a Commercial Tree by Charles Curtis	(p42-44)
Pony Breeding and Measuring by John Hill	(p45-49)
A Hundred Years Ago: Samuel Chifney from *The Sporting Magazine*	(p50-51)
The Cleverest Blind Man	(p51-53)
The Sportsman's Library: Reviews of *Live Stock Journal Almanack 1907* by James Sinclair; *Modern Sporting Gunnery* by Henry Sharp; *British Dogs at Work* by Croxton Smith; *Annals of the Corinthian Football Club* by Bernard Corbett; *Some Irish Yesterdays* by Enone Somerville	(p53-57)
Lithograph [pinx. Cooper]: *Hunter Brood Mare and Foal*	(facing p55)
The Cause of Overestimation of Athletics by Alan Haig-Brown	(p58-59)
Hunting Fiction by Maud Wynter	(p59-63)
Property in Wild Animals by George Harris	(p63-67)
Our Van [inc. Derby Races; Grafton Hunt; Croome Hounds; Bramham Moor Hunt; Westward Ho! Golf Club; Tanatside Harriers; Obituary of George Lees; Argyllshire Otterhounds; Secunderabad Polo; Australian Anti-Betting Laws]	(p67-85)
Sporting Results	(p85-88)

Issue 564 : February 1907

Portrait [Dickinson] and Biography - William Foster	(p89-91)
A Question of Today by Richard Green-Price	(p92-95)
The Modern Foxhound in the Field by Cyril Stacey	(p96-100)
Panther Shooting from a Tope by Frances Murray	(p100-108)
Lithograph [pinx. Scallon]: *What a Jolting We Had*	(facing p103)
Lithograph [pinx. Scallon]: *Hyena at Work on the Panther's Head*	(facing p105)
Lithograph [pinx. Scallon]: *Staggering With Their Burden*	(facing p107)

[Obituary] Walter Read by Otho Paget (p109-112)
Photograph [Hawkins]: *Walter Read* (facing p111)
Hunting in the Provinces by Edward Cuming (p113-116)
Rustic Youth [verses] (p117)
Games and the Boy by John Russell (p118-120)
The Spruce and Douglas Firs as Commercial Trees by Charles Curtis (p121-125)
Photograph: *A Douglas Fir, New Forest* (facing p123)
Photograph [Rouch]: *Mintagon* (facing p125)
Northern Trained Horses by George Lowe (p125-127)
Photograph [Rouch]: *Brood Mares at Highfield* (facing p127)
Don't Halloa by Thomas Dale (p127)
Notes and Sport of a Dry-Fly Purist by James Englefield (p128-131)
Lord Galway's Hounds by George Lowe (p131-135)
Lawn Tennis Politics by Edward Michell (p135-137)
A Hundred Years Ago: Pigeon Shooting from *The Sporting Magazine* (p138-139)
The Sportsman's Library: Review of *Tarpon Fishing in Mexico and Florida* by Edward
    Churchill (p139-142)
Photograph: *Tarpon Leaping* (facing p141)
Photograph: *The Desperate Tarpon* (facing p141)
Moose Shooting in Northern Ontario by John Piltcher (p143-146)
Moderate Hunting by Hugh Henry (p147-149)
Photograph [Elliott]: *New Forest Staghounds* (facing p151)
Hunting in the New Forest by Frederick Hamilton (p151-153)
Photograph [Hazel]: *Courtenay Tracy's Otterhounds* (facing p153)
The Woodcock in Ireland by Harding Cox (p154-157)
Our Van [inc. Newbury Steeplechase; Ludlow Hounds; Street Betting Bill; Warwickshire
    Hunt; The Motor Union; Obituaries of Alfred Shaw and Henry de Bathe; South
    African Rugby Tour; Polo in Upper Burma; Ugandan Game Laws] (158-174)
Sporting Results (p175-176)

Issue 565 : March 1907

Portrait [Crooke] and Biography - Robert Jardine (p177-179)
Foxes I Have Known by Thomas Dale (p179-184)
The Turf: Its Friends and Its Foes by Richard Green-Price (p185-188)
Grand National Winners by Arthur Meyrick (p188-196)
Engraving [sculp. Hunt]: *The Stone Wall* (facing p191)
Engraving [sculp. Hunt]: *The Finish* (facing p193)
[Review] *Great Golfers in the Making* by Henry Leach (p196-201)
Photograph [Fairweather]: *The Quartette - Alexander Herd, John Taylor, James Braid and
    Harry Vardon* (facing p199)
Sport with the Trout by Paul Taylor (p201-203)
In Fancy's Vale [verses] by William Ogilvie (p203)
Photograph: *Thomas Hills, Jem Hills, Charles Absalom and Harry Bartlett* (facing p205)
Wychwood Forest: When Jem Hills Hunted the Heythrop by Arthur Matthews (p204-206)
Frosty London Evenings by Otho Paget (p207-211)
The Berlin Exhibition of Antlers by John Rowbotham (p211-213)
Photograph: *Hungarian Stag Antlers* (facing p211)
Photograph: *Silesian Stag Antlers* (facing p211)
The Kennel Fox-Terrier by George Lowe (p213-217)
Photograph [Babbage]: *Old Surrey Foxhounds Meet at Marden Park* (facing p217)
The Old Surrey Foxhounds by Charles Frederick (p217-218)
The Grouse Committee's Report by George Teasdale-Buckell (p218-221)

The Sportsman's Library: Reviews of *Five Thousand Miles in a Balloon* by Frank Butler; *White Fang* by Jack London; *Sporting Nonsense Rhymes* by Finch Mason (p222-226)

The Silver Fir as a Commercial Tree by Charles Curtis (p226-229)

Some of Yorkshire's Famous Racers (1700-1800) by George Teasdale-Buckell (p229-234)

Lithograph [pinx. Seymour]: *Old Partner* (facing p231)

Lithograph [pinx. Seymour]: *Bay Bolton* (facing p231)

A Hundred Years Ago: Hounds from *The Sporting Magazine* (p235)

Extra Notes From the Diary of Felix (part 1) (p236-240)

Our Van [inc. The Jockey Club; Gatwick Meeting; Cheshire Hunt; New Forest Beagles; West Hambledon Hounds; County Polo Association; County Cricket Qualification; Ice Skating; Punjab Polo; Ceylon Fishing Club; South African Cricketers] (p240-259)

Sporting Results (p260-262)

Issue 566 : April 1907

Portrait [Elliott] and Biography - John Swire (p263-265)

A Red Letter Day in Wales by Richard Green-Price (p265-268)

A Mixed Catch by Herbert Bromhead (p268-271)

Model Yacht Racing by George Hopcroft (p271-275)

Lithograph [sculp. Hopcroft]: *Typical Models of the Present Day* (facing p273)

Lithograph [sculp. Hopcroft]: *Model of Extreme Type* (facing p275)

Photograph: *Steed Caparisoned for a State Occasion* (facing p277)

The Rajah's Stable by George Cecil (p277-279)

Photograph: *The State Elephant and Embroidered Howdah* (facing p279)

An Average of Sport by William Scarth-Dixon (p280-284)

The Responsibilities of Inheritance (p284-286)

Some Recent Motor Experiments by Sidney Edge (p286-288)

Lottery and His Son by George Teasdale Buckell (p289-294)

Engraving: *Lottery* (facing p291)

Engraving: *Cigar and Lottery* (facing p291)

London Evenings at Eastertide by Otho Paget (p295-298)

[Obituary] Charles Alcock by Otho Paget (p299-300)

A Hundred Years Ago: Cocking from *The Sporting Magazine* (p301)

Photograph [Babbage]: *Hackney Stallion Rosador* (facing p303)

The Spring Horse Shows by George Lowe (p303-310)

Photograph [Babbage]: *Thoroughbred Stallion Flambeau* (facing p305)

Photograph [Babbage]: *Hunter Gelding Fable* (facing p307)

Photograph [Babbage]: *Polo Pony Stallion Spanish Hero* (facing p309)

The Sportsman's Library: Reviews of *Animal Artisans* by Charles Cornish; *The Complete Fisherman* by Walter Gallichan; *Horses, Cattle, Sheep and Pigs* by Townsend Barton; *Grouse Shooting & Deer Stalking* by Evan Mackenzie (p310-313)

Polo Prospects for 1907 by Edward Miller (p313-319)

Photograph [Elliott]: *Egerton Green* (facing p315)

Photograph [Elliott]: *Edward Miller* (facing p315)

The Pinaster as a Commercial Tree by Charles Curtis (p320-322)

Photograph: *The Pinaster* (facing p321)

Sporting Personalities: Quaint Stories of Men of Mark (p323-327)

Photograph: *Edgar Vincent* (on p323)

Photograph: *Henry Hawkins* (on p325)

Photograph: *William Griggs* (on p326)

Night Coaching of Today by Claude Sisley (p328-331)

Our Van [inc. Leicester Meeting; Warwick Races; Obituaries of Charles Pitman (*Baily's* contributor) and Frederick Holland; Cottesmore Hunt; Tedworth Hounds; Essex Hunt Point-to-Point; The Motor Union; National Sporting Club; University Boat Race; Cross Country Running; Nairobi Races] (p332-347)

Sporting Results (p347-350)

Issue 567 : May 1907

Portrait [Elliott] and Biography - Lewis Priestman (p351-354)
The Game Preserver in May by Frank Bonnett (p354-358)
Horse Shows Past and Present by Richard Green-Price (p358-362)
Present Day Athletics by Charles Batchelder (p362-367)
Photograph [Gillman]: *The Twin Brothers Christopher and Noel Chavasse* (facing p365)
Photograph [Wright]: *Arthur Astley* (on p365)
Facts About Famous Jockeys by William Fox-Russell (p367-373)
Photograph: *James Robinson* (on p368)
Photograph: *Patrick Connolly* (on p369)
Photograph: *George Fordham* (on p370)
Photograph: *Thomas Chaloner* (on p371)
Photograph [Chancellor]: *Frederick Archer* (on p372)
The Latest Shooting Problem by George Teasdale-Buckell (p374-377)
Some Aspects of Trout Fishing by James Englefield (p378-380)
Cricket is King [verses] by Alan Haig-Brown (p380)
Scientific Regulation of Road Traffic by John Russell (p381-383)
The Breeding of Steeplechase Winners by Arthur Coaten (p383-392)
Photograph [Rouch]: *Eremon* (facing p385)
Photograph [Reid]: *Thurles* (facing p387)
Photograph [Hailey]: *Jeddah* (facing p389)
Photograph: *James Cleary* (on p390)
Spring Evenings in London by Otho Paget (p392-395)
Sporting Personalities: Quaint Stories of Men of Mark (p395-398)
Photograph: *Cecil Legard* (on p396)
Photograph: *Richard Webster* (on p397)
Photograph: *Lees Knowles* (on p398)
A Hundred Years Ago: Cricket from *The Sporting Magazine* (p399)
Cinderellas of County Cricket by Otho Paget (p400-404)
Predominance of Irish Horses by George Lowe (p404-409)
Photograph: *Gilbert Grace at Bowls* (facing p409)
The Sportsman's Library: Reviews of *The Bowlers Annual* by Gilbert Grace; *Some Old English Inns* by George Burrows; *Modern Side-Saddle Riding* by Eva Christie; *Farming for Ladies* by Edith Park (p409-413)
Photographs: *Hand Holding Reins - Single and Double* (facing p411)
Photographs: *Hand Holding Reins - Awkward and Runaway Horse* (facing p413)
A Rubber at Bowls by William Stonehewer (p413-418)
Photograph [Bailey]: *Southampton Town Bowling Green* (facing p415)
Photograph [Taylor]: *Queen's Park Bowling Green, Glasgow* (facing p415)
Photograph [Gregson]: *William Taylor* (on p415)
Our Van [inc. Aintree Racing; Lincoln Meeting; Grove Hunt; Obituary of George Langley; Kildare Hunt; Sparkford Vale Harriers; County Polo Association; The Motor World; Thames Regatta; Royal North Devon Golf Club; Bombay Cricket Club; Calcutta Polo] (p418-435)
Photographs: *Six-Cylinder Napier Car* (facing p429)
Sporting Results (p436-440)

Issue 568 : June 1907

Portrait [Medrington] and Biography - Reid Walker	(p441-443)
The Temperament of the Racehorse by Henry Pilkington	(p444-448)
For Health and Pleasure by Richard Green-Price	(p448-453)
Photograph [Perestvelle]: *Tapira Valley, Monte, Canary Islands*	(facing p451)
The Game Preserves in June by George Teasdale-Buckell	(p454-458)
Jockeys Who Have Won The Derby by William Fox-Russell	(p459-465)
Photograph: *Alfred Day*	(on p460)
Photograph: *John Daley*	(on p460)
Photograph: *Thomas Cannon*	(on p461)
Photograph: *Henry Custance*	(on p461)
Photograph: *Charles Wood*	(on p462)
The Hoofs of the Horses [verses] by William Ogilvie	(p465)
Otterhunting Prospects by Ludovick Cameron	(p466-469)
Sport and Country Life at The Royal Academy by Otho Paget	(p469-473)
Fisherman, Parr and Wells by George Teasdale-Buckell	(p473-478)
Lithograph [sculp. Hall]: *Fisherman*	(facing p477)
Photograph: *John Wells*	(on p478)
May Cricket by Otho Paget	(p479-482)
Sporting Personalities: Quaint Stories of Men of Mark	(p482-485)
Photograph: *Harold Chaplin*	(on p483)
Photograph: *Sammy Woods*	(on p485)
Shooters Essentials by George Teasdale-Buckell	(p485-488)
The Romance of Gallinule and Pioneer by George Lowe	(p489-493)
Albert Trott by Edward Cuming	(p493)
Richard Wood by Edward Cuming	(p494-495)
Photograph [Whitlock]: *Richard Wood*	(on p494)
Some Midsummer Nights in London by Otho Paget	(p495-499)
The Poplar Family as Commercial Trees by Charles Curtis	(p499-502)
Photograph: *Italian Black Poplar*	(facing p500)
A Hundred Years Ago: Bibury Races from *The Sporting Magazine*	(p502-503)
The Sportsman's Library: Reviews of *Ornithological and Other Oddities* by Frank Finn; *Hints on Horses* by Henry Young; *Notes on the Points of the Horse* by Robert Gilchrist; *Types and Breeds of Farm Animals* by Charles Plumb; *The New Book of the Dog* by Robert Leighton; *The Dog in Health, Accident and Disease* by Frank Barton	(p504-507)
Photograph [Finn]: *A Well Known Figure at the Zoo*	(on p504)
Photograph [Finn]: *A Colonial Visitor*	(on p505)
Our Van [inc. Newmarket Meetings; Chester Races; Cheshire Hunt; Ranelagh Polo; The Motor Club; University Athletics; Ilkley Moor Golf Club; Rangoon Racing; Bengal Lawn Tennis Championships]	(p507-529)
Photograph: *The King's Daimler*	(facing p517)
Sporting Results	(p529-532)

Volume 88, July - December 1907

Issue 569 : July 1907

Portrait of Thomas Bishopp, huntsman	Title page
Portrait [Sherwood] and Biography - John Stewart-Murray	(p1-2)
Goodwood and its Memories by Edward Michell	(p3-9)
Photograph [Rouch]: *View Down the Course at Goodwood*	(facing p5)
Photograph [Rouch]: *Under the Plantation at Goodwood*	(facing p7)

Successful Backers by Henry Pilkington (p10-15)
Leg Before Wicket in 1907 by Edward Bligh (p15-18)
The Young Game in July by George Teasdale-Buckell (p18-21)
An Apostle of Amateurism: Charles Crane by Unite Jones (p22-27)
Photograph [Sands]: *Charles Crane, President of the Rugby Football Union* (facing p25)
Photograph: *Manor House, Birlingham, Pershore* (facing p27)
On the Northern Circuit by John Radcliffe (p28-30)
The Amateur Golf Championship by Gordon McPherson (p31-33)
Current Cricket by Otho Paget (p33-37)
Modern Racehorses by Richard Green-Price (p37-40)
A Hundred Years Ago: Cricket from *The Sporting Magazine* (p40-41)
To the Old Bay Nag [verses] by Ben Benjamin (p42)
Another Shooter's Problem by George Teasdale-Buckell (p43-46)
A Wail from the Wicket by Otho Paget (p47-49)
The International Horse Show by George Lowe (p49-55)
Photograph [Rouch]: *Coker's Rosador and Proserpine* (facing p51)
Photograph [Clarke]: *Cherry Boy and Cherry Girl* (facing p53)
Some Fishing Problems by Ernest Phillips (p55-59)
Sporting Personalities: Quaint Stories of Men of Mark (p59-61)
Photograph [Foster]: *Frederick Byrne* (on p59)
English Coaching Clubs by Horace Wyndham (p61-66)
Photograph [Rouch]: *Edward Colston's Black Brown Team* (facing p63)
Photograph [Rouch]: *Edward Stern's Blue Roan Team* (facing p65)
The Sportsman's Library: Reviews of *Eclipse and O'Kelly* by Theodore Cook; *Notes and Sketches* by George Fothergill; *Cricket and Cricketers* by Frederick Ashley-Cooper; *Grouse Disease* by Adrian Woodruffe-Peacock; *Salmon Fishing* by John Hardy; *Pretty Polly* by Joscelyne Lechmere (p66-69)
The Cannibal Pike by Herbert Blyth (p68-69)
Photographs [Blyth]: *Cannibal Pike* (facing p69)
Dry-Fly Sport by James Englefield (p70-71)
Bisque Taking by Maud Drummond (p72-76)
The Fascination of Minor Sports (p76-78)
Our Van [inc. Harpenden Races; Epsom Meeting; Racehorse Owners' Association; Polo Pony Show; Sandwich Golf; Canadian Hockey; Obituary of Owen McCourt] (p78-94)
Photograph [Rouch]: *Orby* (facing p81)
Photograph [Rouch]: *England Polo Team* (facing p85)
Sporting Results (p95-98)

Issue 570 : August 1907

Portrait [Hawkins] and Biography - Reginald Foster (p99-101)
They're Off, Yet They're On by Richard Green-Price (p102-104)
More Shooting Problems by George Teasdale-Buckell (p105-108)
The South African Cricketers by Otho Paget (p109-111)
Stake Nets on the Solway by Claude Benson (p112-117)
Photographs: *Nets - Distant View and Close Up* (facing p115)
Photographs: *Fish in Net and Fisherman* (on p115)
Causes of British Decadence in Sport by Charles Batchelder (p117-120)
The Yachting Derby by George Hopcroft (p121-125)
Lithograph [sculp. Hopcroft]: *Cowes Regatta in the 1840s* (facing p123)
Lithograph [sculp. Hopcroft]: *Cowes Regatta at the Present Day* (facing p125)
Swordsmanship by Charles Hancock (p126-128)
Is British Golf Declining by Gordon McPherson (p128-130)
An Appreciation of the Grouse by Alan Haig-Brown (p131-132)

Polo and Polo Players by Edward Miller (p133-138)
Current Cricket Topics by Otho Paget (p138-144)
The Game in August by George Teasdale-Buckell (p144-147)
The Peterborough Shows by George Lowe (p148-156)
Lithograph [sculp. Bradley]: *Hertfordshire Sampler* (facing p153)
Lawn Tennis Championships by Wallis Myers (p156-157)
A Hundred Years Ago: Shooting from *The Sporting Magazine* (p158)
Hereditary Racing Qualities of St.Leger Winners (part 1) by Jack Fairfax-Blakeborough (p159-164)
Engraving [sculp. Herring]: *Filho Da Puta* (facing p163)
Engraving [sculp. Turner]: *Blue Bonnet* (facing p163)
Sporting Personalities: Quaint Stories of Men of Mark (p165-166)
Photograph [Hawkins]: *Russell Bencraft* (on p165)
The Sportsman's Library: Reviews of *Sunshine and Sport in Florida and the West Indies* by
        Frederick Afalo; *How to Fish* by Earl Hodgson; *The Complete Golfer* by
        William Butler (p167-170)
Photograph: *Where the Tarpon Jumps* (facing p169)
A Tragedy of Tattersalls [verses] by Cyril Stacey (p170-171)
Rabbit Damage to Underwood by Claremont Clare (p172-175)
The Royal Yachts of England by Horace Wyndham (p176-178)
Our Van [inc. Hurst Park Meeting; Ascot Races; Devon & Somerset Staghounds; University
        Sport; Henley Regatta; Brooklands Motor Racing; Ranelagh Polo] (p178-192)
Photograph: *Coventry Humber Car* (facing p187)
Photograph: *Thornycroft Car* (facing p187)
Sporting Results (p192-196)

Issue 571 : September 1907

Portrait [Elliott] and Biography - Edgar Milne (p197-200)
The First Snipe by Edwin Arnold (p200-202)
From Skei to Sandene by John Bickerdyke (p203-206)
Brow, Bay and Tray by John Page (p206-210)
Angling in Ireland: Lough Corrib by Edwin Arnold (p210-216)
Photograph [Monaghan]: *Hill of Doon* (facing p213)
Photograph [Monaghan]: *Owenriff River* (facing p213)
Photograph [Monaghan]: *Carrarevagh Bay and House* (facing p215)
Photograph [Monaghan]: *Played Out* (facing p215)
The End of the Polo Season by Edward Miller (p216-220)
Hereditary Racing Qualities of St.Leger Winners (part 2) by Jack Fairfax-Blakeborough (p220-224)
Photograph: *William Scott* (on p221)
Photograph [Hall]: *Caller Ou* (facing p223)
Photograph [Hall]: *Surplice* (facing p223)
[Review] *A History of Kent Cricket* by George Harris (p225-229)
Gun Powders and Their Tests by George Teasdale-Buckell (p229-233)
Ballade of Cubhunting [verses] by Robert Churchill (p233)
Current Cricket by Sydney Pardon (p234-237)
The Sportsman's Song [verses] by Alan Haig-Brown (p237)
[Obituary] John Doyle by Eric Parker (p238-240)
Photograph [Hills]: *John Andrew Doyle* (on p238)
The Sportsman's Library: Reviews of *Pedigree of English Thoroughbred Horses* by Laurits
        Jorgensen; *The Spirit of the Links* by Henry Leach; *A Mother's Son* by Charles Fry;
        The Horses of the British Empire by Humphrey de Trafford; *Modern Croquet Tactics*
        by Charles Locock; *The Complete Shot* by George Teasdale-Buckell (p240-242)
Sporting Personalities: Quaint Stories of Men of Mark (p243-244)
A Hundred Years Ago: Stallions from *The Sporting Magazine* (p245)

Among the Crannogs With a Gun by Charles Marsh (p246-252)
The Grouse Season by George Teasdale-Buckell (p253-257)
Public School Cricket in 1907 by William Seton (p257-260)
Scotland's Veteran Caddies by Arthur Grime (p261-269)
Photograph [Spence]: *John Carey* (facing p263)
Photograph [Spence]: *Bob Pringle* (facing p265)
Our Van [inc. Mersey Stakes; Brighton Cup; Culmstock Otterhounds; Obituary of Robert
            Podmore; Gun Dog League; Scarborough Town Golf Club; Scottish Motor
            Trials; Auckland Racecourse Bookmakers] (p269-283)
Photograph: *Mercedes Racing Car* (facing p279)
Photograph: *Daimler Racing Car* (facing p279)
Sporting Results (p283-288)

Issue 572 : October 1907

Portrait [Burton] and Biography - Charles McNeill (p289-292)
Game and Deer in October by George Teasdale-Buckell (p292-296)
Two Famous Hunts by George Lowe (p296-300)
Whaling as a Sport by John Russell (p300-306)
Photograph: *The Bjorn - An International Class of Whaler* (facing p303)
Photograph: *Whalers Discharging at the Refinery* (facing p303)
The Cricket Season of 1907 by Otho Paget (p306-310)
Waltoniensis by Mary Fair (p311-316)
Photograph: *Fishing in the Highlands - I* (on p311)
Photograph: *Isaac Walton's Country - On the River Itchen* (on p312)
Photograph: *Fishing in the Highlands - II* (facing p315)
Photograph: *Bringing a Fish Ashore to be Weighed* (facing p315)
To a Racehorse [verses] by Alan Haig-Brown (p316)
Nerve in Jockeys by William Fox-Russell (p317-321)
Photograph: *Frank Buckle* (on p319)
Photograph: *John Singleton* (on p319)
[Review] *Horses of the British Empire* by Humphrey de Trafford reviewed by Richard
            Green-Price (p321-324)
Fly-Fishing in Reservoirs by John Taylor (p325-327)
The Ornamental in Planting by Charles Curtis (p327-330)
Photograph: *Tree Planting - Firs, Laurel, Yews* (facing p329)
Photograph: *Tree Planting - Thujas* (facing p329)
Hints on Breaking Pointers and Setters by George Garrow-Green (p330-332)
The Veteran [verses] by William Ogilvie (p332)
A Hundred Years Ago: Pigeon Shooting from *The Sporting Magazine* (p333-334)
A Rural Revolution by George Teasdale-Buckell (p334-337)
The Sportsman's Library: Reviews of *Dogs* by Harding Cox and *The Horse* by Frederick Barton (p337-338)
Racquets [verses] by Harold Rudd (p339)
Sporting Personalities: Quaint Stories of Men of Mark (p340-341)
Polo Ponies I Have Known by Thomas Dale (p341-346)
[Obituary] Edmund Burton by Arthur Meyrick (p347-351)
Lithograph [pinx. Cutler]: *Edmund Burton* (facing p349)
The Farmer-Dealer by Lilian Bland (p351-355)
Our Van [inc. Redcar Stakes; York Meeting; Doncaster Cup; Meynell Hunt; Obituaries of
            Edgar Lubbock and Vincent Herman; Market Harborough Horse Show; County
            Polo Association; Motoring Illustrated; Plumpton Coursing; Henley Regatta;
            Seaford Golf Club; Australian Rugby Union] (p355-374)
Photographs: *Brooklands Motor Racing Circuit - Experiments of Wind Resistance* (facing p367)
Sporting Results (p374-378)

Issue 573 : November 1907

Portrait [Graham] and Biography - Richard Verney (p379-380)
Red Deer and the Highlands by George Teasdale-Buckell (p381-385)
The Professional Influence on Games by Frederick Aflalo (p385-388)
Polo, Punctuality and Popularity by Edward Miller (p388-390)
Tufts of Turf by William Fox-Russell (p390-395)
Photograph: *Thomas Jennings* (on p393)
Photograph: *John Osborne* (on p393)
The Art of Fly-Tying [Illustrated] by Joseph Adams (p395-402)
[Obituary] Henry Hawkins by Edward Cuming (p402-403)
[Review] *Hounds Please* by George Lowe reviewed by Richard Green-Price (p404-407)
Autumn Evenings in London by Otho Paget (p408-413)
Gunpowders: Good and Bad by George Teasdale-Buckell (p413-417)
The Old Mare's Foal [verses] by William Ogilvie (p418)
The Great Fox Family by George Lowe (p419-421)
A Hundred Years Ago: Shooting from *The Sporting Magazine* (p422)
The Sportsman's Library: Reviews of *Big Game Shooting on the Equator* by Francis Dickinson; *Jock of the Bushveld* by Percy Fitzpatrick; *Two Dianas in Somaliland* by Agnes Herbert; *The Life of Old Tom Morris* by William Tulloch; *The Diary of Master William Silence* by Dodgson Madden; *A Practical Guide to the Game Laws* by Charles Row (p423-428)
Photograph: *Burchell's Zebra* (facing p425)
Photograph: *Tommy - The Tame Zebra* (facing p425)
Photograph: *An Ipmala Buck* (facing p427)
Photograph: *A Water Buck on Lake Naivasha* (facing p427)
Baily's Hunting Directory 1907-08 by Edward Cuming (p428)
The Ornamental in Planting by Charles Curtis (p429-432)
Photograph: *A Sentinel - The Golden Cypress* (on p430)
Sporting Personalities: Quaint Stories of Men of Mark (p433-435)
Five Stouthearted Horses (part 1) by George Teasdale-Buckell (p435-440)
Engraving [sculp. Herring]: *Touchstone* (facing p437)
Engraving [sculp. Herring]: *Bay Middleton* (facing p439)
Hunt Changes [including Obituaries of Mark Rolle, German Shepherd, Foster Milliar, Thomas Garth and Edward Stanley] by Edward Cuming (p440-445)
Our Van [inc. Ayr Racecourse; Newbury Autumn Cup; Quantock Staghounds; Exmoor Foxhounds; Motor Union; Mid-Annandale Coursing; St.Andrews Golf; Poona Polo; British East Africa Turf Club] (p445-464)
Photograph: *Daimler Car* (facing p455)
Photograph: *Landaulet Argyll Car* (facing p455)
Sporting Results (p464-468)

Issue 574 : December 1907

Portrait [Chancellor] and Biography - Edmond Fitzmaurice (p469-470)
Point to Point Racing by Richard Green-Price (p471-473)
Game in December by George Teasdale-Buckell (p473-477)
The Worth of the Foxhound by George Lowe (p477-480)
Alone With Hounds [verses] by William Ogilvie (p481)
Photograph [Hailey]: *The White Knight* (facing p483)
The Equine Hero of 1907 by Edward Cuming (p482-485)
Photograph [Sherborn]: *Harry Sadler* (on p482)
Photograph [Rouch]: *Radium* (facing p485)
The Art of Angling (part 1) by Joseph Adams (p486-492)
Photograph: *Bottom Fishing Reels* (on p487)

Photograph: *Floats for Bottom Fishing* (on p490)
Playing the Game by Vincent Blue (p492-493)
Some Progress With Powders by George Teasdale-Buckell (p493-496)
Reflections on the Past Trout Season: (part 1) by Ernest Phillips (p497-500)
Reflections on the Past Trout Season: (part 2) by James Englefield (p500-502)
Five Stouthearted Horses (part 2) by George Teasdale-Buckell (p502-507)
Engraving [pinx. Turner]: *Harkaway* (facing p505)
Engraving [pinx. Herring]: *Hetman Platoff* (facing p505)
The Sportsman's Library: Reviews of *The New Book of the Dog* by Robert Leighton;
          Foxhunting Recollections by Reginald Graham; *The Man-Eaters of Tsavo* by
          John Patterson; *My Racing Adventures* by Arthur Nightingall (p508-513)
Photograph: *Henry Howard and Reginald Graham* (facing p511)
Photograph: *"His Length was Nine Foot Eight Inches"* (on p512)
A Hundred Years Ago: Hunting from *The Sporting Magazine* (p513-514)
Sporting Personalities: Quaint Stories of Men of Mark (p514-515)
Photograph [Rouch]: *Desmond* (facing p517)
The Premier Stallions of the Year by Arthur Coaten (p516-523)
Photograph [Parsons]: *Gallinule* (facing p519)
Photograph [Parsons]: *Orme* (facing p521)
Photograph [Newman]: *Charles Cavendish and George Capell* (facing p523)
[Obituary] Charles Cavendish by Heneage Bagot-Chester (p523-524)
Planting for Covert [with Diagrams] by Charles Curtis (p525-527)
Tupgill, Middleham (part 1) by George Fothergill (p528-532)
Lithograph [pinx. Fothergill]: *Tupgill House, Middleham* (on p528)
Lithograph [pinx. Fothergill]: *Town Square, Middleham* (on p529)
Thomas Bishopp by Edward Cuming (p533)
Our Van [inc. Newbury Meeting; Middle Park Plate; Liverpool Cup; Obituary of John
          Kincaid-Smith; Cottesmore Hunt; Cattistock Hounds; Cambridge University
          Staghounds; East Sussex Hunt; Motor Union; Altcar Coursing; Sunningdale Golf;
          Upper India Golf; Kashmir Cricket; New York Hunting] (p533-550)
Photograph: *Daimler Car* (facing p545)
Photograph: *Crossley Car* (facing p545)
Sporting Results (p550-552)

Volume 89, January - June 1908

Issue 575 : January 1908

Portrait [Hailey] of William Higgs, jockey Title page
Portrait [Kirk] and Biography - Alwyn Greville (p1-2)
Foxhounds in India by Thomas Dale (p3-6)
Sport in West Wales by Richard Green-Price (p7-11)
Photograph [Rouch]: *Missel Thrush* (facing p9)
The Art of Angling (part 2) by Joseph Adams (p11-16)
Photograph: *Five Chub Flies* (on p14)
Photograph: *The Weir Chub Pool* (on p15)
Autumn Polo Meetings by Edward Miller (p17-19)
An Imperial Venture at Cricket by Sydney Pardon (p20-22)
Tupgill, Middleham (part 2) by George Fothergill (p23-27)
Lithograph [pinx. Fothergill]: *Norman Scott* (on p23)
Lithograph [pinx. Fothergill]: *Bibiani* (facing p25)
A Hundred Years Ago: St.Leger Stakes from *The Sporting Magazine* (p28)
Extra Notes From the Diary of Felix (part 2) (p29-35)
William Somervile: Poet and Sportsman by Hugh Henry (p35-42)

Sporting Personalities: Quaint Stories of Men of Mark (p43-45)
Photograph: *James Keene* (on p43)
The Foibles of Fashion by George Lowe (p45-48)
Planting in its Relation to Sport by Charles Curtis (p49-51)
The Sportsman's Library: Reviews of *Live Stock Journal Almanac 1908* by James Sinclair; *Days Stolen for Sport* by Philip Geen; *Newfoundland and its Untrodden Ways* by John Millais; *The Popular Bridge Player* by Edwin Anthony; *Everyday Farriery* by William Day; *In the Land of the Beautiful Trout* by Arthur Johnson; *Notes on the Chase of the Wild Red Deer* by Charles Collyns; *The Complete Mountaineer* by George Abraham; *Real Diabolo* by Charles Fry; *Some Nature Biographies* by John Ward; *Who Goes Racing* by Thomas Crosland (p51-56)
Photograph: *Pike Ve-Baiting Tackle* (on p53)
The Oldest Home of Racing and Sport: A History of Chester Races (part 1) by Charles Batchelder (p57-62)
Engraving [pinx. Hall]: *Joe Miller* (facing p61)
The Perils of Cliff Climbing (p63-68)
Our Van [inc. Derby Meeting; Manchester Racing; Gimcrack Club Dinner; Cambridge University Steeplechasing; Quorn Hunt; Isle of Man Tourist Trophy Motor Race; Cinque Ports Golf Club; Jubbulpore Polo; Brunswick Foxhound Club] (p68-88)
Photograph: *Daimler Car* (facing p79)
Photograph: *Mercedes Car* (facing p79)
Sporting Results (p89-90)

Issue 576 : February 1908

Portrait [Davey] and Biography - Teasdale Hutchinson (p91-93)
The Duties of Hunt Servants by Richard Green-Price (p93-96)
Photograph [Elliott]: *Thomas Smith* (on p94)
The G[entleman] R[ider] and the Grand National by Edward Cuming (p96-99)
Photograph: *Cambridge University Draghounds* (facing p101)
The Oxford and Cambridge Drag Hunts and the Eton Beagles by Pack Ford (p100-111)
Photograph: *Frederick Freake* (facing p103)
Photograph: *Lawrence Ronaldshay* (facing p103)
Photograph: *Lionel de Rothschild* (facing p103)
Photograph: *Pista Jarmay* (facing p103)
Photograph: *George Foster, Richard Faber, Edward Hanbury, Charles Scott* (facing p105)
Photograph: *Morres Nickalls* (facing p107)
Photograph: *Richard Pape* (facing p107)
Photograph: *William Pearson* (facing p107)
Photograph: *Robert Brassey* (facing p107)
Photograph: *Edward Hanbury* (on p107)
Photograph: *Stewart Menzies* (facing p109)
Photograph: *George Kekewich* (facing p109)
Photograph: *Holland Gilbey* (facing p109)
Photograph: *Ian Straker* (facing p109)
The Olympic Games in London by Theodore Cook (p112-120)
Test Match Troubles by Otho Paget (p121-123)
The Art of Angling (part 3) by Joseph Adams (p124-129)
Photograph: *A Bream Swim* (on p124)
Photograph: *Shoulder-Strap Net with Knuckle-Joint Closed* (on p125)
Photograph: *Shoulder-Strap Net Open* (on p125)
The Oldest Home of Racing and Sport: A History of Chester Racing (part 2) by Charles Batchelder (p130-134)
Wintry Nights in London by Otho Paget (p134-137)
A Hundred Years Ago: The Burton Hunt from *The Sporting Magazine* (p138)

The Belgian Crew and the Olympic Regatta by Guy Nickalls (p139-141)
Lithograph [pinx. Alken]: *Gay Lass* (facing p141)
Trotting Mares Past and Present by John Hill (p141-143)
The Sportsman's Library: Reviews of *George Morland, His Life and Works* by Walter Gilbey; *The British Thoroughbred Horse* by William Allison; *Winners of the Past* by Charles Meek (p143-147)
Loatland Wood [verses] by Harry Cumberland-Bentley (p147-149)
Sporting Personalities: Quaint Stories of Men of Mark (p150-151)
The Trend of the Science of the Shotgun by George Teasdale-Buckell (p151-155)
The Planting of Hedges by Charles Curtis (p155-158)
Photograph: *An Ineffective Hedge* (on p156)
Winter Croquet and the Art of Breakmaking by Maud Drummond (p159-164)
Our Van [inc. York Race Committee; Fernie's Hounds; West Norfolk Hunt; Hurlingham Club Polo; Royal Eastbourne Golf Club; Obituaries of Charles Absolon, Edward Hanlon and John Radcliffe (*Baily's* contributor); Lucknow Polo; Christchurch (NZ) Jockey Club] (p164-180)
Sporting Results (p181-182)

Issue 577 : March 1908

Portrait [Kevis] and Biography - Charles Wyndham (p183-184)
Point-to-Point Racing by Edward Cuming (p185-190)
The April Trout by Paul Taylor (p190-192)
The Saddling Bell by Richard Green-Price (p192-195)
The Art of Angling (part 4) by Joseph Adams (p195-201)
Photograph: *Where Tench Feed* (on p197)
Photograph: *The Home of the Carp* (on p199)
General George Hanger (p201-204)
Engraving [sculp. Springaguth]: *George Hanger* (facing p203)
Archer and After by Charles Batchelder (p205-209)
Photograph: *George Barrett* (on p205)
Photograph: *Samuel Loates* (on p205)
Photograph: *Frederick Barrett* (on p206)
Photograph: *Mornington Cannon* (on p208)
A Day's Jack Fishing by Arthur Brown (p209-211)
Harriers by George Teasdale-Buckell (p212-216)
Shooting in Northern Nigeria by Edward Wilcox (p216-218)
The Planting of Osiers for Sport and Profit by Charles Curtis (p218-221)
A Hundred Years Ago: Foxhounds from *The Sporting Magazine* (p222-223)
Ashes and Dust of Cricket by Otho Paget (p223-225)
Foxhounds: Potent and his Progeny by George Lowe (p225-229)
Photograph: *Charles Murray* (facing p229)
Photograph: *Henry Moreton* (facing p229)
Photograph: *Nigel Kingscote* (facing p229)
Photograph: *Charles Fitzhardinge* (facing p229)
The Sportsman's Library: Reviews of *History of Shorthorn Cattle* by James Sinclair; *My Life in the Open* by William Ogilvie (p229-235)
Sporting Personalities: Quaint Stories of Men of Mark (p235-236)
More Tufts of Turf by William Fox-Russell (p236-241)
Unorthodox Sport by William Parlour (p241-244)
The Joys of the Open Road by William Parkes (p245-247)
A Cornish Trout Stream by John Tregarthen (p247-252)

Our Van [inc. Newbury Meeting; Paisley Racecourse; Belvoir Hunt; Obituaries of Thomas Vigors (Ashplant of *The Sportsman*), Thomas Brooks, Charles Boyce, William Selby, Sydney Crosfield and George Walker; Quorn Huntsman; Cannes Polo; Motoring; Newcastle Livestock Show; Indian Golf] (p252-271)

Photograph [Gray]: *Beeston Humber Car* (facing p265)

Photograph: *Dennis Car* (facing p265)

Sporting Results (p272-274)

Issue 578 : April 1908

Portrait [Elliott] and Biography - Edward Rawnsley (p275-277)

Quick and Slow Huntsmen by Thomas Dale (p277-281)

Lithograph [pinx. Reynolds]: *Banastre Tarleton* (facing p283)

General Sir Banastre Tarleton (p282-285)

Shooting Schools and Gun Fitting by George Teasdale-Buckell (p285-289)

The Development of Modern Athletics by Abel Chapman (p289-295)

Famous Military Riders by Arthur Meyrick (p295-303)

Photograph: *George Knox* (facing p297)

Photograph: *Hope Johnstone* (facing p297)

Photograph: *Arthur Hughes-Onslow* (facing p297)

Photograph: *Roderick Owen* (on p298)

Photograph [Ferneley]: *John White on Euxton* (on p299)

Photograph: *George Middleton* (on p300)

The Sportsman's Library: Reviews of *England's Oldest Hunt* by Jack Fairfax-Blakeborough; *Shorty McCabe* by Sewell Ford; *My Alpine Jubilee* by Frederic Harrison; *With the MCC to New Zealand* by Philip May (p303-305)

The Horse of the Belvoir [verses] by George Fothergill (p306)

Lithograph [pinx. Fothergill]: *The Horse of the Belvoir* (p307)

Concerning Grayling by James Englefield (p308-311)

An Officer's Stable Statistics by Williams Wynn (p311-315)

Wanted: Masters of the Fox-Hounds by Richard Green-Price (p315-318)

The Art of Angling (part 5) by Joseph Adams (p318-325)

Photograph: *A Pike Pool on the Stour* (on p319)

Photograph: *Selected Tackle* (on p321)

Photograph: *Silex Reel* (on p323)

Photograph: *Telescopic Gaff and Registered Safety Ring* (on p324)

International Cricket by Otho Paget (p325-327)

Spring Evenings in London by Otho Paget (p327-329)

A Hundred Years Ago: Hunting from *The Sporting Magazine* (p329-330)

Sporting Personalities: Quaint Stories of Men of Mark (p330-331)

The Spring Horse Shows by Gerald Ricardo (p332-341)

Photograph: *Copper King* (facing p335)

Photograph [Babbage]: *President Roosevelt* (facing p337)

Photograph [Babbage]: *Broadwood* (facing p339)

Photograph [Babbage]: *Arthur* (facing p341)

Has Golf Improved by Gordon McPherson (p341-343)

Bird Nesting in India by Edwin Arnold (p344-347)

Ashes and Dust of Cricket: A Response by Pelham Warner (p347-348)

Our Van [inc. Grand Military Meeting; Warwick Steeplechasing; Atherstone Hunt; Obituary of Hugh Owen; Polo and the Railway Companies; Eton College Athletics; Puckeridge Hunt Master; University Boat Race; Cross-Country Running; Bradford Harriers] (p349-364)

Sporting Results (p365-366)

Issue 579 : May 1908

Portrait [Beresford] and Biography - John Montagu (p367-370)
Early Hunter Races by Abel Chapman (p370-374)
Gallant Greys, Gone and Forgotten by William Fox-Russell (p375-379)
Lithograph [pinx. Cooper]: *Grey Momus* (facing p377)
Lithograph: *Grey Trentham* (facing p379)
Croys on Salmon Rivers by Henry Johnston (p380-389)
Photograph: *Low Croy Throwing Stream on to Four Croys* (facing p383)
Photograph: *A Stone Croy* (facing p383)
Photograph: *A Wooden Croy* (on p383)
Lithograph [pinx. Paton]: *St.Simon* (facing p389)
The Story of St.Simon by Edward Cuming (p389-390)
Croquet's New Openings by Maud Drummond (p390-394)
Are Our Athletes Pothunters by Lawrence Levy (p394-395)
A Hill Fox [verses] by William Ogilvie (p396-397)
Some Fatal Accidents in the Hunting Field by Willoughby Maycock (p398-403)
The Sportsman's Library: Reviews of *Thomas Coke of Norfolk* by Anna Stirling; *Camping* by Thomas Holding; *Otters and Otterhunting* by Ludovick Cameron; *A Melton Monologue* by Diana Crossways; *His Final Flutter* by Henry Potts; *The Diseases of Animals* by Nelson Mayo; *The One Dog and the Other* by Frances Slaughter; *Elementary Lectures on Veterinary Science* by Henry Thompson (p403-404)
Some Thoughts Upon Home Forestry by Charles Curtis (p405-408)
Photograph: *Waste Land Planted With Assured Success* (facing p407)
Photograph: *The Same Class of Land Planted* (facing p407)
Sporting Personalities: Quaint Stories of Men of Mark (p409-412)
Photograph: *John Corlett* (on p410)
Photograph: *George Hodgman* (on p410)
Now and Then: A Staffordshire Farm (part 1) (p412-415)
The Art of Angling (part 6) by Joseph Adams (p415-421)
Photograph: *Punjaub Wire Paternoster* (on p416)
Photograph: *Devon, Spoon and Phantom* (on p417)
Photograph: *Halcyon Spinner* (on p418)
Photograph: *Hardy's Spoon for Lough Pike* (on p419)
A Hundred Years Ago: Dotterel from *The Sporting Magazine* (p422)
Chasers and their Breeding by Abel Chapman (p423-428)
Photograph [Rouch]: *Bushey Park* (facing p427)
Photograph: *St.Gris* (on p427)
The Dusty Ashes of Defunct Cricket Tours by Otho Paget (p429-431)
Our Van [inc. Aintree Steeplechasing; Puckeridge Hunt Presentation; Essex Hunt Point-to-Point; Axe Vale Hounds; County Polo Association; Motor Yacht Club; Sandhurst Athletics; Boxing at Eton; Obituaries of William Foster, George St.Quintin, James Forshaw, Edwin Foster, Ronald Greville, Edward Reynolds and Arthur Griffiths (*Baily's* contributor); Nice Golf Club; Gujarat Pigsticking; Rhodesia Hunt] (p432-454)
Photograph: *Puckeridge Hunt Cup* (on p437)
Photograph: *Daimler Car at the top of Buttertubs Pass* (facing p447)
Photograph: *Auxiliary Brooke Cruiser* (facing p447)
Sporting Results (p455-458)

Issue 580 : June 1908

Portrait [Howard] and Biography - Russell Walker (p459-462)
Our Old Racecourses by Richard Green-Price (p463-466)
Two Remarkable Derbyites by Willoughby Maycock (p467-468)

Mares of Mark and Merit (part 1) by George Teasdale-Buckell (p469-475)
Lithograph: *Penelope* (facing p471)
Engraving: *Eleanor* (facing p473)
Lithograph [pinx. Hopcroft]: *The First Spin of the Season 1908* (facing p477)
The Opening of the Yachting Season by George Hopcroft (p476-480)
Lithograph [pinx. Hopcroft]: *The First Spin of the Season 1858* (facing p479)
Racquets by Henry Rudd (p481-483)
Publicity in Sport by Edwin Smith (p483-486)
To a Steeplechaser at Grass [verses] by William Ogilvie (p486)
Sport and Country Life at The Royal Academy by Edward Cuming (p487-489)
A Master of Foxhounds by Claremont Clare (p490-494)
Lithograph: *George Colomb* (on p491)
The Art of Angling (part 7) by Joseph Adams (p495-502)
Photograph: *Where Perch Lie* (on p495)
Photograph: *Horn, Headed and Rubber Phantom* (facing p497)
Photograph: *Minnow, Spoon, Halcyon and Minnow Fly* (facing p497)
Photograph: *The Old Mill Pool* (on p497)
Photograph: *A Winter Pool* (on p499)
Now and Then: A Staffordshire Farm (part 2) (p502-506)
A Hundred Years Ago: Cricket from *The Sporting Magazine* (p507-508)
Photograph [Myers]: *Sydney Smith* (facing p509)
Photograph [Myers]: *Laurence Doherty* (facing p509)
[Review] The Art and History of Lawn Tennis: *The Complete Lawn Tennis Player* by
        Wallis Myers (p508-513)
Photograph [Myers]: *George Hillyard* (facing p511)
Photograph [Myers]: *Arthur Gore* (facing p511)
Photograph [Myers]: *Beales Wright* (on p511)
The Future of County Cricket by Otho Paget (p513-514)
Summer Evenings in London and Shepherd's Bush by Edward Cuming (p515-518)
[Obituary] Edward Bligh (*Baily's* contributor) by Edward Cuming (p518-520)
Photograph: *Edward Bligh* (on p519)
The Sportsman's Library: Reviews of *Farm-Cottage, Camp and Canoe in Maritime Canada*
        by Arthur Silver; *Modern Argentina* by William Koebel (p520-521)
Sporting Personalities: Quaint Stories of Men of Mark (p522-523)
William Arnold Higgs by Edward Cuming (p524)
Our Van [inc. Lewes Meeting; Epsom Races; Hurlingham Polo Manager; Obituaries of Gordon
        Renton, James Blyth, William Kenyon-Slaney and Harry Custance; Egyptian
        Golf; Olympic Games Preview; Calcutta Racing; Delaware Hunt] (p525-543)
Photograph: *Alexander Duncan* (on p539)
Sporting Results (p544-546)

This volume is the largest in the history of Baily's Magazine

Volume 90, July - December 1908

Issue 581 : July 1908

Portrait [McNeille] of William Boore, huntsman Title page
Portrait [Guy] and Biography - Thomas Kirkwood (p1-2)
Masters of Hounds on Motors by Edward Cuming (p3-7)
The Cult of the Hound by Walter Greswell (p8-12)
Photograph [Greswell]: *Dignified Inimitable Grace* (facing p11)
Photograph [Greswell]: *Wistful Upturned Faces* (facing p11)
A Troublesome Tigress by Henry Pilkington (p12-16)

Mares of Mark and Merit (part 2) by George Teasdale-Buckell   (p17-23)
Engraving [pinx. Herring]: *Queen of Trumps*   (facing p19)
Photograph [Rouch]: *Signorinetta*   (facing p21)
The Opening of the Otterhunting Season by Ludovick Cameron   (p24-27)
Experiences of a Screwdriver   (p28-32)
The Art of Angling (part 8) by Joseph Adams   (p33-40)
Photograph: *Perfect Trout Reel*   (on p34)
Photograph: *Amateur Rod-Making*   (on p35)
Photograph: *Jam Knot for Attaching Line to Gut*   (on p36)
Photograph: *The Double Water Gut Knot*   (on p36)
Photograph: *The Buffer Gut Knot*   (on p37)
[Review] *Advanced Golf* by James Braid   (p40-43)
Photograph: *The Ball Has Just Left the Club*   (facing p40)
Photograph: *Passing the Opponents Ball*   (facing p40)
Photograph: *Running to the Hole*   (facing p40)
Photograph: *Stance and Address*   (on p42)
Photograph: *Backswing*   (on p42)
Photograph: *The Stroke Successful*   (on p42)
Sporting Personalities: Quaint Stories of Men of Mark   (p44-46)
Photograph: *Walter Seton-Karr*   (on p44)
Photograph: *Norman Brookes*   (on p45)
Mallet and Ball [verses] by William Ogilvie   (p47)
A Hundred Years Ago: Breeding from *The Sporting Magazine*   (p48)
Recent Polo by Arthur Coaten   (p49-52)
Tips from Dreams and Omens by William Fox-Russell   (p53-55)
The Sportsman's Library: Reviews of *The Senses of Insects* by Auguste Florel; *How to Trap and
        Snare* by William Carnegie; *Forty Seasons of First-Class Cricket* by Richard
        Barlow; *The Horse, Its Selection and Purchase* by Frank Barton; *The Dapple Grey*
        by Nat Gould; *The Condition of Hunters* by Frank Barton; *Foxhunting Past and
        Present* by Richard Carlisle   (p56-58)
Cricket Notions by Sydney Pardon   (p59-62)
Further Thoughts on Forestry by Charles Curtis   (p63-66)
A Note of Warning to Big Game Hunters   (p66-68)
Our Van [inc. Chester Races; Knavesmire Meeting; Masters of Fox-Hounds Association;
        Albrighton Hunt; Devon & Somerset Staghounds]   (p69-78)
Sporting Intelligence [inc. Skiff Racing Association; Sandwich Golf; Obituaries of [Old] Tom
        Morris, Garrett Moore, Charles Hoare, John Jones, Denzil Onslow, Robert Lang,
        Montagu Turner, William Hardy, Algernon Rutter and Marcus Martin; Stepney
        Spare Wheel; Southern Football League]   (p79-84)
Photograph: *Stepney Flange*   (on p82)
Sporting Results   (p84-88)

Issue 582 : August 1908

Portrait [Gillman] and Biography - Victor Child-Villiers   (p89-90)
Staghounds of Today on Exmoor by Edward Cuming   (p91-97)
The Poetry of Grouse and Grouse-Shooting by Frank Bonnett   (p98-100)
Wild Dayrell and Littlecote by George Teasdale-Buckell   (p100-106)
Photograph [Righton]: *Littlecote House*   (facing p103)
Lithograph [pinx. Hall]: *Wild Dayrell*   (facing p105)
Twenty Bores by Harry Cumberland-Bentley   (p107-109)
Memorable Yacht Races by George Hopcroft   (p110-114)
Lithograph [pinx. Hopcroft]: *The Henrietta in the Ocean Race of 1866*   (facing p113)
Lithograph [pinx. Hopcroft]: *Race Between Britannia and Vigilant 1874*   (facing p113)

Lithograph [pinx. Hopcroft]: *Dauntless and Cambria Racing Across the Atlantic 1870* (facing p113)
Lithograph [pinx. Hopcroft]: *New Moon During the Royal International Yacht Club Race 1865* (facing p113)
The Art of Angling (part 9) by Joseph Adams (p115-121)
Photograph: *How to Cast - Forward Action* (on p118)
Photograph: *How to Cast - Backward Action* (on p120)
Photograph: *How to Attach Fly to Casting Line* (on p121)
Deerstalking in New Zealand (p122-125)
Some Cricket Topics by Otho Paget (p126-128)
Fencing: Epee-Play by Charles Hancock (p128-131)
Photograph [Rouch]: *Harness Horse Radiant* (facing p131)
Lessons of the International Horse Show by Gerald Ricardo (p131-136)
Photograph [Babbage]: *Londesborough & Londsdale* (facing p133)
Photograph: *Giovanni Volpini* (facing p135)
Photograph: *Raoul Daufresne* (facing p135)
Photograph: *Gino di Morpurgo* (facing p135)
Photograph: *Galo Febrel* (facing p135)
The Sportsman's Library: Reviews of *The Racecourses of Great Britain* by Frederick Bayles; *Elements of Angling* by Hugh Sheringham; *The Country Gentleman's Estate Book* by William Broomhall; *English Bird Life* by Knight Horsfield; *The Complete Oarsman* by Rudolf Lehmann; *Veterinary Pathology* by Alice Hayes; *The Romance of The Derby* by Edward Moorhouse; *Small Holdings and Allotments* by George Johnston and *The British Yearbook of Agriculure and Agricultural Who's Who* by James Shepherd (p136-140)
Photograph: *Rudders Ancient and Modern* (on p137)
A Hundred Years Ago: Horse Sale from *The Sporting Magazine* (p141-142)
All Night on the Thames in a Punt by James Englefield (p142-146)
Sporting Personalities: Quaint Stories of Men of Mark (p146-147)
The Cream of Polo by Edward Miller (p148-152)
Forest Fires by Charles Curtis (p152-155)
The Peterborough Foxhound Show by George Lowe (p155-161)
Lithograph [pinx. Bradley]: *Donovan* (facing p157)
Our Van [inc. Manchester Racecourse; Ascot Meeting; Newbury Races; Skibbereen Otterhounds; Ranelagh Hound Show] (p161-167)
Sporting Intelligence [inc. University Sport; Henley Regatta; Prestwick Golf; Obituaries of Joseph Wright, Frederick Stanley and Alec Waugh; Criccieth Golf Club; Dulverton Foxhounds] (p167-173)
Sporting Results (p174-178)

Issue 583 : September 1908

Portrait [Elliott] and Biography - Arthur Gore (p179-181)
Tales of Tithing by Abel Chapman (p181-187)
Horsemanship by Frank Wedge (p188-192)
Stories of Old Jockeys by Gerald Ricardo (p192-196)
Photograph: *Harry Constable* (facing p195)
Photograph: *Thomas Ashmall* (facing p195)
A Day with the Small Hawks by James Harting (p196-202)
Racing in the State of New York by Belmont Purdy (p202-206)
The Art of Angling (part 10) by Joseph Adams (p207-213)
Photograph: *The Test - A Dry Fly Chalk Stream* (on p208)
Photograph: *The Itchen, Abbots Barton* (on p210)
Photograph: *The Bourne - Chalk Stream* (on p211)
Photograph: *The Avon – A Dry Fly Stream* (on p212)

A Hundred Years Ago: Game from *The Sporting Magazine* (p214)
The Olympic Games by Theodore Cook (p215-227)
Photograph: *Melvin Sheppard* (facing p219)
Photograph: *Clarence Kingsbury* (facing p219)
Photograph: *John Hayes* (facing p219)
Photograph: *George Larner* (facing p219)
Photograph: *Harold Wilson* (facing p219)
Photograph: *Raymond Ewry* (facing p219)
Polo: Looking Ahead by Archibald Charlton (p228-232)
[Obituary] Henry Lambe (p230-231)
International Cricket by Sydney Pardon (p232-234)
Oak in Youth and Age by Charles Curtis (p235-239)
Photograph: *A Monarch of the Forest* (facing p237)
Photograph: *Young Oak Plantation* (facing p239)
Taking Him Up [verses] by William Ogilvie (p239)
The Sportsman's Library: Reviews of *The Rules of Sport* by Theodore Cook; *The Love of his
    Life* by Harry Cumberland-Bentley; *Bush Life* by Dougal Ferguson; *Running and
    Cross-Country Running* by Alfred Shrubb; *Fifty Years a Fighter* by Jem Mace;
    Hints on Lameness in Horses by Charles Gregory and *A History of The Olympiads*
    by Theodore Cook (p240-241)
Sporting Personalities: Quaint Stories of Men of Mark (p241-242)
Trout Fishing on the Bushman's River by Henry Rowan-Robinson (p243-249)
Photograph: *Sylvia Brocklebank's Road Team* (facing p249)
A Workman-Like Coach Team by Gerald Ricardo (p249)
The Silks of the Turf by George Teasdale-Buckell (p250-251)
Our Van [inc. Newmarket Meeting; Goodwood Cup; Exmoor Staghunting; West Somerset
    Hounds; Cattistock Hunt] (p251-257)
Sporting Intelligence [inc. Grouse Disease Enquiry; Olympic Rowing; Blackheath Golf
    Tournament; Obituary of Robert Watson; Ormond Hunt; Bangalore Polo] (p258-262)
Sporting Results (p262-266)

Issue 584 : October 1908

Portrait [Lafayette] and Biography - Lees Knowles (p267-270)
Puppies and Cubs by Richard Green-Price (p270-273)
Round the Outsides: In Hedgerow and Spinney by Frank Bonnett (p274-276)
One View of Deer Stalking by John Bristow-Noble (p276-282)
Photograph [Valentine]: *Deer Stalking - Waiting for the Ponies* (facing p279)
Photograph [Valentine]: *Deer Stalking - The Return* (facing p281)
A Review of the 1908 Yachting Season by George Hopcroft (p283-288)
Lithograph [pinx. Hopcroft]: *The Twenty-Three Metre Yachts of 1908* (facing p285)
Public School Cricket in 1908 by Archibald Charlton (p288-291)
The Art of Angling (part 11) by Joseph Adams (p292-299)
Photograph: *Dry Fly Fishing - An Underhand Cast* (on p293)
Photograph: *Spinners for Natural Bait* (on p294)
Photograph: *Thames Flight for Natural Bait* (on p295)
Photograph: *Galway River - The Crib White Trout Pool* (on p296)
Photograph: *Lough Corrib – A Trolling and Dapping Lough* (on p297)
The Puppy Show by Edward Cuming (p300-303)
Some Exciting Narrow Escapes by Lester Arnold (p303-306)
The County Cricket Circus by Otho Paget (p307-310)
The Best Horse by George Teasdale-Buckell (p311-312)

The Sportsman's Library: Reviews of *The Horse in History* by Basil Tozer; *Bulldogs and Bulldog Men* by Henry Cooper; *How to Attract and Protect Wild Birds* by Martin Hiesemann; *The Book of The Horse* by Frank Barton; *Walks and Climbs around Arolla* by Walter Larden; *Trout Waters of England* by Walter Gallichan; *Everybody's Book of the Dog* by Frederick Gresham; *Record of the Olympic Games* by William Will; *First Aid to Dogs* by Gordon Stables; *Trout Waters* by Wilson Armistead (p313-315)
The Ballyuppan Harriers and Their Great Run by Hugh Henry (p315-320)
Arboretums and Nature Study by Charles Curtis (p320-322)
A Hundred Years Ago: Boxing from *The Sporting Magazine* (p323)
Polo in the Himalayas by Peter Bairnsfather (p324-327)
Sporting Personalities: Quaint Stories of Men of Mark (p327-328)
Enemies of the Trout by Morgan Watkins (p329-331)
Outdoor Life in America by Belmont Purdy (p332-333)
Cricket Pugilists by William Wilmott-Dixon (p334-339)
The Mallard by Alan Haig-Brown (p339-341)
Our Van [inc. Yorkshire Oaks; Doncaster Meeting; Devon & Somerset Staghunt; Badminton Hunt; Meath Hounds; New Forest Deerhounds] (p341-347)
Sporting Intelligence [inc. Perthshire Grouse; St.Andrews Golf; Obituaries of William Blenkiron, Octavius Hammond, William Day, Gustavus Briscoe, Charles Fownes and Thomas Harveyson; Racing in New York] (p347-351)
Sporting Results (p351-354)

Issue 585 : November 1908

Portrait [Russell] and Biography - James Pender (p355-357)
The Hunting Man's Budget by Thomas Dale (p357-362)
Some Great Road Matches by Edward Cuming (p363-365)
Old Friends in New Places by George Teasdale-Buckell (p366-370)
My Friend the Fox by Alan Haig-Bown (p371-373)
Splint in Horses by William Tweedie (p373-380)
[Review] England's Oarsmen: *Thomas Doggett Deceased* by Theodore Cook (p380-386)
Lithograph [pinx. Rowlandson]: *The Race for Doggett's Coat and Badge* (facing p383)
Lithograph: *John Broughton* (facing p385)
Remarkable Golf Feats by Horace Wyndham (p387-389)
Polo Pony Misfits and the Racecourse by Archibald Charlton (p389-392)
The Art of Angling (part 12) by Joseph Adams (p392-399)
Photograph: *Ballynahinch Salmon and White Trout River* (on p393)
Photograph: *Salmon Fishing in the Shannon at Castleconnell* (on p394)
Photograph: *Castleconnell Salmon Flies* (on p395)
Photograph: Galway Salmon Flies (on p397)
Gallant Lord Chesham [verses] by Harry Cumberland-Bentley (p400-401)
Mixed Shooting on the Niger (p401-403)
[Review] *The Complete Foxhunter* by Charles Richardson (p403-407)
Photograph: *Harper* (facing p405)
Photograph: *Lord Harrington's Hounds* (facing p407)
Sporting Personalities: Quaint Stories of Men of Mark (p407-408)
A Hundred Years Ago: Cranborne Chase Foxhounds from *The Sporting Magazine* (p409)
Autumn Evenings in London by Otho Paget (p410-413)
The Sportsman's Library: Reviews of *Trout Fishing in Cape Colony* by Dumaresq Manning; *British Terriers* by John Maxtee, *The Ross Bird-Stalker* by Charles Dixon; *Angling and Art in Scotland* by Ernest Briggs; *Horses and Horse Racing* by Thomas Day, and *Baily's Hunting Directory 1908-09* by Edward Cuming (p414-416)
An Indian Sportsman's Ordinary Days by Lester Arnold (p417-420)

Tufts of Turf by William Fox-Russell (p421-425)
Hunt Changes by Edward Cuming (p425-430)
Our Van [inc. Manchester Racing; Newbury Meeting; North Cumberland Hunt; Atherstone
        Hounds; Exford Stables; York & Ainsty Hunt] (p431-434)
Sporting Intelligence [inc. Oxford University Rugby; Hampshire County Cricket Club;
        Amateur Athletic Association; Pytchley Hunt Memorial; Cromer Golf Club;
        Obituaries of Owen Williams, John Wheeler and Patrick McConville;
        Queensland Bookmakers; New South Wales Polo] (p435-439)
Sporting Results (p440-442)

*For the first time, **Baily's** are using photographs from the **Sport & General** press agency*

Issue 586 : December 1908

Portrait [Whitlock] and Biography - Richard Heygate (p443-445)
Masters of Hounds on the Etiquette of Hunting Dress by Edward Cuming (p445-450)
Early Hunting Pictures (part 1) by Richard Green-Price (p450-454)
Lithograph [pinx. Alken]: *Gone Away* (facing p453)
Successful Sires of the Season by Abel Chapman (p454-461)
Photograph [Rouch]: *St.Frusquin* (facing p457)
Photograph [Rouch]: *Missel Thrush* (facing p459)
Parson Dove by Willoughby Maycock (p461-465)
Lithograph [pinx. Maycock]: *Parson Dove* (facing p465)
The Art of Angling (part 13) by Joseph Adams (p466-473)
Photograph: *The Moy Salmon River, Ballina* (on p467)
Photograph: *A Salmon Pool in the River Maigne, Adair* (on p468)
Photograph: *Galway Salmon River* (on p470)
Photograph: *The Prawn - Mounted and Threaded* (on p471)
Reporting Upon Woodlands by Charles Curtis (p473-475)
Hunting From the Train by Charles Higgins (p476-477)
Photograph [Elliott]: *Bosworth Smith* (facing p479)
[Obituary] Reginald Bosworth Smith by Herbert Hewett (p478-481)
The New Point-to-Point Rules by Edward Cuming (p482-488)
Fly-Fishing Notes and Sport by James Englefield (p488-493)
Sporting Personalities: Quaint Stories of Men of Mark (p493-495)
Weeding Out for Golf Championships by Gordon McPherson (p495-497)
A Hundred Years Ago: Jockey Annuity from *The Sporting Magazine* (p498)
Oarsmen Ancient and Modern (part 1) by George Teasdale-Buckell (p499-506)
Photograph [Field]: *Ernest Barry* (facing p501)
Photograph [Field]: *George Towns* (facing p503)
The Sportsman's Library: Reviews of *Two Dianas in Alaska* by Agnes Herbert; *Birds of the
        Plains* by Douglas Dewar; *Betting in Excelsis* by Thomas Day; *Three Jovial
        Puppies* by James Shepherd; *Glanders* by William Hunting; *Thomas Ken and
        Izaak Walton* by Edward Marston (p507-509)
Will Boore by Edward Cuming (p509-510)
Our Van [inc. Sandown Park Racing; Aintree Meeting; South Dorset Hunt; New Forest
        Buckhounds; North Warwickshire Hunt; Woodland Pytchley Country] (p510-515)
Sporting Intelligence [inc. Oxford University Rugby; Mid-Surrey Golf Club; Olympic Games
        Finals; Polo Pony Society; Woodland Pytchley Hunt Master; Obituaries of Elliott
        Lees, Herbert Crosse, John Watson and Henry Boden; New South Wales
        Cricket Allowances; New Zealand Turf Club] (p515-520)
Sporting Results (p521-522)

Volume 91, January - June 1909

Issue 587 : January 1909

Portrait [Waters] of James Braid, golfer   Title page
Portrait [Lafayette] and Biography - Arthur Plunkett   (p1-3)
Young Hounds and Foxes in Big Woodlands by Thomas Dale   (p3-8)
The Etiquette of Hunting Dress by Edward Cuming   (p8-10)
Early Hunting Pictures (part 2) by Richard Green-Price   (p10-14)
Engraving [pinx. Ferneley]: *The Quorn Hunt*   (facing p13)
An Old Cricket Match Card by Otho Paget   (p14-18)
Lithograph: *Ware versus County, July 1785*   (facing p17)
The Huntsman's Horse [verses] by William Ogilvie   (p19)
Photograph [Coster]: *The Hailsham Harriers*   (facing p21)
The Chase of the Hare by Frank Bonnett   (p21-24)
Photograph [Coster]: *In Full Cry*   (facing p23)
In Memoriam: Henry Boden and John Watson by Edward Cuming   (p24-30)
Lithograph [pinx. Cutler]: *Henry Boden on Equality*   (facing p27)
Photograph [Lafayette]: *John Watson*   (facing p29)
Photograph [Salter]: *Original Polo Stick*   (on p30)
English Thoroughbreds by George Lowe   (p31-34)
Otterhunting Past by Ludovick Cameron   (p35-37)
Oarsmen Ancient and Modern (part 2) by George Teasdale-Buckell   (p37-43)
Photograph [Field]: *Harry Blackstaffe*   (facing p39)
Photograph [Stuart]: *James Renforth*   (on p39)
Photograph [Stuart]: *Harry Kelley*   (on p40)
Photograph [Stuart]: *Robert Bagnall*   (on p41)
Deer Farming in the United States by Abel Chapman   (p43-46)
Coursing: Its Romantic History by William Lamonby   (p46-53)
Lithograph [pinx. Jolley]: *Effort*   (on p47)
Engraving [sculp. Hacker]: *Master M'Grath*   (facing p49)
Lithograph [pinx. Cooper]: *Mocking Bird*   (on p50)
The Sportsman's Library: Reviews of *Some British Birds* by Edward Thomas; *Show Dogs* by
          Theodore Marples; *Camp Fires on Desert and Lava* by William Hornaday;
          Dogs by Harding Cox   (p53-59)
A Hundred Years Ago: Hunting from *The Sporting Magazine*   (p59-60)
Among the Potholes of Lancashire by Claude Benson   (p60-66)
Photograph: *Outside Gable Hole*   (facing p63)
Photograph: *Thornton Force*   (facing p63)
Photograph: *Rumbling Hole*   (facing p63)
Sporting Personalities: Quaint Stories of Men of Mark   (p67-68)
For Our Poultry Fund [verses] by Edward Cuming   (p68-69)
Travel in Garhwal, Himalayas by Henry Pilkington   (p70-74)
Our Van [inc. Derby Meeting; Doncaster Races; Blackmore Vale Hunt; Grafton Hounds;
          Cottesmore Hunt   (p74-80)
Sporting Intelligence [inc. Cambridge University Steeplechases; Deal Golf; International
          Swimming Federation; Hackney Horse Show; Yorkshire Cricket; Birchfield
          Harriers; Obituaries of John Thornton, Harry Barnato, Reginald Selous and
          George Hollington; Secunderabad Polo; Australian Tennis]   (p80-87)
Sporting Results   (p88-90)

Issue 588 : February 1909

Portrait [Ellis] and Biography - William Tyrwhitt-Drake   (p91-93)

The Gimcrack Club Dinner by Richard Green-Price   (p93-96)
The Past Partridge Season by Alexander Blyth   (p97-98)
Photograph: *Melton Constable White Partridges*   (on p98)
The Best Sporting County by George Teasdale-Buckell   (p99-103)
Hunting in Olden Times by Thomas Lister   (p103-105)
Field Memorials to Sportsmen by Henry Archer   (p106-112)
Photograph [Archer]: *Whyte-Melville's Grave, Tetbury Churchyard*   (on p107)
Photograph [Archer]: *George Middleton's Memorial, Kineton*   (on p108)
Photograph [Archer]: *John Speke's Stone, Wadswick*   (on p109)
Photograph [Archer]: *George Cavendish's Memorial, Brixworth*   (facing p111)
Photograph [Archer]: *King William Rufus's Stone, Minstead, New Forest*   (on p111)
[Review] Twici's Art of Venery: *The Art of Hunting* by Alice Dryden, reviewed by William
         Baillie-Grohman   (p113-115)
George Verrall by Edward Cuming   (p116-121)
Photograph [Bolton]: *George Verrall*   (facing p119)
American Foxhunting by Belmont Purdy   (p121-125)
Parson Dove by Cave Humfrey   (p125-126)
Diana - The Consoler [verses] by Eustace Frith   (p127-128)
A Hundred Years Ago: Poaching from *The Sporting Magazine*   (p129)
The Complete Master of Hounds by George Lowth   (p130-134)
[Review] *Anglo-French Horsemanship* by John Swire   (p134-137)
Photograph [Delton]: *Handling a Dangerous Rearer*   (facing p137)
The Hunting Inns of Cheshire by Alexander Lainson   (p137-145)
Photograph: *The Bear's Head, Brereton*   (facing p139)
Photograph: *The Swan Inn, Tarporley*   (facing p139)
Photograph: *Bluecap Inn, Sandiway*   (facing p141)
Photograph [Littler]: *Smoker Inn, Plumbley*   (facing p141)
Photograph: *The Famous Hound Bluecap*   (on p141)
The Sportsman's Library: Reviews of *Stalks Abroad* by Harold Wallace; *Spanish History* by
         Henry Watts; *Modern Spain* by Martin Hume; *The Nun Ensign* by Catalina de
         Erauso; *Bridle Roads of Spain* by George Cayley; *Shooting in China* by
         Thomas Jernigan   (p145-150)
Photographs [Wallace]: *Some Typical New Zealand Deer Heads - I*   (facing p147)
Photographs [Wallace]: *Some Typical New Zealand Deer Heads - 11*   (facing p147)
[Review] *When Diamonds Were Trumps* by Reginald Herbert   (p150-151)
Trout Fishing in the Bushman's River by Richard Sawyer   (p152-153)
Sporting Personalities: Quaint Stories of Men of Mark   (p153-154)
A Sporting Causerie by Gerald Ricardo   (p155-159)
Slaves of the Track [verses] by William Ogilvie   (p160)
The National Hunt Committee and Sham Hunters by Edward Cuming   (p161-164)
Our Van [inc. Gimcrack Dinner; Barnstaple Staghounds; Fernie's Hounds; Norfolk Harriers;
         West Somerset Hunt]   (p165-170)
Sporting Intelligence [inc. Animal Painters; University Sport; Spring Horse Shows;
         Knebworth Golf Club; Obituaries of Harry Crawford, James Gunter, Philip
         Muntz (*Baily's* contributor), Gilbert Kennedy, Henry Parry, William Waller,
         Frederic Morgan and Edwin Couch; North Staffordshire Hounds; Old Trafford
         Cricket Ground; Rufford Hunt; Lucknow Polo]   (p170-178)
Sporting Results   (p179-180)

Issue 589 : March 1909

Portrait [Howard] and Biography - Gordon Canning   (p181-182)
Shooting Management by Alexander Blyth   (p183-184)
Foxhunting by Charles Frederick   (p184-188)

Hints for Polo Combination (part 1) by Walter Buckmaster (p188-193)
The Cost of Golf by Gordon McPherson (p193-202)
Photograph: *Willingdon (Eastbourne) Golf Links* (facing p197)
Photograph [Dixon]: *Open Golf Championship at Prestwick* (facing p199)
Lady Masters of Hounds by Maud Wynter (p202-207)
Engraving [pinx. Hall]: *Lord Lyon* (facing p207)
More Stories of Old Jockeys by William Fox-Russell (p207-209)
Engraving [pinx. Hall]: *Lord Clifden* (facing p209)
The Grand National Horse [verses] by William Ogilvie (p210)
The Grayling Fishing Season by James Englefield (p211-216)
[Obituary] Charles Perrot-Noel (p216-218)
Aspects of Amateur Boxing by John Lynch (p219-221)
Some Memorable Dead Heats by George Teasdale-Buckell (p221-223)
Rural Cottages by Charles Curtis (p224-226)
Photograph: *A Haunt of Ancient Peace* (on p225)
Spring Trouting in North Devon by Paul Taylor (p227-228)
Sporting Personalities: Quaint Stories of Men of Mark (p228-230)
Fifty Years of Wire by Edward Cuming (p230-235)
Frosty Nights in London by Otho Paget (p235-239)
A Hundred Years Ago: The Pytchley Stakes from *The Sporting Magazine* (p240-241)
The Sportsman's Library: Reviews of *On Safari* by Abel Chapman; *A Motor Flight Through France* by Edith Wharton (p241-244)
A Word on Sport and Games by Hugh Henry (p245-249)
Shooting in Rain by Maitland Stewart (p249-252)
Our Van [inc. Worksop Steeplechase; Ribblesdale Buckhounds; Blackmore Vale Hunt; Quorn Hunt Committee; Hampshire Hunt] (p252-256)
Sporting Intelligence [inc. Hunter Certificates; Tedworth Hunt; Edinburgh Golf Courses; West Middlesex Ladies Golf Club; Obituaries of Joseph Bailey, Henry Johnson, James Gordon and Henry Waring; Allahabad Polo] (p257-262)
Sporting Results (263-264)

Issue 590 : April 1909

Portrait [Lafayette] and Biography - Walter Cazenove (p265-266)
Hints for Polo Combination (part 2) by Walter Buckmaster (p267-271)
The Sport of Kings in Early Days by Thomas Lewis (p272-273)
Boxing as a Clean Sport by Edward Michell (p274-278)
Photograph [Seaman]: *John Summers* (facing p277)
Old Time Rowing [with Posters] by Guy Nickalls (p279-285)
Lithograph: *The Boat Race in the Thirties* (facing p281)
Lithograph: *Countess of Salisbury's Regatta & Promenade* (facing p283)
Lithograph: *Life on the Water* (facing p283)
Greyhounds for Sport by Charles Conquest (p284-285)
The Gentleman Salmon Poacher by Cave Humfrey (p286-288)
The Trout-Brook in April by Arthur Sharp (p288-290)
Thoroughbreds as Hunter Sires by William Fox-Russell (p290-296)
Engraving [pinx. Herring]: *Hobbie Noble* (facing p293)
Engraving [pinx. Hall]: *Caractacus* (facing p295)
Fencing for Women by Frances Slaughter (p297-303)
Photograph [Window]: *Clara Woolner* (on p298)
Photograph [Porter]: *Millicent Hall* (on p299)
Photograph [Porter]: *Julia Johnstone* (on p299)
Photograph [Towers]: *Rose Edwardes* (on p300)
Photograph [Vandyke]: *Daphne Milman* (on p300)

The Influence of Arabian Poetry on the Arab Horse by Thomas Dale (p303-310)

Creatures I Have Tamed and Taught by Athol Maudslay (p310-314)

A Hundred Years Ago: The Essex Hunt from *The Sporting Magazine* (p315)

The Ibex of Portugal by Robert Dunkin (p316-319)

Photograph: *The Last Portuguese Ibex* (on p317)

Sporting Personalities: Quaint Stories of Men of Mark (p319-321)

The Sportsman's Library: Reviews of *The Old-Time Parson* by Peter Ditchfield; *Highways and Byways of Surrey* by Eric Parker; *George Borrow: The Man and His Work* by Robert Walling (p321-324)

The Spring Horse Shows by Gerald Ricardo (p324-330)

Photograph [Babbage]: *Signal* (facing p327)

Photograph [Babbage]: *Ormeton* (facing p329)

[Obituaries] In Memoriam: Douglas Baird, Edward Bateman, Hirst Sitwell, George Maclachan, Bogislav von Heyden-Linden, Henry Chandler, William Allsopp, Sydney Buxton and Charles Payne (p330-336)

Our Van [inc. Turf Legislation; Exmoor Staghunting; Rothschild's Staghounds; North Shropshire Hounds; Southwold Hunt; Galway Blazers; South Dorset Hunt; Obituary of Florence Bampfylde] (p336-342)

Sporting Intelligence [inc. University Point-to-Point; Lincoln Racecourse; St.Andrews Old Golf Course; Waterloo Cup; Limerick Race Company; National Sporting Club; Indian Polo Association] (p342-347)

Sporting Results (p347-348)

Issue 591 : May 1909

Portrait [Lafayette] and Biography - William Filgate (p349-351)

Hindrances to Hunting by Edward Cuming (p351-355)

Cast Chasers and Point-to-Point Races by Edward Cuming (p356-358)

The Grand National by Edwin Smith (p359-363)

Photograph [Pirou]: *James Hennessy* (facing p361)

Photograph [Rouch]: *Lutteur* (facing p363)

The Polo Season of 1909 by Edward Miller (p364-366)

The Yachting Prospects for 1909 by George Hopcroft (p366-370)

Lithograph [pinx. Hopcroft]: *Shamrock* (facing p369)

Three Good Old Sportsmen by Frank Bonnett (p370-374)

Photograph: *George Lane-Fox* (on p371)

Photograph: *John Anstruther-Thomson* (on p373)

The Breeding of Steeplechase Stock by James Cameron (p375-378)

Photograph [Rouch]: *Enthusiast* (facing p377)

A Chime of the Cotswold Hunt [verses] (p379-380)

In Search of Trout by Charles Lane (p381-386)

Photograph: *Our First Luncheon Spot* (on p382)

Photograph: *Where a Large Trout was Lost* (facing p384)

Photograph: *A Typical Birch Bark Canoe* (facing p384)

Photograph: *At the Outlet of Lake Nipigon* (on p385)

Marathons by William Fox-Russell (p386-388)

A Hundred Years Ago: Hunting from *The Sporting Magazine* (p389)

The Sportsman's Library: Reviews of *A Holiday in Connemara* by Stephen Gwynn; *Sunset Playgrounds* by Frederick Aflalo; *The Balance of Nature* by George Abbey; *Salmon Scales* by Arthur Hutton, and *Stock Owners' Manual* by Frank Barton (p390-391)

The Modern Haunts of the Giraffe by Henry Bryden (p391-395)

Sporting Personalities: Quaint Stories of Men of Mark (p396-397)

Some Notable Stayers by George Teasdale-Buckell (p398-404)

Engraving [pinx. Herring]: *Faugh-A-Ballagh* (facing p401)

Engraving [pinx. Hall]: *Julius*   (facing p403)
Easter Evenings in Town by Otho Paget   (p405-408)
The Unexpected in Sport by Lester Arnold   (p408-411)
Old Sporting Books by Arthur Chesterman   (p412-419)
Photograph [Rouch]: *Duke of Sparta*   (facing p419)
Our Van [inc. Lincoln Meeting; Newbury Spring Cup; Pytchley Hunt; South Devon Hunt
            Week; Courtney Tracy Otterhounds]   (p419-424)
Sporting Intelligence [inc. University Boat Race; University Athletics; Obituaries of John
            Russell (*Baily's* contributor), Alexander Ramsay, Henry Constable, James
            Douglas, Charles Hancock (*Baily's* contributor), William Leader, James Hill,
            Francis Wyberg, Joseph Gibson and William Jervis; Amateur Boxing;
            Indian Polo Association]   (p424-430)
Sporting Results   (p430-432)

Issue 592 : June 1909

Portrait [Chidley] and Biography - Robert Yerburgh   (p433-434)
Race Clubs by Richard Green-Price   (p434-437)
Famous American Guides by Lincoln Wilbar   (p437-442)
[Reviews] Golf Leaders and Legislators: *Great Golfers in the Making* and *The Spirit of the
            Links*, both by Henry Leach; *Advanced Golf* by James Braid, all reviewed by
            William Fox-Russell   (p442-450)
Photographs: *Stance; Top of Swing; Finish*   (on p445)
Photograph: *A View on the Links at Leamington*   (on p447)
Photograph [Dixon]: *Herbert Fowler*   (facing p449)
Stockwell and Vedette by George Lowe   (p450-454)
The Promise of May to Cricketers by Otho Paget   (p454-455)
Three Pillars of the Turf by George Teasdale-Buckell   (p456-462)
Engraving [pinx. Hall]: *Thormanby*   (facing p459)
Engraving [pinx. Hall]: *Andover*   (facing p459)
Engraving [pinx. Hall]: *Virago*   (facing p461)
Engraving [pinx. Davis]: *Mameluke*   (facing p461)
Sport and Country Life at The Royal Academy by Edward Cuming   (p463-466)
More Field Memorials to Sportsmen by Henry Archer   (p466-470)
Nesting by the River by Joseph Adams   (p470-474)
Photograph: *Swans - On Guard*   (facing p470)
Photograph: *Wild Duck's Nest in Rushes*   (facing p472)
Photograph: *Moorhen's Nest*   (facing p472)
Photograph: *Dabchick's Nest Uncovered*   (facing p472)
Photograph: *Teal's Nest*   (facing p472)
A Hundred Years Ago: An Obituary from *The Sporting Magazine*   (p475)
The Sportsman's Library: Reviews of *Swimming* by Archibald Sinclair; *Hockey and Lacrosse*
            by Stanley Christopherson; *Fights Forgotten* by Henry Sayers; *The Opinions
            of a Betting Man* by Thomas Dey; *Auction Bridge* by Harold Browning;
            British Mountaineering by Claude Benson; *British Military Prints* by Ralph
            Nevill; *Modern Golf* by Arnold Vaile; *Trout Fishing* and *The Angler's Season*
            both by William Hodgson; *Sports Philosophy* by Robert Routledge; *Hints for
            Polo Combination* by Walter Buckmaster   (p476-481)
Photograph: *The Vardon Grip with Both Hands*   (facing p479)
Photograph: *The Vardon Grip Looking From the Hole*   (facing p481)
Trout Fishing in Reservoirs by Ernest Phillips   (p481-486)
Sporting Personalities: Quaint Stories of Men of Mark   (p486-489)
I Remember by Athol Maudslay   (p490-492)
A Few Facts in Forestry by Charles Curtis   (p492-493)

James Braid Golf Champion by Edward Cuming | (p494)
Our Van [inc. Lancashire Steeplechase; Epsom Meeting; Esher Plate; Croome Hounds; Tickham Hunt; Cattistock Hunt; Polo at Rugby] | (p495-501)
Sporting Intelligence [inc. University Sport; Zambesi Regatta; Royal & Ancient Golf Club; Football Antiquity; Obituaries of Ralph Faber, Joseph Wostinholm, Thomas Lunn and Henry Holroyd; Greyhound Racing; Argentine Horses] | (p502-509)
Sporting Results | (p509-512)

Volume 92, July - December 1909

Issue 593 : July 1909

Portrait of Arthur Thatcher, huntsman | Title page
Portrait [Russell] and Biography - Peter Walker | (p1-2)
Fox Preserving in Summer by Thomas Dale | (p3-7)
A Few Words to the Australian Cricketers by Herbert Hewett | (p7-10)
Loyal Heart [verses] by William Ogilvie | (p11)
Photograph [Rouch]: *Minoru* | (facing p13)
The King's Derby by Edward Cuming | (p12-17)
Photograph [Hailey]: *Richard Marsh* | (facing p15)
Photograph: *Hall Walker* | (on p15)
Photograph [Hailey]: *Herbert Jones* | (on p16)
[Review] *Essex in the Twentieth Century* by Charles Benham | (17-20)
Photograph: *Down Hall, Harlow* | (facing p19)
Photograph: *Hassobury, Bishop's Stortford* | (facing p19)
Photograph: *Hylands, Widford* | (on p19)
The First Months of the Trout Season by James Englefield | (p20-25)
Lithographs [pinx. Hopcroft]: *The Five Yachts of King Edward* | (facing p25)
Royal Yachts Past and Present by George Hopcroft | (p25-29)
Lithographs [pinx. Hopcroft]: *The Six Yachts of Queen Victoria* | (facing p27)
Cricket Notes by Otho Paget | (p29-32)
[Obituary] Richard Green-Price (*Baily's* contributor) by Edward Cuming | (p32-34)
Photograph: *Richard Green-Price* | (on p33)
The Sportsman's Library: Reviews of *Rambles in Sussex* by Frederick Brabant; *A Record of Field Trials* by Walter Baxendale; *The Olympic Games* by Theodore Cook; *The Law Affecting Dogs* by William Freeman; *Club Bridge* by Archibald Dunn; *Beautiful Joe* by Marshall Saunders; *Highways and Byways of Surrey* by Eric Parker; *Scotch and Irish Terriers* by John Maxtee; *Live Stock Breeds and Management* by Primrose McConnell | (p34-35)
Wire Fencing [with Sketches] by Charles Curtis | (p36-38)
Sporting Personalities: Quaint Stories of Men of Mark | (p39-40)
Midsummer Nights in London by Otho Paget | (p41-43)
Game Preservation Problems in Africa by Harold Bindloss | (p43-48)
A Hundred Years Ago: Captain Barclay from *The Sporting Magazine* | (p49)
Photograph: *Peep Bo* | (facing p51)
The International Horse Show by George Lowe | (p50-53)
Photograph: *Broadwood* | (facing p53)
Polo by Archibald Charlton | (p54-60)
Photograph: *Charles Chetwynd-Talbot & Frank Belville* | (facing p57)
Photograph [Rouch]: *Arthur* | (facing p59)
Pig [Sticking] by Douglas Oliver | (p61-63)
Some Thoughts on Poaching by Charles Batchelder | (p64-65)
Gun Clubs by Arthur Bentley | (p66-67)
A Big Game Hunt in British Columbia by Lincoln Wilbar | (p68-70)

Our Van [inc. York Races; Somersetshire Stakes; Manchester Cup; Exford Stables;
        Shropshire Hunt] (p71-72)
Sporting Intelligence [inc. Thames Regattas; Zambesi Regatta; Irish Army Point-to-Point;
        Muirfield Golf; Obituaries of Harry Everard and Daniel Cooper; Australian Tote;
        Californian Polo] (p73-78)
Sporting Results (p79-80)

Issue 594 : August 1909

Portrait [Mayall] and Biography - Bernard Forbes (p81-82)
Foxhunting, Harehunting and Other Sports on Exmoor by Thomas Dale (p83-89)
Humours and Dangers of a Racing Stable by William Fox-Russell (p90-98)
Polo by Archibald Charlton (p99-109)
Photograph: *John Watson* (on p99)
Photograph: *American Polo Team* (facing p103)
Photograph [Rouch]: *English Polo Team* (facing p105)
Photograph [Rouch]: *America Saves Well* (facing p107)
Photograph: *Exciting Play Near the Board* (facing p107)
The Wet-Fly Angler in July by Arthur Sharp (p109-111)
The Varsity Cricket Match by Otho Paget (p112-113)
The Future of Racquets by Eustace Miles (p114-115)
Doncaster Races by Ernest Phillips (p116-122)
Photograph [Scott]: *Doncaster Enclosure and Course* (facing p119)
A Hundred Years Ago: Galloways from *The Sporting Magazine* (p123)
Photographs: *John Cotterell, Henry Coventry, Edward Heygate, Arthur Turner, Allen Hughes
        and William Britten* (facing p125)
The Sportsman's Library: Reviews of *The Gentle Art of Angling* by Joseph Adams; *History
        of Herefordshire Cattle* by James Macdonald; *The Evolution of British Cattle*
        by James Wilson (p124-127)
Sport Versified [verses] by Athol Maudslay (p128-130)
Sporting Personalities: Quaint Stories of Men of Mark (p130-133)
Photograph: *Charles Pulley* (on p132)
Photograph: *Migel Martinez de Hoz* (on p132)
Song of the Vale of Belvoir [verses] by Lionel Musters (p133)
Test and Other Cricket by Herbert Hewett (p134-136)
The Peterborough Shows by George Lowe (p137-144)
Photograph [Babbage]: *Red Sea* (facing p139)
Lithograph [pinx. Bradley]: *Warwickshire Trickster* (on p141)
August and the Gunner by Frank Bonnett (p145-148)
Our Van [inc. Ascot Meeting; Newbury Races; Newmarket *Pari-Mutuel*; Warwickshire
        Hunt, Sparkford Vale Harriers; Obituary of Neven du Mont] (p148-153)
Sporting Intelligence [inc. Henley Regatta; Polo Ponies at Gloucester; Obituaries of William
        Peech, Henry Sadleir-Jackson, Henry Hawley, Frederick Monk and William
        Payne; *Golf Illustrated* Gold Vase; Alexandra Park Racing; Minor Counties
        Cricket; Indian Football; Gibraltar Polo] (p153-159)
Photograph [Ullyett]: *Harry Vardon* (on p156)
Sporting Results (p159-162)

Issue 595 : September 1909

Portrait [Dickinson] and Biography - Henry Lascelles (p163-165)
On Turf Handicapping by Edward Cuming (p166-169)
Thoughts on Distemper in Hounds by Thomas Dale (p169-171)
The Modern Harrier by George Lowe (p172-177)
Photograph: *North Montgomery Harriers* (facing p175)

Photograph: *Ransom* (on p176)

[Obituary] Arthur Guillum Scott by Walter Gilbey (p178-180)

Photograph [Russell]: *Arthur Scott* (facing p178)

Turf Nomenclature by Seymour Ramsdale (p181-183)

The Wildness of Partridges by Alan Haig-Brown (p183-185)

The Polo Season by Archibald Charlton (p185-188)

Test Matches by Herbert Hewett (p189-191)

Photograph [Clinch]: *Jevogla Falls, New Brunswick* (facing p193)

Salmon Fishing in New Brunswick by Douglas Clinch (p193-197)

Photograph [Clinch]: *Miramichi River, New Brunswick* (facing p195)

The Working Terriers of England and Scotland (part 1) by William Tweedie (p197-202)

[Review] *Gentlemen Riders Past and Present* by John Maunsell-Richardson (p203-207)

Lithograph: *Viscount Tredegar and his Hounds* (facing p205)

Tufts of Turf by William Fox-Russell (p207-209)

Our Waste Land and its Classification by Charles Curtis (p209-212)

Photograph: *A Type of Waste Land* (on p210)

A Hundred Years Ago: Sailing from *The Sporting Magazine* (p213)

The Sportsman's Library: Reviews of *Sporting Guide to Nova Scotia* by Edward Breck; *The Young Naturalist* by Percival Westell; *Notes on Shooting in the British Isles* by Arthur Hood; *Hunting* by William North (p214-215)

County Cricket by Edward Clayton (p216-219)

Photograph [Foster]: *Kent Cricket Team* (facing p219)

The Romance of the Beaver by Lincoln Wilbar (p220-222)

Sporting Personalities: Quaint Stories of Men of Mark (p223)

Photograph: *Cuthbert Quilter* (on p223)

An Autumn Day with the Gun in Japan by Harold Parlett (p224-228)

The Arts of Ease and Happiness in Sport by George Teasdale-Buckell (p228-229)

Dogs I Have Known (part 1) by Bird Thompson (p230-232)

Our Van [inc. Dullingham Plate; Goodwood Gold Cup; Exmoor Deer Hunt; North Staffordshire Hounds; Cattistock Hunt; Obituary of Henry Wardell; Hawkstone Otterhounds] (p233-237)

Sporting Intelligence [inc. Pointer Club; Thames River Club; Hazelwood Moor Grouse; Calcutta Cup Golf; Royal Yacht Squadron; Brooklands Time Trial; American Polo] (p238-242)

Sporting Results (p242-244)

Issue 596 : October 1909

Portrait [Bassano] and Biography - William Cooke (p245-246)

The Late Test Matches by Richard Williams (p247-249)

Test Match Cricket by Frederick Spofforth (p249-251)

Photograph: *Woodcock Brooding* (facing p253)

Photograph: *Woodcock Crouching* (facing p253)

Protective Mimicry in Game Birds and Wildfowl by Hector Macpherson (p252-256)

Photograph: *Ptarmigan Leaving Nest* (facing p255)

Photograph: *Red Grouse Creeping Up to Nest* (facing p255)

The Hunter's Moon [verses] by William Ogilvie (p257)

The Working Terriers of England and Scotland (part 2) by William Tweedie (p258-266)

A Basket of Grayling by Joseph Adams (p266-272)

Photograph: *Where Grayling Feed* (on p267)

Photograph: *The Meadow Reach* (on p269)

Photograph: *The Bridge Pool* (on p271)

The Cultivation of the Laurel in Kent by Otho Paget (p273-275)

Billiard Handicaps by John Buchanan (p275-276)

A Hundred Years Ago: Cricket from *The Sporting Magazine* (p277)
The Lessons of the Polo Season by Archibald Charlton (p278-280)
What Helps the Master of Fox-Hounds by Robert Dunkin (p280-283)
Public School Cricket in 1909 by Abel Chapman (p283-288)
A Review of the Yacht Racing Season by George Hopcroft (p288-292)
Lithograph [pinx. Hopcroft]: *Handicap Racing in the Solent* (facing p291)
Lithograph [pinx. Hopcroft]: *White Heather & Cicely* (facing p291)
Autumn Evenings in London by Otho Paget (p292-297)
Curious Things in Racing Results by William Fox-Russell (p298-301)
A Delectable Day by Arthur Browne (p301-304)
The Sportsman's Library: Reviews of *A Wasted Life* by Dyke Williamson; *The Keepers' Book* by Peter Mackie; *The British Motor Tourist* by Upcott Gill; *Hound and Horn in Jed Forest* by Scott Anderson; *Teddy Whistler's Yarns* by Thomas Dey; *Equine Eugenics* by Francis Ram; *The Kea* by John Marriner (p304-305)
Sporting Personalities: Quaint Stories of Men of Mark (p306)
Dogs I Have Known (part 2) by Bird Thompson (p307-309)
Our Van [inc. Jockeys; Stockton Races; Ebor Meeting; Doncaster Stakes; Quantock Stags; Pytchley Hunt; Fitzwilliam Hounds; North Herefordshire Hunt; Obituary of Percy Browne] (p309-318)
Photograph [Rouch]: *Bayardo* (facing p313)
Sporting Intelligence [inc. American Polo; Irish Golf; Blackpool Golf Club; Obituaries of Jack de Clifford, Henry Waring, Philip Hartigan, William Peech, Henry Studdy, Charles Rowell and Harry Boyton; Polytechnic Harriers, Twickenham Rugby Ground; Hungarian Gentlemen Riders' Association] (p319-321)
Sporting Results (p322-324)

Issue 597 : November 1909

Portrait [Elliott] and Biography - George Lane-Fox (p325-326)
Concerning Scent by Henry Bryden (p327-329)
Bankside Reflections on a Blank Day by Abel Chapman (p330-336)
Photograph: *The Run Below Aire Bridge* (facing p333)
Photograph: *A Series of Pools Below the Falls* (facing p333)
Photograph: *A Good Pool in May* (facing p335)
Photograph: *Below the Falls* (facing p335)
The Druid by Caroline Dixon (p336-341)
Engraving [sculp. Alais]: *Henry Hall Dixon* (on p338)
Tufts of Turf [inc. Obituary of Frederick Page] by William Fox-Russell (p341-345)
Engraving [pinx. Hall]: *Voltigeur* (facing p343)
Engraving [pinx. Hall]: *Kettledrum* (facing p343)
Sportsmen Afoot [verses] by William Ogilvie (p346-347)
Sport in Basutoland by Mervyn Bosworth-Smith (p347-351)
The Working Terriers of England and Scotland (part 3) by William Tweedie (p351-353)
Engraving: *The Forerunner of the Barmaid* (facing p355)
[Review] *Inns, Ales and Drinking Customs of Old England* by Frederick Hackwood (p354-358)
Photograph: *The Sign of The Five Alls* (on p356)
More Curious Results in Racing by William Fox-Russell (p359-362)
Engraving: *Sultan* (facing p361)
Engraving: *The Old Mare* (facing p361)
Eight Days Dry-Fly Fishing by James Englefield (p362-365)
Birds for the Table: Past and Present by Watkin Watkins (p365-372)
Engraving [sculp. Beckwith]: *Setter & Pheasant* (facing p367)
Engraving [sculp. Hacker]: *Retrieving Mallard* (facing p367)
Hunt Changes by Edward Cuming (p372-377)

Dogs I Have Known (part 3) by Bird Thompson (p378-379)

Autumn Evenings in London by Otho Paget (p380-382)

Foxes and the Utility Poultry Club by Frank Bonnett (p382-385)

A Hundred Years Ago: Foxhunting from *The Sporting Magazine* (p386)

Sporting Personalities: Quaint Stories of Men of Mark (p387-388)

The Sportsman's Library: Reviews of *Hunting* by William North; *The Modern Veterinary Adviser* by Gerald Leighton; *Billiards* by John Roberts; *Auction Bridge* by Archibald Dunn; *The Grizzly Bear* by William Wright (p389-390)

Our Van [inc. Budapest Racecourse; Newmarket Meeting; Devon & Somerset Staghounds; Blackmore Vale Hunt; Obituaries of Frank Cross and Thomas Powell; East Antrim Staghounds; East Sussex Hunt] (p391-397)

Sporting Intelligence [inc. Retriever Trials; University Captains; Royal & Ancient Golf; Test Match Receipts; Obituaries of Arthur Guillemard and George Lowe (*Baily's* contributor); All-England Angling Championship; New York Athletic Club] (p397-402)

Sporting Results (p402-404)

Issue 598 : December 1909

Portrait [Lafayette] and Biography - Ventura Misa (p405-407)

Ware Wheat! What's the Damage (p407-410)

Mobilization Horses by Herman Lewis (p410-416)

The Felsted Run by Walter Gilbey (p416-421)

Lithograph [pinx. O'Brien]: *Leaden Wash* (facing p419)

Lithograph [pinx. O'Brien]: *Evelyn Wood Climbing a Tree Over the River Chelmer* (on p420)

Bloodstock Breeding Honours of the Year by Archibald Charlton (p422-428)

Photograph [Rouch]: *Cyllene* (facing p425)

Photograph [Fall]: *Sundridge* (facing p427)

Fiction or Grouse by Charles Batchelder (p429-433)

Athletics and Sport in Wild Places by George Teasdale-Buckell (p433-440)

Photograph [Woodley]: *Eskdale Hounds in Full Cry Across Crags* (facing p435)

Photograph [Woodley]: *Eskdale Hounds on Dry Ghyll* (facing p435)

Photograph [Woodley]: *Tommy Dobson* (on p435)

Photograph [Woodley]: *The Pole Vault - A Northern Professional Sport* (on p436)

Photograph [Woodley]: *Tommy Dobson and Will Porter* (on p437)

Photograph [Woodley]: *The Hound Trail - Ready to Start* (on p438)

Decadence or Change of Taste by George Burrows (p440-443)

Winter Evenings in London by Otho Paget (p444-449)

The Carted Deer by Thomas Dale (p449-454)

Whyte-Melville [verses] by William Ogilvie (p455)

A Hundred Years Ago: Pigeon Shooting Club from *The Sporting Magazine* (p456)

Sporting Personalities: Quaint Stories of Men of Mark (p457-459)

Photograph: *Cecil Haverson* (facing p461)

The Sportsman's Library: Reviews of *British Sport Past and Present* by Edward Cuming; *The Billiard Book* by Mavis Warren; *British Mountain Climbs* by George Abraham (p460-464)

Photograph: *The Pillar Rock* (facing p463)

Arthur Thatcher by Edward Cuming (p464-465)

Our Van [inc. Kempton Park Races; Knockany Stud; Blackmore Vale Hunt; Kildare Hounds; Obituaries of Frederick Usher, Lloyd Baker, John Brooke, Joseph Scott-Plummer and Edward Fenwick] (p465-472)

Sporting Intelligence [inc. Cambridge University Deerhunt; County Polo Association; Edinburgh Golfers; Weybridge Golf Club; Sheffield Otter Swimming Club; Obituaries of William Philpotts, Cyril Hillyard, Frederic Langstaff, William Pollock, George Smart, William Frith, Richard Wainwright and Luke Greenwood; Irish Turf Club; Yorkshire Cricket Council; South African Rugby Union]   (p473-479)

Sporting Results   (p479-480)

Volume 93, January - June 1910

Issue 599 : January 1910

Portrait [Hawkins] of Jack Hobbs, cricketer   Title page
Portrait [Heyman] and Biography - Thomas Gallwey   (p1-3)
The Organization of Foxhunting by Robert Dunkin   (p3-9)
Dandy White by Robert Ball   (p9-12)
Photograph: *William Inman White*   (on p11)
A Masterless Pack by Harding Cox   (p12-14)
Photograph: *The Hunting Dog*   (on p13)
Prehistoric British Ponies [with Sketches] by Cossar Ewart   (p15-25)
Lithograph: *The Steppe Type - Mongolia*   (facing p17)
Lithograph: *The Siwalik Type - Sumatra*   (facing p17)
Lithograph: *The Forest Type - Iceland*   (facing p19)
Lithograph: *The Plateau Type - North Africa*   (facing p19)
Lithograph: *The Plateau Type - Europe*   (facing p21)
The Youngster to Suit [verses] by Henry Pilkington   (p26)
Advance of Golf in Ireland by Lionel Hewson   (p27-29)
An Afternoon with the Woodpigeons   (p30-34)
Cambridge Drag Hunt Prosecution [* *Worth reading* *]   (p34-37)
The Reflections of a Fox [verses] by Robert Churchill   (p37)
A Mixed Bag by Abel Chapman   (p38-42)
The Flyfisher's Rod   (p42-43)
A Hundred Years Ago: Cottesmore Hunt from *The Sporting Magazine*   (p44)
Jack Burge [introduction and verses] by Francis Hayes   (p45)
The Spirit of Foxhunting by Eric Parker   (p46-48)
[Review] The Vitality of the Thoroughbred: *Horse Breeding in Theory and Practice* by Burchard von Oettingen   (p49-50)
[Review] *Sporting Stories* by William Wilmott-Dixon   (p51-53)
Last Season's Otterhunting by Ludovick Cameron   (p54-56)
The Sportsman's Library: Reviews of *Lake Victoria to Khartoum* by Francis Dickinson; *Live Stock Journal Almanac 1910* by James Sinclair; *The Six-Handicap Golfer* by Harold Hilton; *Modern Riding* by Noel Birch; *Breaking and Training Dogs* by Henry Dear; *Book of the Goat* by Holmes Pegler; *My Pets* by Alexandre Dumas; *Jack Carstairs of the Power House* by Sydney Sandys; *The Morphia Habit* by Oscar Jennings   (p57-59)
Sporting Personalities: Quaint Stories of Men of Mark   (p60-62)
Photograph: *Hugh Lowther*   (on p60)
Photograph: *John Maunsell-Richardson*   (on p61)
Photograph: *Gilbert Greenall*   (on p61)
Photograph: *Victor Cavendish*   (on p62)
Photograph: *George Coventry*   (on p62)
The Badger and Badgerhunting by Alfred Pease   (p62-63)
Record Moose-Heads by Lincoln Wilbar   (p64-68)
Photograph [Wilbar]: *Alaskan Moose Head*   (on p65)
Photograph [Wilbar]: *New Brunswick Moose Head*   (on p66)

Photograph [Wilbar]: *New Brunswick Moose* (on p67)

Dogs I Have Known (part 4) by Bird Thompson (p69)

Our Van [inc. Aintree Meeting; Manchester Races; Kildare Hounds; Warwickshire Hunt; Obituary of Martin Powell; Cambridge University Steeplechases] (p70-76)

Sporting Intelligence [inc. Oxford University Rowing; Obituaries of Frederick Hassall, Harry Barker, Edward Cardwell, Charles Merry, Frederick Finlay, Denis Shanahan, Herbert Langham and Robert Dow; Mid-Kent Golf Club; Worcestershire County Cricket Club; South Shropshire Hounds; Pytchley Hunt; Melbourne Cricket Club] (p77-82)

Sporting Results (p83-84)

Issue 600 : February 1910

Portrait [Abraham] and Biography - James Lowther (p85-86)

The Making of a Pack by Harding Cox (p87-91)

Speed and the Grand National [with Diagrams] (p92-96)

A Rambling History of English Lacrosse by Charles Thomas (p96-100)

Photograph: *United Kingdom Lacrosse Team* (facing p99)

Hunt Disputes by Edward Cuming (p101-105)

Yachting: The America's Cup Controversy by George Hopcroft (p106-110)

Lithograph [pinx. Hopcroft]: *Reliance* (facing p109)

Lithograph [pinx. Hopcroft]: *Showing Reliance Under-Water Body* (facing p109)

A Week's Shooting in British East Africa by John Patterson (p110-113)

The Neglect of the Pike by Alan Haig-Brown (p113-115)

Tufts of Turf by William Fox-Russell (p115-118)

An Historic Bet by Bromehead Soulby (p118-120)

The Hireling [verses] by William Ogilvie (p121)

Engraving [pinx. Herring]: *Sweetmeat* (facing p123)

Engraving [pinx. Herring]: *Mincepie* (facing p123)

Happy Nomenclature by George Teasdale-Buckell (p122-125)

Engraving [pinx. Herring]: *Longbow* (facing p125)

Engraving [pinx. Hall]: *Queen Bertha* (facing p125)

Pig by Maxwell McTaggart (p126-129)

Another Mixed Bag by Abel Chapman (p129-130)

A Hundred Years Ago: The Four-in-Hand Club from *The Sporting Magazine* (p131)

The Reprieve by Herbert Hewett (p132-134)

Winter Nights in London by Otho Paget (p134-138)

Some South African Cricket by Sydney Pardon (p139-140)

The Sportsman's Library: Reviews of *Skiing* by Rickmer Richards; *The Estate Manager* by Richard Henderson; *Garryowen* by Henry Stacpoole; *In the Grip of the Nyika* by John Patterson (p140-141)

Sporting Personalities: Quaint Stories of Men of Mark (p142-143)

Dogs I Have Known (part 5) by Bird Thompson (p143-146)

The Right of Pannage by Charles Curtis (p146-148)

Our Van [inc. Gimcrack Club Dinner; North Warwickshire Hunt; Hunt Servant Changes; Obituary of Henry Judd; Meath Hunt; Ward Union Staghounds] (p149-156)

Sporting Intelligence [inc. Oxford University Aero Club; Irish Horses; Spring Horse Shows; Polo Ponies; Obituaries of Herbert Langham, Alice Gifford, Hercules Blincko, William Hodgson, George Rodney, Charles Strickland, Garrett Taylor, Billy Wittem, Timothy Desmond and Edward Spencer Mott ('Nathaniel Gubbins` of *The Sporting Times*); Golf Championship of India; Australian Boxing] (p157-164)

Sporting Results (p164)

Issue 601 : March 1910

Portrait [Young] and Biography - Archibald Orr-Ewing (p165-166)

Foxhound Puppies at Home and at Walk by Harding Cox (p166-172)
Causes of Decline of Cup Racing by Richard Seymour-Ramsdale (p173-177)
Lithograph: *Charles Bunbury* (facing p177)
Charles Bunbury and Bellario by George Teasdale-Buckell (p177-182)
Engraving [pinx. Sartorius]: *Goldfinder* (facing p179)
Engraving [pinx. Sartorius]: *Tortoise* (facing p179)
Engraving [pinx. Sartorius]: *Bellario* (facing p181)
Engraving [pinx. Sartorius]: *Pilgrim* (facing p181)
The Quorn and South Quorn by Edward Cuming (p182-187)
[Review] *Life History and Habits of the Salmon* by Peter Malloch (p187-191)
Photograph: *Two Male Forty Pound Salmon Unspawned* (facing p189)
Photograph: *Sea-Trout* (facing p191)
Polo Ponies and their Prices by Archibald Charlton (p192-196)
A Hundred Years Ago: Skating from *The Sporting Magazine* (p197)
Engraving [pinx. Cooper]: *The Earth-Stopper of Old* (facing p199)
The Earth-Stopper: His Duties by Frank Bonnett (p198-200)
[Review] *Wisden's Cricketers' Almanack 1910* by Sydney Pardon (p200-202)
Some Notes from Old Show Rings by William Parlour (p203-208)
Devonshire Fishing by Paul Taylor (p208-212)
Cricket Topics [inc. Obituary of Thomas Hearne] by Herbert Hewett (p212-215)
Sporting Personalities: Quaint Stories of Men of Mark (p215-216)
On The Tan [verses] by William Ogilvie (p216)
The Billiard Room by John Buchanan (p217-224)
Badgers and Badgerhunting by Alfred Pease (p224-226)
The Popularity of Plebeian Pastimes by Gerald Ricardo (p226-228)
Repeated Racehorse Names by Edward Cuming (p229-231)
Engraving [pinx. Sartorius]: *Charles Sidley's True Blue* (on p230)
Engraving [pinx. Sartorius]: *Looby* (facing p233)
Old Match Horses (part 1) by Frank Bonnett (p232-234)
Our Van [inc. Inspector of Flat-Racing Courses; Atherstone Hunt; North Northumberland
        Hounds; Brighton & Brookside Harriers; Essex Hunt] (p235-239)
Photograph [Newman]: *Mary Fitzmaurice and her Father* (on p237)
Sporting Intelligence [inc. Carlisle & Silloth Golf Club; Obituaries of Alfred Brewer, Edward
        Morant, John Page, Felix Fielding and William Rainbird; York & Ainsty Hounds;
        Royal Forth Yacht Club; Matthew Webb Memorial] (p239-243)
Sporting Results (p243-244)

Issue 602 : April 1910

Portrait [Elliott] and Biography - Charles Cavendish-Bentinck (p245-246)
Reasons for Masters' Resignations by Edward Cuming (p247-252)
The Kennel and Kennel Management by William Fox-Russell (p253-257)
Lithograph [pinx. Duncan]: *Teal Sailing Past Decoys* (facing p259)
Duck Shooting over Decoys by Stanley Duncan (p258-264)
Lithograph [pinx.Duncan]: *Shoveler Coming in to Decoys* (on p261)
Lithograph [pinx.Duncan]: *Mallards* (facing p263)
The Brook Angler in April by Arthur Sharp (p264-267)
Polo in 1910 by Archibald Charlton (p268-269)
The Scottish Curler by John Kerr (p270-273)
Engraving [pinx.Stubbs]: *Protector* (facing p273)
Engraving [pinx. Stubbs]: *Sweetbriar* (facing p273)
Old Match Horses (part 2) by Frank Bonnett (p273-277)
Engraving: *Hambletonian* (facing p275)
Engraving: *Silverlocks* (facing p275)

Is Duelling Sportsmanlike by Frederick Aflalo (p277-280)
Shootings and their Managements by Thomas Dale (p280-282)
Poultry Keeping and the Preservation of Foxes by Barrington Horne (p282-285)
On Teaching Horses to Jump by Henry Pilkington (p285-289)
A Memory of the Woodland Pytchley [text and verses] (p290-291)
The Spring Horse Shows by William Parlour (p291-297)
Photograph [Babbage]: *Akbar* (facing p295)
Photograph [Babbage]: *Broadwood* (facing p297)
The Boat Race by Walter Woodgate (p298)
A Hundred Years Ago: Four-in-Hand from *The Sporting Magazine* (p299)
The Home of the Rock Pigeon by Maitland Stewart (p300-302)
Cricket in South Africa by Herbert Hewett (p303-305)
Sporting Personalities: Quaint Stories of Men of Mark (p305-306)
Peter Beckford's Thoughts on Hunting (p306-311)
The Sailor Side by William Fox-Russell (p312-317)
Our Van [inc. Sandown Park Meeting; Grand Military Gold Cup; North Bucks Harriers; Hertfordshire Hunt; Obituaries of William Gwynne and Robert Thoyts; Percy Hunt; East Essex Hounds; Bexhill Harriers] (p317-321)
Sporting Intelligence [inc. University Rugby; Council of Ladies Golf Union; County Polo Association; Obituary of Thomas Taylor; Lucknow Polo; Middlesex Hunt of Massachusetts] (p321-324)
Sporting Results (p325-326)

Issue 603 : May 1910

Portrait [Cleer] and Biography - Robert Barkley (p327-330)
Members of the Hunt and their Duties by William Fox-Russell (p330-336)
Days among the Salmon in Connemara by Joseph Adams (p336-343)
Photograph: *The Colonel's Pool* (facing p339)
Photograph: *Galway Pier - The Bridge Pool* (facing p339)
Photograph: *Galway Pier - A Spring Cast* (facing p341)
Photograph: *The Pool by the Wood* (facing p341)
St.Andrews Links: Legal Actions by Bromehead Soulby (p343-348)
Means of Helping the Masters of Hounds by Edward Cuming (p348-352)
Yachting Prospects for 1910 by George Hopcroft (p352-356)
Lithograph [pinx. Hopcroft]: *The Big Schooners in the Solent* (facing p355)
Lithograph [pinx. Hopcroft]: *A Yacht Yard in Spring* (facing p355)
[Obituary] John Harris of Liskeard by Percy Percival (p357-362)
Photograph: *John Harris* (on p358)
Photograph: *Charles Faultless* (on p359)
Photograph: *Bill Gilliver* (on p360)
A Fox Covert in May [verses] by William Ogilvie (p362)
Fish and Fishing in Brackish Water by Frederick Aflalo (p363-366)
A Hundred Years Ago: Epping Hunt from *The Sporting Magazine* (p367)
[Obituary] Thomas Dobson by Yerburgh Dixon (p368-369)
Some Studies in Black by William Wilmott-Dixon (p369-376)
Is Duelling Unsportsmanlike by Claude Champion de Crespigny (p376-377)
Polo Notes and News by Archibald Charlton (p378-381)
Spring Evenings in London by Otho Paget (p381-384)
Sporting Slang and its Derivation by George Burrows (p385-386)
Old Time Racing Connections by William Fox-Russell (p386-389)
[Obituary] James Tomkinson by Edward Cuming (p389-393)
Photograph: *James Tomkinson* (facing p391)
Poultrykeeping and the Preservation of Foxes by Barrington Horne (p392-393)

Our Van [inc. Lincolnshire Handicap; Nottingham Races; Newbury Spring Cup; South
        Shropshire Hunt; Lamerton Hounds; Exmoor Sport; High Peak Harriers;
        Dartmoor Otterhounds] (p393-400)
Sporting Intelligence [inc. University Boat Race; Oxford University Drag Hunt; Hallamshire
        Athletic Harriers; Biarritz Golf; West Surrey Golf Club; Obituaries of William
        Curgeven, Samuel Salt, Harcourt Turner, John Wallington, Archibald Ayde and
        James Pawson; Knockany Stud; New Jersey Polo] (p401-408)
Sporting Results (p408-410)

Issue 604 : June 1910

Portrait [Aylward] and Biography - Richard Rycroft (p411-412)
The Late King as a Sportsman by Edward Cuming (p413-418)
Photograph: *King Edward VII with Minoru* (facing p415)
Hunt Horses and their Riders by William Fox-Russell (p418-424)
Point-to-Point Racing by William Scarth-Dixon (p424-428)
Foxhunting and Poultry Compensation by Barrington Horne (p428-433)
Lithograph: *Squire Osbaldeston* (facing p433)
Two Hundred Miles on Horseback in 439 Minutes by Edward Cuming (p433-435)
The Oxford and Cambridge Drag Hunts by Charles Brantsen (p435-437)
A True Story of the Indian Turf (part 1) by William Tweedie (p437-440)
Sport and Country Life at the Academy by James Shepherd (p440-443)
The Romantic Story of a Despised Stallion by Gerald Ricardo (p443-447)
Lithograph [pinx. Herring]: *Blacklock* (facing p445)
Some Free Fishing and an Allegory by Bernard Tonkin (p447-450)
Recent Racquets by Harold Rudd (p450-453)
The Feast of Football by James Bentley (p453-456)
Is Duelling Sportsmanlike by Frederick Aflalo (p456-457)
Polo en Passant by Archibald Charlton (p458-460)
A Hundred Years Ago: Whip Club from *The Sporting Magazine* (p461)
Fresh Phases of Cricket by Herbert Hewett (p462-464)
Reminiscences of Somaliland by Henry Pilkington (p464-467)
The Sportsman's Library: Reviews of *Science from an Easy-Chair* by Ray Lankester; *An
        Invitation to the Woods* by Philip Oyler; *Minor Tactics of the Chalk Stream* by
        George Skues; *A History of Birds* by William Pycraft; *The Roarer* by Nat Gould;
        Hounds Gentlemen Please by William Forbes (p467-469)
Sporting Personalities: Quaint Stories of Men of Mark (p470-471)
John Berry Hobbs by Edward Cuming (p471-472)
Our Van [inc. Greenham Stakes; Doveridge Handicap; Hurst Park Meeting; Cricklade (Vale of
        White Horse) Hounds; Eastbourne Hunt] (p473-480)
Sporting Intelligence [inc. Cambridge University Lawn Tennis Club; Stourbridge Golf Club;
        Obituaries of Robert Barkley, George Pettitt, John Fraser, John Craig, James
        Galway, William Everitt, Felix Calvert, Philip Chaloner, John Wallington, Thomas
        Winship, Alexander Giles and Henry Bean; Football Association Wage Limit;
        Sydney Grade Cricket; Riviera Tennis] (p480-487)
Sporting Results (p488-490)

Volume 94, July - December 1910

Issue 605 : July 1910

Portrait [Holt] of Charles Gillson, huntsman Title page
Portrait [Lafayette] and Biography - Merrik Burrell (p1-3)
On the Influence of Hound Shows on Foxhunting by William Fox-Russell (p3-8)

Co-operative Game and Fish Preservation by Henry Pilkington   (p9-13)

Jockeys and their Statistics by George Teasdale-Buckell   (p13-18)

Lithograph: *Frederick Archer*   (on p15)

Photograph [Sherborn]: *Frederick Allsopp*   (on p15)

Photograph [Sherborn]: *Thomas Cannon*   (on p15)

Photograph [Sherborn]: *Joseph Plant*   (on p17)

Photograph: *George Nelson*   (on p18)

In Praise of Wrestling by William Calderwood   (p19-22)

Irish Polo by Archibald Charlton   (p23-26)

The Infinite Varsity of Sport by Frederick Aflalo   (p27-29)

A True Story of the Indian Turf (part 2) by William Tweedie   (p29-36)

Polo en Passant by Archibald Charlton   (p36-40)

Current Cricket Chat by Herbert Hewett   (p40-44)

Foals [verses] by William Ogilvie   (p45)

A Hundred Years Ago: Harness Racing from *The Sporting Magazine*   (p46)

The International Horse Show by Gerald Ricardo   (p47-48)

The Sportsman's Library: Reviews of *Motor Routes of France* by Gordon Home; *The Principles of Heredity Applied to the Racehorse* by John Robertson; *Letters of a Modern Golfer* by Henry Leach; *The Chance of a Lifetime* by Nat Gould; *Lawn Tennis for Ladies* by Dorothea Lambert-Chambers   (p49-52)

Photograph: *Douglas versus Sutton at Wimbledon*   (facing p51)

A New Inland Golf Course at Bishop's Stortford by Charles Batchelder   (p53-57)

Photograph [Babbage]: *Massy Driving at the Start*   (facing p55)

Photograph [Babbage]: *Braid Playing at the Ninth Green*   (facing p55)

Types of the Belvoir Kennel by Charles Batchelder   (p57-58)

Lithograph [Bradley]: *Belvoir Vulcan*   (facing p57)

Lithograph [Bradley]: *Belvoir Rallywood*   (facing p57)

Trout Fishing at Night by Ernest Phillips   (p58-62)

Sporting Personalities: Quaint Stories of Men of Mark   (p62-63)

Hits by Bad Missers by Lincoln Wilbar   (p64-67)

Some Curious Racing Laws and Customs by Yerburgh Dixon   (p68-71)

Our Van [Somersetshire Stakes; Knavesmire Plate; Epsom Meeting; Kempton Park Races]   (p72-76)

Photograph [Rouch]: *Lemberg*   (facing p75)

Sporting Intelligence [inc. Cambridge University Boat Club; Henley Regatta Review; National Hunt Committee Meeting; Masters of Foxhounds Association; Kelso Golf Club; Reigate Hound Show; Obituaries of James Hallows, John Hammond and Spencer Maul; Brighton Lawn Tennis]   (p77-82)

Sporting Results   (p83-84)

Issue 606 : August 1910

Portrait [Elliott] and Biography - Samuel Scott   (p85-87)

Cubhunting and Condition by William Fox-Russell   (p88-94)

The Schooling of Horses by John Swire   (p95-96)

A Red-Letter Day on the Moy by Joseph Adams   (p97-104)

Photograph: *River Moy - Top of the Garden Wall*   (facing p99)

Photograph: *River Moy - The Streams and Ridge Pool*   (facing p99)

Photograph: *River Moy - The Ash Tree Pool*   (facing p101)

Photograph: *Upper Moy - Rating a Fish in Hag's Pool*   (facing p101)

Memorable Boat-to-Boat Contests by George Hopcroft   (p104-108)

Lithograph [pinx. Hopcroft]: *Race Between Valkyrie III and Ailsa 1895*   (facing p107)

Lithograph [pinx. Hopcroft]: *Torpid Defeating Thought 1864*   (facing p107)

A True Story of the Indian Turf (part 3) by William Tweedie   (p109-114)

Raft Fishing in Norway by Edward Almack   (p114-117)

Four Famous Yorkshire Mares by George Teasdale-Buckell (p117-122)
Engraving [pinx. Herring]: *Cyprian* (facing p119)
Engraving [pinx. Hall]: *Songstress* (facing p119)
Engraving [pinx. Herring]: *Miss Letty* (on p121)
A Survey of the Shooting Field by Eric Parker (p122-127)
Polo of the Month by Archibald Charlton (p127-135)
Photograph [Roach]: *Oxford Polo Team* (facing p133)
A Hundred Years Ago: A Duel from *The Sporting Magazine* (p136)
Current Cricket Chat by Herbert Hewett (p137-141)
An Old Fashioned Twelfth by Alan Johnson (p142-145)
[Review] *History of Aberdeen-Angus Cattle* by James Sinclair (p145-146)
The Peterborough Shows by William Scarth-Dixon (p147-154)
Lithograph [pinx. Bradley]: *The Fitzwilliam Rector* (on p150)
Our Van [inc. Ascot Meeting; Hurstbourne Stakes; Bibury Cup; Devon & Somerset Staghounds;
        Quorn Hunt; Eastbourne Hunt] (p154-161)
Sporting Intelligence [inc. Henley Regatta; University Sporting Results; British Open Golf
        Championship; Park Langley Golf Club; Dublin Horse Show; Heavyweight
        Boxing; Obituaries of Charles Rolls, Frederick Furnivall, Mordecai Sherwin,
        James Smith, Eyre Hussey and George Chatterton; Chiddingfold Hunt; Quetta
        Hounds; Denmark Derby] (p162-169)
Sporting Results (p169-170)

Issue 607 : September 1910

Portrait [Reinhold] and Biography - Humphry Sturt (p171-173)
The Perils of the Pack by William Fox-Russell (p173-178)
Long Distance Rides by Eric Parker (p179-182)
The Sportsman's Busy Day by Harold Macfarlane (p183-187)
Lithograph [pinx. Barenger]: *Tapster* (facing p187)
[Review] Early Eighteenth Century Melton: *Records of the Old Charlton Hunt* by Charles
        Gordon-Lennox (p187-191)
Engraving [pinx. Barenger]: *The Colonel* (facing p191)
Running off Dead Heats by William Fox-Russell (p191-195)
Engraving [pinx. Hall]: *Brown Duchess* (on p192)
Engraving [pinx. Hall]: *Tim Whiffler* (on p193)
Hunting the American Wolf by Lincoln Wilbar (p195-199)
Photograph [Wilbar]: *Spoils of the Chase* (facing p197)
Various by Alan Haig-Brown (p200-201)
Popularity of Croquet by Frederick Aflalo (p202-204)
Experiences with the Illingworth Reel by Harry Cumberland-Bentley (p204-208)
Photograph: *Position for Casting With the Illingworth Casting Reel* (on p205)
Photograph: *Putting the Line into the Eye* (on p206)
Photograph: *Position for Winding in and Playing Fish* (on p207)
Photograph: *Tackles and Methods of Baiting for use with Illingworth Casting Reel* (on p208)
English Horses in the Grand Prix by Willoughby Maycock (p209-213)
Probable Effects of No Offside on Polo Pony Breeding by Thomas Dale (p213-215)
Four in Hand [verses] by William Ogilvie (p216)
A Hundred Years Ago: Horncastle Fair from *The Sporting Magazine* (p217)
Sporting Personalities: Quaint Stories of Men of Mark (p218-220)
Photograph: *Walter Winans* (on p218)
Photograph: *John Kerr* (on p219)
Photograph: *Frederick Wilkinson* (on p219)
Photograph: *William Foster* (on p219)
Photograph: *Nigel Colman* (on p219)

Polo of the Month by Archibald Charlton (p220-226)
Current Cricket Chat by Herbert Hewett (p226-230)
John Jorrocks, MFH by Eric Parker (p230-232)
A Day's Elephant Hunting by Henry Pilkington (p232-235)
Our Van [inc. Eclipse Stakes; Goodwood Meeting; West Somerset Hounds; Berwickshire Hunt;
    Obituary of George Luttrell] (p236-241)
Sporting Intelligence [inc. Marlow Regatta; London Rowing Club; Coursing Review;
    Chislehurst Golf Club; Obituaries of Poyntz Spencer, Ernest Simson, Thomas
    French, Thomas Purkiss, Benjamin Ellam, David Burrin, Harry Luff, Claude
    Champion de Crespigny (sr) and James Tomkinson; Hampton Court Palace
    Tennis Club; Cambridge University Drag Hunt] (p242-247)
Sporting Results (p248-250)

Issue 608 : October 1910

Portrait and Biography - Ailwyn Fellowes (p251-253)
The Fox and the Poultry Yard by William Fox-Russell (p253-257)
Horse Racing and Horse Breeding (part 1) by William Tweedie (p257-261)
The Enthusiasm of Foxhunting by William Fox-Russell (p261-263)
A Review of the 1910 Yachting Season by George Hopcroft (p263-268)
Lithograph [Hopcroft]: *Fifteen Metre Yachts Racing off Ryde* (facing p265)
Lithograph [Hopcroft]: *Part of the Anchorage off Ryde during the Regatta Week* (facing p265)
Polo by Archibald Charlton (p268-271)
Bobcat Hunting in Nova Scotia by Lincoln Wilbar (p271-275)
Photograph [Wilbar]: Two Bobcat (on p273)
Cricket Chat by Herbert Hewett (p276-281)
Curiosities in Inn Signs by George Teasdale-Buckell (p281-285)
Autumn Horse Shows by Gerald Ricardo (p285-289)
Photograph: *Hunter Kelly* (facing p287)
Photograph [Rouch]: *Hunter Zealot* (facing p289)
A Hundred Years Ago: Dumfries Shooting from *The Sporting Magazine* (p290)
Public School Cricket in 1910 by Abel Chapman (p291-294)
The Irish Polo Fortnight by Archibald Charlton (p295-298)
[Review] *Forty Years of a Sportsman's Life* by Claude Champion de Crespigny (p299-307)
Photograph: *John Astley* (facing p301)
Photograph: *Percy Douglas* (facing p303)
Photograph: *Claude Champion de Crespigny* (facing p305)
Fifty Years of Stockton Races by William Scarth-Dixon (p307-312)
Sporting Personalities: Quaint Stories of Men of Mark (p313-314)
Photograph: *Edward Stanley* (on p313)
The Sportsman's Library: Reviews of *Grouse and Grouse Moors* by George Malcolm; *Arms
    and Ammunition* by Dudley Wilson; *An Open Creel* by Hugh Sheringham;
    Jungle Byways in India by Edward Stebbing; *The Keeper's Book* by Jeffrey
    Mackie; *The Book of the Dry Fly* by George Dewar; *All on the Irish Shore* by
    Edith Somerville; *The Black Bear* by William Wright; *Echoes of Sport* by Hilda
    Murray; *The Lucky Shoe* by Nat Gould (p314-318)
Our Van [inc. Lewes Meeting; Stockton Racing; Doncaster Cup; Devon & Somerset
    Staghounds; Cattistock Hunt; Woodland Pytchley Hounds; South Notts Hunt;
    Lamerton Hounds] (p318-324)
Sporting Intelligence [inc.Welsh Golf Championship; Sheringham Golf Club; Ducks on
    Trout Streams; Obituaries of Allen Hill, Frank Gillard, Edward Fisher and
    Ernest Trubshaw; American Lawn Tennis Championship; Angling in
    New Zealand (p325-329)
Sporting Results (p329-330)

Issue 609 : November 1910

Portrait [Howard] and Biography - John Fullerton (p331-333)
The View Halloa by William Fox-Russell (p333-337)
American Polo [inc. Obituary of James Swan] (p337-341)
The Racing Tout at Work by Horace Hutchinson (p341-344)
Photograph: *Touts on the Ditch at Newmarket* (facing p343)
Photograph: *Cantering Work, Glencairn, Dublin* (facing p343)
Old Shooting Songs by William Parlour (p344-347)
Winter Yachting by Francis Cooke (p348-349)
Horse Racing and Horse Breeding (part 2) by William Tweedie (p350-355)
[Billiards] Red Losing Hazard by Sydenham Dixon (p355-357)
Horse Breeding in Ireland by Richard Preston (p357-361)
[Obituary] Edwin Sachs by Sydenham Dixon (p362-364)
Photograph: *Edwin Sachs* (on p362)
At the End of the Trout Season by James Englefield (p364-365)
The Opening Meet [verses] by William Ogilvie (p366)
Polo: Its Increase and Development by Archibald Charlton (p367-368)
Some Golf Problems by Gordon McPherson (p369-375)
[Obituary] Patteson Nickalls by Edward Cuming (p375-379)
Photograph [Lafayette]: *Patteson Nickalls* (facing p377)
Photograph: *Tarporley Hunt Cup* (facing p379)
The Sportsman's Library: Reviews of *Racing Cups* by Walter Gilbey; *The Aviator's Companion* by Dick Farman; *Salmon Scale Examination* by Arthur Hutton; *Mountain Adventures at Home and Abroad* by George Abraham; *Life and Sport on the Norfolk Broads* by Oliver Ready; *Game Preserver's Journal* by Philippa Esdaile; *Aigrettes and Birdskins* by Harold Smith; *The Channel Islands of California* by Charles Holder; *African Game Trails* by Theodore Roosevelt; *An Irish Cousin* by Edith Somerville; *Vyner's Notitia Venatica* revised by Cuthbert Bradley; *Lectors* by Denholm Armour; *Rambles in Surrey* by Charles Cox (p379-384)
Photograph: *Charles Holder and Tuna* (facing p383)
A Hundred Years Ago: Cavalry Horses from *The Sporting Magazine* (p385)
Stray Thoughts on Angling by Frederick Aflalo (p386-390)
Hunt Changes [inc. Obituaries of John Hasell, John Francis, Frederick Usher and George Walker] by Edward Cuming (p390-395)
Our Van [inc. Ayrshire Handicap; Manchester Meeting; Windsor Races; Badminton Hunt; Old Berkeley Hounds; Taunton Vale Hunt; Review of *Baily's Hunting Directory 1910-11*] (p395-405)
Sporting Intelligence [inc. University Rugby; Monte Carlo Golf Club; Portslade Links; Obituaries of Ernest Harding, Emily Schwind, Claud Chamberlain, Thomas Loates and William Bailey; Blencathra Foxhounds] (p405-411)
Sporting Results (p411-412)

Issue 610 : December 1910

Portrait [Russell] and Biography - Horatio Hutchinson (p413-417)
Efficiency of the Modern Standard of Foxhounds by William Fox-Russell (p417-422)
Haunts of Snipe and Woodcock by Henry Pilkington (p422-425)
The Amateur Rider and his Mounts (part 1) by Harding Cox (p425-429)
Catching Conger with Rod and Line by Frank Verney (p429-435)
Photograph [Verney]: *Two Conger Caught with Rod and Line* (facing p433)
How and Where to Hunt on £20 a Year by Claremont Clare (p436-439)
More Golf Problems by Gordon McPherson (p439-448)
Lithograph: *Some Noted Golf Club Badges* (on p441)
Photograph [Drake]: *James Sherlock* (on p443)

Photograph [Vandyke]: *George Duncan* (on p445)
Successful Sires of the Year by Archibald Charlton (p449-455)
Photograph [Rouch]: *William the Third* (facing p451)
Photograph [Rouch]: *John O'Gaunt* (facing p453)
Horse Racing and Horse Breeding (part 3) by William Tweedie (p455-460)
The Joys and the Songs of the Open Road by George Teasdale-Buckell (p460-463)
A Hundred Years Ago: Partridges from *The Sporting Magazine* (p464)
The Sportsman's Library: Reviews of *Good Sport with Famous Packs* by Cuthbert Bradley; *The King's Favourite* by Nat Gould; *War, Police and Watchdogs* by Edwin Richardson; *The Fisherman's Companion* by Edward le Breton-Martin; *A Natural Method of Training* by Edwin Checkley; *The Real Charlotte* by Edith Somerville; *A Vagabond in the Caucasus* by Stephen Graham; *A Gamekeeper's Notebook* by Owen Jones; *The Book of Migratory Birds* by William Halliday; *Anecdotes of Big Cats and Other Beasts* by David Wilson (p465-469)
Photograph [Firth]: *Shere Village* (facing p467)
Outlaws and Rebels by William Ogilvie (p470-472)
Charles Gillson by Edward Cuming (p472)
Our Van [inc. Newmarket Meetings; Brighton Autumn Handicap; Newbury Races; Quorn Hunt; Tedworth Hounds; Woodland Pytchley Hunt; Seavington Harriers] (p473-482)
Sporting Intelligence [inc. Carmarthenshire & Pembrokeshire Otter-Hounds; Hurlingham Polo Rules Committee; Oxford University Rowing; Hollingbury Park [Brighton] Golf Club; Obituaries of Leonard Roberts-West, John Maycock, William Clay, Arthur Turner, Francis Hatzfeldt, William Anderson and Francis Teck; North German Breeders Association] (p483-488)
Sporting Results (p488-492)

Joseph Shorthouse

273

Volume 95, January - June 1911

Issue 611 : January 1911

Portrait [Hailey] of Herbert Jones, jockey	Title page
Portrait [Faulkner] and Biography - George Ormsby-Gore	(p1-3)
Discipline In and Out of the Kennel by William Fox-Russell	(p3-7)
Famous Bags of Snipe by Abel Chapman	(p7-10)
The Amateur Rider and His Mounts (part 2) by Harding Cox	(p11-17)
Shore Shooters and Shore Shooting by Stanley Duncan	(p17-25)
Photograph: *A Shot From the Hut*	(facing p19)
Photograph: *Retrieved a Mile From Across the Mudflats*	(facing p19)
Photograph: *A Shore Shooters Bag*	(on p20)
Photograph: *Mallard and Sheld Duck*	(on p21)
How Shall we Test our Cricket by Herbert Hewett	(p25-27)
Gimcrack, Crab and Pietri by George Teasdale-Buckell	(p27-34)
Engraving [sculp. Roberts]: *Gimcrack when in Training*	(facing p29)
Engraving [sculp. Scott]: *Gimcrack as a Stallion*	(facing p31)
Oxford University Drag Hunt by Cameron Gull	(p35-40)
Photograph [Gillman]: *A Meet at Woodstock*	(facing p37)
Photograph [Gillman]: *Voltelin Heath*	(on p37)
Photograph [Gillman]: *The Pack*	(facing p39)
Photograph [Gillman]: *The New Kennels*	(facing p39)
About Dead Heats by William Scarth-Dixon	(p41-44)
Winter Evenings in London by Otho Paget	(p44-48)
A Hundred Years Ago: The Wiltshire Hunt from *The Sporting Magazine*	(p49)
The Sportsman's Library: Reviews of *The Unwritten Laws of Foxhunting* by Charles McNeill; *Live Stock Journal Almanac 1911* by James Sinclair; *Farm Stock One Hundred Years Ago* by Walter Gilbey; *The Life of Disraeli* by William Monypenny; *Encyclopaedia of Sports and Games* by Henry Howard; *The Game of Roulette* by Victor Silberer; *Deck and Home Golf* by John Macdonald; *With Boat and Gun in the Yangtze Valley* by Henling Wade; *The Golf Courses of the British Isles* by Bernard Darwin	(p50-58)
The Choice of a Country Residence by Athol Maudslay	(p58-60)
Ideal Physical Culture by Victor Holloway	(p60-63)
Our Van [inc. Lincoln Meeting; Grand Sefton Steeplechase; Manchester Handicap; Dumfriesshire Hunt; South Dorset Hounds; York & Ainsty Hunt]	(p63-72)
Sporting Intelligence [inc. University Sport; Calcutta Turf Club; Rules of Golf Committee; Spring Horse Shows; Obituaries of Ethel Crossman, Hugh Scott, Thomas Higgins, John Lawson, Joseph Houldsworth, Northey Hopkins, Jack White, Thomas Humber, Alderman Batchelor and Jem Mace; Biggleswade Harriers; Four Burrow Hunt; Argentine Jockey Club; New York Horse Show]	(p72-81)
Sporting Results	(p82)

* Edward Cuming relinquished the deputy editorial chair at the end of 1910 and the issue below was his successor's first effort. Changes are immediately noticeable especially in the writers of articles and the fact that most are named instead of hiding behind nom-de-plumes, nicknames or initials *

Issue 612 : February 1911

Portrait [Elliott] and Biography - Godfrey Morgan	(p83-86)
Pheasants: High or Low by Harcourt Gold	(p86-88)
The Scottish Hunt by Ruaraidh Erskine	(p89-91)
The Sportsman in Corsica by John Dodington	(p91-95)

A New Yacht Racing Class by Francis Cooke (p95-97)

The Unsuspected Drag by Thomas Dale (p97-101)

Photograph [Elliott]: *Reginald Doherty* (facing p103)

[Obituary] Reginald Doherty by George Burrows (p102-103)

Gypsy Jack by Finch Mason (p104-108)

The Cougar by Lincoln Wilbar (p109-114)

Photograph [Wilbar]: *The Cougar in Action* (facing p111)

An Australian Impression of Hunting by Dirk Swincott (p114-119)

A Relic of a Decayed Industry by Arthur Sharp (p119-123)

Photograph [Sharp]: *Duck Decoy as Seen From Bank* (on p121)

Photograph [Sharp]: *Sight House of Decoy Showing Peephole* (on p122)

Some Big Fish Records (part 1) by Ernest Phillips (p124-128)

Some Thoughts on Wild Duck by Alan Haig-Brown (p129-131)

The Sportsman's Library: Reviews of *Farm Stock One Hundred Years Ago* by Walter Gilby; *Life Story of a Tiger* by Augustus Mockler-Ferryman; *The Car* by Geoffrey Osborn; *The Hunting Horn* by Ludovick Cameron (p131-133)

Lithograph: *A Stage Waggon a Hundred Years Ago* (facing p133)

Three Pillars of the Turf (part 1) by George Teasdale-Buckell (p134-140)

Engraving: *James Merry* (on p135)

Photograph [Sherborn]: *Matthew Dawson* (on p136)

Engraving: *Robert Peck* (on p136)

Engraving [pinx. Hall]: *Thormanby* (on p138)

A Hundred Years Ago: Obituary of Peter Beckford from *The Sporting Magazine* (p140-141)

Rough Shooting by Richard Black (p141-145)

Lord Lonsdale and the Cottesmore by Himself (p146-148)

Our Van [inc. National Hunt Committee; Midlands Steeplechase; Kempton Park Meeting; Meynell Hunt; Waterford Hounds; Hailsham Harriers; Warwickshire Beagles; Obituaries of Gilbert Willoughby, Arthur Wrottesley, Walter Corbet, William Woddrop, William Parkin, Henry Carden, John Murphy, William Wood, Francis Grant, Alfred Brocklehurst, John Morgan, Rose Price, James Bullingham, John Carr, Luther Martin, John Morris, George Charleton and Harry Lush] (p149-156)

Sporting Intelligence [inc. University Rugby; Country Polo Players; Spring Horse Shows; Welsh Golf; Obituaries of Frederick Whitting, James Harradine, Charles McJerrow, Andrew Mair, Mildred Meux, Thomas Blinks, Thomas Kirkwood, John Widger, Joseph Pratt, Thomas Brocklebank, Alexander Rowley and William Thurlow; Chiddingfold Hunt; German Derby; Russian Wrestling] (p157-165)

Sporting Results (p165-166)

Issue 613 : March 1911

Portrait [Dickinson] and Biography - Robert Brassey (p167-169)

On Nerves in Sport by Claye Shaw (p169-175)

The Old Pytchley Sort by Thomas Dale (p175-180)

The Old Order and the New in Grouse Shooting by William Tweedie (p180-182)

Amongst Cornish Conger: A Night in the Open by Edwin Arnold (p183-186)

Three Pillars of the Turf (part 2) by George Teasdale-Buckell (p186-192)

Engraving: *Joseph Hawley* (on p187)

Engraving [pinx. Hall]: *Pero Gomez* (facing p189)

Engraving [pinx. Hall]: *Blue Gown* (facing p189)

Engraving [pinx. Hall]: *Thomas Chaloner* (on p190)

Engraving: *Richard Naylor* (on p191)

Forty Minutes on the Grass [verses] by William Ogilvie (p192-193)

The English Foxhound Abroad by William Fox-Russell (p194-197)

Early Trouting in the West Country by Paul Taylor (p197-199)

A Chat over Wisden's Cricketers' Almanack by Herbert Hewett (p199-203)

[Obituary] A Famous Yacht Master: Charles Barr by Francis Cooke (p203-204)

Snipe Shooting by George Garrow-Green (p205-207)

Field Trials by Frederick Gresham (p207-211)

Engraving: *Partridge Shooting One Hundred Years Ago* (on p209)

Some Big Fish Records (part 2) by Ernest Phillips (p211-215)

A Hundred Years Ago: A Wager from *The Sporting Magazine* (p216-217)

Three Notable Days for Grayling by James Englefield (p217-218)

Alcibiade's Grand National by Finch Mason (p219-222)

The Sportsman's Library: Reviews of *The Polo and Riding Pony Stud Book* by Walter
  Buckmaster; *A Great Coup* by Nat Gould; *Swiss Mountain Climbs* by
  George Abraham, (p222-223)

[Review] *The Broad Highway* by Jeffrey Farnol (p223-227)

Some Deals in Horseflesh by William Smith (p227-230)

Our Van [inc. Staffordshire Handicap; Windsor Racing; Newbury Meeting; Tipperary Hunt;
  New Forest Hounds; Silverton Hunt; Hurworth Hounds] (p231-241)

Sporting Intelligence [inc. University Rowing; Aquatic Notes; Hurlingham Polo Committee;
  Blackpool North Shore Golf Club; Obituaries of Frederick Taylor, David
  Wauchope, Ralph Slazenger, Arthur Birch, George Grey, Edward Flint, Frank
  Ritchie, Fenwick Cumberlege, John Mirehouse, John Christy, Harry Parry,
  Gordon Smith, Thomas French, Charles Dilke, William Wills, James Gardner,
  Philip Martineau, Harry Graham and William Walker; Royal Thames Yacht Club;
  Frog Shooting in Canada; American Wrestling] (p241-251)

Sporting Results (p252)

Issue 614 : April 1911

Portrait [Maull] and Biography - Laurence Dundas (p253-254)

What Length Do You Ride by Maxwell McTaggart (p255-259)

Engraving [sculp. Babbage]: *Horse and Rider* (on p259)

Nimrod's Life and Times by Aylmer Field (p260-270)

Engraving [pinx. Maclise]: *Nimrod* (on p261)

Lithograph [pinx. Maclise]: *Nimrod* (on p263)

Lithograph [sculp. Lewis]: *Melton Breakfast - Nimrod Writing* [incorrectly captioned] (facing p265)

Lithograph [pinx. Caldecott]: *Nimrod's Birthplace* (facing p267)

Photograph: *Nimrod's Snuffbox and Tobacco Jar* (facing p267)

The Coming Yachting Season by Francis Cooke (p271-273)

What the Fisherman Owes His Gillie by Frederick Aflalo (p273-277)

The Effect of Motor Traction on Country Life by Athol Maudslay (p277-281)

The Last of the Buggies by William St.Aubyn (p281-286)

All the Running [verses] by William Ogilvie (p286-287)

How Railway Companies Help Sport by George Burrows (p288-294)

A Hundred Years Ago: Shotgun Safety from *The Sporting Magazine* (p295-297)

Lithograph: *The King of the Kennel* (facing p297)

[Review] Sporting Illustrations: *Twenty Sporting Designs* by George Fothergill (p297-299)

Lithograph [pinx. Fothergill]: *Peterborough Weathergage* (on p298)

Spring Horse Shows Reviewed by Gerald Ricardo (p299-307)

Photograph [Babbage]: *Berrill* (facing p303)

Photograph [Babbage]: *Monarch* (facing p305)

Polo Prospects by Archibald Charlton (p308-309)

March Evenings in London by Otho Paget (p309-314)

The Sportsman's Library: Reviews of *The Mystery of Golf* by Arnold Haultain; *Deer Hunting
  in Norfolk* by John Harvey, and *The Green Book of London Society* by Douglas
  Sladen (p314-316)

The Charm and Development of Bowls by James Manson (p316-320)

Our Van [inc. Gatwick Meeting; Salford Handicap Steeplechase; Cheltenham Racing; Fernie's Hunt; Essex Staghounds; Grafton Hunt] (p321-328)

Sporting Intelligence [inc. University Matches; Mid-Surrey Golf Club; Altcar Coursing Club; French Greyhound Club; Fly Fishers' Club; Obituaries of William Murdoch and George Nichols] (p329-334)

Sporting Results (p335-338)

Issue 615 : May 1911

Portrait [Vowles] and Biography - William Waldegrave (p339-340)

How do we Stand for Stayers by Seymour Ramsdale (p341-344)

The Mental Aspect of Golf by Claye Shaw (p344-350)

Epsom, Durdans, Amato and The Pump by George Teasdale-Buckell (p350-355)

Photograph: *The Amato Inn at Epsom* (facing p353)

Photograph: *The Grave of Amato* (facing p353)

Photograph: *The Grave of Illuminata* (on p353)

Yachting Season Prospects by Francis Cooke (p356-357)

Otter Hunting in South Devon (part 1) by Edward Davies (p358-363)

Horsemanship at the International Show by John Swire (p363-364)

Harvey Covey: An Old Time Jockey by Gerald Ricardo (p364-367)

Photograph [Hawkins]: *Harvey Covey* (on p365)

Under the Circumstances by Hugh Henry (p367-371)

Amateur Golf International Statistics by Harold Macfarlane (p372-376)

A Hundred Years Ago: Horse Poisoning from *The Sporting Magazine* (p377)

Search for the Champion County by Harold Hewett (p378-383)

At Cheltenham Once More by Finch Mason (p383-386)

Polo Notes and News by Archibald Charlton (p386-389)

The Sportsman's Library: Reviews of *Rugby School* by Hill Hardy; *Modern Development of the Dry Fly* by Frederick Halford; *Agricultural Writers 1200-1800* by Donald McDonald; *The Adventures of James Capen Adams* by Theodore Hittell; *Horse Mastership* by Frederick MacCabe (p389-395)

Photograph: *The Webb Ellis Tablet at Rugby School* (on p390)

Engraving [pinx. Babbage]: *The Epitome of the Art of Husbandry* (facing p393)

On Building Stables by William Malden (p395-400)

Sporting Days in Ireland by Henry Pilkington (p400-403)

Cheetah Hunting in India by Frederick Joy (p403-406)

Our Van [inc. Lincolnshire Handicap; Liverpool Meeting; Warwick Races; Cheshire Hunt; North Warwickshire Hounds] (p406-416)

Photograph [Rouch]: *Glenside* (facing p409)

Sporting Intelligence [inc. University Boat Race; Press Golfing Society; East Herts Golf Club; Dibbing; Hounds in America; Hallamshire Cross-Country Harriers; Obituaries of John Hickey, Richard Botterill and Percy Dale; Easton Fox Harriers; Army Rugby Cup; Chester Race Company] (p416-423)

Sporting Results (p424-426)

Engraving [sculp. Babbage]: *Horse at Auction* (on p426)

Issue 616 : June 1911

Portrait [Montano] and Biography - Everard Hambro (p427-428)

International Horse Show by Maxwell McTaggart (p429-433)

Engraving [sculp. Babbage]: *Equestrian Jumping* (on p433)

[Adam] Lindsay Gordon and His Friends by Edith Humphris (434-441)

Lithograph: *Lindsay Gordon* (on p435)

Photograph: *Jem Edwards* (on p436)

Photograph: *Thomas Pickernell* (on p437)

Photograph [Williams]: *Jem Edwards' Grave and Stephen Miles* (on p438)

Ascots of the Past by Eric Wood (p442-453)

Lithograph: *The Ascot Cup* (on p443)

Engraving: *An Early Grandstand* (on p444)

Lithograph: *The Duke of Cumberland* (on p445)

Lithograph: *Queen Anne* (on p446)

Lithograph: *The Oatlands Stakes* (on p448)

[Review] *The History of the Linlithgow and Stirlingshire Hunt* by James Rutherford (p454-458)

Lithograph [pinx. Gordon]: *William Ramsay* (facing p454)

Lithograph [pinx. Nasmyth]: *The Death of the Fox* (facing p456)

Homing Pigeons: Their Racing Value by Percy Percival (p458-462)

Photograph: *Red Cheq Cock* (on p460)

The Turf Poisoners by Henry Archer (p462-468)

Engraving: *Daniel Dawson* (on p464)

Sport and Country Life at the Academy by George Burrows (p468-471)

At the Beginning of the Dry-Fly Season by James Englefield (p472-475)

Otter Hunting: Opening of the Season by Ludovick Cameron (p475-477)

The Melton Hunt Breakfast by Willoughby Maycock (p477-482)

Polo *En Passant* by Archibald Charlton (p482-485)

Balls and No-Balls by Herbert Hewett (p485-488)

A Hundred Years Ago: Prize Fighting from The Sporting Magazine (p489-490)

The Sportsman's Library: Review of *King Edward VII as a Sportsman* by Alfred Watson (p490-493)

Coronation Nights in London by Otho Paget (p493-497)

Herbert Jones: The King's Jockey by George Burrows (p497-498)

Our Van [inc. Kempton Park Meeting; Hyde Park Plate; Hurst Park Races; Lamerton Foxhounds; Avon Vale Hunt; Tiverton Staghounds; Galway Blazers] (p498-505)

Sporting Intelligence [inc. Cambridge University Boat Club; Lytham St.Anne's Golf Club; Public Schools Racquets Championship; Spey Bay Golf Club] (p505-509)

Sporting Results (p510)

Volume 96 : July - December 1911

Issue 617 : July 1911

Portrait [Bourne] of John Turner, huntsman Title page

Engraving [sculp. Babbage]: *Mare and Foal* (on Illustrations page)

Portrait [Debenham] and Biography - Walpole Greenwell (p1-2)

The Goodwood Cup by George Teasdale-Buckell (p3-13)

Engraving: *The Goodwood Cup* (on p3)

Engraving [pinx. Herring]: *Priam* (on p5)

Engraving [pinx. Hall]: *Van Tromp* (on p7)

Engraving [pinx. Hall]: *Vauban* (on p9)

Horsemanship in the Seventeenth Century by Eric Parker (p13-16)

King George as a Country Gentleman by Edward Cuming (p17-19)

The Riddle of the Rainbow Trout by Ernest Phillips (p19-24)

Small Yacht Racing in the Solent by George Hopcroft (p24-28)

Lithograph [pinx. Hopcroft]: *The First Match of the Season* (facing p25)

Lithograph [pinx. Hopcroft]: *A Trial Trip* (facing p25)

An Irish Country Show by Henry Pilkington (p28-31)

The Year's Racquets by Harold Rudd (p31-35)

The Month's Polo by Archibald Charlton (p35-40)

The Childwickbury Stud by Sidney Galtrey (p41-48)

Photograph [Rouch]: *Sunstar* (facing p43)

Photograph [Fall]: *Your Majesty* (facing p45)
Current Cricket by Herbert Hewett (p48-53)
Openboat Racing by Francis Cooke (p53-55)
A Hundred Years Ago: Wroxham Water Cup from *The Sporting Magazine* (p55-56)
The Idylls of Angling by Alan Johnson (p56-62)
The Sportsman's Library: Reviews of *The Aeroplane* by Claude Grahame-White and *Yacht Racing for Amateurs* by Francis Cooke (p63-66)
Photograph: *King Edward in Hunting Costume* (facing p65)
Photograph: *King Edward and Horse* (facing p65)
Photograph: *An Evening Flight* (on p65)
Photograph: *Flying at Dusk* (on p66)
Our Van [inc. Newmarket Meeting; Bath Racing; Great Northern Handicap; Coronation Epsom Week; Reigate Hound Show; Devon & Somerset Staghounds; Masters of Foxhounds Association] (p67-76)
Sporting Intelligence [inc. Jesus College Cambridge Rowing; Regatta Previews; Rules of Golf Committee; Coombe Hill Golf Club; Obituaries of Edward Mills Grace and William Dunn; Surrey Lawn Tennis; Shooting in Hungary] (p76-82)
Sporting Results (p82-84)

Issue 618 : August 1911

Portrait [Vandyke] and Biography - John Bankes (p85-86)
Yacht Racing by Athol Maudslay (p87-89)
The Sea Angler's Bird Friends by Frederick Aflalo (p90-92)
Sport and the Scottish Peasant by Ruaraidh Erskine (p93-97)
Racing in British Guiana by William Benson (p98-102)
Photograph: *Grandstand, Durban Racecourse, Demerara* (on p98)
Photograph: *Ben Bubble* (on p99)
Photograph: *Creole Bohemian* (on p100)
Otter Hunting in South Devon (part 2) by Edward Davies (p102-107)
Current Cricket by Herbert Hewett (p107-112)
Idlewood [verses] by William Ogilvie (p112)
The Wet-Fly Angler in August by Arthur Sharp (p113-115)
Eccentricities of Spin and Swerve in Golf, Cricket and Lawn Tennis by Percy Vaile (p116-124)
Photograph: *How Spin of Pull is Obtained* (on p118)
Polo *En Passant* by Archibald Charlton (p124-129)
Peterborough Foxhound Show by William Scarth-Dixon (p129-136)
Lithograph [pinx. Bradley]: *Meynell Waverley* (on p131)
International and Royal Shows by Gerald Ricardo (p137-143)
Photographs: *Geoffrey Brooke on Alice* (facing p139)
Photograph [Rouch]: *Flame* (facing p141)
Photograph [Rouch]: *Gaythorn* (facing p141)
International Yacht Racing by Francis Cooke (p143-145)
A Hundred Years Ago: Grouse Shooting from *The Sporting Magazine* (p145-146)
On Matters Shooting by Frank Bonnett (p146-152)
Our Van [inc. Manchester Cup; Gatwick Races; Ascot Meeting; Northumberland Plate; Alexandra Park Racing; Bibury Club Meeting] (p153-159)
Sporting Intelligence [inc. University Sport; Henley Regatta; Irish Amateur Golf Championship; Sandwich Golf Club; Obituaries of Harold Steel and George Race; Wimbledon Lawn Tennis Championships] (p160-163)
Sporting Results (p164-166)

Issue 619 : September 1911

Portrait [Elliott] and Biography - Edward Stern — (p167-168)
The Chivalry of the Turf by Finch Mason — (p169-171)
Reminiscences of Sport in Ireland by Henry Pilkington — (p171-174)
[Obituary] A Veteran of the Chase: George Race — (p174-179)
Photograph [Mooring]: *George Race* — (on p175)
The Cultivation of Wild Duck by Harwood Brierley — (p179-184)
After Elephant in Sierra Leone and French Guinea by George Wills — (p184-191)
Photograph: *A Kill to be Proud of* — (on p187)
Foxhunting and the Humanities (part 1) by George Powell — (p191-194)
The Angler and the Otter by Eric Parker — (p194-197)
Some Effects of Racing by Gerald Ricardo — (p197-201)
A Hundred Years Ago: Partridge Shooting from *The Sporting Magazine* — (p201-202)
The England Team for Australia by Herbert Hewett — (p202-206)
The Partridge by Frank Bonnett — (p206-212)
Amato by George Burrows — (p213)
Engraving [sculp. Powell]: *Amato* — (on p213)
County Cricket by Herbert Hewett — (p214-216)
Horses Fighting by George Burrows — (p217-218)
Lithograph [pinx. Laporte]: *Arab Horses Fighting* — (on p217)
Polo by Archibald Charlton — (p218-223)
The Sportsman's Library: Reviews of *Cricket Hints for Youngsters* by Herbert Farmer; *The Simplicity of the Golf Swing* by James Macbeth; *Men of the Day* by Leslie Ward, and *Angling for Coarse Fish* by Charles Cook — (p223-225)
The Preservation of Soaks and Marshes by William Stewart — (p225-229)
Our Van [inc. Leopardstown Meeting; Ayr Racing; Gratwicke Stakes; Sussex Handicap; Exmoor Staghunting; New Forest Hounds; Southdown Hunt; Belvoir Foxhounds] (p230-240)
Sporting Intelligence [inc. Grouse Reports; Molesey Regatta; Wildernesse Golf Club; Obituaries of Charles Bristowe, Patrick Cowley and Edward Norris; Redcar Clerk of Course] — (p240-244)
Sporting Results — (p244-246)
Engraving [sculp. Babbage]: *Another Mare and Foal* — (on p246)

Issue 620 : October 1911

Portrait [Elliott] and Biography - Charles Pulley — (p247-249)
Racing in Upper Burma by Charles Higgins — (p249-253)
The Cost of Yachting by Francis Cooke — (p253-254)
Recollections of a Gallant Soldier and Sportsman by Arthur Meyrick — (p255-258)
Photograph [South]: *George Wombwell* — (on p255)
Reflections on the County Cricket Championship by Otho Paget — (p259-262)
Dry Fly Fishing in an Abnormal Summer by James Englefield — (p263-264)
Sport in the Rocky Mountains by Joseph Adams — (p265-273)
Photograph: *Duck Shooting in Saskatchewan* — (facing p266)
Photograph: *Buffaloes in the Rockies* — (facing p266)
Photograph: *On the Trail to Mount Robson* — (on p269)
Photograph: *Camp Scene on Grand Fish River* — (on p271)
Public School Cricket of the Year by Abel Chapman — (p274-277)
Pheasant Shooting and its Future by Eric Smyth — (p278-283)
A Hundred Years Ago: Pugilism from *The Sporting Magazine* — (p283-284)
Polo by Archibald Charlton — (p284-288)
Foxhunting and the Humanities (part 2) by George Powell — (p288-291)
A Morning after Bear in the Central Provinces — (p292-296)
Personal Observations of Birds by William Halliday — (p297-300)

Dublin Horse Show Reflections by William Scarth-Dixon (p300-302)

Cricket of 1911 by Herbert Hewett (p303-308)

Autumn Grayling and the Trout Fisher by Arthur Sharp (p308-311)

The Sportsman's Library: Reviews of *Motor Routes of England [West] and Wales* by Gordon
        Home; *Stalks in the Himalaya* by Edward Stebbings (p312)

Our Van [inc. Leicester Meeting; Stockton Races; Yorkshire Oaks; West Cumberland Hounds;
        Quorn Hunt] (p313-323)

Sporting Intelligence [inc. Canadian Drag Hunts; Welsh Golf Championship; Fly Fishers'
        Club; Obituaries of William Warner, Charles Lock, Robert Brooks, William
        Williams and William Carruthers; English Sculling Championship] (p323-327)

Sporting Results (p327-328)

Issue 621 : November 1911

Portrait [Lafayette] and Biography - Roylance Court (p329-331)

Modern Foxhunting by Thomas Dale (p332-337)

Yachting in 1911 by Francis Cooke (p337-342)

White and Scarlet [verses] by William Ogilvie (p342-343)

The Red Tag for Grayling and Dace by Paul Taylor (p343-344)

Hunt Changes by Edward Cuming (p345-362)

Photograph [Bassano]: *William Wailes-Fairbairn* (York & Ainsty) (on p347)

Photograph [Bullingham]: *Harry Malet* (Tedworth) (on p348)

Photograph [Mudford]: *Ian Heathcote-Amory* (Tiverton) (on p349)

Photograph [West]: *Arthur Blakiston* (Lamerton) (on p350)

Photograph: *Norman Loder* (Southdown) (on p351)

Photograph [Bartlett]: *Herbert Connop* (United) (on p352)

Photograph [Good]: *Archibald Pape* (Silverton) (on p353)

Photograph [Russell]: *John Molyneux-McCowen* (Chiddingfold) (on p354)

Photograph [Willoughby]: *George Tongue* (East Essex) (on p355)

The Cheshire Hunting Poet [Rowland Egerton-Warburton] by Arthur Lainson (p362-366)

Some Notes on Foxhunting by Eric Parker (p366-368)

[Review] *Baily's Hunting Directory 1911-12* [with Masters' Autographs] by Edward Cuming (p369-371)

A Hundred Years Ago: Horse Breaker from *The Sporting Magazine* (p372)

Top Hamper (part 1) by Athol Maudslay (p373-375)

The Passing of the Big Horn by Lincoln Wilbar (p376-380)

The Rabbit by Alan Haig-Brown (p380-382)

Mild Sport in Northern Natal by Rosamond Southey (p382-385)

The Sportsman's Library: Reviews of *Golf for the Late Beginner* by Henry Hughes; *Partridge
        and Partridge Manors* by Aymer Maxwell; *Sea Fishing* by Charles Minchin (p386-387)

Sir George Wombwell and the Grand Military Cup by George Burrows (p387-388)

Autumn Evenings in London by Otho Paget (p388-393)

Late Polo Season Renewed by Archibald Charlton (p393-396)

Photograph: *Some Different Styles of Polo Sticks* (on p395)

Our Van [inc. Doncaster Meeting; Leicester Racing; Ayrshire Handicap; Nottingham Races;
        South & West Wilts Hunt; South Oxfordshire Hounds; Obituary of Richard
        Bower; Empire Swimming Championships] (397-407)

Sporting Intelligence [inc. Kintore Golf Club; Purchase of Hoylake Golf Course; Obituaries
        of Thomas Sherman, Thomas Rider, George Verrall, Edward Whymper, Rajendra
        Cooch-Behar, Henry Tomlinson and Charles Lawes-Wittewronge; Tully Stud;
        Pytchley Hounds; Blencathra Hunt] (p407-411)

Sporting Results (p411-412)

Issue 622 : December 1911

Portrait [Baker] and Biography - Herbert Straker   (p413-415)
On Temperament in Sport by Claye Shaw   (p415-418)
Hunting Songs by Orton Bradley   (p419-427)
The Racing Season of 1911 by Thomas Pinch   (p428-435)
Photograph [Russell]: *Edward Stanley*   (on p429)
Photograph [Rouch]: *Willonyx*   (facing p431)
Photograph: *Charles Howard*   (on p431)
Photograph [Allen]: *Samuel Darling*   (on p432)
Photograph [Hailey]: *Charles Trigg*   (on p434)
Polo Legislation by Archibald Charlton   (p435-437)
Swallows by Walter Gilbey   (p438-441)
Happenings in the Hunting Field by Finch Mason   (p441-443)
Successful Thoroughbred Sires by Abel Chapman   (p444-451)
Photograph [Hailey]: *Tredennis*   (facing p447)
Photograph [Rouch]: *Forfarshire*   (facing p449)
Hunt Presentations [with Autographs] by Edward Cuming   (p451-457)
Photograph: *George Walters*, Huntsman, Beaufort's Hounds   (on p454)
Photograph: *Edwin Short*, Huntsman, Cheshire Hunt   (on p455)
Trout in the Bredheimsvand by Abel Chapman   (p457-462)
How Billy Scott Lost and Found His Nerve by Hugh Henry   (p462-468)
A Hundred Years Ago: Packs of Harriers from *The Sporting Magazine*   (p468-469)
The Sportsman's Library: Reviews of *Baily's Hunting Directory* by Edward Cuming; *Essays on Various Subjects* by John Doyle; *The Adventures of James Capen Adams* by Theodore Hittell; *Dan Russel the Fox* by Edith Somerville; *My Book of Little Dogs* by Townend Barton; *Casuals in the Caucasus* by Agnes Herbert; *An Open Creel* by Hugh Sheringham   (p469-471)
John Turner by George Burrows   (p472)
Our Van [inc. Cheveley Park Stakes; Lingfield Meeting; Rutland Handicap; Newbury Races; Morpeth Hunt; South Dorset Hounds; Heythrop Hunt]   (p472-479)
Sporting Intelligence [inc. Oxford University Athletic Club; Rowing Reports; Walton Heath Golf Club; West Sussex Hunt; Obituaries of William Onslow, Herbert Lewis, James Williams and William Delacombe; Wilfred Rhodes Benefit]   (p479-483)
Sporting Results   (p483-484)

Volume 97, January - June 1912

Issue 623 : January 1912

Portrait [Hawkins] of Sidney Barnes, cricketer   Title page
Portrait [Florian] and Biography - John Heathcote-Amory   (p1-3)
Stray Leaves of Sport (part 1): Eton in the Sixties by Finch Mason   (p3-8)
Lithographs [pinx. Mason]: *Eton Personalities*   (facing p5)
Lithograph [pinx. Mason]: *The Wise Man of Eton*   (facing p7)
Yacht Racing Rules by Francis Cooke   (p9-11)
Vanguard and His National by Gerald Ricardo   (p11-15)
Lithograph [pinx. Sextie]: *Vanguard*   (facing p13)
[Review] *Billiards* by Edward Mardon reviewed by John Buchanan   (p15-19)
Woodcock by Frank Bonnett   (p20-28)
Photograph [Grabham]: *Woodcock on Nest Amongst Dog's-Mercury*   (on p21)
Photograph [Grabham]: *Woodcock on Nest Among Dead Bracken*   (on p23)
Photograph [Grabham]: *Nest and Eggs of Woodcock*   (on p24)
Photograph [Grabham]: *Woodcock on Nest Amongst Bluebells*   (on p25)

Top Hamper (part 2) by Athol Maudslay (p28-30)

Sports of the Multitude by Frederick Aflalo (p30-34)

To A Favourite Retriever [verses] by Alan Haig-Brown (p34)

The Sportsman's Library: Reviews of *Live Stock Journal Almanac 1912* by James Sinclair; *A Winter Sport Book* by Reginald Cleaver; *Modern Polo* by Edward Miller; *The Money Moon* by Jeffery Farnol; *Vinton's Show Record 1911* by George Burrows; *The Phantom Horse* by Nat Gould; *Tommy White-Tag the Fox* by Francis Pitt; *London Stories* by Wilfred Whitten; *My Guest of the Arab Horse* by Homer Davenport; *Yachting and Cruising for Amateurs* by Frank Cowper; *Babes in the African Wood* by Gorell Barnes; *Derby Chart* by Edward Moorhouse; *Rifle, Rod and Spear in the East* by Edward Durand; *The Complete Billiard Player* by Charles Roberts; *From Pillar to Post* by Cecil Lowther; *The Golfer's Pocket Tip Book* by George Fox; *Notes on Shoeing for Horse Owners* by Victor Scratchley; *Sport on the Rivieras* by Eustace Reynolds-Ball; *River and Sea Fishing in the South of Europe* by Charles Payton; *Letters From China* by Sarah Conger; *The Book of the Horse* by Douglas Phillott; *Tee Shots and Others* by Bernard Darwin; *An Angler at Large* by William Cane; *Fleming's Veterinary Obstetrics* by John Craig; *My Life Among the Wild Birds in Spain* by Willoughby Verner (p35-42)

A Sportsman [verses] by Michael Hope (p43)

The Martin by Walter Gilbey (p44)

Photograph: *The Martin* (on p44)

A Hundred Years Ago: Rifle Shooting from *The Sporting Magazine* (p45-46)

Marylebone Cricket Club Team in Australia by Herbert Hewett (p46-48)

The Rural Exodus of Sports and Pastimes by Henry Pilkington (p49-53)

Lithograph [pinx. Towne]: *Newton Races 1831* (facing p55)

[Review] *Animal Painters of England* by Walter Gilbey (p55)

The Australian Horse-Breaker by William Ogilvie (p56-60)

Winter Nights in London by Otho Paget (p61-63)

[Review] The Rule of the River: *The Gentle Art* by Henry Lamond (p63-64)

Our Van [inc. Lincoln Meeting; Aintree Racing; Midland Counties Handicap; Cottesmore Hunt; Tiverton Foxhounds; Ledbury Hunt Committee; Grove Hunt] (p65-71)

Sporting Intelligence [inc. Christ Church College Football; Hurlingham Polo Fixtures; Croham Hurst Golf Club; Gimcrack Club Dinner; Worcestershire County Cricket Club; Obituaries of William Cowell-Davies, Cuthbert Quilter, James Trotter, William Jones, James Cole, George Coatsworth, James Daly, Henry Beresford, William Grantham, Henry Ingilby, Hubert Oxley, Robert Weiss, George Lewis, John Hoskyns, Frederick Thellusson and Samuel Sadler; Nova Scotia Moose Hunting] (p71-79)

Sporting Results (p79-80)

Issue 624 : February 1912

Portrait [Dickinson] and Biography - John Curre (p81-82)

The Development of Racecourses by Gerald Ricardo (p83-96)

Engraving: *Fear Nought* (on p85)

Engraving: *An Old Stud Card* (facing p87)

Engraving [pinx. Chalon]: *Quiz* (facing p89)

Engraving [pinx. Corbould]: *Oatland Stakes at Ascot* (facing p89)

Lithograph [pinx. Towne]: *Maghull Racecourse* (facing p93)

Engraving [pinx. Turner]: *Effie Deans* (facing p95)

Engraving [pinx. Hall] *Rhedycina* (facing p95)

Olympic Yacht Races by Francis Cooke (p96-98)

The Grudge in Shooting by Lincoln Wilbar (p98-103)

February Pike by Ernest Phillips (p103-106)

The Dogs of St.Bernard Hospice by Charles Batchelder (p106-111)

Photograph [McLeish]: *A Monk of St.Bernard with Dog* (facing p109)

Photograph [McLeish]: *The Summit of the Great St.Bernard Pass* (facing p111)

Stray Leaves of Sport (part 2): Hunting by Finch Mason (p111-118)

Lithographs [pinx. Mason]: *Old Days in the Vale of Aylesbury* (facing p115)

Lithograph [pinx. Mason]: *After a Run With the Baron - At Leighton Station* (facing p117)

A Hundred Years Ago: A Chase from *The Sporting Magazine* (p119-120)

Marylebone Cricket Club Cricketers in Australia by Herbert Hewett (p120-123)

Light Horse Shows by Merrik Burrell (p123-125)

The Sportsman's Library: Reviews of *An Introduction to Foxhunting* by Edward Hobson; *Reminiscences of An Old 'Un* by Frank Streatfeild; *The Mahatma and the Hare* by Rider Haggard; *The Practical Science of Billiards* by Charles Western; *Heroes and Heroines of the Grand National* by Finch Mason; *A Yachtswoman's Cruises* by Maude Speed; *An Angler at Large* by William Caine (p126-129)

Two Masters of the Circus: Astley and Ducrow by Forbes Sieveking (p129-136)

[Review] *Ranching, Sport and Travel* by Thomas Carson (p136-139)

Reynard [verses] by Alan Haig-Brown (p139)

The Possibilities of Fen Shooting by John Harvey (p140-142)

The Schooling Ground [verses] by William Ogilvie (p142)

Our Van [inc. National Hunt Rules; Nottingham Meeting; Didcot Handicap; Belvoir Hunt; Ward Union Hounds; Essex Staghounds; Hertfordshire Hunt; East Devon Hounds] (p143-151)

Sporting Intelligence [inc. Cambridge University Ice-Hockey; Calcutta Golf; Spring Horse Shows; Uddingston Cricket Club; Obituaries of Taylor Sharpe, Thomas Holmes, James Clarke, Ernest Benzon, Reginald Duff, Charles Duncombe, William McGregor, James Newsome, Medhurst Troughton, Otway Cuffe and John Banwell; Boxing Champions' List] (p152-158)

Sporting Results (p158-160)

Issue 625 : March 1912

Portrait [Elliott] and Biography - Francis Champion (p161-163)

Foxhunters, Farmers and Damage by Thomas Dale (p163-167)

Stray Leaves of Sport (part 3): Racing by Finch Mason (p168-174)

Lithographs [pinx. Mason]: *Flowers Plucked at Newmarket in the Seventies* (facing p171)

Lithograph [pinx. Mason]: *The Glossy Peer* (facing p173)

The Handicapping of Yachts by Francis Cooke (p174-176)

Coverts for Sport by Frank Bonnett (p176-185)

Photograph [Smith]: *Good Timber but no Undergrowth* (on p179)

Photograph [Smith]: *A Well Protected Boundary* (on p181)

Photograph [Smith]: *The Ideal Place for Pheasants* (on p182)

Photograph [Smith]: *Good Cover - Bracken and Birch* (on p183)

[Obituary] John Maunsell-Richardson by Finch Mason (p185-190)

Photograph: *John Maunsell-Richardson in 1873* (on p187)

Photograph: *John Maunsell-Richardson in 1907* (on p189)

Granite and Tarred or Treated Roads by Athol Maudslay (p190-193)

Ladies and the Show Ring by Gerald Ricardo (p193-203)

Photograph [Rouch]: *Grand Viscount* (facing p195)

Photograph: *Catalina and Woodhatch Ruth* (facing p195)

Photograph: *Children's Class Competitors* (on p195)

Photograph: *Exhibiting Shetland Ponies in Harness* (on p196)

Photograph [Babbage]: *Bleddfa Telltale* (facing p196)

Photograph [Babbage]: *Halcyon* (facing p196)

Photograph [Rouch]: *Piccolo* (on p198)

Photograph: *Grey Mist* (facing p198)

Photograph: *Coaching Event at Ranelagh* (on p200)

Photograph: *Grey Ladies' Hacks - I* (facing p200)

Photograph: *Grey Ladies' Hacks - II* (facing p200)

Photograph [Lafayette]: *Blafor* (on p202)

The Ashes Recovered by Herbert Hewett (p204-207)

The Sportsman's Library: Reviews of *The Noble Science* by Delme Radcliff; *The Age and Growth of Salmon and Trout in Norway* by Knut Dahl; *Couch Fires and Primrose Ways* by Marriott Watson; *Practical Rabbit Keeping* by George Townsend; *Poems of the Chase* by Reginald Graham, (p207-210)

Foxhunting: The Old Order and the New (part 1) by Charles Batchelder (p211-213)

River Pollution and Sport by Arthur Sharp (p213-215)

A Hundred Years Ago: Hounds for Lisbon from *The Sporting Magazine* (p215-216)

Engraving [Babbage]: *Horse and Foal in Stables* (on p216)

An Old Man [verses] by William Ogilvie (p217)

Helping Out Light Horse Breeding by Wickham Boynton (p218-221)

Other Beasts of Burden by Abel Chapman (p222-228)

Our Van [inc. Windsor Meeting; Manchester Racing; Wigston Steeplechase; Romney Marsh Foxhounds; Belvoir Hounds; Cotley Harriers] (p228-233)

Sporting Intelligence [inc. Oxford University Beagles; Polo in India; German Open Golf; Torquay Golf Club; Gloucestershire County Cricket Club; Obituaries of William Oakeley, William von Schroder, Beiby Lawley, James Burroughes, Caroline Chaworth-Musters, Edward Ayers, William Ashe, Fletcher Cruickshank, James Joicey, James Meredith, William Marshall, Winifred Peck, George Johnstone and Henry Smurthwaite (*Baily's* contributor); Clifton Park Racecourse Company; Weald of Kent Harriers; West Cumberland Otterhounds; Chelmsford Golf Club] (p234-241)

Sporting Results (p242)

Issue 626 : April 1912

Portrait [Collings] and Biography - Charles Leveson-Gower (p243-244)

Some Likely Cheap Sires by Seymour Ramsdale (p244-248)

Brook Trouting in April by Arthur Sharp (p248-252)

The Yachting Season by Francis Cooke (p252-254)

Ancient Hackneys and an Author by Gerald Ricardo (p255-262)

Engraving: *The Darley Arabian* (facing p257)

Engraving [pinx. Hall]: *Flying Childers* (facing p259)

Engraving [pinx. Stubbs]: *Mambrino* (facing p259)

Engraving: *Hazard* (on p260)

Engraving: *Danegelt* (on p261)

Hands by Eric Parker (p262-264)

Billiard Breaks and Averages by John Buchanan (p264-269)

Our National Terriers by Harding Cox (p269-275)

Photographs: *National Terriers* (facing p271)

Farmers in the Hunting Field by Thomas Dale (p276-280)

Polo Prospects by Archibald Charlton (p281-283)

A Coursing Causerie by Hole O'Lyne (p284-287)

Engraving [sculp. Hunt]: *Captain Spencer and Sunbeam* (on p285)

Lithograph [pinx. Langley]: *Famous Greyhounds of the Past - King Pepin, Kitty Fisher, King Cob* (on p287)

The Flags on the Fences [verses] by William Ogilvie (p288)

A Hundred Years Ago: Prize Fighting from *The Sporting Magazine* (p289-290)

Gilbert Greenall's Mastership by Cuthbert Bradley (p290-293)

Engraving [pinx. Bradley]: *Frances Greenall riding Blue Skin* (on p291)

Some Thoughts on Cricket by Herbert Hewett (p293-296)

The Spring Horse Shows by George Teasdale-Buckell (p296-300)

Spring Evenings in London by Otho Paget (p300-305)

The Sportsman's Library: Reviews of *The Ox and its Kindred* by Richard Lydekker; *Athletics* by Edward Ryle; *Hockey* by Eric Green; *County Polo Association* by Walter Buckmaster and *The Art of Worm-Fishing* by Alexander Mackie (p305-306)

Notes on the Brown Hare by Abel Chapman (p307-312)

Our Van [inc. Thames Handicap Steeplechase; United Services Meeting; Ludlow Racing; York & Ainsty Hounds; Pytchley Hunt; Grafton Hounds] (p312-320)

Sporting Intelligence [inc. Oxford University Torpid Races; Belgian Golf; Obituaries of Percy Percival, William Storer, John Wingrove-Smith, Charles FitzGerald, George Pritchett, Hamilton Day and Miles I'Anson; American Athletics; East Kent Foxhounds] (p320-324)

Sporting Results (p325-326)

Issue 627 : May 1912

Portrait [Elliott] and Biography - Gordon Foster (p327-328)

Derby Tips and Tipsters by Henry Allen (p328-334)

Foxhunting: The Old Order and the New (part 2) by Charles Batchelder (p334-338)

Stray Leaves of Sport (part 4): Steeplechasing in the 60s & 70s by Finch Mason (p338-343)

Lithograph [pinx. Mason]: *Stable Companions* (facing p341)

Lithograph [pinx. Mason]: *The Grand National 1871* (on p342)

The May-Fly: Then and Now by Paul Taylor (p344-345)

The Show-Dog in the Field by Harding Cox (p346-350)

More Spring Horse Show Lessons by George Teasdale-Buckell (p350-357)

Photograph [Babbage]: *Kings Courtship* (facing p353)

Photograph [Babbage]: *The Snob* (facing p355)

Photograph [Babbage]: *Vivid* (facing p357)

Photograph [Babbage]: *Mavourneen II* (facing p357)

The Billiard Season 1911-12 by Sydenham Dixon (p357-361)

Photograph [Lafayette]: *John Nugent* (on p360)

Photograph: *Edgar Thomas, Henry Virr & Sydenham Dixon* (on p361)

Yachting in the Solent by Francis Cooke (p362-364)

The Whisperer [verses] by William Ogilvie (p365)

Triangular Cricket Contests by Herbert Hewett (p366-368)

A Hundred Years Ago: Quick Driving from *The Sporting Magazine* (p368-369)

Some Stories of the Grand National by Tom Pinch (p370-379)

Photograph [Hopkins]: *Arthur Nightingall* (on p371)

Photograph [Bourne]: *Roderic Owen* (on p371)

Photographs: *Grand National Winners* (facing p373)

Photograph [Rouch]: *Jerry M* (facing p379)

Photograph [Hughes]: *Charles Assheton-Smith* (on p379)

Roman [verses] by George Fothergill (p380-381)

Lithograph [pinx. Fothergill]: *Every Sweet Must Have Its Bitter* (on p380)

Lithograph [pinx. Fothergill]: *Better To Have It Than Hear Of It* (on p380)

Lithograph [pinx. Fothergill]: *Better To Sit Still Than Rise Up & Fall* (on p381)

Lithograph [pinx. Fothergill]: *Naithing Venture, Naithing Win* (on p381)

Our Roads by Athol Maudslay (p382-384)

Our Van [inc. Great Cheshire Steeplechase; Anglesey Point-to-Point Races; Rendlesham Hurdle Handicap; Bramham Moor Hunt; Norwich Staghounds; Puckeridge Hunt Point-to-Point Races] (p385-396)

Sporting Intelligence [inc. University Boat Race; Southern Counties Cross-Country
        Championship; North Warwickshire Hunt; Warwickshire County Cricket Club;
        Wembley Park Golf Club; Obituaries of Harry Peel, Charles Williams, Henry
        Crawshaw, Thomas Tristram, Alexander Kinloch, Ralph Ashton, Mervin
        Dunnington-Jefferson, Frank Riley-Smith, John Coupland, Horace Regnart,
        William James, James Coats, Thomas Winter, Louisa Scott, Frances
        Carrick-Buchanan, Charles Kinahan and Thomas Reibey; *Angler's Guide
        Annual*; North Durham Foxhounds]   (p396-403)
Sporting Results   (p404-406)

Issue 628 : June 1912

Portrait [Elliott] and Biography - William Dobson   (p407-408)
Thoughts on Riders and Horses by Finch Mason   (p409-412)
The Genial Guide by Lincoln Wilbar   (p412-416)
Stray Thoughts on Hunting by Frederick Aflalo   (p416-418)
International Yachting by Francis Cooke   (p419-421)
A Chat about Horses by Gerald Ricardo   (p421-427)
Engravings: *American Horses*   (facing p423)
A Shooting Expedition in Basutoland (part 1) by Mervyn Bosworth-Smith   (p428-433)
Bird Sanctuaries by Charles Batchelder   (p433-437)
Photograph [Webb]: *A Nightingale's Nest*   (on p434)
Photograph [Webb]: *A Robin's Nest*   (on p435)
Photograph [Webb]: *A Turtle Dove's Nest*   (on p436)
Photograph [Webb]: *A Blackbird's Nest*   (on p436)
Fresh Water Racing by George Hopcroft   (p437-441)
Lithograph [pinx. Hopcroft]: *Yachting on the Norfolk Broads*   (facing p439)
Lithograph [pinx. Hopcroft]: *Thames Half-Raters*   (facing p439)
Lithograph [pinx. Hopcroft]: *A Windermere Yacht of the Old Type*   (facing p439)
Summer Evenings in London by Otho Paget   (p441-445)
A Hundred Years Ago: A Shooting Match from *The Sporting Magazine*   (p445-446)
Sport and Country Life at the Royal Academy by George Burrows   (p446-450)
Polo by Archibald Charlton   (p450-454)
Test Match Cricket by Herbert Hewett   (p454-456)
Racquets by Harold Rudd   (p456-461)
Sidney Barnes by George Burrows   (p461-462)
Our Van [inc. Newbury Meeting; Lingfield Racing; Chester Cup; Berwickshire Hounds;
        Tipperary Hunt Master; South Devon Hunt]   (p463-470)
Sporting Intelligence [inc. University Golf; Wimbledon Town Golf Club; Obituaries of Hans
        Hamilton, Walter Clopton-Wingfield, Gerald Halifax, John Daley, Alfred Dryden,
        William Fife-Cookson, John Neligan and John Blacklock; Dartmoor Point-to-Point;
        Avon Vale Hunt; Royal Harwich Yacht Club]   (p470-476)
Sporting Results   (p476-478)

Volume 98, July - December 1912

Issue 629 : July 1912

Portrait of William Batchelor, huntsman   Title page
Portrait [Thomson] and Biography - Mark Lockwood   (p1-2)
Foxhounds: Their Development by Walter Gilbey   (p3-13)
Engraving [sculp. Babbage]: *Trojan*   (facing p5)
Lithograph: *Craven Vagabond*   (facing p9)
Lithograph [pinx. Bradley]: *Meynell Waverley*   (on p11)

A Recent Shooting Trip in Central Asia by Abbot Anderson (p13-19)
Photograph: *On The Way to Gulche* (on p14)
Photograph: *Descent of Kurdin Pass* (on p15)
Photograph: *Tien Shan - Glaciers at Top of Khmpura Sir* (on p16)
Photograph: *Ibex Shot in Agiars Nala* (on p17)
Photograph: *Tien Shan - Twelve Pointer Wapiti* (on p18)
Evolution of the Racing Yacht by Francis Cooke (p20-22)
Condition in Polo Ponies by Thomas Dale (p22-25)
What Should Pheasant-Rearing Cost by Frank Bonnett (p25-35)
Photograph [Grabham]: *Trap for Catching Up Wild Pheasants* (on p26)
Photograph [Grabham]: *Rearing Pens in the Field* (on p27)
Photograph [Grabham]: *Trap for Catching Up Pheasants* (on p28)
Photograph [Grabham]: *Young Pheasants in the Ride* (on p29)
Photograph [Smith]: *A Healthy Batch of Young Pheasants* (on p30)
Photograph [Grabham]: *Feeding the Young Pheasants* (on p31)
Photograph [Smith]: *Broody Hens Pegged Up for Their Morning Feed* (on p32)
A Shooting Expedition in Basutoland (part 2) by Mervyn Bosworth-Smith (p35-39)
A Hundred Years Ago: Game Association from *The Sporting Magazine* (p39-41)
Photograph: *Hatley Park, Cambridge* (facing p41)
The Sportsman's Library: Reviews of *Chances of Sports of Sorts* by Thomas St.Quintin; *Distance and Cross-Country Running* by John Hardwick; *The Economics of Feeding Horses* by Harold Woodruff; *Bowls* by George Burrows (p41-47)
Lithograph: *Valentine Baker* (facing p43)
Lithograph [pinx. Pil]: *Thomas St.Quintin* (facing p45)
Current Cricket by Herbert Hewett (p48-53)
Polo by Archibald Charlton (p54-59)
Photograph [Underwood]: *Sprite* (facing p57)
How a Busy Man may Keep Fit by Victor Howard (p59-61)
Snipe and Countryside Notes in Malabar by Charles Higgins (p61-64)
The Ponies [verses] by William Ogilvie (p64)
Our Van [inc. Kempton Park Meeting; York Races; Windsor Castle Handicap; West Carbery Hunt; Hares & Rabbits Act; Masters of Foxhounds Association; Obituaries of Richard Kemble, Richard Bower and Herbert Allcroft; Hunt Secretaries' Association; Hunt Servants' Benefit Society; Reigate Hound Show; Masters of Basset Hounds Association] (p65-76)
Sporting Intelligence [inc. University Sailing; Le Touquet Golf Club; Obituaries of Jock Campbell, Richard Grosvenor and Cecil Lord; German Hunting Book] (p77-79)
Sporting Results (p79-80)

Issue 630 : August 1912

Portrait [Hawkins] and Biography - Frank Foster (p81-83)
Shooting Jottings by Arthur Blyth (p83-85)
The Range of the Grouse by Frank Bonnett (p85-91)
Queen Bess in the Hunting Field by William Baillie-Grohman (p92-102)

This article looks at hunting books from 1486 onwards. It includes Boke of St.Albans by Juliana Berners; The Noble Arte of Venerie or Hunting which has been filched line for line from Jacques du Fouilloux's famous work La Venerie, through to Gaston de Foix's The Master of Game

Lithograph: *The Booke of Hunting - The Report of a Huntsman Upon the Fight of a Hart* (on p96)
Lithograph: *The Booke of Hunting - The Prince Takes the Deer With a Sharp Knife* (on p98)
Lithograph: *The Booke of Hunting - The Princess Takes the Deer With a Sharp Knife* (on p99)
Cowes Regatta by Francis Cooke (p102-104)

Trout Among the Tarns by Ernest Phillips   (p105-110)

[Obituary] George Bonnor by Herbert Hewett   (p110-113)

Photograph [Hawkins]: *George Bonnor*   (facing p110)

Coarse Fish and the Flyrod by Arthur Sharp   (p113-117)

What's Wrong With Lord's by Harry Tate   (p117-118)

Luck and the Unexpected in Yacht Racing by George Hopcroft   (p119-123)

Lithograph [pinx. Hopcroft]: *The Defeat of Sappho in 1868*   (facing p121)

Lithograph [pinx. Hopcroft]: *Volunteer and Thistle*   (facing p121)

Lithograph [pinx. Hopcroft]: *Madge in American Waters*   (facing p121)

Lithograph [pinx. Hopcroft]: *Vigilant and Britannia*   (facing p121)

[Obituary] Tom Richardson by Herbert Hewett   (p123-126)

The Sportsman's Library: Reviews of *Pheasants in Covert and Aviary* by Frank Barton;
         Batsmanship by Charles Fry; *The Light Side of Horses* by Charles Richardson;
         Fox Hunting From Shire to Shire by Cuthbert Bradley   (p126-127)

Current Cricket by Herbert Hewett   (p127-134)

Polo by Archibald Charlton   (p134-138)

Stray Leaves of Sport (part 5): Suburban Meetings in the 60s by Finch Mason   (p138-143)

Lithograph [pinx. Mason]: *Croydon in the Sixties*   (facing p143)

Lithograph [pinx. Mason]: *That Old Beeswing - Harrow Steeplechases*   (facing p143)

Peterborough Hound Show by William Scarth-Dixon   (p143-150)

Lithograph [pinx. Bradley]: *Byron*   (on p147)

Our Van [inc. Newbury Races; Gatwick Meeting; Ascot Royal Hunt Cup; Alexandra Park
         Racing; Southdown Hunt; Crawley & Horsham Hounds; Goathland Hunt]   (p150-157)

Sporting Intelligence [inc. Cambridge University Swimming; Henley Regatta; Irish
         Cockfighting; Wimbledon Tennis Championship; Obituary of William Ford]   (p157-161)

Sporting Results   (p161-162)

Issue 631 : September 1912

Portrait [Lafayette] and Biography - Alfred Mackintosh   (p163-164)

What Game Shall I Play by Claye Shaw   (p165-171)

September and Sports by Arthur Sharp   (p171-174)

Sportsmen in Mufti by Finch Mason   (p175-180)

Lithograph [pinx. Mason]: *Sportsmen in Mufti 1870*   (facing p177)

Lithograph [pinx. Mason]: *Tom Wallace - A Sketch in St.James Street*   (facing p179)

A Red-Letter Day Among Grayling by Paul Taylor   (p180-181)

The Two Hunters [verses] by William Ogilvie   (p182-183)

Supremacy in Games and Sport by Hugh Henry   (p183-186)

New Views on Old Questions by George Teasdale-Buckell   (p186-189)

One of the Real Old School by Edward Cuming   (p190-191)

Photograph: *Henry Jackson*   (on p190)

What of the Pony for the Army by Charles Stanhope   (p191-196)

Shortage of Good Retrievers by Alan Haig-Brown   (p196-198)

Wild Ducks for Sport by Charles Batchelder   (p199-205)

The Courage of the Grizzly by Lincoln Wilbar   (p205-208)

Photograph [McGuire]: *Old Ephraim*   (on p207)

I Go A-Fishing by Arthur Hamilton   (p208-212)

The Sportsman's Library: Reviews of *Dry Fly Fishing in Border Waters* by Frederick Fernie;
         Ten Thousand Miles Through Canada by Joseph Adams   (p212-213)

Current Cricket by Otho Paget   (p213-216)

Polo by Archibald Charlton   (p216-219)

A Hundred Years Ago: Hurling from *The Sporting Magazine*   (p219-220)

The Position of British Yachting by Francis Cooke   (p221-223)

The Triangular Cricket Tournament by Herbert Hewett   (p224-226)

Our Van [inc. Bibury Club Meeting; Pontefract Races; Goodwood Racing; New Forest
        Buckhounds; Hertfordshire Hunt] (p226-236)
Sporting Intelligence [inc. Leander Rowing Club; University Sporting Results Table; French
        Golf; Westmeath Polo; Obituaries of Andrew Lang, Philip Barthropp, Kendall
        Burnett, James Adams and Alfred Downer] (p237-240)
Sporting Results (p241-242)

Issue 632 : October 1912

Portrait [Lafayette] and Biography - George Bullough (p243-244)
The Debt of the Naturalist to the Sportsman by Thomas Dale (p245-249)
Wickets at Lord's by Robert Walker (p249-250)
Hunt Presentations by Edward Cuming (p251-254)
Engraving [sculp. Babbage]: *Horse and Rider* (on p254)
Yachting in 1912 by Francis Cooke (p255-258)
Partridge Shooting in Ireland by George Garrow-Green (p258-260)
Ovis Ammon Shooting in Tibet by Frederick Bailey (p260-267)
Photograph: *The Trophies* (on p261)
Photograph: *Dead Ovis Ammon* (on p262)
Photograph: *Shepherd Boys* (on p263)
Photograph: *Camp at a Tibetan Village* (on p264)
Public School Cricket in 1912 by Abel Chapman (p268-272)
Salmon Fishing in Norway by Arthur Browne (p272-274)
[Review] The Druid and His Works: *The Druid Sporting Library* (p275-282)
Engraving [sculp. Alais]: *The Druid - Henry Hall Dixon* (on p277)
Polo: The International Team by Archibald Charlton (p283-285)
Forr'ad On [verses] by Michael Hope (p285)
A Hundred Years Ago: Suffolk Punches Horses from *The Sporting Magazine* (p286-287)
The Status of a Grouse Season by George Teasdale-Buckell (p287-293)
County Cricket in 1912 by Herbert Hewett (p293-299)
The Sportsman's Library: Reviews of *Sport in the Olden Time* by Walter Gilbey; *The Complete
        Yachtsman* by Brooke Heckstall-Smith; *The Book of the All-Round Angler* by
        John Bickerdyke; *A Member of Tatts* by Nat Gould (p299-301)
Photograph: *Position of Crew Running Before the Wind* (on p300)
The Carp by Ernest Phillips (p301-305)
Tales of Jockeys and Others by Gerald Ricardo (p305-309)
Our Van [inc. Lewes Meeting; Nottingham Races; Stockton Racing; Ebor Handicap; Devon
        & Somerset Staghounds; Pytchley Hunt] (p309-317)
Engraving [sculp. Babbage]: *Horse in Stable* (on p317)
Sporting Intelligence [inc. Prestatyn Golf Club; Royal Porthcawl Links; Obituaries of Edwin
        Wallace, Henry Cavendish, John Heathcote, Humphrey Marriott, Charles Brand,
        Charles King, Charles Race, Frederick Woodward and Henri Saussereau; Ostende
        Yachting] (p318-320)
Sporting Results (p320-322)

Issue 633 : November 1912

Portrait [Lafayette] and Biography - Robert Williams-Wynn (p323-325)
On Showing Pheasants by Frank Bonnett (p326-333)
Hunt Changes by Edward Cuming (p333-349)
Photograph [Allen]: *Owen Philipps* (on p335)
Photograph [Elliott]: *Frederic Lambart* (on p335)
Photograph [Clarke]: *Edward Turton* (on p337)
Photograph [White]: *William Burton* (on p337)
Photograph [Bennett]: *James Twinberrow* (on p339)

Photograph [Langfier]: *William Pretty* (on p339)
Photograph [Barnett]: *Yalden Thomson* (on p341)
Photograph: *Hume Chaloner* (on p341)
Photograph [Elliott]: *Kirby Stapley* (on p343)
Photograph [Elliott]: *Edith Somerville* (on p343)
Photograph [Hills]: *Robert Wilson* (on p344)
Photograph [Lafayette]: *Emerson Herdman* (on p345)
Autumn Days in Norfolk by Henry Pilkington (p349-351)
Between the Flags by William Scarth-Dixon (p352-359)
Baily's Hunting Directory 1911-12 [with Autographs] by Edward Cuming (p359-364)
Photograph: *George Salkeld* (on p362)
Photograph: *James Brown* (on p362)
Photograph: *The Roman Foxhounds Going to Draw* (facing p362)
Photograph: *A Meet of the Roman Foxhounds* (facing p362)
Poultry Claims by Edward Cuming (p364-367)
Polo En Passant by Archibald Charlton (p367-369)
The Sportsman's Library: Reviews of *The Complete Bowler* by James Manson; *My Hunting Day Book* by Wilhelm Ernst; *Things I Can Tell* by Derrick Westenra; *Reptiles, Amphibians and Fishes* by Joseph Cunningham, and *The Anglo-Indians* by Alice Perrin (p369-375)
Distemper in Puppies by Edward Cuming (p376-377)
The Huntsman [verses] by Michael Hope (p377)
Yachting in the Solent by Francis Cooke (p378-380)
A Hundred Years Ago: The Royal Hunt from *The Sporting Magazine* (p381)
London Evenings by Herbert Hewett (p382-387)
Our Van [inc. Doncaster Racecourse; Warwick Races; Ayr Meeting; New Forest Foxhounds; South Staffordshire Hunt; Harrington's Hounds] (p387-396)
Sporting Intelligence [inc. University Hockey Blues; Bath Water-Polo; Northumberland Swimming Club; Sunningdale Golf; Obituaries of John Savile, Augustus Orlebar and John Rolls; Blencathra Hounds] (p396-400)
Sporting Results (p400-402)

Issue 634 : December 1912

Portrait [White] and Biography - William Burton (p403-404)
Masters of Hounds and the New Point-to-Point Race Rules by Edward Cuming (p405-417)
The Racing Season of 1912 by Charles Richardson (p417-421)
Photograph [Hailey]: *Prince Palatine* (facing p419)
Photograph [Hailey]: *Craganour* (facing p421)
The Rescue of the Bison by Abel Chapman (p422-427)
[Review] *Adam Lindsay Gordon* by Edith Humphris; *The Poems of Adam Lindsay Gordon* by Douglas Sladen; *Poems of Adam Lindsay Gordon* by Henry Frowde (p428-432)
Photograph: *The Mecca of Australian Literature* (on p429)
Lithograph: *Tom Oliver on Birmingham* (facing p431)
A New Yachting Association by Francis Cooke (p433-435)
The Trout Season of 1912 by James Englefield (p435-438)
A Christmas Shooting Trip in North China by Abbot Anderson (p438-445)
Photograph: *Camels on the March Crossing a Frozen River* (on p439)
Photograph: *Chinese Inn, North Shansi* (on p440)
Photograph: *Chinese Inn Yard* (on p442)
Photograph: *The Caravan* (on p443)
Psychology and Golf by Arthur Hamilton (p445-450)
Yonder He Goes [verses] by William Ogilvie (p450)
Some Memorable Thoroughbred Sires by Gerald Ricardo (p451-454)

A Hundred Years Ago: Foley Hunt Club from *The Sporting Magazine* (p454-455)
A Study of Hound Work by Thomas Salter (p455-459)
[Reviews] *Chronicles of the Houghton Fishing Club* by Herbert Maxwell; *Angling Memories and Maxims* by Edward Barnard (p459-462)
Lithograph [pinx. Smith]: *Dining Tent of the Houghton Fishing Club* (facing p461)
Will Batchelor by George Burrows (p462)
Our Van [inc. Berkshire Handicap; Houghton Week; Criterion Stakes; Belvoir Hunt; Burton Hounds; Badminton Hunt] (p463-471)
Sporting Intelligence [inc. Oxford University Coxwainless Fours; Manchester Golf Links; Lancashire County Cricket Club; Obituary of Thomas Conneff] (p471-473)
Sporting Results (p474)

John Corlett

Volume 99, January - June 1913

Issue 635 : January 1913

Portrait [Hailey] of Albert Whalley, jockey	Title page
Portrait [Vandyke] and Biography - Alexander Bruce	(p1-3)
The Restocking of Pheasant Coverts by Frank Bonnett	(p3-10)
The New Point-to-Point Rules by George Burrows	(p10-15)
The Dangers of the Alps by George Abraham	(p15-22)
Photograph [Abraham]: *Great Crevasse on the Way Up Mont Blanc*	(facing p17)
Photograph [Abraham]: *A Great Ice Tower on Mont Blanc*	(on p18)
Photograph [Abraham]: *On the Crest of the Weisshorn*	(facing p21)
Curling Words and Phrases by Bertram Smith	(p23-25)
[Review] Golf Greens and How to Keep Them: *The Book of the Links* by Martin Sutton reviewed by Charles Batchelder	(26-31)
Photograph: *Edward Ray Driving*	(facing p29)
Photograph: *Bunkers at Ganton*	(facing p29)
Lithograph [Wilkinson]: *Lengthening of Golf Courses*	(facing p31)
[Obituary] Thomas Pickernell [aka] 'Mr Thomas'	(p31-34)
Hunt Wire and Boy Scouts by Godfrey Bosvile	(p34-38)
On Shows and Coaching by Gerald Ricardo	(p38-47)
Photographs: *Two Coaching Event Starts*	(facing p41)
Photographs: *Two Coaching Event Finishes*	(facing p41)
Engraving [sculp. Babbage]: *Coaching in the Olden Times*	(facing p43)
Photograph: *Four Back to the Road Again*	(facing p45)
Photograph: *A Feature of Olympia Horse Show is its Decorations*	(on p45)
Photograph: *The French Military Display Team*	(facing p47)
A Hundred Years Ago: Stag Hunt at Epping from *The Sporting Magazine*	(p47-48)
Foxhunting and Poultry-Keeping by Bramston Horne	(p49-53)
The Sportsman's Library: Reviews of *Live Stock Journal Almanac* by James Sinclair; *Sport in the Olden Times* by Walter Gilbey; *Coarse Fishing* by Hugh Sheringham; *Triangular Cricket* by Edward Sewell; *Left in the Lurch* by Nat Gould; *Ten Years of Motors and Motor Racing* by Charles Jarrott	(p53-55)
The Path to the Stable [verses] by William Ogilvie	(p56)
A New Sporting Gun by Arthur Blyth	(p57-58)
Photograph: *Over and Under Gun*	(on p57)
Winter Nights in London by Herbert Hewett	(p58-62)
The Winter Roach by Ernest Phillips	(p62-66)
Our Van [inc. Lincoln Meeting; Chatsworth Handicap; Warwick Races; Cottesmore Hunt; Ledbury Huntsman; Silverton Foxhounds; Eastbourne Hunt]	(p66-73)
Sporting Intelligence [inc. Cambridge University Sculls; Pytchley Hunt; Glamorganshire Golf Club; Leicestershire County Cricket Club; Obituaries of Alfred Smith, William Verney, John Wright, Joseph Flint, George Fenwick, Thomas Cradock, Augustus Orlebar, Stewart Bell, Lambert Nicholls, William Crofts and Frederick Allsopp; Belvoir Hunt; Tipperary Hounds; West Cumberland Foxhounds]	(p73-79)
Sporting Results	(p79-80)

Issue 636 : February 1913

Portrait [Bassano] and Biography - Montagu Cholmeley	(p81-83)
Some Facts in the Psychology of Sport by Claye Shaw	(p83-89)
The Alterations in the Rules of Point-to-Point Races by Richard Meysey-Thompson	(p89-95)
New Racing Yachts for 1913 by George Hopcroft	(p95-98)
Lithograph [pinx. Hopcroft]: *The German Emperor's 'Meteor'*	(on p96)
Lithograph [pinx. Hopcroft]: *The American Yacht 'Westward'*	(on p97)

Revolver Shooting by Edward Almack (p98-102)
Clinker: His Steeplechase Exploits by Gerald Ricardo (p102-107)
Lithograph [pinx. Ferneley]: *Clinker* (facing p102)
Kismet [verses] by Francis Monckton (p107)
Jack Gloomfell's Dream by Hugh Henry (p108-111)
Modern Steeplechasing by George Burrows (p112-115)
On Training Showjumpers by Gilbert Chesterton (p115-119)
Photograph: *Practice in the Ring at Olympia* (on p116)
Photograph: *Eight Jumping Scenes at Olympia* (facing p119)
The Death of a Boar [verses] by Ralph Ousley (p120)
[Review] *Hunting in the Olden Days* by William Scarth-Dixon (p121-128)
Engraving [pinx. Bailey]: *The Quorn Hunt* (facing p123)
Lithograph: *John Mytton* (facing p125)
Engraving: *Thomas Drake* (facing p127)
Passing of the Big Cutter by Francis Cooke (p128-130)
The Protection of Wild Birds by Abel Chapman (p131-136)
A Hundred Years Ago: Prize Fighting from *The Sporting Magazine* (p136-137)
Caveat Emptor (p137-140)
The Old Rector by Hugh Henry (p140-142)
The Sportsman's Library: Reviews of *How to Play Golf* by Harry Vardon; *The Art of Golf* by Josh Taylor; *Sport in Five Continents* by Alfred Leatham; *The Bow-Wow Book* by Coulson Kernahan; *The Life of Benjamin Disraeli* by William Monypenny; *An Introduction to Foxhunting* by Edwin Hobson; *The Arab Horse the Thoroughbred and the Turf* by James Boucaut, and *A Reckless Owner* by Nat Gould (p142-145)
Our Van [inc. Nottingham Meeting; Windsor Racing; Plumpton Races; Meath Hunt; Haldon Harriers; Burton Hunt; Cattistock Dog Pack] (p146-153)
Sporting Intelligence [inc. University Rugby; Obituaries of Charles Travess, James Keene, William Matthews, Vernon Wilcock, James Frame and Clem Barton; Oakley Hounds; Meynell Hunt; Royal North Devon Golf Club; Rakospalota Racecourse] (p154-159)
Sporting Results (p159-160)

Issue 637 : March 1913

Portrait [Jarvis] and Biography - Oswald Riley (p161-162)
Thoughts on the Future of Foxhunting by Thomas Dale (p162-168)
The Art of the Decoy Man by Frank Bonnett (p169-177)
Photograph: *The Entrance to a Pipe* (on p171)
Photograph: *A View of the Other Side of the Pipe* (on p173)
Trouting in March by Arthur Sharp (p177-181)
Auction Bridge - Club Statistics (p181)
Photograph: *London Fire Brigade's Horse Escape* (facing p183)
The Fashion in Greys by George Teasdale-Buckell (p183-190)
Photograph: *Two Greys of Eastern Origin* (facing p185)
Photograph [le Roy]: *Two Grey Boulannaise Horses* (facing p185)
Photograph: *A Medley of Greys seen at Olympia* (facing p187)
Photograph: *Arab Stallion 'Zoowar'* (on p187)
Photograph: *A Percheron Stallion* (on p188)
Photograph: *Grey Highland 'Garron'* (on p189)
Photograph: *Fred Archer's Early Home* (on p190)
Some Boat Race Facts [inc. Obituary of Ernald Lane] by Walter Woodgate (p191-193)
All in the Game [verses] by William Ogilvie (p194)
Point-to-Point Race Rules by George Burrows (p195-199)
The Glorious Uncertainty by Charles Richardson (p199-201)
A Hundred Years Ago: Renfrewshire Harriers from *The Sporting Magazine* (p202-203)

In Praise of Boxing by Norman Clark (p203-204)
Crooked Powder by Lincoln Wilbar (p205-208)
Fishermen's Fads by Clifford Cordley (p209-212)
London Evenings by Herbert Hewett (p212-217)
London Riverside Amusements in the Time of Queen Elizabeth by Culling Gaze (p217-222)
Old Athletic and Cycling Champions by Charles Batchelder (p223-224)
Our Van [inc. Purley Handicap Steeplechase; Lingfield Meeting; Manchester Racing; Obituary of Thomas Isaac; South Down Hunt; West Norfolk Hounds; South Shropshire Hunt; Surrey Union Hounds] (p225-233)
Sporting Intelligence [inc. Essex Hunt; Flint & Denbigh Hounds; Tarporley Hunt; Yorkshire County Cricket Club; Castle Bromwich Golf Course; Obituaries of Charles Winn, Frederick Holman, Frank Shuttleworth, Thomas Elliott and James Arrowsmith; New Zealand Rugby] (p234-240)
Sporting Results (p240)

Issue 638 : April 1913

Portrait [Elliott] and Biography - Norman Loder (p241-244)
Woodland Monarchs by Bonnycastle Dale (p244-250)
Photograph: *The Head of a Moose* (on p245)
Photograph: *The Fate of a Mountain Goat in British Columbia* (on p247)
Photograph: *A Head of a Bighorn Sheep* (on p249)
Archery and all about it by Maud Drummond (p250-256)
Photograph: *Brooks King* (facing p253)
Coaching as a Sport by Valentine Elwy (p256-260)
Photograph: *Richmond Horse Show Coach Judging* (facing p259)
Yachting in 1913: A Forecast by Francis Cooke (p260-263)
The Ponies of Great Britain by George Teasdale-Buckell (p263-271)
Photograph [Babbage]: *Bleddfa Shooting Star* (on p264)
Photograph: *Highland Pony 'Gometer'* (on p265)
Photograph [Chapman]: *Welsh Mountain Mare 'Hawddgar Dewdrop' and her Foal* (facing p267)
Photograph [Babbage]: *Polo Pony Mare 'Vivid'* (on p267)
Photograph: *Shetland Pony 'Thoreau'* (facing p268)
Photograph: *Fell Pony Stallion 'Goblin'* (facing p268)
Photograph [Cassells]: *Shetland Ponies in their Wild State* (on p270)
Photograph: *Child's Pony 'Pretty Polly'* (on p271)
The End of the Season [verses] by William Ogilvie (p272)
Sport in the Fatherland by James Dodington (p272-274)
The Wet-Fly Angler in April by Arthur Sharp (p275-277)
Sport in the Wilds of Yorkshire by William Leighton (p278-281)
Tis An Otter We're Hunting Today [verses] by Francis Monckton (p282)
Polo En Passant by Archibald Charlton (p283-285)
A Hundred Years Ago: Tom Cribb from *The Sporting Magazine* (p285-286)
Cross-Country Running (p286-288)
The Spring Horse Shows by Gerald Ricardo (p288-297)
Photograph [Babbage]: *Shire Stallion 'Champion's Goalkeeper'* (on p289)
Photograph [Babbage]: *Hackney Stallion 'Hopwood Viceroy'* (on p292)
Photograph [Babbage]: *Kings Courtship* (facing p295)
[Obituary] Godfrey Morgan, Viscount Tredegar by George Burrows (p297-300)
Photograph: *Godfrey Morgan* (on p298)
The Sword Duel in England by Abel Chapman (p300-306)
Netting of Duck and Snipe in Burma (p307-308)

Our Van [inc. Manchester Races; Ludlow Racing; Grand Military Meeting; Eton College
        Beagles; Pytchley Hunt; Shire Horses; Ullswater Foxhounds; Cottesmore Hunt;
        Obituary of Edward Baldock]   (p309-316)
Sporting Intelligence [inc. University Boat Race; Bramham Moor Hounds; Bar Golfing
        Society; Obituaries of Jimmy Sinclair and Francis Buckland; Waterloo Cup]   (p316-319)
Sporting Results   (p319-320)

Issue 639 : May 1913

Portrait [Bartlett] and Biography - Herbert Connop   (p321-322)
A National Polo Association by Archibald Charlton   (p323-327)
Guideless Mountaineering by George Abraham   (p328-332)
Photograph [Abraham]: *Nearing the Col Du Geant*   (facing p329)
Photograph [Abraham]: *Midst the Snow Wreathed Glacier Des Bossons*   (facing p331)
The First Royal Yachtsman by George Hopcroft   (p333-337)
Lithograph [pinx. Hopcroft]: *Typical Yachts of Charles II's Reign*   (facing p335)
[Review] *Hounds in Old Days* by Walter Gilbey   (p337-341)
Lithograph [pinx. Taylor]: *A Hunting Scene*   (facing p339)
Lithograph [pinx. Reinagle]: *The Harrier*   (facing p341)
The Sport of Horse Showing by George Teasdale-Buckell   (p341-343)
Photograph: *A London Van Horse* [W.H.Smith & Son]   (on p342)
Photograph [Fall]: *Heavy Van Trios* [Messrs Schweppes]   (on p343)
Point-to-Point Races by George Burrows   (p344-346)
Red Letter Days on the Erne by Joseph Adams   (p347-354)
Photograph: *The Erne - A Pool at Belleek*   (on p349)
Photograph: *River Erne - The Doctor's Pool*   (on p350)
Photograph: *The Rapids*   (on p351)
Photograph: *Assaroe Falls*   (on p353)
Incident and Poetry of Otterhunting by Jack Fairfax-Blakeborough   (p354-357)
The Playing of Games by Charles Batchelder   (p357-358)
Rooks and Rook Shooting by Frank Bonnett   (p359-363)
Yachting in the Solent by Francis Cooke   (p363-366)
Trout and Minnow by Ernest Phillips   (p366-370)
A Hundred Years Ago: Cricket from *The Sporting Magazine*   (p370-371)
The Sportsman's Library: Reviews of *Ranelagh and its Times* by Cyril FitzGerald; *The
        Complete Horseman* by William Scarth-Dixon; *Verb Sap on Going to West Africa*
        by Alan Field; *Bloodstock Breeders' Review* by Somerville Tattersall   (p372-375)
Polo Notes and News by Archibald Charlton   (p375-376)
Seagoing Canoes by Athol Maudslay   (p377-381)
Fox Farming in Canada by Harold Bindloss   (p381-386)
Our Van [inc. Cheltenham National Hunt; Newbury Meeting; Liverpool Racing; Studbrook
        Harriers; West Cumberland Hounds; Blankney Hunt]   (p386-393)
Photograph: *Francis Hurt with his Hounds*   (on p392)
Sporting Intelligence [inc. Cambridgeshire Hunt; East Essex Hounds; Cattistock Hunt;
        Puckeridge Point-to-Point Races; University Gymnastics; Cornwall Golf;
        Mid-Surrey Golf Club; Obituaries of Norman Christie, Harry Wallis, John Rich,
        William Chatterton, Henry Salwey and George Hodgman; Polo at Ranelagh;
        Essex County Cricket Club; John Peel Lecture]   (p393-398)
Photograph [Harley]: *George Hodgman*   (on p397)
Sporting Results   (p398-400)

Issue 640 : June 1913

Portrait [Scattola] and Biography - Alfred Cox   (p401-402)
Women in Sport by Claye Shaw   (p403-410)

Sport on the Borders of the Gobi Desert by John Anderson (p410-416)
Photograph: *The Bag of Ovis Heads* (on p411)
Photograph: *Mongol Herds and Camp* (on p413)
Photograph: *A Derelict Ovis Head* (on p415)
The Luckiest Winner of the Derby by George Teasdale-Buckell (p416-419)
Engraving [sculp. Herring]: *Merry Monarch* (on p417)
On Spurs and Spurring by William Scarth-Dixon (p419-422)
Photograph: *Stanley Water Fishing* (on p423)
A Good Catch by Woodley Burrows (p423)
Play the Game [verses] by Cyril Stacey (p424)
The Fortunes of Fishing by Charles Cassels (p425-431)
Photograph [Gordon-Lennox]: *Spey Salmon* (on p426)
Photograph: *Loch Leven Trout* (on p427)
Photograph [Bridge]: *Test Trout* (on p429)
My First Lion by Frederick Davis (p432-434)
Influence of International Polo on Polo and Pony Breeding by Thomas Dale (p434-437)
Racquets Reviewed by Harold Rudd (p437-443)
Photograph: *Basil Foster* (facing p439)
Photograph [Hawkins]: *Alan Luther* (on p441)
Photograph [Bremner]: *Archibald Muir* (on p441)
A Hundred Years Ago: The Derby from *The Sporting Magazine* (p444-445)
[Obituary] Tatton Sykes by George Burrows (p445-447)
Engraving: *Doncaster* (on p446)
Bona-fide Hunt Anomaly by George Burrows (p447-449)
Polo Government and Other Topics by Archibald Charlton (p450-458)
Albert Whalley by George Burrows (p458-459)
Our Van [inc. Newbury Meeting; Epsom Races; Great Surrey Handicap; Esher Cup; Chester Cup] (p459-464)
Sporting Intelligence [inc. University Racquets; Sporting Pictures; Woodland Pytchley Hounds; Zetland Hunt; Dunster Petty Sessions Case; Betting Inducements Bill; Hoylake Golf Course; Obituaries of Harry Cumberland-Bentley (*Baily's* contributor), Thomas Jayes, Charles Newton-Robinson, Raymond Etherington-Smith, Alexander Apcar, William Wingfield, John Barnes and Charles Rose; Torbay Yacht Club; Colne Valley Hunt] (p464-471)
Sporting Results (p472)

Volume 100, July - December 1913

Issue 641 : July 1913

Portrait [Burton] of Arthur Fisher, huntsman Title page
Portrait [Elliott] and Biography - Arthur Nicholson (p1-2)
July and the Trout Fisher by Arthur Sharp (p3-6)
Yachting: The America's Cup by Francis Cooke (p6-10)
Hounds at Reigate by Gerald Ricardo (p10-13)
Rotten Row in the Sixties by Finch Mason (p13-19)
Lithograph [pinx. Mason]: *Though Lost to Sight, In Memory Clear* (facing p15)
Lithograph [pinx. Mason]: *Ginger Stubbs* (facing p17)
The Pistol Duel in England by Abel Chapman (p19-26)
The Cobs [verses] by William Ogilvie (p26)
Olympic Games in the Cotswolds by Valentine Elvy (p27-28)
A Day with the Mole Catcher by Chisholm Mitchell (p29-34)
Lithograph: *Mole Catcher at Work* (on p30)
Lithograph: *Mole Trap Set* (on p32)

Lithograph: *Very Destructive Beast* (on p34)
Flighting [verses] by Francis Monckton (p34)
Sport and Work on the Zambesi by Herbert Harrington (p35-40)
Photograph: *View on the Zambesi near Feira* (on p36)
Photograph: *Scaly Ant-Eater Caught near Feira* (on p37)
Photograph: *The Author's Home at Feira* (on p38)
Photograph: *The Zambesi at Luangwa Junction* (on p39)
Cricket Notes by Herbert Hewett (p40-43)
A Buck Jumping Contest by George Burrows (p43-45)
Photograph: *A Bucking Horse Fails to Unseat an Expert Rider* (facing p45)
Photograph: *An Exciting Second in a Buck-Jumping Contest* (facing p45)
Photograph: *Dancing Buck-Jumper* (on p45)
A Hundred Years Ago: Shooting Match from *The Sporting Magazine* (p45-46)
Woman and Sport by Gerald Ricardo (p47-50)
Photograph: *Ladies Parliamentary Golf Match* (facing p49)
Polo: Current Events by Archibald Charlton (p51-55)
A Famous Hackney's Birthplace by Thomas Axon (p55-58)
Engraving [sculp. Webb]: *Marshland Shales* (on p56)
Photograph: *Parish Church of Walpole St.Peter, Norfolk* (on p57)
Photograph: *Stable Yard at St.Peter's Lodge* (on p58)
Willow Grouse Shooting in Newfoundland by John Seigne (p59-61)
King Charles I and Sunday Sports by Edgar Thomas (p61-65)
Gallows and Inns by George Teasdale-Buckell (p65-67)
Our Van [inc. Kempton Park Meeting; Hurst Park Plate; Newmarket Stakes; Four Burrow
         Hunt; Wilton Hounds; Worcestershire Hunt; Point-to-Point Rules; Obituary of
         Letilia Ames; Northern Counties Otterhounds] (p67-75)
Sporting Intelligence [inc. University Lawn Tennis; Thames Regattas; Masters of Foxhounds'
         Association; Frinton Golf Club; Obituaries of George Cotterill, Hamilton
         Ferrier-Kerr, William Binnie, Thomas Davies, Charles Kohler, John Cooper and
         George Dawson] (p76-79)
Sporting Results (p80)

Issue 642 : August 1913

Portrait [Howard] and Biography - Walter Raphael (p81-84)
The Grouse Shooting Outlook by Frank Bonnett (p85-89)
The Banshee by Arthur Fisher (p90-92)
Days in Bogland by Henry Pilkington (p92-94)
Too Old for Sport by Robert Lyle (p94-96)
The Natural Habits of the Pheasant by Arthur Horwood (p97-102)
Photograph [Crooke]: *A Sitting Pheasant* (on p98)
Photograph [Crooke]: *Hatching-Out Day* (on p99)
Photograph [Crooke]: *A Study in Light and Shade* (on p100)
Photograph [Crooke]: *Pheasant's Nest Among Bracken* (on p101)
Photograph [Crooke]: *Pheasant's Nest Among Sedges* (on p101)
An August Trout [verses] by Francis Monckton (p102)
The Bonnie Purple Heather by Maitland Stewart (p103-106)
Rifle Shooting by Edward Almack (p107-108)
The Ubiquitous Pony by Gerald Ricardo (p108-118)
Engraving [pinx. Landseer]: *His First Leap* (on p109)
Engraving: *A Child's Shetland Pony* (on p110)
Engraving [sculp. Babbage]: *A Real Good Old-Fashioned Shooting Pony* (on p112)
Photograph: *A Ready-Made and Stylish Polo Pony* (on p113)
Engraving [sculp. Palfrey]: *Polo Pony Mares and Their Foals* (on p114)

Photograph: *A Typical Welsh Pony*   (on p115)
Photograph: *A Spanish Vineyard Pony Loaded with Grapes*   (on p117)
The Flyfisher and Coarse Fish by Arthur Sharp   (p119-124)
The Making of Wickets by Harry Tate   (p124-126)
A Hundred Years Ago: Essex Hunt from *The Sporting Magazine*   (p126-127)
Cricket Notes by Herbert Hewett   (p127-129)
Current Polo by Archibald Charlton   (p129-133)
Photograph [Rouch]: *Inter-Regimental Polo Cup Presentation*   (facing p131)
The County Polo Association by Archibald Charlton   (p134-136)
Peterborough Foxhound Show by William Scarth-Dixon   (p137-145)
Lithograph [pinx. Bradley]: *The Linlithgow & Stirlingshire Factor*   (on p141)
Our Van [inc. Newbury Races; Ascot Meeting; Northumberland Plate; Alexandra Park
         Racing; Amory's Harriers; Masters of Hounds' Point-to-Point Association;
         Staintondale Pack]   (p145-155)
Sporting Intelligence [inc. Henley Regatta; Jockey Club Annual General Meeting Report;
         Hoylake Golf; Obituaries of Frederic Johnstone, Charles Cotes, Henri
         Delamarre, Alfred Lyttelton and Arthur Cecil; Galloway Races]   (p155-160)
Sporting Results   (p161-162)

Issue 643 : September 1913

Portrait [Russell] and Biography - Francis Baring   (p163-165)
The Coaching Revival by Wodehouse Garland   (p165-174)
Photograph [Rouch]: *'The Reynard' Passing Kempton Park*   (on p167)
Photograph [Rouch]: *Alfred Vanderbilt on the Brighton Road*   (on p169)
Partridges in 1913 by Frank Bonnett   (p174-178)
The Trout Brook in September by Arthur Sharp   (p179-183)
Yacht Races Lost through Trifles by George Hopcroft   (p184-187)
Lithograph [pinx. Hopcroft]: *The Neglect of Some Trifling Stay*   (facing p187)
Some Thoughts on the Treatment of Horses Feet by Thomas Dale   (p188-192)
Cricket Weeks by Harold Rudd   (p193-199)
Polo by Archibald Charlton   (p199-202)
Gunpowders by Arthur Blyth   (p203-205)
Rifle Shooting - A Reply   (p205-207)
Cricket Notes [with Obituaries of Bertie Evans and Stanley Cody] by Herbert Hewett (p207-213)
Tufts of Turf by Gerald Ricardo   (p214-217)
The Bird of the Shires by Arthur Horwood   (p218-222)
Photograph [Crooke]: *Partridge Nest Built on Dyke Bank*   (on p220)
Photograph [Crooke]: *Dead at his Post*   (on p221)
The Gamest Fish that Swims by Ernest Phillips   (p222-228)
Our Van [inc. Bibury Club Meeting; Lingfield Park Racing; Leicester Races; Liverpool Cup;
         Cheshire Hunt; Belvoir Hounds]   (p228-238)
Sporting Intelligence [inc. Welsh Hounds; West Middlesex Golf Course; Obituaries of
         Thomas Harman, Ralph Knox, Harold Hawke, Robert Brice, Potts Chatto and
         John Smart; Heythrop Hunt; Pytchley Hounds; Sculling Championship;
         Ribblesdale Buckhounds]   (p238-241)
Sporting Results   (p241-242)

Issue 644 : October 1913

Portrait [Elliott] and Biography - George Child   (p243-246)
Measurement of Polo Ponies by Thomas Dale   (p247-252)
Past Yachting Season by Francis Cooke   (p252-257)
Photograph: *Carina*   (facing p255)
Distemper in Foxhounds by Edward Cuming   (p257-259)

Thoughts on Covert-Shooting by Frank Bonnett (p260-265)

The Druid [verses] by William Ogilvie (p266)

Evolving the Exmoor Pony by Gerald Ricardo (p267-269)

Photograph: *Exmoor Brood Mare and Foal* (facing p269)

End of the Horse Show Season by George Teasdale-Buckell (p269-273)

Photograph [Lafayette]: *Barney* [Dublin Champion Cup Winner] (on p271)

Photograph: *Judging Hunters at Dublin Show* (on p272)

Some Notes on the Cambridgeshire by William Scarth-Dixon (p273-276)

Public School Cricket in 1913 by Abel Chapman (p277-280)

Photograph [Hills]: *Geoffrey Wilson* (on p278)

Photograph [Saunders]: *George Whitehead* (on p278)

Oliver Goldsmith's Animated Nature by Ernest Clarke (p280-284)

The Sportswoman's Summer by Robert Lyle (p284-289)

October Cubbing: A Morning on Foot (p289-293)

The Sportsman's Library: Reviews of *Sporting Recollections of An Old 'Un* by Frank Streatfield; *The Story of the King's Highway* by Sidney Webb; *The Salmon Rivers of Scotland* by Augustus Grimble; *The Salmon Rivers of England & Wales* by Augustus Grimble; *An Irish Gentleman* by Maurice Moore; *Recovering the Ashes* by Jack Hobbs; *High Pheasants* by Ralph Payne-Gallwey; *Motor Ways in Lakeland* by George Abraham; *Inland Golf* by Edward Ray (p293-300)

Photograph: *The Estuary of The Dart* (facing p294)

Lithograph: *Coranna* (facing p296)

Photograph: *A Mountain Road in Lakeland* (on p298)

Photograph [Abraham]: *A Typical Scene in Lakeland* (facing p298)

Home and International Polo by Archibald Charlton (p301-304)

[Review] *Women in the Hunting Field* by Amy Menzies (p304-307)

Our Van [inc. Northern Circuit Racing; Nottingham Meeting; Windsor Castle Handicap; Stockton Races; Exmoor Foxhounds; St.Columb & Newquay Hounds; Axe Vale & Cotley Harriers; Obituaries of Charles Clapp and John Lawrence; Portia Beagles] (p307-316)

Sporting Intelligence [inc. Barclays of Ury; Dornoch Golf; Criccieth Golf Club; Obituaries of James Lonsdale, Robert Willoughby, Evelyn Ellis and John Cooper; Bramham Moor Hounds] (p317-320)

Sporting Results (p320-322)

Issue 645 : November 1913

Portrait [Laib] and Biography - Henry Lewis (p323-324)

Maintaining Britain's Athletic Supremacy by Theodore Cook (p325-328)

Lithograph [pinx. Fothergill]: *Better to Sit Still than Rise Up and Fall* (on p328)

Hunt Changes in 1913 by Edward Cuming (p329-345)

Photograph [Weston]: *Jane Portal* (on p331)

Photograph [Harper]: *Frederick Milbank* (on p332)

Photograph [Laib]: *Henry Hawkins* (on p333)

Photograph [King]: *Gratwicke Heasman* (on p333)

Photograph [May]: *Edward Phillips* (on p334)

Photograph [Holloway]: *Delamere Bouth* (on p335)

Photograph: *Gerald Burgoyne* (on p335)

Photograph [Harrison]: *Frederick Gibbes* (on p337)

Photograph [Harrison]: *Stafford Hotchkin* (on p339)

Photograph [Brown]: *Charles Rickard* (on p339)

Photograph [Illingworth]: *Edward Molyneux* (on p341)

Photograph: *Beaufort's Hounds near Badminton* (facing p341)

On Historic Ground by Arthur Fisher (p345-348)

An Old Friend [verses] by Francis Monckton (p348)

Morality in Sport [part 1] by Claye Shaw (p349-356)
*[*This is only the second time in the history of **Baily's** that the Editor states that he does not agree with the contributor*]*

River or Lake by Abel Chapman (p356-363)
Photograph: *Trout on the Upper Rauma, Sudbrandsdal, Norway* (on p357)
Photograph: *Large Trout on the River Tivy, Wales* (on p358)
Photograph: *Borte Lake, Telemark, Norway* (on p359)
Photograph: *Trout Reach on the River Tivy, Wales* (on p361)
[Review] *The Polo Calendar of the Indian Polo Association* reviewed by Archibald Charlton (p363-365)
Yearling Sales: Then and Now by Gerald Ricardo (p365-369)
Baily's Hunting Directory 1913-14 by Edward Cuming (p370-371)
The Sportsman's Library: Reviews of *First Steps to Golf* by George Brown; *The Game Fishes of the World* by Charles Holder; *Westley Richards Gunmakers* by Leslie Taylor; *Pheasants and Covert Shooting* by Aymer Maxwell; *The Complete Athletic Trainer* by Scipio Mussabini; *My Game Book* by Alan Haig-Brown; *Riding and Driving for Women* by Belle Beach, and *The Hunting Year* by William Scarth-Dixon (p372-377)
Photograph [Graham]: *Bunkered - The Stance Required* (facing p372)
Photograph [Graham]: *Niblick - Halfway Back* (facing p372)
Photograph [Graham]: *Niblick - Top of Swing* (facing p375)
Photograph [Graham]: *Niblick - The Finish* (facing p375)
The Royal Cutter's Return by George Hopcroft (p377-380)
Lithographs [pinx. Hopcroft]: *Eight Memories of the Britannia* (facing p378)
Autumn Evenings in London by Herbert Hewett (p380-385)
End of the Polo Season by Archibald Charlton (p386-388)
Our Van [inc. Doncaster Meeting; West of Scotland Foal Stakes; Newbury Autumn Cup; Exe Valley Hounds; Vale of White Horse (Cricklade) Hunt] (p388-396)
Sporting Intelligence [inc. Oxford University Boxing Club; Middlesbrough Swimming Club; Brighton & Hove Golf Club; Obituaries of Albert de Rutzen, Frank Hardy and Charles Stokes; Culmstock Otterhounds; Knighthood for Willoughby Maycock (*Baily's* contributor); Alderley Edge Bowls] (p397-400)
Sporting Results (p401-402)

Issue 646 : December 1913

Portrait [Lafayette] and Biography - Henry Lopes (p403-404)
Lithograph [pinx. Fothergill]: *Every Sweet Must Have Its Bitter* (on p404)
Baily's Hundredth Volume by Charles Batchelder (p405-412)
Engraving: *Henry Rous* (on p406)
Engraving: *Tatton Sykes* (on p406)
Engraving: *Joseph Hawley* (on p407)
Engraving: *Richard Naylor* (on p407)
Photograph: *John Wells* (on p408)
Engraving: *James Merry* (on p408)
Engraving: *Robert Peck* (on p408)
Photograph: *Thomas Cannon* (on p409)
Photograph: *John Daley* (on p409)
Photograph: *Harry Custance* (on p409)
Photograph: *George Fordham* (on p409)
Photograph: *Henry Chaplin* (on p410)
Photograph: *George Coventry* (on p410)
Photograph: *Charles Stanhope* (on p411)
The Hunting Tradition by Henry Bryden (p412-416)
Lithograph [Hailey]: *George Montagu* (on p413)

Lithograph: *Francis North* (on p413)

Photograph: *William North* (on p414)

Photograph: *Dudley North* (on p415)

The Straight Goer [verses] by William Ogilvie (p416)

Sport and Work on the Zambesi by Hubert Harrington (p417-420)

Photograph: *Baboon Shot for Thieving off Native Land* (on p418)

Photograph: *Native with a Two-Man Elephant Gun* (on p419)

Bunkered: Famous Golfers in Difficulties by Harold Macfarlane (p421-425)

Successful Sires of the Racing Season by Abel Chapman (p425-432)

Photograph [Rouch]: *Roi Herode* (facing p427)

Photograph [Rouch]: *Santoi* (facing p429)

Photograph [Rouch]: *Corcyra* (facing p431)

The Aftermath [verses] by Henry Pilkington (p432)

Morality in Sport (part 2) by Claye Shaw (p433-437)

The Oldest Pack of Hounds in Ireland (p438-441)

Photograph: *Duhallow Foxhounds - Nigel Baring, Master* (on p439)

Photograph: *Duhallow Foxhounds - John Longfield, Master* (on p439)

Photograph: *Duhallow Foxhounds - Stephen Grehan* (on p439)

The Perch as a Game Winter Fish by Arthur Sharp (p442-444)

The Sportsman's Library: Reviews of *The Corinthian Yachtman's Handbook* by Francis Cooke;
My Dog Friends by Maud Earl; *Dogs* by Frank Barton; *Rob Roy - The Story of a
Stag* by Theodore Tharp; *Fox and Hounds* by Edward Cuming; *Coaching Days* by
Edward Cuming; *Covert and Field Sport* by Edward Cuming; *Wild Life Across the
World* by Cherry Kearton; *Sport in Art* by William Baillie-Grohman; *The Shetland
Pony* by Charles Douglas; *The Romantic Side of Racehorse Breeding* by Edward
Moorhouse; *Athletics in Theory and Practice* by Ernst Hjertberg (p445-452)

Silhouette: *Hounds Crossed the Waveny Brook for the Second Time that Day* (facing p446)

Engraving [sculp. Tasniere]: *Stoning A Stag At Bay* (on p449)

Engraving [sculp. Gribelin]: *Shooting Flying* (on p450)

Polo Ponies Past and Present by Archibald Charlton (p452-456)

Assumed Names in Racing by George Burrows (p456-458)

Arthur Fisher by George Burrows (p459)

Our Van [inc. Kempton Park Meeting; Newmarket Racing; Liverpool Steeplechases; Quorn
Hunt; Hailsham Harriers] (p459-468)

Sporting Intelligence [inc. Oxford New College Rowing; Camberley Heath Golf Club;
Point-to-Point Dispute; Jockey Arrangements; Aldershot Command Golf Club;
Obituaries of George Wombwell, Gerald Paget, Henry Hope, Albert Gaudron and
Richard Carter; Waterloo Cup Winner] (p468-473)

Sporting Results (p473-474)

Volume 101, January - June 1914

Issue 647 : January 1914

Portrait [Hailey] of Frederick Templeman, jockey — Title page

Portrait [Swaine] and Biography - William Higson (p1-2)

The Foxhunter's Dream [verses] by George Scheu (p2)

Tarporley Hunt Club by George Teasdale-Buckell (p3-16)

Photograph: *Swan Hotel, Tarporley* (facing p5)

Lithograph: *Blue Cap* (facing p5)

Engraving: *Hound Race at Newmarket in 1762* (facing p6)

Lithograph: *Cheshire Hunt 1842* (facing p8)

Lithograph: *Rowland Egerton-Warburton* (facing p12)

Photograph: *Sandiway Head Hotel - 'The Blue Cap'* (on p14)

The Horse Show Outlook by Gerald Ricardo (p16-23)
Photograph: *William Moore and his Road Team* (facing p16)
Photograph: *Dorothy Chapman on one of her Winners* (facing p18)
Photograph: *Edward Stern Lover of Both Harness and Saddle* (facing p18)
Photograph: *Four Scenes from the East Berkshire Horse Show* (facing p21)
Fred Archer by Gerald Ricardo (p23-34)
Photograph [Shaw]: *House in Cheltenham where Archer was Born* (on p24)
Photograph: *Kings Arms at Prestbury* (on p25)
Photograph [Hailey]: *Archer's Home in Newmarket* (on p26)
Photograph [Sherborn]: *Portrait of Archer* (facing p26)
Lithograph: *Evelyn Boscawen* (on p28)
Lithograph: *James Machell* (on p28)
Lithograph: *Thomas French* (on p29)
Photograph [Sherborn]: *Matthew Dawson* (on p29)
Lithograph [pinx. Adam]: *The Mighty Ormonde* (facing p30)
Lithograph: *Archer in Royal Colours* (on p32)
[Obituary] Alfred Stedall by George Burrows (p35-37)
Lithograph [pinx. Ellis]: *Alfred Stedall* (facing p37)
How we Lost the America's Cup by Francis Cooke (p37-40)
The Sportsman's Library: Reviews of *Live Stock Journal Almanac 1914* by James Sinclair;
          Songs of Sports and Pastimes by Cyril Stacey; *Winter Sports in Switzerland* by
          Edward Benson; *Inland Golf* by Edward Ray (p41-47)
Photograph [Babbage]: *Four Typical British Light Horses* (facing p42)
Photograph: *A Practice Skiing Ground* (facing p44)
Photograph: *Sunny Corner, St.Moritz Bobsleigh Run* (facing p47)
The New Masters of Hounds Point-to-Point Committee by George Burrows (p47-52)
Motors and Hunting by Stuart Menzies (p52-54)
Some Sporting Epitaphs by Edgar Thomas (p54-56)
Quis Separabit [verses] by John Lang (p56)
In Tight Places by William Fox-Russell (p57-62)
Our Van [inc. Derby Racing; Warwick Races; Manchester Meeting; Meath Hounds; Croome
          Hunt; Biggleswade Harriers; Obituaries of Hollwey Steeds, William Christie
          and William Fitzsimons] (p63-72)
Photograph: *Henry Nevill* (on p69)
Photograph [Cuddy]: *William Fitzsimons* (on p71)
Sporting Intelligence [inc. Oxford University Trial Eights; Jockey Club Starter; Gimcrack Dinner;
          York & Ainsty Hunt Memorial; Dublin Golf Club; American Polo Cup; Obituaries
          of George Sayers, Otto Scavenius, George Lyttelton, Edward Higginson, Spencer
          Austen-Leigh, Charles Blake, William Erskine, Berkeley Paget, Frank Lewis,
          William Ansorge, Thomas Burns, Henry Venn and Patrick O'Donnell;
          Boddington Harriers; Bendigo Show; Review of *Northern Sport and Sportsmen*
          by Jack Fairfax-Blakeborough and Preview of *Annals of the Billesdon Hunt* by
          Frederick Palliser de Costobadie] (p72-79)
Sporting Results (p79-80)

Issue 648 : February 1914

Portrait [Elliott] and Biography - Marmaduke Furness (p81-83)
Lithograph [pinx. Fothergill]: *Better To Have It Than Hear Of It* (on p83)
Hunt Clubs and What They are Doing by Edward Cuming (p84-89)
After Ibex in Central Asia by Percy Etherton (90-96)
Photograph [Etherton]: *Crossing the Roof of the World - En Route to Thian Shan* (facing p90)
Photograph [Etherton]: *Crossing the Roof of the World - Yaks* (facing p90)
Photograph [Etherton]: *Kalmuk Hunter* (facing p93)

Photograph [Etherton]: *Two Ibex Horns*   (facing p93)
Photograph [Etherton]: *Three More Ibex Horns*   (on p99)
The Burro in Sport by Lincoln Wilbar   (p97-102)
Photograph: *The Burro*   (on p99)
Tufts of Turf by William Fox-Russell   (p102-110)
Lithograph: *John Herring*   (on p103)
Engraving [pinx. Turner]: *Don John*   (facing p104)
Engraving [pinx. Turner]: *Little Wonder*   (facing p104)
Engraving [pinx. Hall]: *Julius*   (facing p106)
Engraving [pinx. Hubbard]: *Nimrod*   (facing p106)
Engraving [sculp. Babbage]: *Out for an Early Morning Spin*   (on p110)
Varsity Men Famous in Hockey by Edward Thomson   (p111-117)
Photograph [McKenzie]: *Arthur Leighton*   (facing p112)
Photograph [Hensman]: *Francis Stocks*   (facing p112)
Photograph [Gillman]: *Frederick Stocks*   (facing p112)
Photograph: *William Smith*   (facing p112)
Photograph: *Henry Tennent*   (on p115)
To Hunting Farmers [verses] by George Fothergill   (p117)
On Chauffeur Troubles by Stuart Menzies   (p118-119)
Fish Culture and Sport by Arthur Sharp   (p120-124)
Photograph: *Stocking A Burn With Trout*   (on p121)
A Spanish Game Preserve   (p124-131)
Photograph: *A Journey to a Spanish Game Preserve*   (facing p126)
Photograph: *A Consultation by the Wayside*   (facing p126)
John Leech, Sportsman by Abel Chapman   (p131-136)
Lithograph [pinx. Leech]: *No Consequence*   (facing p132)
Lithograph [pinx. Leech]: *Made Horses*   (facing p134)
Sam Darling by Sydenham Dixon   (p137-142)
Photograph [Allen]: *Samuel Darling*   (on p137)
Masters of Hounds Point-to-Point Committee by George Burrows   (p142)
[Obituary] William Tailby by George Burrows   (p142-144)
Photograph: *William Tailby*   (on p143)
Our Van [inc. Nottingham Steeplechasing; Gatwick Racing; Cheltenham Meeting; Seavington
          Harriers; Atherstone Hunt; New Forest Buckhounds; Egerton-Warburton Poetry;
          Coaching Revival]   (p144-154)
Sporting Intelligence [inc. Essex Hunting Reminiscences; Yorkshire Golf Union; Durban
          Golf Course; Obituaries of Alfred Savigear, Alexander Brown, Bramwell Davis
          and Michel Ephrussi; Blackburn Rovers Football; Thanet Hunt]   (p154-159)
Sporting Results   (p159-160)

Issue 649 : March 1914

Portrait [Howard] and Biography - Alfred Pease   (p161-163)
Two Famous Irish Horses by Ernest Clarke   (p163-166)
A Missing Chapter in Bramham Moor History by William Scarth-Dixon   (p166-169)
Royalty in the Hunting Field by Edward Cuming   (p170-175)
With Skis in Sweden by Nicholas Jarvis   (p175-182)
Photograph: *A View of Lake Äre*   (on p176)
Photograph: *Äre Ski Jump*   (facing p176)
Photograph: *Sailing on Skates*   (facing p176)
Photograph: *A Group of Little Laplanders*   (on p178)
Photograph: *Laplanders Sledge*   (facing p178)
Photograph: *Pony Skiing*   (facing p178)
Photograph: *Ice Yachting in Sweden*   (facing p180)

Photograph: *Ice Yacht Showing Passenger Accommodation* (facing p180)
Coursing: Some Training Quarters by William Lamonby (p183-187)
The Trout Brook in March by Arthur Sharp (p187-191)
Shooting in the Yangtse Valley by John Seigne (p191-193)
When to Sell your Car by Stuart Menzies (p193-195)
Single-Handed Cruising by Francis Cooke (p195-199)
Aintree Calls [verses] by William Ogilvie (p199)
Matthew Hale by Charles Batchelder (p200-202)
Photograph [Tear]: *Matthew Hale* (facing p200)
Some Coaching Reminiscences by Wodehouse Garland (p203-209)
Lithograph [Yuarde]: *The Post Boy* (facing p205)
Photograph: *Tilling's Magnet* (facing p204)
Photograph: *Vanderbilt's Venture* (facing p206)
Lithograph [pinx. Henderson]: *The Travelling Post* (facing p209)
The Starting Difficulty by Sydenham Dixon (p210-213)
[Review] Racing: *Songs of Sports and Pastimes* by Cyril Stacey (p214-215)
Lithograph [Mason]: *Ever Had Instructions From An Owner* (on p214)
Lithograph [Mason]: *Gone Into the Ring* (on p215)
A Plea for the Red-Leg by Frank Bonnett (p216-221)
The Master of the Horse [verses] by George Fothergill (p221-222)
Engraving: *One of the Old School* (on p222)
Our Van [inc. Lincolnshire Handicap; Haydock Park Races; Palatine Steeplechase; Warwick Meeting; Belvoir Hunt; Dartmoor Hounds; Old Surrey Hunt] (p223-232)
The Sportsman's Library: Reviews of *An Agricultural Faggot* by Richard Rew; *The Salmon Rivers of England and Wales* by Augustus Grimble; *Sport and Nature in the Himalayas* by Peter Bairnsfather; *Vices in Virtues and Other Vagaries* by Thomas Longueville (p232-233)
Sporting Intelligence [inc. University Football; Worcestershire Hunt Club; Assumed Names in Racing; United States Polo Association; Mid-Surrey Golf Club; Obituaries of George Dobell, Edward Mitchell ('Captain Coe' of *The Star*), William Moberly, Wightman Wood and Nicholas Snow; Greyhound *Coupe de Fontenoy* Meeting; Review of *Wisden's Cricketers' Almanack*; Tasmanian Yacht Club] (p233-238)
Sporting Results (p238-240)

Issue 650 : April 1914

Portrait [Howard] and Biography - Ferdinand Hanbury (p241-242)
George Stevens by Claye Shaw (p243-249)
Photograph [Shaw]: *Headstone at Cleeve Hill* (facing p244)
Photograph [Shaw]: *Obelisk in Cheltenham Cemetery* (facing p246)
Lithograph [pinx. Garrard]: *A Cover Hack* (on p249)
The Southcourt Stud by George Teasdale-Buckell (p250-257)
Photograph: *Leopold de Rothschild* (facing p250)
Photograph: *St.Frusquin's Box at Southcourt* (facing p253)
Photograph: *St.Frusquin* (facing p252)
Photograph: *St.Amant* (facing p255)
Photograph: *Radium* (facing p254)
The Spread of Polo by Archibald Charlton (p257-259)
Easter by the Waterside by Ernest Phillips (p259-262)
Shooting the Rooks in May by Aitken Oldfield (p262-265)
Photograph: *The Rook* (on p262)
Shooting in the Fayoum, Egypt by Alfred Herbert (p266-272)
Pugi by Hugh Mallin (p272-274)
The Enjoyment of Motor Touring by Stuart Menzies (p275-277)

A Yachting Holiday by Francis Cooke (p277-280)
Photograph [Cooper]: *Outward Bound* (facing p279)
Photograph [Cooper]: *A Fine Sailing Breeze* (facing p279)
Coaching Clubs of the Past by Victor Wilson (p280-283)
A Forty Pound Fighter [verses] by George Skues (p284)
A Problem in Ethics by Sinclair Carr (p285-289)
The Spring Horse Shows by Gerald Ricardo (p289-301)
Photograph [Babbage]: *Champions Goalkeeper* (facing p291)
Photograph [Babbage]: *Hopwood Viceroy* (facing p290)
Photograph [Babbage]: *Beckingham Lady Grace* (facing p292)
Photograph [Babbage]: *Cudham Marjorie* (facing p295)
Photograph [Babbage]: *Torchfire* (facing p297)
Photograph: *Antonius* (on p297)
Photograph [Babbage]: *Birk Gill* (facing p299)
Baiting of Wild Beasts in the Tower of London by Culling Gaze (p302-304)
Our Van [inc. Thames Handicap Steeplechase; Manchester Racing; Grand Military Meeting; Hurst Park Races; Goathland and Staintondale Hunts' Dispute; Quorn Hunt; South Shropshire Hounds] (p305-313)
Sporting Intelligence [inc. University Gymnastics; Boxing Finances; Obituaries of Gilbert Elliot, Frank Haines, Frederick Halford (*Baily's* contributor), Henry Pilkington (*Baily's* contributor) and Ernest Dresden; San Francisco Yacht Race; Selby & District Hunting Committee] (p313-318)
Photograph: *Gilbert Elliott* (facing p317)
Sporting Results (p318-320)

Issue 651 : May 1914

Portrait [Elliott] and Biography - Frederick Lambart (p321-323)
Yachting Season Outlook by Francis Cooke (p323-326)
Wanted A Lightweight Jockey by George Teasdale-Buckell (p327-334)
Engraving: *Jem Robinson* (on p328)
Photograph [Hailey]: *Herbert Randall* (on p329)
Photograph: *Alfred Day* (on p330)
Engraving: *Thomas Challoner* (on p330)
Photograph [Hailey]: *Elijah Wheatley* (on p331)
Photograph: *Charles Wood* (on p332)
Photograph: *George Barrett* (on p332)
Photograph: *Thomas Ashmall* (on p333)
The Mexican and his Cockfight by Frederick Kennedy (p334-336)
Photograph: *A Mexican Cock-Fighter* (on p334)
Photograph: *Mexican Cock-Pit* (facing p334)
Photograph: *A Glimpse of Mexican Life* (facing p334)
The Trout Stream in May by Arthur Sharp (p337-341)
Photograph: *Trout Fishing* (on p339)
Testing the America's Cup Yachts by George Hopcroft (p341-345)
Lithograph [pinx. Hopcroft]: *The Sloop 'Mischief' 1881* (facing p342)
Headmasters as Athletes by Harold Macfarlane (p345-351)
Coaching Then and Now by Gerald Ricardo (p351-357)
Lithograph: *The Oxford and Cheltenham Coach* (facing p352)
Photograph: *Coaching as a Spectacle* (facing p354)
Sport in the Wilds of Yorkshire by William Leighton (p357-362)
A Houseboat Trip in China by John Seigne (p362-367)
Photograph [Seigne]: *Picturesque Houses Overhanging the Waterway* (facing p362)
Photograph [Seigne]: *A Stone and Wooden Bridge* (facing p362)

Photograph [Seigne]: *A Maze of Traffic in the Narrow Canal of the Village* (facing p362)
Photograph [Seigne]: *The Outskirts of a Village* (facing p362)
Photograph [Seigne]: *Ready to Land* (on p365)
Photograph [Seigne]: *The Morning's Bag* (on p365)
Photograph [Seigne]: *Houseboat Entering the City Moat* (on p366)
Art of Brook Fishing with the Worm in Clear Water by George Garrow-Green (p368-371)
Horses in War by Cameron Gull (p372-377)
Marking of Trees for Felling by Charles Curtis (p377-379)
Enemies of Fish and Fish Spawn by John Smith (p379-383)
Avoidable Dangers in Motoring by Stuart Menzies (p383-385)
Polo Notes and News by Archibald Charlton (p385-386)
Our Van [inc. Cheltenham Steeplechases; Lincoln Races; Aintree Meeting; Nottingham
         Spring Handicap; Atherstone Hunt; West Kent Harriers; Linlithgow &
         Stirlingshire Hunt] (p387-397)
Photograph [Rouch]: *Sunloch* (facing p388)
Sporting Intelligence [inc. University Boat Race; Sandy Lodge Golf Club; Obituaries of
         Frank Sharpe, Piers Egerton-Warburton, John Close-Brooks, Frederick Howey,
         Sydney Day, Henry Williams-Wynn, John Lempriere, George Hodgson and
         Hubert von Herkomer; Chester Race Company] (p397-399)
Sporting Results (p400)

Issue 652 : June 1914

Portrait [Beresford] and Biography - Stephen Christy (p401-402)
Point-to-Point Racing and the National Hunt Committee by George Burrows (p403)
Polo Notes and Gossip by Archibald Charlton (p404-406)
Voltigeur and The Flying Dutchman by George Teasdale-Buckell (p407-417)
Engraving [pinx. Hall]: *Voltigeur* (facing p408)
Engraving: *The Flying Dutchman* (facing p410)
Lithograph: *Voltigeur Winning the Doncaster Cup* (facing p412)
Engraving [pinx. Hall]: *Elnathan Flatman* (facing p414)
Engraving [pinx. Hall]: *Job Marson* (facing p417)
Dun Colour in Horses by Henry Farnie (p418-420)
An Old Chester Cup and Some Stories by William Scarth-Dixon (p420-424)
Racquets at Queen's and Prince's by Harold Rudd (p424-430)
Photograph: *John Manners* (on p425)
Photograph [Elliott]: *Edgar Baerlein* (on p427)
Photograph: *John Strachan* (on p429)
Photograph: *Laurence Monier-Williams* (on p429)
Wilderness Camps by Lincoln Wilbar (p431-434)
The Call of the Pointer by John Nicholson (p434-438)
Photograph: *Head Studies of Pointers* (facing p434)
Photograph: *The Pointer is Useful in Sport* (on p437)
The Care of Motor Tyres by Stuart Menzies (p438-440)
Ben Capell by Cuthbert Bradley (p440-443)
Engraving [pinx. Bradley]: *Ben Capell* (facing p440)
Centreboards and Sliding Keels by George Hopcroft (p444-446)
Lithograph [pinx. Hopcroft]: *Five Centre-Boards* (facing p444)
The Sportsman's Library: Reviews of *Golf* by Arnaud Massy; *The Foxhound of the
         Twentieth Century* by Cuthbert Bradley; *Field Studies of Some Rarer British
         Birds* by John Walpole-Bond; *Wild Game in Zambesia* by Reginald Maugham;
         The Image of War by Robert Dunkin (p447-452)
Photograph: *A Fine Bag of Lion* (facing p450)
Frederick Templeman by George Burrows (p452)

The Angler in Wales by Walter Gallichan (p453-455)

Our Van [inc. Kempton Park Meeting; Manchester Steeplechases; Westminster Plate; Chiddingfold Hounds; Waterford Hunt; Exmoor Staghunting; Worcestershire Hunt; Border Counties Otterhounds] (p455-465)

Sporting Intelligence [inc. Oxford University Athletes in Philadelphia; Regatta Previews; English Bowls Association; Obituaries of Alexander Park, Frank Wedge, William Lucas, Robert Frost-Smith, Joseph McCormick, William Foster and Arthur Duller; Bishop's Stortford Golf Club; American Real Tennis; Review of *The History of the Muskerry Foxhounds* by John Lindsay; New York Yacht Club] (p466-471)

Sporting Results (p471-472)

Volume 102 : July - December 1914

Issue 653 : July 1914

Portrait [Gillman] of George Baker, huntsman — Title page

Portrait [Smith] and Biography - John Philipps (p1-3)

Masters of Hounds Point-to-Point Committee by George Burrows (p3-4)

Masters of Foxhounds Association Annual General Meeting Report (p4-11)

Polo Notes and News by Archibald Charlton (p11-14)

Wapiti Hunting in Central China by Percy Etherton (p14-19)

Photograph [Etherton]: *Asiatic Roedeer from Thian Shan* (facing p14)

Photograph [Etherton]: *Camp in the Thian Shan* (facing p14)

Photograph [Etherton]: *A Fourteen-Pointer Asiatic Wapiti* (on p17)

Photograph [Etherton]: *Fording a River in the Thian Shan Mountains* (on p18)

The Public Schools and Henley by Claude Holland (p19-24)

The Oldest English Race Meeting by Jack Fairfax-Blakeborough (p24-27)

The Trout-Fisher in July by Arthur Sharp (p28-31)

Teaching Children to Ride (part 1) by Eva Christy (p32-36)

Photograph: *Maud Preece on Silver Grey* (facing p32)

Reigate Hound Show by William Scarth-Dixon (p36-41)

Photograph: *Lord Willoughby de Broke at Reigate* (facing p36)

Photograph: *Rhetoric* (on p39)

The Maunsell-Richardson Memorial Pavilion (p42)

Photograph: *Harrow Memorial Pavilion* (facing p42)

County Cricket by Herbert Hewett (p44-49)

Free Fishing by Clifford Cordley (p49-51)

Motorists at Wayside Garages by Stuart Menzies (p52-53)

America's Cup Prospects by Francis Cooke (p54-57)

Our Van [inc. Newmarket Meeting; Gatwick Races; York Racing; Epsom Meeting; Manchester Cup] (p57-66)

Photograph: *Durbar II* (facing p61)

Photograph: *Herman Duryea* (on p62)

Photograph: *Thomas Murphy* (on p63)

More Coaching Reminiscences by George Hardwick (p66-68)

Sporting Intelligence [inc. Masters of Foxhounds Meeting; Hunt Secretaries' Association Annual General Meeting; Hunt Servants' Benefit Society Annual General Meeting; Pytchley Hunt; Sandwich Golf; Obituaries of Alice Lister, Edith Cay, Eustace Barlow, Reginald Foster, John Heathcoat-Amory and Elizabeth Tute; Wharfedale Agricultural Show] (p69-76)

Sporting Results (p76-78)

Issue 654 : August 1914

Portrait [Turner] and Biography - Thomas Wickham-Boynton (p79-81)

The Highest Climbs in the World by George Abraham (p82-89)
Photograph [Sella]: *Below Kabru* (facing p82)
Photograph [Sella]: *High Camp Below Kangchenjunga* (facing p86)
Captain Barclay of Ury by Culling Gaze (p89-92)
Teaching Children to Ride (part 2) by Eva Christy (p93-98)
Photograph: *Sylvia Kaye on Ping Pong* (facing p94)
Photograph: *Jean Douglas-Hamilton on Dainty* (facing p96)
The Record Lightweight Jockey by George Teasdale-Buckell (p99-102)
Photograph: *John Kent* (facing p100)
The Ocean Passage by George Hopcroft (p103-105)
The Twelfth [verses] by Alan Haig-Brown (p106)
The Moorland Stream in August by Arthur Sharp (p107-111)
[Obituary] Allan Gibson Steel by Herbert Hewett (p111-114)
Photograph [Hawkins]: *Allan Steel* (facing p112)
Too Much Wimbledon by Herbert Bourke (p114-116)
Motoring Makeshifts by Stuart Menzies (p117-119)
Cricket Notes and News by Herbert Hewett (p119-126)
Photograph [Hawkins]: *Johnny Douglas* (facing p120)
Photograph [Hawkins]: *Bernard Bosanquet* (facing p122)
Grouse and Grouse Shooting by Frank Bonnett (p126-130)
Horses and Hounds at Peterborough by William Scarth-Dixon (p130-139)
Photograph [Babbage]: *Luxury* (facing p133)
Lithograph [pinx. Bradley]: *Fitzwilliam Wiseman* (facing p134)
Polo Notes and News by Archibald Charlton (p139-143)
Foxes and Fowls in Parliament by Thomas Dale (p143-145)
Our Van [inc. Calcutta Turf Club; Newbury Races; Ascot Meeting; Gosforth Park Racing; Blackmore Vale Hunt; Devon & Somerset Staghounds; Bexhill Hounds; South Oxfordshire Hunt] (p145-153)
Sporting Intelligence [inc. Cambridge University Sporting Successes; Belgian Golf; Hallamshire Golf Club; Obituaries of Charles Blacklock, Joseph Brain and Francis Egerton; Christie's Hunting Auction; Wimbledon Lawn Tennis Championship; Lightweight Boxing; Hurlingham Club Polo] (p154-157)
Sporting Results (p157-158)

Issue 655 : September 1914

Portrait [Fry] and Biography - Robert McKergow (p159-161)
War and Sport by George Burrows (p162-165)
Three Great Polo Captains by Thomas Dale (p165-172)
Photograph [Lafayette]: *John Watson* (facing p166)
Photograph: *Harry Whitney* (facing p168)
Photograph: *Walter Buckmaster* (facing p170)
Some Prominent Breeders of Livestock by George Teasdale-Buckell (p173-180)
Photograph: *Charles Gordon-Lennox* (facing p175)
Photograph: *Francis Baring* (facing p175)
Photograph: *Ailwyn Fellowes* (facing p175)
Photograph: *Digby Willoughby* (facing p175)
Photograph: *George Coventry* (facing p175)
Photograph: *Gilbert Greenall* (facing p175)
Photograph: *Arthur Nicholson* (facing p175)
Photograph: *Watkin Williams-Wynn* (facing p175)
Photograph [Bartlett]: *George Herbert* (on p175)
Photograph: *Thomas Green* (on p176)
Photograph: *Leopold Salomons* (facing p176)

Photograph: *Robert Whitworth* (facing p176)
Photograph: *Romer Williams* (facing p176)
Photograph: *Charles Coltman-Rogers* (facing p176)
Photograph: *Albert Hickling* (facing p176)
Photograph: *Alexander Bowie* (facing p176)
Photograph: *Thomas Simpson* (facing p176)
Photograph: *Durbin Montefiore* (facing p176)
Photograph: *Walter Bourne* (on p178)
Photograph: *Frank Bibby* (on p178)
[Obituary] Eustace Loder by George Burrows (p180-183)
Photograph [Lafayette]: *Eustace Loder* (facing p180)
The Insurance of Motorcars by Stuart Menzies (p183-185)
Public School Cricket at Lord's by Herbert Hewett (p185-188)
Tufts of Turf by William Fox-Russell (p188-192)
Photograph: *John Osborne* (on p189)
September Shooting Prospects by Frank Bonnett (p192-195)
Our Van [inc. Bibury Club Meeting; Newmarket Racing; Sandown Park Races; Leicester Oaks; Goodwood Plate; Drogheda Memorial Stakes; Waterford Hunt; Dartmoor Otterhounds; North Tipperary Hunt] (p196-201)
Sporting Intelligence [inc. University Boxing Blues; Wingfield Sculls; Farmers' and Poultry Keepers' Bill; Olympia Horse Show; Obituaries of William Forbes and Henry Strutt; French Golf; Prestwich Golf Club] (p201-204)
Sporting Results (p204-206)

Issue 656 : October 1914

Portrait [Howard] and Biography - Robert Strawbridge (p207-208)
Hunting's Contribution to the War by Edward Cuming (p209-218)
Poultry Damage and What is Paid per Year by George Burrows (p219-226)
On the Influence of Sport on the English Cavalry Horse by Thomas Dale (p227-229)
Covert Shooting and the War by Frank Bonnett (p230-233)
The Value of Pony Blood by Edward Moorhouse (p234-239)
Photograph [Babbage]: *Polo-Bred Filly 'Black Fashion'* (facing p234)
Photograph [Babbage]: *Polo-Bred Gelding 'Sunrise'* (facing p234)
Photograph: *Four Varied Uses of Ponies* (facing p236)
Photograph: *Welsh Mountain Ponies and Cobs* (on p238)
The Sportsman's Library: Reviews of *Reminiscences* by Sam Darling; *Mixed and Rough Shooting* by Frank Bonnett; *Golf for Women* by George Duncan; *Trout in Lakes and Reservoirs* by Ernest Phillips and *The Motor Routes of Germany* by Henry Hecht (p239-241)
Our Van [inc. Irish Turf Club; Brighton Meeting; Gatwick Races; Folkestone Meeting; Seaton Delaval Stakes; Tiverton Staghounds; Tickham Hunt; Warwickshire Hounds] (p242-247)
Sporting Intelligence [inc. Rowing in Chester; Hurlingham Polo; Ulster Yacht Club; Grouse Season; Obituaries of Victor Brooke, Charles Browning, Henry Hughes-Onslow, Eric Wright and Robert Mitchell; Hainault Forest Golf Club; Yonkers Handicap Race] (p247-252)
Sporting Results (p252-254)

Issue 657 : November 1914

Portrait [Bassano] and Biography - Edwin Alderson (p255-256)
Hunt Changes in 1914 by Edward Cuming (p257-269)
The Age for Entering Colts to their Work by Henry Farnie (p270-272)
Skyline Tommy [verses] by William Ogilvie (p273)
A Fortnight's Shooting in the Yangtsze by Percy Etherton (p274-275)

The Mexican Horse by Trevor Roller   (p276-277)
In Khaki [verses] by Michael Hope   (p277)
[Review] Turf Tales Retold: *Reminiscences* by Sam Darling   (p278-280)
Turf Nomenclature by Seymour Ramsdale   (p281-283)
Baily's Hunting Directory 1914-15 by Edward Cuming   (p283-285)
Photograph [Allen]: *Owen Philipps*   (on p284)
Photograph [Clarke]: *Edmund Turton*   (on p284)
Photograph: *Frederic Lambart*   (on p285)
The Sportsman's Library: Reviews of *The Complete Curler* by John Grant; *British
          Mountaineering* by Claude Benson; *Golf Stories* by Gerald Batchelor; *Wild Life
          in the Woods and Streams* by Charles Palmer; *How to Dress Salmon Flies* by
          Thomas Pryce-Tannatt; *Minor Tactics of the Chalk Stream* by George Skues;
          The Shotgun and Its Uses by Frank Bonnett, and *The Cottesbrooke Pedigree
          Book* by Robert Brassey   (p286-289)
Photograph [Myron]: *The Tee-Ringer at Work*   (facing p286)
Photograph [Winchester]: *Preparing to Play*   (facing p286)
Photograph [Lunn]: *Delivering the Stone*   (facing p286)
Our Van [inc. Jockey Club Ruling; Doncaster Races; Warwick Meeting; Newmarket Racing;
          Fitzwilliam Hounds; Meynell Hunt; Obituaries of John Seabrook and William
          Coates; Hertfordshire Hunt]   (p290-296)
Sporting Intelligence [inc. Obituaries of Charles Assheton-Smith, Mary Oakeley, Norman
          de Crespigny, George Knight, Evelyn Bradford, George Springfield, Riversdale
          Grenfell, James Huggan, Mockler Ferryman, John Manners, Charles Banbury,
          Jean Bouin, William Fuller-Maitland, Frederick Allfrey, Charles Sills, Charles
          D'Alton, Wilfred Brownlee, Arthur Tree, Bransby Cooper, James Haggin,
          William York and William Tweedie (*Baily's* contributor); Kerry Beagles; Masters
          of Foxhounds Association; Polo Statuette]   (p296-301)
Photograph [Hughes]: *Charles Assheton-Smith*   (on p296)
Sporting Results   (p302)

Issue 658 : December 1914

Portrait [Lafayette] and Biography - Alfred Miller   (p303-304)
Surtees and Mr Sponge by Hugh Henry   (p305-310)
The Sporting Mind (part 1) by Claye Shaw   (p311-314)
The Racing Year of 1914 by Thomas Pinch   (p315-318)
Polo Players in War Time and Obituary List by Archibald Charlton   (p319-322)
[Obituary] Walter Gilbey by George Burrows   (p323-328)
Lithograph [pinx. Orchardson]: *Walter Gilbey*   (facing p324)
George Baker by George Burrows   (p328)
Our Van [inc. Bloodstock Breeders; Kempton Park Racing; Middle Park Plate; Lingfield Park
          Meeting; Tedworth Hunt; Tipperary Hounds; Cottesmore Hunt; Pytchley
          Hounds]   (p329-335)
Sporting Intelligence [inc. Oxford University Drag Hunt; Obituaries of Maurice Battenberg,
          William MacNeill, Thomas Cunningham, Alastair Gwyer, William Christie,
          Edmund Antrobus, Lachlan Gordon-Duff, Hugh Sandbach, Musgrave Wroughton,
          Hugh Shields, Francis Lambton, Francis Mackworth, Francis Waller, James Browning,
          Gordon Wilson, Lionel Hawkins, William Wyndham, George Brooke, Aymer Maxwell,
          Stephen Christy, Bartholomew Mullins, Francis Alexander, William
          Montagu-Douglas-Scott and Richard Mather; Brecon Hounds; Lichfield Beagles;
          Ribblesdale Buckhounds; Aspull Harriers; Ardnamurchan Forest Stags; Professional
          Golfers Association; Greyhound Club of France]   (p335-341)
Sporting Results   (p342)

Volume 103, January - June 1915

Issue 659 : January 1915

Portrait [Brookes] of Reginald Reynolds, huntsman — Title page
Engraving [sculp. Babbage]: *Horses Leaving Stables* — (on Illustrations page)
Lithograph [pinx. Best]: *A Ginger-Red Cock* — (facing p1)
Portrait [Howard] and Biography - Ivor Guest — (p1-4)
Gone to the War [verses] by Michael Hope — (p4)
The Sporting Mind (part 2) by Claye Shaw — (p5-9)
Bears by Duncan Oliver — (p9-11)
The Showing of Horses by George Teasdale-Buckell — (p12-17)
Lithograph [pinx. Ferneley]: *Sambo* and *Pilot* — (facing p12)
Photograph: *A Summer Show-Ring Scene* — (on p15)
[Obituary] John Barker by George Burrows — (p18-21)
Photograph: *John Barker* — (facing p18)
The Elsenham Stud Sale by Tresham Gilbey — (p21-23)
Future Horse Supplies by James Sinclair — (p24-26)
Photograph [Babbage]: *Victory II* — (facing p24)
Photograph [Babbage]: *Ver Vigorous* — (facing p24)
Polo Players at the War and Obituary List by Archibald Charlton — (p27-30)
Melmerby Fell [verses] by George Rimington — (p30-31)
Our Van [inc. Manchester Racing; Lincoln Meeting; Lancashire Handicap; Stevenstone Hunt; Lamerton Hounds; Croome Hunt; Ward Union Hunt] — (p32-40)
Sporting Intelligence [inc. University Rowing; Obituaries of George Docker, Stirling Stuart, Francis Annesley, Frederick Pemberton, Archer Windsor-Clive, Francis Monckton (*Baily's* contributor), Arthur Collins, Mervyn Crawshay, Gordon Wilson, Henry Parnell, Bernard Gordon-Lennox, Lewis Robertson, Robert Flint-Drake, Cecil Wood, Howard St.George, Robert Page, Harold Whitaker, Henry Chinnery, George Vize, Charles Henderson, John Crichton, John Grant, Alexander Baltazzi, Harry Kelley and Sidney Jacobs; Review of *Rugby Football Annual*; Bath Swimming Club; Tanatside Harriers] — (p40-47)
Sporting Results — (p48)

Issue 660 : February 1915

Portrait [Adams] and Biography - Eric Palmer — (p49-50)
To the World's Foe [verses] by Michael Hope — (p50)
Some Masters of the Cheshire Hounds by George Teasdale-Buckell — (p51-56)
The Highland Pony by Coltman Rogers — (p57-60)
Photograph [Reed]: *A Group of Highland Ponies* — (facing p59)
Doctor Syntax by Edward Cuming — (p60-62)
Curling as an Indoor Game by Bertram Smith — (p63-66)
Engraving [sculp. Babbage]: *Trotting* — (on p66)
Panthers and their Ways (part 1) by George Armour — (p67-68)
Derby Winners and What has Become of Them by Thomas Pinch — (p69-73)
Engraving [sculp. Babbage]: *Stallion* — (on p73)
The Sportsman's Library: Reviews of *Through the Brazilian Wilderness* by Theodore Roosevelt; *Agriculture, Theoretical and Practical* by John Wrightson; *Jungle Sport in Ceylon* by Marcus Millett; *From Jungle to Zoo* by Ellen Velvin; *The Champion* by Howard Whitehouse — (p74)
You Keep the Ball A'Rolling [verses] by John Walters — (p75)
Engraving [sculp. Babbage]: *Farrier at Work* — (on p75)
Bags, Ancient and Modern by Harold Macfarlane — (p76-79)

Our Van [inc. National Hunt Stewards; Hurst Park Steeplechase; Kempton Park Meeting; Manchester Handicap Steeplechase; Burton Hounds; York & Ainsty Hunt; Obituary of Montague Cholmeley; Sinnington Hunt] (p80-87)

Sporting Intelligence [inc. Obituaries of Percy Illingworth, Arthur Jones, Henry Grosvenor, William Thomson, Charles Brackley, George McLaughlin, Thomas Goodgames, Alfred Smith, William Willmott-Dixon (*Baily's* contributor), John Wright, Bedford Ogden, Samuel Roberts, Frank Beevor, Francis Oakeley, Walter Lloyd, Hugh Taylor, Archibald Trotter, Radolph Persse, Arthur Murray-Smith and William Newton; Spring Horse Shows; Essex Hunt; Reviews of Annuals] (p87-95)

Photograph: *Where Are They Now* (on p93)

Sporting Results (p96)

Issue 661 : March 1915

Portrait [Elliott] and Biography - Charles Kidd (p97-99)

Foxhunting at the Front by Ashford White (p99-100)

Sportsmen Who have Heard the Call by Gerald Ricardo (p101-106)

The Past Shooting Season and the Future by Frank Bonnett (p107-108)

The Slow Hunting Basset by Alan Sealy (p109-111)

Photograph: *Sandringham Valour* (on p110)

The Man that Counts [verses] by Michael Hope (p111)

Contrasts by George Teasdale-Buckell (p112-119)

Engraving [sculp. Herring]: *Bay Middleton* (facing p112)

Engraving [sculp. Herring]: *Touchstone* (facing p116)

Engraving: *Doncaster* (on p119)

The Patriot [verses] by Cyril Stacey (p120-122)

Joseph Osborne - His Books by George Burrows (p123-125)

Engraving [pinx. Turner]: *Harkaway* (on p125)

Panthers and Their Ways (part 2) by George Armour (p126-128)

Should we Establish Remount Depots by Gerald Ricardo (p128-130)

Our Van [inc. Staffordshire Handicap; Gatwick Races; Norbiton Steeplechase; Warwick Meeting; Puckeridge Hunt; Ludlow Hounds; New Forest Foxhounds; Ledbury Hunt] (p131-139)

Sporting Intelligence [inc. Oxford University Drag Hunt; Obituaries of Charles Taylor, Piers St.Aubyn, Percy Kendall, George Chaworth-Musters, Charles Worsley, Frederick Turner, Charles Stewart, William Duncombe, Thomas Miller, Edwin White, William Grieves, Frederick Steele, Charles Shafto, Samual Hoare, Francis Monkland, Joseph Easby, Percy Illingworth and Thomas Perry; Elsenham Stud Sale] (p140-145)

Sporting Results (p145-146)

Issue 662 : April 1915

Portrait [Goath] and Biography - Gilbert Popplestone (p147-148)

Dispatch Riders and Military Rides by Harold Macfarlane (p149-152)

Dishonoured [verses] by Michael Hope (p152)

Sportsmen Who Have Heard the Call by Gerald Ricardo (p153-156)

Should Racing be Stopped by George Burrows (p156-158)

A Notable Polo Pony Stud by Arthur Coaten (p159-160)

Photograph: *Brood Mare 'Actress'* (on p159)

The Spring Horse Shows by Gerald Ricardo (p161-169)

Photograph [Babbage]: *Blaisdon Jupiter* (facing p163)

Photograph [Babbage]: *Birk Gill* (facing p163)

Photograph [Babbage]: *Himan* (facing p165)

Phorograph [Babbage]: *Golf Ball* (facing p165)

Photograph [Babbage]: *Repeat II* (facing p167)
Photograph [Babbage]: *Spanish Hero* (facing p167)
Photograph [Babbage]: *Adbolton Kingmaker* (facing p169)
Photograph [Babbage]: *Terrington Modish* (facing p169)
Photograph [Babbage]: *Tissington Bauble* (on p169)
The First Trout by Ernest Phillips (p170-172)
[Review] *The Shire Horse* by Albert Frost (p173-174)
[Review] *The Complete Golfer* by Harry Vardon (p175-178)
Our Van [inc. Birmingham Meeting; Thames Steeplechase; Rendlesham Hurdle Handicap; Uttoxeter Races; Quorn Hunt; Vale of Lune Harriers; Crawley & Horsham Hunt; North Devon Otterhounds] (p179-185)
Sporting Intelligence [inc. Cambridge University Rowing; Warwickshire Hunt Poultry Fund; County Polo Association; Obituaries of George Cadogan, Hamilton Labat, Robert Lucas-Tooth, George Nutting, William Travers, Richard Turk, Cloudesley Marsham, Joseph Dexter, Henry Gray, James Chuter, George Bell, William Eden, George Hodgkinson, Martin Buckle, William Morgan, John Coke, William Burbidge, Charles Daft, Audley Thursby, Brian Osborne, George Newstead, Edward Nash, Rowland Beech, Arundell Neave, Kenneth Powell and Eric Gilbey; Waterloo Cup; Limerick Racecourse; Gloucestershire County Cricket Club; Racquets] (p186-194)
Sporting Results (p194)

Issue 663 : May 1915

Portrait [Whaley] and Biography - William Gresson (p195-196)
The Last Day [verses] by Peggy Grant (p196)
What Hunting Men Have Done for Britain by Edward Cuming (p197-225)
Photograph: *Foxhunting at the Front* (facing p198)
Photograph: *Godfrey Heseltine* (on p201)
Photograph [Elliott]: *Frederick Wingfield-Digby* (on p203)
Photograph: *Gerald Burgoyne* (on p204)
Photograph [Bartlett]: *Herbert Connop* (on p205)
Photograph: *Esmond Morrison* (on p215)
The Sportsman's Battalions by George Burrows (p225-228)
A Sporting Pike by Ernest Williams (p228-230)
Our Van [inc. Cheltenham National Hunt Steeplechases; Wolverhampton Meeting; Newbury Races; Durham Plate; Holderness Hunt; Dartmoor Hounds; Ludlow Hunt Farmers] (230-238)
Sporting Intelligence [inc. New College & Magdalen Beagles; Obituaries of Herbert Tyrwhitt-Drake, Herbert Ethelston, Douglas Pennant, William Montgomery, Gordon Wilson, William Stackhouse, Samuel Cockerell, Wyndham Halswell, Nathan Rothschild, Archibald Paterson, John Ornsby, John Godwin, John Toppin, Robert Vyner, Andrew Stoddart, Thomas Parrington and Mackenzie Ross; Warwickshire Hounds; Old Fold Manor Golf Club] (p238-244)
Sporting Results (p244-246)

Issue 664 : June 1915

Portrait [Howard] and Biography - Edmund Turton (p247-248)
Yachtsmen and the War by Francis Cooke (p249-251)
The Last of the Old School by Alexander Chalmers (p252-256)
Our Roads by Athol Maudslay (p256-257)
Engraving [pinx. Stubbs]: *Eclipse* (facing p259)
Walter Gilbey's Sporting Pictures by William Roberts (p259-264)
Engraving [pinx. Sartorius]: *Stag Hunt* (facing p261)
Engraving [pinx. Alken]: *The Leicestershire Steeplechase* (facing p263)

Engraving [pinx. Marshall]: *Barrington Price and Hunter* (facing p262)

Teddington by George Burrows (p265-266)

Engraving [sculp. Hacker]: *Teddington* (on p266)

The Horse in Peace and War by Henry Callaby (p267-270)

George Bentinck by George Teasdale-Buckell (p270-274)

Reginald Reynolds by George Burrows (p274)

Our Van [inc. Greenham Stakes; Epsom Meeting; Newmarket Races; Chester Cup; New Forest Hounds; Surrey Staghounds; Brighton Harriers; Poonah Polo] (p275-282)

Sporting Intelligence [inc. University Cricket; Masters of Harriers and Beagles Association; Obituaries of Gilchrist Maclagan, Gerald Kirk, Wilfred Onions, Eric Samuel, Henry Warren-Davis, Albert Snellgrove, James Duffy, Alexander Todd, Ronald Poulton-Palmer, Anthony Wilding, Henry Tomkinson, Henry Biron, James Rankin, William Walters, John Johnson, Stanley Duckett, Andrew Greig, George Breed, Frederick Reynolds and Thomas Mitchell; Essex County Cricket Club; Scottish Football Association; Ludlow Hunt] (p282-287)

Sporting Results (p287-288)

Volume 104, July - December 1915

Issue 665 : July 1915

Portrait [Hayman] of William Back, huntsman Title page

Portrait [Howard] and Biography - Ian Heathcote-Amory (p1-2)

Lithograph: *A New Study of Gimcrack* (facing p1)

Famous Sportsmen Fallen by George Burrows (p3-5)

The Turf in Story (part 1) by George Teasdale-Buckell (p6-18)

Engraving: *Flying Childers* (facing p10)

Engraving [pinx. Seymour]: *Old Partner* (facing p10)

Engraving [pinx. Cooper]: *Grey Momus* (facing p12)

Engraving [pinx. Sartorius]: *Goldfinder* (facing p16)

Engraving [pinx. Sartorius]: *Bellario* (facing p16)

Has the Speed of Racing Yachts Increased by George Hopcroft (p19-21)

[Review] *The Complete Science of Fly Fishing and Spinning* by Frederick Shaw (p22-28)

Photographs: *Four Scenes - Netting a Fish* (facing p22)

Photograph: *Salmon Rod in the Spey Throw* (facing p24)

Photograph: *A Chalk Stream - The Test Below Romsey* (facing p26)

Photograph: *Teepee in the Rockies* (facing p26)

The Cards of Fate [verses] by Peggy Grant (p28)

Australian Horses by Thomas Dale (p29-30)

Life of the Wild Duck by Arthur Horwood (p30-34)

Photograph [Crook]: *A Nest of Wild Duck* (on p31)

Some Methods of Destroying Pike by Ernest Phillips (p34-36)

Our Van [inc. Newmarket Spring Meeting; Gatwick Races; Windsor Handicap; Baldoyle Derby; Cessation of Racing; Tedworth Hunt; Carlisle Otterhounds] (p36-39)

Sporting Intelligence [inc. Oxford University Bumping Races Centenary; Masters of Foxhounds Association; Hunt Secretaries' Association; Hunt Servants' Benefit Society; Obituaries of Victor Villiers, Montague Cholmeley, Stephen Christy, George Brooke, Ralph Nevill, Charles Forster, Butt Miller, Philip Evans-Freke, Francis Grenfell, Basil Maclear, David Bain, Harry Berry, Martin McNally, George Winfield, Philip Thomas, Dennett Davies, Julian Grenfell, Ferdinand Marsham-Townshend, Sylvester Rait-Kerr, William Bird, Alwyne Hobson, James Pearson, Charles Martin, John Isaac, George Blake, Stewart Duckett, Edward Chandos-Leigh, Robert Fergusson and Robert Balfour; Elsenham Pictures Sale; *Anglers Guide for 1915*; Northern Rugby Union; *Shooters Yearbook for 1915-16*] (p40-48)

Sporting Results (p48)

Issue 666 : August 1915

Portrait [Mendelssohn] and Biography - Reginald Hill (p49-50)
The Grouse in Wartime by Frank Bonnett (p51-53)
Memories - Wartime and After by Arthur Sharp (p53-55)
The Turf in Story (part 2) by George Teasdale-Buckell (p56-73)
Lithograph: *Gimcrack* (facing p58)
Lithograph: *Shark* (facing p58)
Engraving: *Eleanor* (facing p60)
Lithograph: *Grey Trentham* (facing p62)
Lithograph [pinx. Towne]: *Newton Races, 1831* (facing p64)
Engraving [pinx. Herring]: *Hobbie Noble* (facing p66)
Engraving [pinx. Hall]: *Lord Lyon* (facing p68)
Engraving [pinx. Hall]: *Wild Dayrell* (facing p70)
Thief of the World [verses] by Herbert Thomas (p73)
Sporting Trips of the Water Poet by Culling Gaze (p74-79)
Trout in Burns by Sinclair Carr (p79-81)
The Little Brown Trout [verses] by Cyril Stacey (p81-82)
Shooting Incidents True and Otherwise by Alan Haig-Brown (p82-84)
Our Van [inc. Newmarket Meeting; Wilton Hunt; Staghunting; Goathland Otterhounds; Cottesmore Hunt; Carlisle Otterhounds; Boddington Harriers] (p84-90)
Sporting Intelligence [inc. Public Schools Rowing; Australian Sculling; Obituaries of Robert Kingslake, John Graham, Ivor Davies, James Simpson, James Boswall, Richard Somers-Smith, Victor Trumper, John Corlett and William Dunne; Sale of the Gilbey Library; Income Tax on Sires] (p90-98)
Sporting Results (p98)

Issue 667 : September 1915

Portrait [Lafayette] and Biography - Harry Greer (p99-102)
The Partridge's Prospects by Frank Bonnett (p103-105)
Future of Foxhunting by William Scarth-Dixon (p105-108)
Some Permanent Lines of Foxhound Blood by Thomas Dale (p109-111)
With Fly Rod and Creel in September by Arthur Sharp (p112-115)
The Turf in Story (part 3) by George Teasdale-Buckell (p115-126)
Engraving [pinx. Hall]: *Thormanby* (facing p116)
Engraving [pinx. Hall]: *Vauban* (facing p116)
Engraving [pinx. Herring]: *Priam* (facing p118)
Engraving [pinx. Hall]: *Brown Duchess* (facing p118)
Engraving [pinx. Herring]: *Filho da Puta* (facing p120)
Engraving [pinx. Hall]: *Mincepie* (facing p120)
Engraving [pinx. Turner]: *Blue Bonnet* (facing p122)
Engraving [pinx. Herring]: *Hetman Platoff* (facing p122)
Engraving [pinx. Hall]: *Van Tromp* (facing p124)
Engraving [pinx. Hall]: *Queen Bertha* (facing p124)
Sports Forgotten (p126-131)
Still Game [verses] by Peggy Grant (p131-132)
Engraving [sculp. Babbage]: *Horses Galloping* (on p132)
Our Van [inc. Newmarket Racing; New Forest Hunt; Pytchley Show; Grove Hunt; Devon & Somerset Staghounds] (p133-138)

Sporting Intelligence [inc. University Hurdling; Eton College Beagles; Obituaries of Robert
        Raper, Gerald Grenfell, Frank Tarr, David Taylor, Alan Marshal, Thomas Allen,
        Patrick Blair, Frederick Aston, Henry Steel, George Lambert, Finch Mason (*Baily's*
        contributor), David Arnott, George Eyre, John Milton and Charles Littlefield;
        John Corlett's Residence; American Polo]   (p139-145)
Sporting Results   (p146)

Issue 668 : October 1915

Portrait [Elliott] and Biography - Kirby Stapley   (p147-149)
Hunting Must Be Carried On by George Burrows   (p149-155)
Shooting in War Time by Arthur Blyth   (p155-156)
Pheasant Shooting Prospects by Frank Bonnett   (p157-159)
Golfers and the War by Robert Howard   (p159-161)
A Racing Causerie by Gerald Ricardo   (p161-166)
Hockey Men with the Colours by Edward Thomson   (p166-168)
The Timid Hare in Folklore and Superstition by Jack Fairfax-Blakeborough   (p169-174)
From Pink to Khaki [verses] by Michael Hope   (p174)
The Romance of the Canoe by Lincoln Wilbar   (p175-178)
Our Van [inc. Jockey Club Directive; Newmarket Meetings; Leopardstown Races; New Forest
        Buckhunting; Devon & Somerset Staghounds; Cottesmore Cubhunting; South
        Oxfordshire Hunt]   (p178-185)
Hunting Notes From All Quarters by Edward Cuming   (p185-187)
Sporting Intelligence [inc. Oxford University Drag Hunt; Obituaries of Henry Steward, David
        Bedell-Sivright, Arthur Dingle, Edmund Turton, Cecil Palmer, Henry Dyas,
        Herbert Steward, Robert Fellowes, Henry Cholmondeley-Pennell (*Baily's*
        contributor), Ralph Johnston, John Lee and Penn Sherbrooke; Irish Horse
        Ownership; Finch Mason Appeal]   (p187-193)
Sporting Results   (p194)

Issue 669 : November 1915

Portrait [Kay] and Biography - John Thursby   (p195-198)
On the Value of Sport in War by Claye Shaw   (p199-203)
The Second Horseman [verses] by Michael Hope   (p204)
Hunt Changes in 1915 by Edward Cuming   (p205-215)
Photograph: *Samuel Hardy*   (on p207)
Photograph [Vandyke]: *Warwickshire Hunt Horse Show*   (facing p208)
Photograph: *Charles Brindley*   (on p211)
Norwegian Ponies by Henry Bryden   (p215-218)
Photographs: *Norwegian Ponies at Pasture*   (facing p216)
A Fatal Year for Sport by William Holland   (p219-221)
Ode to a Favourite Retriever [verses]   (p221-222)
Baily's Hunting Directory 1915-16 by George Burrows   (p223-224)
Our Van [inc. Racing Interregnum; *The Sportsman*'s Editorial; The Racecourse Association;
        Curragh Meeting; Atherstone Hunt; Quorn Hounds]   (p224-232)
Hunting Notes and News by George Burrows   (p232-234)
Sporting Intelligence [inc. Yale University Rowing; New York Rowing Association; Obituaries
        of Alfred Baldry, Richard Lewis, Thomas Gaskell, Maurice Lippins, Frederick
        Hyslop, Harold Wright, William Wallace, Walter Dickson, Ernest Deane, Guy
        Napier, Bernard Holloway, Thomas Bucknill, Albert Spalding, William Chivers,
        Charles Morris and Oswald Bainbridge; Yardley Stud]   (p234-241)
Sporting Results   (p242)

Issue 670 : December 1915

Portrait [Gabell] and Biography - Malcolm Fox (p243-246)
Hunting Songs by Ernest Pulbrook (p246-251)
Twins and Prolific Breeders by Gerald Ricardo (p251-255)
A Prominent Southern Courser by Alan Sealy (p255-258)
Photograph [Fry]: *William Smith* (facing p256)
Night Fishing for Sea Trout by Joseph Wheeldon (p259-262)
A Remarkable Year's Racing by Charles Richardson (p262-265)
[Obituary] Morland Greig by Henry Bryden (p265-266)
William Back by George Burrows (p267)
Our Van [inc. Newmarket Meetings; Curragh Racing; Albrighton Hunt; Staintondale Hounds; Quorn Hunt; Sinnington Hounds] (p267-274)
Hunting Notes and News by George Burrows (p274-275)
Sporting Intelligence [inc. Oxford University Boxing; Yale University Athletics; Review of *The Recollections of a Bishop* by George Browne; Obituaries of Geoffrey Davies, Douglas Lambert, Herbert Lumb, Ralph Hemingway, Francis Bacon, Geoffrey David, Henry Alexander, Morland Greig; Gilbert Grace, Peter Walker, James Sinclair (editor of *The Agricultural Gazette* and *The Live Stock Journal*), Thomas Corns, James Griffiths, Gerald Hazlitt and Dicky Lockwood] (p275-282)
Sporting Results (p282)

Volume 105, January - June 1916

Issue 671 : January 1916

Portrait [Chapman] of William Boore, huntsman Title page
Portrait [Edge] and Biography - David Davies (p1-2)
Peter Beckford and *Thoughts Upon Hunting* by Hugh Henry (p3-9)
After Wild Pigs in Corsica by Edwin Arnold (p10-14)
Hall Walker's Gift of a National Stud by George Burrows (p14-20)
Home on Leave by Michael Hope (p20)
Future Horse Breeding: Review of *The Live Stock Journal Almanac* by George Burrows (p21-23)
Photograph: *Larkspur* (facing p22)
Photograph: *Royal Sovereign* (facing p22)
A Man Made Lake by Scudamore Jarvis (p24-27)
The Irish Terrier by Alan Sealy (p27-30)
Photograph [Allison]: *Modern Irish Terrier* (on p29)
Our Van [inc. National Hunt Committee; Middleton Hunt; Hunter Sires; Cottesmore Hounds; Brocklesby Hunt; Ledbury Hounds; Foxhunting in Cumberland] (p30-37)
Sporting Intelligence [inc. Oxford University Point-to-Point Steeplechases; Amateurism in American Universities; Obituaries of George Gosling, Spencer Ponsonby-Fane, Frank Hesham, Arthur Jaques, Geoffrey Davies, Harold Springthorpe, Lynedoch Mackenzie, Richard Webster, Louis Hall, Charles Lambert, Robert Gomes, James Ryan, Walter Lovejoy, John Braithwaite and Harry Varley; County Cricket Accounts; Belgian Racehorses; Tod Sloan Deported; John Corlett's Will; New Brunswick Big Game Season; Austrian Derby; Lingfield Park Clerk of Course] (p37-48)
The Sportsman's Library: Reviews of *The Winning Shot* by Jerome Travers; *Billiards* by Thomas Reece; *How to Lay Out Suburban Home Grounds* by Herbert Kellaway; *Wonders of Animal Life* by Walter Berridge; *The Story of a Hare* by John Tregarthen; *The Life Story of an Otter* by John Tregarthen; *Modern Horse Management* by Reginald Timmis (p39-40)
Sporting Results (p48)

Issue 672 : February 1916

Portrait [Foulsham] and Biography - Charles Menzies (p49-50)
The Case for Hunting by Frederick Webster (p51-56)
Polo: Past Present and Future by Archibald Charlton (p56-58)
A Nation of Horsemen by Gerald Ricardo (p59-68)
Photograph [Babbage]: *Annuity* (facing p61)
Photograph [Parsons]: *Grand Slam* (facing p62)
Photograph [Parsons]: *Wilton Drummer* (facing p62)
Photograph [Babbage]: *Soft Answer* (facing p64)
Photograph [Babbage]: *Sudbourne Bellman* (facing p64)
Photograph [Parsons]: *Lunesdale Stockman* (facing p66)
Photograph [Parsons]: *Marden Lilac* (facing p66)
A Coursing Chat by Alan Sealy (p69-74)
Engraving [sculp. Scott]: *Miller* (facing p70)
Engraving [pinx. Snow]: *Tomboy and Bran* (facing p70)
Colonel Trelawny's Hunting Song by Maitland Kelly (p74)
An 1814 Devonshire Staghunt [verses] by James Savile (p75-76)
Our Van [inc. Gatwick Races; Lingfield Park Meeting; New Forest Buckhounds; Woodland
    Pytchley Hounds; Blankney Hunt; Cottesmore Hunt; Ledbury Hunt Farmers] (p77-87)
Photograph [Babbage]: *Norbury Park Pedigree Shire Horse Sales* (facing p83)
Sporting Intelligence [inc. Oxford University Boat Club; Spring Horse Shows; Obituaries of
    Charles Newcombe, Henry Field-Etherington (of *Yachting Monthly*), Edward
    Lawson (of *The Daily Telegraph*), Edgar Price (author of *With Horn and Hound
    in Wales*) and Samuel Haigh; Yarmouth Angling; Norfolk & Suffolk Bowls Union;
    Clare Harriers; Walton Heath Golf Links; Reviews of *Ayres Cricket Companion*
    and *Abnegation* by Amy Menzies] (p87-96)
Photograph [Thomson]: *Edward Lawson* (on p92)
Sporting Results (p96)

Issue 673 : March 1916

Portrait [Lafayette] and Biography - Jerry Rohan (p97-98)
The Horsemanship of the Soldier by Frederick Webster (p99-107)
The Coming of the Thoroughbred Horse by Thomas Dale (p108-110)
Swimming Horses by Cyril Stacey (p110-117)
Winter: The Alehouse Door by Robert Dunkin (p117-120)
Lithograph [pinx. Morland]: *Winter - The Alehouse Door* (facing p118)
Women and Sport by William Holland (p120-122)
Choosing a Line by Pack Ford (p122-125)
Heron Hawking by James Harting (p125-126)
Are Sportsmen Jealous by Eric Parker (p126-129)
Our Van [inc. Revised Racing Fixtures; Racecourse Association Steeplechase; Windsor
    Meeting; Gatwick Races; Blankney Hounds; North Shropshire Hunt;
    Cumberland Foot Packs; Worcestershire Hunt] (p129-135)
Sporting Intelligence [inc. Oxford University Drag Hunt; Avon Vale Hounds; Hound Trailing
    Association; Obituaries of Robert Filmer, John Clemson, Edward Almack (*Baily's*
    contributor), George Dewar, Francis Roberts, Hugh Mosman, Frank Streatfeild
    (*Baily's* contributor), Assheton Biddulph, John Leslie and John Beattie; National
    Pony Stud Book; Jockey Club Sporting Pictures; Yorkshire County Cricket Club] (p135-144)
Sporting Results (p144)

Issue 674 : April 1916

Portrait [Russell] and Biography - William Palmer (p145-147)

War Horses (part 1) by Frederick Webster (p147-158)
Lithograph [pinx. Lucas]: *Modern War Horse 'Syrea'* (facing p148)
Lithograph [pinx. Babbage]: *The War Horse of Old* (facing p152)
Lithograph: *A Light of Other Days* (facing p156)
Engraving [sculp. Babbage]: *War Horse and Foal* (on p158)
The Individual Exploits of Foxhounds by Thomas Dale (p159-161)
London's Light Horse Shows by Gerald Ricardo (p161-167)
Photograph [Babbage]: *Birk Gill* (on p163)
Photograph [Babbage]: *Gilgandra* (on p165)
Photograph [Babbage]: *Naughty Girl* (on p166)
Photograph [Babbage]: *Burton Bluebell II* (on p167)
[Obituary] A Famous Athlete: Godfrey Shaw (p167-170)
With A Nine Foot Rod in April by Arthur Sharp (p170-172)
Sport in Wales a Thousand Years Ago (p172-177)
Our Van [inc. Gatwick Meeting; Lingfield Park Racing; Woldingham Hurdle Race; Surrey
         Steeplechase; Badworth Hunt; Blackmore Vale Hounds; Croome Hunt] (p178-185)
Photograph [Babbage]: *Black Beauty* (on p183)
Sporting Intelligence [inc. Public School Sport; Cambridge University Rugby; William Caffyn
         Reminiscences; Obituaries of Harold Bache, Rollo Atkinson, Norman Wentworth,
         Edwin Bonner, James Covey, George Pragnell and Robert Benson; Doncaster
         Racing Prints; Cheriton Otterhunt; Yacht Racing Association, Badsworth Hounds,
         Cotswold Hunt and Hackney Horse Society Stud Book] (p185-191)
Irish Blood Stock by Herbert Hewett (p189-190)
Photograph [Babbage]: *Blacksmith* (on p190)
Photograph [Babbage]: *Bury* (on p191)
Sporting Results (p192)

Issue 675 : May 1916

Portrait [Howard] and Biography - Owen Philipps (p193-195)
War Horses (part 2) by Frederick Webster (p195-202)
Photograph: *Orfold Blue Blood* (facing p196)
Photograph: *London Champions - Shire Mare and Shetland Pony* (facing p196)
Photograph: *An Ideal Stallion* (facing p198)
Photograph: *An Ideal Pony* (facing p200)
Hunting in Wartime with the Cottesmore and Cheshire by Cuthbert Bradley (p202-206)
Lithograph [pinx. Bradley]: *Hall Walker Mounted on Buttercup* (facing p204)
[Obituary] Thomas Barnard by George Burrows (p206-207)
Should the Dog Tax be Increased by Frederick Aflalo (p208-210)
Some Fishing Facts by Ernest Phillips (p210-212)
The Sportsman Naturalist by George Teasdale-Buckell (p212-216)
Snipe Shooting in Ireland by George Garrow-Green (p216-221)
Some Reindeer Notes by Abel Chapman (p221-224)
Our Van [inc. Colwell Park Meeting; Windsor Races; Lincolnfield Handicap; New Forest
         Hounds; Bramham Moor Hunt; Bedale Hounds; Obituary of Pemberton Barnes;
         Quarme Harriers] (p224-232)
Sporting Intelligence [inc. University Rugby; Midland Counties Amateur Athletics Association,
         Cambridge University Rowing; Thames Rowing Club, Obituaries of James
         Strachan-Davidson, Charles Austen-Leigh, Louis Phillips, Harry Shute, Gerald
         Smith, Robert Smyth, Lawrence McCreery, South Norton, Loftus Bushe-Fox,
         Louis Salkeld, Alfred Crawshay, John Louch, Arthur Heal, George Holden, Joseph
         Cribb and Newton Rhodes; Heaton Park Golf; Yorkshire Derby; Carlisle
         Otterhounds; Westmeath Hounds] (p232-241)
Cricketiana by William Holland (p237-238)

Use of Dogs in War [from the *Pall Mall Gazette*] (p238-239)

Horses to Ride by Herbert Hewett (p240-241)

Sporting Results (p242)

Issue 676 : June 1916

Portrait [Howard] and Biography - George Herbert (p243-245)

Photograph: *Shire Horse* (on p245)

Deeds of the Cavalry by Frederick Webster (p246-255)

Lithograph [pinx. Lucas]: *Officer's Charger 'Sailor'* (facing p246)

Photograph: *Hunter Mare and Foal* (facing p248)

Famous Huntsmen: Thomas Oldacre by Henry Bryden (p256-261)

Lithograph [Colebrook]: *Thomas Oldacre* (facing p256)

The Coming of the Pari-Mutuel by George Burrows (p262-265)

The Amateur Whipper-in by Charles Tindall (p266-269)

Fred Archer by George Teasdale-Buckell (p270-272)

Our Van [inc. Craven Meeting; Newbury Races; Linlithgow & Stirlingshire Hunt; New Forest
Buckhounds; South Shropshire Hunt; Dartmoor Otterhounds] (p272-280)

William Boore by George Burrows (p281)

Sporting Intelligence [inc. Baron Pierre de Coubertin's Pronouncement on 1920 Olympic
Games; Obituaries of Kenelm Digby, Thomas Colmore, Alastair Morley-Brown
(of *The Sporting Life*) Andrew Ross, Thomas Horan, Frederick Browning,
William Auld, Robert Watson (of *The Sporting Life*) and Donald Dinnie; Queen's
Club Tennis Coach] (p281-286)

Sporting Results (p286)

Volume 106, July - December 1916

Issue 677 : July 1916

Portrait of Jack Doe, huntsman Title page

Lithograph [pinx. Fothergill]: *Every Sweet Must Have Its Bitter* (facing Contents page)

Portrait [White] and Biography - Ewen Goff (p1-5)

Yacht Racing Before and After the War by George Hopcroft (p5-8)

Lithograph [pinx. Hopcroft]: *American Defenders, Resolute and Vanitie* (on p6)

Lithograph [pinx. Hopcroft]: *Race Between the Two Shamrocks* (on p7)

Deeds of the Royal Artillery by Frederick Webster (p9-16)

Summer Trouting by Arthur Sharp (p17-20)

Fishing Yarns by Ernest Phillips (p20-23)

The Lighter Side of Cricket by William Holland (p23-26)

A Japanese Hunter by Henry Parlett (p26-31)

Our Van [inc. Windsor Racing; Newmarket Meeting; Gatwick Races; Carlisle Hunt; Eastbourne
& East Sussex Hounds, Surrey Union Hunt; Stevenstone Hounds] (p32-39)

Sporting Intelligence [inc. University Field Sports, Cambridge University Boxing Blues;
Obituaries of Bouverie Talbot, George Rathbone, Charles Mullins, Gerald Fowler,
Charles Fisher, Ronald Lagden, Dudley Aldin, Alexander Crawford, Harry
Chinnery, Cecil Abercrombie, Frederick Batty-Smith (of *The Sportsman*), John
Wilson, James Pickup, Gerald Fowler, Ernest Sharp, Henry Perkins (former *MCC*
Secretary), Robert Watson (of *Sporting Life*) and Mason Scott; Masters of
Foxhounds Association; Review of *Conformation in Horses* by Daniel Wilkinson;
Brooklands Speed Record; Matlock & Cromford Angling Association; Chester
Race Company; South Molton Harriers; Mellbrake Hunt] (p39-47)

Sporting Results (p47-48)

Issue 678 : August 1916

Portrait [Howard] and Biography - Thomas Baring (p49-51)
Deeds of the Royal Engineers by Frederick Webster (p52-59)
Hunting Recollections of Golden Days by Thomas Dale (p60-62)
The Perfect Retriever (p62-65)
Wild Shooting in Spain by Abel Chapman (p65-67)
The Yeomen of England [verses] by Frederick Webster (p67)
The Rugby Game by Edward Sewell (p68-72)
Ancient Chess Books by Edgar Thomas (p72-78)
Our Van [inc. Leopardstown Meeting; Dublin Plate; Lingfield Park Racing; Newbury Meeting;
  Belvoir Hunt; Military Exemption for Hunt Servants; Dartmoor Otterhounds] (p79-85)
Sporting Intelligence [inc. Public School Rowing; Obituaries of Cecil Gold, Henry Crichton,
  William Booth, Evelyn Lintott, Francis Gillespie, John Ryan, John Wilson, Frank
  Hannam, Rowland Fraser, Robert Somers-Smith, Guy Crawford-Wood (of *The Field*),
  Oswald Wreford-Brown, Arthur Isaac, Stanley Millar, Thomas McCormick, Arthur
  Atkinson ('Sandy Hollows' of *Golf Illustrated*), Robert Pillman, John Williams,
  William Filgate and Harry Carter; Hong Kong Derby; Jockey Club Fixtures; Review
  of *Shooter's Yearbook*; West Somerset Foxhounds] (p86-95)
Photograph [Weston]: *Cecil Gold* (on p88)
Sporting Results (p95-96)

Issue 679 : September 1916

Portrait [Howard] and Biography - Henry Boileau (p97-99)
Deeds of the Infantry by Frederick Webster (p100-107)
Outdoors in September by Arthur Sharp (p108-111)
What the Women of England are Doing (p111-115)
Photographs: *What the Women are Doing* (facing p112)
Photograph: *A Lady Herdsman* (on p114)
End of an Era in the History of Cowes Regatta by George Hopcroft (p115-118)
Doncaster and the St.Leger by William Oldfield (p118-127)
Lithograph: *Anthony St.Leger* (on p119)
Photograph: *St.Leger Course in 1916* (on p121)
Lithograph: *St.Leger Course in 1826* (on p121)
Photograph: *Doncaster Racecourse on St.Leger Day* (facing p122)
Photograph: *The Paddock at Doncaster Racecourse* (facing p124)
Our Van [inc. National Hunt Committee; Gatwick Meeting; Newmarket Racing; Curragh
  Races; Lingfield Park Stakes; New Forest Buckhounds; Ossory Hunt] (p127-132)
Sporting Intelligence [inc. Drag Hunting; Rugby in Public Schools; Obituaries of Harold
  Freeman, Geoffrey Barclay, William Burns, Thomas Hamer, Frederick Longstaff,
  Ernest Shorrocks, Eric Milroy, Foster Cunliffe, Percy Anthony, David Gaussen,
  Richard Thomas, Percy Jeeves, William Church, John Williams, Strawson Wilson,
  Charles Pritchard, James Crabtree, Harold Brassey, Leslie Cheape, Alfred Lubbock,
  Fergus Suter, Charles Hughes, Robert Walkington and Arthur Ridley; Chester Races;
  Hertfordshire Hounds; Woman Scorer at Lord's; Grouse Shooting] (p132-143)
Sporting Results (p144)

Issue 680 : October 1916

Portrait [Wakefield] and Biography - Leopold de Rothschild (p145-152)
Photograph: *St.Frusquin* (facing p146)
Photograph: *St.Amant* (facing p150)
The Carry On of Hunting by Edward Cuming (p152-161)
Deeds of the Medical Service by Frederick Webster (p161-169)

The Ideal Winning Record by Harry Parker (p169-171)
Farmers can Help Bloodstock Breeding by Ernest Franklyn (p171-172)
Sport and the War by William Fox-Russell (p173-178)
Some Famous Cricket Matches by William Holland (p179-181)
Our Van [inc. Lingfield Races; Newbury Meeting; Leopardstown Racing; Phoenix Park Plate; East Sussex Hunt; West Cumberland Otterhunt] (p182-186)
Sporting Intelligence [inc. South Oxfordshire Hunt; American Hurdling; Obituaries of John Robinson, Vivian Byrne-Johnson, Stanley Richards, John King, Christopher Collier, Kenneth Hutchings, Horace Thomas, William Phillpotts Williams (*Baily's* contributor) and William Cardwell; Cheshire Hunt; Tynedale Hunt; Cockfield Agricultural Show] (p186-192)
Sporting Results (p192)

Issue 681 : November 1916

Portrait [Howard] and Biography - Alfred Pearson (p193-195)
Lithograph [Fothergill]: *Better to Sit Still Than Rise Up and Fall* (on p195)
Hunt Changes in 1916 by Edward Cuming (p196-204)
Photograph: *Samuel Slater and the Exmoor Hounds* (facing p196)
Photograph: *Roger Cunliffe* (on p199)
Photograph [Sutcliffe]: *William Danby* (on p199)
Photograph: *Edward Tozer* (on p200)
Photograph: *Hilda Brunskill* (on p201)
Photograph: *Constance Morgan* (on p201)
[Obituary] Charles Duncombe by Alan Sealy (p204-208)
Photograph: *Charles Duncombe* (facing p204)
[Review] *The South Devon Hunt* by Edward Tozer (p209-217)
Lithograph: *Martin Haworth's Hounds* (facing p210)
Photograph: *Jack Russell* (facing p210)
Photograph: *Cup Presented to Thomas Westlake* (on p215)
Buck Hunting in the New Forest by Thomas Dale (p218-221)
Baily's Hunting Directory 1916-17 by George Burrows (p221-222)
Ronald Poulton-Palmer [verses] (p222)
In a Remount Depot by Ernest Franklyn (p223-224)
Our Van [inc. National Hunt Fixtures; Jockey Club Report; Bury St.Edmunds Handicap; Curragh Meeting; New Forest Buckhunting; Melton Hunt; Atherstone Hunt Servants; High Peak Harriers] (p225-232)
Photograph: *Thomas Newman* (on p230)
Hunting Notes and News by Edward Cuming (p232-233)
Sporting Intelligence [inc. Eton College Beagles; Obituaries of Rupert Inglis, Thomas Milvain, Wyndham Thomas, Bertram Evers, Gilbert Bogle, Thomas Rowlandson, Arthur Marston (of *The Fishing Gazette*), Frederick Goldberg, Robert Walker, George Fawcett, William Denison, Frank Farrands, Thomas Milvain, Denys Dobson] (p233-241)
Sporting Results (p241-242)

Issue 682 : December 1916

Portrait [Brigham] and Biography - Charles Brook (p243-247)
[Obituary] Auberon Herbert by Thomas Dale (p247-250)
Photograph [Russell]: *Auberon Herbert* (facing p249)
Turf and Stud in 1916 by Arthur Coaten (p250-258)
Photograph [Rouch]: *Fifinella* (facing p251)
Photograph [Rouch]: *Hurry On* (facing p255)
Deeds of the Yeomanry by Frederick Webster (p258-265)
On Sport After the War by Claye Shaw (p265-270)

Thoughts on Remounts by Ernest Franklyn (p271-272)

Half Bred Racing by George Burrows (p272-274)

Our Van [inc. Clearwell Stakes; Newmarket Racing; Curragh Meeting; New Forest Staghounds; Newmarket & Thurlow Hunt; South Devon Hounds; Haldon Harriers; Eastbourne & East Sussex Hounds] (p274-281)

Sporting Intelligence [inc. University Appointments; Obituaries of Alfred Humphry, Frederick Norman, Gordon Southam, Henry Bentinck, Henry Keigwin, Francis Oddie, Arthur Davis, Danny Maher, John Sloughgrove, George Vize and Henry Coke; Jockey Club Pari-Mutuel; Hunting and Racing in France; Cock-Fighting in Ireland; Kildare Hounds; Cotswold Hunt; Sinnington Hunt] (p281-291)

Sporting Results (p292)

Frederic Halford

Volume 107, January - June 1917

Issue 683 : January 1917

Portrait [Smith] of William Hale, huntsman	Title page
Portrait [Elliott] and Biography - Isaac Burns-Lindow	(p1-5)
Eaton and the Turf by Durbin Montefiore	(p5-11)
Engraving [sculp. Herring]: *Touchstone*	(facing p6)
Lithograph: *Ormonde*	(facing p8)
Photograph [Parsons]: *Orme in the Eventide of Life*	(facing p10)
[Review] Masters on £700 a year: *Hunting Notes from Holderness* by Frank Reynard	(p12-16)
Foxhunters and Fences by Charles Frederick	(p16-19)
Engraving [sculp. Babbage]: *Going Home*	(on p19)
[Obituary] Charles Green by George Burrows	(p20-22)
Photograph: *Charles Green*	(on p21)
Deeds of the Territorials by Frederick Webster	(p23-31)
Our Van [inc. Windsor Steeplechase; Newbury Meeting; Newmarket Bloodstock Sales; South Oxfordshire Hunt; Croome Harriers; Berkeley Hunt]	(p31-37)
Sporting Intelligence [inc. University Rugby; Oxford University Golf Club; Reviews of *The Live Stock Journal Almanac* by George Burrows and *Vinton's Agricultural Almanac* by Edward Moorhouse; Shire Horse Council Secretary; Obituaries of Noel Newton, Charles Green, Lewis Lodge; Frederick Kelly; Allen Palmer, Alfred Maynard, Leonard Moon, Percy Woodland, Attwood Torrens, Edward Pennell-Elmhirst (*Brooksby of The Field*), Henry Dent, George Thompson, Charles Fitzharding, Ralph Payne-Gallwey (*Baily's* contributor), Frederick Babbage (*Baily's* engraver/photographer), William Snook and Thomas Dyke (*Stud Book* author)]	(p38-48)
Photograph: *Archibald Charlton*	(on p41)

Issue 684 : February 1917

Portrait [Langfier] and Biography - Richard Verney	(p49-52)
Boadicea and her Owners by Charles Prior	(p53-63)
Lithograph: *Charles Knightley*	(facing p54)
Tis Knightley [verses] by Frederick Litchfield	(on p55)
Engraving [pinx. Alken]: *Camel*	(facing p58)
A Prisoner of War [verses] by Maud Wynter	(p63)
Deeds of the New Armies by Frederick Webster	(p64-72)
Engraving [sculp. Babbage]: *Two Horses*	(on p72)
Fiftieth Anniversary of a Famous Yacht Race by George Hopcroft	(p73-76)
Lithograph [pinx. Hopcroft]: *Schooners Vesta, Henrietta and Fleetwing*	(facing p74)
Some Forgotten Coursing Grounds by Alan Sealy	(p77-81)
Lithograph: *The Great Caledonian Meeting at Ardrossan*	(facing p78)
Sport with Irish Trencher-Fed Packs by Jack Fairfax-Blakeborough	(p81-85)
The Missing Master of Foxhounds [verses] by William Williams	(p85)
Our Van [inc. Hawthorn Hill Meeting; Gatwick Racing; Purley Steeplechase; Tiverton Hounds; York & Ainsty Hunt; Sinnington Hounds; Fitzwilliam Hunt]	(p86-91)
Sporting Intelligence [inc. Oxford University Polo Club; Obituaries of Charles Hobhouse, James Round, William Jenkins, Robert Yerburgh, Reginald Mowbray, William Curtis, Frederick Selous, John Nason, Henry Euren, Thomas Harrison and William Curtis; South Staffordshire Hunt; London Spring Horse Shows]	(p91-96)

Issue 685 : March 1917

Portrait [Lafayette] and Biography - Richard Ker	(p97-99)

Engraving [sculp. Babbage]: *Jumping a Fence*   (on p99)
Future Light and Heavy Horse Breeding by Durbin Montefiore   (p100-110)
Photograph: *Percheron Mare Number Four*   (facing p102)
Photograph: *Percheron Mare Number Ten*   (facing p102)
Photograph [Babbage]: *Morston Cider Cup*   (facing p104)
Photograph [Babbage]: *Chirkenhill Forest Queen*   (facing p104)
Engraving [sculp. Babbage]: *The Old Earth Stopper*   (facing p106)
Lithograph: *A Stage Waggon of 1817*   (facing p108)
Deeds of the Indian Army (part 1) by Frederick Webster   (p110-118)
Hunting in Snow and Frost by Jack Fairfax-Blakeborough   (p118-121)
[Obituary] Charles Stanhope by Charles Batchelder   (p122-127)
Lithograph [pinx. Bradley]: *Charles Stanhope on Ali Baba*   (facing p124)
Our Van [inc. Jockey Club Committee Meeting; Windsor Races; Lingfield Park Meeting;
          South Notts Hounds; Berkeley Hunt; Tipperary Hounds; Blankney Hunt]   (p128-134)
Sporting Intelligence [inc. Magdalen College Cricket Ground; Racehorse Owners, Breeders
          & Trainers Association; Rearing of Pheasants; Obituaries of Thomas Western,
          John Fryer, Robert Hull, Henry Ashington, Harold Sloan, Grattan Lushington,
          William Jenkins, Paget Bowman, Frank Penn, William Copeland, Edwin Tyler,
          Robert I'Anson, James Veitch and Hugh McCoull; Liverpool Hunt Club;
          Yorkshire County Cricket Club]   (p134-144)

Issue 686 : April 1917

Portrait [Howard] and Biography - Logan Kidston   (p145-148)
The Spring Horse Shows by George Teasdale-Buckell   (p149-158)
Photograph [Parsons]: *Champion's Clansman*   (facing p150)
Photograph [Parsons]: *Roycroft Forest Queen*   (facing p150)
Photograph: *Pallingham*   (facing p152)
Photograph: *Rathurde*   (facing p152)
Photograph: *Dandy Peter*   (facing p154)
Photograph: *Bush Girl*   (facing p154)
Photograph: *Adbolton Bountiful*   (facing p156)
Photograph: *Adbolton Kingmaker*   (facing p156)
Some Horse Breeding Puzzles by William Scarth-Dixon   (p159-162)
Jockeys in Adversity by William Allison   (p162-164)
Deeds of the Indian Army (part 2) by Frederick Webster   (p165-172)
A Substitute for Trout Fishing by Ernest Phillips   (p173-177)
Goodbye Old Bay [verses] by William Williams   (p177)
Our Van [inc. Lingfield Park Meeting; South Notts Hunt; Quorn Hounds; Blankney Hunt] (p178-182)
Sporting Intelligence [inc. Cambridge University Drag Hunt; Light Horse Breeding; English
          Swimming; Obituaries of Robert Jessen, Charles Adams, Andre Slocock, Keith
          Eltham, Norman Barnfather, George Chetwynd, Gervas Wells-Cole, Cecil Willett,
          Christopher Brown, John Donahoo, Frank Allan, Robert Martin, John Reynolds,
          William Atkins, Arthur Tidy and Frederick Hardy; *Ayres Lawn Tennis Almanack*;
          Wisden's Cricketers' Almanack; South Herefordshire Foxhounds; Eton College
          Beagles; Meynell Hunt]   (p182-192)
Photograph: *Peace Dove*   (facing p185)
Photograph: *Imperial*   (facing p185)

Issue 687 : May 1917

Portrait [Gunn] and Biography - Roger Cunliffe   (p193-196)
Nature and Sport at the Back of the Front by Jack Fairfax-Blakeborough   (p196-199)
The Future of the Cricket Nursery by Edward Thompson   (p200-203)
Deeds of the Canadians by Frederick Webster   (p204-210)

Studies in the Pedigrees of King's Premium Horses by John Drage (p211-222)
Boat Race Reminiscences by William Holland (p222-225)
Our Van [inc. Newmarket Gold Cup; Windsor Races, Gatwick Meeting; Essex Steeplechase; Meynell Hunt; Brampton Harriers; Belvoir Hunt; Puckeridge Hounds] (p225-230)
Sporting Intelligence [inc. Eton College Beagles; Obituaries of Charles Bulkeley-Johnson, Alister Kirby, Basil Thomas, Charles Vigurs, Thomas Nelson, Arthur Flett, Albert Jackson (of *Angler's News*), Bryn Lewis, Frederick Webb, Frederick Elers, Robert Crawford and Tobias Field; Reviews of *For An Ideal* by Frederick Webster, *The National Stud* by George Fothergill, *The National Pony Stud Book 14* and *Weatherby's Races Past for 1916*; Devon & Somerset Staghounds; Royal Cruising Club] (p231-240)
Sporting Results (p240)

Issue 688 : June 1917

Portrait [Swaine] and Biography - Hedworth Meux (p241-246)
A Sporting Lincolnshire Worthy by Charles Prior (p247-256)
Photograph: *Pishey Snaith* (facing p248)
Engraving [pinx. Corbet]: *Theon* (facing p252)
The Development of the Rugby Game by Edward Sewell (p256-265)
Deeds of the Australians by Frederick Webster (p265-271)
Our Van [Newmarket meeting] (p272-275)
Sporting Intelligence [inc. Boat Race Medal; Public Schools Athletic Championships; Stoppage of Racing; Jockey Club Reaction; Half-Bred Horse Breeding; Obituaries of John Scott, Thomas Bumpsted, John Will, Harold Goodwin, Bertram Fawcett, Robert Powell, Walter Forrest, David Watt, Brinsley Lewis, Frank Carr, William Pickup, Albert Wade, William Thomas, Arthur James and William Shalders; Salford Harriers; Otter Hounds; William Hale Biography; Review of *Cycling for Health* by Frank Bowden] (p276-288)
Scroll for The King of the Kennel [verses] by George Fothergill (facing p284)
Sporting Results (p288)
Jockey Club Deputation to the Prime Minister (p288)

Volume 108, July - December 1917

Issue 689 : July 1917

Portrait of Frederick Wood, huntsman Title page
Portrait [Elliott] and Biography - Herbert Lord (p1-4)
An Artist's Recollections of Solent Yacht Racing by George Hopcroft (p4-10)
Lithograph [pinx. Hopcroft]: *First Shamrock* (facing p4)
Lithograph [pinx. Hopcroft]: *Fourth Shamrock* (facing p6)
Lithograph [pinx. Hopcroft]: *Reliance* (facing p8)
Lithograph [pinx. Hopcroft]: *Thunderclouds over the Solent* (on p10)
Deeds of the South Africans by Frederick Webster (p11-19)
[Obituary] Leopold de Rothschild by George Burrows (p19-23)
Photograph [Howard]: *Leopold de Rothschild* (on p21)
Future of Lawn Tennis by Henry Bourke (p24-26)
Piscator in Khaki by Charles Stevenson (p27-29)
Cricketiana by William Holland (p30-32)
Road Travel Past and Present by Ernest Pulbrook (p33-35)
Racing Traditions by William Scarth-Dixon (p35-38)
Our Van [inc. Suspension of Racing; Carlisle Otterhounds; Crowhurst Hounds; American Masters of Foxhounds Association] (p38-41)

Sporting Intelligence [inc. University Athletics and Rowing; Eton School-Pulling; Obituaries of Valentine Fleming, William Grandage, Frank Reay, Thomas Arthur, Isaac Bentham, Harry Blacklidge, John Raphael, Roylance Court, Somerville Gurney, Francis Gulston, John Page and Frank Wise; Horse Breeding and Racing]   (p41-48)

Issue 690 : August 1917

Portrait [Howard] and Biography - Richard Gosling   (p49-52)
The Old Huntsman [verses] by William Williams   (p52)
[Review] The Chase and its Essayists: *The Book of Sports* (part 1) by John Carleton   (p53-63)
Lithograph [pinx. Maclise]: *Charles Apperley*   (on p55)
Engraving [pinx. Laporte]: *Hold Hard*   (facing p56)
Lithograph: *William Somervile*   (on p59)
Deeds of The Royal Flying Corps by Frederick Webster   (p64-70)
The Second Horse in the Derby by Henry Platt   (p71-76)
A Missing Chapter in Bramham Moor History by William Scarth-Dixon   (p76-81)
Waiting [verses] by Norman Innes   (p82)
Our Van [inc. Baldoyle Racing; Curragh Meeting; Waterford Stakes; Limerick Races; Machynlleth Foxhounds; Atherstone Hunt]   (p83-87)
Sporting Intelligence [inc. Public School Sport; Racing Resumed; Review of *The Life of William Beresford* by Amy Menzies; Hay from Golf Courses; Obituaries of John Raphael, Atherton Brown, Harry Pallett, William Alston, Thomas Newman and Thomas Cannon; Coney Island Jockey Club; Review of *Shooters Yearbook 1917-18*; Royal Yacht Squadron]   (p88-96)
Sporting Results   (p96)

Issue 691 : September 1917

Portrait [Howard] and Biography - Bower Ismay   (p97-102)
Cock Fighting by George Teasdale-Buckell   (p102-109)
Lithograph [pinx. Best]: *Ginger Red Fighting Cock*   (on p105)
Lithograph [pinx. Best]: *Birchen Yellow Fighting Cock*   (on p107)
Engraving [sculp. Babbage]: *Herne Hill Cycling*   (on p109)
[Review] The First of September: *The Book of Sports* (part 2) by John Carleton   (p110-112)
[Review] *Sixty Years on the Turf: The Life and Times of George Hodgman* by Charles Warren   (p112-115)
Lithograph: *George Fordham*   (on p113)
The Old Hound [verses] by William Williams   (p115)
Deeds of the Padres by Frederick Webster   (p116-122)
The Derby Winner: A Study in Pedigree by James Cameron   (p123-125)
The Foxhunter's Alphabet [verses] by John Carleton   (p125)
Our Van [inc. Tattersall's Committee Judgment; Curragh Meeting; Newmarket Racing; Windsor Races; Manchester Meeting; New Forest Buckhounds; West Cumberland Hounds]   (p126-131)
Sporting Intelligence [inc. Obituaries of Arthur Jelf, Gurney Little, Charles Wilson, Lawrence Blencowe, Herbert Wilson, William Clement (of *Bell's Life*), Alfred Taylor, James Henderson, Edgar Mobbs, James Zimmerman, John Bott, Logie Leggatt, George Quin, William Ewbank and Frederick Wood; Amateur Swimming Association]   (p131-142)
[Obituary] Thomas Cannon by George Burrows   (p137-140)
Photograph: *St.Amant*   (facing p139)
Photograph [Sherborn]: *Thomas Cannon*   (on p139)
Photograph: *Mornington Cannon*   (on p140)
Sporting Results   (p142-144)
Engraving [pinx. Cooper]: *The Earth Stopper*   (facing p142)

Issue 692 : October 1917

Portrait [Desgranges] and Biography - Claud Portman (p145-148)
Some Great Handicap Performances by Henry Platt (p149-153)
When Yachts were Yachts by George Hopcroft (p154-158)
Lithograph [pinx. Hopcroft]: *Yachts of the Seventies* (facing p154)
Lithograph [pinx. Hopcroft]: *The Racing Fleet* (facing p156)
A Famous Coursing Reunion by Alan Sealy (p159-161)
Some Stockton Memories by Jack Fairfax-Blakeborough (p162-165)
Photograph [Parsons]: *Patricia* (on p165)
Deeds of the Scottish by Frederick Webster (p166-171)
Now Lucy Wears the Breeches by Cyril Stacey (p172-173)
Photograph [Ellis] *Lucy* (facing p172)
Our Van [inc. Windsor Races; Suffolk Stakes; Stockton Meeting; Leopardstown Racing; Hunt Horse Rations; New Forest Buckhounds; Croome Hunt; Hailsham Hunt] (p174-179)
Late Hunting Notes by Edward Cuming (p179-180)
Hockey's Roll of Honour by Herbert Bourke (p181-183)
Sporting Intelligence [inc. Obituaries of Henry Cook, David Westacott, Robert Elliott, Charles Arnold, Daniel Davies, Edwin Banks and Frederick Kidd; Irish Cock-Fight; Horse Breeding in Denmark; Haydock Park Racecourse; Tiverton Foxhounds] (p183-191)
Engraving [pinx. Turner]: *Cheering in Covert* (facing p190)
Sporting Results (p192)

Issue 693 : November 1917

Portrait [Howard] and Biography - George Lambton (p193-197)
The Great Twin Brethren by Sydenham Dixon (p198-203)
Photograph: *St.Frusquin* (facing p198)
Engraving [sculp. Babbage]: *Hare* (on p203)
The Brain Power of the Horse by Jack Fairfax-Blakeborough (p204-208)
Hunt Changes in 1917 by Edward Cuming (p208-214)
Deeds of the Irish by Frederick Webster (p214-221)
Baily's Hunting Directory 1917-18 (p222-223)
Our Van [inc. Newmarket Meetings; Windsor Racing; Enniskillen Plate; Ayr Races; Limerick Meeting; Rationing of Hunters; Devon & Somerset Staghounds; South Cheshire Hounds; Instow Harriers; Quorn Hunt] (p223-232)
Photograph: *George Lambton and Canyon* (on p225)
Engraving [pinx. Turner]: *Blue Bonnet* (facing p226)
Hunting News: Late Hunting Notes by Edward Cuming (p232-233)
Sporting Intelligence [inc. University Rugby; Obituaries of Richard Lewis, Robert Manners, Arnold Dargie, Theodore Rixon, Joseph Gibbs, John Murray, Henry Vane, Charles Radclyffe, Louis Borissow and Benjamin Wardill; Honolulu Swimming; Crickhowell Harriers; Machynlleth Foxhounds] (p233-239)
Sporting Results (p240)

Issue 694 : December 1917

Portrait [Downey] and Biography - Charles Paget (p241-244)
Gay Crusader's Year by Arthur Coaten (p245-249)
The Difference Between Sports and Games by Claye Shaw (p250-255)
Deeds of the Welch by Frederick Webster (p256-264)
Sporting England in 1987 by Jack Fairfax-Blakeborough (p264-270)
Our Van [inc. Rous Memorial Stakes; Leopardstown Meeting; Curragh Racing; Vale of White Horse Hounds; East Kent Hunt; Brighton Beagles; East Sussex Hunt] (p270-278)

Sporting Intelligence [inc. Obituaries of Norman Kennedy, Lancelot Driffield, Edwin Latheron, Samuel Grimshaw, Donald McLeod, Ernest Waymouth, Thomas Spittle, Allan Steel, Duncan Mackinnon, John Tetley, Richard Rail, George Hope, William Odell, David Gallaher, Frederick Griffiths, Thomas Longboat, Colin Blythe, Claude Holland (*Baily's* contributor), George Cayley, William Denison, Harry Trott, Walter Richards, Bob Fitzsimmons, Arthur Wise and Arthur Anderton; Tattersall's Park Paddocks; Derwent Hunt; Durban Golf] (p278-288)

Sporting Results (p288)

Volume 109, January - June 1918

Issue 695 : January 1918

Portrait of Samuel Gillson, huntsman Title page

Portrait [McNeille] and Biography - Francis Greville [including a review of *Memories of Sixty Years*] (p1-8)

Photograph: *Francis Greville* (facing p4)

Shape in the Horse's Head by James Cameron (p9-10)

Staying Powers of Modern Hunters by Ernest Robinson (p11-13)

Engraving [pinx. Barraud]: *Who-Whoop* (on p13)

A Plea for Old Customs by William Parlour (p14-16)

[Review] Future of Pedigree Stock Breeding: *The Live Stock Journal for 1918* by George Burrows (p17-19)

Deeds of the Brigade of Guards by Frederick Webster (p19-30)

Our Van [inc. Manchester Meeting; Curragh Racing; York & Ainsty Hunt; Cheshire Hounds; Essex & Suffolk Hunt; New Forest Hounds] (p30-36)

Sporting Intelligence [inc. Obituaries of Arnold Draper, Robert Ward, Miles Atkinson, Evelyn de Rothschild, Norman Lowe, Ivan Laing, Frederick Wheatcroft, Frederick Atkinson, Harold Garnett, John Griffiths, Charles Blake, Wynne Griffith and John Allen; Gypsies and Racing; Ullswater Foxhounds; National Pony Society; Carlisle Horse and Nag Bells; Vesta Rowing Club; Staintondale Hunt] (p36-46)

Lithograph: *A Group of Polo Ponies* (facing p46)

Sporting Results (p48)

Issue 696 : February 1918

Portrait [Russell] and Biography - Waldorf Astor (p49-54)

Notable Newmarket Matches 1860-85 by Henry Platt (p54-61)

Deeds of the Royal Navy (part 1) by Frederick Webster (p61-71)

The Demon Bowler by William Holland (p71-73)

George IV and the Turf by William Lamonby (p73-75)

Notable King's Premium Horses by George Teasdale-Buckell (p76-80)

Lithograph [pinx. Cooper]: *William Worley* (facing p78)

Our Van [inc. Devon & Somerset Staghounds; New Forest Foxhounds; Percy Hunt; Pytchley Hounds] (p81-85)

Lithograph [pinx. Laporte]: *Made A Cast* (facing p82)

Sporting Intelligence [inc. Obituaries of Stephen Steyn, Roland Gibbons, Herbert Sants, Harry Watts, Neville Wells-Cole, Leonard Colbeck, Albert Brassey, Harry Luke, George Littlewood, Richard Howard-Brooke and David Russell; Winter Bathing; Early Cheshire Hunting; Bagdad Racing; Croome Hounds; Louth Foxhounds] (p85-96)

Issue 697 : March 1918

Portrait [Lafayette] and Biography - Cecil Anderson-Pelham (p97-99)

Some Sporting Memories and Reflections by Jack Fairfax-Blakeborough (p99-103)

Spectral Hounds and Huntsmen by James Cameron (p103-107)
Deeds of the Royal Navy (part 2) by Frederick Webster (p108-120)
Knur and Spell by William Leighton (p121-126)
The Wilderness Blanket by Lincoln Wilbar (p127-130)
Our Van [inc. Windsor Meeting; Crawley Steeplechase; Woodland Pytchley Hunt; Heythrop
       Hounds; Masters of Foxhounds Association] (p130-136)
Sporting Intelligence [inc. Obituaries of Alan Balfour, Percy Thornton, Harvey Staunton,
       Leonard Colbeck, Ralph Thurgar, Lockett Agnew, John Sullivan, Edward Wilson,
       Richard Fort, Edward Brown, John Miller, Charles Frith (editor *The Irish Field*),
       Frederick Stedman, Michael Pigg, Thomas Dunning (of *The Sportsman*) and
       Henry Stubberfield; Review of *A Third of a Century with the High Peak Harriers*
       by Robert Nesfield; Lanark Silver Bell] (p136-144)

Issue 698 : April 1918

Portrait [Howard] and Biography - William Fuller (p145-148)
Newmarket Spring Stallion Shows by Gerald Ricardo (p149-153)
Photograph [Parsons]: *Rickford Coming King* (facing p151)
Photograph [Parsons]: *Harboro Nulli Secundus* (facing p151)
Photograph: *Star of Kildare with Henry Hoare, Martin Burrell and Alexander Campbell* (facing p153)
Derby Pluralists by Henry Platt (p154-162)
Lithograph: *Charles Bunbury* (facing p154)
Some Records of Great [Real] Tennis Players (p162-164)
Deeds of the Royal Navy (part 3) by Frederick Webster (p165-169)
The Story of The Godolphin Arabian by William Scarth-Dixon (p169-173)
The Diary and Letters of John Hervey (part 1) by Charles Prior (p174-178)
Our Van [inc. Lingfield Park Meeting; Sandown Park Races; Berkshire Handicap Hurdle Race;
       Whaddon Chase Hunt; Review of *The Foxhound Kennel Stud Book* by Henry
       Preston; South Devon Hunt] (p179-184)
Sporting Intelligence [inc. Marylebone Cricket Club Matches; Public Schools Athletics; Eton
       Steeplechase; Obituaries of John Campbell, Ralph Erskine, George Lamond,
       Francis Knowling, Cecil Legard, Richard Fort, James Fairrie, Malcolm Fox,
       Septimus Cooke, Frederick Sellers; Billy Madden; Thomas Dowling and Percy
       Maynard; Review of *Wisden's Cricketers' Almanack*] (p185-192)

Issue 699 : May 1918

Portrait [Barnett] and Biography - Somerville Tattersall (p193-199)
The Diary and Letters of John Hervey (part 2) by Charles Prior (p199-207)
Future of Light Horse Breeding by Durbin Montefiore (p208-210)
The Last of the Champions by Norman Clark (p211-221)
Deeds of the Royal Navy (part 4) by Frederick Webster (p222-227)
Our Van [inc. Sandown Park Meeting; Baldoyle Races; Gatwick Racing; Lancashire
       Steeplechase; Birmingham Spring Handicap; Old Berkeley Hunt; Blackmore
       Vale Hounds] (p227-232)
Sporting Intelligence [inc. University News; Obituaries of James Newton-Digby, Malcolm
       Fox, Thomas Hughes, Reginald Pridmore, Noel Humphreys, Alan Haig-Brown
       (*Baily's* contributor), George Hawksley, Walter Tull, Douglas Tosetti, Thomas
       Kingdom, Harold Hodges, William Hutchison, Alfred Parsons, Lawrence le
       Fleming, Hubert Turtill, William Manning, John Willoughby, Alan Lupton,
       Richard Burge, Charles Mitchell, William Dale, James Walker and Daniel Doyle;
       Light Horse Breeding; Arab Horse Society; Lancaster Cricket Club] (p232-240)

Issue 700 : June 1918

Portrait [Elliott] and Biography - William Tatem	(p241-245)
An Old Stable Door by Willoughby Maycock	(p246-250)
Photograph: *The Old Stable Door*	(facing p246)
Photograph: *The Paddock at Lubenham*	(on p249)
In Defence of the Sportsman by Claye Shaw	(p250-258)
Deeds of the Royal Navy (part 5) by Frederick Webster	(p259-265)
Influences of the Eaton Stud by George Teasdale-Buckell	(p265-271)
Our Van [inc. Lewes Meeting; Newmarket Races; Curragh Racing; Derwent Hounds; Devon & Somerset Staghounds; East Kilkenny Hounds; Review of *Meadow Brook Yearbook*]	(p271-277)
Sporting Intelligence [inc. Public Schools Athletic Championships; Obituaries of Reginald Hands, Charles Awdry, Ronald Sanderson, Stephen Steyn, Noel Humphreys, William Tyldesley, Frank Cochran, Arthur Harrison, George Hope, Joseph Bulcock, Hugh Malcomson, Sidd Stagg and Walter Dickson (of *The Pink 'Un*); Great Twin Shorthorns; Bloodstock Breeding; Melbrake Hounds; Kent County Cricket Club; English Percheron Horse Society]	(p277-285)
Lithograph [pinx. Booth]: *Bracelet*	(facing p283)
Lithograph [pinx. Booth]: *Necklace*	(facing p283)
Sporting Results	(p285-288)
Engravings and Verses: *The Portraiture of Squirril*	(facing p286)

Volume 110, July - December 1918

Issue 701 : July 1918

Portrait of Stephen Donoghue, jockey	Title page
Portrait [Swaine] and Biography - Hugh Gray-Cheape	(p1-4)
A Race Meeting in Egypt by Sydenham Dixon	(p4-6)
The Greatest Race in the World by Henry Platt	(p7-10)
Some Doncaster Eccentrics by Edgar Thomas	(p10-15)
A Sportsman's Notebook in France by Jack Fairfax-Blakeborough	(p16-20)
A Gallant Grey by James Cameron	(p21-23)
Deeds of the Royal Navy (part 6) by Frederick Webster	(p24-29)
A Sportsman's Cottage by Alan Sealy	(p29-32)
A Celebrated Norfolk Hackney by Ernest Robinson	(p33-34)
Engraving [pinx. Corbet]: *Phenomenon*	(on p33)
Cricket [verses] by William Williams	(p34)
Our Van [inc. Newmarket Meetings; Phoenix Park Races; Haydock Park Racing; Manchester Meeting]	(p35-41)
Engraving: *Quiz*	(facing p36)
Engraving: *Fearnought*	(facing p36)
Sporting Intelligence [inc. Obituaries of George Rudd, Egerton Wright, John Luff and Frederick Ames; Light Horse Breeding; Warwickshire County Cricket Club; British Boxing Board of Control]	(p41-47)
Sporting Results	(p48)

Issue 702 : August 1918

Portrait [Sutcliffe] and Biography - William Danby	(p49-51)
The Roebuck: Its History and Hunting by William Watts	(p51-55)
The Dean (Devon) Hunt 1776-1803 by Charles Perry-Keene	(p55-58)
The Old Master of Foxhounds [verses] by William Williams	(p58)
Memorable Dead-Heats (part 1) by Henry Platt	(p59-65)

The Story of Ormonde by George Burrows (p65-70)
Deeds of the Royal Navy (part 7) by Frederick Webster (p71-74)
Royalty and Cricket by William Holland (p74-76)
The Antiquity of Tennis by Edgar Thomas (p76-81)
Our Van [inc. Newmarket Gold Cup; Curragh Meeting; Exeter Stakes; Southdown Hunt; Colne
       Valley Harriers] (p81-87)
The Horse for Today [verses] by Stanhope Rodd (p87)
Sporting Intelligence [inc. Cambridge University Lawn Tennis; Obituaries of Hugh McIlwaine,
       William Cook, Conilh de Beyssac, Henry Persse, William Robinson, Samuel
       Mordan, Charles Marriott, Clive Phillipps-Wolley, William Baird and Ernest
       Cheston; Review of *A Sporting and Dramatic Career* by Alfred Watson;
       Auckland Park Club, Johannesburg] (p88-95)
Photograph [Hambling]: *Sudbourne Senora* (facing p92)
Photograph [Hambling]: *Refornmer* (facing p92)
Photograph: *Eastern Duchess* (facing p95)
Photograph: *Eastern Harriett* (facing p95)
Sporting Results (p95-96)

Issue 703 : September 1918

Portrait [Mayall] and Biography - Malcolm Little (p97-100)
Hermit's Derby: A Problem by Willoughby Maycock (p100-101)
Why Baseball Fails in its Appeal by Frank Carruthers (p102-104)
Public Schools Rowing by Reginald Rowe (p105-106)
The Silver Age of Foxhunting at Melton by Thomas Dale (p107-110)
Duck Shooting in the Punjab by Lester Arnold (p111-113)
Old Slaves of the Race Track (p113-117)
A Lindsay Gordon Sketch by Edith Humphris (p118-127)
Deeds of the Royal Navy (part 8) by Frederick Webster (p127-131)
Our Van [inc. Limerick Junction Meeting; Zetland Plate; Curragh Biennial Stakes; Newmarket
       Races; New Forest Buckhounds; Burton Hunt] (p132-137)
Sporting Intelligence [inc. Duke's Meadows; Public Schools Shooting; Obituaries of Michael
       Donaldson, Henry Macintosh, Charles Marriott, Eric Harper, David Jennings,
       Frederick Champion, William Elliott, Michael Lynch and Richard Glyn; Pytchley
       Hounds] (p137-142)
Photographs [Rouch]: *Cowslip, Rosette of Orleans, Pioneer's Noble and Goddington
       Foxglove* (facing p142)
Sporting Results (p144)

Issue 704 : October 1918

Portrait [Howard] and Biography - Ernest Wingrove (p145-148)
We'll All Go A'Hunting Today [verses] by William Williams (p148)
When and Where was Shooting on the Wing First Practised by William Baillie-Grohman (p149-154)
Lithograph: *Venetian Noblemen Bringing Down Wildfowl* (facing p150)
Hunters I Have Known by Maxwell Angas (p154-156)
Racing in France: Not Under Rules by Jack Fairfax-Blakeborough (p157-159)
Confession [verses] by Norman Innes (p160)
Deeds of the Royal Navy (part 9) by Frederick Webster (p161-165)
Adventure With a Tiger by Lester Arnold (p165)
An Early Morning Jackal Hunt by Lester Arnold (p166-168)
Amateur Association Footballers by Herbert Hewett (p168-170)
Camp Life on a Texan Prairie by Lincoln Wilbar (p170-175)
Memorable Dead-Heats (part 2) by Henry Platt (p175-181)

Our Van [inc. Leopardstown Races; Newmarket Meeting; Carlisle Otterhounds; North
        Shropshire Hunt; Eggesford Hounds; West Cumberland Otterhounds]   (p182-186)
Sporting Intelligence [inc. Heythrop Hounds; Obituaries of Allan Morris, George Pollard
        and Cecil Humphries; Flapping Meetings Banned; Grafton Hunt]   (p187-192)
Sporting Results   (p192)

Issue 705 : November 1918

Portrait [Howard] and Biography - Richard Meysey-Thompson   (p193-200)
Hunting Season of 1918-19 by Edward Cuming   (p200-210)
Lord Chaplin and Hermit's Derby by George Burrows   (p210-211)
Horse Breeding Disappointments by James Cameron   (p212-214)
Customers I Have Known by Thomas Dale   (p214-217)
The Inner History of Minting by Richard Meysey-Thompson   (p217-223)
Sportsmen I Have Met by Charles Perry-Keene   (p223-226)
Our Van [inc. Curragh Meeting; Boscawen Post Stakes; Norwich Handicap; New Forest
        Staghounds; Croome Hounds; Tynedale Hunt]   (p227-231)
Sporting Intelligence [inc. Oxford University Polo Ground; Cambridge University Athletics;
        Obituaries of Philip Barnett, Oscar Muntz, Gerard Dicconson, Octavius Fane,
        Roland Gordon, Oswald Samson, Benjamin Uzzell, Charles Adamson, Charles
        Hatfeild, Thomas Truman, Joseph Dines, Walter Sutherland, William Grant,
        Frederick Twigg, Arthur Widdop, Alfred Hartley, Evan Hanbury, Joseph Parker,
        John Bentley, Gerald Vaughan, William Henley and Collingwood Bertram;
        Review of *The America's Cup Races* by Herbert Stone]   (p232-239)
Sporting Results   (p240)

Issue 706 : December 1918

Portrait [Owen] and Biography - Arthur Hussey   (p241-242)
A Sunday Hunt by William Fawcett   (p243-246)
Feeding Time by Harding Cox   (p247)
Quaint Beliefs of the Country   (p248-250)
The Landseer Terrier by George Rope   (p251-254)
Turf and Stage by Charles Richardson   (p255-257)
Ascot in its Adolescence by William Allison   (p257-259)
The Old Marley Drain [verses] by Wyndham Roebuck   (p260-261)
Travelling in the Olden Days by John Wright   (p261-264)
Our Van [inc. Newmarket Meeting; Curragh Races; Rutland Handicap; York & Ainsty Hunt;
        Enfield Chase Hounds; Oakley Hunt; Meath Hounds]   (p265-271)
Sporting Intelligence [inc. Henley Regatta Stewards; Obituaries of Harold Hodges, Frederick
        Rickaby, Arthur Du Boulay, Sophia Barrett, George Whitehead, Henry Farrer,
        Gordon White, Arthur Stone, Cyril Eiloart, Frank Smith, Jules Forgues, Reginald
        Schwarz, Daniel Woolfall, Edward Pryse, John Dugdale, William Worsley, Albert
        Collison and Alfred Gathorne-Hardy; Lord's Tennis Court; Putney Regatta]   (p271-282)
Photograph [Parsons]: *Champions Goalkeeper*   (facing p280)
Photograph [Parsons]: *Pendley Goalkeeper*   (facing p280)
Sporting Results   (p282)

Arthur Griffiths

Volume 111, January - June 1919

Issue 707 : January 1919

Portrait of Victor Smyth, jockey — Title page
Portrait [Histed] and Biography - Aubrey Wallis-Wright — (p1-5)
The Reconstruction of Racing by Sydenham Dixon — (p5-9)
The Rebuilding of Hunting and Polo by Thomas Dale — (p10-14)
Sport in our New England by Frank Carruthers — (p14-18)
War on Woodpigeons by Eric Franklyn — (p18-22)
Sporting Prospects in the Cameroons by John Durham — (p22-27)
[Obituary] Jack Martin by Robert Dunkin — (p28-31)
The Sporting Past: An Old Diary by Jack Fairfax-Blakeborough — (p31-34)
Our Van [inc. Newmarket Sales; Woodland Pytchley Hunt; Belvoir Hounds; Cottesmore Hunt; Fernie's Hounds; Quorn Hunt; Tipperary Hounds; Calpe Hunt, Tedworth Hunt] — (p34-39)
Sporting Intelligence [inc. Cambridge University Rugby; Army Sport Control Board; University Hockey; Obituaries of Charles Russell, Richard Sutton, Michael Moran, Charles Fitzroy, Frederick Aflalo (*Baily's* contributor), Wildman Cattley, Christopher Wilson and Bob Travers; Bloodstock Prices; Thoroughbred Breeders Association; Military Sport; Royal Ulster Yacht Club; Revival of Polo; Altcar Coursing Club; Lawn Tennis Association] — (p40-48)

Issue 708 : February 1919

Portrait [Elliott] and Biography - Charles Wodehouse — (p49-53)
To Reclaim the Old Hunting and Country Spirit by Jack Fairfax-Blakeborough — (p53-55)
The Status of Amateur Boxing After the War by Norman Clark — (p56-58)
Racing Rhymes and Prophecies by Henry Platt — (p58-66)
Selecting the Brood Mare by Durbin Montefiore — (p66-68)
The [Press] Room by George Teasdale-Buckell — (p68-72)
(This article puts names to many racing nom-de-plumes)
Hack Hunters I Have Known by Thomas Dale — (p72-76)
In Jungle Byeways by Philip Etherton — (p77-80)
Our Van [inc. Leopardstown Steeplechase; Manchester Meeting; Wolverhampton Races; Oxenholme Staghounds; Cheshire Hounds; Ullswater Pack; Ledbury Hunt] — (p80-86)
Sporting Intelligence [inc. University Billiards; Spring Horse Shows; County Polo Association; Review of *The Live Stock Journal Almanac* by George Burrows; Obituaries of John Rohde, David Fenton, Robert Harries, Arthur Gould, Sidney Baker, Harvey du Cros and George Bowen; Japanese Football] — (p87-95)
Photograph: *Officers' Chargers* — (facing p88)
Photograph: *Utility Horses* — (facing p88)
Photograph [Parsons]: *Paymaster* — (facing p90)
Photograph [Parsons]: *His Majesty* — (facing p90)
Sporting Results — (p96)

Issue 709 : March 1919

Portrait [Bassano] and Biography - Donald Fraser — (p97-100)
Cricket Reform by Russell Walker — (p100-102)
Sport and the Ministry of Health by Claye Shaw — (p102-105)
Sport Ten Years Hence by Edward Thomson — (p105-106)
Encouraging Amateur Athletics by George Teasdale-Buckell — (p107-109)
The Sporting Spirit by Hugh Henry — (p110-112)
Can We Have Too Many Foxes by Thomas Dale — (p113-115)
Revival in Bowls by Charles Batchelder — (p115)

The Ethics of Trout Fishing by Alan Johnson (p116-117)
Sporting Personalia by Jack Fairfax-Blakeborough (p118-121)
Goose Driving in Macedonia by Abel Chapman (p121-122)
Past Championship Tennis Matches by Evan Noel (p123-125)
[Review] *A Short Treatise of Hunting* by Thomas Cockaine (p125-129)
Our Van [inc. Jockey Club Meeting; Sandown Park Races; Gatwick Meeting; Windsor Racing; Kilkenny Hunt; South Bucks Hounds; Hampshire Hunt] (p130-135)
Sporting Intelligence [inc. British Chess Federation; Obituaries of Frederick Gorst, William Fletcher, William Gabain, Charles Rought, James Larnach, Edward Booker, William Beatty, Alonzo Drake, Charles McLeod, Thomas Coulson and Thomas Pride; County Polo Association; County Cricket Advisory Committee; Amateurs in Rugby; Rowing Regattas; International Cyclists Union; Altcar Coursing; Golf Union of Ireland] (p136-144)
Sporting Results (p144)

Issue 710 : April 1919

Portrait [Weston] and Biography - Berkeley Sheffield (p145-147)
The Future of Hill Hunting by Jack Fairfax-Blakeborough (p148-150)
The Trout-Fisher in April by Arthur Sharp (p151-154)
Yacht Racing Reform by Francis Cooke (p154-156)
Jim Bailey, Essex Huntsman by George Burrows (p157-162)
Photograph: *James Bailey* (facing p160)
The Romance of the Grey by Adair Dighton (p162-165)
Racquets by Harold Rudd (p166-168)
The Spring Horse Shows by Gerald Ricardo (p168-173)
Photograph [Parsons]: *Generosity* (facing p168)
Photograph: *Blaisdon Draughtsman* (facing p168)
Photograph: *Sober Wisdom* (facing p170)
Photograph: *Sir Galahad* (facing p170)
The Golf-Ra by Arthur Horsley (p173-176)
Our Van [inc. Walton Steeplechase; Leopardstown Racing; Wolverhampton Meeting; Haydock Park Races; New Forest Buckhounds; East Essex Hounds; Norwich Staghounds; Border Hunt] (p176-181)
Sporting Intelligence [inc. London University Rowing Club; Hertfordshire Cricket; Polo at Hurlingham; Public Recreation Grounds; Obituaries of Henry Anderson, William Bolitho, Martin Burls, Edward Bishop, Thomas Ball, Henry Sparrow, Thomas Irvine, John Smythe, Horace Cheston, William Fryer and James Whitehead; Review of *The Life of Frederick Selous* by John Millais; Belgian Jockey Club] (p181-191)
Sporting Results (p191-192)

Issue 711 : May 1919

Portrait [Elliott] and Biography - Joseph Williams (p193-197)
Homing Instinct of the Horse by Jack Fairfax-Blakeborough (p197-198)
May Foxes and Fox Brushes by Charles Batchelder (p199-201)
Great Classic Upsets 1861-1918 by Henry Platt (p201-207)
The Responsibility of the Public Schools to Sport by Frederick Webster (p208-215)
Photograph: *Eton College Sports - One Hundred Yards Race* (facing p208)
Photograph: *Eton College Sports - Long Jump* (facing p210)
The Earls of Derby and the Turf by Adair Dighton (p216-219)
Inns of Memory by Alan Johnson (p220-222)
The Brown Rat in the Coverts by Arthur Sharp (p223-225)

Our Van [inc. Warwick Races; Lullenden Steeplechase; Lincoln Meeting; Leicester Racing; North Shropshire Hunt; Avon Vale Hounds; Peterborough Hound Show; Tedworth Hunt; Fowey Harriers; South Staffordshire Hunt] (p225-232)

Sporting Intelligence [inc. Inter-University Sports; Obituaries of Alexander Eccles, Henry Hanbury, Edward Oakeley, Stella Temple and Guy Parsons; Henley Regatta Committee; County Polo Association; Inter-Services Rugby; Yacht Racing Association; Barnstaple Hunt Club; Clifton Cricket Festival; Northern Counties Otterhounds] (p233-238)

Photograph [Parsons]: *Gartly Lancer* (on p238)
Sporting Results (p239-240)

Issue 712 : June 1919

Portrait [Bassano] and Biography - Walter Gilbey [II] (p241-243)
Cowes Castle and its Connection with Yachting by George Hopcroft (p244-246)
Engraving [sculp. Sparrow]: *Cowes Castle* (facing p244)
Temperament and the Boxing Ring by Norman Clark (p247-249)
The Trout Fisher in Mayfly Time by Arthur Sharp (p249-251)
Public Schools Racquets Championship by Harold Rudd (p252-255)
Well Defined Tracks in Bloodstock Breeding by Robert Brooke (p256-257)
Angling and the Classics (part 1) by Edgar Thomas (p257-261)
Heat Racing (part 1) by William Scarth-Dixon (p262-266)
Amateur Tennis Championship by Wallis Myers (p267-268)
Our Van [inc. Alexandra Handicap; Curragh Meeting; Catterick Bridge Racing; Epsom Races; Polo Programme; Obituary of Walter Smythe; Vale of Aylesbury Hounds; New Forest Hunt Club; Percy Hounds; Hampshire Hunt; Taunton Vale Hounds] (p268-278)
Sporting Intelligence [inc. University Rowing; Whaddon Chase Hounds; Ivo Bligh Illness; Sunday Games Association; Jockey Club Finance Meeting; Obituaries of William Paget, Alfred Cox, Seth Waring, Kenelm Pepys, James Gairdner, William Middlebrook and Harry Wood; Wellington Polo Club] (p278-282)
Sporting Results (p282-284)

Volume 112, July - December 1919

Issue 713 : July 1919

Portrait [Rouch] of Edgar Crickmere, jockey Title page
Portrait [Smith] and Biography - Richard Ord (p1-4)
Trouting in Summer by Arthur Sharp (p4-8)
A Tudor Game Licence by Henry Symonds (p8-10)
The 1880 Test Match by William Holland (p10-12)
Old Sporting Servants by Jack Fairfax-Blakeborough (p12-16)
Rowland Prothero by George Burrows (p16-18)
Photograph [Elliott]: *Rowland Prothero* (facing p16)
The Question of the Olympic Games by Frederick Webster (p18-21)
The House of Grosvenor and the Turf by Adair Dighton (p22-25)
The Evening Flight by Maud Wynter (p25-27)
Angling and the Classics (part 2) by Edgar Thomas (p27-29)
Heat Racing (part 2) by William Scarth-Dixon (p30-31)
Our Van [inc. Hurst Park Meeting; Somerville Stakes; Knavesmire Races; Bath Racing; Roehampton Polo; Hurlingham Polo Pony Show] (p31-40)
Photograph [Rouch]: *Grand Parade* (facing p34)
Photograph [Rouch]: *Paper Money* (facing p34)

Sporting Intelligence [inc. University Baseball; Tanatside Harriers; Tiverton Foxhounds; West
            Cumberland Otterhounds; John Peel Manuscript Auction; Epsom Racecourse;
            Glasgow Golf; Obituaries of Arthur Hillyard, William Goodall, James Rothery,
            Robert Chambers, Walter Slade and John Garratt; Chester Races Finances; Army
            Polo Association]   (p41-45)
Sporting Results   (p46-48)

Issue 714 : August 1919

Portrait [Swaine] and Biography - Roland Forestier-Walker   (p49-50)
My Gun-Bearer by Frederick Webster   (p51-54)
The Red Grouse at Home by Arthur Horwood   (p54-56)
What is Woman's Place in Sport   (p57-59)
Old Fighters Features by Norman Clark   (p59-60)
August and the Fly-Fisher by Arthur Sharp   (p61-66)
Stories of the St.Leger by William Herbert   (p66-69)
Hunters at Peterborough by Gerald Ricardo   (p69-71)
English Compared with American Athletes by Lees Knowles   (p72-74)
The Shorthorn's Place in Literature by Charles Batchelder   (p74-77)
Our Van [inc. Baldoyle Derby; Manchester Meeting; Ascot Races; Curragh Meeting; Gosforth
            Park Racing; Grand Prix de Paris; Bibury Club; Military Cup Polo]   (p77-86)
Photograph [Rouch]: *Irish Elegance*   (facing p78)
Photograph [Rouch]: *Champion Polo Cup Presentation*   (facing p84)
Sporting Intelligence [inc. University Cricket; Henley Rowing; Oxford Inter-Collegiate
            Cricket; Jockey Club Annual General Meeting; County Polo Association;
            Wimbledon Lawn Tennis, Bloodstock Sales at Newmarket; Obituaries of Henry
            Phillips and William Cummings; Queens Club Tennis; Leyton Cricket Ground;
            Cleveland Foxhounds]   (p86-93)
Photograph [Rouch]: *Optimistic & Illumination*   (facing p88)
Photograph [Parsons]: *Morston Cider Cup*   (facing p88)
Sporting Results   (p94-96)

Issue 715 : September 1919

Portrait [Howard] and Biography - Joseph Pease   (p97-101)
The Lure of the Partridge by Arthur Horwood   (p101-104)
Sport-Ember by Arthur Sharp   (p104-107)
Some Famous Matches by Adair Dighton   (p107-110)
Peter Hawker at Keyhaven by John Vaughan   (p110-115)
The African Native as a Sportsman by John Mitford   (p115-120)
The Ways of the Trout by Arthur Sharp   (p120-122)
[Review] *The Life of a Great Sportsman* by Mary Richardson   (p122-126)
Our Van [inc. Lingfield Races; Leicestershire Oaks; Curragh Meeting; Liverpool Cup;
            Goodwood Plate; Army Polo; Cowdray Park Polo; Grafton Hounds]   (p126-134)
Sporting Intelligence [inc. Oxford University Water Polo; Obituaries of William Tyrwhitt-Drake,
            Ernest Ingleby, Nat Gould, Richard Barlow, Edward Clark, David Gregory, George
            Waddington, Edmund Driscoll, William Griffin and Gregor MacGregor; The
            Totalisator; Manchester Athletic Club; Naval Racquets; Dunstable Golf Club;
            Minor Counties Cricket Association]   (p135-141)
Sporting Results   (p142-144)

Issue 716 : October 1919

Portrait [Howard] and Biography - Francis Willey   (p145-146)
The Hunt Puppy Show by George Collins   (p147-149)

[Obituary] Squire (William Tyrwhitt-) Drake (p149-151)
[Obituary] Gregor MacGregor by William Holland (p152-156)
Photograph [Hawkins]: *Gregor MacGregor* (facing p152)
Marshal Soult by Lees Knowles (p156-157)
The Eyes in Boxing by Norman Clark (p158-159)
County Cricket in 1919 by William Holland (p159-163)
Photograph [Hawkins]: *Yorkshire County Cricket Club Team* (facing p160)
Scientific Application of Brains to Sport by Frederick Webster (p163-166)
October by Lorna Collard (p167)
General Paine and the Boston Cup Defenders by George Hopcroft (p168-170)
Public School Cricket by Evan Noel (p171-173)
Amusements of Olden Days by John Wright (p173-176)
Some Famous Greyhound Sales by Adair Dighton (p177-179)
Our Van [inc. Nottingham Meeting; Stockton Racing; Great Yorkshire Stakes; Curragh
        Meeting; Doncaster Races; Quantock Staghounds; East Cornwall Foxhounds;
        Haldon Harriers] (p180-186)
Sporting Intelligence [inc. Cambridge Trinity College Beagles; Review of *Rowing at Henley*
        by Theodore Cook; Bloodstock Prices; Sinnington Hunt; Obituaries of Margaret
        Inge, James Beesley, Hugh Doherty, Charles Fernie, William Coryton, William
        Caffyn and Charles Beresford; Irish Golf Championship; Yorkshire County
        Cricket Club Finances] (p187-191)
Sporting Results (p191-192)

Issue 717 : November 1919

Portrait [Lafayette] and Biography - Rooke Rawlence (p193-195)
The Management of Fox Coverts by William Wroughton (p196-202)
Hunt Changes in 1919 by Edward Cuming (p203-208)
Farming and Foxhunting by Edward Cuming (p208-210)
Building An A1 Nation by Frederick Webster (p210-213)
The English Style of Boxing by Norman Clark (p213-216)
The Temperament of the Thoroughbred by Jack Fairfax-Blakeborough (p216-218)
The Sportsman's Library: Reviews of *Success in Athletics* by Frederick Webster; *The
        Biography of W.G.Grace* by Martin Hawke; *The Principles of Horsemanship* by
        Francois Baucher; *Cavalry Horsemanship and Horse Training* by Blacque Belairs;
        My Kingdom for a Horse by William Allison; *Light Horses - Breeds and
        Management* by William Blew; *Maeterlinck's Dogs* by Georgette Maeterlinck;
        Come Duck Shooting With Me by Herbert Gardner; *The Swing in Golf* by
        Alan Quartermain (p219-222)
Voltigeur versus Flying Dutchman by Richard Meysey-Thompson (p222-223)
The Pheasant at the Covert Side by Arthur Horwood (p223-227)
Queen of the Seasons [verses] by Norman Innes (p228)
Our Van [inc. Curragh Races; Ayr Meeting; Newbury Races; Leicester Meeting; South Notts
        Hunt; Worcestershire Hounds; South Oxfordshire Hunt; Hailsham Harriers] (p229-236)
Photograph [Rouch]: *Swynford* (facing p230)
Photograph [Rouch]: *Arthur D* (facing p230)
Photograph [Rouch]: *Black Prince* (facing p232)
Photograph [Rouch]: *Marcia* (facing p232)
Hunting and Farming by Seymour Bathurst (p236)
Sporting Intelligence [inc. Royal & Ancient Golf Club; Compulsory Purchase of
        Hurlingham Ground Deferred; Belvoir Hunt; Obituaries of William Portman,
        William Escott, Frank Laver, Herbert Winfield and Ernest Halliwell; Army
        Cross-Country Association; New York Yacht Club; Ribblesdale Buckhounds] (p237-239)
Sporting Results (p239-240)

Issue 718 : December 1919

Portrait [Thurlock] and Biography - Dennis Readett-Bayley	(p241-243)
Manners in the Hunting Field by George Collins	(p244-246)
Sydenham Dixon: An All-Round Sportsman by Henry Platt	(p247-254)
Photograph [Elliott]: *Sydenham Dixon* [Son of The Druid]	(facing p248)
Light on the Lowth Cricket Mystery by William Holland	(p254-259)
Individual Courage in Hounds by Jack Fairfax-Blakeborough	(p259-262)
Next Year's America's Cup Problem by George Hopcroft	(p262-265)
The Chub: A Fine Winter Fish by Arthur Sharp	(p266-270)
Baily's Hunting Directory 1918-20	(p270-271)
Our Van [inc. The Cesarewitch; Newcastle Meeting; Jockey Club Cup; Cottesmore Hunt; North Shropshire Hounds; Tarporley Hunt Club]	(p271-279)
Sporting Intelligence [inc. International Polo; Hunt Changes; Sculling Championship; Obituaries of James Woodburn, Edward Wainwright, John Doig, John Curre and Roger Walker; Review of *The Rugby Football Annual* by Charles Marriott; North Hereford Hounds; South Hereford Hunt]	(p280-284)
Sporting Results	(p284)

Volume 113, January - June 1920

Issue 719 : January 1920

Portrait [Rouch] of Frederick Rees, jockey	Title page
Portrait [Russell] and Biography - David Beatty	(p1-5)
The Whaddon Chase Dispute by George Burrows	(p5-8)
The Poacher by Claye Shaw	(p8-17)
Broughton's Mark by Norman Clark	(p17-19)
[Obituary] Maud Cheape by Jack Fairfax-Blakeborough	(p19-22)
A Day on Patrol in Rhodesian Wilds by James Lamburn	(p22-29)
[Review] An Annual For All Country Gentlemen: *The Live Stock Journal Annual for 1920*	(p30-33)
Our Van [inc. Leicester Meeting; Derby Cup; Warwick Races; Quorn Hunt; Cattistock Hounds; East Dorset Hunt; Blencathra Hounds]	(p33-41)
Sporting Intelligence [inc. University Rugby; Jockey Club Racing Reforms; Gimcrack Dinner; County Polo Association; Brocklesby Hounds; Obituaries of Kinross Arber, Arthur Litteljohn, Samual Reade, Charles Innes-Ker, William McTaggart and W.C.Pack Ford (*Baily's* correspondent); Antwerp Olympic Games; The Trainers' Federation]	(p41-48)
Sporting Results	(p48)

Issue 720 : February 1920

Portrait [Howard] and Biography - Walter Wiggin	(p49-50)
Masters of Hounds Point-to-Point Committee by Ulric Thynne	(p51-56)
Whaddon Chase Dispute by Rooke Rawlence	(p56)
The New Generation of Golfers by Frank Carruthers	(p57-60)
The National Hunt Steeplechase by Adair Dighton	(p61-64)
British Wild Geese by Arthur Horwood	(p65-68)
The Old Hound [verses] by William Williams	(p68)
Fishing for Pike in Winter by Alan Johnson	(p69-71)
Record Breaking by Frederick Webster	(p71-74)
The Last of the Sporting Drums by Norman Clark	(p74-80)
Our Van [inc. Plumpton Races; Haydock Park Racing; Ramsgate Handicap Steeplechase; Cheltenham Meeting; Manchester Steeplechase; Bedale Hunt; Chilworth & Stoneham Harriers; Isle of Wight Foxhounds; Percy Hounds; Norwich Staghounds]	(p80-89)

America Polo Cup by Thomas Dale (p89)

Sporting Intelligence [inc. Oxford University Athletic Club; Ranelagh Polo; Obituaries of
Charles Kinsky, John Roberts, William Ward, Lee Pilkington, Joseph Bennett,
Frank Cullen and Thomas Crossland; Yorkshire County Cricket Club; Welsh Rugby;
Football Association International Conference; Review of *Horse and Hound* by
William Williams] (p90-93)

Sporting Results (p93-96)

Issue 721 : March 1920

Portrait [Barnett] and Biography - Gerald Mildmay (p97-98)
With the Fell Packs by Charles Parry (p98-100)
The Hound and His Nose by Richard Clapham (p100-103)
Duck-Netting in Japan (p103-105)
The Boat Race by Herbert Hewett (p105-108)
An Open Air Profession by Frederick Webster (p108-111)
[Review] *The Life of Ronald Poulton* (-Palmer) by Edward Poulton (p112-113)
The Sportsman's Library: Reviews of *Skating* by Alfred Crawley; *The Art of Health* by James
Long; *How Jerusalem was Won* by William Massey; *Wild Sports and Natural
History of the Highlands* by Charles St.John and *Fifty Years of Golf* by Horace
Hutchinson (p114-115)
Plover and Their Ways by Arthur Horwood (p116-119)
[Review] *John Porter of Kingsclere* by Edward Moorhouse (p120-124)
Defender of the America's Cup by George Hopcroft (p125-128)
Our Van [inc. Rangoon Turf Club; National Hunt Rules; Staines Steeplechase; Nottingham
Meeting; Fernie Hunt; Blankney Hounds; Davies Hounds at Llanwrog] (p128-137)
Sporting Intelligence [inc. University Golf; Obituaries of Thomas Leader, Frederick Horsfall,
Thomas Harrison, Clement Archer and Wilberforce Eaves; Polo Handicapping;
Lawn Tennis at Schools; Review of *The Racing Calendar for 1919*; Hunting as a
Profession; Essex Hounds; Olympic Games; Royal Cinque Ports Golf Club;
Royal Caledonian Curling Club] (p138-142)
Grey Patch [verses] by William Williams (p141)
Sporting Results (p143-144)

Issue 722 : April 1920

Portrait [Bassano] and Biography - Douglas Haig (p145-150)
The Corinthian Age by Henry Archer (p150-154)
The Hound and His Feet by Richard Clapham (p154-157)
Sidelights on Spring Fly Fishing by George Garrow-Green (p157-159)
Whaddon Chase Settlement by George Burrows (p160-162)
Jim Bailey's Retirement by Tresham Gilbey (p162-164)
Racquets by Henry Rudd (p164-167)
Hounds Please Gentlemen by George Roller (p167-169)
Woodpigeon Flocks by Arthur Horwood (p169-171)
A Study of the Greyhound by Harding Cox (p172-175)
Life in a Training Stable by Jack Fairfax-Blakeborough (p175-178)
London's Spring Horse Shows by Gerald Ricardo (p179-183)
Our Van [inc. Ludlow Meeting; Newbury Races; Cheltenham Handicap Steeplechase; Rufford
Hunt; Albrighton Hounds; Beaufort Hunt; Suffolk Hounds] (p183-188)
The English Football Cup by Herbert Hewett (p188)
Sporting Intelligence [inc. Stamford Bridge Football; Yacht Racing; Scottish Ladies Golf;
Oxford University Athletics; Obituaries of Herbert Hutchinson, David Morgan,
Walter Greene, Shawe Taylor and Richard Ord; Puckeridge Hunt; Somerset
County Cricket Club] (p189-190)

To Diana [verses] by William Williams (p189)
Sporting Results (p191-192)

Issue 723 : May 1920

Portrait [Lafayette] and Biography - Arthur Turner (p193-194)
The Outlook for Regimental Polo by Archibald Charlton (p195-199)
New Golf Teachings by Frank Carruthers (p200-202)
A Plea for a Length Class by George Hopcroft (p202-205)
Trail Hounds and Hound Trailing by Richard Clapham (p205-208)
Some Famous Anglers by Ernest Phillips (p209-213)
Point-to-Point Racing: Some Suggestions by George Burrows (p213-215)
Presentation to Jim Bailey by Tresham Gilbey (p215-216)
Adventurer by William Scarth-Dixon (p217-220)
Clouds: Their Meaning for the Angler by Charles Stevenson (p220-222)
An Admirable Crichton of the Victorian Era by Charles Kent (p222-226)
Our Van [inc. The Southern Case; Lincolnshire Handicap; Grand National; Brocklesby Stakes; Hursley Hunt; Stevenstone Hounds; South Durham Hunt; High Peak Harriers] (p227-235)
To Finish the Season [verses] by Norman Innes (p235)
Sporting Intelligence [inc. University Boat Race; Review of *The Common Sense of Coaching* by Harcourt Gold; Puckeridge Hunt Presentation; Hurlingham Club Polo Rules Committee; Obituaries of Austin Miller, West Fenton (editor of *The World*), Edward Holmes and Caroline Dixon (widow of The Druid); General Stud Book; South Shropshire Hounds] (p236-238)
Sporting Results (p239-240)

Issue 724 : June 1920

Portrait [Langfier] and Biography - Cecil Lowther (p241-244)
The New and the Old Pugilism by Claye Shaw (p245-252)
Racquets: A Revival by Henry Rudd (p252-256)
Amateur Billiards: Past and Present by Arthur Mainwaring (p257-259)
On Foot With Foxhounds by Charles Race (p259-263)
Countryside Fun by Jack Fairfax-Blakeborough (p264-265)
The Amateur Tennis Championships by Wallis Myers (p265-267)
Light Casts by Morgan Watkins (p267-269)
Our Van [inc. Oadby Plate; Lancashire Handicap Steeplechase; Newbury Racing; Chester Meeting; Tickham Hunt Point-to-Point Races; Sparkford Vale Harriers; Ranelagh Polo Pavilion; Cheltenham Polo Club] (p269-280)
Sporting Intelligence [inc. Pennsylvania University Athletics; Oxford University Boat Club; Stoke Poges Golf Club; Obituaries of John Madge, William Macpherson and Frank Summers; Brighton Coaching] (p280-281)
Sporting Results (p282-284)

Volume 114, July - December 1920

Issue 725 : July 1920

Portrait of Frank Bullock, jockey Title page
Portrait [Elliott] and Biography - John Butcher (p1-4)
Sport on the Rhine by Horace Wyndham (p4-6)
Polo in 1920 by Thomas Dale (p6-8)
Hunt Disputes: Whaddon Chase and Essex Union Hunts by George Burrows (p8-10)
Memories of Point-to-Point Racing by Trevor Roller (p10-11)
Otter Hunting in the Fell Country by Richard Clapham (p12-15)

Jerry Milne by George Collins (p15-18)
Who's Who in Yachting by George Hopcroft (p18-21)
Trout Flies and Fancies by Arthur Sharp (p21-25)
Boxing: Cultivating the Raw Material by Norman Clark (p25-27)
Vanished Names in Horse Breeding by Jack Fairfax-Blakeborough (p28-31)
Masters of Hounds Point-to-Point Committee by George Burrows (p31-32)
A Lucky Experience with Roe by Morgan Watkins (p32-36)
Do Foxes Kill Lambs by Charles Batchelder (p37-39)
Our Van [inc. Newmarket Stakes; York Races; Manchester Cup; Epsom Meeting; American Army Polo Team; Aldershot Polo] (p39-47)
Sporting Intelligence [inc. Royal Portrush Golf Club; Sheringham Golf; Obituary of Alexander Sinclair] (p48)
Sporting Results (p48)

Issue 726 : August 1920

Portrait [Howard] and Biography - Frank Barbour (p49-51)
The Trout of Blagdon by Ernest Phillips (p52-54)
A Huntsman's Reminiscences by James Cockayne (p55-57)
The Polo Season of 1920 by Thomas Dale (p57-61)
Photograph [Rouch]: *Seventeenth Lancers Polo Team* (facing p58)
Wild Duck by Arthur Horwood (p61-64)
The Hound at Walk by Richard Clapham (p64-69)
Photograph [Rouch]: *Lady Margaret* (facing p67)
Photograph: *Rackette* (facing p67)
Will Dale by George Collins (p69-72)
An Unlucky Horse by Jack Fairfax-Blakeborough (p73-74)
Beverley: An Historic Racing Centre by Jack Fairfax-Blakeborough (p74-79)
Small Trout Streams by Arthur Sharp (p79-81)
Hunters and Hounds at Peterborough by Gerald Ricardo (p82-86)
Our Van [inc. Newbury Meeting; Ascot Stakes; Royal Hunt Cup; Northumberland Plate; Alexandra Park Races; Dumfriesshire Otterhounds] (p86-93)
Sporting Intelligence [inc. University Polo; Oxford University Lawn Tennis Club; Henley Regatta; Wimbledon Lawn Tennis; Deal Golf; Obituaries of Arthur Tempest, Thomas Aldridge and Henry Fitzwilliam; Naval Racquets] (p94-96)
Sporting Results (p96)

Issue 727 : September 1920

Portrait [Swaine] and Biography - George Hastings (p97-99)
Starting Prices and Winning Chances by Henry Rudd (p99-102)
Defensive Hitting in Boxing by Norman Clark (p102-104)
Hare Hunting Versified by Henry Bryden (p105-106)
The True Spirit for Cubhunting by George Collins (p107-109)
The Recent America's Cup Races by George Hopcroft (p109-110)
Today's Partridge Problems by Arthur Horwood (p110-113)
Wire in the Hunting Field by Frank Bonnett (p113-115)
Photograph [Parsons]: *Tracery* (facing p117)
Billiards: Some Historical Notes by Edgar Thomas (p117-120)
The Sire of Eclipse by James Cameron (p120-123)
Engraving [sculp. Scott]: *Eclipse and Shakespeare* (facing p120)
The Close of the Polo Season by Thomas Dale (p124-126)
The Modern Foxhound by Charles Richardson (p126-130)
September Sea-Trout by Arthur Sharp (p130-132)

Our Van [inc. Newmarket Meeting; Leicester Races; Liverpool Plate; Goodwood Racing;
        Devon & Somerset Staghounds; Albrighton Hunt] (p132-139)
Sporting Intelligence [inc. Obituaries of Walter Winans, John Shuter, Ryder Richardson,
        George Nevill and John Gilmour; Wingfield Sculls; Rufford Hunt; Review of
        Modern Bowls by George Burrows; Harriers & Beagles Association] (p140-142)
Night in the Wood [verses] by William Williams (p141)
Sporting Results (p142-144)

Issue 728 : October 1920

Portrait [Howard] and Biography - Robert Hermon-Hodge (p145-147)
Some Hunt Changes by Edward Cuming (p147-151)
Hunting Types: The Novice by Michael Hope (p151-152)
Hunting Horns and Horn Music by Thomas Dale (p152-155)
A Nation of Stock Breeders by Charles Batchelder (p155-159)
Photograph: *Blue Tit* (on p159)
On Grayling and Grayling Flies by Arthur Sharp (p160-163)
Confessions of a Poacher by Jack Fairfax-Blakeborough (p164-165)
Should the America's Cup Rules be Altered by George Hopcroft (p166-168)
The View Halloa by Charles Richardson (p169-172)
Coverts for [Wood]Cock by James Harting (p172-178)
The First Australian Tour by William Holland (p178-179)
Our Van [inc. Nottingham Races; Folkestone Meeting; Redcar Handicap; Great Yorkshire
        Stakes; Ludlow Hunt; South Oxfordshire Hounds; Exford Horse Show;
        Obituary of Monte Waterbury] (p180-188)
Sporting Intelligence [inc. International Athletics; Obituaries of Joseph Pickersgill, George
        Marriner and Egerton Castle; St.Andrews Golf; English Arab Horse Society;
        Bramham Moor Hunt] (p188-190)
Sporting Results (p190-192)

Issue 729 : November 1920

Portrait [Elliott] and Biography - Hugh Cholmondeley (p193-194)
Economy in Foxhunting by Thomas Dale (p195-198)
Hunting Types: The Master by Michael Hope (p198-200)
Baily's Hunting Directory 1920-21 by George Burrows (p200-201)
Hunt Changes in 1920 by Edward Cuming (p201-204)
Old Kate by Sydenham Dixon (p204-205)
Photograph [Rouch]: *Old Kate with William Allison* (facing p204)
The Boxer's Greatest Asset by Norman Clark (p206-207)
Hunting Cries [verses] by Norman Innes (p207)
Post-War Foxhunting by George Collins (p208-211)
To Open the Season [verses] by William Williams (p211)
The Breeding of Polo Ponies by James Cameron (p212-213)
The Sportsman's Library: Reviews of *My Fighting Life* by Georges Carpentier; *Memories of the
        Shires* by Otho Paget; *Foxhunting on the Lakeland Fells* by Richard Clapham and
        Old Village Life by Peter Ditchfield (p213-215)
Austria's Government-Bred Horses by George Burrows (p216-217)
November Afield by Arthur Sharp (p217-219)
Two Famous Rugby Clubs by Edward Sewell (p219-224)
An Old Hunting Diary and the Evolution of a Pack of Hounds by Jack Fairfax-Blakeborough (p224-228)
The Height of Polo Ponies by Thomas Dale (p228-231)
Our Van [inc. Hornsey Plate; Ayr Races; Boscawen Stakes; Kempton Park Meeting; Bramham
        Moor Hunt; West Somerset Hounds; Croome Hunt] (p231-237)

Sporting Intelligence [inc. Camberley Heath Golf Club; Turf Fraud Trial; Obituaries of
         Chevalier Ginistrelli, Thomas Morgan and William Senior (*Baily's* contributor);
         East Waterford Foxhounds; Hawkstone Otterhounds; West Kent Hounds; Review
         of *Round About Egypt* by Alexander Horsley]   (p237-239)
Sporting Results   (p239-240)

Issue 730 : December 1920

Portrait [Pannell] and Biography - Algernon Burnaby   (p241-243)
Mixed Sport in Central Wales by Charles Richardson   (p243-247)
The Christmas Partridge by William Malden   (p248-250)
Hunt Terriers by Richard Clapham   (p251-253)
Hunting Types: The Follower by Michael Hope   (p253-255)
Britain's Forestry by William Schlich   (p256-257)
Brains at Play by Ernest Bergholt   (p258-261)
Frank Bullock by Sydenham Dixon   (p262-263)
[Review] *Hunting the Fox* by Richard Verney   (p264-265)
The Joy of Winter by John Wright   (p265-266)
Old Age at the Covertside [verses] by George Fothergill   (p266)
One Side of Bull Fighting by Trevor Roller   (p267-272)
Our Van [inc. Newmarket Meeting; Curragh Racing; Newbury Autumn Handicap; Milton
         Hounds; West Norfolk Foxhounds; Bedale Hunt; Widford Beagles]   (p272-279)
[Obituary] William Selby-Lowndes by George Burrows   (p278-279)
Photograph [Newman]: *William Selby-Lowndes*   (on p278)
[Obituary] John Ryder by George Burrows   (p280)
Sporting Intelligence [inc. Live Stock Prices; Obituaries of Alec Watson, Walter Woodgate
         (*Baily's* contributor) and Thomas Springfield; Essex Staghounds; Dulverton Hunt;
         West Somerset Foxhounds; High Peak Harriers; Fettes Rugby]   (p280-283)
Sporting Results   (p283-284)

Eustice Miles

Volume 115, January - June 1921

Issue 731 : January 1921

Portrait [Roach] of Bernard Carslake, jockey	Title page
Portrait [Hoppe] and Biography - Lionel Robinson	(p1-4)
The Value of Pedigree in Foxhound Breeding by George Collins	(p5-9)
Hunting Types: The Huntsman by Michael Hope	(p9-11)
Baily's Hunting Directory 1920-21 by George Burrows	(p11)
Live Stock Journal Annual 1920 by George Burrows	(p12)
The Irony of Fate [verses] by George Fothergill	(p12)
The Laying-Up Season by George Hopcroft	(p13-15)
Death of His Old Grey Mare [verses] by George Fothergill	(p15)
The Olympic Games: Shall We Go On by Frederick Webster	(p16-18)
Wild Goose Shooting by Stanley Duncan	(p18-21)
Small Packs by Richard Clapham	(p22-24)
Of Warwickshire Lads [verses] by George Fothergill	(p24)
The Great Little Champion by Norman Clark	(p25-34)
A Month's Leave in India by George Birks	(p34-36)
Our Van [inc. Liverpool Meeting; Manchester Races; Kenilworth Handicap; Warwickshire Hunt; Louth Hounds; Ward Union Staghounds; Whaddon Chase Hunt Dispute]	(p36-44)
Sporting Intelligence [inc. Open Golf Championship; Irish Hunters; York Race Committee; Westminster Tennis; Obituaries of Thomas Wadlow, Rawson Robertshaw and Harry North; Oxford University Rowing; Cambridge University Athletic Club; Record Football Transfer Fee]	(p44-47)
Sporting Results	(p47-48)

Issue 732 : February 1921

Portrait [Elliott] and Biography - William Standish	(p49-50)
Polo Topics by Thomas Dale	(p51-55)
What is An Amateur by Frederick Webster	(p55-58)
The Siamese Sportsman by George Cecil	(p58-60)
Racing Reforms by Charles Richardson	(p60-65)
An Imported Buckjumper by George Fothergill	(p65-67)
Virago by Adair Dighton	(p68-69)
The Angler in Flood Time by Charles Stevenson	(p70-71)
Elephants by Mervyn Beech	(p72-75)
Foxhunting with Harriers by Richard Clapham	(p76-77)
Hunting Types: The Lady Follower by Michael Hope	(p78-80)
Squash by Frederick Wilson	(p80-83)
Our Van [inc. Manchester Handicap Steeplechase; Strawberry Hill Hurdle Race; Newbury Meeting; Cottesmore Hunt; Hursley Hunt; Blackmore Vale Hounds; Tavistock Harriers]	(p83-91)
Sporting Intelligence [inc. Essex Hunt Dispute; Whaddon Chase Pack; Obituaries of Reginald Graham, John Thursby, Edmond Blanc, Thomas Osborne, Alfred Dixon, Meredith Brown, Hue Williams, Joseph O'Sullivan, Joseph Jefferson, Frank Townsend, John Simpson and Robert Moorhouse; American Golf Tour; Sperling Harriers; North Shropshire Hunt; Quarme Harriers]	(p91-96)
The Season [verses] by William Williams	(on p92)

Issue 733 : March 1921

Portrait [Bacon] and Biography - Frederic Straker	(p97-99)
End of the Whaddon Chase Dispute by George Burrows	(p100-104)

Polo in England in 1921 by Edward Miller (p104-105)
Foxhounds and Fencing by Richard Clapham (p106-108)
The Psychology of Sport by John Wright (p109-111)
Golf in Italy by Horace Wyndham (p111-113)
India's Native Farriers by George Cecil (p113-115)
America's Golf Challenge by Frank Carruthers (p115-118)
The Literature of Hunting by Thomas Dale (p118-121)
Hunting Types: The Whip by Michael Hope (p121-123)
The New Rating Rule by George Hopcroft (p123-126)
A Gentleman and a Sportsman by Jack Fairfax-Blakeborough (p127-129)
Racquets by Henry Rudd (p130-132)
Our Van [inc. Burstow Handicap Steeplechase; Kempton Park Meeting; Windsor Racing;
     North Hertfordshire Hounds; Norwich Staghounds; New Forest Buckhounds] (p132-139)
Norris Midwood of the National Pony Society by George Burrows (p140)
Photograph: *Norris Midwood* (on p140)
Sporting Intelligence [inc. Obituaries of William Westenra, William Gunn, William Timmis,
     Clive Wilson, James Hoyland, Charles Hunter, William Codgbrook and
     Graham Prentice; Betting in France; Sculling Presentation; Yorkshire County
     Cricket Club] (p141-143)
Sporting Results (p144)

Issue 734 : April 1921

Portrait [Collings] and Biography - George Bellville (p145-146)
What to Look for in the Polo Pony by Walter Buckmaster (p146-148)
[Obituary] Herbert Hewett by George Burrows (p149-150)
The Unconscious Mind in Sport and Games by Claye Shaw (p151-157)
Foxhunting with Beagles at Aldershot by George Fothergill (p158-162)
The Whip in Racing by William Fox-Russell (p162-164)
Fox Tales by George Collins (p164-166)
The Quins by Edward Sewell (p167-169)
The Spring Horse Shows by William Scarth-Dixon (p170-172)
The Hesseltines of Hambleton by Jack Fairfax-Blakeborough (p172-177)
April Afield by Harding Cox (p178-180)
Our Van [inc. Birmingham Races; Gloucester Hurdle Race; Leicester Meeting; Heythrop
     Hounds; Southwold Hunt; Obituary of Godfrey Meynell; North Cotswold Hunt;
     Mid-Kent Hounds; Downham Harriers; Glamorganshire Hunt] (p181-188)
Sporting Intelligence [inc. Pytchley Hunt Point-to-Point; Obituaries of John Brocklehurst,
     Edward Mashiter, Schofield Haigh, Charles Leslie and Percy La Touche;
     Southwold Hounds; Review of *Wisden's Cricketers' Almanack*] (p188-192)
Morning in the Woods [verses] by William Williams (on p191)
Sporting Results (p192)

Issue 735 : May 1921

Portrait [Bassano] and Biography - Charles Stewart (p193-196)
Sport in May by Harding Cox (p197-200)
Point-to-Point Racing and its Royal Patrons by Edward Cuming (p200-204)
Muntz's Robin Red [with verses] by George Fothergill (p204-206)
Edward Rawnsley by George Collins (p206-208)
An Elephant Drive in the Indian Hills by George Cecil (p208-210)
Hail and Au Revoir [verses] by Norman Innes (p210)
The Forward Seat by Hugh Henry (p211-214)
Headwork in Boxing by Norman Clark (p214-216)
Rejuvenating His Majesty's Britannia by George Hopcroft (p216-219)

Lithograph [Hopcroft]: *Britannia in 1920 Rig* (on p217)
Lithograph [Hopcroft]: *Britannia in 1893-94 Rig* (on p217)
India's Native Vets by George Cecil (p219-222)
The Warthog and Bushpig by Morgan Watkins (p222-224)
Caddie Stories by Horace Wyndham (p225-228)
Our Van [inc. Staffordshire Steeplechase; Grand Military Gold Cup; Brocklesby Stakes; Aintree Meeting; Fernie Hunt; Tickham Hounds; Essex & Suffolk Hunt; Linlithgow & Stirlingshire Hounds; Essex Staghounds] (p228-236)
Sporting Intelligence [inc. Obituaries of Charles Barclay, William Badco, Charles Sawyer, Charles Liversidge, Ronald Oswald, Peter Hansell and Charles Page; Cannes Tennis; Grove Hounds; Catterick Bridge Races] (p236-237)
Sporting Results (p237-240)

Issue 736 : June 1921

Portrait [Russell] and Biography - Clive Behrens (p241-243)
International Polo Match Prospects by Thomas Dale (p244-249)
Photograph [Rouch]: *Vivian Lockett* (facing p244)
Photograph [Rouch]: *Devereux Milburn* (facing p246)
The Forward Seat (p250-251)
Can Carpentier Win by Norman Clark (p251-256)
Tommy Lye: A Middleham Retrospect by George Fothergill (p256-264)
Lithograph: *Wrapper Inscribed by William Harry* (on p257)
The Racquets Season by Henry Rudd (p265-269)
Bernard Carslake by Edmund Cuming (p269)
Notable Test Cricket Matches by William Holland (p270-272)
Golf in the Mountains of Ceylon by George Cecil (p272-274)
Our Van [inc. Government Withdraws Ban on Racing; Association of Owners, Breeders and Trainers; Horse Boxes; Newmarket Meeting; Kempton Park Racing; Cattistock Hunt; Cheshire Hounds; South Durham Hunt] (p275-280)
Sporting Intelligence [inc. Marylebone Cricket Club President; Queen's Club Tennis; County Cricket Record; Obituaries of Lawrence Cotton, Edward Roper, John Wood ('Hyme' of *The Field*), Percy Christopherson, Arthur Mold and Samuel Darling; Tattersall's Sales; All England Tennis Club; Review of *Meadow Brook Club Yearbook*] (p281-284)
The Angler [verses] by William Williams (on p282)
The Peaceful Wood [verses] by William Williams (on p282)
Sporting Results (p284)

Volume 116, July - December 1921

Issue 737 : July 1921

Portrait [Rouch] of Joseph Childs, jockey Title page
Portrait [Rouch] and Biography - Faudel Phillips (p1-3)
First Polo Test and its Lessons by Thomas Dale (p3-7)
Photograph [Rouch]: *American Polo Team* (facing p4)
Photograph [Rouch]: *English Polo Team* (facing p4)
Sport in British East Africa by George Cecil (p7-9)
The Fight for the Ashes of Cricket by William Holland (p10-13)
The Man in the Box by Jack Fairfax-Blakeborough (p14-16)
Angling in Still Waters by Arthur Sharp (p17-19)
Old Time Hoghunting in India by Horace Wyndham (p20-22)
Fly Fishing for Summer Chub (p22-25)

Early Lady Jockeys by Charles Batchelder (p25-28)
A Remarkable Old Time Sportsman by Edgar Thomas (p28-30)
Prize Fighting and Modern Boxing by Norman Clark (p31-33)
Formosa by Charles Richardson (p33-35)
Old Stagers on the Turf by Adair Dighton (p35-36)
Our Van [inc. Government Consent to Racing; Newmarket Stakes; Manchester Meeting; Epsom
        Racing; England Polo Team; Indian Regimental Polo; Quorn Hunt Kennels] (p36-43)
Sporting Intelligence [inc. American Polo Association; Hoylake Golf; Hertfordshire Hunt;
        National Hunt Committee] (p43-44)
Sporting Results (p45-48)
Photograph [Rouch]: *Belle of All* (facing p46)
Photograph [Rouch]: *Handselleta* (facing p46)

Issue 738 : August 1921

Portrait [Spalding] and Biography - Brian Allott (p49)
International Polo Match and After by Thomas Dale (p50-54)
Weight in Polo by Frederick Rouse (p54-57)
Deep Sea Racing Yachts by George Hopcroft (p57-59)
Wild Elephant Hunting in Ceylon by George Cecil (p60-61)
The Little Trout of the Mountains by Alan Johnson (p61-63)
Foxhunting Quakers by George Fothergill (p64-68)
Lithograph [pinx. Whittaker]: *Flintoff Leatham on Screwdriver* (on p67)
Horse and Hound at Peterborough by William Scarth-Dixon (p68-72)
Jim Smith of Brocklesby by George Collins (p72-77)
The Lost Ashes of Cricket by William Holland (p77-78)
The Mugger [Crocodile] by George Cecil (p78-82)
James Pigg's Forelder John by Jack Fairfax-Blakeborough (p83-84)
Our Van [inc. Ascot Meeting; Northumberland Plate; Carlisle Racecourse; Nottingham Races;
        Bibury Club Meeting; Worcester Racing] (p85-90)
Sporting Intelligence [inc. Harvard/Yale Universities versus Oxford/Cambridge Universities
        Athletics Meeting; Polo Test Reflections; Henley Regatta; Wimbledon Lawn
        Tennis Championships; Yorkshire Golf Championship; Obituaries of Morton
        Lucas, Charles Dawson, John Strong and Edward Hobson; Walker's Harriers] (p91-94)
Photograph [Parsons]: *Lady Millie* (facing p92)
Photograph [Parsons]: *Mathias* (facing p92)
Sporting Results (p95-96)

Issue 739 : September 1921

Portrait [Lafayette] and Biography - Loftus Bates (p97-99)
The Opening Meet by Trevor Roller (p99-100)
Notes on Managing Foxhounds by Reginald Corbet (p101-107)
Sport in Malaya by George Cecil (p108-110)
Science in Polo by Frederick Rouse (p111-114)
Grayling Lures by Arthur Sharp (p114-117)
Grouse and Drought by Arthur Horwood (p117-120)
Sporting Terminology by Jack Fairfax-Blakeborough (p120-122)
Foxhounds for Otterhunting by Richard Clapham (p123-125)
Evolution of the Marconi Rig by George Hopcroft (p125-128)
Our Van [inc. Racing Dates from *Town Topics*; Newmarket Racing; Ayr Meeting; Curragh
        Races; Goodwood Cup; Dartmoor Otterhounds; Polo at Rugby; Cowdray Park
        Polo] (p128-140)
Photograph [Lafayette]: *Macanna* (facing p130)
Photograph: *Filly* (facing p130)

Photograph: *Pamber Ugly Duckling* (facing p134)
Photograph: *Suffolk Ewes* (facing p134)
Photograph: *Resolute II* (facing p138)
Photograph: *Doune Monarch* (facing p138)
The Grey Fox [verses] by William Williams (p140)
[Obituary] A Story of William Craven by George Fothergill (p141)
Sporting Intelligence [inc. Live Stock in England; Arthur Mailey's Cricket Feat; Cottesmore
        Hounds; Warwickshire Hunt] (p141-142)
Sporting Results (p143-144)

Issue 740 : October 1921

Portrait [Rouch] and Biography - Atherton Brown (p145-147)
Thomas Lipton and the America's Cup by George Hopcroft (p147-150)
A Coursing Causerie by Adair Dighton (p150-152)
Snipe and Their Habits by Arthur Horwood (p153-156)
What is Scent by Richard Clapham (p156-158)
Engraving [sculp. Babbage]: *The Earthstopper* (facing p158)
East African Campaign Shooting Memories by Morgan Watkins (p160-163)
The Prince as an Athlete by George Burrows (p163-164)
The Woodcock by Frank Bonnett (p164-168)
Lions by Mervyn Beech (p168-171)
Snipe in West Africa by Morgan Watkins (p172-174)
Athletic Paris by George Cecil (p175-177)
Anticipations [verses] by Norman Innes (p178)
The Angler's Inns by Eric Parker (p179-181)
Our Van [inc. Stockton Meeting; Ebor Handicap; Manchester Races; Wilton Hounds;
        Puckeridge Hunt; Heythrop Hounds] (p182-186)
The Australian Cricketers by William Holland (p187)
Sporting Intelligence [inc. Warner and Thornton Cricket Presentations; Doncaster Yearling
        Sales; Cumberland Hunt Point-to-Point Races; North Foreland Golf Club; Welsh
        Open Golf; Obituary of Nat Robinson] (p187-191)
The Vixen [verses] by William Williams (on p190)
Sporting Results (p191-192)

Issue 741 : November 1921

Portrait [Bacon] and Biography - John Rogerson (p193-196)
Hunt Changes in 1921 by Edward Cuming (p196-205)
Baily's Hunting Directory 1921-22 by George Burrows (p205-206)
Some Famous Fox Coverts by Thomas Dale (p206-209)
Hunts and Hunters I Have Known (part 1) by Michael Hope (p210-212)
On Digging Out by Richard Clapham (p212-215)
Reynard in Rome by Horace Wyndham (p215-217)
The London Scottish by Edward Sewell (p217-220)
Bargains in Greyhounds by Adair Dighton (p220-222)
A Bengal Tiger Shoot by George Cecil (p222-226)
Henry Mellish by Arthur Sharp (p227-229)
Our Van [inc. Baldoyle Races; Ayr Meeting; Jockey Club Stakes; Curragh Racing; Puckeridge
        Hounds; Teme Valley Hunt; County Down Staghounds] (p230-238)
Sporting Intelligence [inc. Samuel Darling's Will; Obituaries of Ernest Cassel and Percy de
        Paravicini; English Ladies Golf Championship; Stockholm Athletics] (p238-239)
November [verses] by William Williams (p238)
Sporting Results (p240)

Issue 742 : December 1921

Portrait [Elliott] and Biography - Dennis Boles	(p241-242)
Notes on Wire Removal by Robert Lambert	(p242-246)
Foxhunting First and Forever by George Fothergill	(p246-249)
A Note on Seventeenth Century Foxhunting by Edward Cuming	(p249-250)
The Medical and Surgical Aspect of Sports and Games (part 1) by Claye Shaw	(p250-256)
Woodcock Shooting on Irish Mountains by George Garrow-Green	(p257-259)
Trout for Sport by Arthur Sharp	(p259-262)
Yachting Season of 1921 by George Hopcroft	(p262-264)
Hunts and Hunters I Have Known (part 2) by Michael Hope	(p265-267)
Our Van [inc. Middle Park Plate; Sandown Park Racing; Alexandra Park Meeting; Newbury Autumn Handicap; Isle of Wight Hounds; Aldershot Staff College Hunt; Golden Valley Hounds; South Tetcott Hunt]	(p267-277)
Hunting Men and Fences by George Fothergill	(p277-278)
The Old Huntsman [verses] by William Williams	(p278)
Sporting Intelligence [inc. Hunting Etiquette; Straker's Brood Mares; Reviews of *The Widford Beagles* by John Pawle and *Baily's Hunting Directory 1921-22*; Obituaries of Richard Moore, Charles Loates and Gilbert Kennedy; Army Sports Control Board; Monmouthshire Foxhounds]	(p278-280)
Sporting Results	(p281-284)

Volume 117 : January - June 1922

Issue 743 : January 1922

Portrait [Rouch] of George Archibald, jockey	Title page
Portrait [Swaine] and Biography - Joseph Watson	(p1-3)
Professional Influence in Golf by Frank Carruthers	(p3-6)
The Medical and Surgical Aspect of Sports and Games (part 2) by Claye Shaw	(p7-10)
Herefordshire Hindhunting by Clifford Cordley	(p11-17)
Old Time Racing in India by Horace Wyndham	(p18-19)
The History of Archery as a Sport by Kennedy Bell	(p20-21)
Hunts and Hunters I Have Known (part 3) by Michael Hope	(p22-24)
Early Morning Hunting Fixtures by Jack Fairfax-Blakeborough	(p24-27)
Drake's Game and its Progress by George Teasdale-Buckell	(p27-29)
Tiger Shooting in India by George Cecil	(p29-31)
Shikar in Himalayan Forests by Alan Davis	(p32-35)
The Hunt Dinner [verses] by William Williams	(p35)
Our Van [inc. Lincoln Races; Grand Sefton Steeplechase; Warwick Meeting; Lingfield Park Racing; Grove Hunt; Eglinton Hounds; Woodland Pytchley Hunt; East Sussex Hounds; Zetland Hunt]	(p36-43)
Sporting Intelligence [inc. Review of *The Live Stock Journal Annual 1922*; Gimcrack Dinner and Pari-Mutuel; Hunt Servants and Insurance; Taxing Amateur Sport; Obituaries of Thomas Worton, Gerald Ricardo (*Baily's* contributor), William Jarvis, William Baillie-Grohman (*Baily's* contributor) and Peter Kemp; Heythrop Hunt; Review of *The Shooter's Yearbook*]	(p43-48)

Issue 744 : February 1922

Portrait [Howard] and Biography - George Dundas	(p49-52)
Famous Lightweight Greyhound Bitches by Adair Dighton	(p52-54)
Britain's Chance in Sport in 1922 by George Hopcroft	(p55-57)
Rugby Football in the Sixties by Edward Sewell	(p58-60)
American Foxhounds by Richard Clapham	(p61-63)

Sport, Games and Mr Pepys (part 1) by Edgar Thomas (p63-67)
Hunts and Hunters I Have Known (part 4) by Michael Hope (p67-69)
Winter Fishing in Canada by Bernard Houghton (p70-76)
Somerset Signs by Lorna Collard (p76-78)
A Gymkhana in the Tanganyika Territories by Gerald Ambrose (p78-81)
Golf in Hungary by Horace Wyndham (p81-83)
How They Race in Ceylon by George Cecil (p83-84)
Our Van [inc. Lingfield Park Steeplechases; Twickenham Hurdle Handicap; Hurst Park Racing; Manchester Meeting; West Norfolk Hunt; Essex Staghounds; Obituaries of Frederick Cheshire, William Smith and Reginald Hill; East Essex Foxhounds] (p84-92)
Sporting Intelligence [inc. Hurlingham Committee Ruling; County Polo Association; Rules of Golf Committee; Obituaries of Ephraim Lockwood, Frederick Martin, Henry Ripley and Edgar Barnett; New Zealand Sculling; Tynedale Hunt; Burton Hunt] (p92-95)
Reynard's Dream [verses] by William Williams (p94)
Sporting Results (p96)

Issue 745 : March 1922

Portrait [Howard] and Biography - Lionel Holliday (p97-100)
New and First Hand Voltigeur Memories by Jack Fairfax-Blakeborough (p100-105)
Long Shots Which Have Won at Altcar by Adair Dighton (p106-108)
Hunts and Hunters I Have Known (part 5) by Michael Hope (p108-110)
Sport, Games and Mr Pepys (part 2) by Edgar Thomas (p110-114)
Racquets An Experimental Season by Henry Rudd (p115-117)
The Wit of the Whipper-in by Thomas Dale (p117-121)
Francolin-Shooting in West Africa by Gerald Ambrose (p121-124)
Has the Standard of Professional Golf Improved (p124-125)
Spring Trout Fishing by Arthur Sharp (p125-128)
Racing in Egypt by George Cecil (p128-129)
The Football Association Cup by William Holland (p130-131)
Our Van [inc. Middlesex Hurdle Handicap; Sandown Park Meeting; Gatwick Races; Sinnington Hunt; Warwickshire Hounds; Worcestershire Hunt; West Somerset Hounds; South Durham Hunt; Obituaries of Cameron Douglas, Francis Mew, Jack Scott and Matthew Muir] (p132-139)
Sporting Intelligence [inc. Hertfordshire Foxhounds; Professionalism in Sport; Civil Service Sport; Reviews of Chasing and Racing by Harding Cox; Rough Shooting by Richard Clapham; Melbreak Hunt; International Polo; North Warwickshire Hounds; Obituaries of Arthur Fludyer, William Elsey, Thomas Gardner and Frederick Patton; Yorkshire County Cricket Club; Ystrad & Pentyrch Hounds; Vesta Rowing Club] (p139-144)
Young Grey Fox [verses] by William Williams (p142)
Foxhunting in Rome [verses] by William Williams (p143)

Issue 746 : April 1922

Portrait [Rouch] and Biography - David Davies (p145-147)
An April Idyll by Arthur Sharp (p148-150)
Wild Fowling in Britain by Arthur Horwood (p150-153)
Old Time Coursing Clubs by Adair Dighton (p153-154)
The Old Pink Coat [verses] by Norman Innes (p155)
Stolen Sport in Ireland by John Durham (p155-162)
The Proverbs of Sport and Play by Clifford Cordley (p162-164)
Dogs in India by George Cecil (p164-166)
[Obituary] John Porter by George Burrows (p167-170)
The Right Stamp of Hunter by Alan Hickling (p171-172)

Popularity of Bowls by George Teasdale-Buckell (p172-174)
London's Spring Horse Shows by Thomas Dale (p175-181)
Our Van [inc. Lingfield Park Races; Manchester Meeting; Cheltenham National Hunt
      Steeplechase; Bicester Hunt; New Forest Hounds; Goodwood Hunt; Essex
      Union Hounds] (p181-188)
Playing Cricket to a Finish by Stanley Jackson (p189)
Rugby Football in North-Western Canada by George Dewe (p189)
Sporting Intelligence [inc. Melbourne Cup; Obituaries of William Saxby, Joseph Watson, John
      Rowell and James Davidson (*Baily's* Contributor); Shire Horse Society; Malton
      & Ryedale Otterhounds; Review of *Wisden's Cricketers' Almanack 1922*] (p190-191)
Sporting Results (p192)

Issue 747 : May 1922

Portrait [pinx. Ward] and Biography - Charles Thornton (p193-197)
Generalship in Boxing by Norman Clark (p197-201)
The Yachting Outlook for 1922 by George Hopcroft (p201-204)
[Obituary] Robert Gosling by George Burrows (p205-206)
An Afternoon's Goose Driving by Kenneth Dawson (p207-209)
The Golf Championships by Frank Carruthers (p210-212)
The Chester Cup by Adair Dighton (p212-215)
County Cricket by William Holland (p215-217)
The Mayfly Trout by Arthur Sharp (p218-219)
The Racquets Championship by Henry Rudd (p220-221)
The Grand National and Its Critics by Jack Fairfax-Blakeborough (p221-225)
Point-to-Point Races by Edward Cuming (p225-228)
Our Van [inc. Lincolnshire Handicap; Liverpool Spring Cup; Holderness Hunt; Stanton Drew
      & Wells Foxhounds; Hursley Hunt; Berkshire Staghounds; Hunter's Certificates] (p228-235)
Sporting Intelligence [inc. Obituaries of Russell Walker, William Cobbold, John Eliot, Miall
      Green, Edward Clayton, Joseph Cannon and Frederick Bodington; Grand
      National injuries; Reviews of *Dry Fly Fishing* by Robert Bridgett, *Book of the
      Otter* by Richard Clapham, *Terriers* by Darby Matheson; *Terriers for Sport*
      by Pierce O'Connor; West Essex Golf Club; University Boat Race; Modern
      Boxing; Inter-Varsity Sports] (p235-238)
Sporting Results (p239-240)

Issue 748 : June 1922

Portrait [Howard] and Biography - Robert Wilmot (p241-242)
A Visit to Harwood Stud by Lewis Birch (p242-247)
Photograph [Rouch]: *Gainsborough* (facing p244)
More Golden Eagles by William Jepson (p247-250)
A Reed Buck Stalk by Morgan Watkins (p250-254)
Cricket in India by George Cecil (p254-255)
The Racquets Season by Henry Rudd (p256-260)
The Dover Road in 1812 by Culling Gaze (p260-265)
Grey Horses of Note on the Turf by Alfred Pullin (p266-268)
Current Polo Gossip by Frederick Rouse (p269-271)
Our Van [inc. Epsom Meeting; Alexandra Park Racing; Hurst Park Races; Great Cheshire
      Handicap; Ripon Meeting; Haydock Park Handicap] (p271-277)
Sporting Intelligence [inc. National Hunt Jockeys Insurance; Obituaries of Charles Kendall,
      Ernest Brutton, Thomas Ventress, Alec Timms, Harry Crichton, Arthur Yates and
      Charles Hutchings; Army Golf Championships; Essex Foxhounds; Review of
      A Gallery of Games by Kenneth Bird] (p278-282)
The Angler [verses] by William Williams (p279)

Sport and Language from *The Manchester Guardian*   (p279-280)
Sporting Results   (p282-284)

Volume 118, July - December 1922

Issue 749 : July 1922

Portrait [Rouch] of Charles Elliott, jockey   Title page
Portrait [Howard] and Biography - James Graham   (p1-2)
Record Times and Limits of Endurance by Claye Shaw   (p3-11)
Houghton Fishing Club Centenary by George Burrows   (p12-13)
Current Polo Topics by Frederick Rouse   (p13-18)
Photograph [Rouch]: *Argentine Polo Team*   (facing p14)
Photograph [Rouch]: *Isaac Bell and Walter Buckmaster*   (on p17)
Some Cricket Reflections by William Holland   (p19-20)
Exmoor in the Sixties by Clifford Cordley   (p21-23)
Kestrels and Game by William Jepson   (p23-25)
Rabbit Shooting with a Rifle by John Durham   (p26-30)
Which is the Fastest Rig by George Hopcroft   (p30-33)
Some Coarse Fish Fly Takers by Kenneth Dawson   (p34-35)
On Staying by William Scarth-Dixon   (p36-39)
Our Van [inc. Birmingham Meeting; Lewes Races; Redcar Racing; Salford Borough Handicap;
         Gatwick Meeting]   (p39-45)
Sporting Intelligence [inc. Badger Hunt in London; Obituaries of Digby Willoughby and
         Charles Lyttelton; Polo Ponies]   (p45-47)
The Ex-Huntsman [verses] by William Williams   (p46)
Sporting Results   (p47-48)

Issue 750 : August 1922

Portrait [Howard] and Biography - Edward Miller   (p49-51)
How British Golf has Declined by Frank Carruthers   (p52-54)
On a Wicklow Trout Stream by John Durham   (p55-57)
Thoughts on Preserving and Showing Game by Lewis Birch   (p58-61)
A Last Shoot in Salonika by Kenneth Dawson   (p61-64)
A Mystery of Old Cowes by George Hopcroft   (p64-67)
Current Polo Topics by Frederick Rouse   (p67-72)
Women as Cricketers by William Holland   (p72-74)
The Game of Bowls by Edgar Thomas   (p74-81)
Horse and Hound at Peterborough by William Scarth-Dixon   (p81-86)
Our Van [inc. Ascot Meeting; Newcastle Races; Sandringham Stakes; Nottingham Races; Bibury
         Cup; Pontefract Meeting; Old Newton Cup]   (p87-93)
Sporting Intelligence [inc. National Association of Equine Breeding Societies; Henley Regatta;
         Obituaries of Hesketh Pritchard, Percy Latham, Harold Janion, Tudor Williams
         and James Brown; Argentine Polo Ponies; Bucks Otterhounds]   (p93-95)
The Angler's Inn [verses] by William Williams   (p94)
Sporting Results   (p96)

Issue 751 : September 1922

Portrait [Speaicht] and Biography - Hugh Grosvenor   (p97-98)
Eve of British-American Cup Contest by George Hopcroft   (p98-101)
Bass Fishing by John Durham   (p101-105)
A Duck Shoot at Constantinople by Kenneth Dawson   (p105-108)
A Weasel Hunt by Nicholas Sedgwick   (p108-109)

Memories of Wild Beasts by Morgan Watkins (p109-112)
Tom Moody by Richard Darwall (p112-116)
Billiards by Sydenham Dixon (p116-119)
The Wisdom of Walton by Clifford Cordley (p120-121)
Current Polo Topics by Frederick Rouse (p122-124)
London's Ancient Duelling Grounds by Edgar Thomas (p125-129)
The Brighton Road by Dorking in 1812 by Culling Gaze (p129-134)
Our Van [inc. Soltykoff Stakes; Newmarket Summer Handicap; Hurst Park Plate; Sussex Stakes; Brighton Cup; Lewes Races] (p134-140)
Sporting Intelligence [inc. Doggett's Coat and Badge; Obituaries of Francis Wethered, Martin Rucker, Joseph Davis and Frank Euren; Brooklands Motor Racing; Review of *The Sealyham Terrier* by Theodore Marples; Comment on *Newmarket and Arabia* by Roger Upton] (p140-143)
The Trout [verses] by William Williams (p141)
Sporting Results (p143-144)

Issue 752 : October 1922

Portrait [Collings] and Biography - Henry Lopes (p145-147)
A Famous Mountain Foxhound Pack by Richard Clapham (p147-149)
Old Hounds by Oulton Gorse (p149-151)
Venatic Customs and Superstitions by Charles Roberts (p151-154)
Review of the Yacht Racing Season of 1922 by George Hopcroft (p155-158)
The Lure of the Pike by John Durham (p158-160)
Jackel Hunting in Mesopotamia by Henry Perch (p160-161)
Cricket in 1922 by William Holland (p161-163)
Limits of Endurance by Frederick Webster (p164)
Countries [verses] by Norman Innes (p165)
Streatlam Abbey Stud Memories by Charles Batchelder (p166-169)
Engraving: *Queen of Trumps* (facing p166)
Engraving: *Fisherman* (facing p168)
Racecourse Slang by Jack Fairfax-Blakeborough (p170-171)
Coat Colour in Thoroughbreds by Richard Sternfeld (p172-173)
The Opening Day by George Collins (p174-176)
[Review] *Sport in the Nineteenth Century* by George Trevelyan (p176-178)
Old October by Arthur Sharp (p178)
The Barb Horse by James Cameron (p179)
[Review] Orme from *Memories of Men and Horses* by William Allison (p179-180)
Our Van [inc. Leopardstown Meeting; Nottingham Breeders Stakes; North Surrey Handicap; Yorkshire Oaks; Haydock Park Races; Ebor Handicap; Badminton Hunt; Exmoor Hounds] (p181-187)
Photograph: *Casterway* (facing p187)
Photograph: *Lady Grace* (facing p187)
Sporting Intelligence [inc. National Stud; Sledmere Yearlings; Obituaries of Vivian Crawford, James Whipp, John Osborne, Charles Archer, Wilfrid Blunt, William Wakefield and Charles Rumsey; London's Duelling Grounds] (p188-191)
Photograph: *Butterpat* (facing p188)
Photograph: *Skiplam Pride* (facing p188)
Sporting Results (p192)

Issue 753 : November 1922

Portrait [Elliott] and Biography - Edwin Stanyforth (p193-195)
Hunt Changes in 1922 by Edward Cuming (p196-206)
Goodall's Practice with Foxhounds by Henry Bentinck (p207-211)

November's Legacy by Jack Fairfax-Blakeborough (p211-213)
The British Pheasant and its Adaptability to Modern Covert Shooting by Alan Horwood (p213-216)
Stalking the Tahr by Alan Davis (p216-220)
[Obituary] Charles Wade: A Famous Three-Quarter Back (p220-221)
A November Day by Arthur Sharp (p221)
Baily's Hunting Directory 1922-23 by George Burrows (p222-223)
Horses Coughing by Claye Shaw (p223)
Arab Horse Endurance Test by Albert Frost (p224)
Government Light Horse Breeding Scheme by George Burrows (p225-226)
Our Van [inc. Doncaster Meeting; Warwick Races; Yarmouth Racing; Ayr Meeting; New Forest Buckhounds; Ullswater Hounds; Derwent Hunt; Goodwood Hounds] (p226-235)
Sporting Intelligence [inc. Argentine Polo; South & West Wilts Hunt; Review of *Rugby Football* by David Gent; Obituaries of Charles Brindley and Herbert Robertshaw] (p235-237)
A Foxhunting Tale [verses] by William Williams (p236)
Sporting Results (p238-240)

Issue 754 : December 1922

Portrait [Bassano] and Biography - Ulric Thynne (p241-243)
The Art of Riding to Hounds by Charles Richardson (p244-246)
In a Stone Wall Country by Richard Clapham (p246-248)
Some Old Hunting Clubs by Richard Darwall (p248-250)
British Six-Metre Yachts in America by George Hopcroft (p250-253)
The Angler in Winter by John Durham (p253-256)
Cock Shooting by Arthur Sharp (p256-258)
Snipe by William Malden (p258-260)
Wasps Rugby Football Club by Edward Sewell (p261-263)
Sporting Ceylon by George Cecil (p263-265)
Backgammon: Its Story by Edgar Thomas (p266-270)
Our Van [inc. Cheveley Park Stakes; Prix du Conseil Municipal; Northumberland Handicap; Jockey Club Cup; Milton Hunt; Tarporley Hunt Club; Cheshire Hounds; South Dorset Hunt] (p270-278)
The Football League by William Holland (p279-280)
Sporting Intelligence [inc. National Pony Society; Moorland Gaming; Jockey's Accident Fund; Garth Hunt; Bicester Hounds; Axe Vale Harriers; Sinnington Hounds; Obituaries of Henry Lopes, Walter Tosswill, Walter Gordon-Lennox, Harry Watkins, John Dene, James Graham, William Standish and Sidney Tindall; Review of *Float and Fly* by Samuel Looker] (p280-283)
Sporting Results (p284)

Volume 119, January - June 1923

Issue 755 : January 1923

Portrait of Jack Hobbs, cricketer	Title page
Portrait [Howard] and Biography - Frederick Reynard	(p1-3)
Foxhound Characteristics by Richard Clapham	(p3-5)
The Great Turf Army by Jack Fairfax-Blakeborough	(p6-9)
Void Nominations and Other Turf Reforms by Charles Richardson	(p10-13)
[Obituary] Marcus de la Poer by George Burrows	(p14-16)
Photograph: *Marcus de la Poer*	(facing p14)
[Obituary] Luke White by George Burrows	(p16-17)
Downstream Worming: An Experiment in Trout Fishing by Eric Parker	(p18-19)
Wildfowling in Winter by Arthur Sharp	(p20-22)
Bygone Amusements by John Wright	(p22-24)
The Fourteen-Pointer of Altnaquhair by Charles Batchelder	(p25-28)
Some Fishing Memories of Constantinople by Kenneth Dawson	(p28-31)
Old Wayside Inns and Their Signboards (part 1) by William Williams	(p31-34)
Our Van [inc. Lincoln Racing; Aintree Meeting; Leicestershire Handicap; Manchester Races; Ledbury Hunt; Warwickshire Hounds; Cambridgeshire Hunt; Ward Union Staghounds; Meath Hunt]	(p35-41)
A Memory of George Lohmann by William Holland	(p41-42)
Polo in London in 1923 by Frederick Rouse	(p42-43)
Sporting Intelligence [inc. Bloodstock Prices; Turf Statistics; Hunters Improvement Society; Thoroughbred Stallion Show; Obituaries of Willoughby Maycock (*Baily's* contributor), George Hales, James Forsyth, Richard Lant, Eustace White, Lachlan Maclean and Charles Hawkins; Widford Beagles; West Drayton Golf Club]	(p43-47)
Racing Results	(p47-48)

Issue 756 : February 1923

Portrait [Howard] and Biography - James Dugdale	(p49-52)
Hunt Point-to-Point Steeplechases by George Collins	(p53-55)
Qualifying for a Hunter's Certificate by George Collins	(p55-57)
Them Stinking Vi'lets by George Collins	(p57-58)
Foxhunting on the Skyline by Richard Clapham	(p58-59)
An America's Cup Suggestion by George Hopcroft	(p59-62)
Some Turf Loving Parsons by Jack Fairfax-Blakeborough	(p62-67)
Engraving [pinx. Hall]: *Lord Lyon*	(facing p62)
A Morning's Punt Gunning by Eric Parker	(p67-69)
The Earls of Sefton and Coursing by Adair Dighton	(p70-71)
An Unlucky Day in Macedonia by Kenneth Dawson	(p71-74)
An Old Cumberland Sportsman by William Scarth-Dixon	(p75-80)
Engraving [sculp. Hunt]: *At The Stone Wall Jump*	(facing p76)
Old Wayside Inns and Their Signboards (part 2) by William Williams	(p80-85)
Our Van [inc. Kildare Hunt; Limerick Hounds; New Forest Buckhounds; Avondale Hounds; Essex Union Hunt; Cottesmore Hounds; Cheshire Hunt; North Herefordshire Hounds]	(p86-90)
Sporting Intelligence [inc. International Polo Rules; Pegasus Club; Fitzwilliam Hounds; Reviews of *The Curse of the Lion* by Frederick Webster, *Record Bags and Shooting Records* by Hugh Gladstone, *Hockey* by Stanley Shoveller, *On The Green* by Samuel Looker, *The Chase* by Samuel Looker, *The Black Shadow* by Frederick Webster; *How to Box* by Norman Clark; Football Association Cup; Obituaries of John Benson, Norman Bailey, Barron Kilner, Henry Ladell, Joseph Dodds, Ernest Gostling, William Grischotti, Southwell Fitzgerald, Harry Ladell and Gerald Winter]	(p91-95)

Archie [verses] from *The Morning Post*   (p92)
Goal [verses] by William Williams   (p93-94)
Racing Results   (p95-96)
Whaddon Chase Mastership   (p96)

Issue 757 : March 1923

Portrait [Scottor] and Biography - Richard Colvin   (p97-99)
Elephant Hunting in Namaqualand by Horace Wyndham   (p99-101)
The Venice of the North by Frederick Webster   (p102-106)
Mid-Ocean Angling by Charles Halcombe   (p106-109)
The Care of Sporting Guns by Eric Parker   (p109-110)
The Rustic Angler by Alan Johnson   (p110-111)
A Lay of the South Oxfordshire [verses] by Hanbury Williams   (p112-114)
With Rod and Creel in April by Arthur Sharp   (p115-117)
Current Polo Topics by Arthur Coaten   (p117-119)
Racquets Championship by Henry Rudd   (p119-120)
[Review] The Old Style in Boxing: *How to Box* by Norman Clark   (p120-124)
A Morning's Shore Shooting by Eric Parker   (p124-128)
Our Van [inc. Lincolnshire Handicap; Newbury Meeting; Birmingham Races; Cheshire
          Foxhounds; North Durham Hunt; Wilton Hounds; Cattistock Hunt; Essex
          Staghounds]   (p128-140)
Engraving [pinx. Hall]: *Voltigeur*   (facing p128)
Engraving: *The Flying Dutchman*   (facing p130)
Sporting Intelligence [inc. Whaddon Chase Dispute; Review of *A Sportsman at Large* by
          Harding Cox; Eden Fishery Board; Yorkshire County Cricket Club; Aldershot
          Command Beagles; Obituaries of Arthur Kinnaird, Frank Bibby, James Tyldesley
          and Kenneth McAlpine; Waterloo Cup]   (p140-144)
March to November [verses] by William Williams   (p141)
Racing Results   (p144)

Issue 758 : April 1923

Portrait [Smith] and Biography - Arthur Miller   (p145-146)
The End of the Season [verses] by Norman Innes   (p146)
Hunting Problems by Richard Reed   (p147-150)
The Yachting Outlook by George Hopcroft   (p150-153)
London's Spring Horse Shows by William Scarth-Dixon   (p153-158)
Photograph [Rouch]: *Morella III*   (facing p154)
Photograph [Rouch]: *Little Captain*   (facing p154)
Photograph [Rouch]: *Reform*   (facing p156)
Photograph [Rouch]: *Good Mark*   (facing p156)
Army Racquets by Henry Rudd   (p159-160)
In Praise of the Otter by John Drage   (p160-162)
Venturesome Voyages by Francis Cooke   (p162-164)
Hunting with Basset Hounds by Eric Parker   (p164-165)
Pheasant Rearing by Richard Darwall   (p165-166)
Cricket in Coomassie by George Cecil   (p167-169)
Science and Art in Sport by Claye Shaw   (p169-177)
Shakespeare and Sport by Clifford Cordley   (p178-182)
Our Van [inc. Hurst Park Meeting; Derbyshire Steeplechase; Cheltenham National Hunt
          Races; Fernie Hounds; Old Surrey & Burstow Hunt; Sperling Harriers; Braes of
          Derwent Hounds; Vale of Lune Harriers]   (p183-188)

Sporting Intelligence [inc. Thoroughbred Show; County Polo Association; Obituaries of Robert Ladell, Southwell Fitzgerald, David Cassells, John Hoare, George Cholmondeley, Jerry Rohan, Alfred Lewis, John Edwardes, Nigel Freer, Alfred Taylor, George Bean, John Morland, Thomas Lote and Hamilton Kinglake; Reviews of *Show Collies* by William Baskerville; *Wisden's Cricketers' Almanack* by Sydney Pardon]   (p188-192)
The Boat Race [verses] by William Williams   (p191)
Reynard [verses] by William Williams   (p191)
Death of the Old Hunter [verses] by William Williams   (p191)
Racing Results   (p192)

Issue 759 : May 1923

Portrait [Waterford] and Biography - Ian Bullough   (p193-194)
The Polo Season by Arthur Coaten   (p194-200)
[Review] *The Principles of Horsemanship* by Francois Baucher   (p197)
Hunting Pace Past and Present by Richard Reed   (p200-202)
Hunting Accidents by Hugh Henry   (p202-204)
A Brace in May by Richard Clapham   (p205-206)
A Lucky Trespass by Eric Parker   (p206-208)
The Fish Poacher and His Methods by Richard Darwall   (p208-210)
Yacht Racing with Economy by Francis Cooke   (p210-213)
Golf in Nice by Horace Wyndham   (p213-215)
Becalmed in Mid-Ocean by Charles Halcombe   (p215-217)
A Forgotten Island by Frederick Webster   (p218-221)
Amateur Racquets Championship by Henry Rudd   (p221-223)
Wildfowling Memories of Macedonia by Kenneth Dawson   (p224-226)
Our Van [inc. Brocklesby Stakes; Liverpool Spring Cup; Nottingham Meeting; Atherstone Hunt; Cambridgeshire Hounds; Tring Draghounds; Essex Hunt Point-to-Point; East Essex Hunt; Middlesex Farmers Staghounds]   (p226-236)
[Review] *Anglo-French Horsemanship* by John Swire   (p227)
[Review] *The Horse as Comrade and Friend* by Everard Calthorp   (p230)
Sporting Intelligence [inc. Widford Beagles; Boroughbridge Agricultural Society; Obituaries of Billy Shaw, William Whineray, James Walker, O'Grady Delmege, George Herbert, Donald Macgregor, William Donaldson, Arthur Curnick, George Parfrement and Charles Crump; Punchestown Meeting]   (p236-239)
The Old Hunter [verses] by William Williams   (p238)
Racing Results   (p240)

Issue 760 : June 1923

Portrait [Tear] and Biography - Ernest Pretyman   (p241-243)
Jack Hobbs by George Burrows   (p243)
Polo by Arthur Coaten   (p244-248)
Heredity in Sport by Frank Bonnett   (p249-251)
The Perfect Batsman by Thomas Pelham   (p251-252)
Odd Thoughts on the Fox by Richard Clapham   (p253-254)
Environment and Trout by Arthur Sharp   (p255-256)
Early Yacht Races and Opening Cruises by George Hopcroft   (p256-258)
Public School and University Racquets by Henry Rudd   (p259-262)
Otterhunting by Clifford Cordley   (p262-264)
Pike Fishing near London by Eric Parker   (p264-266)
A Nigerian Race Meeting by George Broun   (p266-267)
Some Famous Surrey Cricketers by William Holland   (p268-270)
The Romantic Life of Jack Mytton by Richard Darwall   (p270-273)

Our Van [inc. Pontefract Races; Newbury Cup; Nottingham Spring Handicap; Derby Racing;
       Chester Meeting; Esher Cup] (p273-280)
Sporting Intelligence [inc. Obituaries of Dick Stovin, Robert de Winton and Walter
       Coggeshall; St.Anne's Golf Tournament; English Bowling Association; West
       Lancashire Golf Club] (p280-282)
Engraving: *Newton Gold Cup 1831* (facing p280)
Racing Results (p283-284)

Volume 120, July - December 1923

Issue 761 : July 1923

Portrait of Bernard Carslake, jockey — Title page
Portrait [Howard] and Biography - Charles Fitzroy (p1-4)
[Obituary] Henry Chaplin by George Burrows (p4-9)
Photograph [Rouch]: *Henry Chaplin* (facing p4)
[Obituary] A Champion of Other Days: Arthur Chambers by Edward Sewell (p10-13)
Polo by Arthur Coaten (p14-19)
Photograph [Rouch]: *Walter Buckmaster and Charles Lowther* (facing p14)
Tennis by Wallis Myers (p19-20)
Our Billiard Champions by Sydenham Dixon (p21-24)
Current Cricket Chat by Thomas Pelham (p24-28)
Trout of the Lochs by Arthur Sharp (p28-29)
The Himalayan Wild Boar by Alan Davis (p29-32)
Advance of British Golf by Frank Carruthers (p32-35)
Cock and Quail in Constantinople by Kenneth Dawson (p36-39)
Our Van [inc. Newmarket Stakes; Middlesex Handicap; Bath Racing; Manchester Meeting;
       Salisbury Races; Kempton Park Racing] (p39-44)
Sporting Intelligence [inc. Jockey Club Presentation; Obituaries of John Chiene, Charles Lewis,
       Hugh McCalmont and Thomas Baring; Amateur Golf Championship] (p45-46)
Racing Results (p46-48)

Issue 762 : August 1923

Portrait [Elliott] and Biography - Frederick Robinson (p49-51)
Polo by Arthur Coaten (p52-56)
August Shooting by Eric Parker (p57-61)
Sailing Rules at Cowes by George Hopcroft (p61-64)
A Morning at Errebodde, Ceylon by Kenneth Dawson (p65-66)
Concerning Lobs by William Holland (p66-67)
Current Cricket Chat by Thomas Pelham (p68-70)
Hustling in Sweden by Frederick Webster (p70-74)
Bucking Horses by George Bosvile (p74-76)
[Obituary] Henry Platt by Sydenham Dixon (p76-77)
Stapleton Park Traditions by Jack Fairfax-Blakeborough (p77-79)
[Review] *Thoughts on Hunting* by Will Smith (p79-81)
[Review] *Open Air Pig Breeding* by Moses Rowlands (p82)
Horse and Hound at Peterborough by William Scarth-Dixon (p83-87)
Our Van [inc. Chantilly Races; Beverley Meeting; Ascot Hunt Cup; Rous Memorial Stakes;
       Newcastle Races; Carlisle Racing; Waterbeach Handicap] (p87-94)
Sporting Intelligence [inc. Obituaries of Arthur Willey, Arthur Hartley, Richard Sykes and Alfred
       Shelton; Peshawar Vale Hunt; Tattersall's Newmarket Sales; Inter-Universities
       Athletics] (p94-95)
Racing Results (p96)

Issue 763 : September 1923

Portrait [Elliott] and Biography - Clarence Bruce	(p97-99)
Sporting Dress by Ashton Agar	(p99-100)
Cubhunting by Charles Frederick	(p100-101)
Hunters Horns by Richard Darwall	(p102-103)
Jolly Huntsman Wind Your Horn [verses]	(p104)
Partridge Shooting on the Marshes by Eric Parker	(p105-107)
The Dearth of Personality in Modern Sport by Durbin Montefiore	(p108-110)
September and the Fly Fisher by Arthur Sharp	(p110-112)
Badger Hunting by Starlight by Douglas Gordon	(p113-116)
Shore Shooting by Kenneth Dawson	(p116-119)
The Leedes Family and their Stud by Jack Fairfax-Blakeborough	(p120-125)
Polo by Arthur Coaten	(p125-131)
Current Cricket Chat by Thomas Pelham	(p131-133)
Our Van [inc. Harrington Handicap; Salisbury Meeting; West Riding Plate; Ayr Races; Eglinton Meeting; Drogheda Memorial Stakes; Chesterfield Cup; Puckeridge Hounds; Devon & Somerset Staghounds]	(p133-141)
Sporting Intelligence [inc. Review of *Amid The High Hills* by Hugh Fraser; The Porcellian Club; Blackheath Rectory Field Cricket; Obituary of Arthur Michell; Tonbridge School Memorial Pavilion; Spey Bay Golf Club; Copenhagen Athletics]	(p141-143)
Racing Results	(p143-144)

Issue 764 : October 1923

Portrait [Elliott] and Biography - Francis Mildmay	(p145-147)
Pheasant Shooting Prospects by Eric Parker	(p148-152)
Hunt Point-to-Point Steeplechases by Jack Fairfax-Blakeborough	(p153-155)
The Yacht Racing Season by George Hopcroft	(p155-158)
Pike and Pike Fishing by Arthur Sharp	(p159-161)
Our Light Hearted Cricket Heroes by Thomas Pelham	(p162-163)
Jottings About Snipe by John Mansfield	(p163-165)
Late Polo Season Reviewed by Arthur Coaten	(p165-171)
Famous Sporting Brotherhoods by Archibald Charlton	(p171-174)
A Sunday Shoot in Salonika by Kenneth Dawson	(p174-178)
Our Van [inc. Brighton Races; Lewes Handicap; North Sea Stakes; Stockton Meeting; Jigginstown Plate; Doncaster Meeting; North Herefordshire Hounds; South & West Wilts Hunt]	(p178-187)
Sporting Intelligence [inc. Channel Swimming; Obituaries of Horace Farquhar, George Lockett, William Beach, James Walker and Henry Waldock; Reviews of *The Alsatian Wolfdog* by George Horowitz; *Memories of Sporting Days* by Red Heather; Sussex County Cricket Club]	(p188-189)
Racing Results	(p190-192)

Issue 765 : November 1923

Portrait [Elliott] and Biography - John Gibbon	(p193-195)
Hunt Changes by Edward Cuming	(p195-199)
Sidelights on Old Time Foxhunting (part 1) by George Collins	(p200-202)
Hunting the Stag by Edward Cuming	(p203-204)
Baily's Hunting Directory 1923-24 by George Burrows	(p205)
Coursing by Guy Broun	(p206-208)
The Good Sportsman [verses] by Norman Innes	(p208)
Mark Cock (part 1) by Eric Parker	(p209-210)
Bustard Shooting in West Africa (part 1) by Gerald Ambrose	(p211-215)

Out of the Storied Past (part 1) by Charles Thomas (p215-218)
Foxhunters of Yesterday and Today by William Fawcett (p219-221)
Sports Ancient and Modern by Florence Baillie-Grohman (p221-222)
Premier British Sportswomen by Frederick Lees (p222-224)
Members of Parliament Famed in Sport by William Holland (p224-226)
British Polo Teams in America by Arthur Coaten (p226-230)
Polo Pony Breeding by Frederick Rouse (p230-231)
Our Van [inc. Alexandra Park Races; Irish Turf Club Cup; Yarmouth Racing; Ayr Meeting; Leicestershire Stakes; Caledonian Hunt Cup] (p231-235)
Sporting Intelligence [inc. Obituaries of Thomas Dale (*Baily's* contributor), Erskine Crum, John Williams, William Close, Frederick Robinson and Joseph Green; Women Jockeys; Windsor Meeting; Royal and Ancient Golf Club] (p236-239)
Racing Results (p239-240)

Issue 766 : December 1923

Portrait [Hoppe] and Biography - John Upton (p241-242)
Rugby Football Centenary by Edward Sewell (p242-244)
Lady Anglers by Thomas Pelham (p245)
Sidelights on Old Time Foxhunting (part 2) by George Collins (p246-249)
Mark Cock (part 2) by Eric Parker (p249-251)
Bustard Shooting in West Africa (part 2) by Gerald Ambrose (p251-255)
Out of the Storied Past (part 2) by Edgar Thomas (p255-257)
The Dairy Shorthorn by Horace Regnart (p258-260)
Photograph: *Lily Charter* (facing p258)
Photograph [Parsons]: *Rickerscote Leader* (facing p258)
The Correct Seat by Michael McTaggart (p260-262)
Outdoor Show Jumping by William Scarth-Dixon (p262-263)
What is Horse Power by Oscar Seyd (p263-265)
Photograph: *Tibberton Leader* (facing p264)
Photograph [Parsons]: *Roycroft Forest King* (facing p264)
Tax on Betting by George Burrows (p266-267)
Our Van [inc. Nottinghamshire Handicap; Haydock Park Meeting; Cheveley Stakes; West Riding Handicap; Middleton Hounds; Zetland Hunt; Hurworth Hounds; Taunton Vale Hunt; Obituaries of Meyrick Angel and Sidney Hough] (p267-276)
Follow Oh! Follow the Fleet Footed Hare [verses] (p276)
Sporting Intelligence [inc. Reviews of *Physical Energy* by Billy Wells, *Modern Polo* by Edward Miller, *Age of the Horse* by Ludo Frateur, *Seamanship for Yachtsmen* by Francis Cooke, *Vinton's Agricultural Almanac 1924*; *Baily's Hunting Directory 1923-24*; Notable Harness Horses; Artists' Rifles; The Hare [verses]; Obituaries of Thomas Willis ('*Milroy*'), Frank Ashley, Angus Stuart, Thomas Hockin, Joseph Widger, Alfred Lucas, Allan Arthur and William Stevens; Colquhoun Sculls; Bucks Otterhounds; High Peak Harriers] (p277-282)
Racing Results (p282-284)

Volume 121, January - June 1924

Issue 767 : January 1924

Portrait of Charles Smirke Title page
Portrait [White] and Biography - Harold Hambro (p1-2)
The Three-Year-Olds of 1924 by Sydenham Dixon (p2-5)
Organising a Hunt Point-to-Point by Jack Fairfax-Blakeborough (p6-9)
Foxhunting in Wales by Richard Darwall (p9-12)

The Economics of Sport (part 1) by Claye Shaw (p13-18)
A Big Class Yachting Year by George Hopcroft (p18-21)
A Rum 'Un to Follow; A Bad 'Un to Beat by George Collins (p21-24)
Dealing and Schooling by George North (p24-28)
[Obituary] William Grant by George Fothergill (p28-29)
[Review] An Annual for Sporting Farmers: *Live Stock Journal Annual 1924* by George Burrows (p29-31)
Hunt Team Classes at Shows by William Scarth-Dixon (p31-33)
Persian Sport by George Cecil (p33-34)
Sea Trout in Brooks by George Garrow-Green (p34-35)
Our Van [inc. Lincoln Racing; Derby Cup; Liverpool Races; Warwick Meeting; Jockey
          Championship; North Herefordshire Hunt; Hawkstone Otterhounds; Point-to-Point
          Fixtures] (p36-43)
The Editor's Bookshelf: Reviews of *Fantasies & Impromptus* by James Agate; *Memories* by
          Walter Long; *Game Birds and Wild Fowl* by Archibald Thorburn; *Collected
          Poems* by John Masefield (p44-45)
Obituaries: Quintin Dick, Richard Verney, Lindsay Hogg, Frederick Slingsby, Martin Gurry,
          Robert Reid, Algernon Anthony, Thomas Cunnington and Patrick Cullinan (p45-47)
Miscellaneous: Stipendiary Stewards; Bombay Pioneers Cyclists; Royal & Ancient Golf Club (p47)
Racing Results (p48)

Issue 768 : February 1924

Portrait [Elliott] and Biography - Alfred Goodson (p49-50)
Managing a Hunt Point-to-Point by Jack Fairfax-Blakeborough (p50-54)
Large or Small Hounds by Harding Cox (p55-56)
Some Famous Brood Mares by Sydenham Dixon (p56-60)
British Golf Prospects in 1924 by William Knight (p60-63)
Motor Matters by Oscar Seyd (p64-65)
Come Away to the Heath [verses] (p66)
The Sporting Hare by Charles Cordley (p67-69)
Fish Ponds by Alan Horwood (p69-70)
The Olympic Games by George Hopcroft (p70-71)
The Economics of Sport (part 2) by Claye Shaw (p71-74)
Some Notable Foxhounds by Richard Darwall (p75-76)
Headmasters as Athletes by Frederick Webster (p77-82)
Odd Thoughts About the Otter by Noel Sedgwick (p82-84)
Some Curious Channel Crossings by Alan Austen-Leigh (p84-86)
Our Van [inc. Molesey Steeplechase; Manchester Meeting; Hurst Park Races; Derwent Hunt;
          Burton Hounds; Beaufort Hunt] (p87-91)
Hunt Point-to-Point Steeplechases (p91-92)
Sporting Intelligence [inc. London Spring Horse Shows; Polo Trials; Obituaries of Francis
          Greville, Geoffrey Bennet, George Villiers, Ernest Paget, Sydney Callaway,
          Frederick Wheldon, George Haines, John Lambie, Ernest Irish, Billy Miske,
          Nathaniel Cockburn, William Radford, Edward Buxton and Henry Harries; Troon
          Golf Club] (p92-95)
Racing Results (p96)

Issue 769 : March 1924

Portrait [Bale] and Biography - Ambrose Gorham (p97-99)
Spring [verses] by Henry Pilkington (p99)
Officials at Point-to-Point Meetings by Jack Fairfax-Blakeborough (p100-101)
My Collection of Hunting Horns by George Collins (p102-106)
The America's Cup by Francis Cooke (p107-109)
The 1924 Polo Season by Arthur Coaten (p110-112)

Foxhunting on Foot by Frederick Hughes (p112-115)
Gentlemen Riders in the Grand National by Charles Richardson (p115-117)
The Saltby Plate by Charles Prior (p117-120)
Photograph: *The Saltby Plate* (facing p118)
Motor Matters by Oscar Seyd (p120-122)
Concerning Blues by William Holland (p122-124)
Cormorant Fishing in Japan by George Cecil (p124-126)
Rabbit Beagling by Frank Bonnett (p126-128)
[Obituary] Norris Midwood by Arthur Coaten (p129-130)
Photograph: *Norris Midwood* (on p129)
Our Van [inc. Pytchley Hunt; Wylye Hounds; Bilsdale Hunt; Middleton Hounds; Bicester Hunt; North Herefordshire Hounds] (p131-137)
Hunt Point-to-Point Steeplechases (p137-138)
Sporting Intelligence [inc. Obituaries of Hugh Dawnay, Edward Lawson, Frank Thurlow, Frank Wright, Henry Tubb, Thomas Baxter, John Rawlin, Auguste d'Arenberg and Frank Tandy; Reviews of *Dogs and I* by Harding Cox, *Yarns Without Yawns* by Harding Cox; *Partridges From Czechoslovakia* by Carlton Hunting; Queen's Club; Farne Islands Sanctuary; Widford Beagles; Yacht Racing Association; Cricket County Championship; Spring Shows; Neuadd Fawr Foxhounds] (p139-144)
Racing Results (p144)

Issue 770 : April 1924

Portrait [Elliott] and Biography - William Lambarde (p145-146)
The Thoroughbred Horse by Percy Ricketts (p146-152)
Some Stories Told by William I'Anson by Jack Fairfax-Blakeborough (p153-157)
London's Spring Horse Shows by William Scarth-Dixon (p158-167)
Photograph [Parsons]: *Cowage Clansman* (facing p158)
Photograph [Parsons]: *Herontye Buscot* (facing p158)
Photograph [Rouch]: *Gleadthorpe Selection* (facing p160)
Photograph [Rouch]: *Erfyl Lady Grey* (facing p160)
Photograph [Rouch]: *Crosbie* (facing p162)
Photograph [Rouch]: *Piave* (facing p162)
Photograph [Rouch]: *Wild Tint* (facing p164)
Photograph [Rouch]: *Waiting Maid* (facing p164)
Future of Coaching by Wodehouse Garland (p167-169)
Heu Gaze: An Otterhunting Song [verses] (p170)
Touchstone and Other Queries by Richard Darwall (p171-172)
Springtime Trout by Arthur Sharp (p172-173)
Some Lesser Known Duels by Edgar Thomas (p173-178)
Robert Smith Surtees by William Kerr (p179-181)
Motor Topics by Oscar Seyd (p182-183)
The New Racquets Season by Henry Rudd (p184-185)
Our Van [inc. New Century Steeplechase; Newbury Meeting; Gatwick Races; Derwent and Sinnington Hunts Amalgamation; Llandinam Show; South Notts Hunt] (p185-190)
Hunt Point-to-Points (p190-191)
Sporting Intelligence [inc. Yacht Racing Association; Jockey Club Meeting; Obituaries of Peter Hardwick and Walter Money; Chiddingfold Hunt; Waterloo Cup; Reviews of *Wisden's Cricketers' Almanack 1924* by Sydney Pardon; *Loch Fishing in Theory and Practice* by Robert Bridgett] (p191-192)

Issue 771 : May 1924

Portrait [Rouch] and Biography - Malise Graham   (p193-194)
From An Indian Jungle by Percy Etherton   (p195-198)
Paris Anglers by George Cecil   (p199-200)
The First Cricket Club by William Holland   (p201-202)
The Little Bay Mare [verses] by John Moore   (p202)
My Friends of the Hill Streams by Kenneth Dawson   (p203-205)
Puppies [verses] by Norman Innes   (p205)
Scent by Charles Tremlett   (p206-207)
Beagling in Lakeland by Mary Fair   (p208)
Spearing and Bobbing for Eels by Guy Broun   (p209-211)
Britain's Rarest Mammal: The Pine Marten by Richard Clapham   (p212-213)
Some Recollections of Pre-War Days in Rural England by George North   (p214-217)
Chester's Veteran Rowing Men by Richard Martin   (p217-219)
The Coming Polo Season by Arthur Coaten   (p219-221)
Amateur Championship and Varsity Racquets by Henry Rudd   (p221-223)
Motor Matters by Oscar Seyd   (p224-225)
Our Van [inc. Lincolnshire Handicap; Aintree Meeting; Windsor Races; Belvoir Hunt;
         Bathurst Hounds; Garth Point-to-Point Races; East Essex Hunt; United
         Yorkshire Hunts' Sweepstakes; Puckeridge Farmers' Race]   (p226-235)
Sporting Intelligence [inc. Reviews of *Field Sports of the Month* by Thomas Moreton;
         Green Peas at Christmas by William Wilson; International Polo; Obituaries of
         George Thorneycroft, Stephen Finney, George Campbell, Charles Wright, George
         Tickell, William Gardiner, Walter Humphreys, Jesse Hide and Frank O'Keefe;
         University Golf; University Boat Race; Rugby Union County Championship;
         Cirencester Polo Club]   (p236-239)
Racing Results   (p239-240)

Issue 772 : June 1924

Portrait [Bassano] and Biography - Arthur Blake   (p241-242)
Some Famous Fast Bowlers by William Holland   (p242-244)
Early Days of Cricket by Thomas Pelham   (p244-246)
The Fitting-out Season by George Hopcroft   (p246-248)
The Past Billiards Season by Sydenham Dixon   (p249-251)
Summer [verses] by Henry Pilkington   (p251)
A Review of the Hunting Season by Jack Fairfax-Blakeborough   (p252-255)
Motor Matters by Oscar Seyd   (p255-257)
Public Schools Racquets Championship by Henry Rudd   (p257-259)
Polo Topics by Arthur Coaten   (p259-260)
The Poonch Road to Kashmir by Charles Nasmyth   (p261-263)
Golf under Difficulties by George Cecil   (p263-266)
Old Village Games by Arthur Sharp   (p266-268)
My First Waterbuck by Gerald Ambrose   (p268-271)
Badger Baiting by Noel Sedgwick   (p272-273)
Our Van [inc. Leicester Races; Newbury Spring Cup; Lancashire Steeplechase; Newcastle
         Handicap; Catterick Meeting; Pontefract Plate]   (p274-280)
My Charger [verses]   (p281)
Sporting Intelligence [inc. Obituaries of Lowry Cole, John Board, George Street, Richard
         Mecredy, Alfred Mackenzie, Edward Holmes, Sidney Graystone, John Clayton,
         Henry Townshend, Charles Horley, William Fulford and Thomas Erskine;
         Wembley Football Association Cup Final; Polo Show at Ranelagh; Review of
         Lawns for Sports by Reginald Beale; New Forest Hunt Club; London & Southern
         Counties Cricket Conference; Jockey Club Annual General Meeting]   (p281-284)

Racing Results (p285-288)

Volume 122 : July - December 1924

Issue 773 : July 1924

Portrait [Rouch] of Thomas Pryor, jockey | Title page
Portrait [Lafayette] and Biography - Beauvoir de Lisle | (p1-2)
The Evolution of the Racing Yacht by Francis Cooke | (p2-7)
Doncaster and Ascot by Richard Darwall | (p7-9)
The True Story of Hermit by Sydenham Dixon | (p10-11)
Athletic Training by George Teasdale-Buckell | (p11-14)
Polo Topics by Arthur Coaten | (p14-16)
Motor Matters by Oscar Seyd | (p16-18)
Barbel Fishing by Arthur Sharp | (p18-19)
July Joys by Clifford Cordley | (p20-21)
Cricket and Evolution by Thomas Pelham | (p22)
Lutra the Brave [verses] by Henry Baines | (p23)
Gun Dogs by Harding Cox | (p24-26)
The Tennis Season by Wallis Myers | (p26-27)
Clear Water Worm Fishing by George Garrow-Green | (p27-30)
A Question of Pedigree by William Scarth-Dixon | (p31-33)
A Celebrated Charger | (p33-35)
Our Van [inc. Lewes Racing; Chester Cup; Bedford Stakes; Epsom Meeting; Bath Races; Wiltshire Handicap; Woodcote Plate] | (p35-41)
Sporting Intelligence [inc. Reviews of *Sunshine and the Dry Fly* by John Dunne, *The Principles and Practice of Fly and Bait Casting* by Reginald Hughes, *Through Central France to the Pyrenees* by Maude Speed, *Robert Smith Surtees* by Edward Cuming, *Cricket Old and New* by Archibald MacLaren, *Cricket Form at a Glance in this Century* by Home Gordon, *The Amateur's Derby* by Harding Cox; *Sport on Fell, Beck and Tarn* by Richard Clapham; Covering of Cricket Pitches Ruling; British Ladies Open Golf; Obituaries of Ludovick Bligh, Bower Ismay, Ernest Robson, Tankerville Chamberlayne, Edward Hobson, Thomas Illsley, Edward Finch, Frank Thomas and George Wootton; Carlisle Otterhounds; Cumberland Cockfighting] | (p41-46)
Cricket [verses] by William Williams | (p42)
Racing Results | (p46-48)

Issue 774 : August 1924

Portrait [Poole] and Biography - Gerald Lousada | (p49)
The International Polo Team by Arthur Coaten | (p50-51)
Grouse Shooting Prospects by Alan Horwood | (p51-53)
Grouse Differences by Alan Horwood | (p53-55)
Otter Hounds and Welsh Foxhounds by Charles Richardson | (p56-62)
Motoring Matters by Oscar Seyd | (p63-64)
Memories of Thirsk Races by Jack Fairfax-Blakeborough | (p64-67)
Wicketkeeping and Wicketkeepers by Thomas Pelham | (p67-69)
Angling in the Isle of Skye by Joseph Adams | (p70-73)
An Indian Hunting Ground by Lester Arnold | (p74-77)
Stonewallers and Sloggers by William Holland | (p78-81)
Horses and Hounds at Peterborough by William Scarth-Dixon | (p81-86)
Our Van [inc. Hurst Park Races; Yarmouth Meeting; Manchester Cup; Ascot Stakes; Curragh Racing; Grand Prix de Paris; Jockey Club Elections] | (p87-93)

Sporting Intelligence [inc. Obituaries of Willie Fernie, Frederick Wilson, Dyke Wilkinson,
       James Fraser and Francis Ricardo] (p94)
Racing Results (p95-96)

Issue 775 : September 1924

Portrait [Rouch] and Biography - Geoffrey Brooke (p97-98)
September's Delights by George Burrows (p98-99)
The First of September [verses] by Henry Baines (p99)
A Lame St.Leger Winner by Jack Fairfax-Blakeborough (p100-101)
Reforming County Cricket by Thomas Pelham (p101-102)
North versus South in Yacht Racing by George Hopcroft (p103-105)
A Morning With the Errebodde Hunt by William Fawcett (p105-106)
Golf at Budapest by George Cecil (p107-108)
Falconry and Wembley by Edward Michell (p108-110)
Autumn [verses] by Henry Pilkington (p110)
Polo in West Africa by Guy Broun (p111-113)
Hunt Uniforms by William Fawcett (p113-118)
Photograph: *Hean Climax* (facing p114)
Photograph [Parsons]: *Broadheath* (facing p114)
Today's Countryside Problems (p118-120)
Walking by George Teasdale-Buckell (p120-123)
Photograph: *Violet* (facing p120)
Photograph [Parsons]: *Theale Eveline* (facing p120)
Rustic Rabbiting by Guy Broun (p123-125)
The Byerley Family and their Turk by Jack Fairfax-Blakeborough (p125-127)
Sportsmen's Epitaphs (p127-129)
The Gliding of Hawks by Guy Broun (p130)
The Hatching Season by Noel Sedgwick (p131-132)
Our Van [inc. Dukeries Plate; Bibury Club Meeting; Pontefract Races; Lingfield Park Plate;
       Ayr Racing; Goodwood Stakes; Chesterfield Cup] (p132-137)
Jim Crack [verses] by Henry Baines (p138)
Sporting Intelligence [inc. Milton Hounds; Shorthorn Breeding; Obituaries of George Cook
       and Walter Langlands; Rugby Football Union Secretary; Welsh Pony & Cob
       Society; Galway Blazers Hunt] (p138-142)
Racing Results (p142-144)

Issue 776 : October 1924

Portrait [Bale] and Biography - Mark Fenwick (p145-147)
Pheasant Shooting Prospects by Eric Parker (p147-149)
On Buying a Gun Dog by Harding Cox (p150-151)
The South Durham Hunt by William Fawcett (p152-153)
Women Golfers of Paris by George Cecil (p154-155)
Some Minor Fights by Edgar Thomas (p156-158)
The Joys of Deer Stalking (p158-161)
Cricket Curiosities by William Holland (p161-163)
Woodcock by Arthur Sharp (p163-164)
Photograph [Parsons]: *Mauricette* (facing p164)
Photograph [Parsons]: *Leda Chablis* (facing p164)
How Points are Scored in Coursing by Guy Broun (p166-167)
Falconry in Ancient Times by Eric Parker (p167-168)
A Review of the Yacht Racing Season by George Hopcroft (p168-171)
The Polo Defeats by Arthur Coaten (p171-173)
Over the Pennines by Cecil Arthington (p174-178)

Photograph [Parsons]: *Balcairn Watchword*   (facing p176)
Photograph [Parsons]: *Priory Norseman*   (facing p176)
Quisting by Eric Parker   (p178-180)
Our Van [inc. Birmingham Races; Brighton Meeting; Redcar Plate; Knavesmire Finances;
          Great Yorkshire Stakes; Grand International d'Ostende; Doncaster Cup]   (p180-187)
Sporting Intelligence [inc. Obituaries of Walter Gilbert, Moreton Frewen, Dario Resta,
          William Churton, David Shaw, Philip Wykeham, Walter Lees and Joseph
          McCormick; Bloodstock Prices; Scarborough Cricket; Rufford Hunt]   (p187-190)
Racing Results   (p190-192)

Issue 777 : November 1924

Portrait [Bale] and Biography - Arthur Mills   (p193)
Polo: The Pony and the Game by Arthur Coaten   (p194-196)
The International Yacht Races of 1924 by George Hopcroft   (p196-199)
Family Packs of Foxhounds by Charles Richardson   (p199-205)
The Sport of Kings by Douglas Gordon   (p206-208)
Fashions in Hunt Clothes by Richard Darwall   (p209-211)
Hunt Changes in 1924 by Edward Cuming   (p212-217)
The Hunted Fox [verses] by Norman Innes   (p217)
Foxhunting in Fiction by Arthur Sharp   (p218)
November by Alan Sealy   (p219-220)
Baily's Hunting Directory 1924-25 by George Burrows   (p221)
Pheasant Shooting of Today by Frank Bonnett   (p222-225)
Grouse Season by Alan Horwood   (p225-228)
Shore Bird Life   (p229-230)
Our Van [inc. Muswell Stakes; Windsor Meeting; Lanark Races; Kingsclere Plate; Newmarket
          Judge's Box; Norwich Handicap; Pontefract Races]   (p230-236)
Sporting Intelligence [inc. Obituaries of Robert Henderson, Horace Marriott, Arthur Trevor,
          James Bush and Walter East; Polo Test Matches; Devon & Somerset Staghounds;
          Review of *The Passing Years* by Richard Verney; Berwickshire Hunt; English
          Ladies Golf Championship]   (p237-239)
Racing Results   (p240)

Issue 778 : December 1924

Portrait [Wilkins] and Biography - Edward Sholto   (p241-243)
Cheshire's Old First Flighters by George Teasdale-Buckell   (p243-247)
The Haydon Hunt by William Fawcett   (p248-250)
Racing in China by John Hasty   (p250-254)
Harehunting Ancient and Modern by Harding Cox   (p254-257)
Hunting the Mighty Boar by Eric Gill   (p258-260)
Winter Shooting in Kashmir by Lester Arnold   (p260-263)
The Deer Stalking Season   (p263-265)
Old Time Yachts by Edgar Thomas   (p266-270)
The First Australian Tour by William Holland   (p270-271)
Winter [verses] by Henry Pilkington   (p271)
Our Van [inc. Newbury Races; Gosforth Park Meeting; Jockey Club Cup; Worcester Racing;
          Lincoln Meeting]   (p272-277)
Sporting Intelligence [inc. Forfeit in Classic Races; Hurlingham Club Taxation; Brooklands
          Motor Racing; Richmond Gold Cup; Obituaries of Ernest Willoughby,
          Marmaduke Salvin and George Jackson; Amateur Weightlifting]   (p277-282)
Racing Results   (p283-284)

Volume 123, January - June 1925

Issue 779 : January 1925

Portrait of Herbert Sutcliffe, cricketer	Title page
Portrait [Swaine] and Biography - Marshall Roberts	(p1)
The English Racehorse by Edgar Vincent	(p2-5)
Photograph [Hailey]: *Hurry On*	(facing p2)
Photograph [Hailey]: *Captain Cuttle*	(facing p2)
Improving British Racing by Charles Richardson	(p6-9)
To the Woodcock [verses] by Henry Baines	(p9)
[Obituary] Henry Somerset by George Burrows	(p10-12)
Photograph: *Henry Somerset*	(facing p10)
Hunting Days: A Wet Day by George Collins	(p12-16)
The Cream of the Shires by Alan Horwood	(p17-19)
Are We On the Eve Of a New Era in Yachting by George Hopcroft	(p19-22)
January Shooting by Eric Parker	(p22-24)
Falconry From the Stream by Nigel Sedgwick	(p25-26)
The Indian Bison by Laurence Maxwell	(p26-32)
Cock-Fighting in Cheshire by George Teasdale-Buckell	(p32-36)
Monster Sea Fish and Their Capture by Alan Horwood	(p36-38)
Enemies of Game by Alan Johnson	(p38-41)
[Review] Pedigree Stock on Our Farms: *Livestock Journal Annual 1925*	(p41-42)
Our Van [inc. Atherstone Handicap; Hampton Court Stakes; Lingfield Park Races; Newmarket Sales; Compton Stud]	(p42-47)
Sporting Intelligence [inc. Obituaries of Alfred Straker, Bert Elphick, Ebenezer Morley, Arthur Thistlethwayte, Frederick Coryton, Edward Garnier, Ian Macdonald and August Belmont; Widford Beagles; Real Tennis]	(p47-48)

Issue 780 : February 1925

Portrait [Bale] and Biography - Seymour Allen	(p49-50)
Loss of Nerve by John Swire	(p50-52)
The International Polo Match by Arthur Coaten	(p52-53)
Hunting Days: A Scenting Day by George Collins	(p54-58)
Polo in West Africa by Hugh Clifford	(p58-60)
Hunting Beyond the Seas by Clarence Bruce	(p60-64)
A Great Huntsman: An Appreciation [Henry Somerset] by Henry Codrington	(p65-68)
Society and the Highlands by Ruaraidh Erskine	(p68-70)
Richard Marsh [King's Trainer at Newmarket] by George Burrows	(p70-71)
Sport in Abyssinia by George Cecil	(p71-72)
Amateur Championship of Squash Racquets by Henry Rudd	(p73-74)
Hunting Appointments [verses] by Henry Baines	(p74)
The Origin of Cards by Alan Shelley	(p75-78)
Getting Even With the Rabbit	(p78-81)
Photograph [Parsons]: *Astronomer*	(facing p83)
Photograph [Parsons]: *Twyford Edgar*	(facing p83)
Blank Days by Claremont Clare	(p83-85)
The Racehorse of the Present Day by Sydenham Dixon	(p85-88)
Our Van [inc. Essex Hunt; Point-to-Point Steeplechases]	(p89-93)
Sporting Intelligence [inc. Army Horses; Obituaries of Arnold Landor, Charles Allen, Richard Barcroft, Charles Cummings, Edwin Diver, William Harford and Thomas Crofton; Cottesmore Hounds; Pytchley Hunt; Santa Ines Polo Club; Ranelagh Polo Management]	(p93-96)

Issue 781 : March 1925

Portrait [Marsh] and Biography - Arthur Harris (p97-99)
The Thoroughbred Horse by Peter Ricketts (p99-104)
Famous Varsity Strokes by William Holland (p104-108)
Hunting Days: A Windy Day by George Collins (p108-112)
Sport and Athletics in Buenos Aires by Alan Wilkinson (p112-113)
Curling by John Grant (p113)
Hunting Handicaps by William Fawcett (p114-116)
Prospects of Thames Fisheries by Noel Sedgwick (p117-118)
Billiards in Cairo by George Cecil (p119)
George Coventry by George Burrows (p120-123)
Photograph [Bustin]: *George Coventry* (on p121)
The Empire Within Our Village by William Holland (p123-125)
The Border by William Fawcett (p125-127)
The Hunter's Horn [verses] by Henry Baines (p127)
The Calcutta Cup by Edward Sewell (p128-129)
Photograph [Parsons]: *Charles II* (facing p131)
Photograph [Parsons]: *Apsam* (facing p131)
Cross Country Running by Frederick Webster (p131-132)
Golf in Switzerland by George Cecil (p132-133)
Our Van [inc. Egerton Stud; Heath Stud; Brocklesby Hounds; Monmouthshire Hunt Club; Old Berkeley Hounds; Bedale Hunt; Essex Hounds] (p134-140)
Sporting Intelligence [inc. Obituaries of James Blyth, James Tinne, Augustus Grimble, John Bridges, Percy Platt, Newton Apperley (*Baily's* contributor); Harry Furniss (*Two Pins Club*), William Lamonby (Coursing Editor *The Field*), James Driscoll and Horace Davenport; Steeplechase Jockey Frederick Rees Presentation; Ranelagh Managers; Grafton Hounds; Grantown Angling Association; Army Golf] (p141-144)

Issue 782 : April 1925

Portrait [Bale] and Biography - George Bennet (p145-148)
A Chat With Old Jim Lillywhite by John Bristow-Noble (p149-153)
Racing in Burma by William Benson (p153-156)
The Billiard Season of 1924-25 by Sydenham Dixon (p156-158)
Polo Topics by Arthur Coaten (p159-161)
[Obituary] Rooke Rawlence (Secretary, Masters of Foxhounds Association) by George Burrows (p162-164)
Photograph [Lafayette]: *Rooke Rawlence* (on p163)
April Fly Fishing by George Garrow-Green (p164-166)
English Public Schools Sports by Frederick Webster (p166-169)
Amateur Photography by Robert Goodsall (p169-171)
Winds: Their Meaning for the Angler by Charles Stevenson (p171-173)
Hunting Days: A Closing Day by George Collins (p174-178)
The Season is Over [verses] by Henry Baines (p178)
Spring Horse Shows by George Teasdale-Buckell (p179-183)
Our Van [inc. Manchester Racing; Staffordshire Hurdles; Chelmsford Meeting; Lingfield Park Steeplechase; Yardley Handicap] (p183-188)
Sporting Intelligence [inc. County Polo Association; National Pony Society; Obituaries of Arthur Smith-Barry, Charles Tatham, Frederic Alderson, Charles Richardson, John Bridges, Charles Appleton, Finlay Kennedy and James McCall; Review of *Hardy's Anglers' Guide*] (p188-191)
Racing Results (p192)

Issue 783 : May 1925

Portrait [Bale] and Biography - Sydney Varndell (p193-196)
Cricket Season Opens by James Catton (p196-198)
Helping the Partridge by Eric Parker (p198-201)
[Obituary] Henry Jones: A Fine Old Essex Sportsman by Charles Bruce (p202-204)
Photograph: *Henry Jones* (facing p202)
How Do They Do It [Poachers] by Richard Jefferies (p204-205)
Kashmir of Old Days by Henry Pilkington (p205-210)
The Future of the Olympic Games by Frederick Webster (p210-214)
The Woodpigeon Pest by Richard Darwall (p214-216)
The Amateur Boxing Championships by Norman Clark (p216-219)
Sport on the Pamirs by Percy Etherton (p220-223)
The 1925 Racquets Championships by Henry Rudd (p223-225)
On Ravens by Guy Selby (p225-226)
Hambledoniana by William Holland (p226-228)
Point-to-Point Races by William Fawcett (p228-231)
Our Van [inc. Lincoln Meeting; Liverpool Grand National; Newbury Races; Nottingham Spring Handicap; Oadby Plate] (p231-235)
Sporting Intelligence [inc. American Army Polo Team; Greyhound Sales; Sunbright Ale [verses]; Haunts of Trout [verses]; Review of *Wisden's Cricketers' Almanack 1925* by Sydney Pardon; East Berkshire Horse Show Society; Meynell Hunt; Portman Hounds; West Cumberland Otterhounds; Holcombe Harriers; Obituaries of Cecil Nickalls, John Rogerson, Adam Scott, Walter Hearne, Walter Ball, James Bristow, Arthur Kemble and Bernard Green] (p235-239)
Racing Results (p240)

Issue 784 : June 1925

Biography - Judith Blunt-Lytton (p241-246)
Photograph [Bassano]: *Baroness Wentworth and Skowronek* (facing p241)
Photograph: *Baroness Wentworth with Arab Mares* (facing p242)
Photograph: *Baroness Wentworth with Arab Foals* (facing p244)
A Hunt Cricket Match by George Collins (p247-252)
Photograph: *Teams - Yarborough's versus Galway's [Cricket]* (facing p248)
Photograph: *Yarborough's and Galway's with Brocklesby Hounds* (facing p250)
Play to the Score by James Catton (p253-254)
Herbert Sutcliffe by George Burrows (p255)
A Cavalry Reverie by Albert Barrow (p256-257)
Polo by Arthur Coaten (p258-260)
The Bards Who Sang the Chase by Ruaraidh Erskine (p260-262)
The Melton Raceday by Alexander Muntz (p263-264)
Sherwood Forest by Derek Wilkinson (p265-266)
Army and Public Schools Racquets by Henry Rudd (p266-268)
The Tennis Championships by Wallis Myers (p268-270)
The Ocean Yacht Race by Francis Cooke (p270-272)
Hints for Novice Golfers by George Duncan (p272-273)
Badger Digging by George Teasdale-Buckell (p274-275)
The Otterhounds [verses] by Henry Pilkington (p275)
Our Van [inc. Kempton Park Racing; Birmingham Races; Epsom Meeting; Curragh Races; Pontefract Plate; Esher Cup; Hurst Park Racing; Chester Cup] (p276-281)
Sporting Intelligence [inc. Obituaries of Herbert Lawford, Philip Godsal, Frank Wilkinson, Charles Smith, Thomas Tyler, Arthur Dunlop and Joseph Holmes; *Pointers and Setters* by Harding Cox; Epsom Racecourse; Goathland Hounds] (p281-282)
Racing Results (p283-284)

Volume 124, July - December 1925

Issue 785 : July 1925

Portrait [Rouch] of Gordon Richards, jockey — Title page
Portrait [Bale] and Biography - Arthur Gilligan — (p1-3)
Polo and the Polo Pony by Tresham Gilbey — (p4-6)
The Otter: The Anglers' Friend by Ludovick Cameron — (p6-9)
The Polo Season by Arthur Coaten — (p10-12)
Grouse on Dartmoor by William Johnson — (p12-13)
History at Lord's by James Catton — (p14-15)
Hunting Days: A Very Unorthodox Day by George Collins — (p16-20)
Le Gros Veneur by George Teasdale-Buckell — (p20-23)
Management of Ducks for Shooting — (p24-27)
Days by Gerald Ambrose — (p28-33)
Tennis Under Difficulties by George Cecil — (p33-34)
Concerning Southpaws by William Holland — (p34-37)
Our Van [inc. Newmarket Meeting; Haydock Park Racing; Bois de Boulogne Races; Sledmere Stakes; Salisbury Cup; Epsom Meeting; Yarmouth Races] — (p37-44)
Sporting Intelligence [inc. South Shropshire Hounds; Obituaries of Edward Hulton, John Bowen-Jones, Thomas Pilkington and Rider Haggard; Middlesex County Cricket Club; Gilbey Sports Meeting] — (p44-46)
Racing Results — (p46-48)

Issue 786 : August 1925

Portrait [Rouch] and Biography - William Baird — (p49-50)
The Polo Season by Arthur Coaten — (p50-53)
An Old Penistone Hound by John Dransfield — (p53-54)
Photograph: *Rumbo* — (on p53)
Pheasants by Noel Sedgwick — (p54-55)
Characteristics of Grouse by Richard Clapham — (p55-56)
The Road Coach [verses] by Ludovick Cameron — (p56)
One Hundred Years of Cowes by George Hopcroft — (p57-58)
A Famous Partridge County by Guy Selby — (p59)
Fish Foes by Clifford Cordley — (p60-62)
Hound Walking by Charles Lloyd — (p62-63)
Set a Thief by Guy Selby — (p63-64)
A Father of the Turf by Jack Fairfax-Blakeborough — (p64-67)
The Hovering of Kestrels by Guy Broun — (p67-68)
The Red Kite by Guy Selby — (p68-69)
The Red Leg by Frank Bonnett — (p69-70)
Cricket Captains Courageous by William Holland — (p71-73)
Newmarket Sales of Bloodstock by Sydenham Dixon — (p74-76)
A Pack of Foxhounds by George Monckton-Arundell — (p76-82)
With Horse and Hound at Peterborough by William Scarth-Dixon — (p82-85)
Our Van [inc. Chantilly Races; Warwickshire Breeders' Plate; Coventry Stakes; Ascot Gold Cup; Northumberland Plate; Curragh Meeting; Cumberland Handicap] — (p86-92)
Sporting Intelligence [inc. Cricket Ball Making; Obituaries of Charles Taylor, William Allison (of *The Sportsman*), Francis Brandt, George Smith (aka Drake) and Frederick Amphlett (of *The Fishing Gazette*); Viking Rowing Club; Philadelphia Sculling] — (p92-94)
Racing Results — (p94-96)

Issue 787 : September 1925

Portrait [Bale] and Biography - Courtenay Warner (p97-99)
An Old Fashioned First of September by Clarence Bruce (p99-102)
Hunting Days: A Cubbing Day by George Collins (p103-107)
Past and Present [verses] by Norman Innes (p107)
Jim Driscoll by Norman Clark (p108-110)
After Wild Geese With a Stalking Horse by Kenneth Dawson (p110-113)
Some of the Chief Difficulties in Dog Breaking by Gerald Ambrose (p113-120)
Sport in Turkey by George Cecil (p120)
Billiards on the Rhine by George Cecil (p121)
Cowes Week by George Hopcroft (p122-123)
Festival Cricket by William Holland (p123-124)
Golf on the Gold Coast by George Cecil (p124-126)
The Polo Season by Arthur Coaten (p126-128)
Some Thoughts on Cricket in 1925 by James Catton (p128-130)
Cycling by James Lightwood (p130-132)
Our Van [inc. Wiltshire Stakes; West Riding Plate; Newmarket Meeting; Ayr Races; Drogheda Memorial Stakes; Leicestershire Oaks; Goodwood Racing; Chesterfield Handicap] (p133-139)
Sporting Intelligence [inc. Obituaries of Percy Gosnell, Eric Oliver, John Bell-Irving, Frederick Hulke and Adam Beck; West Somerset Foxhounds; Review of *Fifty Years of Sport* by Edward Miller; Wingfield Sculls; Palestine Foxhounds; New Editor of *The Sporting Life and Sportsman*; Badsworth Foxhounds] (p140-142)
Racing Results (p142-144)

Issue 788 : October 1925

Portrait [Bale] and Biography - Henry Lascelles (p145-148)
Provincial Polo by Arthur Coaten (p149-151)
The Yachting Season of 1925 by George Hopcroft (p152-154)
Finland's Rise to Athletic Fame by Frederick Webster (p154-155)
Coursing by Guy Broun (p155-156)
Concerning Barracking by William Holland (p156-158)
Hound Trailing by Carter Platts (p158-160)
Ancient and Modern Sporting Terms by Richard Darwall (p160-162)
Pigeon Shooting by Eric Parker (p163)
Golf at Chantilly by George Cecil (p164-165)
The Two Johns [verses] by Henry Baines (p165)
We Are Tolerated by Guy Selby (p166)
Staghunting by Clifford Cordley (p167)
Shooting by Eric Parker (p168-169)
With the Cottesmore on a Bicycle by Alexander Muntz (p169-171)
Round the Outsides by Noel Sedgwick (p171-172)
Billiards in the Congo by George Cecil (p172-173)
The Man Who 'Did' Dr Syntax by Jack Fairfax-Blakeborough (p174-178)
Our Van [inc. Nottingham Meeting; Redcar Races; Stockton Handicap; Hardwicke Plate; Wykeham Handicap; Great Yorkshire Handicap; Ostend Grand International] (p178-186)
Engraving [pinx. Hall]: *Voltigeur* (facing p180)

Sporting Intelligence [inc. Physiology and Sport; Rugby in New Zealand; Tedworth Hounds;
        Bowls Greens; Reviews of *The Racehorse in Training* by William Day, *How to
        Shoot* by Robert Churchill, *A Fellowship of Anglers* by Horace Hutchinson, *Golf
        From Two Sides* by Roger Wethered, *Secrets of the Salmon* by Edward Hewitt,
        The Science of Fly Fishing for Trout by Frederick Shaw, *Malton Memories and
        I'Anson Triumphs* by Jack Fairfax-Blakeborough, *Hunting Songs* by Rowland
        Egerton-Warburton, *The Sport of Our Ancestors* by Richard Verney, *Game Trails
        in British Columbia* by Bryan Williams; *Sporting Days and Sporting Stories*
        by Jack Fairfax-Blakeborough; Obituaries of Arthur Coventry, James Batho,
        Charles Horner, James Complin and Charles Orvis; Nat Gould's Notebook;
        Lincolnshire Cricket; Crowhurst Otterhounds] (p186-191)
Racing Results (p191-192)

Issue 789 : November 1925

Portrait [Bale] and Biography - Paget Steavenson (p193-194)
Hunting Days: An Opening Day by George Collins (p194-198)
The Ground Game Act of 1880 by Frank Bonnett (p199-201)
Fox Cunning by William Fawcett (p202-204)
Hunt Changes by Edward Cuming (p204-209)
Baily's Hunting Directory 1925-26 by George Burrows (p210-211)
[Review] *A Trainer to Two Kings* by Richard Marsh reviewed by Sydenham Dixon (p211-213)
The Limerick Fox [verses] by Henry Pilkington (p214)
Cockers Past and Present by George Rope (p215-216)
The Tynedale Hunt by William Fawcett (p216-219)
The Laying-Up Season by George Hopcroft (p219-220)
Dinghy Racing by Francis Cooke (p220-222)
Ferreting by Noel Sedgwick (p222-224)
Billiards in Turkey by George Cecil (p224-225)
Woodcock Wisdom by Guy Selby (p225-226)
Our Van [inc. Grand Prix de Paris; Curragh Meeting; Yarmouth Racing; Ayr Gold Cup;
        Caledonian Hunt Stakes; Great Eastern Handicap; Lanark Races] (p227-232)
Sporting Intelligence [inc. Reviews of *British Birds* by Archibald Thorburn, *Over the Grass
        by William Ogilvie, *Hunting the Fox* by Richard Verney, *Auction Bridge Play* by
        Manning Foster; *Memories and Hopes* by Edward Lyttelton; Obituaries of
        Eugen Sandow, Thomas Bolitho, Russell Swanwick, William Thompson, Thomas
        Lister, Weston Crocker and Frederic Custance; Kingsclere Racing Stables;
        Llangibby Hunt; Wye Valley Otterhounds; Newmarket Town Plate] (p233-237)
To Open the Season [verses] by William Williams (p236)
Racing Results (p238-240)

Issue 790 : December 1925

Portrait [Collings] and Biography - Seymour Gosling (p241-242)
In John Peel's Country by William Fawcett (p243-247)
Hunting Days: A Lucky Day by George Collins (p248-253)
And Rather Liking It by Charles Simpson (p253-257)
The Christmas Camp in India by George Cecil (p257-258)
Bird Shooting in Northern India by Henry Johns (p259-261)
Sport in Patiala State by Lester Arnold (p261-263)
Playtime in Borneo by George Cecil (p264-265)
Early Days of Football by Charles Batchelder (p265)
Cockfighting in India by George Cecil (p266-268)
Our Van [inc. Newmarket Champion Stakes; Lingfield Park Meeting; Doncaster Foal Plate;
        Jockey Club Cup; Alexandra Park Races; Newbury Autumn Handicap] (p269-275)

Sporting Intelligence [inc. South Herefordshire Foxhounds; Hertfordshire Hunt; Vale of White
     Horse Hounds; The National Stud; Reviews of *The History of the Cheshire Hunt*
     by George Burrows, *A Pack of Hounds* by George Monckton-Arundell, *Hockey:*
     Historical and Practical by Edward Thomson, *The Salmon: It's Life Story* by
     William Menzies, *Mr Jorrock's Thoughts on Hunting* by George Armour, *The*
     Secret of Athletic Training by Harry Andrews, *The Foundations of Golf* by Joseph
     Smith, *Records of the Cheriton Otterhounds* by William Rogers, *Sea Wake and*
     Jungle Trail by Warington Smyth; *Sympathic Training of Horse and Man* by
     Thomas Paterson; Obituaries of Charles Francis, Gilbert Jordan, Bache Cunard,
     Harry Reynolds, George Fosbroke, Thomas Hill, Richard Rycroft, James Leigh
     and William Cleminson; Peshawar Vale Foxhounds]   (p275-281)
Racing Results   (p281-284)

Volume 125, January - June 1926

Issue 791 : January 1926

Portrait of Frederick Archer, deceased jockey   Title page
Portrait [Collings] and Biography - Thomas Hickman   (p1-3)
Test Matches for 1926 by James Catton   (p3-5)
The Racehorse of Today by Sydenham Dixon   (p5-6)
Foxes and Pheasants by Frank Bonnett   (p7-9)
Pioneers of Boxing by Norman Clark   (p10-12)
Yacht Racing in January by George Hopcroft   (p13-14)
Billiards in the Cameroons by George Cecil   (p14)
Herod by Charles Richardson   (p15-16)
A Family of Great Trainers by Nigel Freer   (p17-18)
Sports and Pastimes in Ancient Greece by William Williams   (p18-19)
The Evolution of Football by William Holland   (p20-21)
A Huntsman's Grave   (p22)
A Rum 'Un to Follow [Whyte-Melville]   (p22-23)
Et Ego in Arcadia Fui [verses] by Edward Chase   (p23)
January Afield by Arthur Sharp   (p24-26)
Hunting Days: An Unlucky Day by George Collins   (p26-30)
Hunting Conduct by Alan Horwood   (p30-32)
Famous Hunting Runs by Robert Davies   (p33-36)
Hunting Hints for Newcomers by Edward Cuming   (p36-37)
Our Van [inc. Lincoln Autumn Meeting; Croxteth Handicap; Curragh Races; Hurst Park Stakes;
     Warwick Racing; Sandringham Stud]   (p37-43)
Photograph: *Haselor Clipper Knight*   (facing p38)
Sporting Intelligence [inc. Stipendiary Stewards; New National Hunt Rule; Reviews of *Live*
     Stock Journal Annual 1926 by George Burrows, *Shooting in the Barbary*
     States by Hilton Simpson; *The Stringing of Shot* by Charles Burrard; South
     & West Wilts Hunt; Obituaries of Charles Arthur, Albert Hornby, John Dalton,
     Walter Dorling, Sydney Pardon, Amos Burn (of *The Field*), William Cail, William
     McCanlis and Stamford Hacker; New Editor of *Wisden's Cricketers' Almanack*]   (p43-48)
The Hunt [verses] by William Williams]   (p48)

Issue 792 : February 1926

Portrait [Collings] and Biography - Guy Hargreaves   (p49-50)
Walter Buckmaster by George Burrows   (p51-52)
The Australian Cricket Team by James Catton   (p52-54)
Light Blues and Heavy Blues by William Holland   (p55-56)

Parades at Agricultural Shows by William Scarth-Dixon (p57-58)
That Horsebreaking Bloke [verses] by Henry Pilkington (p59)
Hunt Changes of Twenty Years by Charles Lloyd (p60-61)
Bush-Cow Shooting by Gerald Ambrose (p61-64)
Billiards in Cyprus by George Cecil (p64)
On Breaking and Schooling a Hunter by John Noble (p65-66)
The People's Cricketer by James Catton (p67-68)
Hunting Days: A Frosty Day by George Collins (p68-72)
Five Generations of Hunt Servants (part 1) by George Teasdale-Buckell (p72-75)
There Lay a Fox in Naburn Wood [verses] by Henry Baines (p75)
First Aid to the Horse by William Lyon (p76-78)
A Shorthorn Reverie by Charles Batchelder (p78-81)
Hunt Point-to-Point Steeplechases by William Fawcett (p82-84)
Our Van [inc. Coleshill Steeplechase; Newbury Races; Reigate Handicap; Berkshire Handicap;
        Haydock Park Meeting; Belvoir Foxhounds; Warwickshire Hunt; Zetland Hounds;
        Carmarthenshire Hunt; Cambridgeshire Foxhounds] (p84-91)
Sporting Intelligence [inc. Institute of The Horse; Review of *The Brocklesby Hounds 1746-1925*
        by George Collins; Obituaries of Harry Vassall, George Gee, Leonard Pilkington,
        James Forrest, Harold Reade and John Dickerson; Quorn Foxhounds; Hurworth
        Hunt] (p92-96)
Racing Results (p96)

Issue 793 : March 1926

Portrait [Swaine] and Biography - Samuel Hardy (p97)
Record Average Tay Salmon Catch by Charles Randall (p98-100)
Photograph: *Opening Day of River Tay* (facing p98)
Sporting Metaphors by Eaton Smith (p100)
Hubback by Horace Regnart (p101)
[Obituary] Harry Vassall by Edward Moorhouse (p102-103)
March by Guy Selby (p103-104)
Big Racing Yachts of 1926 by George Hopcroft (p104-106)
Hunting Days: A Bye Day by George Collins (p106-111)
A Morning's Trout Fishing in Natal by John Durham (p111-113)
The Boat Race by Frederick Webster (p113-114)
Pity the Poor Wicketkeeper by James Catton (p115)
Hunting in Wiltshire by John Ravenstone (p116-117)
Famous English Cup Finals by William Holland (p117-119)
Five Generations of Hunt Servants (part 2) by George Teasdale-Buckell (p120-122)
Long Records Among Hunt Servants: The Smiths of Brocklesby by George Collins (p123-125)
The Boxall's Record by William Kell (p125)
Britain's Small Horses by Charles Batchelder (p126-128)
Hindhunting on Exmoor by Clifford Cordley (p128-130)
Our Van [inc. Wigston Steeplechase; Tenby Races; Windsor Meeting; Winchester Steeplechase;
        Essex & Suffolk Hunt; Monmouthshire Hounds; South Oxfordshire Hunt; Garth
        Hounds; Ludlow Hunt] (p130-138)
Sporting Intelligence [inc. Polo Tournaments; Hunters Certificates; Obituaries of Digby
        Jephson, Hugh Locke-King, Abraham Robarts, Edward Rutter, Frederick Reynard,
        Cecil Samuda and Emanuel Harbron; Review of *A Jockey's Profession* by George
        Lambton; Horse Racing in Australia; Newmarket Racecourse Assessment; Masters
        of Otterhounds Association; Derbyshire County Cricket Club] (p138-143)
The Passing Season [verses] by Norman Innes (p140)
Racing Results (p144)

Issue 794 : April 1926

Portrait [Barnett] and Biography - John Cridlan (p145-147)
Riding by Michael Rimington (p147-151)
Australia Armed at all Points by James Catton (p152-154)
Winter Polo by Arthur Coaten (p154-157)
Sport in Ceylon by George Cecil (p157-159)
How to Learn to Hunt by William Fawcett (p159-160)
The Locarno Spirit in Yacht Racing by George Hopcroft (p160-162)
Our Foxhunting Prince [verses] by Richard Clapham (p162)
Hunting Days: A Red Letter Day by George Collins (p163-167)
Anglo-Australian Cricket by William Holland (p167-169)
London Spring Horse Shows by William Scarth-Dixon (p169-174)
Photograph [Rouch]: *Erfyl Lady Grey* (facing p170)
Photograph [Rouch]: *What's Wanted* (facing p170)
Photograph [Rouch]: *London Cry* (facing p172)
The Racquets Season by Henry Rudd (p174-175)
Hunting by Scent by Alan Horwood (p176-179)
Our Van [inc. Ludlow Handicap; Surrey Steeplechase; Colborne Hurdles; Leicester Races; Roehampton Handicap; Plumpton Meeting; Gatwick Racecourse Stand; Bramham Moor Hunt; Warwickshire Hounds; Westmeath Hunt; Hambledon Hounds; West Kent Hunt] (p179-186)
Sporting Intelligence [inc. Turf Changes; Sunday Golf; Tarporley Hunt Club Fire; Reviews of *Rugby Football* by Ronald Cove-Smith, *Show Dogs* by Theodore Marples; *The Breeding of Foxhounds* by Seymour Bathurst; Obituaries of William Murland, William Barry, Thomas Ainslie and Guy Yerburgh; *Live Stock Journal* Show List 1926; Waterloo Cup] (p186-190)
To Finish the Season [verses] by William Williams (p188)
Racing Results (p191-192)

Issue 795 : May 1926

Portrait [Bustin] and Biography - Urian Corbett-Winder (p193-194)
The Coming Polo Season by Arthur Coaten (p194-196)
[Obituary] Harry Fordham by George Burrows (p197-199)
Photograph: *Harry Fordham* (facing p199)
Point-to-Point Racing by William Fawcett (p199-201)
Hunting the Roe in France by George Cecil (p202-207)
English and Australian Cricket by James Catton (p208-209)
Bat versus Ball by Octavius Christie (p209-210)
Those Ashes by William Holland (p211-212)
Billiards in the Seychelles by George Cecil (p213)
Wild Pheasants by Jack Fairfax-Blakeborough (p214-218)
Rink Bowls by George Teasdale-Buckell (p218-219)
Advice to a Huntsman by Harding Cox (p220-222)
Knurr and Spell by Francis Reynolds (p222-223)
Shooting in Mesopotamia by Horace Wingfeld (p224-227)
Our Van [inc. Cheltenham Gold Cup Steeplechase; Hurst Park Races; Grand Military Meeting; Lincolnshire Handicap; Leicester Racing; Burton Handicap] (p228-233)
Song of the Otter Hunter [verses] by Henry Baines (p233)
Sporting Intelligence [inc. Obituaries of John Musker, Frank Iredale, Charles Tindall, Hwfa Williams, Allan Smith and William Watkinson; Jockey Frank Buckle; The Old Fox [verses]; Ullswater Foxhounds; Craven Lodge Club; Cricket [verses]; British Show Jumping Association; Review of *John Wisden's Cricketers' Almanack* by Stewart Caine; National Stud Farm] (p234-238)

The Master Angler [verses] by William Williams (p236)
Racing Results (p238-240)

Issue 796 : June 1926

Portrait [Bassano] and Biography - Herbert Cayzer (p241-242)
Farewell by Tresham Gilbey (p242-246)
Senor de Hoz by Albert Frost (p247-251)
The Jubilee of Lawn Tennis by Wallis Myers (p251-255)
Yachting Prospects for 1926 by George Hopcroft (p255-257)
A Great West Country Sportsman by Henry Bryden (p257-258)
The Hand Rearing of Partridges by Jack Fairfax-Blakeborough (p259-261)
Captains of England (p261-264)
Dogs or Bitches by William Fawcett (p264-265)
Racing in France by George Cecil (p266-267)
Engraving [pinx. Turner]: *Harkaway* (on p267)
Billiards in Albania by George Cecil (p268)
The Puppy Show by Harding Cox (p269-270)
Artificial Earths by Denis Williams (p270-271)
Who Will Keep Wicket by Ap Llewellyn (p272-273)
A Leicestershire Ride by Alexander Muntz (p273-275)
The Old Order Changeth (p275-277)
Racquets by Henry Rudd (p277-279)
Our Van [inc. Greenham Plate; Catterick Bridge Races; Newmarket Meeting; Middle Park Plate; Epsom Spring Meeting; Pontefract Plate; Esher Cup; Hurst Park Stakes] (p279-286)
Engraving: *Penelope* (facing p280)
Engraving [pinx. Hall]: *Tim Whiffler* (on p285)
Sporting Intelligence [inc. Obituaries of Harry Sadler, Aubrey Wallis and John Hargreaves; Trainer John Watson; International Sheepdog Society] (p287)
Racing Results (p287-288)

Gerald Ricardo

Although this Index and Bibliography is about the sporting magazine, the Baily family proved to be of interest to me when researching. One thing which will have been noted is the fact that there are no known photographs of any Baily people. All these years of searching have drawn blanks with the nearest of anyone to Alfred Baily being that of a third cousin twice removed.

Alfred Head Baily (the first of three to have this name) and his elder brother Charles Edward Baily had, in 1832, set themselves up as "printers, stationers and account book manufacturers" with the business quietly establishing itself during the following years.

As the decade progressed so the brothers came to a loose amalgamation with the firm B.B.King of Change Alley. They produced a number of *Rural Life Alamanacks* together (see page six) with the first being published in January 1839. There were also the Thomas Hood *Comic Annuals* (1830-41), A *Naval & Military Almanack* (1840) and a *Sportsman's Annual* (1836) which was all about dogs.

However, it was not all sweetness and light as an unscrupulous individual, William Maxwell, had run up debts with the company by falsely claiming to be a wholesale agent who could supply their stationery to numerous retailers. Maxwell, an Irishman who hailed from Portrush, County Antrim, was duly charged and sent, on 23 May 1839, to Fleet Prison to join other imprisoned debtors. Whatever impact this had on the business is unknown but within two years Alfred's financial situation would improve considerably.

An old friend of the family, Grace Say (1770-1841), was a spinster who lived at Gartley House in Dartford. Her father, Charles, had been a printer based in Bishopsgate and was in business with Alfred's grandfather James Richardson for many years. The families had known and trusted each other which resulted in Grace appointing Alfred as one of the executors of her Will.

Grace was an only child and she had inherited a considerable amount of money, investments, property and land. She died in February 1841, and in her Will she directed her executors to give a number of legacies to local individuals and also to use some of her land fronting Dartford Road for the construction of eight charity almshouses. These were erected the following year and still exist for the purpose of which they were built. They were given Grade II heritage status in 1975.

The total sum of her investments were enormous by the standards and estimates of the day. Alfred inherited an amount which would exceed £2.4 million by today's values. This enabled him to purchase a large property in South Hampstead as well as stables and land in Bushey, Hertfordshire.

The Baily business started to grow and both Alfred and Charles were ready to invest large amounts of money. They obviously considered the Irish railway building projects to be worthy of investment for on 10th July 1846, each brother put £7,500 (at that day's value) into the 'Railway Subscription Contract' for the creation of the "Waterford, Wexford, Wicklow and Dublin Railway Company."

The line was created in stages with the developers also building two large hotels by the stations at Bray and Rathdrum. After the line to Wexford North had been completed, and bonus payments made to shareholders, the brothers cashed in with each making in excess of £10 million (by today's values). With no heavy taxation to worry about Alfred duly purchased his brother's part of the firm as well as land at Berkhamsted and a number of racehorses.

Alfred's eldest son, also called Alfred, went into the family business followed some time later by his brother Percy. It was Percy who seemed to be more of an 'ideas man' as twice in 1879 he registered designs, initially for an "Assegai and Shield Ornament," and then, four months later, for "A Gaiter-Galosh." Ten years later he teamed up with the Chicago based Smiths Biscuit Company with both patenting in their respective countries "... a food in the form of a biscuit or cake which is not only highly nutritious but possesses medicinal and curative qualities."

By then Percy had time on his hands as well as money in the bank. He had taken over the editorship of the Magazine early in 1885, on the death of his father, and continued until both brothers sold all Baily titles to Vinton & Company in late 1888. Percy then moved from the family home setting himself up in business at 199 Euston Road and purchasing a house at 3 Pembridge Gardens in Bayswater. On his death in July 1908, a number of claims were made on his estate which took his Kilburn based solicitors some time to finalise.

Alfred junior appeared to have no aptitude for business for not only did he go through the Vinton money, he also caused A.H.Baily & Company to be made bankrupt in July 1891. His application for a discharge, made the following January was refused on the grounds "... that the bankrupt's assets are not of a value equal to ten shillings in the pound on the amount of his unsecured liabilities." Baily had also committed another offence by, according to court papers, "... he had continued to trade after knowing himself to be insolvent."

The business, still located in Laurence Pountney Hill, closed down a few months later. Alfred junior, his wife Josephine and their eight children then emigrated to Massachusetts. In 1920, one of his daughters-in-law, now living in Nebraska, produced a son who was named Alfred Head Baily. There the trail ends.

Henry Rous